D0206143

A HISTORY OF IOWA

LELAND L. SAGE

A HISTORY OF IOWA

THE IOWA STATE UNIVERSITY PRESS / AMES

1974

LELAND L. SAGE IS A FORMER MEMBER OF THE FACULTY AT THE UNIVERSITY OF Northern Iowa where he taught from 1932 to 1967 and where he now holds the title of Professor of History, Emeritus. His baccalaureate is from Vanderbilt University and his graduate degrees were received from the University of Illinois. He also taught at DePauw University and was a visiting professor at the University of Nebraska and Indiana University. His chief interest as a teacher was in the stimulation of student writing in the field of Iowa history. His own writings include a biography of Iowa's longtime congressman and senator, *William Boyd Allison: A Study in Practical Politics,* published by the State Historical Society of Iowa in 1956, and articles and reviews in various historical journals and encyclopedias, the most important article being "The Clarksons of Indiana and Iowa" *(Indiana Magazine of History,* 1954). He is a member of the Organization of American Historians, the Southern Historical Association, and the State Historical Society of Iowa.

Composed and printed by
The Iowa State University Press

First edition, 1974

Library of Congress Cataloging in Publication Data

Sage, Leland Livingston, 1899–
A history of Iowa.

Includes bibliographical references.
1. Iowa—History. I. Title.
F621.S15 977.7 73–14984
ISBN 0–8138–0840–5

AGAIN TO **MARGARET**, **CAROLYN**, AND ALL OUR FAMILIES

CONTENTS

PREFACE

LIKE EVERY BOOK, THIS ONE ON THE HISTORY OF IOWA HAS A history of its own. During the period devoted to research and writing, sometimes a part-time, sometimes a full-time activity, the author has been asked many times what prospective audience he had in mind for the book. There has never been and there still is no pat answer to this well-taken question. Certainly no particular age group of readers was in mind as the book grew through the years; no vocabulary studies were made to fit the text to any certain group. There was only the assumption of intelligent readers of all ages from nine to ninety who would be interested in the history of their state.

By occupation an instructor in modern European history, a non-Iowan of Southern and Midwestern backgrounds, I began my studies of Iowa history simply as an extracurricular interest in the history and government of a state in which I had chanced to settle and which bid fair to become my permanent home—the kind of natural interest characteristic in varying degrees of most persons possessing a reasonable amount of civic pride. This strictly amateurish reading was begun in the stirring years of the New Deal efforts to rescue Iowa and the nation from the Great Depression, an era which left its mark on nearly all of us who lived through it, and whose stamp, I hope, is on all my pages dealing with the affected times.

As time passed and the range and depth of my reading increased, certain facts began to come clear, chiefly, the startling revelation that absolutely no scholarly general history of the state existed and very few of its leading citizens had been treated in scholarly biographies, and the few which had been written were sadly outdated. For various reasons no professionally trained historian had seen fit to engage himself in the preparation of a complete history of the state. The courtly Benjamin F. Shambaugh, to be sure, who through a long career doubled as professor of Political Science at the University of Iowa and superintendent of the State Historical Society of Iowa, had gathered and edited several volumes of documentary materials (now badly in need of updating) and had written an excellent monograph on the proceedings of the three Iowa constitutional conventions of 1844, 1846, and 1857. Also, he was the prime mover in the launching and perpetuation of a scholarly quarterly journal devoted to Iowa history. Several graduate students in his department and elsewhere published their dissertations and theses as books sponsored by the society or in complete or extracted form as articles in the journal. Occasionally a book or article was published elsewhere—but still the call for a scholarly general history was not answered.

In a sense, Iowa historiography was a victim of the youth of the state. A state whose formal beginnings were as recent as the 1830s could not acquire much of a historical past in just over a hundred years. In addition, the witness of history was often victimized and seldom benefited by the county and state histories of largely commercial motivation which appeared in the 1880s and 1890s. Subscribers, quite often veterans of the Civil War or their proud relatives, subscribed for copies at a pledged amount, those whose portraits accompanied their biographical sketches paying a larger amount than the unpictured. The first but not the last general history of the state was written under this arrangement and published in 1903, a stout four-volume set divided between history and the "mug" pages. The author, Benjamin F. Gue, was a distinguished Iowa newspaper man, politician, religious leader, and public-spirited citizen, who often was writing personal reminiscences in the form of history. His work still finds a place on library shelves and, alas, is cited by hard-pressed students who seldom bother to notice the date of publication or inquire into the author's credentials as a historian.

Bypassing the Reverend Dr. William Salter's little book of 1905, one finds a set similar in form to the Gue work, a three-volume production in 1915 by Johnson Brigham, a librarian and editor of scholarly instincts and interests. This was followed in 1921 by a general history by Cyrenus Cole, a newspaper editor, politician, and raconteur, and in 1931 by a five-volume history from the pen of Edgar R. Harlan, curator of the Iowa State Department of History and Archives, a political appointee. Cyrenus Cole, having been swept out of office by the Roosevelt landslide of 1932, condensed the substance of his previous writings and added a touch of his political sentiments to make a readable but untrustworthy one-volume work, *Iowa through the Years*. Part history and part memoir, unedited and totally lacking in scholarly apparatus, its publication (1940) by the State Historical Society of Iowa can only be characterized as a "mistake." Later, in 1952, William J. Petersen, a professional historian with two excellent books and many scholarly articles to his credit, collaborated in the production of popular history by compiling two volumes of topical narrative to accompany two volumes of pictures and biographical sketches.

So much for the past attempts at writing a narrative history of Iowa. A brief perusal of these works, the titles of which will appear below, will convince the least critical reader that the state deserves better. Many excellent monographs have been published and many excellent theses and dissertations have been prepared at the four universities in the state and elsewhere. Surely Iowa historiography has come of age; it is time to rise above the mugbook and the children's book. A three-step plan properly executed would give Iowa a storehouse of information worthy of the stamp of History. First, we should have *several* scholarly one-volume histories of the state. After these have been subjected to relentless criticism, and a cross-fertilization of subject matter has taken place, they should be followed by a multiauthor *Dictionary of Iowa History,* made up of short identifying sketches of men and women who have contributed in some way to the state's development. Then should come the crowning work, a definitive history in five or six volumes, each to be written by an authority on the period covered. Similar programs have been carried out in other states with marked success.

The present author can only hope that his work is a step in the direction indicated. If the book seems heavily weighted on the side of politics, perhaps a second look will show that I am writing about economic and social politics, using an account of the political process as a vehicle for carrying other aspects of history. Many people have helped me in various ways, and I should like to thank them most cordially. The list could never be complete but first of all I must thank my friend and former colleague, Herman L. Nelson, who wrote the first chapter and drew the maps for the book, and his wife, Margaret Buswell Nelson. For reasons best known to them I also wish to thank Wallace Anderson, Allan G. Bogue, Roger D. Bridges, Iver Christoffersen, Charles and James Hearst, Philip D. Jordan, William C. Lang, Gloria G. Riley-McIntosh, William K. Metcalfe, Ferner Nuhn, Daryl Pendergraft, Erma Plaehn, Leslie Santee, Raymond Schlicher, Merle R. Thompson, Don Whitnah, Don Winters, Brooke Workman, Eva Grace Bonney, Mary Dieterich, Lawrence Kieffer, Gretchen Myers, Verna Ritchie, Edward Wagner, and Janice Wieckhorst. The assistance given by Professor Wallace Farnham of the University of Illinois and Dean Ronald F. Matthias of Wartburg College was of a special nature and I shall be forever in their debt. William J. Petersen and Peter T. Harstad of the State Historical Society of Iowa, Jack Musgrove of the Iowa State Department of History and Archives, and Lida L. Greene of the State Library were unfailing in their response to calls for help, as was Francis Paluka of the Special Collections Department of the University of Iowa Libraries.

State Senator Willard R. Hansen of Cedar Falls kindly loaned maps and informatively discussed matters of state government. The graduate students whose theses I supervised helped me more than I helped them; I have drawn heavily on their writings. Dean Gordon Rhum and the Committee on Research of the University of Northern Iowa provided financial assistance for which I am deeply grateful. I could not count the ways in which my wife, Margaret Pearson Sage, has helped. Finally, I should like to call to remembrance the memories of the late Mildred Throne, Earle Dudley Ross, Emory Hampton English, Irving Harlow Hart, and Horace Van Metre, who helped me in so many ways and who exemplified all that is best in the word "Iowan."

LELAND L. SAGE

A HISTORY OF IOWA

CHAPTER 1 THE BEAUTIFUL LAND

One of the meanings attributed to the Indian word, "Iowa," a word whose original spelling and exact definition are shrouded in uncertainty, is "the beautiful land." Although doubtful as a literal translation or definition of the word, the connotation of beauty is not misplaced. We may entertain the thought that the Indians in Iowa, like many primitive peoples in the world and in time, possessed a sense of beauty, a love for color, an interest in design, a feeling for rhythm in nature. The assumption that the Indians before our time, who were hunters and then farmers, could look at their surroundings and express their delight in the beauty of the land does not strain credibility.

The elements of that land which were helpful to the Indians were also helpful to the men of European descent who first shared with them and then displaced them. Agriculture became a way of life on the American frontier; "Iowaland" became a part of a vast and complex economic system whose demands its people could partially fulfill, with pride of achievement and reasonable rewards. In recent years an urbanized factory system, much of it farm related, has surpassed agriculture in dollar value of its products. But first there was the land. The chief concern of a proper Iowan should be always to understand his land.

No one who lives here
knows how to tell the stranger
what it's like, the land.
I mean the farms all gently rolling
squared off by roads and fences,
creased by streams, stubbled with groves,
a land unformed by the mountain's
height or tides of either ocean,
a land in its working clothes,

sweaty with dew, thick-skinned loam,
a match for the men who ride it.
It breathes dust, pollen, wears furrows
and meadows, endures drouth and flood,
its muscles bulge and swell in horizons
of corn, lakes of purple alfalfa,
a land drunk on spring promises,
half-crazed with growth—I can no more
tell the secrets of its dark depths
than I can count the bushels in a
farmer's eye as he plants his corn.[1]

GLACIATION: IMPACT ON IOWA

A million years ago, perhaps a million and a half, the first of the Pleistocene glaciers began to form. No one knows what factors caused the climate to change, but most glaciologists agree that low summer temperatures and heavy precipitation in solid form are the principal meteorological factors involved in glaciation.[2] In North America the continental glaciers covered an area of more than 1,500,000 square miles, moving from two centers: the Keewatin, located west of Hudson Bay, and the Labradorean Center east of James Bay in Canada. Here the snow failed to melt in the summer and gradually changed to névé, granular snow resembling ice pellets, and then by compaction to glacial ice. Each winter more snow increased the size of the glacier. Once in motion the glacial ice acted like a rasp, a saw, and a file. Sand, gravel, and boulders frozen into the bottom of the ice moved over the land; gradually the tops of hills were scoured away and broken into fragments, and the accumulating debris became a tool used by the glacier to grind away other hills located more distantly from the ice center. The southernmost margin in the United States was in the vicinity of the Ohio and the Missouri rivers.

Everything in the path of the ice was changed. Near the ice center few loose rocks can be found; the land was scoured to bedrock. Along the margin the ice heaped up moraines, changed river courses, and deposited the material frozen in the ice. The marginal zone surrounding a continental glacier is a "glacially deposited area" and may be 500 miles, or near that figure, in width. The deposited material, called drift, is composed of boulders, gravel, sand, silt, and powdered rock and was deposited as a result of the melting of the ice and by rivers coming from or under the ice. Glacial drifts have been extensively studied in the United States and especially in Iowa, since "it is generally conceded that of all the States in the Mississippi Valley, Iowa has the most available evidence from which to interpret the history of the Pleistocene, to classify the deposits which belong to the geological system, and to estimate the duration of the period."[3]

Most geologists agree that there were four stages during the Pleisto-

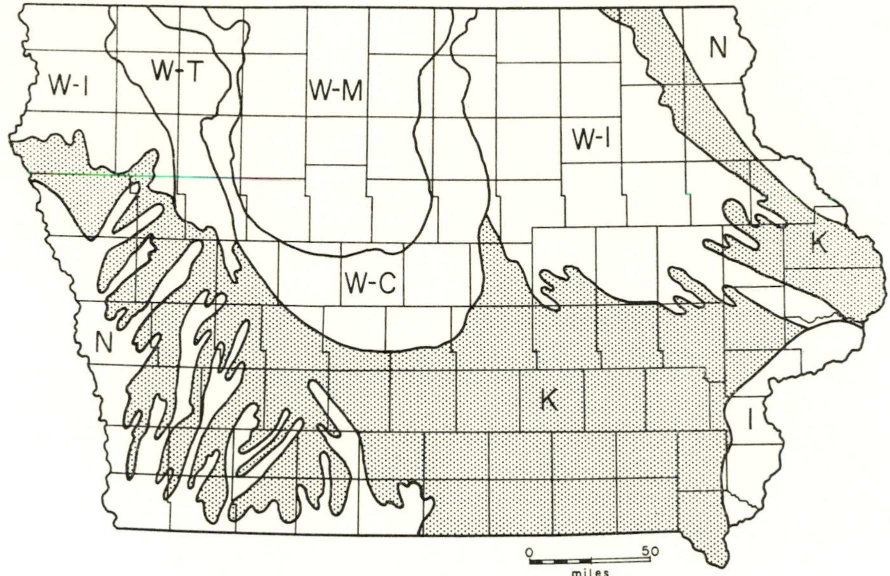

FIG. 1.1. Surface distribution of glacial drifts.

GLACIAL DRIFT	SUBSTAGES	
4th Wisconsin	Mankato	W-M
	Cary	W-C
	Tazewell	W-T
	Iowan	W-I
3rd Illinoian		I
2nd Kansan		K
1st Nebraskan		N

cene time and each of the four is represented in Iowa. The first glacial epoch, the Nebraskan, lasted for some tens of thousands of years, an indefinite figure at best. This Nebraskan ice sheet covered the entire state with ice and it holds a special significance for Iowa. For many years geologists thought that the area in northeastern Iowa, marked "N" on the map (Figure 1.1), was not affected by this glacier, and maps of glaciation can be found which erroneously portray that region as part of the Driftless Area, a portion of Minnesota, Wisconsin, and Illinois that was never covered with ice. Although the topography in northeastern Iowa might lead to this impression, surveys made after 1920 located patches of Nebraskan drift on the highlands and above the rivers, indicating the presence of the Nebraskan ice sheet. It is certain that the ice sheet could not have been very thick; if it had been, a more rounded hill area would have resulted than is evident at present.

Following an interglacial period (the Aftonian), a change in climate caused a new ice sheet to develop. This second one, the Kansan, extended as far south as did the Nebraskan ice sheet, but the northeastern part of Iowa was not covered. When the ice disappeared, a drift averaging fifty feet in depth was left over most of the state. At present the largest extent of exposed Kansan deposit is in the south central and southeastern parts of the state.

The third ice sheet, the Illinoian, pushing west from the Labradorean Center, entered Iowa only in the southeastern part of the state. Here the ice pushed the Mississippi River westward and for a time the river flowed around the western edge of the lobe of ice; when the ice melted, the river returned to its former channel. In the area of the Illinoian ice sheet the drift averages thirty feet in depth.

The Wisconsin glacial epoch, the fourth and last ice sheet, evidently was accompanied by considerable fluctuations of climate, which resulted in advances and retreats of the ice sheet. Four substages of this ice sheet are recognized, though for years the Iowan substage was thought to have been an independent ice epoch and was listed as the last in a line of five. Drift left by the Wisconsin ice sheets is found only in the northern half of the state. The powdered rock, clay, and silt are the parent materials which developed into exceptionally rich soils. For this reason, and also because it is an important period in the development of prehistoric man in Iowa, the Wisconsin epoch will be referred to below.[4]

The interglacial periods between the four successive glacial epochs should not be overlooked. During these years the climate changed, plant life returned and grew on the glacial drift, and soil was formed. In some places buried peat bogs and forests with trees still standing upright have been found, indicating that a considerable length of time elapsed between the glacial periods. These forests grew during an interglacial period and were buried by sand and gravel deposited by streams flowing from a subsequent advancing glacier.

During each interglacial period, loess was deposited on the drift. Loess is windblown buff-colored material composed principally of silt with small amounts of sand and clay, more evident in the bluffs of western Iowa than elsewhere in the state. This is explainable by the actions of rivers flowing from the glacial ice and the forces of winds blowing from the west and southwest. Eastward of the bluffs the loess mantled the drift to depths of ten to fifteen feet. Where loess is found, it is the basis for the development of very good soil in many places throughout the state.[5]

The floodplains of the Mississippi and Missouri rivers show little evidence at present that they were once significantly glaciated. These plains are now covered with alluviums that are considered recent in age. Indeed, the same assertion might well be made relative to the floodplains of the major streams within the state, such as the Des Moines, Cedar, and Iowa rivers.

GEOGRAPHIC DIVISIONS

The characteristics of the present topography of Iowa are the result of glacial ice, rivers, wind, and time. These geologic agents have caused sufficient variation on the surface of the land to permit dividing the state into three geographic divisions: Northeast Iowa, Northern Iowa, and Southern Iowa. In geological terms, most of Northeast Iowa is "maturely dissected." The rivers have deepened their channels to the extent that some of the valley walls are precipitous, and outcrops of nearly horizontal sedimentary rock are common on either side of the valley walls. Many of the valley bottoms are 500 feet lower in elevation than the cliffs on either side. Most of the land is in slope; the small areas of flattish land which can be found are located either in the uplands or the valley bottoms. The region is frequently referred to as the "Switzerland" of Iowa.

Northern Iowa, corresponding with the Wisconsin drift area, is a young glacial plain. Within this section, the area of the Mankato and Cary drifts is flatter as a whole than any other part of the state. (See Figure 1.1.) Tiling is a necessary part of farm management, and drainage ditches are more numerous than in any other part of the state. Thus adequately drained, the cropland becomes highly productive. The main streams have deepened their channels throughout much of the area but smaller streams run only a few feet lower than the surrounding land. Many of the tributaries, containing numerous meanders, slowly wend their way across land of only slight relief. Lakes are commoner in Northern Iowa than elsewhere in the state, many of them formed as a result of blocked river drainage.

The land of Southern Iowa has been subjected to erosion by water for a longer time than that in Northern Iowa. Rivers have deepened their channels; the intervening lands, frequently more than 200 feet higher in elevation than the floodplains, are well drained. Some of the rivers, especially the Des Moines, flow in a meandering course on their floodplains. During a time of flood the river may cut across a meander, isolating a bend in the river and forming an oxbow lake on the floodplain. Like the northeastern part of the state, Southern Iowa is described as a maturely dissected plain. Although one cannot find the precipitous bluffs common in the northeastern part of the state, this section is hillier than Northern Iowa.

CLIMATE

Because of Iowa's midcontinental location and the amount of rainfall, the climate is often described as the "humid continental long summer" type. It is frequently called the best corn climate in all the world. This is the climatic type in the United States where the wind brings moisture from the Gulf of Mexico; adequate rainfall usually comes at

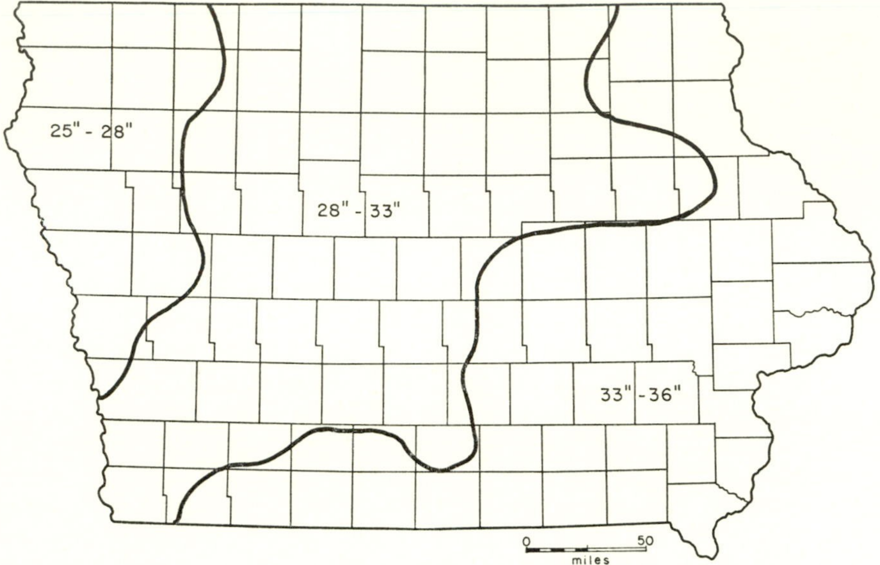

FIG. 1.2. Average annual precipitation.

the right time of the year and the sun assures temperatures high enough for the lush growth of corn during a long growing season. The average annual precipitation ranges from 25 inches in northwestern Iowa to 36 inches in southeastern Iowa. (Figure 1.2.) About 70 percent of the annual precipitation occurs between April 1 and September 30. During the summer months the commoner type of rainfall is the convectional thunderstorm, usually of short duration but copious in quantity. The regularity of the rainfall in its visitation is quite marked, a highly significant factor for agriculture. Seldom do droughts occur and when one does it is usually not widespread. Furthermore, a strong argument could be made for using the term *dry year* in Iowa rather than the word *drought,* because a year during which the rainfall is much below normal is usually preceded and followed by years of normal precipitation.

Since the average monthly temperatures for January and July vary slightly throughout the state, the characteristics of Des Moines will serve as an example. The average monthly temperature in Des Moines for January is 21° F.; the July average is 76° F.[6] Summer days with temperatures in the high 90s are common throughout the state. Such temperatures, accompanied by high relative humidity, result in hot, sultry days with little relief at night, unwelcome to man but providing ideal conditions for growing a crop of corn. In winter, temperatures below freezing are common, while severe cold waves and blizzards are less common. Low temperatures are beneficial in one important respect,

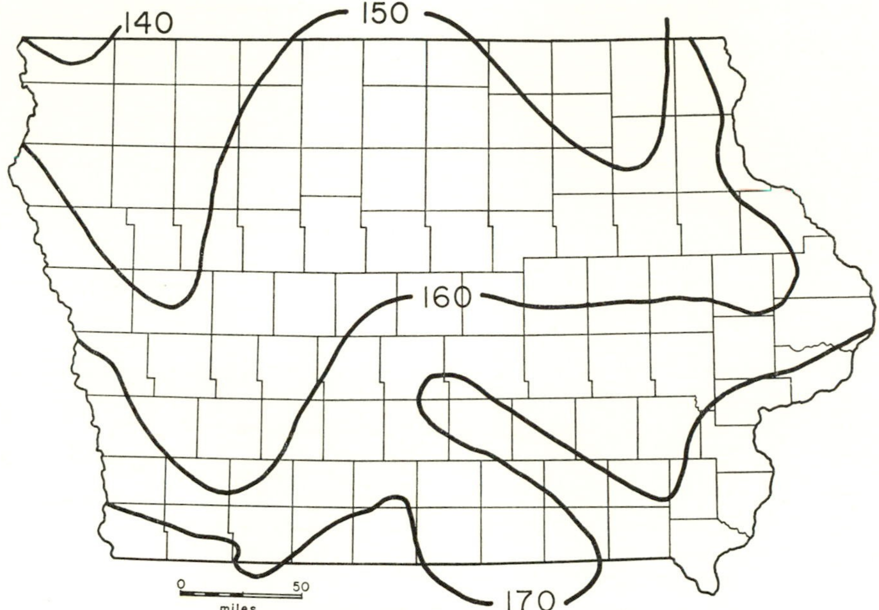

FIG. 1.3. Average number of days without killing frost. (From *Atlas of American Agriculture,* U.S. Government Printing Office, 1936, p. 39.)

however, for during many months the land lies frozen and the soil is neither eroded nor leached.

A map indicating the length of the frost-free season is more easily understood than a lengthy description. (See Figure 1.3.) One hundred and forty days when temperatures are high are ample for corn to mature. Most corn in Iowa will mature in 120 days but a growing season longer than the maturity period may appreciably increase the yield per acre. The date of the last killing frost in spring occurs usually in the two-week period from April 23 to May 7. In the fall the first killing frost generally occurs between October 1 and October 14.[7] Variations occur from year to year and an exceptionally late killing frost in spring or an early killing frost in fall are prospects which disturb the corn farmer's peace of mind. It should be noted that the frost-free period and the length of growing season are not the same for all crops.

Extremes of weather are not unknown in Iowa. A *tornado* or twister, popularly though erroneously called a cyclone, is the most disastrous type of storm during the spring months. Iowa has the dubious honor of having more tornadoes "in proportion to its size than any other state and is second only to Kansas in the total number recorded." Although great devastation takes place along the path of a tornado, property loss in Iowa has been relatively light, "due largely to the fact that no severe tornado has happened to strike any of the larger cities of the state."[8] A heavy snow driven by a strong wind is called a *blizzard,* a word which originated in Iowa.[9] The term is used with some latitude.

SOILS

Most of the pioneers who came to Iowa more than a hundred years ago were attracted by the good soil. Except for outliers of prairie grass in Indiana, Ohio, and Kentucky, the native vegetation of America was a vast deciduous forest extending from the Atlantic Coast to the approximate future boundary of Indiana and Illinois; beyond that line were scattered timber areas. As for Iowa, John Plumbe, Jr., traveler, observer, and author, wrote in 1838 that "probably three-fourths of the Territory is without trees."[10] Although this educated guess is prefaced with the word "probably," it appears to have been one that was reached by a man with a keen eye. Later, more scientific calculations indicate that prairie grass covered 75 to 85 percent of the state, and firmly undergird Plumbe's estimate. (See Figure 1.4.)

The bluestem sod grass association was the dominant type of prairie in Iowa. Big bluestem was common in the valley bottoms where the land was usually moist; little bluestem covered most of the drier hillslopes. Other species of grass and at times a profusion of flowering plants were also a part of this association. It is the height of the grass that is difficult to imagine. To be classified as "tall" grass, the growth must reach a height of five feet; estimates of a height of six to eight feet were common.[11] Such a large percentage of the original prairie has been put under the plow that few acres of native prairie remain. Fortunately, the state has purchased and put under control four sites, and scientific scholars and ecologists are hoping to acquire more examples of unspoiled areas for preservation. The Kalsow Prairie north of Manson has 160 acres which have never been grazed or plowed; Hayden Prairie near Lime Springs has 240 acres which have never been plowed but have been cut for hay. Most of the 160-acre Cayler Prairie just west of Lake Okoboji has never been grazed or plowed, and, like the 25-acre Sheeder Prairie near Guthrie Center, is used regularly by scholars interested in the study of the original prairie vegetation.

Along the rivers the oak-hickory forest was the dominant vegetative type. This forest was composed of various species of oak and hickory, along with some ash, black walnut, elm, and box elder. It has been thought that repeated fires, either the result of lightning or of fires set by Indians to improve the grazing lands, made it impossible for forests to establish themselves on the hilly lands between rivers. In any case the subsurface drainage of water along the floodplains of rivers made

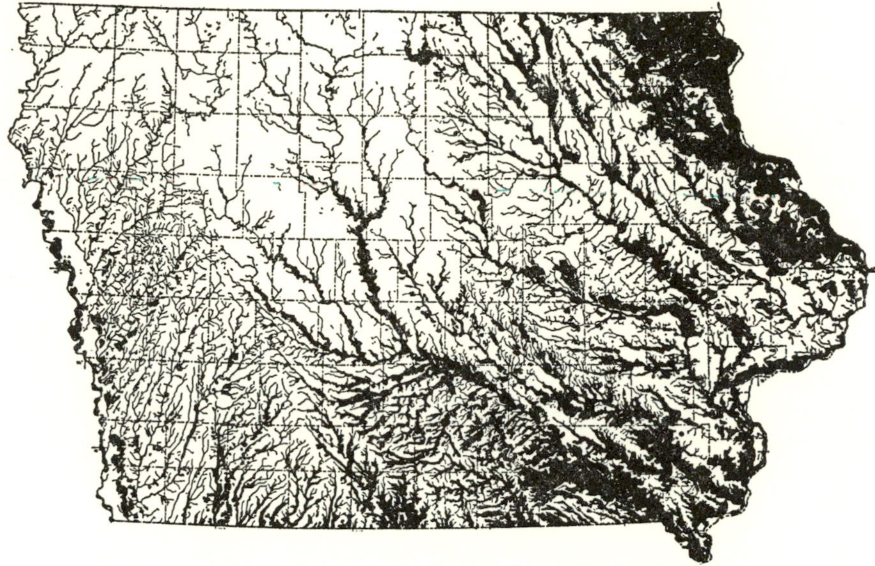

FIG. 1.4. Native vegetation in Iowa. Most of the forests were located along the rivers (area shaded black); the prairie grass covered the rest of the state. (Map courtesy of Iowa Conservation Commission, Des Moines.)

more water available for the forest vegetation than was the case throughout the interfluves of rivers. A forest cover is most often associated with a greater annual rainfall or a greater supply of available water than the amount associated with grass vegetation.

Soil Groups

Allowing for sharp differences of opinion among geologists, it seems safe to date the waning of the Wisconsin glacial epoch at about 8000 B.C. This being the last of the glaciers, it follows that the soils of this area have had about 10,000+ years in which to build themselves—each spring the greening of the prairie, each winter the dying of the grass and other vegetation—a cycle which accounts for the incorporation of the dead matter as humus and the resultant enrichment of the soil. Iowa has been found to possess about 26,000,000 acres of Grade-1 land out of 36,019,000 acres, about one-fourth of all such land in the United States.[12]

Since the climate and the parent materials for soil formation are somewhat uniform throughout the state, the major soil types have marked similarity. A simplified map is given here as indispensable in visualizing the location of the varying soil groups. (See Figure 1.5.)

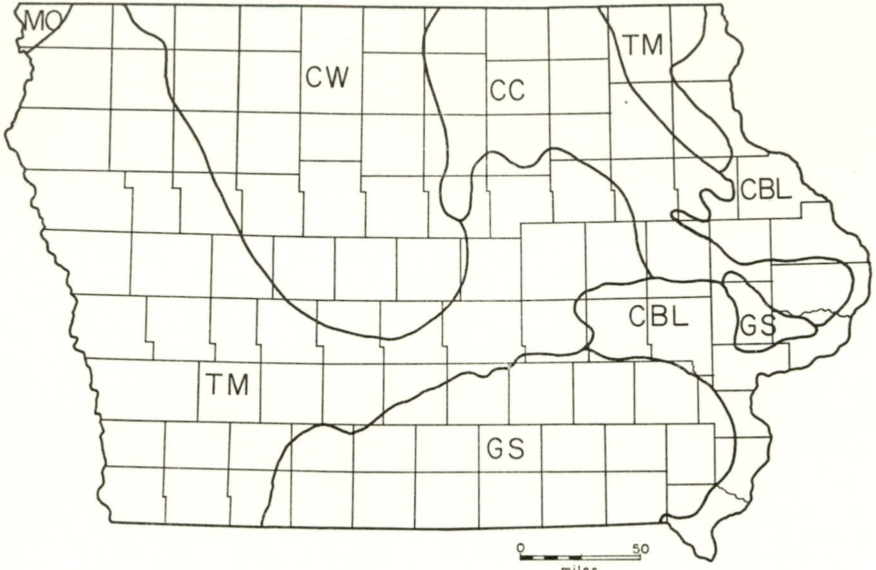

FIG. 1.5. Soils of Iowa. Prairie Soils: CW—Clarion-Webster; TM—Tama-Marshall; CC—Carrington-Clyde. Planosol Soil: GS—Grundy-Shelby. Gray-Brown Podzolic Soil: CBL—Clinton-Boone-Lindley. Chernozem Soil: MO—Moody. (Adapted from the map "Soil Associations of the United States," endpaper in *Soils & Men: Yearbook of Agriculture,* U.S. Government Printing Office, 1938.)

Prairie soils constitute the most familiar type in Iowa, identifiable under three subheads: Clarion-Webster, Tama-Marshall, and Carrington-Clyde. Prairie soils cover a larger portion of the state than any other soil type. These soils developed in moderately humid climates under grass vegetation. The surface layer is deep and rich in humus and nitrogen. They contain a greater amount of the minerals necessary for plant growth than soils which develop under a forest cover. Prairie soils absorb water readily and store water well, and they are easily tilled.

Clarion-Webster soils in Iowa have slightly varying characteristics from the other two, developing as they did on calcareous glacial drift of the late Wisconsin epoch. (Compare Figure 1.5 with Figure 1.1.) Clarion soils occupy the gently rolling hillslopes, while the heavier and blacker Webster soils are found in the more level areas. A considerable area of the Tama-Marshall soils developed on loess that mantles an older glacial drift. These soils are leached of lime carbonates to depths of three feet or more and therefore are slightly acidic in reaction. Carrington-Clyde soils roughly correspond with the eastern part of the early Wisconsin glacial drift. The area abounds in glacial boulders on the surface and in the soil, and the area has more swampy and marshy places than any other in the state.

Planosol soils make up another category. Distinguished by having a well-defined layer of clay or cemented material at depths varying from two to three feet below the surface, the top layer is dark grayish brown or nearly black in color. In Iowa the Grundy-Shelby soils belong to the planosol group. The Grundy soil developed on loess and the Shelby on old glacial drift. Both developed under tall grass vegetation and are consequently rich in humus, but the soil profile is somewhat different from a prairie soil because of the clay layer.

Another type, the gray-brown podzolic soils, has developed under a deciduous forest cover in areas where the annual rainfall ranges from 30 to 37 inches. The amount of humus in these soils is much less than the amount found in prairie soils. Tree roots are obviously not annually incorporated into the humus complex. The forest floor is covered with a thin leaf litter lying on an inch or two of grayish brown humus. Soil reaction is usually medium acidic but the soil responds well to liming. The only example of gray-brown podzolic soils in Iowa is the Clinton-Boone-Lindley area.

The extremely black soil of northwestern Iowa is called *chernozem* soil after the Russian word for black soil, used in the Ukraine to describe their best soil. In the United States this type is found in areas of tall grass vegetation where precipitation ranges from 18 to 26 inches per year. Known in Iowa as the Moody area, it runs from dark brown to almost black in color; it accumulates carbonates at a depth of one to three feet. The lime trait is its principal difference from the Tama-Marshall soils.[13]

AGRICULTURAL AREAS

Iowa is deservedly famous for her corn production, the most important crop in each of the soil areas of the state. One area stands out above all others, the Clarion-Webster soil area, "not surpassed by any other of equal size. . . ."[14] Most of the state is in the Corn Belt but differences within the state warrant division into five agricultural areas. (Figure 1.6.)

Numerous criteria are used for delimiting the areas but the most important is "the basis of soil types." An examination of Figures 1.1, 1.5, and 1.6 reveals a marked similarity between the last two stages of the Wisconsin glacial epoch, the Clarion-Webster soil area, and the large portion named the North Central Grain Area, also called the Cash Grain Area. Because of vast flattish stretches, greater than in any other section of the state, it is ideal for tractor farming. Approximately 85 percent of the total area is in cropland, the most of any agricultural area in the state, and 14 percent is in pasture. Because much of the land is poorly drained, most of it requires heavy tiling to make crop

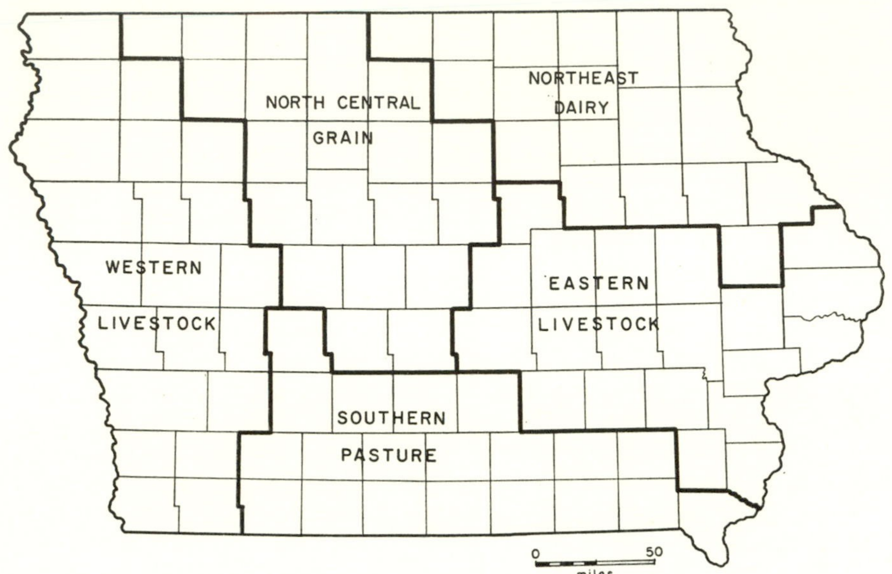

FIG. 1.6. Agricultural areas in Iowa.

production possible, thus furnishing a good illustration of the fact that glacial action alone does not make a good soil. Grain crops will give a greater dollar yield per acre than hay or pasture, thus there is an excess of feed grains for sale and a deficiency of forage. The sale of corn, oats, and soybeans accounts for roughly 30 percent of the farm income, a greater percentage from this source than in any other area of the state, but outstripped by the income from the sale of cattle and hogs, which adds more than 50 percent to the annual regional farm income.

The two areas known as the Western Livestock Area and the Eastern Livestock Area show greater similarity than any other two areas of the state. Slightly more than 70 percent of farm income in the Western Area and more than 80 percent in the Eastern Area are from the sale of livestock and livestock products. In the Western Area the production of beef cattle is more important than the production of hogs, whereas in the Eastern Area the reverse is the case. The ratio of feed grains to pasture, in each area, is about 3 to 1. In the Western Area more feeder cattle are purchased from the grasslands of the Great Plains than in the Eastern Area and a larger percentage of the land is hilly grazing land than in the Eastern Area. In both areas corn occupies approximately 50 percent of the cropland.

The Southern Pasture Area has more hilly terrain than any other section of the state except Northeast Iowa. The hilliest land is commonly devoted to pasture (about 35 percent of the farmland) and to hay crops, since erosion has been and still is a serious problem. Crop yields per acre are lower in this area of the state than in any other, yet the supply of forage feeds and pasture roughly equals the supply of corn, oats, and soybeans. With this balance in livestock feeds, more emphasis is placed on beef cattle than in any other area of the state. In this connection a recent development is the effort to promote a local cow-calf economy to meet the demand for feeder calves. Sheep are raised in the Southern Pasture Area in greater numbers than in any other part of Iowa. Dairying is precluded because the hot dry months of late summer too frequently burn out the pastures.

The Northeast Dairy Area is actually a transitional area between intensive dairying in Minnesota and Wisconsin and the feed grain–livestock farming to the south and west. Much of the hilly terrain is better devoted to pasture and hay crops than to grain crops; any other use would be hazardous. The valleys and the occasional flattish areas are highly productive for corn and small-grain farming. Thus, while dairying is twice as important as in the rest of the state, and has won a name for itself for excellence of product, actually meat production is the leading industry and the chief source of income.

For years Iowa has ranked second to California in the value of farm products sold, yet California is nearly three times as large as Iowa. It may seem incongruous to state that the value of Iowa's agricultural products is worth more each year than all the gold mined in the world each year—yet such is the case. In 1970, for example, Iowa's farm production was valued at $3,929,700,000, while the value of gold mined in that year was estimated at only $1,450,000,000.[15]

WATER RESOURCES: RIVERS

Iowa has been described as "the land between two rivers," the Mississippi and the Missouri satisfying the descriptive phrase. Complete accuracy would require the addition of the Big Sioux as part of the western boundary. Most of the rivers, located in roughly two-thirds of the state, drain into the Mississippi. (Figure 1.7.) Some of these rivers have deepened their channels to bedrock, causing rapids or falls at such places. The tributaries of the Missouri are smaller than those draining into the Mississippi, with relatively fewer falls and rapids. In south central Iowa a small area is drained by the headwaters of tributaries that flow in a southerly direction through the northern part of Missouri and into the Missouri River.[16]

A few enterprising pioneers viewed the falls and rapids on Iowa's rivers as possible sources of power. At the site of a waterfall or rapids, a dam could be built of logs or brush, and rocks. The dam need not be high or the stream large. A head of three or four feet would suffice to furnish power for a sawmill or a gristmill, the two most important

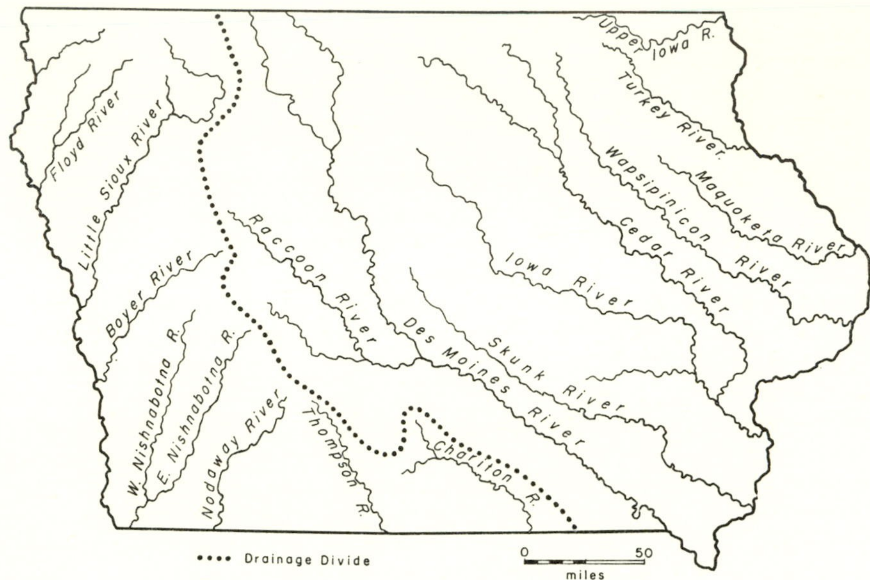

FIG. 1.7. Iowa's major streams. The dotted line is the water divide between the Mississippi River and Missouri River drainage.

users of power in the early days. In modern times the demand for power generated by falls or rapids has decreased but still is appreciable. In 1968 Iowa had fifty-six dams for which licenses from the Iowa Natural Resources Council had been granted. Twenty-three of these were licenses for the production of hydroelectricity but at only twelve sites was electricity being generated. Eleven dams were licensed in the category of electric generation other than hydroelectric (chiefly condenser water), four were licensed to impound water for use in manufacturing, and seven impounded water for a municipal water supply. A few dams have been licensed for river beautification and recreation, the latter use seeming to grow each year.[17]

Periodically one of the rivers in Iowa will flood, causing damage that may run into millions of dollars. The Iowa Natural Resources Council has made a systematic study of the water problems and resources of a number of Iowa's river basins, the first report being published in 1953. These studies have dealt with flood control measures and wise utilization of the available water, including recreational uses. The Corps of Engineers of the United States Army has made similar studies and under its direction a number of federal water resource projects have

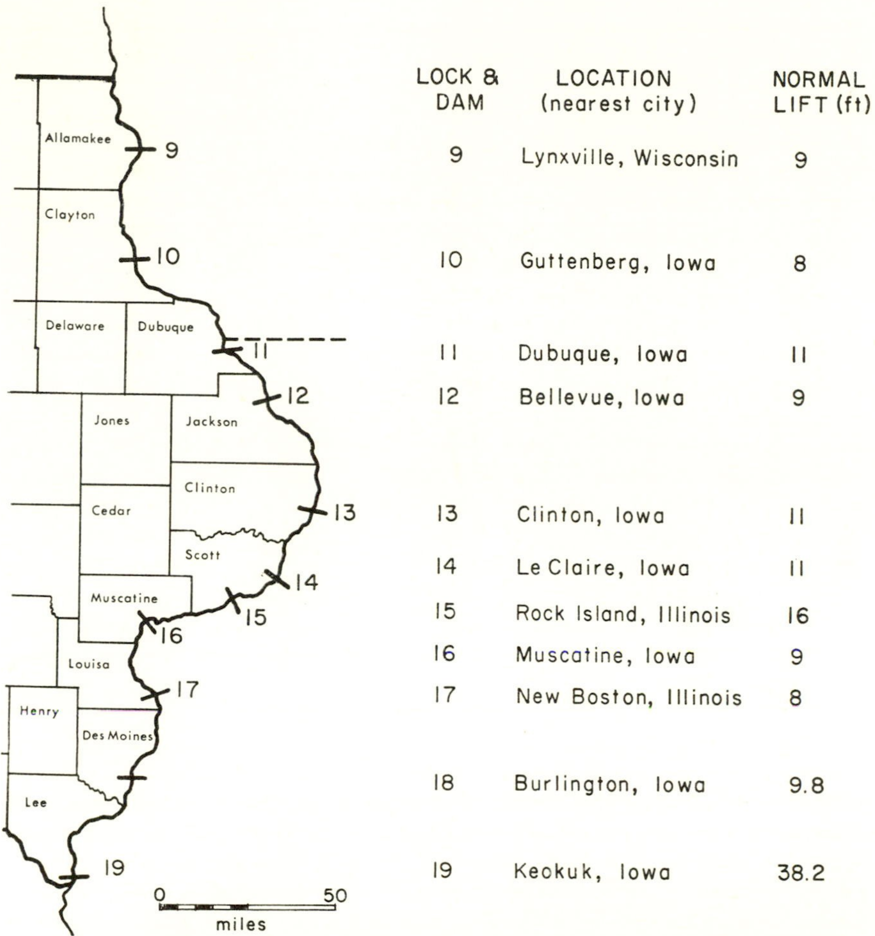

LOCK & DAM	LOCATION (nearest city)	NORMAL LIFT (ft)
9	Lynxville, Wisconsin	9
10	Guttenberg, Iowa	8
11	Dubuque, Iowa	11
12	Bellevue, Iowa	9
13	Clinton, Iowa	11
14	Le Claire, Iowa	11
15	Rock Island, Illinois	16
16	Muscatine, Iowa	9
17	New Boston, Illinois	8
18	Burlington, Iowa	9.8
19	Keokuk, Iowa	38.2

FIG. 1.8. Locks and dams on the Iowa reach of the Mississippi River.

been completed, for example, the Coralville dam on the Iowa River near Iowa City. Others more recently completed are the Red Rock dam on the Des Moines River, near Knoxville, and the Rathbun dam near Centerville, on the Chariton River. Such projects are intended to make Iowa's inland rivers servants rather than masters of the people.[18]

The Mississippi River has long been and still is Iowa's most important water route. The channel has been repeatedly deepened and now a nine-foot channel is in use. Locks and dams have been constructed at a number of points, and dredging, dikes, and revetments assist in maintaining the channel at the proper depth. (See Figure 1.8.) Most notable as an aid to flood control and navigation is the dam at Keokuk, the first to be built on the Upper Mississippi. Construction was authorized in 1905 and its completion in 1913 obliterated the Des Moines River Canal which had been built to circumvent the rapids at the mouth of that river, and which had been in use for thirty-five years. The new lock at Keokuk, completed in 1957, is 1,200 feet long. Here generators produce appreciable amounts of electricity for a vast army of consumers in several states and, additionally, the lock created Lake Keokuk, a recreational area serving people in at least three states.

The Missouri River has long been a problem river. Because of the floods and the meandering course, the river changed its channel often, causing many boundary problems, particularly between Nebraska and Iowa. A series of dams along the river's course in South Dakota, North Dakota, and Montana will permit an even flow of water and a stabilized channel; beneficial effects have already been felt from this gigantic project. Utilizing a channel of nine feet, barges laden with coal, gasoline, molasses, and fertilizer chemicals make the upward journey; grain shipments make up the bulk of the downstream traffic. This increase of river business has done much to bring a new prosperity to towns and cities along the once unreliable course of "Big Muddy," Sioux City being a special beneficiary of the new commerce.[19]

MINERALS

Any treatment of the topic of a state's land and its contents must include a reference, positive or negative, to the mineral resources. The treatment for Iowa can be positive though brief. Lead mining was once considered very important in a small area around Dubuque, long before a city by that name was founded. This field was an extension of the principal deposits in southwestern Wisconsin and northwestern Illinois.[20] Coal was once an important item but now is virtually an extinct business except in a few counties. Gypsum is mined in the Fort Dodge area out of four open mines, and certain clays in the Mason City area are suitable for the manufacture of cement. Limestone deposits were of great value to the pioneers for use in public buildings, dams, and occasionally in home building. Gypsum and cement are the principal current items in the production and sale of mineral products. In 1970 the value of all Iowa minerals sold was $121,000,000, compared with $3,929,700,000 derived from agriculture in the same year.

PREHISTORIC MAN

Those pioneers who moved into Iowa through Ohio, Indiana, Illinois, or Wisconsin, would probably have seen many mounds left by pre-

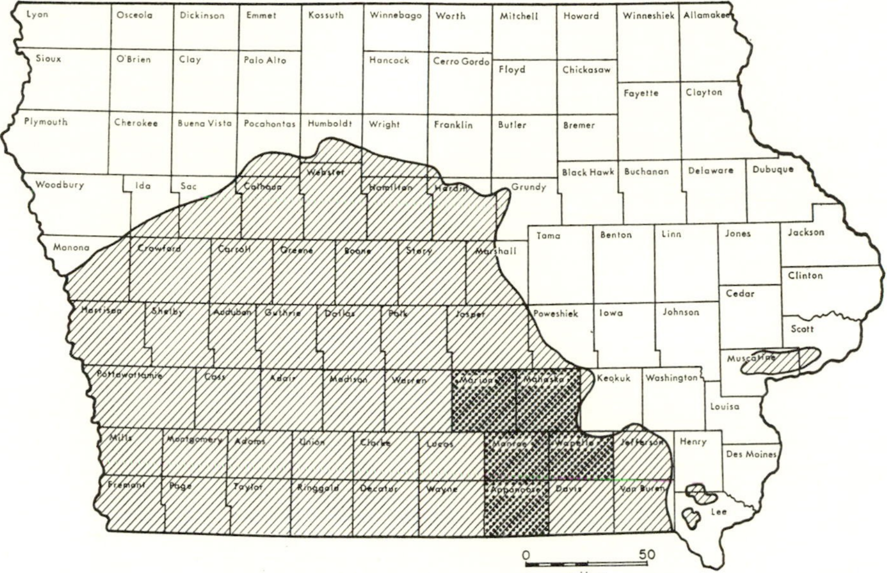

FIG. 1.9. Area underlain by coal (shaded area) and the five coal-producing counties (stippled area).

historic man, including some built as late as the seventeenth century. Crossing the Mississippi, they would have found in Iowa additional though not so many examples of these curious structures. The easy assumption made by the pioneers—and by some men who posed as "scientists" at that time—was that a race of "Mound Builders" of mysterious origin, related to some lost race of antiquity, and much superior to the Indians of the nineteenth century, had built the mounds. Preoccupied as they were with the problem of their own survival, the early settlers took little more than a casual interest in the culture of the people who had lived in "Iowaland" before them. To them a mound was an obstacle, to be destroyed with a plow in a few minutes; if not destroyed, its contents were disarranged so that scientific study would be impaired or made impossible.

Later, study by professional (and amateur) archeologists has led to the rejection of the concept of Mound Builders as the name of a race of prehistoric men. At present, if we may greatly simplify this highly technical subject, scientists regard all North American Indians, including "mound builders," as descendants of the race of men who came from Asia by crossing the Bering Sea at its narrowest point, and over a period of thousands of years spread out over much of the American continent. This migration began about 30,000 years ago, give or take 10,000–20,000

FIG. 1.10. The Pleasant Ridge Group of effigies is located in the south unit of Effigy Mounds National Monument. This group is composed of ten bear mounds (each about 3 feet high and 80 to 100 feet long), three bird effigies, and two linear mounds. (Effigy Mounds National Monument pamphlet, National Park Service, Washington, D.C., 1964.)

years, according to one's source. The name of Paleo-Indians is given to the first known, nomadic hunters and food-gatherers of about 10,000 years ago; next were the ones whom we call Archaic Indians, men of about 8000–1000 B.C., who were moving up to the food-producing stage. Next came the mound builders, about 1000 B.C. up to A.D. 1700, in several subdivisions such as burial mound builders, temple mound builders, and effigy mound builders.[21]

Authorities disagree on the exact order and dating of the cultures which occupied Iowa. In 1938 a distinguished student of Iowa archeology listed five distinct "archeological manifestations" in Iowa: the Woodland, the Hopewell, the Glenwood, the Mill Creek, and the Oneota

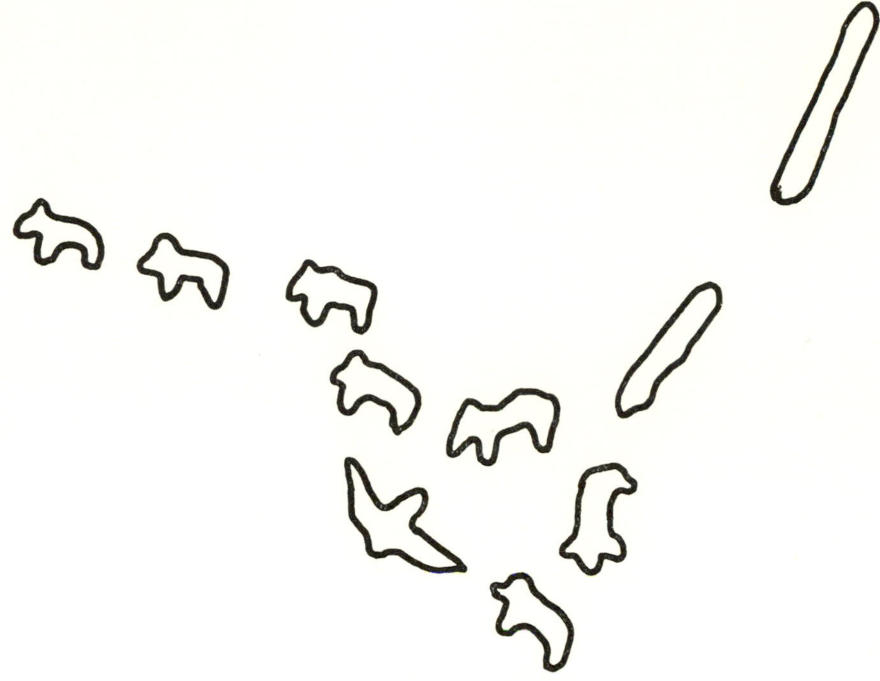

(Upper Iowa). More recent writers seem to prefer to list the Hopewell culture, which originated near Chillicothe, Ohio, as "Middle Woodland," and one writer elevates it to "Woodland-Hopewell co-tradition." It is assigned to a time period of about 200 B.C.–A.D. 400. Generalizing very broadly, one may say that the Woodland and the Oneota are found rather generally over the state; the Hopewell is found along the Mississippi; the Glenwood in Mills County; and the Mill Creek near Cherokee.

It was in the seventeenth century that the line was crossed between prehistoric and historic times in Iowa; the Oneota was at that time the predominant culture; and the Indians in Iowa in the Oneota period were the Ioway and the Oto, chiefly the former.[22]

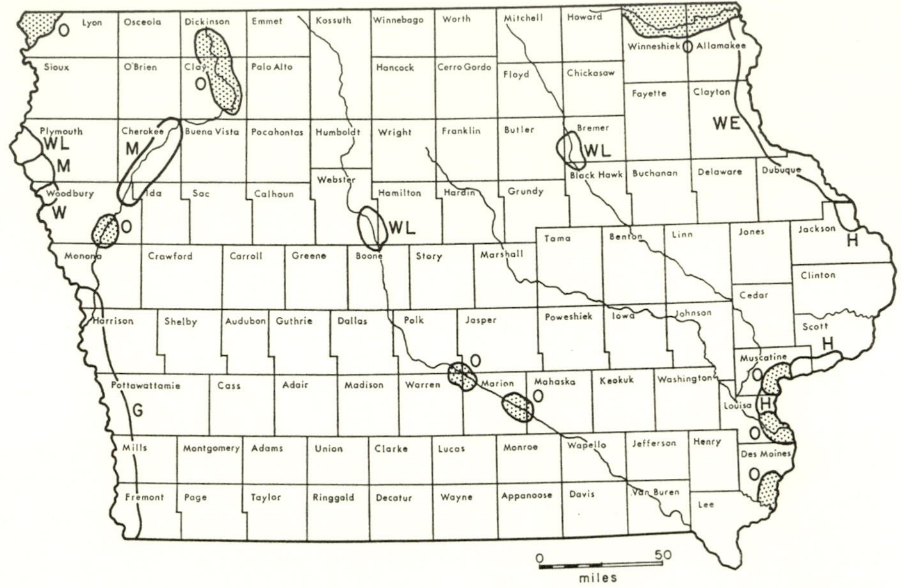

FIG. 1.11. Locations of prehistoric cultures in Iowa (Adapted from maps by Mott and Ruppé.) The areas of the dominant Oneota are stippled for contrast with the less prominent cultures in Iowa.

O–Oneota W–Woodland (statewide)
M–Mill Creek WL–Woodland (linear mounds)
G–Glenwood WE–Woodland (effigy mounds)
H–Hopewell

CHAPTER 2 IOWALAND: INDIAN, FRENCH, SPANISH, AMERICAN 1673-1803

STUDENTS OF INDIAN HISTORY HAVE COUNTED SEVENTEEN TRIBES who occupied land in Iowa's limits at some time in the seventeenth and eighteenth centuries, only a few of whom had any meaningful contact with Iowa as a land or with Iowa's people. This select list would have to begin with the Ioway and add the Sauk and Fox, the Potawatomi, the Winnebago, and the Sioux. The time of their arrival in Iowa cannot be stated with exactness because of the wanderlust inherent in their mixed hunting and agricultural system. Neither can their numbers be more than guessed at. French travelers' estimates, somewhat retrospective, ranged all the way from 1,000 to 8,000 for the Ioway-Oto tribes,[1] a spread so elastic as to be meaningless. Of this we may be fairly certain: when Jolliet and Marquette made their historic journey down the Mississippi, they paddled for many days before they saw any Indians—and these were Illinois (Peorias), merely over-the-river visitors engaged in a hunting expedition.

THE IOWAY

If the French explorers had made inland journeys, they would almost certainly have encountered the Indians known to us as the Ioway, later known by the accepted modern spelling of the state's name, Iowa. According to the best evidence, they came into the future Iowa from the Illinois country and lived in the Upper Iowa River region, later wandering or being driven into the Lake Okoboji area, on into the pipestone country of southwestern Minnesota, southward along the Missouri to the Platte, eastward into Missouri, and northward into the Des Moines River valley. Such movements can be traced only with approximation, not exactness. Allusions to the Ioway appear in the journals of French travelers and imperial officials. At the end of the century, we find mention of an Ioway chieftain named Mauhawgaw, the father of Mahaska (White Cloud), the most famous of all Ioways, whose wife was the beautiful Rantchewaime.

Far from being the largest or most powerful tribe in the annals of Iowa, the Ioway officially closed their Iowa sojourn in 1838 when they sold their lands between the Mississippi and the Missouri rivers and south of the line assigned to the Sioux and Sauk and Fox as a dividing line in 1825, plus all the lands they had claimed under the treaties of 1824, 1830, and 1836. In spite of their lackluster record as an occupying power in the seventeenth century when they controlled all of Iowa except the small areas occupied by the Oto, and despite their declining strength at the time of their departure from Iowa, Iowans must take some interest in this tribe because presumably here is the source of the name of the state. The name appears in a bewildering variety of spellings and uncertain pronunciations: Pahoutet, Paoutet, derived from Pahutchae, meaning "Dusty Faces" or "Dusty Noses," the name the Ioway gave to themselves; Aiaoia, Aioinouea, Ayoes, Ayavois, Ayubha, Ayuez, Ayauway, Ayouway, Iowai, Ioway—and, at last, simply Iowa,[2] which in turn can be pronounced in many ways. Nothing could be more uncertain and really meaningless than speculation on the meaning of the word to the natives. Suffice it to say that the name has been traced to the river which bears the name, and from that to the Ioway Indians who gave their name to the river, presumably because it was their favorite residence. Such an explanation requires an exercise of great faith. In view of the wide travels of these people, who can assure us that the Iowa was their preferred river or place of residence? If so, at what spot? How does one explain the source of the name Iowa for a county in the Territory of Michigan, and later in the Territory of Wisconsin when that entity was lopped off from Michigan? The name was used there long before it was given any widesepread use in Iowa and it is still in use today.

OTHER INDIAN TRIBES

The Sauk and Fox Indians, of the Algonquian language division, are closely identified with Iowa's history, more so than the Ioway. They were originally and always remained independent tribes which became federated but not united, in or just before 1735, in the face of a French threat to their existence. The French had pursued them across the Mississippi, intending to punish them for the murder of some minor officials. Their objective in federating was a more efficient defense system; the arrangement represents an advanced form of political and social planning not often found in Indian tribal government.

Their original home was in Wisconsin; they moved to Iowa near the turn of the eighteenth century by way of northwest Illinois. Their first important venture into history was their involvement in a conference held at St. Louis in 1804 where five of their chiefs joined others in signing a momentous treaty, repudiated by their war chief, Black Hawk, which ceded their residential lands east of the Mississippi and some hunting grounds on the west side to the United States. The most famous Sauk chieftains were Appanoose; Pashepaho; Keokuk, whose exaggerated nickname of "The Watchful Fox" misleads the unwary; and Black Hawk, technically a war chief rather than a full-fledged tribal chief, but more influential than any other leader. The Fox chiefs of greatest fame were Poweshiek, Taimah, and Wapello. By the time Chief Keokuk had risen to supremacy over the federation in the 1820s, the Fox who followed his leadership were more inclined toward cooperation with the white settlers and with white authority than were the Sauk, resulting in the weakening of the alliance.[3]

The most virile, warlike, and indomitable of all the Indians who spent some time on Iowa soil were the Dakotas, better known as the Sioux. More definitely associated with Wisconsin, Minnesota, and the Dakotas than with Iowa, they hunted and fought their way across southern Minnesota and northern Iowa. This powerful tribe was divided into several subtribes, the most important in Iowa being the Santee, the Sisseton, and the Wahpeton. Their residence here began in the early 1700s but their significant Iowa contacts began in the 1830s, coinciding with the first advances of the white man across the Great River, bringing about an almost inevitable confrontation at many places, with dire consequences for both peoples. They were the last Indians to make treaties surrendering Iowa soil to the United States.[4]

Among other tribes of some prominence in Iowa history, mostly in the nineteenth century, were the Winnebago, brought from their home in Wisconsin as unhappy wards of the United States to the Neutral Ground in northeast Iowa. Once numerous and powerful, they lost out completely before the aggressions of the whites in Wisconsin and degenerated into a poverty-stricken condition. In the eyes of the whites they became a troublesome and almost obnoxious set of neighbors, with a reputation for thieving and begging. Even so, the tribal name and the names of some of their leaders have been chosen as badges of honor by Iowa towns and counties, notably Chief Waukon-Decorah and Chief Winneshiek.[5]

The Potawatomi (modernized as Pottawattomie) have a story which has points of similarity with the Winnebago experience. Of Algonquian stock, they originated in the Lake Michigan region and gradually moved westward. They probably did not suffer as much at the hands of the whites as did the Winnebago but they too were forced to leave their homelands in the 1830s. The national government settled them on lands in the western part of the future Iowa and built a fort south of Fort Atkinson (Fort Croghan) to house their protectors. After a few years of fruitless effort, during which the Belgian Jesuit missionary,

Father Pierre-Jean de Smet, labored to teach them and to convert them to Christianity, the experiment in "protection" was given up in 1847 and the Potawatomi were moved to Kansas, probably unregretted then but honored later by the choice of their name for the second largest county in the state.[6]

Other Indians who had some connection with Iowa, however brief and fleeting, were the Otoes, Pawnees, and Missouris, who should be listed if for no other reason than to clarify reference to them by various travelers in the Iowa region and by the explorers Lewis and Clark. While they undoubtedly hunted throughout southern, central, and western Iowa, their chief habitat was west of the Missouri River. The Otoes deserve special mention because of their inclusion with the Iowa(y) in the Oneota archeological record. Some of the members of the Illinois Confederation, the Ottawa-Huron, Miami-Wea, Kitchigama, Kickapoo, and Chippewa, all had fleeting contacts with the lands on this side of the Mississippi.[7]

Thus we see that actually very few Indians lived in Iowa's future boundaries before the time of the Louisiana Purchase. Any notion that the land was lived on by Indians in some regular and consistent pattern, as our farms or timber and mineral preserves today fill in a given area in shoulder-to-shoulder fashion, must be abandoned as unrealistic. On the contrary, the life style of the Woodlands and Plains Indians was in natural conflict with the concept of a closed, settled country. The Indian life style was based on the institution of the seasonal hunt, an event to be looked toward and prepared for throughout the year. If these seasonal ventures, which in large part determined the good or bad standard of living for a given tribe of Indians, came into conflict with similar plans of other tribes, warfare was the usual result, a fact of life so commonplace that fighting seemed to be the real vocation of most tribes. The intervals between hunts were short periods of sedentary life to allow the squaws to engage in women's work of gardening, harvesting, and preservation of the produce, and looking after the creature comforts, such as they were, of all members of the tribe. Just as the medieval European manor was economically based on the idea of supporting as many armed knights on horseback as possible, so the Indian economy was built around the idea of supporting as many armed and mounted braves as possible.

In a society whose economy was based on such complete dependence on nature, the one thing to be desired above all else was an open and free country in which animal life of the forest and plain, river and lake, and wild fruits, nuts, and herbs in the wooded areas, could multiply in abundance to reward the hunter and food-gatherer. If ever the Indians became totally a food-providing instead of a food-gathering people, by learning to control the soil and domesticate the animals, a revolution would have been wrought which would have changed the entire pattern of Indian-white relations. Such a development was not in sight in the seventeenth or eighteenth centuries.

The first white men who came in as businessmen, that is, as trappers and fur traders, did not want to change the Indian social system, strange as this statement may sound to modern ears. If these trappers and traders were to flourish, there must be two worlds: one, the wild and free country which could produce peltries, which would be their stock in trade; the other, the world of consuming society which could purchase their offerings. The Indian was not *their* enemy, as he was to later generations of American settlers of the West; on the contrary, the Indian was their associate in business. Of course, such a limited social and economic system could not long endure against the oncoming rush of the white settlers.

Certain hard facts about Indian life should be noticed. Within the tribe their existence was peaceful, happy, and full of harmony. After allowances are made for superficial differences created by time and place, one is more impressed by similarities than differences between their attitude toward the problems of social living and ours. Home and family life were central to their scheme of existence as they are to ours. Husbands and wives followed a definite plan of division of labor, a plan which at first glance seems unfair to the wives but which is defensible when all things are considered. Children yielded obedience and received instruction up to a recognized period in their lives. Their "schools" and methods of instruction were probably superior to ours in terms of results obtained. Their religious thought was not as complex, far-reaching, and subtle as ours, but it dealt with their problems of personal living and gave them a sense of satisfaction.

As noted above, a regrettable feature of their lives was the vast amount of intertribal warfare before the coming of the white man. What would have been the outcome of all this fighting, if uninhibited by the whites, cannot be said with assurance. Perhaps "superior" and "inferior" rankings would have asserted themselves, and "master" and "slave" rankings would have become commonplace. Second, it is agreed that a weakness for whisky was a greater factor in Indian deterioration than any other force. Finally, warfare between Indians and whites was the extreme form of adjustment between the conflicting forces, whose relations were ordinarily peaceful.[8]

EUROPEAN CONTACT WITH "IOWA"

Jolliet and Marquette

The dominance of the trans-Mississippi lands by the Ioway and other Indian tribes was challenged in the late seventeenth century. On

June 17, 1673—or June 15, according to respectable authority—Louis Jolliet, a woodsman, trapper, explorer, and mapmaker, and Father Jacques Marquette, S.J., a priest-missionary in the service of God and country, and their five companions moved out of the Wisconsin River into the broad Mississippi. For the first time in recorded history the land of the future state of Iowa was brought under the gaze of men of European descent. The sphere of influence of "New France" had now been extended nearly a thousand miles from Quebec and some four thousand miles from Paris.

More important than the details of time and place is the question of motivation, though never completely answerable. Why was Jolliet sent to this region? Many writers present the story as an example of an explorer's personal desire to find an unknown river and to follow the urge to build up a trade in furs, at best, an incomplete explanation. It was a government project, though financed as a private profit-making venture. Mere curiosity about a fabled river, even one which reputedly led to the South Seas and China, hardly satisfies one's sense of realism. As for an increased fur trade, there was no shortage of furs; in some years there was a surplus, and the immediate sources of supply were more than adequate for the time being. Yet these are the points on which historians have harped since Francis Parkman, that master of romantic history, set the pattern.

Recent scholars, using a method and a line of reasoning unknown to Parkman, have opened up a totally new approach to the subject. In their analysis,[9] New France was the object of much study and thought on the part of Louis XIV after he took over the direction of his empire in 1663, and even greater study on the part of Jean-Baptiste Colbert, his Minister of Marine. Remarkably well informed and possessed of a realistic understanding of a land which he knew only by report, Colbert had very definite ideas about the kind of colony he wanted New France to be: a small, compact, but viable part of a mercantilistic French Empire now scattered from Canada to India, an empire whose goal was self-sufficiency.

The weakness of New France as a part of the French Empire in the seventeenth century was that its local economy was much too narrow, in spite of the efforts of Colbert and his ambitious intendant, Jean Talon, to broaden its base. The fur trade was out of balance as compared with agriculture, timbering, mining, and fishing. In short, Quebec was built on a one-crop economy, the fur trade, and this was an inadequate basis for an importing and exporting unit within the French Empire or for supporting a well-rounded society. Such a society could not furnish recruits for the imperial army and navy, use French currency on a large scale, pay heavy taxes into the French royal treasury, and in a thousand ways fit itself into a worldwide political and economic organization.

The empire grew, and Quebec grew, in spite of Colbert's policy. The bonds of his tightly knit colony along the St. Lawrence were broken down by far-ranging fur traders and by explorers and missionaries who were braving the unknown, bringing back stories of their findings and of claims which they had made in the name of France. Jean Nicolet had gone as far as the present site of Green Bay in 1634; in 1641 the Jesuits had planted a mission and given it a name which was destined to become famous, Sault Sainte Marie; Father Claude Allouez had established a mission on Chequamegon Bay in Lake Superior, where he also acted as a copper scout for the officials at Quebec; Grosseilliers and Radisson, the most daring of all, had gone all the way to what is now Minnesota; in 1671 Daumont St. Lusson and Nicolas Perrot had met with representatives of fourteen tribes at Sault Sainte Marie and claimed all their lands for Louis XIV, and then cavalierly handed back the whole lot in exchange for a pile of beaver skins. Every explorer brought back information based on what he had heard as well as what he had seen. Most exciting of all were the reports and descriptions of a great river somewhere to the west, by the name of Michisippi or some variation thereof. Father Claude Dablon, the superior of the Jesuits, had heard so much and in such detail that in 1670 he was able to compile a fairly good description of the Mississippi River without having ever seen it!

Other pressures were forcing the French out of their narrow confines. The English had managed to plant themselves on both sides of the French settlements, a situation which the French could never allow to stand unchallenged. On the north, English outposts were on Hudson Bay; on the south, they had displaced the Dutch in the Hudson River valley from Manhattan to Albany. As if these flanking operations were not enough, there was constant danger from the Iroquois. The French had two alternatives: they could try to defeat the English and their Iroquois allies, and drive them away entirely, or they could fight a holding action and at the same time expand their own territory to the west and south of the Lakes. If the latter strategy could be successfully employed, the English could be pinned against the Atlantic seaboard and a co-existence policy might be possible.

The end of Colbert's rigid policy of a tight, compact colony around Quebec and Montreal was in sight. He had always allowed for two exceptions to his policy: (1) other lands were subject to seizure if there was danger of their falling into the hands of an enemy nation, thereby hurting French trade; (2) any possibility of the discovery of an ice-free route into New France was always welcome. A leading historian of the subject states: "Ironically, it was Colbert himself who allowed the floodgates to French western expansion to be opened."[10] If this reasoning is correct, the Jolliet expedition to the country beyond the Lakes was not merely a quest for a mysterious river nor an effort to increase the fur trade, nor were the explorations of his contemporary, La Salle, so intended. Jolliet and his coexplorers in the king's service were advance agents of imperialism. They were helping their country multiply its resources, promoting better relations with the Indians, and, if the plans for an expanded and strengthened empire worked out, contributing to the policy of containment of the hated English along the eastern seaboard. This is not to deny the importance of looking for a great river or enlarging the fur trade; it is merely to enlarge the frame of reference and put the matter in a more significant setting.

The role of the intendant of New France, Jean Talon, in planning and sponsoring the exploratory expedition headed by Louis Jolliet has not been sufficiently noticed. All too many writers and others have given the impression that Jolliet was a volunteer, self-directed explorer, and many have erroneously given Father Jacques Marquette equal or superior billing as an actor in the drama of the expedition. Actually, Talon selected Jolliet as one who had won local fame as a woodsman and mapmaker. Forced to finance his own trip, Jolliet formed a profit-sharing company and out of the list of partners selected five men to be his companions and boatmen on the voyage.[11] A seventh person was to be a priest-missionary, a customary provision on most French and Spanish exploratory ventures. Father Jacques Marquette, S.J., then stationed at St. Ignace, was the man selected by his immediate superior, Father Claude Dablon, head of the Jesuit order in Quebec. A man of undoubted zeal and great devotion to his calling, and a master of several Indian languages, he eagerly accepted the call to serve with Jolliet.

On May 17, 1673, Jolliet and his six companions pushed off from St. Ignace, Father Marquette alternating as a passenger on the two barks. Going around the northern shore of Lake Michigan, then south into Green Bay, on to the mouth of the Fox River in the present city of Green Bay, the route can be followed on the accompanying map. (Figure 2.1.) Up to this point it was the very same route followed by Jean Nicolet in 1634. Venturing into the Fox River took courage, although Nicolet had dared to do it on his memorable journey. Threading their way onward, they came to a point where the river became very shallow. Friendly Indians of the Mascouten (Muscatine) tribe gave information to Jolliet, some of it inaccurate, and others of the Miami tribe were there to guide the party over a portage of a short distance (through present-day Portage, Wisconsin, of course), 2,700 paces by Father Marquette's reckoning, 1.28 miles by modern measurement, and then out onto the waters of the Meskouing (Wisconsin) River. The date of departure was recorded as June 14, 1673. When they came to the Great River, with its enormous bluffs covered with magnificent foliage, it was "with a joy I cannot express," in the words attributed to Father Marquette. The now-accepted date is June 17, 1673, though some have figured it as June 15, a figure which would invalidate June 14 as the departure date.[12]

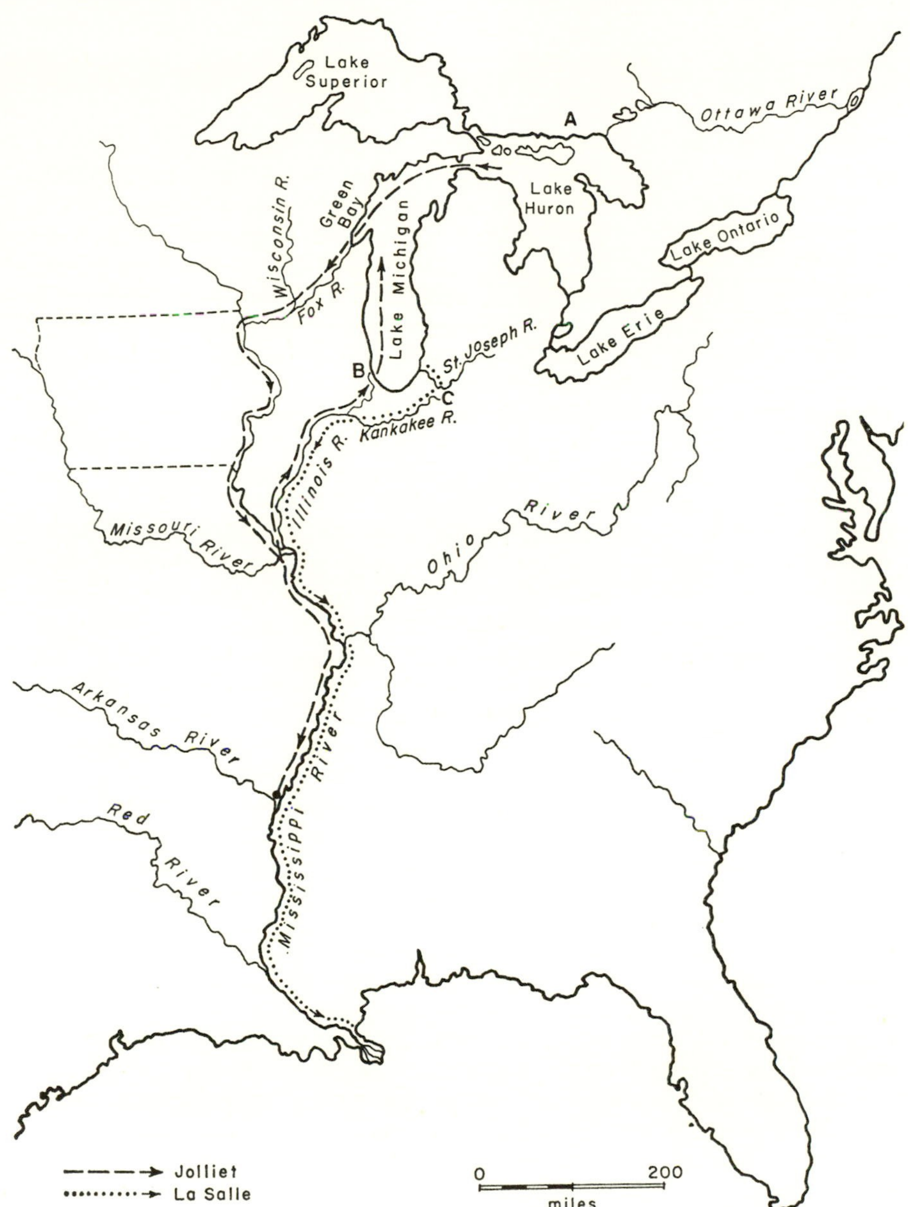

FIG. 2.1. This map shows the routes used by Jolliet and Marquette on their journey to the Mississippi, southward to their turning point (Arkansas River), and return by way of the Illinois and Des Plaines rivers, the Chicago Portage, and Lake Michigan. In addition, it shows the route used by La Salle on his journey in 1682.

Key to the letters on the map:

A–Indicates without detail the portage complex of the Mattawa River, Lake Nipissing, the French River, and Georgian Bay, portages used by all travelers, including Jolliet and Marquette, going from Montreal to the Lake Michigan–Green Bay area.

B–The Chicago Portage.

C–The portage between the St. Joseph and Kankakee rivers, used by La Salle.

The "land across the river," as it seemed to the French explorers, could now appear on accepted maps, by implication a part of the French Empire. But Jolliet's instructions called for exploration of the destination of the river. Apparently making the trip south by slow stages, considering that they had the current with them, Louis Jolliet and Father Marquette went ashore on June 25, a date to be taken on faith but long since proclaimed as the official date of the first European presence on Iowa soil. Once presumed to be at the mouth of the Des Moines River by Marquette's reckoning, modern opinion holds that the landing was at the mouth of the Iowa River, near a spot known today as Toolesboro.[13] Attracted, so the story goes, by the discovery of footprints in the mud, the leaders were eager to see the owners of these markings. After walking several miles inland, the two men came upon Indians of the family known as Peorias, of the Illinois or Illini tribe, who treated them with great kindness.

After prolonged council meetings with their generous hosts, the two men returned to the river and led their party farther south. After narrow escapes from hostile Indians, and many a close call from disaster on the treacherous river, they finally reached a point where a large tributary, known to us as the Arkansas, emptied into the Great River. By this time they were convinced that they had solved the mystery of their river, that it led only to the Gulf of Mexico, not to the South Sea and to Cathay; furthermore, they heard that the mouth of the river was in the hands of their hated enemies, the Spanish. Rather than risk death at the hands of either the Spanish or Indians more hostile than any so far met, Jolliet reluctantly gave up the plan to go to the mouth of the river and set about the return journey. He boldly changed the route by following the Illinois River to the Des Plaines, then a portage to the Chicago River and on into the waters of Lake Michigan; then north to Sturgeon Bay and by portage to the friendly waters of Green Bay. Near the present town of De Pere, Father Marquette left the party to go to the St. Xavier Mission while Jolliet and some others went on to Sault Sainte Marie for the winter, which he spent in studying and amplifying his notes and making a copy for safekeeping at the Jesuit Mission there.

The following spring (1674) Jolliet set out for Quebec. In the dangerous waters of the Ottawa River, almost at the end of his journey, his canoe capsized. Jolliet alone of his crew was saved; the metal chest containing his notes and maps was lost along with all other mementoes of his trip. Thus it was that the most authentic evidence of this historic expedition of thousands of miles, fraught with meaning for the future, was lost. By a matching stroke of misfortune, even the copy or copies which Jolliet had left in deposit at Sault Sainte Marie were destroyed in a fire. As a consequence of these two mishaps, Jolliet's description of the trip rests upon the notes and maps reconstructed from memory and from oral testimony which he could put into the records at Quebec on affidavit.

As for Father Marquette, because of the physical exhaustion after the ordeal of the journey and the illness resulting from an abused digestive system, and because of the priority he gave to a return mission to the Illinois country, his records were not immediately turned over to his superiors. Many historians, though not all, think that the account of the Mississippi expedition attributed to him was not wholly his own but an ensuing reconstruction of his notes by his superior, Father Dablon. For this reason and others, a bitter dispute has raged and still smolders, principally among Jesuit historians, as to Marquette's place in history.[14]

Beyond cavil is the superb spectacle of the seven men against the unknown, breaking down the barriers of time, space, and uncertainty, yet a few summary comments may be in order. First, the definition of the relationship between Jolliet and Father Marquette should be reinforced. Louis Jolliet was the undisputed commander and leader of the expedition—only sentiment or a lack of realism could create the image of the two as leaders with equal authority, much less mention Marquette in the first place. Second, the whole Jolliet-Marquette story, like the Columbus story, is beset with uncertainties, vagueness, and unanswerable questions. The uncertain timetable of key dates, left in uncertainty because of the failure to keep an official logbook, or the loss of same; the lack of complete certainty about the exact place of landfall in Iowa; the loss of Jolliet's records; the debate over Father Marquette's journal, which at best has to be corrected as to the measurement of distances—all these create annoying problems in the assessment of historical evidence. Still another question is whether Jolliet officially took possession in the name of France of the lands which he "discovered" in 1673.[15] Nevertheless, despite the eventual failure of France's North American imperial policy, this is an important chapter in French history—and thus to Iowa.

La Salle's Claims for France

It was left to another to make the first formal claim to the Mississippi Valley: Robert Cavelier, Sieur de la Salle, better known to history simply as La Salle, a man whose great vanity and ambition were not matched by ability and character; indeed, even his sanity has been questioned. La Salle was chosen as an explorer by Talon's successor as the governor of New France, Count Frontenac. The wreck of La Salle's ship, the *Griffon,* and other difficulties consumed two years of precious time and threw the whole undertaking into jeopardy. At last, in 1682, he was able to leave Fort Miami on the St. Joseph, make it to the Illinois River, then to the Mississippi and finally to the Gulf of Mexico, the first on record to go from Canada to the Gulf and make a northern entrance into that body of water. On the basis of his exploits, La Salle hoisted the French flag and claimed the river and its valley for France, giving the area the meaningful name of Louisiana in honor of Louis XIV, who had supplied the financial and moral support necessary for success.[16] The French now had their vastly expanded empire. Under their rule, other places—not Iowa—became centers of French power, wealth, and culture. In view of the eventual importance of Prairie du Chien as Wisconsin's second oldest settlement, it was Iowa's special misfortune that this important French outpost was not located on the Iowa side of the river; it might have become the first white settlement on Iowa soil.

The apparent though not real indifference of the French to their trans-Mississippi claims can be explained in three words: wars of imperialism. The French were simply overwhelmed with their commitments elsewhere. The early wars of imperialism must be passed over here. The student of Iowa history cannot ignore, however, the results of two wars: the Seven Years' War (1756–1763), and the War of the American Revolution. The ultimate meaning of these wars reaches to the Iowa country. By their victories the British gained a great advantage in the struggle for global domination then in progress, even though the French were shrewd enough to make a secret transfer of their lands west of the Mississippi to Spain in 1762 to prevent their falling into British hands, a transfer publicly acknowledged in the Treaty of Paris in 1763. A final decision as to possession of the lands between the Alleghenies and the Mississippi was postponed, but it was clear that either the British or their successors, either as conquerors or natural heirs, would control its settlement. The fate of Iowa was involved to this extent: the final owners of the trans-Allegheny lands would most likely be the eventual owners of the trans-Mississippi lands as well.

"Iowa" during Spanish Control over the West

If signs of French cultural impact on Iowa are scarce, those of Spanish relation are even harder to find. Three large land grants were made but there were no associations with Spanish culture. One grant was to Julien Dubuque, a French-Canadian, who in 1785 came into the lead-mining country of northern Illinois, southwestern Wisconsin, and Dubuque County, Iowa (to use their modern names for purposes of clear identification), and soon established himself as a business tycoon in mining and trading. By making virtual slaves out of Indian women and old men of the Fox tribe, he prospered as only a monopolist can prosper; his trading activities went as far south as St. Louis and as far north as Prairie du Chien. In 1796 he secured from the Spanish government at St. Louis a document which he took to be a legal grant for thousands of acres of land. Later, he fell on to bad times and gave a deed to seven-sixteenths of his holdings to a St. Louis creditor, Auguste Chouteau. In spite of this desperate forestalling action, he died a bankrupt in 1810. Even so, he lives on in history through his namesakes, the city and county of Dubuque, while the Chouteau name disappeared into oblivion when the heirs found that their title was worthless.

Another grant went to one Louis Honore Tesson of St. Louis, whose lands near Montrose became famous for an apple orchard which he planted in fulfillment of the terms of his grant. The orchard lived on in historical fame; the man himself disappeared from view. Still another grant went to Basil Giard, who, like Julien Dubuque, for many years simply appropriated and enjoyed the usufruct of thousands of acres of land across the river from Prairie du Chien. Eventually, Giard asked the Spanish imperial officials in 1800 for a legal grant, but his petition was not acted on during the remainder of Spanish tenure at St. Louis. American officials denied the claim in 1807 but in 1816 Giard's persistent heirs secured a congressional validation of their title.[17]

THE LOUISIANA PURCHASE

One must force himself to remember that we are dealing with lands which included the future Iowa at a time of such momentous events as the War of the American Revolution and the French Revolution and its consequent wars. Strange as it may seem, the future of Iowa was affected by these wars. For example, although the British in 1783 surrendered their claims to the lands east of the Mississippi River, they did not actually hand over the lands to Americans. After Great Britain became involved in the French Revolutionary Wars in 1793, the United States found itself able to make two treaties which had great effect on the West. In Jay's Treaty the British promised to end their policy of supporting Indian attacks on the whites in the West and Northwest; the other, the Treaty of Greenville in 1795, marked the formal recognition of American control in the Northwest. A third treaty, with the Spanish, secured unrestricted navigation of the Mississippi and the right of deposit at New Orleans, and a promise not to incite the Indians to further attacks on the whites. Thus the way was opened for a population explosion into the lands of the Southwest and the West.

In a sequel to these events, making up a story so familiar as not to require retelling here, Napoleon reclaimed the Mississippi Valley from the Spanish in 1800, made plans for its conquest which he could not carry out, and then sold not only New Orleans but a vast and undetermined area west of the river to the United States. The empire which we had bought to get a city included the future Iowa.[18]

CHAPTER 3 IOWALAND AS AMERICAN TERRITORY 1803–1832

So great is the apparent logical sequence, the impression persists that the Louisiana Purchase spawned the explorations of the Missouri River and its borderlands by Lewis and Clark. Nothing could be further from the facts. For twenty years previous to the Purchase, Thomas Jefferson had been trying to organize an expedition to explore "Louisiana"; he wanted to know about the geography, the Indians, and the strength of the Spanish and the British forces there. At least three men had been offered the leadership of an expedition—George Rogers Clark, John Ledyard, and André Michaux—but nothing came of the offers. Sometime in 1802, acting in great secrecy, Jefferson, now president, offered his friend and secretary, Captain Meriwether Lewis, the chance to become a maker of history, and Lewis accepted. Captain Lewis was authorized to pick his own companion and adjutant, finally settling on Lieutenant William Clark, "Captain" Clark only by courtesy since the Senate refused to approve the recommended raise in rank.[1]

THE LEWIS AND CLARK EXPEDITION

Jefferson charged Lewis to investigate the extent of the Missouri River, gathering data as he proceeded; to search for the sources and learn if the Missouri, probably in conjunction with some other river, might afford a feasible route to the Pacific; to study the people and the country along the way, cultivate good relations with the natives, and study the possibility of trade in furs and other goods. Obviously the Iowa of our day would not be heavily involved in the findings except in a negative way. Monumental as was the feat of Lewis and Clark, their triumphant achievement touched Iowa only peripherally. Measured mathematically, the number of miles of Iowa shoreline which they touched or looked upon was only a small proportion of their total journey. The first specific entry in Captain Clark's journal which can be identified with a later-to-be Iowa is an item dated July 18, 1804, when they crossed the parallel of 40° 30′.[2] From this point as they made their way north there are frequent allusions to the serpentine meanderings of the river; on one memorable day they logged 20½ miles against the current, only to find that twelve of those miles had taken them to a point which they could have covered in 370 yards of land travel.

There are references to the physical appearance of part of Iowa's future "Western Slope," to the Indians of the area, and to the possibilities of settlement and development. One such passage which has caused some confusion in the writings of historians was the entry for August 3 which describes a place "which we call Council Bluff a Spot well Calculated for a Tradeing establishment . . . ," a spot which should not be mistaken for present-day Council Bluffs, Iowa. The reference was to a spot about twenty-five miles north of Omaha and on the west (Nebraska) side of the river.[3] Another entry which could mislead is the statement that the Little Sioux River empties into Spirit Lake, whereas the river actually bypasses the lake by an appreciable distance.[4] On this point the two captains departed from their usual skeptical approach and relied on the word of a traveler-interpreter, Dorion, without checking his report.

Iowans do not overlook the fact that the only member of the expedition who lost his life, Sergeant Charles Floyd, died while the group was on Iowa soil. He was buried near the juncture of the Missouri and "a Small river without a name to which we name & call Floyds River. . . ."[5] The exemplary young soldier has been remembered by Iowans in a variety of ways. "Floyds River" is still known by his name but Iowans call it, less colorfully, the Floyd River. A town a few miles downstream from the burial site was given a name in his honor, Sergeant Bluff, and a county in northeastern Iowa was given his name when it was formed. The supreme tribute came in 1900 when a splendid monument was erected on a commanding site near the burial place, within the present southern limits of Sioux City, testifying that Iowans are proud that Iowa was touched by this expedition, a necessary part of the process of the winning of the West.[6]

ZEBULON MONTGOMERY PIKE'S EXPLORATION OF THE MISSISSIPPI RIVER

Another explorer of interest to Iowans, the first to make a formal investigation of our future eastern border, was Lieutenant Zebulon M. Pike, a twenty-six-year-old officer in the United States Army. Leaving St. Louis in August 1805, his instructions were "to take the course of the River," note the weather and the resources along the way, collect statistics about the Indians, conciliate the Indians and bring some of their chiefs to St. Louis for a council, select sites for forts, and explore the Mississippi to its source unless freezing weather should drive him home before this could be accomplished.[7]

The information which he gathered jibes well with that which has accumulated through later years. For example, his description of the rapids near present-day Keokuk, then known as the "De Moine Rapids," gives an accurate picture of the hazards of navigation presented by that passage of water until modern engineering could provide relief. Farther up the river Pike found two likely sites for forts, both within the limits of present-day Burlington, Iowa. One, which he described in well-deserved glowing phrases, is today the site of scenic Crapo Park; the other is only a mark on a map.[8]

Continuing his northward thrust, at or near modern Dubuque he came upon the shrewd and clever Julien Dubuque, from whom he elicited guarded replies to a written questionnaire, answers which revealed the magnitude of Dubuque's business ventures even though Pike thought the replies "seemed to carry with them the semblance of equivocation."[9] About ninety miles farther upstream, Pike came to the mouth of the Wisconsin River, and then the village of Prairie du Chien, where he was hospitably received by the leading citizens. In the company of his hosts he searched for a suitable place for a fort, first looking on the Wisconsin River, then visiting the west side of the Mississippi, where he discovered a spot on a high bluff which impressed him very favorably, and which he carefully marked out as to location and distances. Unfortunately for the future Iowa, when army officials came to make the decision for the location of the fort, they placed it on the Wisconsin side of the river, near Prairie du Chien. A few years later the site on the Iowa side acquired the name of Pike's Hill, today affectionately known as Pike's Peak. Pike's continuing travels up the river in a search for its sources, although not directly related to Iowa history, make up a legitimate concern of Iowans because of their proprietary interest in the great river which has contributed so much to their history.[10]

Pike has been criticized for the ineptness of his dealings with the Indians. It is true that he did not produce any Indians in St. Louis for a council nor did he make any treaty arrangements which could eventuate in Indian alliances. As for sites for forts, the ones which he recommended were not approved, much to Iowa's and the nation's loss. The Burlington sites would have been infinitely superior to the one at Fort Madison selected by Meriwether Lewis, and the site on Pike's Hill would have been far more commanding than the one later chosen for Fort Shelby (later Fort Crawford) on the flood-ridden plain at Prairie du Chien. It would seem a bit condescending to conclude, as some have done, that his expedition was a "failure."[11]

THE EVOLUTION OF "LOUISIANA"

The explorations of Lewis and Clark, and Pike, made many people in the eastern and southern states aware of the existence of the territory newly acquired from France, and directed the attention of some toward the prospect of settling across the Mississippi. Such an event would have effects on the Iowa of the future. The process of settlement cannot be described, however, until two premises are established: first, that the government of the United States of America insisted on a formal policy of treaty relationship with the Indians, the same as with the French, the Spanish, or any other foreign power. By a policy announced in 1791, we followed the rule that all lands acquired from the Indians must be "legally" acquired from them by a treaty-making process. However much this policy might seem to some to have been a cover for hypocrisy and abuse, at least it was a policy. Second, before our government could give title to any purchaser or grantee, whether speculator, settler, or absentee landlord, it must first perfect its own title by the aforesaid treaty, and then must carry out a survey, a division, and a public auction (or make a congressional grant), before it could pass on the title to a presumable legal recipient, whoever that might be. Even though certain lands might be occupied before this legalizing process had taken place, the persons occupying the land (squatters) could not get a proper title until all the formalities had been met, or later rescued by a congressional preemption act.

We did not actually take possession of the newly purchased lands until March 10, 1804. Before any legal settlement of "Louisiana" could take place, therefore, many intervening steps must be taken by the government. Congress had not been inattentive to the problem of territorial government inherited from the French with the bill of sale. On March 26, 1804, just fourteen days after the transfer of the lands took place in a ceremony in St. Louis, Congress completed action on a bill which divided the entire area, vaguely defined as it was, into two parts:[12] the Territory of Orleans, reaching up to the parallel of 33°, and the District of Louisiana, that vast, largely unknown land mass out of which the future Iowa and all or parts of twelve other states would ultimately be carved.

The Territory of Orleans was almost ready for self-government; the region to the north was barely more than a name. To give it some substance and a semblance of law, this District of Louisiana was assigned to the governor and judges of the Indiana Territory for supervision. Except for an occasional piece of business at the office of the superintendent of Indian affairs at St. Louis, it is doubtful if the Indiana officials took much notice of its ward.[13] Such a piece of business was not long in making its appearance.

THE TREATY OF 1804 WITH THE SAUK AND FOX

This Indian treaty was the first in a long series of transactions with the Sauk and Fox. In itself a humdrum affair, it contained a portent for the future. A sordid incident made up of Indian quarrels and murders led to the application of the formula, described above, for extracting lands from the Indians. President Jefferson, for the first time, insisted on observing the formula to the last detail. Earlier he had prodded Governor William Henry Harrison of the Indiana Territory to make land cession treaties with as many tribes and as soon as possible. For two years Harrison negotiated by offering annuities and other rewards but with little success. Then the Sauk fell victim to an act by some of their own impetuous young braves. During a small war with the Osages, four young Sauk warriors, carried away by their enthusiasm, murdered and scalped three white persons, throwing all the whites of the area into a fit of terror at the prospect of a general massacre, at the same time alarming the older Indians who feared a wholesale reprisal.

By the red man's code, the whole tribe should pay for a crime with lands, money, or other gifts, thus gaining the release of the guilty person or persons, whereas the white man's code demanded "an eye for an eye and a tooth for a tooth." It was while both whites and reds were in this state of mind that a few chiefs from the Sauk and their Fox allies visited St. Louis and were asked to "touch their goose quills" to a treaty which signed away a vast body of lands in Illinois north and west of the Illinois River, and smaller slices of Wisconsin and Missouri. In return, Governor Harrison pledged his government to pay an annuity of $600 to the Sauk and $400 to the Fox, plus immediate gifts of well over $2,000, and generously conceded that the Indians were to be allowed to live and hunt on these lands until possession was taken by the United States, at some unspecified future date.[14] Small wonder that this concession created an impression among the Indians that they had never really sold their lands. The reader who already knows something of American history will recognize that here, unwittingly, were sown the seeds of the Black Hawk War of 1832.

FURTHER TERRITORIAL DEVELOPMENTS

Indicative of a rapid growth of population in the area just north of New Orleans was the decision in 1805 to change the status of the District of Louisiana. By an act of Congress, March 3, 1805, the district was given the new name and the new status of the Territory of Louisana, removing the necessity of assignment to the Territory of Indiana.[15] On March 3, 1807, Congress took further notice of the growth of settlement by passing the important though little noticed antisquatting law, "an Act to prevent settlements being made on lands ceded to the United States, until authorized by law." This act specifically exempted those whose claims were in the hands of the commissioners, as already provided, or who had occupied lands ceded to the United States by treaty with a foreign nation or ceded by a state to the United States.[16] It is easy to see that it would be virtually impossible for the federal government to enforce such an act, but it was necessary to have such a law as the legal basis for the eviction of trespassers.

As the years went by after the momentous Purchase of 1803, it soon became evident that a new enemy had taken the place of the French. This new enemy was the British, not as outright opponents in the field but as gadflies harassing Americans in every possible way, principally by a steady effort to turn the Indians of the Mississippi Valley against the Americans and to pledge the Indians as allies in case of war. Our counteracting policy took various forms: we could try to out-bargain the British; we could bribe Indian chiefs by inviting them to Washington for conferences with the Great White Father; and we could build and maintain forts at strategic places and occasionally march companies of soldiers through the countryside in an effort to impress the Indians and intimidate them into inaction. Our ultimate decision was that all three options should be used or any combination thereof as might seem advisable.

One such fort among the dozens eventually built in execution of this policy was Fort Madison, the first after the erection of the fort at Prairie du Chien. The site was chosen in 1808 with great difficulty, and then the choice proved to be a major blunder, an ill-starred venture from the first move to the last. The problem of defense was complicated by the policy of maintaining "factories" (so called for the word "factor" used as a title for the government agent) for trade with the Indians. The "Indian factory system," initiated in 1795 and abandoned in 1822, was really a series of warehouses and salesrooms set up in an effort to create a government monopoly in the fur trade as a protection of the Indians from the practices of ruthless white traders.[17] Common sense dictated the protection of a factory by a fort. Out of this scheme of things comes the sad tale of Fort Madison.

ESTABLISHMENT AND LOSS OF FORT MADISON

Both Zebulon M. Pike and Meriwether Lewis ignored the mouth of the Des Moines River as a site for a factory and its protecting fort. Instead, Lewis chose a spot at the head of the Des Moines River rapids, and a Colonel Thomas Hunt was delegated to construct the buildings. After his sudden death, his successor, Lieutenant Alpha Kingsley, selected a new site some ten miles to the north, the worst strategic choice possible. A ridge gave protection to any Indian outposts which might be set up, while on the west there was a ravine through which enemies could approach the fort unseen. The young lieutenant was never to see his fort seriously tested. A confrontation with threatening Indians in 1809 was frustrated; a little later he went on a furlough, never to return to the fort.

Captain Horatio Stark, Kingsley's successor, stayed on until 1812. Stark's replacement, Lieutenant Thomas Hamilton, had the misfortune to take over just as the War of 1812 was getting under way. Now the propaganda and the long years of playing up to the Indians paid off for the British. Never able to persuade a majority of the Sauk, Fox, Ioways, and other tribes to come over completely to their side, the British were able to secure the services of Black Hawk and a few of his Sauk, aided by a small number of Fox, while elsewhere a few Winnebago fought on their own. In September 1812 Black Hawk began an attack on Fort Madison and the factory adjacent to it. After two days of fighting in which the Indians definitely had the best of it, Lieutenant Hamilton decided to burn the factory at a favorable time when the flames would not spread to the fort itself. After this had been done, Hamilton was on the verge of surrendering the fort itself, since it was there primarily to protect the factory. Relief arrived, however, and the Indians voluntarily retired from this particular siege because of a shortage of ammunition.

In 1813, in spite of an extension of the fort's blockhouses, the Indians under Black Hawk renewed the attack. This time Lieutenant Hamilton took it on himself to destroy the fort and evacuate his men. A trench was dug from the fort all the way to the riverbank under cover of darkness. Boats were loaded with supplies and the garrison troops crawled through the trench to the boats, after which the torch was applied to the fort. When the surprised Indians caught on to what had happened, the boats were safely moving downstream.[18]

Thus ended the existence of the fort and factory—and Iowa's contact with the War of 1812. The white forces had been brought to a humiliating defeat by an error in judgment by a fledgling lieutenant who chose the poor location for the fort. An unhappy consequence of the episode was the false sense of strength which the Indians would derive from the American white man's retreat in the face of an Indian attack.

FURTHER TERRITORIAL EVOLUTION

Iowaland's status as part of a frontier buffer zone for the Louisiana country underwent a decided change in 1812. In this year the Territory of Orleans was admitted into the Union as the state of Louisiana, and the Territory of Louisiana was renamed as the Territory of Missouri. The first governor (1813–1820) of the new territory was that same Captain William Clark who had originally seen most of his province, including the borderlands along the Missouri River of the future Iowa, as the colleague of Captain Meriwether Lewis in 1804–1806. Therefore, in a somewhat romanticized sense, Iowa might claim William Clark, now a brigadier general, as one of her early governors. In his companion role as superintendent of Indian affairs for a vast trans-Mississippi area, with headquarters at St. Louis, from 1807 to 1838, General Clark's authority in the Iowa region was very real.[19]

Other territorial and state organizing developments soon followed. The one of greatest consequence to Iowa was the admission of Missouri under the provisions of the famous Compromise of 1820 whereby among other things Missouri was admitted as a slave state but slavery was *forever* excluded from the remaining portion of the Louisiana Purchase north of the line of 36° 30′.[20] Forever is a strong word but it did not seem to daunt the thinkers of 1820. At least the troublesome question of the expansion of slavery could be laid aside for a few years. Obviously the people of another generation would have to deal with the problem again. So little did the remainder of the former Territory of Missouri command the attention of Congress that for the time being the entire area was left in a sort of limbo, a curiosity, almost a freak, a land without a government or governmental status. The matter drifted on this way for thirteen years until the oversight was corrected in 1834 by an act which extended the Territory of Michigan westward to include not only the future Wisconsin but the future Iowa, and much of Minnesota and the Dakotas.[21]

Some activities did take place in this region, in spite of its seeming neglect. As mentioned above, a fort known as Cantonment Missouri was built on the Nebraska side of the Missouri at the Council Bluff site eulogized by Lewis and Clark. Such a fort could serve as a defense post for the eastern side of the river as well as the western side, and also serve as a destination point for travelers going across "Iowa" as well as those coming up the Missouri River from St. Louis. One such traveler-explorer in the region was an army officer named Stephen Harriman Long, who almost certainly crossed a good part of Iowa on his trip to the Rocky Mountains in 1819–1820. More certain, and of considerably more importance, was the expedition of Lieutenant Stephen Watts Kearny in 1820. He was sent out by his commander, General Henry Atkinson, on a mission to establish contact with the great Sioux chieftain, Wabasha, on the Upper Mississippi. As the map in Figure 3.1 clearly shows, he crossed Iowa on a diagonal line leading from Cantonment Missouri (soon to be renamed Fort Atkinson) to present-day Winona, Minnesota, where he found the great chief and held a council with him. Kearny's findings were confined at the time to his diary and a routine army report.[22] Still another traveler of some note, though of little actual importance to Iowa, was the enterprising Italian explorer, Giacomo Constantino Beltrami, who made the trip up the Mississippi to practically

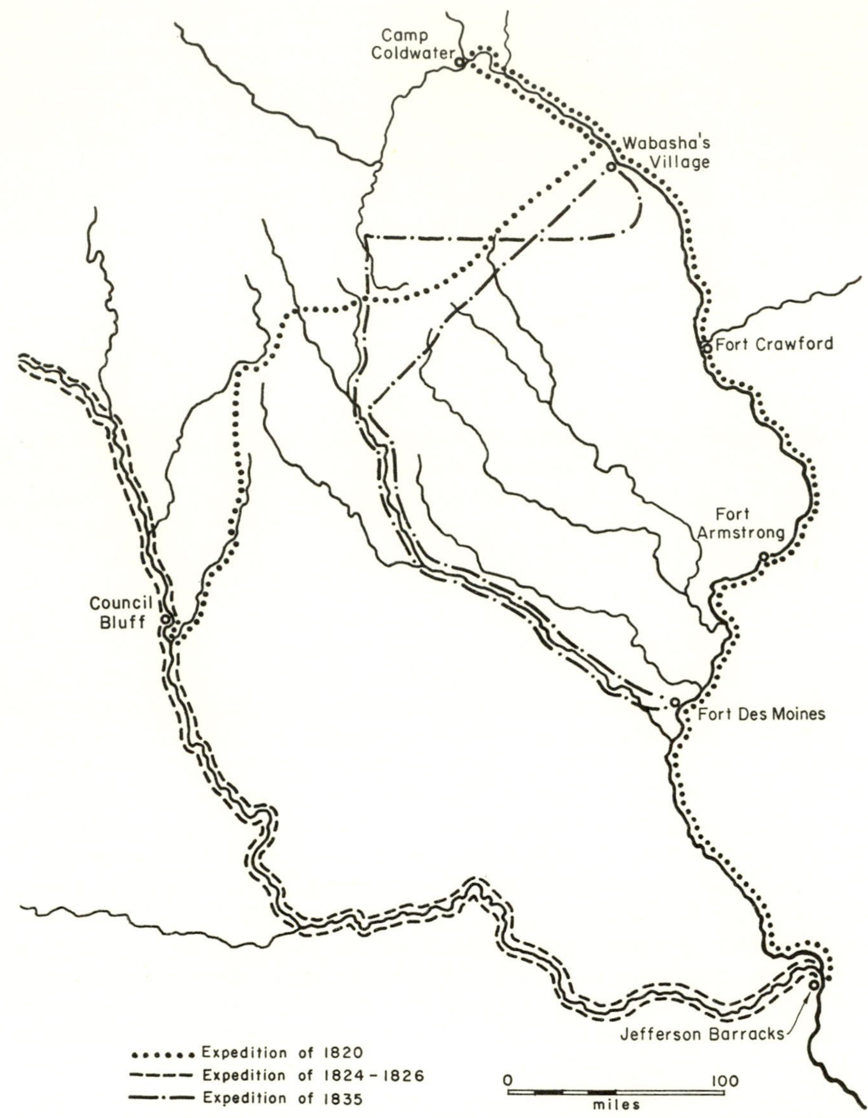

FIG. 3.1. Routes of Stephen Watts Kearny's expeditions in "Iowaland"—1820, 1824–1826, 1835.

the same headwaters reached by Lieutenant Zebulon Pike. Beltrami's account of his trip contains some interesting allusions to the sights and the wildlife along the banks of the river making up Iowa's eastern border, but there is no record of significant inland journeys into the Iowa area.[23]

Further indications of activity in the Iowa of the future may be found. In 1824 the United States purchased a large tract of land from

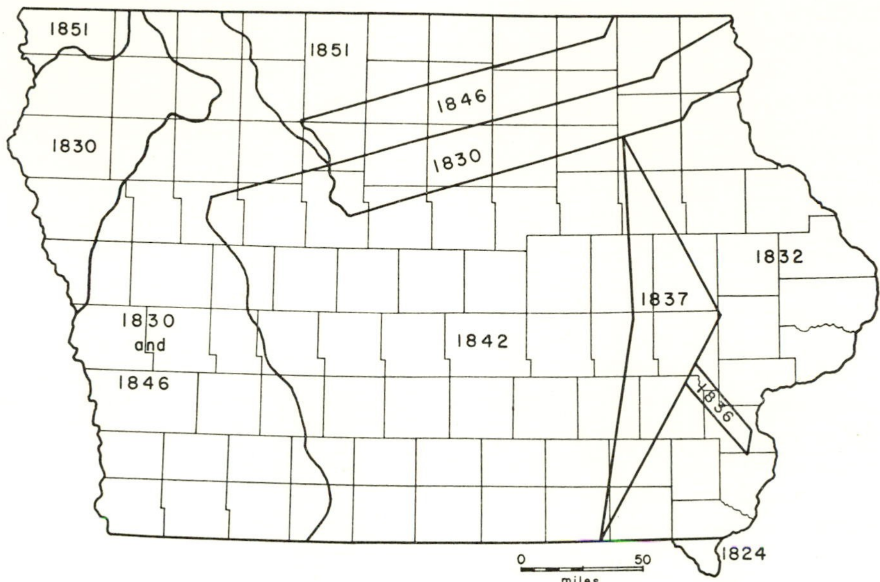

FIG. 3.2. Indian cessions by treaties of 1824, 1830, 1832, 1836, 1837, 1842, 1846, 1851.

the Sauk and Fox, including a small parcel which acquired some fame as the "Half-Breed Tract." Perhaps the emphasis on the name is entirely misplaced—only brief references to half-breeds are made in the treaty of 1824, and an examination of other treaties with other Indians in other places shows that it was a common thing to include a paragraph of items to be provided for the children of white fathers and Indian mothers. This treaty was not unique in any way except perhaps for the abuses later connected with it.[24] The tract covered 119,000+ acres, a good part of present-day Lee County, Iowa, and consisted of that curious little triangle of land dangling between the Mississippi and Des Moines rivers, jutting into Missouri. (See Figure 3.2.) When this land came into the Iowa domain, it brought with it the Indian village of Puckeshetuk, destined to become one of Iowa's most colorful cities, Keokuk.

Evidence of the existence of illegal white settlers abounds. Temporary preemption laws passed by a lenient Congress were intended for their benefit; these were put on a permanent basis in 1841. We may certainly deduce that these legislative notices in the 1830s of the presence of white settlers west of the Mississippi were not taken without considerable justification. The most spectacular case of aggressiveness was the effort of Lucius Langworthy and his workers to take over the Mines of Spain in 1830. After the death of Julien Dubuque in 1810, the Indians held on to and worked these mines. The Langworthy group jealously eyed them from their huts on nearby islands in the river and finally used force to dispossess the Indians, only soon to be themselves driven off from their stolen properties by federal troops under Major Stephen W. Kearny, who was by chance on his way from St. Louis to Fort Crawford. Forced back into Illinois, it would not be many years until the Langworthy brothers would become settlers in the town of Dubuque and take their places as leading citizens of that community. More important than the attempt to deprive the Indians of their mines is the record left by Lucius Langworthy of an attempt to draw up some articles of self-government by these rugged individuals. A committee of five was appointed to draw up a document, the resultant framework of government being styled "The Miners' Compact." It was chiefly concerned with the division of property so as to keep the peace among these rough and ready frontiersmen. Each man was allotted a piece of ground two hundred yards square; to retain it he had to work it at least one day out of six. The document was dated June 17, 1830, and is an interesting example of an attempt at frontier law and order.[25]

In another walk of life, we find the first school (1830) on record in Iowa; others may have existed but did not gain notice. A one-room school was set up by Dr. Isaac Galland of the Keokuk region, a man of dubious character, as we shall see, but one who thought enough of his children to employ one Berryman Jennings, a Kentuckian, as a tutor for them. The school was located in a hamlet named after the frontier doctor; the replica of the little building now on view was perforce erected on a spot near the original building site, not on the original site itself.

THE INDIAN REMOVAL POLICY

Highly indicative of the remoteness and apparent uselessness of the trans-Mississippi area in the early 1820s was the willingness of Presidents Monroe and Jackson to turn the region over to the Indians. In 1824, and again in 1825, Monroe recommended such a removal policy to Congress, but without success; President Jackson had better luck in 1830. Contrary to the general reputation of this famous frontier soldier and Indian fighter, Jackson was on this occasion, to the best of his knowledge, acting in the interest of the Indians. The purpose of his Emigration Policy, or Indian Removal Policy, was the avoidance of conflict between the races. By separating them, the whites to stay on the eastern side of the Mississippi, the Indians to be removed to the western side, plenty of land would be available for both. The Eastern Indians—for examples, the Seminoles in Florida, the Cherokees in Georgia, the Delawares in Ohio—would be given specific areas of land in the New World and would be assisted to move. A further theoretical assumption was that the Eastern Indians, partly civilized, would act as a mollifying influence on the "wild" Indians of the West. Such a policy, however imperfect it may seem to us, shows that the white man's government could devise a formal Indian policy that was something more than mere land-grabbing.[26]

A law of May 28, 1830, specified that the region west of Missouri and Arkansas was to be reserved for the Indians, an area from the Red River up to the Platte; additions to the north were made later. Iowa and the future Texas, neither in the "Indian Territory," as the restricted area was popularly called, were immediate beneficiaries;[27] American pioneers did not bother their government with protests as long as good land was available somewhere.

Such a policy of division, a form of the "separate but equal" doctrine, did not last long. By a series of treaties with the Indians, the United States was able to secure title to the lands of the West, including the lands out of which Iowa would be formed. In 1825 and 1830 American officials caused great councils to be held at Prairie du Chien and by various means emerged with treaties in the white man's favor. In the 1825 document the future Iowa was only an indirect beneficiary: the principal objective of this council was to divide the land into equitable shares for the various tribes. For example, the Sioux were assigned to an area north of the Upper Iowa River and running all the way out to the Big Sioux; the Sauk and Fox and the Ioway were to stay south of the Upper Iowa. The Sauk and Fox also agreed to relinquish "to the tribes interested therein," all their claims to land east of the Mississippi.[28]

The demarcation line of 1825 did not prove to be a sufficient barrier to hostilities, and five years later another council was needed. This time a more drastic remedy was adopted. A buffer zone along the line of the Upper Iowa River was created; the Sioux agreed to stay twenty miles north of that line and the Sauk and Fox would stay twenty miles south of it. This forty-mile zone soon acquired the popular name of the "Neutral Ground." In it a fort would be built for the purpose of housing a military contingent which would police the area and keep the Indians from each other's throats.

Of much more importance because of more enduring effects and because of great benefits to Iowa was the clause in the 1830 treaty which provided for a cession of Sioux lands and others. This cession of the future corner on the northwest and the western side of the state is always shown on the maps of Indian grants to the United States but the explanatory background of the council of 1830, given above, seldom accompanies the illustration. The cession began at the upper fork of the Des Moines River and extended to the Big Sioux or Calumet River, ran down to the Missouri state line, then eastward for a distance and on to the Grand River, then to the Boyer River, and back to the Des Moines. In exchange for this tremendous piece of real estate, now the location of many of Iowa's most productive agricultural and industrial counties, the United States pledged itself to pay annual sums over a period of ten years amounting to $205,132 each year—$170,000 in cash, $30,000 for educational purposes, and $5,132 in gifts for immediate distribution—a rare bargain by any standards.[29] (See Figure 3.2.)

THE BLACK HAWK WAR, 1832

As one studies the treaty documents emanating from the councils of 1804, 1816, 1824, 1825, and 1830, one can see a definite pattern taking shape: encroachment, conflict, negotiation, and settlement, always in favor of the United States government as it took the part of the advancing waves of settlers. The Iowa of the future was the beneficiary of these treaties and others to come.

The most basic and most helpful dispossession of the Indians, from the viewpoint of Iowa, was the one arranged in the Black Hawk Purchase Treaty, September 21, 1832, concluding the Black Hawk War between the national government and the Sauk and Fox, primarily that portion of the Sauk following the Sauk war chief, Black Hawk, whose following was called the British Band, because of his alliance with the British in Canada. It is one of the ironies of history that this little war, so important and rewarding to Iowa, did not originate in Iowa but in Illinois; that the fighting did not take place in Iowa but in Illinois and the Wisconsin portion of Michigan Territory; yet the penalty paid by the Indians benefited Iowa, not Illinois or Wisconsin.

The war has usually been described either in highly sentimental language apotheosizing Chief Black Hawk, whose autobiography set the style for this interpretation, or in lighthearted phrases ridiculing the Illinois frontier militia and the United States Army regulars alternately chasing and running away from redskinned warriors who were encumbered by their wives and children, or sometimes running away from imagined opponents. If one looks more deeply, he may find an episode which illustrates all the phases of frontier conflict between Indians and whites. "The 'war' itself resulted in part from vacillation, slow communication, treachery, political opportunism, and the rashness of frontier militia" is the verdict of a keen student of Indian affairs and biographer of the commander of the United States regulars.[30] All these points are well taken as immediate causes of the war, but not the basic causes: relentless pressure by the land-hungry whites on the Indian holdings, and the failure of the Emigration, or Indian Removal, Policy.

A very important corollary of that policy was the assumption that the Indian tribes would give up their wars against one another and live in neighborly peace. This assumption proved to be too generous; the Sauk and Fox to the south and the Sioux to the north were not ready for such idealism. They hated each other, and the Sauk and Fox plainly feared the Sioux, as well they might. Here is the setting for a vital point: Chief Keokuk was ready to believe that the American whites would help his people against the Sioux; Black Hawk, the Sauk war chief, was not so trustful. In short, Black Hawk's fears made him resist the Emigration Policy, and he became the spokesman for the dissenting minority of his people, ready, if necessary, to fight the Sioux *and* the Americans. Chief Keokuk, by contrast, was the leader and spokesman for those who would cooperate ("collaborate") with the outsider (the whites) and resign themselves to the best fate possible, probably dependency in a white man's world.[31] Black Hawk had his reasons. Behind his war of 1832 lay twenty-eight years of friction, marked by undeviating resistance to American white pressures. He had dissented from the Treaty of 1804; he had fought us at Fort Madison; he had accepted anti-American aid from the British; and now he was proudly ready to go it alone against us, whereas Keokuk and others were willing to place their trust in American friendship and possible assistance.

In the 1820s the whites had begun to encroach on the Rock River lands, causing much friction. As a partial solution, lands along the Iowa River in the future Iowa were set aside for the exclusive use of the Sauk and Fox. Not satisfied, Black Hawk and his followers insisted on returning in the spring of 1830 and again in 1831 to their former homes, fields, and hunting grounds in the Saukenuk region of Illinois, and complained loudly that the whites were intruders, not only taking their lands but destroying their burial grounds.

Under this cover of charge and countercharge, General Edmund P. Gaines, commander of the Western District, made what should have been the final settlement of the whole ugly business. On June 30, 1831, Black Hawk "touched the goose quill" to the so-called Corn Treaty in which he committed his people to retire to their assigned lands along the Iowa River, to accept the authority of Chief Keokuk, to abandon all contacts with the British, and to agree to let the United States build military and post roads in the area.[32] There were also oral promises of reimbursement for the corn and other crops they were about to abandon. Among the sad might-have-beens of history, then, is the thought that if this agreement had been honorably observed, there would have been no Black Hawk War.

Unfortunately, a series of little incidents created a war situation, in this case a war made up of a few skirmishes, capped by one bloody and disgraceful slaughter which illustrates war at its worst. The incidents were slight when viewed separately but somehow ran together in such a way as to push both sides into a "war." One of the more notable was the bad advice given to Black Hawk by a young chief, Neapope, who claimed to have promises of help from the British; this was followed by equally bad advice from the Winnebago Prophet, and by others who promised aid. Many persons less vain and less childish than Black Hawk would have yielded to such flattery and cajolery and Neapope's outright deception. Chief Keokuk pled in vain that it would be foolish for a handful of braves, with their squaws and children tagging along, to make war against the Long Knives, even proposing the extreme logical conclusion that the warriors should put their dependents to death and then go on to their inevitable defeat and extinction, a course of action which they rejected.

The whites then compounded the troubles by denying Chief Keokuk's request to go to Washington and negotiate with the Great White Father, a mistake charged up to William Clark. "Then and there, despite his promises to the contrary, the old Sac [Black Hawk] decided to return to Saukenuk in the spring."[33] True to Keokuk's warnings, Black Hawk and his people crossed the Mississippi, on April 6, 1832, and straggled toward the rendezvous with the Winnebago on the Rock River, forty miles from Saukenuk. There was only one clear charge to be made against Black Hawk: he had led his followers across the river to their old haunts in violation of the Corn Treaty of 1831. In spite of the desertion or nonappearance of his allies and promised allies, Black Hawk haughtily rejected all calls for a return to his Iowa River lands, and moved farther up the Rock River. General Atkinson was left with no choice but to send troops after him—"and so the war came."

"Battles" of the Black Hawk War

It has seemed more important by far to explain the causes of the war and the eventual results than to elaborate on the skirmishes that made up the fracas. In the words of a leading authority on the subject, "The Black Hawk War of 1832 was barely a war. It lasted but fifteen weeks. It cost the lives of but seventy settlers and soldiers."[34] This recently corrected number of fatalities is significantly smaller than the original estimate of two hundred as given by earlier writers.

In retrospect, the conflict has elements of both farce and tragedy, and therefore it may be called a tragicomedy. There were skirmishes at several places in northern Illinois and southern Wisconsin. Black Hawk's goal was to get across the Mississippi and vanish into the freedom of the wide open spaces beyond; General Atkinson's strategy called for blocking the crossing of the river. The attempted crossing at the mouth of the Bad Axe River was the climax of the little war. Atkinson's forces were supplemented by a gunboat and by Sioux Indians who gleefully helped to butcher the Sauk as they tried to swim across the river. Black Hawk escaped to the north but was soon apprehended, along with his companion and evil counselor, Neapope.

The Purchase Treaty of 1832

The victors first dealt with the Winnebago,[35] then summoned spokesmen for the Sauk and Fox, principally Chief Keokuk, to Fort

Armstrong on Rock Island to hear the dictated terms of peace on September 21, 1832. Black Hawk, now a humiliated prisoner at Jefferson Barracks, St. Louis, was not allowed to attend or even to send advice. General Winfield Scott was the spokesman for the United States, hence the name long used for the treaty lands, "Scott's Purchase." A better name for the white man's prize might have been "Black Hawk's Folly." The only lands which the Sauk and Fox could surrender were those along the Iowa River. These must now be given up, though the bitter pill was sweetened by small payments of money and added benefits. The forfeited lands were carefully marked off as follows: beginning at a point on the Mississippi at the Sauk and Fox northern boundary line of 1830, running fifty miles to the west; then south to the Red Cedar of the Iowa River, forty miles from the Mississippi; then on a straight line to a point on the northern boundary of Missouri, fifty miles from the Mississippi; then up the western side of the Mississippi to the starting point. (See Figure 3.2.) A segment of four hundred square miles was reserved for the use of Chief Keokuk and his followers as a reward for their neutrality.

For all these lands the monetary cost to the United States was trivial. The government would make thirty annual payments of $20,000, and further provide blacksmithing services, forty barrels of tobacco and a like amount of salt per year, and assume Indian debts of $40,000. Two sections of land were awarded to the famous half-breed interpreter and mediator, Antoine Le Claire. A very specific point was made that these lands were not to be used by the Sauk and Fox for hunting grounds or for planting. Black Hawk and others were held as hostages; supplies were to be issued to the widows and children of those killed in the war; rewards would be given to those Indians who gave information about mines or minerals which proved to be of value.[36]

The Purchase Treaty did *not* provide for the opening up of these lands to settlers; this provision was there by inference only. Since the Indians had to "remove from the lands ceded" by the following June 1, 1833, the natural assumption would be that settlers would be allowed to come in after that date. With the removal of the soldiers who were guarding the frontier, such proved to be the case. At the price of $640,000 in cash and a few lives lost on each side, the United States—not Iowa—thus became the owner of a vast amount of good land. The nucleus for another state had been secured.

CHAPTER 4 PRETERRITORIAL AND TERRITORIAL IOWA 1833–1838–1846

THE REMOVAL OF THE FORMAL BARRIERS ON JUNE 1, 1833, TO settlement in "Scott's Purchase" found hundreds, soon thousands, of potential settlers ready to cross the river (or come up from the south) and dash into the former Indian lands in search of choice holdings. Evidence of the flow of newcomers is furnished by a sheriff's census taken in 1836, in which 10,531 people were enumerated; also by the records of settlement in and incorporation of towns along the Mississippi and in nearby inland locations. The site of an Indian camp or a trading post of earlier days, or a fording place on a creek or river, was a made-to-order location for a town. Dubuque, Bellevue, Muscatine, Burlington, Fort Madison, and Keokuk are well-known places which trace their formal beginnings all the way back to 1833; Davenport, Fairfield, Mount Pleasant, and Keosauqua soon followed as spots on the map. Sometimes the business of platting the townsite and the legal act of incorporation had to wait for several years after actual settlement while local officials got around to the technicalities of dealing with territorial officials.

An incident such as the Patrick O'Connor-George O'Keaf affair in 1834 and the Massey-Smith family feud in 1835 revealed the need for a system of law and order that could go beyond vigilante justice. The apparently brutal and senseless killing of O'Keaf by O'Connor was followed by a recourse to the forms of a jury trial, but one fears that O'Connor was foredoomed before a word was spoken in his defense; in the other episode, the Massey and Smith families took offense at each other and at least three revenge killings followed without resort to any court of justice.[1]

A PART OF THE TERRITORY OF MICHIGAN, 1834

Partially in recognition of the rapid flow of settlers into the land across the river, and the need for some show of law and order, Congress

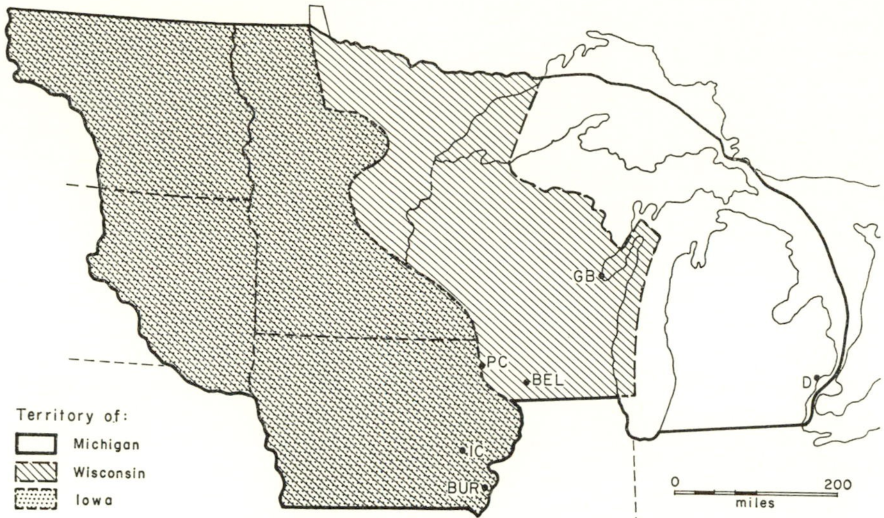

FIG. 4.1. This map indicates the western border of the state of Michigan after 1836; the Territory of Michigan as it was from 1834 to 1836, when it included all of the present Wisconsin and Iowa, plus much of Minnesota and the Dakotas; the Territory of Wisconsin, 1836 to 1838 and from 1838 to 1848; the Territory of Iowa, 1838 to 1846.

Bur–Burlington
IC–Iowa City
PC–Prairie du Chien
Bel–Belmont
GB–Green Bay
D–Detroit

passed a law in 1834 putting the remnants of the old Territory of Missouri, plus Wisconsin, in the Territory of Michigan. Since the Iowa portion of the old Missouri Territory had been neglected and really abandoned since 1821, it was as a waif that Iowa was dropped into the lap of Michigan. Such an arrangement, a makeshift at best, did not long endure, but it helps to account for the legal fact that in 1834 the Territorial Council of Michigan, on recommendation of Governor Stevens T. Mason, took the first step toward the governmental organization of the country immediately beyond the Mississippi which is now Iowa: the creation of two counties, Du Buque and De Moine. Both counties were perpetuated throughout these early years until their eventual division into the several counties familiar to us.[2]

CHRISTIAN MISSIONS

The energetic activity of Catholics, Methodists, and Congregationalists in carrying out missions to the vanguard of migrants from the East and South was not only a mitigating factor in Iowa frontier life but a long step toward the creation of the numerical and influential advantage achieved by these three groups. Organized religion made its formal appearance in this new era of Iowa history when Father Felix Charles Quickenborne came from St. Louis to a hamlet called Puckeshetuk (Keokuk) in 1832 and on to Dubuque in 1833, where he heard masses and performed baptisms and blessed marriages. Father Quickenborne organized the parish of Saint Raphael and drew up plans for a log church building. In 1835 Father Samuel Mazzuchelli came to Dubuque and took charge of the parish. An architect in his own right, he abandoned the plans for a simple log structure and prepared a plan for a stone edifice which was built under his supervision. In 1836 the bishop of St. Louis sent Father Matthew Condamine to Dubuque, the "first priest officially appointed to any place in what is now the State of Iowa." In 1838 Bishop Mathias Loras and Father Joseph Cretin arrived and the diocese of Dubuque came into being, and Saint Raphael's Church became the cathedral church of that diocese. A bishop's palace was built which would serve as the home of a staff of clergymen and also as a seat of Saint Raphael's Seminary, the first diocesan college in Iowa. Other parish churches were built as fast as towns were established along the Mississippi and at interior points.[3]

The Methodists seem to have the honor of having been the first Protestants to enter the Iowa mission field. In just less than six months after the frontiers were removed, the famous Methodist leader, Peter Cartwright, then of Illinois, having evangelized all the way from Kentucky to that state, sent a minister named Barton Randle to Dubuque. Here he soon had the satisfaction of leading his little flock and interested outsiders in the building of what has been accepted as the first church in Iowa. The next establishment was in Burlington ("Flint Hills"), where a prominent layman, Dr. William R. Ross, assisted a minister, Barton Cartwright, in the church's ministry to the people, culminating in the erection of an edifice which was destined to gain some fame as "Old Zion." Soon other towns and villages were ministered to and congregations were organized. Until a special building could be set aside as a house of worship, services might be held in a home, a barn, an empty store, a schoolhouse, or out of doors, following a tradition going back through Peter Cartwright to Asbury to John Wesley himself.

It is almost a truism to say that the Methodist system of "circuits" and "circuit riders" was an asset to this church in carrying the church's message to the widely scattered people of the frontier. This is undoubtedly true, but perhaps of greater importance was the willingness to use local preachers and lay ministers of limited educational backgrounds during the first generation or two of frontier life. A point of Methodist history not usually brought into the story of Iowa in this era of prestatehood is that this was the period during which the church was riven by the struggle over slavery and slaveholding which reached its bitter climax in 1844–1845, coinciding almost exactly with Iowa's attainment of statehood. The Plan of Separation was followed by complete schism and the organization of the Methodist Episcopal Church, South, in 1845, the result being that these early years going on over into 1846 and beyond were marked by an emphasis on antislavery, in some cases on Abolitionism, especially in those towns where New Englanders and York Staters were numerous. The church organization in Iowa was first put under Illinois Methodist officials, whose antislavery sentiment was vigorously expressed. The General Conference of 1844, the national governing body of the church, authorized and organized an Iowa Conference which held a meeting at Iowa City on August 14–19 under Bishop Thomas A. Morris, with a total membership of 5,431 members and 61 ministers, this at a time when the territory's population was about 90,000 people. This early numerical strength plus the good fortune of added strength through migration of other thousands, and leadership of the first order by clergy and laymen, help to account for a denominational influence of great importance to an understanding of Iowa history.[4]

The Congregational Church's entrance into the Iowa mission field was an outgrowth of a joint partnership with the Presbyterians under a working agreement known as the Plan of Union, which lasted from 1801 to 1837. With financial support from the American Home Missionary Society, the two denominations progressively extended the missionary field from New England and New York in perfect unison with the westward movement; now its leaders were ready for one more extension by crossing the river from Illinois, just as a few years later some would be ready to move from Iowa into the Nebraska country and Dakotah Territory. The halcyon days of easy partnership between Congregationalists and Presbyterians were coming to an end just as the first moves into the Half-Breed Tract and the Black Hawk Purchase were being made.

Two men stand out as leaders of the mission to the Iowa District: Asa Turner and Julius A. Reed. These two men and others scouted the country across the river from their Illinois posts in Quincy and Warsaw, earning the endearing name of "Prospectors" in church annals; they and others who came to stay in Iowa were called "The Patriarchs." Asa Turner accepted a call to the tiny New England settlement at Denmark, near Burlington, and established unofficial headquarters for Iowa Congregationalism at his church and the highly rated academy, which drew students from many states. In 1843 he issued a call for help which was answered by nearly a dozen seminarians in Andover, Massachusetts, who formed the "Iowa Band," emulating the "Yale Band" which did so much for Illinois.[5]

In these early years of activity in Iowa, Congregational missioners rode from place to place, even from home to home, like Methodist circuit riders, carrying their ministry to the scattered settlers. But one has only to read the letters of William Salter, a prominent member of the

Band, to sense the desire to settle down in one place, where a well-educated clergyman of fastidious tastes could found and lead a separate and independent church in keeping with Congregational polity. The typical congregation would constitute a social and cultural elite which would sponsor and support higher education, literary societies, and lecture courses, and follow their inclination to regulate the morals of the whole society, hence their support of the temperance movement, antigambling laws, and, most important of all, the antislavery movement.[6]

STEPHEN WATTS KEARNY AND ALBERT MILLER LEA

Turning to more mundane affairs, we find that in the summer of 1835 Lieutenant Colonel Stephen Watts Kearny, USA,[7] was ordered to take a company of 150 Dragoons from his recently constructed Fort Des Moines, near Montrose, on a march through the Indian country west of the Mississippi. Kearny was authorized to investigate possible sites for a new and permanent fort near the junction of the Des Moines and Raccoon rivers, and to pay a visit to Chief Wabasha, a Sioux chieftain. Kearny's route may be easily traced on the map given in Figure 3.1. The long roundabout march was of little military significance but yielded a serendipitous dividend in the form of a booklet entitled *Notes on the Wisconsin Territory; Particularly with Reference to the Iowa District, or Black Hawk Purchase*. It was privately published by the author, Lieutenant Albert M. Lea, Kearny's able assistant and next in command. In the words of the editor of the 1935 reprint, "the supreme significance of Lieutenant Lea's book is the fact that it fixed the name of Iowa upon the country that was to become the Territory of Iowa in 1838 and the State of Iowa in 1846."

Definitely the first book about Iowa, the little book has been compared to a Chamber of Commerce extravaganza because of its enthusiastic and uncritical praise of the area. Lieutenant Lea had a vivid imagination and a facile pen—the Iowa District did not suffer at his hands. Oddly enough, it is Minnesota rather than Iowa which has honored Albert Lea with a place name. His book can be read in a matter of minutes. After a matter-of-fact opening statement about the geographical limits of the district, and the settlers before and after June 1, 1833, Lea launched into a glowing account of the climate, the beauty of the countryside, and a discussion of the minerals and the farm produce which the district was capable of yielding. The lead was the finest in the United States, so he said; the soil and the stands of timber were praised in extravagant terms. He flatly asserted the population to be about sixteen thousand at the end of 1835, only a "little more than two years after the first settlement was made." Most of these settlers had come during 1835, in Lea's opinion, a purely impressionistic conclusion, and an equally great rush of settlers was predicted for 1836. He named Ohio, Indiana, Illinois, Kentucky, and Missouri as the states which had sent most of the early arrivals, another piece of guesswork on his part, based on impressions and hearsay, but one upheld by later census figures. His guess of sixteen thousand or so for the population was about five thousand over the 1836 count.[8]

BURLINGTON, IOWA DISTRICT: CAPITAL OF WISCONSIN TERRITORY

In 1836 the probability of the admission of Michigan as a state reached the point where only the usual boundary dispute, this one with Ohio, stood in the way. Governor Robert Lucas of Ohio, soon to be appointed as the first territorial governor of Iowa, managed to keep the prized Toledo area for Ohio. As the quarrel raged, Congress agreed in early 1836 to detach the lands west of Lake Michigan and place them in a new territory to be called Wisconsin. A measure creating such a territory, including the District of Iowa, became law on April 20, 1836.[9] (See Figure 4.1.)

A leading question of the moment was the choice of a capital for the new territory, a choice likely to be extended as the capital of the ultimate state of Wisconsin. For the moment a hamlet was created near Platteville, given the name of Belmont, and designated as the seat of government. It was so lacking in the amenities of civilized living that the lawmakers demanded a quick removal to some other place, pending the selection and development of a permanent capital city. This procedure was so cleverly manipulated (but not so honestly) by James Duane Doty, a frontier lawyer and land speculator, that the "City of the Four Lakes" (Madison) was chosen, much to the enrichment of speculator Doty and those who supplied the votes. As a part of these hectic negotiations and dealings, Burlington, De Moine County, Iowa District, was chosen as the second temporary capital of Wisconsin Territory—and there were some who hinted that Burlingtonians were among those who helped to supply the votes which Doty needed for his pet project, much to the chagrin of people in Dubuque and other places who were contenders for the honor of selection.[10] One can only speculate as to the effect on the future of Wisconsin and Iowa if Dubuque had been chosen. As it turned out, only one regular session and one special session of the Wisconsin Territorial Legislature met at Burlington. A building was constructed by one Jeremiah Smith, Jr., for the special purpose of housing the meetings of the legislature. When "Smith's Capitol" was burned to the ground, the remaining sessions were held in rooms over commercial buildings. The only business transacted which was of interest to Iowans was the splitting of De Moine County into seven new units.[11]

INDIAN AFFAIRS

In the meanwhile, the Indian problem hung on in spite of the well-intended Removal Act of 1830 and the "peace" following the defeat of Black Hawk in 1832. Secretary of War Lewis Cass was much perturbed by the abuses practiced on the Indians and so was General William Clark, the Indian superintendent at St. Louis. Fortunately, some members of Congress were willing to listen to their recommendations and secure their enactment. In one act a thorough reorganization of the administration of Indian affairs was provided; in another, the Intercourse Act of June 30, 1834, much stricter rules governing trade, especially the sale of alcoholic liquors, were written into law.[12] A third bill for the creation of a completely separate Indian state in the West was defeated.

In the area of the future Iowa taken from the Sauk and Fox in 1832, white-Indian relations deteriorated rather than improved despite the abject surrender of the Indians and the reforms of 1834. In theory the Black Hawk Purchase was justified because the area would serve as a buffer between the whites on the eastern side of the Mississippi and the Indians west of the purchase boundaries. This beautiful theory was nullified by two factors: the pressure of white population expansion (as squatters) against the western border of the purchase, and the existence of the 400-square-mile Keokuk's Reserve, which created friction rather than peace as the whites cast covetous glances at the choice land, making them regret their generosity of 1832. Moreover, the tendency of the Sauk and Fox to break up into factions over Keokuk's claims to supreme authority was a source of dissension. Some of the tribesmen revered him for his leadership against the Sioux but others could not forget his role as the white man's friend and collaborator during the Black Hawk War.

In a further effort to improve white-Indian relations, a council was arranged for September 1836 at Rock Island. On this occasion Chief Keokuk, resigning himself to reality, proposed the sale of his private holdings to the white man's government. Colonel Henry Dodge's counterproposal was a startling one: to buy *all* the Sauk and Fox lands in "Iowa" and move the owners south to the banks of the Missouri River. Dodge's proposition was too overwhelming, even for Keokuk, and it was firmly rejected. Instead, the ensuing treaty of September 28, 1836, provided that the whites would have to be content with the purchase of 256,000 acres of land (see Figure 3.2) for $30,000 cash, plus ten annuities of $10,000 each, plus the absorption of Sauk and Fox debts in the amount of $48,458.87½. In addition, a few more thousands of dollars were parceled out for the support of half-breed children, and $9,341 for the purchase of horses for the Indians.[13] The total cost came to about $200,000, averaging about 75 cents per acre for land resalable at $3 an acre, according to Colonel Dodge's calculations.

The very next year Henry Dodge won his battle for more land, though in a roundabout way. When the Sauk and Fox suffered a defeat by the Sioux, and proposed an alliance with the Oto, Potawatomi, and Iowa, the officers of the American Fur Company were alarmed by the prospects of a general Indian war. Agents of the company then urged the government to call a council in Washington, much to the delight of the Indians who had learned to enjoy the fleshpots of the cities of the East. The council was held in October 1837 and accomplished the all but final ruination of the Sauk and Fox. For something like 1.5 million acres of land just west of the Purchase of 1832 (see Figure 3.2) the United States agreed to pay $100,000 by absorption of the just debts of the Indians to the traders, $28,500 in goods "suited to their wants," $24,000 for fencing and ploughing the lands on which the Indians were to live, $10,000 for laborers' wages over a five-year period, $4,500 for horses, $1,000 for adjustment of a claim, and, finally, the interest on $200,000 to be invested in stocks.[14] For a total of $375,000 the United States thus acquired a parcel of choice land for the future use of white settlers, and brought about the almost total extinction of the Sauk and Fox in this region. That these particular Indians were generally very friendly to the whites, especially under Chief Keokuk's leadership, seems to be a fact that was overlooked.

CREATION OF A SEPARATE TERRITORY OF IOWA, 1838

The population of the District of Iowa as of 1836 was counted by the sheriffs and their deputies in the two counties, De Moine and Du Buque, and was reckoned to be 10,531; all estimates for 1837 and 1838 showed a continuing growth. The eager ones began to talk of separation from the Territory of Wisconsin almost as soon as that territory was formed, and the selection of Madison was assured as its capital. Those who had business to transact at the capital said the distance from the Iowa District to the City of the Four Lakes was too great. Burlingtonians and their neighbors were the first to take steps looking toward a new status for the Iowa District. The first meeting of any importance was held in Burlington on September 6, 1837, when De Moine County citizens met there and resolved that each of the seven counties of the area should hold a county meeting and elect three delegates to a convention to be held in Burlington in November. That convention met on November 6 and of course supported the separate status. (See Figure 4.1.) The very same argument used earlier by Delegate George W. Jones in favor of the division of Michigan was used now against Wisconsin.[15] Stress was laid on the point that a large and growing population was being neglected—for example, in the past sixteen months only one session of court had been held west of the river.

The Wisconsin territorial legislature generously memorialized Congress to pass the necessary legislation. The House of Representatives began the process by instructing its Committee on Territories to inquire into the expediency of a new territory for that part of the Territory of Wisconsin "lying west of the Mississippi and north of the State of Missouri." On February 6, 1838, the committee reported a bill to divide Wisconsin and establish a Territory of Iowa. For some reason the debates did not begin until June 5.[16] A few members of the House put up a token opposition, chiefly Waddy Thompson, Jr., of South Carolina, who wanted to make the creation of a Territory of Iowa conditional upon the annexation of Texas, a natural view for a Southern Democrat. Isaac Bronson of New York and Ebenezer Shields of Tennessee were the principal defenders of the proposition to proceed at once with the organization of the territory. The bill making up the Organic Law of the Territory of Iowa was passed in the House on June 6; the Senate concurred, and the bill was signed by President Martin Van Buren on June 12, 1838, to go into effect on July 4.[17] The area included would be not only the "District of Iowa" but all of the future Iowa, most of the future Minnesota, and parts of the Dakotas as well. (See Figure 4.1.)

Territorial Government

Contrary to natural expectations, and to distinguished authority, the laws of Iowa were not patterned after those of the Territory of Wisconsin. The first governor of Iowa Territory urged the Legislative Assembly "to adapt all our laws to suit the situation and interests of the Territory, without reference to the laws of Wisconsin or Michigan." A little later Governor Henry Dodge of Wisconsin Territory advised his Legislative Assembly to ask permission from Congress to change their terms of office from four years and two years to two years and one year, as provided in the territorial charter of Iowa for its legislators. Basically, however, the Iowa charter owes much to the Wisconsin document.[18]

Under the act of 1838, the governor of the territory was to be appointed by the president of the United States and confirmed by the Senate. President Van Buren first offered the governorship to General Henry Atkinson, a natural choice in view of his long and successful experience as an officer on frontier assignments and his role as commander of United States troops in the Black Hawk War. For some reason or reasons he promptly turned down the post; his biographer can only speculate on the matter because Atkinson left no clues to his thinking. It may have been because he wanted more duty in the West; it may have been that the small salary ($1,500 as governor, plus $1,000 as superintendent of Indian affairs) was not attractive; it may have been because he did not want to give up the pleasures of St. Louis society.[19] He might have made a good governor—this we can never know. We do know that he was a totally different type from the one to whom the president next offered the place: the aggressive and forceful Robert Lucas of Ohio, recently governor of that state for two terms, 1832–1836. Lucas accepted the post and thus assured the infant territory the experienced, firm, and courageous leadership which was needed. He chose Burlington as his temporary residence until the new territorial government could be completely organized.

The second officer of the territory, and replacement for the governor in case of his death, removal, resignation, or absence, was the secretary of the territory, an officer somewhat comparable to a lieutenant governor and secretary of state combined. The position was given to William B. Conway, a young and ambitious Pennsylvania Democrat. Because of a clash in personalities and differing concepts of authority between Lucas and Conway, the governor had to show great firmness if the prerogatives of the office of governor were to be upheld. Conway suffered an ignominious defeat in his schemes to replace Lucas. In the fall of 1839 he died, leaving his financial accounts in bad order, apparently a defaulter to the extent of $3,000. It might be added that Lucas had his troubles with the Legislative Assembly as well, mainly over the right of veto. He maintained his right but had to concede the power of the assembly to override his veto with a two-thirds vote.[20]

Important offices which were filled by presidential appointment, by and with the advice and consent of the Senate, were three judgeships on the Supreme Court of the territory, plus a territorial attorney and a territorial marshal. The personnel of the Court was a matter of great concern in view of the importance of setting the proper legal precedents for the territory, some of which would affect the future state of Iowa as well. No territory was ever more fortunate than Iowa in this respect. The chief justiceship was given to Charles Mason, a resident of Burlington, a graduate of West Point at the head of his class and later trained in the law in New York City. The other two places went to Joseph Williams of Muscatine and Thomas S. Wilson of Dubuque. Chief Justice Mason was called on to codify the territorial laws at the request of Governor Lucas. His superlative performance of this task set a high standard for all such future works, and ranks as a formative influence in early Iowa history. Justices Wilson and Williams ably carried their share of the judicial burden.[21]

The Legislative Assembly was to consist of two houses: a council of thirteen members and a House of Representatives of twenty-six members, the former with two-year terms and the latter with one-year terms. The governor was authorized to arrange a census and on such basis apportion the first council and House accordingly, and set the first elections; after that the assembly would have the power to draw its own district lines and provide for elections. In addition, the governor was authorized to choose the first legislative meeting place, the equivalent of choosing the temporary capital of the territory. After visiting Dubuque, where he was lavishly entertained, and Davenport, the residence of Secretary Conway and strongly favored by him, Governor Lucas returned to Burlington and announced his choice of that place as the seat of government until the designation of some other place by the Legislative Assembly.[22]

BURLINGTON AS THE CAPITAL

The territorial capital remained at Burlington for three years, though not without grumbling in some quarters. The legislators were dissatisfied with the inadequate halls which were available for meeting places, though one wonders where else in the new territory one might have found better facilities. "Smith's Capitol," used by the Wisconsin territorial legislature until it was lost by fire, was never replaced by a structure specifically designed as a capitol. Such construction would have been physically impossible on such short notice; also it must be remembered that Burlington was only a temporary capital of Wisconsin Territory and the town fathers now had every reason to believe that its place as the capital of Iowa Territory would be equally tentative. After the fire the Wisconsin solons met in vacant rooms in business buildings; now the Iowa Legislative Assembly made some slight improvement, perhaps, by meeting in the little Methodist Church of the community, known to later Iowans as Old Zion. The sessions of 1838 and 1839 used this building, as well as the special session of July 1840. After that, for the third regular session, the council met in St. Paul's Catholic Church while the representatives continued to use the Methodist building.[23]

A NEW TERRITORIAL CAPITAL: IOWA CITY

In his first message to the Legislative Assembly, Governor Lucas proposed the selection of three disinterested men of "known integrity and weight of character . . . to fix upon a place" for a territorial capital. Many towns at once began to seek designation as the capital and various resolutions were offered. The town of Mount Pleasant almost became the winner of the competition. Her rivals, unable to secure the prize for themselves, after sharp debate and close roll calls finally forced the passage of a resolution on January 3, 1839, for the selection of three commissioners, all or a majority of whom were to meet at the hamlet of Napoleon (in Johnson County) on May 1 and "proceed to locate the Seat of Government at a most eligible point within the present limits of Johnson county."

It was not to be done as simply as the resolution suggested. Governor Lucas was hard to satisfy on certain details but finally assented on January 21, taking on faith some matters to be cleared up as they went along. Worse yet, on the appointed day of May 1 only one of the three commissioners, Chauncey Swan, was present at the spot known as Napoleon, at best a hamlet of one house and one trading post. Just why the other two commissioners had not taken their duties more seriously is a point which has never been explained. One, Robert Ralston, was known to be out of reach in Des Moines County; the other, John Ronalds, was supposedly at his home some thirty-five miles away. Unless Ronalds could be found and brought to Napoleon, any action taken by Swan alone would be illegal. The story goes, supported by tradition, that a certain Philip Clark volunteered to ride to Ronalds's home and remind him of his assignment and his duty. With some allowance for dramatic effects that make up a good story, the result was that a few minutes before midnight, perhaps after a bit of tampering with Chauncey Swan's watch, Clark produced his man just in time to be sworn in by the local JP before the agonizing day came to an end.

The next day the two men began a search which ended about two miles from Napoleon. On the banks of the Iowa River they found a place which satisfied them. Officially designated on May 4 as "Section 10 of North Township 79 of Range 6 west of the 5th Principal Meridian," its name, Iowa City, had already been provided by legislative fiat. Petty details aside, the worthwhile point about the selection in 1839 is that a spot was selected by these rough and ready frontiersmen which offered great possibilities for both functional and aesthetic development. Nature not only provided a beautiful setting, if properly handled, but natural building stone was close at hand and also a navigable river as an artery of transportation, a great asset in those days.

Most fortunate of all was the choice of an architect and builder of great ability and impeccable taste, John Francis Rague, of Springfield, Illinois. Designer and builder of the Illinois capitol, he and his work somehow became known to Commissioner Chauncey Swan, who awarded him the contract for the Iowa building. For this, Iowans have learned to be thankful, although now it is known that the original building was much smaller and less imposing than the present enlarged structure.[24]

The building which Rague designed required two years for construction. As it took form, other developments took place. A town was platted and lots were auctioned off from time to time, the money going into the territorial treasury's general fund. Far-seeing individuals with a bit of ready cash were there to take advantage of their opportunity; less prescient ones would later curse their luck or lack of foresight. Two hundred and six lots were sold in 1839 for $26,739.75; in 1840 sales ran to thirty-eight lots for $7,077; in 1841, the sales amounted to twenty-eight lots for $9,031.[25]

In December 1841 the seat of government was moved to the clearing on the banks of the Iowa River even though the new Stone Capitol was not yet completed. The legislature in its first meeting in Iowa City had to make do with a frame building named after its builder, Walter Butler. The Stone Capitol was ready for use in December 1842. In the meanwhile other signs of growth were apparent. River traffic on the Iowa River was encouraged and was attempted for many years to come. Inland travel was contemplated and a road was laid out from Dubuque to Iowa City as part of a larger project authorized by Congress for a road from Dubuque to the Missouri border. A settler named Lyman Dillon was employed to break the Dubuque-Iowa City trail for such a road by ploughing a furrow as straight as a team of oxen could be driven and the topography would allow.[26]

BOUNDARY DISPUTE WITH MISSOURI

These constructive developments were not the whole story of the new territory. In 1839 Governor Robert Lucas, an old hand at fighting over disputed boundaries, found himself involved in a dispute over the exact location of the boundary line between the state of Missouri and the Territory of Iowa. This line, as finally determined, involved a disputed segment of some 2,600 square miles. There was great excitement and talk of "war" when a Missouri sheriff attempted to collect taxes in an area not previously regarded as Missouri's "sovereign" soil. Governor Lilburn W. Boggs of Missouri justified this on the grounds of a recent survey by Joseph C. Brown in 1837, describing a line from some ripples in the Des Moines River, near Keosauqua, to the northwest corner of Missouri.

The quarrel was not originated by Iowans. Before there was ever a Territory of Iowa there was a legal question: "What is the correct northern boundary of Missouri?" This question might have come before the courts at any time after 1821, the year of Missouri's admission into the Union with an admittedly tenuous northern boundary line. Missouri might have been challenged by the Territory of Michigan, or vice versa, between 1834 and 1836, or by the Territory of Wisconsin, or vice versa, between 1836 and 1838. As a matter of fact, the state of Missouri took the initiative and filed suit against the latter in 1837 to determine the proper boundary but that territory was divided in 1838 before the suit could be tried, and the Territory of Iowa inherited the suit.[27]

The squabble went back to 1808 when the Osage Indians ceded all their lands north of the Missouri River, but without exact northern limits. In 1816 a certain John C. Sullivan surveyed the Osage boundaries for the federal government. He started at the spot where the Kansas (Kaw) River flows into the Missouri, ran a line 100 miles due north, then ran a line due east, so he thought, to the Des Moines River, a line henceforth known as the Sullivan Line or The Old Indian Boundary. Some years later it was learned that his line veered slightly to the north so that it was several miles off course by the time it reached the Des Moines River.

The heart of the matter lay in the interpretation of the words, "rapids of the River Des Moines," used in the Missouri enabling act of March 6, 1820. Here the northern boundary line was described as a parallel of latitude running through the "rapids of the River Des Moines, . . . making the said boundary line to correspond with the Indian [Sullivan] boundary line"; thence to the middle of the channel of the "said River Des Moines," then down that river to the Mississippi. In 1821 Missouri was admitted with the vague understanding that such a line had been created. Later it would be revealed that the words, "rapids of the River Des Moines," were rooted in ignorance of the exact geography of the region but for years all the actions of Missouri and the territories of Michigan, Wisconsin, and Iowa were based on its acceptance.

After the Black Hawk Purchase Treaty of 1832, incoming settlers raised questions as to the exact location of the line. The question became more acute after the Platte Purchase of 1836 whereby Missouri added six counties to her northwestern corner by purchasing lands from Indians.[28] In December 1836 Missouri asked to have the northern boundary resurveyed. The line was run for Missouri by Joseph C. Brown. He searched the Des Moines River from its mouth upstream and found a few ripples in the river at the Great Bend, about 63 miles from its mouth, near the hamlet of Keosauqua, in Van Buren County. From this point he ran a line due west to the western boundary which Sullivan had established in 1816, and on to the Missouri River, providing, presumably, a northern boundary for the counties which Missouri had just acquired by the Platte Purchase. If the Brown Line could have been made to stand up all the way to the Missouri River, Iowa's loss would have been greater than in the Keosauqua area, because of the difference in the fertility of the land in the two areas.

The Brown Line, generally accepted as definitive by Missourians, was about thirteen miles north of the Sullivan Line. On hearing of the Missouri action, a Burlington convention drew up a petition to Congress, asking for a new survey; also, as explained above, Missouri went to the Supreme Court against the Territory of Wisconsin. Although the Court did nothing, the Congress and the president, Martin Van Buren, were not slow to act. Just six days after the Territory of Iowa was established, an act was passed to set up a three-man boundary commission, one man for each party concerned. Major Albert M. Lea was appointed as the United States Commissioner to ascertain the correct line; Governor Lucas appointed Dr. James Davis of Des Moines County; Missouri's Governor Boggs did not act.

Major Lea failed in this case to come up with an acceptable solution to the problem. He demonstrated that there were four possible

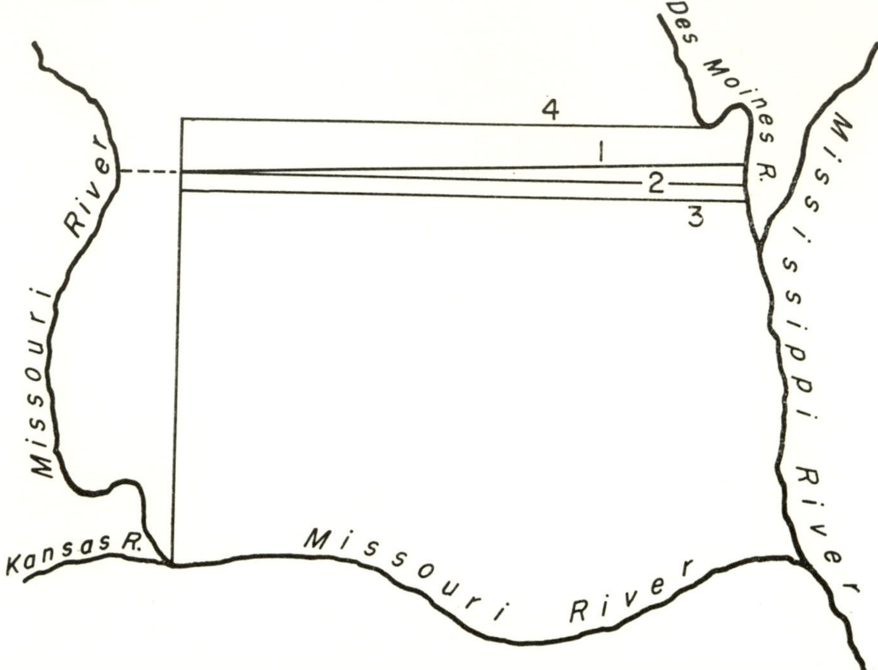

FIG. 4.2. A map to illustrate the border dispute between the Territory of Iowa and the state of Missouri. This map is based on a map which appears in 7 Howard (U.S. Reports), 660. The key to the numbers on the map is as follows:

1. Indian Line as surveyed by Sullivan in 1816.
2. Correct east-west line, which Sullivan should have followed, and which would have been the correct southern boundary of Iowa.
3. Line claimed by Iowa but not allowed.
4. Line claimed by Missouri (the Brown Line, 1837).

lines (see Figure 4.2), and chose the Sullivan Line as the most equitable, but pointed out that the law did not permit him to make a decision as to an official boundary. He threw out Line 2 completely as being neither legal nor equitable; either Line 3 or Line 4 would fulfill the terms of the law, so he said, but he refused to state his preference.[29]

On February 16, 1839, Missouri's legislature extended the jurisdiction of Missouri to the Brown Line. In August Sheriff Uriah Gregory of Clark County, Missouri, went into Van Buren County, Territory of Iowa, to levy and collect taxes. The sheriff visited the Farmington area and tactfully explained his mission and went home in the face of a hostile reaction. A lengthy series of letters, resolutions, proclamations, and conferences came to exactly nothing. Sheriff Gregory returned in November for a showdown.

Several hundred Missouri militiamen were prepared to engage in deadly combat with Iowa frontiersmen, organized as a United States Marshal's *posse comitatus* to defend their "sacred soil." Governor Lucas held that he was powerless in a dispute between the United States and a state. An added source of bad feelings was the act of some Missourians, nameless to history, in cutting down three or four "bee trees," stored with honey, giving rise to the label of The Honey War for the entire boundary dispute. When the Iowa troops were assembled, they were marched southward, only to find that the "enemy" had withdrawn. The appeal to force had been avoided and all agreed to return the dispute to Congress.

The matter dragged on for years. Iowa Territory's able delegate to Congress, Augustus C. Dodge, very properly pointed out that it was not only the land that was at stake—if Missouri were permitted to use the Brown Line, several thousand people who had thought that they were settling north of Missouri would be forced to move from a state whose laws permitting slavery were abominable and unbearable to them.[30] Finally came the struggle of Iowans in 1844–1846 to gain admittance as a state. After providing for the admission of Iowa by an act of August 4, 1846, Congress directed both states to take their boundary question to the Supreme Court for a final and definitive decision. Suit was brought in 1847; the case was heard and decided in 1849. A unanimous Court held that the Sullivan Line had been accepted by Missouri authorities and by United States officials all through the years, particularly in making treaties with the Indians. The Court sat down hard on Iowa's attempt to gain a line south of the Sullivan Line, using the same reasoning. It also firmly held that the northern boundary of Atchison and Nodaway counties in Missouri must be an extension of the Sullivan Line due west to the Missouri, not the Brown Line.[31]

The Court decreed that a new commission should be set up to make a true and correct survey of the line, with special attention to the establishment of the northwest corner of Missouri, to be marked with a cast-iron pillar, and the line to be marked with pillars of stone and cast iron planted every ten miles. The commission reported in 1850 that the work had been completed; a final decree was issued in 1851 and the matter was laid to rest.[32]

SQUATTERS ASSOCIATIONS: LEGEND OF THE CLAIM CLUBS

It is easy to exaggerate the importance of the Black Hawk Purchase when describing the whole series of land acquisitions which total up to "Iowa"—Cyrenus Cole is only the most prominent writer, not the only one, alas, who has erroneously conveyed the thought that these lands constituted the "indemnity that became Iowa."[33] Actually, the lands that became Iowa were acquired in a long series of treaties running from 1824 to 1851. Once acquired, the lands had to be surveyed, and government land offices had to be opened and auctions conducted before valid titles could be obtained. Before the first land offices were opened in 1838, thousands of settlers and speculators had put down claims to lands. All such claimants were trespassers, "permissible trespassers," perhaps, until the Preemption Act of 1841 wiped the slate clean and gave them a chance to make a new start. In the frontiersman's vocabulary, these trespassers were "squatters."

For their own protection and aggrandizement, the squatters formed clubs and virtually took the law into their own hands, or bent the law to suit their needs. Probably no story has been repeated more often, with greater relish, than the tale of these hardy frontiersmen, honest and God-fearing men, who came into the Iowa country (and other prospective territories and states) a few jumps ahead of the government surveys, staked out their claims for future redemption, and then banded together in "claim clubs" for mutual protection of their claims against Eastern speculators, later extending the clubs into self-governing societies which became training schools for democratic government. The moral of such stories was that all "good" people were members or supporters of such clubs, and all who did not join or support them were self-evident allies of the outsiders, who meant only to make a quick profit and then skip the country, leaving to others the more mundane but "patriotic" tasks of improving the lands and the communities which would grow up. Earlier writers authenticated this story and asserted that such clubs were common in eastern and central Iowa before the government land offices were set up.[34]

New criteria of historical generalization and new methods of research have made it possible for specialists in this field to draw a much clearer and more accurate picture of the actual operations of such clubs. If this is to be done, land acquisition must be viewed as an economic process, not a moral issue; second, the researcher must be willing to spend long eye-straining hours in musty court records, studying the resale records and not just the original sale prices. Such study, augmented by close examination of the standard county histories, has revealed that there were only 26 claim clubs in the whole of Iowa, rather than the 100 or more as previously estimated. Such study further reveals that the activities of club members were not nearly so innocent and so noble as they have been pictured. Members exceeded the amount of land (one quarter section) allowed by law, dealt wildly in claims, and not infrequently failed to register their entries when the government land office was opened. Sometimes the members themselves took the role of speculators against real farmers who wanted to file claims on vacant lands; members used the clubs to "extort tribute from latecomers to the community rather than prevent jumping of legitimate claims."[35]

In addition to these findings, a study of a larger scale of operations by the giants in the field of investment has conclusively shown that the heaviest speculators generally operated through local land agents; that they operated frequently by mail rather than by personal visitation, thus giving business to local realtors; that they were interested in finding purchasers as soon as possible rather than in tying up land (and their own money) for long periods of time, hoping for the big rise and the big kill in speculative gains; that they paid their full share of taxes and sometimes more; that their rate of profit was not exorbitant; that they performed such services as advertising the land and offering travel assistance, thus attracting settlers into a new country; that they loaned money to prospective purchasers and often carried them on the books for the first lean year or two on the land, all this in a time when banking services, as we know them, were not available. In short, while the speculators were not angels, they were law-abiding capitalists rather than bloodsucking absentee landlords or fly-by-night hucksters. It is hard to envision the actual settlement of the land under frontier conditions without the performance of their role.[36]

THE UNITED STATES AND LAND DISPOSAL

The first land offices were put into operation in 1838 at Burlington and Dubuque. In 1842 offices were opened in Fairfield and Marion to augment the work in the older districts. In 1843 a district was laid out with headquarters at Iowa City; in 1852 added districts were set up around offices in Chariton, Fort Des Moines, and Council Bluffs. In 1855 districts were marked out around Fort Dodge, Sioux City, and Decorah; in 1856 an office was opened at Osage to supplement the Decorah operations.

Iowa lands were either sold or given away in the proportions shown in Table 4.1.[37]

Thus a generous government disposed of some 36,000,000 acres of land which eventually came under the name of Iowa. The fact of overwhelming importance is that a good third of the land was bought for cash, while more than a third was given away in the form of military bounties—a total of 73.4 percent of all the lands in Iowa falling into these two categories. Many of the military bounty lands found their way into the hands of speculators, sometimes by the honest purchase of the warrants from soldiers who did not want to go west to take up their lands, sometimes, no doubt, by questionable transactions. Generous Congresses gave out the military land warrants with a lavish

TABLE 4.1: Disposal of Iowa lands

	(%)
Cash sales	33.7
Military bounties	39.7
Agricultural college scrip locations	0.7
Homesteads	2.5
Timber claims	0.1
Miscellaneous	0.1
State grants:	
Swamp and saline lands	3.4
Educational grants	4.9
Internal and river improvements and public buildings	3.2
Railroad construction grants	11.7
	100.0

hand as a reward or aid to those who had served the country in its major wars and in its campaigns and skirmishes against the Indians. Such warrants were given out along with the discharges at the time of separation from the service, and were assignable. Fortunate indeed was the veteran who took his warrants and immediately came out to Illinois or Iowa or some other fertile state to cash in on his bonus by trading in the warrants for good black land, for future use or for sale. The veteran who held on to his warrant or his land stood to gain in a time of constantly rising land values. Not all were so provident—or so lucky.

One of the marvels of Iowa history is the speed with which Iowa was settled. With due allowances for inaccuracies and incompleteness, the census figures for 1836 for the Iowa District show 10,531; for 1838, 22,859; for 1840, 43,116. In 1844 the count was 75,150 and in 1846, the year of statehood, the figure was 96,088.

INDIAN AFFAIRS

By 1840 our national government had arrived at a new and seemingly definitive Indian policy: a policy of isolation, or "concentration," based on the supposition that the Indians would benefit by isolation from the debasing effects of contact with the white man. The commissioner of Indian affairs, T. Hartley Crawford, approved this policy, justifying it as a recognition of the rights of advancing white settlers! In his opinion the whites should not be held back by the presence of a "people not amenable to their laws, whose wild and savage character renders them dangerous neighbors." Governor James Duane Doty of Wisconsin Territory said about the same thing. No great powers of discernment are needed to see that the white man was more concerned with his own interests than with the rights or welfare of the Indians.[38]

The Neutral Ground Experiment

It is in this light that the "protective" policy of putting the Winnebago Indians into the Neutral Ground in northeast Iowa, originally set aside in 1830, should be judged. Ostensibly our government was gathering these nearly helpless Indians into a protected buffer zone, policed by soldiers who would ward off the ferocious Sioux on the north and the aggressive Sauk and Fox on the south. Unfortunately the peace-keeping plan did not work out very well. First of all, the Winnebago were loath to leave their familiar and beloved haunts in Wisconsin and strong pressure had to be applied to get them to move. Somehow the job was done in 1840. As a symbol of its power to police the Indians, the government built a fort on the Turkey River at a point about fifty miles inland from the Mississippi, naming it for General Henry Atkinson, the great Indian fighter and might-have-been first governor of the Iowa Territory. The poor Winnebago now found themselves oppressed by their foes and badgered by their friends. It must be admitted that the reluctant Winnebago made very poor wards and poorly disposed clients. It would be only a few years until another move would have to be made.[39]

Treaties of 1842 and 1846

In 1842 the government made its last deal with the Sauk and Fox in Iowa. The superintendent of Indian affairs at St. Louis joined the great trading interests and the squatters in urging the purchase of their lands and the removal of the Indians before Iowa attained statehood, "after which he would be powerless to protect them from the Whites, whom he characterized as rapidly increasing in numbers and depravity."[40] Years of mistreatment by white squatters, by unscrupulous traders who deliberately took advantage of the Indian taste for "firewater," and of their ignorance of fair values, finally paid off: the red men were brought to the point of nonresistance by the pressures exerted against them. Perhaps Chief Keokuk's desire to please the whites and gain glory for himself made it a little easier to close the deal but one should remember that his role was not decisive in policy-making.

The negotiations were prolonged. The treaty was almost arranged in 1841 but the white spokesmen overreached themselves, and John Beach, the government agent for the Sauk and Fox, was able to hold out for a fairer deal. Governor John Chambers of the Territory of Iowa acted as the representative for the United States; for the Indians, Keokuk and Appanoose for the Sauk, and Poweshiek and Pashepaho for the Fox. By the treaty made at the Indian Agency on October 11, 1842, these Indians ceded their lands in the Territory of Iowa to the United

States in return for a home to be selected by the president somewhere on the Missouri or its tributary waters. In addition, they received $800,000 in cash, annuities of 5 percent of that amount, and the government assumed Indian debts of $258,566, a figure which might have been $321,566 if Governor Chambers had not fought so well for the smaller amount. The governor agreed that the Indians might remain in the area east of the Red Rocks until May 3, 1843, and just beyond that line for three more years while they prepared for the transfer to their new home somewhere in the cheerless expanse known as the Indian Territory.[41]

In June 1846, at the very time when the final details of Iowa statehood were being arranged, the Potawatomi sold a vast area of land to the national government for $850,000, an area including all of their lands "north of the Missouri River, embraced in the Territory of Iowa." Next, the United States bought out the claims of the Winnebago to the Neutral Ground, and all other Winnebago claims based on the Treaty of September 15, 1832, made at Fort Armstrong. This deal cost the United States $150,000 plus $40,000 for their hunting privileges, and a grant of 800,000 acres of land north of the St. Peters (Minnesota) River. The actual removal did not take place until 1848, after which Fort Atkinson could be abandoned. Thus, as Iowa entered the Union, only two small parcels of land within the state remained in the hands of Indians, in this case the doughty Sioux. The purchase of their lands could await an opportune time.[42]

MORMON AFFAIRS

During the years of Iowa's territorial status, at the very time when a chief concern was the need for an increase in population, the Mormons made their appearance in the southeastern corner of the territory. Perhaps their coming just at this time was not unrelated to Iowa's frontier condition in the early 1840s. For years the Saints had been in search of peace and complete freedom of worship, moving from New York to Kirtland, Ohio, to northwest Missouri, where they received and returned many a hard blow. From their troubles in Missouri they fled again, this time to Quincy, Illinois, as a temporary refuge.[43] It had become obvious that the peace and freedom they wanted would be found only in a remote region undesired by others, in which they could build a community according to their own beliefs.

Although Joseph Smith, the Prophet and leader, was in jail at Liberty, Missouri, his lieutenants and followers at Quincy proceeded to look for lands in Illinois and Iowa Territory on which they might settle. For the leaders the question of the hour was whether another attempt should be made to gather the faithful in a new Zion or simply to disperse and carry on as individuals. While in this very unsettled state of mind, it was their fortune to come into contact with a colorful frontier land speculator, Dr. Isaac Galland, whom we have already met as the originator of Iowa's first school. The doctor was a dealer in lands on both sides of the river. Ingratiating himself with the Mormon leaders at Quincy, and with Joseph Smith himself after the Prophet escaped from jail, Dr. Galland sold several hundred acres of land on the Illinois side to the Saints, near the paper towns of Commerce and Commerce City, and thousands of acres in Lee County, Iowa Territory, in the area known as the Half-Breed Reservation. (See Figure 3.2.) The fast-talking doctor seemed very confident of being able to deliver an unclouded title to the Half-Breed Lands which he was offering; others were not so certain of titles in an area which a distinguished scholar has called "a land purchaser's nightmare."[44]

A decision was quickly made and announced by Joseph Smith as a doctrinal point that a gathering of the Saints was to be made on each side of the river: the one on the Illinois side was no longer to be called by the worldly name Commerce but by a biblical word, Nauvoo, meaning "beauty and repose"; the settlement on the Iowa side was given the awkward name Zarahemla, a word taken from the *Book of Mormon*. The Prophet himself set up his residence on the Illinois side, which, of course, guaranteed the advantage to Nauvoo. In spite of the hostility of the gentiles in the area, Mormon converts flocked to the Illinois village from far and near, especially people from the depressed cities of Eastern United States and victims of the Industrial Revolution in Great Britain. Nauvoo quickly grew into a city of 20,000 souls, the largest in Illinois just then, whereas Zarahemla struggled along and finally faded out as a stake of Zion. Thus narrowly did Iowa miss the distinction of becoming for a time the chief residence of the Saints. Even so, the day of their departure from this rapidly developing region for still another Zion would only have been postponed briefly.

As for the arrogant claim that Iowans believed in religious tolerance and therefore were ready to give to the Mormons that fair treatment which had been denied them elsewhere, the whole idea needs reexamination. For proof of such exalted virtue on the part of Iowa's citizens, a letter by Governor Robert Lucas is referred to, in which promises of welcome and fair treatment were made. Actually, the query which elicited the letter or letters from the territorial governor (which have never been found by researchers) was part of Dr. Galland's campaign to unload some of the lands he claimed to own or represent. The year was 1840; certainly the governor would not knowingly antagonize these industrious people or any other prospective settlers who were so badly needed. It should be added that Governor Lucas was not necessarily representative of the people of Iowa Territory as to Christian virtues; most gentiles took every opportunity to make derogatory remarks about the Saints. Even so, Governor Lucas made a guarded response of some sort which Dr. Galland, in typical promoter's style, expanded into a "testimonial" to the "good character" of the Mormons and the inference that all "Iowans" would be kind to these good but unfortunate people. At the time, only a few people in this one remote county of the territory were involved in the matter in any way. There were no "Iowans" as of 1840 in any meaningful sense of the word.[45]

It is not difficult to account for the hostility of the gentiles, who made up a majority of the people in Hancock County, Illinois, except in Nauvoo itself. Here we have the age-old story of the sufferings of a minority group at the hands of a majority, with the Mormon minority in a provocative role because of their claims to be God's chosen people. Other factors were the ever-present tendency of a majority to assert their superiority, aggravated by jealousy of the economic success of the minority group; suspicion of the minority group's clannishness; resentment of their demands for preferential treatment from the state, which, if granted, would create a state within a state; Mormon adherence to the antidemocratic principle of complete authority for the leader; and the accusation that the sect believed in and practiced polygamy. Finally, the Saints were suspected of involvement in the murder of Colonel George Davenport.

After years of troubles at Nauvoo, Joseph Smith's announcement of his presidential candidacy in 1844, and Mormon destruction of a newspaper owned by apostates who were critical of Joseph Smith and the doctrine of polygamy, seemed to be the climax of all their arrogant acts as seen through the eyes of the gentiles. The Prophet and his brother Hyrum were arrested and taken for safekeeping to a jail in nearby Carthage. An enraged mob, fed on rumors of an attempted jail delivery, attacked the jail and murdered the prisoners, thus turning the Prophet into a Mormon martyr. No effective move was made by either state or federal government to intervene for the protection of the prisoners or to punish the assassins. After some in-fighting among the faithful, the mantle of Joseph Smith was assumed by Brigham Young, though not without protest. In 1845 gentile persecution of the Saints threatened to bring on a bloody civil war. Finally, Brigham Young promised the Illinois governor's agents that the Mormons would evacuate Nauvoo the following spring.[46] Since their new Zion had to be somewhere in the West, Iowa was certain to be involved, as part of a route westward if nothing else.

The first move in the flight from Nauvoo was across the Mississippi to the obscurity of a camp seven miles inland on Sugar Creek, near Montrose, Iowa Territory. Beginning in the dead of winter, February 4, 1846, following plans which had been made and rehearsed for months, the Saints succeeded in crossing the river with few losses. On Sugar Creek the vanguard could finish their preparations for the journey into the unknown. The table of organization emphasized a chain of com-

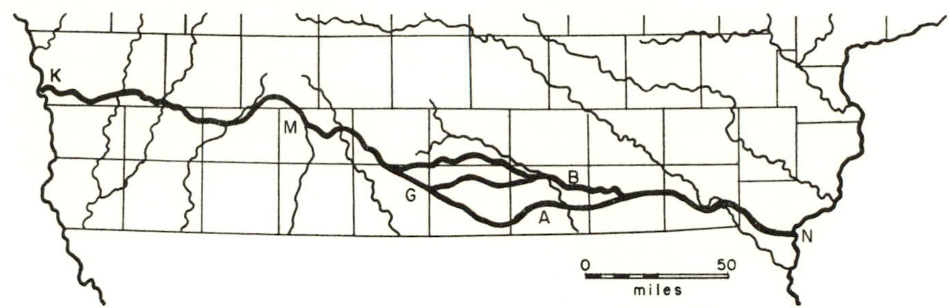

FIG. 4.3. The Mormon trails across southern Iowa, 1846–1856. Map adapted from Wallace Stegner, *A Gathering of Zion* (New York: McGraw-Hill, 1964).

N—Nauvoo, Ill. K—Kanesville (now Council Bluffs)
G—Garden Grove A—1846 route
M—Mount Pisgah B—Alternate routes used after 1846

The reader may also want to consult Figure 1.7 to find the names of the rivers indicated in the above map.

mand employing the leadership principle. Supplies were collected, wagons were built or repaired, oxen and drivers trained, and a thousand and one other details attended to, all with remarkable efficiency and cheerfulness of spirit, in spite of the bitter cold. Finally, on February 25 and 28, detachments of restless members were allowed to lead out, with the main force following on March 1. As fast as these vacated the Sugar Creek base, others crossed over from Nauvoo, made their final preparations, and followed at intervals until late in the year.

With courage and patience in long-suffering, which perhaps only religious zeal could inspire and sustain, the Saints made their way across Iowa. (See Figure 4.3.) The Mormon Trail went from Sugar Creek to Farmington, staying north of the Des Moines River until the crossing at Bonaparte, then generally followed the route of modern Highway 2 westward. Brigham Young wrote to Governor James Clarke for permission to plant temporary camps across Iowa Territory, but by the time he received the governor's favorable answer in September, their principal camps had already been established. The first one along the way was Richardson's Point, a little west of Farmington; the second one was near Centerville. The third, strategically the most important of all, was at Garden Grove. The next was Mt. Pisgah, very important to them but now nonexistent except for a Mormon cemetery at nearby Talmage, in Union County. The last stop in Iowa Territory was at a spot on the Missouri, where a ferry was operated by Peter Sarpy, an agent and trader for the American Fur Company. A camp was made here to serve as a base while waiting for turns on Sarpy's ferry, which carried its passengers across Big Muddy to a spot called Bellevue. Eventually the Mormons were stretched out along the Missouri from this place northward for fifteen miles to a spot at which they established their own ferry directly across from their permanent camp, "Winter Quarters," in the northern part of present Omaha. (Long years later a bridge near the old ferry route would be named in their honor.)

These shifting scenes of activity have caused some confusion and controversy among later generations. It seems safe to say that the first members of the advance guard to reach the river referred to the entire region as the Bluffs, as did other early travelers along the river. To their first camp the Saints gave the name Miller's Hollow, probably in deference to George Miller, the first leader to leave Sugar Creek, on February 25. Another name soon came into use, Kanesville, in honor of a certain Thomas Kane who befriended them as intercessor with President James K. Polk. After a time these names gave way to Council Bluffs City and this to the present name.[47]

The Mormon Battalion

One famous but not well-understood item in Iowa-Mormon history was the recruitment of the Mormon Battalion to serve in the current war with Mexico. As they were on the trek across Iowa, just beyond the Nodaway River the Saints were alarmed by the approach of an emissary of the United States, Captain James Allen, who proved to be a messenger with a requisition for 500 Mormon recruits for service against Mexico. The details of the ensuing negotiations may be followed in the diary of Hosea Stout, a captain in the Mormon Guards.[48] More than most, Captain Stout was convinced that the request for the services of the young men was only a ruse whereby the government could ruin the Mormon cause—until he found that one no less than Brigham Young, the "Lion of the Lord," had *initiated* a deal to furnish the soldiers, for whom the government would pay wages directly to the Mormon treasury. The young men did not volunteer, as is so often said or implied; Brigham Young sold their services as much as ever Swiss parents sold their sons as European mercenaries. If there was no protest, it was because the transaction was in keeping with the Mormon custom of the collective use of their resources. The deal was made at a time when the financial woes of the Saints were at their peak and there is no doubt that the money earned was the margin between starvation and life for many who spent the winter of 1846–1847 at Winter Quarters. As matters turned out, the military service was of no consequence. The "troops" were assembled at Council Bluffs and sent on a march through the Southwest all the way to California, many taking their wives with them as "laundresses." A trusted official was sent after them to collect their wages in gold and bring the money back to Brigham Young for distribution.

Consequences of the Mormon Exodus

A number of material things give witness to the Mormon March across Iowa. Not just one, but three basic routes were opened for travel. The first hundred miles west of Nauvoo cannot be credited to their path-breaking; after that distance they were truly on their own and by trial and error they found the best routes across the territory. From Bloomfield west they marked out their first road, the southern one, always avoiding a misstep into the land of their Missouri enemies. Later they found a way to follow the ridges and higher ground north of the Chariton River. At the site of the modern town of Chariton, the marchers could strike out in a westerly direction and proceed until they approached the bluffs on the Missouri, where a slight shift to the north-west would be necessary. (Present-day Highway 34 pretty well follows this portion of their route.) Still later they marked a third route between the other two, so as to utilize their station at Garden Grove. Wherever they traveled they left their trail markings for the benefit of those who would come later; bridges were built or the best fording places were discovered, improved, and marked, often at a high cost in effort and sometimes in lives. Clearings were made; wells were dug; fields and gardens planted, always with a thought for those who would come afterwards.[49]

Mormons have been credited with having enough influence with the Iowa legislature to secure the passage of a law which forbids prosecution for bigamy except on the complaint of the aggrieved wife, a doubtful honor if true. Most of all the Mormons left the heroic example of men and women willing to endure any amount of suffering, even death, to achieve what they believed in. Rain and mud, sleet and snow, heat and cold, prairie fires, drought, floods, disease, poor food and sometimes no food at all, attacks by wolves and rattlesnakes, unkind treatment from people along the way—in short, every form of suffering imaginable was met and conquered. Not every person was equal to the strain but most of them were heroes, the women most of all. Only the artless memoirs of those who survived can do justice to the trials and traumatic experiences which these people endured and over which they triumphed.

Those who trekked in the third and fourth groups were the most pitiful of all because of their sufferings in Nauvoo at the hands of their gentile enemies. In September 1846, the anti-Mormons came in as an organized militia and expelled the few remaining Saints with a cruelty known only to religious fanaticism. Most of those who managed to survive the horrors of the trip arrived in Kanesville in a pitiful condition and it was impossible for even so dominant and resourceful a leader as Brigham Young to prepare his followers for an immediate continuation of the exodus to the West. Most of the Saints spent the fall and winter in camp at Winter Quarters; a few stayed on the Kanesville side of the river.

Theological Dissension

The remainder of the Mormon story is peripheral to Iowa history except for the subsequent story of the Separatists who formed the Reorganized Church of Jesus Christ of Latter Day Saints. This dissident group has an extended history of its own, but like several breakaway groups, differed primarily on two doctrinal points: succession to the Prophet, and the rejection of the doctrine of polygamy. The preparation for this fragmentation of the Saints can be traced by the knowledgeable all the way back to their experience at Nauvoo;[50] the experiences along the route of the exodus are sufficient to account for the discontents of the actual participants. Those who remained in Iowa instead of going on with Brigham Young tended toward an independence of conduct which found temporary leadership in the persons of James Jesse Strang and the Prophet's brother, William Smith, but a more permanent leader in the Prophet's son, Joseph Smith III. This son and his mother, Lucy Mack Smith, had remained in Nauvoo in and after 1846, a minor miracle in itself. The dissents only vaguely expressed since the Prophet's death in 1844 over leadership and polygamy now opened up a great gulf between the groups. In 1852, having meanwhile founded and built up his base in Utah, President Young sought to end the division and ordered all true believers to journey at once to their new Zion, now ambitiously called the State of Deseret.

James Jesse Strang refused to leave his "Kingdom" near Beloit, Wisconsin, and Lyman Wight, who had defected during the trek, led his followers all the way to Texas. All in all, nineteen dissenting or apostatized groups have been counted. The group of greatest interest to Iowans, the Strangites, gradually shifted their allegiance to Joseph Smith III. Wherever he might be residing for the moment, that was their Zion. He was at first disinclined to take the leadership but gradually roused himself to accept the honor, about 1855. The Strang group now moved from Ohio to Plano, Illinois, near Aurora, and continued to publish a paper. In the 1870s a move was made to establish headquarters somewhere in southern Iowa. The first migrants chose a hamlet known as Pleasanton, strangely close to the Missouri line. The first order of the day was land speculation, an interest which opened up a new locality to which they moved and which they named Lamoni. This was in 1879. In 1880 they began the operation of a publishing house in Lamoni; in 1881 the town was platted. As the Reorganized Church of Jesus Christ of Latter Day Saints they have since flourished. In 1895 they set up Graceland College, which now draws students from all over the world. In spite of the loss of the headquarters of the church to Independence, Missouri, in 1904, the town has maintained its prestige as a cultural center of their church. It is this group of Saints and this town which most Iowans have in mind when they think of Mormonism, a not altogether accurate assumption inasmuch as the Reorganized Church rejects the word "Mormon" and repudiates any and all association with Brigham Young, his followers, and their teachings.[51]

THE HANDCART EXPEDITIONS

The dramatic successes of the missionary programs of the Utah-based Saints in the Eastern states and in Great Britain and Scandinavia sent streams of converts to the new Zion after 1847. Many of these faithful traveled by ship to New York or other ports and then made their way by rail to Chicago and then on to Iowa City where the rails reached their end in 1855. Others came from Europe by ship to New Orleans and then came by steamer to Keokuk to begin their westward overland trek from the Gate City. An acute observer in Keokuk, himself a gentile, has left a glowing account of the good order and the efficient organization in the Mormon camp just outside that town in 1853.[52]

The use of handcart expeditions for the difficult journey across undeveloped Iowa and the rougher country beyond was not a demonstration of religious fervor for its own sake. The plan of using handcarts was first mentioned in 1852 but postponed until 1855, when the order came to prepare the carts for use in 1856. No one denied that their use was an economy measure, brought on by the unexpected success of the missions. The handcart method of travel was not as inefficient, certainly not as absurd, as some have made it out to be. This technique of travel was continued through 1857, 1858, 1859, and 1860 for Utah-bound companies, and by missionaries on their eastward journeys to the Missouri River crossing points. Even on the earlier expeditions men, women, and young people, in fact, all but the very young and the very old, preferred to walk alongside their ox-drawn wagons which could not make more than two miles per hour. Most of the handcart travelers carried only the barest necessities while ox-drawn supply wagons brought along the bulky articles such as barrels of flour and salt. Only the inexcusable blunder of those who sent out two handcart expeditions late in 1856 has given this mode of travel such a bad name. Over two hundred poor souls paid with their lives for this mistake in judgment.[53]

CHAPTER 5 FROM TERRITORY TO STATEHOOD 1844–1846

While the territorial period of Iowa history was eventful, opinion was mixed on the subject of readiness for statehood. Some were ready soon after 1838 to apply for the higher status; others seemed reluctant whenever the subject was taken up. An interesting theoretical question arises here: Should the people of a territory be prepared for statehood before giving them this status, or should full responsibility for self-government be thrust upon them and allowance be made for learning while doing?

UNSUCCESSFUL ADVOCACY OF STATEHOOD, 1839–1842

Certainly the first two territorial governors of Iowa acted on the assumption that the latter course was correct. In November 1839 Governor Lucas proposed that the assembly should ask Congress to authorize a call for a constitutional convention. He was forced to admit that Iowa as a state would have to pay her own expenses, but argued for statehood anyhow. Ohio, Indiana, Illinois, and Michigan had lagged during territorial days but had made a faster growth after the attainment of statehood, so he said, implying that Iowa would also prosper if she sought and gained statehood for herself. The governor's poor logic triumphed over his wisdom. The statement might have been true for the other territories but was not necessarily true for Iowa. Governor Lucas was so confident that the assembly would adopt his proposal that he additionally suggested the boundaries which he thought appropriate for the new state. Much to the governor's disappointment, the proposal was turned down, but the suggested boundary lines survived as a memorial to his name.

The question soon bobbed up again. Acting this time on its own initiative, the Committee on Territories in the national House of Representatives reported favorably on a bill to give Iowa authorization to hold a constitutional convention. This was sufficient encouragement for Governor Lucas. When the Legislative Assembly met in special session in July 1840, he again brought up the subject but this time asked the lawmakers to submit the question to the people. His advice was followed, but in the regular annual elections, held in August, the proposition was decisively defeated, 2,907 to 937. After this rejection the matter was dropped as national politics took the spotlight, notably the elections of 1840 which brought a Whig victory.

In 1841 Robert Lucas, Democrat, was replaced by an appointee of the new Whig president, William Henry Harrison, who named a Kentucky Whig, John Chambers, to the office. Although a member of the antistatehood party of the moment, Chambers broke with party politics and in his first annual message of December 1841 asked the assembly to submit the proposition to the people again. After much debate the governor's proposal was passed, and in August 1842 the people voted for a second time on the issue, again sending it to defeat. Since the Democrats were presumably the majority party and, presumably, the party in favor of statehood, the unexpected defeat is difficult to explain. The old English method of viva voce voting, used on this occasion, consisting of an open declaration of one's vote for or against a candidate or a proposal, makes analysis of the voting almost impossible.

The arguments which were the stock in trade of the politicians of the time were much the same as those used in more recent times. Those favoring statehood appealed to pride and to the natural desire to participate in national elections and help to determine the fate of the country. The greater costs and higher taxes under state government were countered by assurances that the Distribution Act of 1841 would provide more money than was necessary for Iowa's share of expenses. In addition, the state would receive five hundred thousand acres of land for use or sale. Also, Iowa must seize the chance to come in now, as a nonslave state paired with Florida as a slave state, rather than see Wisconsin Territory do this if Iowans failed to act favorably.

The Whig opponents of statehood appealed most of all to the fear of a greater tax burden if federal funds that now paid for territorial government were lost. Another telling argument was the accusation that the Democrats, the majority party in Iowa, wanted a state government merely to give ex-Governor Lucas and ex-Territorial Judge Joseph Williams an opportunity to get back into office. One Whig, Ralph P. Lowe, not suspecting that he himself would one day be elected governor, asserted that the territory had no men who were qualified for officeholding. Later revelations would bring out that the Whigs were dragging their feet in the hope that they soon would build up a firm majority and control the state.[1]

THE CONSTITUTIONAL CONVENTION OF 1844

By February 1844 the Territorial Assembly had overcome its reluctance to go along with the idea of statehood. An election for delegates to a state constitutional convention was set up for August in connection with the regular annual election. In this election the Democrats won two-thirds of the memberships in a convention to be held in Iowa City on October 7, 1844.

Some interesting and perhaps significant data about the delegates have been prepared by Professor Benjamin F. Shambaugh. Seventy-three members were elected but only seventy-two took part in the work of the convention. Of these, fifty-one were Democrats and twenty-one were Whigs. Twenty-six members had been born in the South (an undefined term as used here), twenty-three in the Middle States, ten in New England, ten in the Old Northwest, and one each in Germany, Scotland, and Ireland. Thirteen came to Iowa from Pennsylvania, eleven from Virginia (decades before the split-off of West Virginia), nine from New York, eight from Kentucky, eight from Ohio, six from North Carolina, six from Vermont, and one each from Massachusetts, Connecticut, New Hampshire, Maine, New Jersey, Tennessee, Indiana, and Illinois. None was from the Deep South, and forty-six were from distinctly non-Southern states, counting the three Europeans. The average age was close to forty years. The occupation most heavily represented was farming, with forty-six; next came the legal profession with nine. There were five physicians, three merchants, two mechanics, two miners, two millwrights, one printer, one miller, and one civil engineer. No data were given on the educational background of the members.

Many safeguarding reservations have to be made about such data before any useful generalizations can be deduced from them. The point about place of birth is, in itself, of no importance. Far more important would be information on a man's formative years, thus indicating the sources of his ideas. Information as to his age at the time of his migration to Iowa would be of great value. The previous place of residence, as given, is of little importance unless it could be shown that one had actually participated in or closely observed state government in his previous home state. A minor dissent should be raised as to the implied influence of one's profession or business. Five times as many members were farmers as lawyers. Does this guarantee that the farmer members thought only of the agricultural interest? It could be assumed that a lawyer, a merchant, a physician, or any other nonfarm member would be directly interested in the prosperity of his farmer clients and customers. Have we any assurance that the nonfarmers had no sideline investments in farming?

The most serious objection to Shambaugh's data is his easy generalization about the regional origins of the members. Presumably, the twenty-six from the "South" would have certain attitudes toward the Negro and about slavery—but one should inquire further. Which "South" did these men come from? North Carolina, Virginia, and Kentucky are given as the Southern states but many parts of these states do not qualify as "Southern" as the term is most frequently used. It is completely unrealistic to describe as "Southern" the Appalachian-Blue Ridge sections of the three states named; their culture is greatly different from that of the Deep South. Many men left those three states to go north or west because of their ideas and beliefs about slavery which clashed with those held in the Deep South. Unless further geographical and personal information is given, Shambaugh's data are of little value.[2]

THE CONSTITUTION OF 1844

The framework of the proposed state government was very simple. The convention gave the governor a two-year term, after serious consideration of a four-year term of office. His veto power was similar to that of the nation's chief executive. The legislative branch was made up of the usual two houses, a House of Representatives and a Senate, with two- and four-year terms, respectively. The judges of the State Supreme Court would be named by the General Assembly and the district court judges elected by the people. The range of suggested salaries for governor ran from $600 to $1,200; the compromise figure was $800. Other offices were scaled accordingly, the state treasurer coming out at the bottom of the list at $300, an open invitation, it would seem, to fraud and defalcation.

IOWANS DISCOVER THE NEGRO QUESTION

On the question of the status and rights of Negroes, convention members and many of their constituents proved themselves to be no more and no less liberal than their contemporaries throughout the country. The Missouri Compromise may have saved Iowa from slavery; it had not saved the Negro—in Iowa or elsewhere—from a status of inferiority. In this era there was little disposition to think of the Negro as a human being. It is almost startling to find the convention members seriously considering a proposition to exclude Negroes from residence in the state; startling, that is, until one recalls that the biological science of that day taught that the Negro belonged to a lower order of beings than the white man. Even advanced thinkers who believed in abolition of chattel slavery were not ready for the idea of Negro equality.[3]

It is in this light that the report of a select committee on the "admission of people of color on the same footing as white citizens" must be considered. Couching their report in language which today seems ludicrous, the committee said they could "never consent to open the doors of our beautiful State and invite him to settle our lands. The policy of other States would drive the whole black population of the Union upon us." The results would take the form of a "train of evils" which would be "incalculable." Another member was heard to say: "The people of Iowa did not want Negroes swarming among them," and the Dubuque delegate, Lucius H. Langworthy, was instructed to work for a constitutional prohibition of Negro residence. Even so, the convention did not go along with the committee report. For one thing, one member reminded the others that such a provision might prevent the admission of Iowa as a state. Whatever the reasons, the report was laid on the table.[4]

BANKS AND POLITICS

Another prominent issue before the convention was the banking question. Men of the Iowa frontier were afraid of banks—as well they might have been, in the light of the theory and practice of banking in that era. It was the power of note issue that most banks abused. Banks and bankers were almost totally unregulated in some states; the expression, "wildcat" banks, is not only colorful but accurate as a description of many institutions. The depositor's chief security lay in the honesty of his banker, and even an honest banker might be pulled down by dishonest or unwary colleagues in the profession. Small wonder, then, that there was much debate and much vehement denunciation of bankers and their ways. Whigs generally were in favor of leaving the matter of charter and regulation to the General Assembly; conservative Democrats did not want to freeze the restrictions on banks by putting them in the constitution, changeable only by constitutional amendment; radical Democrats were fiercely opposed to the establishment of any and all banks of issue. Even the conservative Democrats split hairs over their position.

The upshot of the great debate on banks was a rather elaborate six-point compromise. The General Assembly was empowered to charter "corporations" (a word used at the time to designate banks). Each act of incorporation was to have a time limit of twenty years, after which the legislature must renew the charter. Stockholders' liability for a corporation's debts was provided. No bank could be incorporated without submission of the charter to the voters of the state for a yea or nay vote, and the General Assembly could revoke all charters which it had granted. Finally, the state could not become a stockholder in any bank.[5]

THE BOUNDARIES PROBLEM

In terms of future effect, the most meaningful subject taken up by the delegates was the boundary problem. In fact, it became the villain

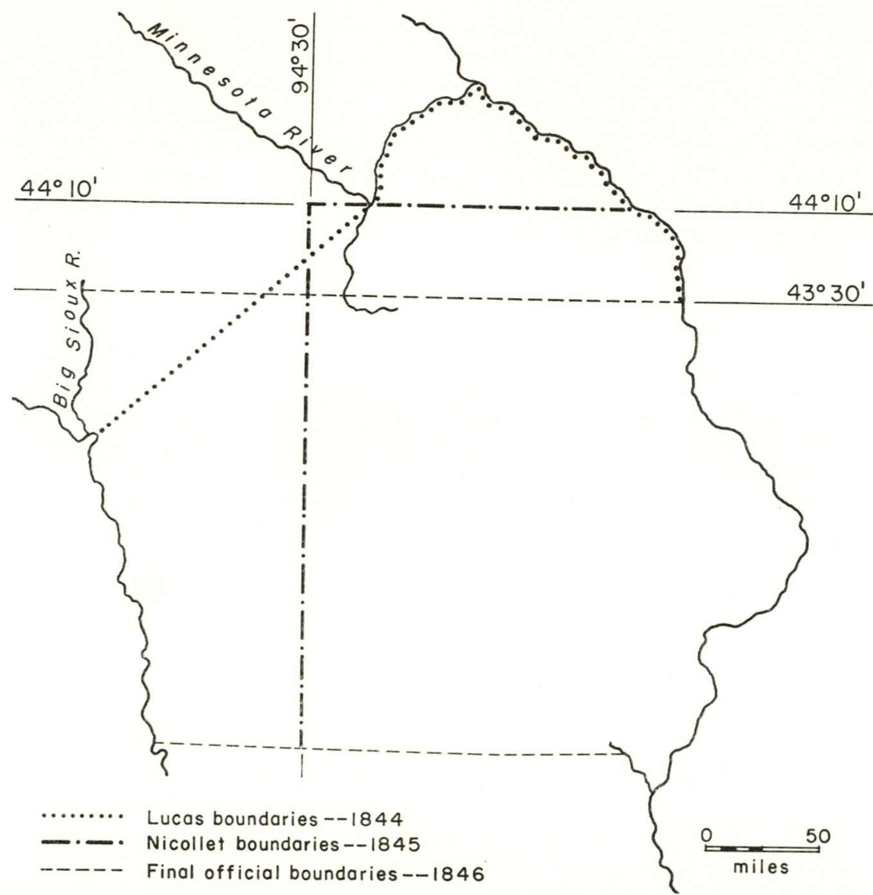

FIG. 5.1. A map to illustrate the boundary problem which delayed the admission of Iowa to statehood.

in the piece, a problem so serious that it held up Iowa's admission as a state for some time. Governor Lucas, in his first recommendation of statehood, as far back as 1839, had recommended certain far-flung lines. Now the convention's committee on boundaries, led by the former governor, recommended them to the convention. Henceforth known as the Lucas Boundaries, they would have enclosed an area roughly equivalent to present Iowa and a great deal of Minnesota. A close study of the map given in Figure 5.1 reveals that the key difference from the later official lines is in the northern boundary. Lucas would have this line run from the mouth of the Big Sioux River where it empties into the Missouri and would run "in a direct line to the middle of the main channel of the St. Peters [Minnesota] River, where the Watonwan River [according to Nicollet's map] enters the same"; then down that river to its intersection with the Mississippi.

Having drawn up a constitution with these basic provisions, the convention adjourned on November 1, 1844. The document was forwarded to Congress and presented on December 9 for acceptance. (It had been specifically provided that the document was to go to Congress first and then to the voters of the territory in April 1845, by which time Congress would presumably have acted.) In Congress the question of acceptance hung not on the general merits of the framework of self-government contained in the document but on the effect that the admission of Iowa would have on the slavery question. The arguments turned largely on the question of the size of the state as it might affect the future balance of free and slave states. Antislavery people wanted the unorganized area west of the Mississippi cut up into as many states as they could persuade Congress to devise, thus creating more potential votes in Congress against slavery; proslavery people wanted just the opposite, of course, and favored the Lucas boundaries for Iowa. Never questioning the future status of Iowa as a free soil state, an enabling act was prepared which coupled Florida as a slave state with Iowa to be the offsetting free soil state, the first time that the admission of two states was ever provided for *in the same act.* (The idea of balancing free and slave states had been used in the case of Missouri and Maine but their admission was dealt with in separate acts.) Although such balancing was never officially admitted to be a way of keeping equality in the Senate between the free and slave states, it was well known that such was the result intended and obtained. In this way an antislavery amendment to the Constitution could be blocked.

It so happened that an alternative to the Lucas boundaries, though not originating as an alternative, had been put before the public. The suggestion was set forth in a report in 1843 by Joseph N. Nicollet, the famous French-American engineer, geologist, and explorer, on his travels and observations in the region west of the upper reaches of the Mississippi. In January 1845 a second edition of his report had been published. His study had been made for the United States Geological Survey and as such had no connection whatever with the political geography involved in the question of Iowa's boundaries—indeed, there is no reason to assume that Nicollet and Lucas were competitors in the game of state architecture. Nicollet, reasoning purely on his observations on the courses of rivers and the topography of the vast area which he had studied, fancifully described what he thought to be the proper divisions for five hypothetical states. For one state he accepted the Mississippi as an eastern boundary, and the Sullivan Line on the south. For a western boundary for his unnamed state he suggested the line of longitude 17°30′ west of Washington, D.C. (94°30′ longitude west of Greenwich), running northward from the Missouri border to the junction of the Watonwan (Blue Earth) River and the St. Peters River. For a northern boundary he would run a line due east from the junction of the two rivers to the Mississippi.[6] The butt of sarcasm then and later, the Nicollet boundaries for "Iowa" might appear to the unbiased observer of a later day to be just as logical as those proposed by Governor Lucas.

Although neither proposal was to prevail, there was a time when the Nicollet lines appeared to be a sure winner. The antislavery elements in Congress put up most of the opposition to the admission of Iowa with the "large" boundaries; they must be credited with the long view into the future as they argued for the division of the West into several states which could make up a regional counterweight between the North and South, as described above, and thus save the Union. It was Representative Alexander Duncan of Ohio who proposed the substitution of the smaller Nicollet boundaries for the Lucas lines and it was Representative Samuel F. Vinton who advanced the argument that the creation of oversized states would eventually deprive the West of its fair share of power in the government of the nation.

The pleas for a small state prevailed. The House substituted the Nicollet lines for the Lucas boundaries, passed the bill for admission in that form, as did the Senate without hesitation, and President John Tyler, just one day before his term would expire, signed the act admitting Iowa and Florida into the Union, on March 3, 1845. The act qualified the admission of Iowa on the acceptance of the Nicollet boundaries in the forthcoming election of April 1845.[7] On their part, the Iowa fathers of the constitution of 1844 had reserved the right to "ratify or reject any conditions Congress may make to this Constitution after the first Monday in April next." Thus it can be argued on technical ground that *Iowa was admitted into the Union,* but with mutual reservations, by the act of Congress, March 3, 1845. The Nicollet boundaries as specified by Congress were not then known to be so highly objectionable to Iowans, and it was a reasonable assumption that the people of the territory would accept them rather than run the risk of defying Congress by insisting on the Lucas lines. This was the position taken by Iowa's territorial delegate to Congress, Augustus Caesar Dodge, of Burlington. Very likely many persons prematurely spoke of "Iowa" as a "new" state in the Union.

REJECTION OF STATEHOOD, 1845

It must not be forgotten that a warm debate had been going on for several months, highly partisan in nature, with nearly all Democrats in favor of ratification of the document as it had come from the hands of the convention, and nearly all Whigs against it. The debate had covered several real issues, chiefly the banking question, and had not emphasized the topic of boundaries. Both parties were in favor of a large state and no one doubted that the Lucas boundaries would be accepted. Now in March 1845 the Congress delivered its bombshell and the ratification or rejection test was coming in April!

The Democrats were in a truly bad situation. Should they reverse themselves and urge the voters to accept the smaller boundaries? Many of their leaders could not bring themselves to this position but one who did so was their acknowledged chieftain: Augustus Caesar Dodge. It was his advice that Iowans might as well vote for the document with the Nicollet lines because he was convinced that Congress would never change its collective mind on this subject. Three young Democrats have been honored for swinging the vote against ratification: Theodore S. Parvin, Enoch W. Eastman, and Frederick D. Mills. The names of Shepherd Leffler and James W. Woods should be added to the list, Leffler as the president of the 1844 convention carrying more weight than the others. Their efforts apparently changed some Democratic votes, and these, plus practically the whole Whig strength, carried the day for a negative vote, though by the narrow margin of 996 votes, 7,019 to 6,023. This small margin makes one conclude that many Iowans were either defeatist in the matter, as was Congressional Delegate Dodge, or agreeable to the Nicollet boundaries—or just plainly indifferent.[8]

Not only was the margin in the April election a small one; a second referendum was taken in August, over Governor Chambers's veto, and again the proposition lost, though by a smaller margin. There were doubtless many reasons for the closeness of the vote. Two might be cited: the opposition of the Whigs to the "hard money" features of the document, and the strategic policy of delay as advocated by the Whigs' behind-the-scenes leader, William Penn Clarke of Iowa City, a lawyer and newspaper man. Clarke insisted that if the Whigs could hold out for a while they would soon attain a majority of the electorate and could then secure a constitution of their own making—one that would permit banks and banking.[9]

CONGRESS RECONSIDERS THE BOUNDARY QUESTION

The Whig strategy of delay was of no avail. On December 3, 1845, Governor James Clarke, the Burlington editor and Democratic leader who succeeded Chambers as a James K. Polk appointee, urged the assembly to renew the fight for admission. On December 19 Delegate Augustus Caesar Dodge, pursuant to his instructions of an earlier date, submitted to Congress a bill which proposed the repeal of those portions of the admission act of March 3, 1845, which had modified the 1844 boundary requests, and proposed a return to the original proposal. He added that he had learned a lesson from the people of Iowa and that there was no use to suggest anything less than the "large state" boundaries. Backing up the governor and the delegate, the Iowa Territorial Legislative Assembly completed an act on January 17, 1846, setting a date in April for the election of delegates to a new convention which would meet on the first Monday in May.[10]

There was a way out of the difficulty. On March 27, 1846, more than a month before the Iowa convention was to meet, Representative Stephen A. Douglas of Illinois, chairman of the House Committee on Territories, reported an amended bill which set the western boundary as the Missouri-Big Sioux rivers and the northern boundary at 43°30′. It would be of great interest to know the full story behind this display of initiative by Douglas. In the absence of explicit information, it is possible to say only that Douglas had made himself the recognized authority in Congress on territorial matters and that he frequently acted without consultation with other members of his committee. His current interest in organization of a Territory of Oregon had led him to make a study of the territorial charters of Indiana, Illinois, Michigan, and Iowa; of these, he found the Iowa charter the "most perfect." In drawing up a bill for a Territory of Oregon he had used the Iowa charter as a model, changing only a few details to fit the needs of that distant region. These special considerations, plus the natural desire to see the Middle Western territories brought into statehood as soon as possible, would seem to go far toward explaining Douglas's interest in hastening statehood for Iowa.[11]

THE CONVENTION OF 1846

In April 1846 elections were held for the selection of delegates to the constitutional convention, the Democrats securing twenty-two delegates, the Whigs ten. Of these winners, eight were repeaters from the 1844 sessions. The delegates met at Iowa City on May 4, with thirty men present. The convention's Committee on Preamble and Boundaries recommended to the convention the adoption of the very same boundaries which had been favorably reported in March by Douglas and his Committee on Territories! After some jockeying back and forth, on May 14 the convention adopted the Douglas lines by a vote of 19 to 13.[12] Considering the difficulties of communication in 1846, the coordination between Congress in Washington and the convention in Iowa City takes on a wondrous aspect. With the boundary problem seemingly on the way to solution, the convention made few changes in the rest of the document. One very important change in procedure from the 1844 experience was a provision for a referendum to the voters of Iowa *before* the document was submitted to Congress.

This did not prevent Congress from going ahead with its own consideration of the boundaries. On June 8 the Douglas bill was debated in the House sitting as a Whole House on the State of the Union. The arguments of 1845 were repeated and a few weak efforts were made to change the Douglas lines. Representative Julius Rockwell of New York, a Whig, proposed the line of 42° as a northern boundary, which for some strange reason certain people in Dubuque had requested, and Representative Samuel F. Vinton of Ohio, who in 1845 had tried to secure a small state, now tried to get the line placed at 43°. Douglas was adamant on the line of 43°30′ and so was Delegate Augustus Caesar Dodge, who with new-found courage virtually defied Congress to offer any other boundary.

The man who came to Iowa's rescue after Douglas had done his best was James B. Bowlin, a representative from Missouri. It was his happy thought to keep the Douglas line on the north but to do so by an amendment calling for *all* the boundaries as adopted by the Iowa constitutional convention in May. On June 9 the boundaries bill as amended by Bowlin passed the House and on August 1 it passed the Senate. If there had been a telegraph line between Iowa City and Washington it would seem safe to say that now the president was working in collusion with the compromise forces: on August 3 the people of Iowa gave the new document with the line of 43°30′ endorsement by the paper-thin margin of only 456 out of a total of 18,528 votes, 9,492 to 9,036; on August 4 President Polk signed the act.[13] The Whigs had won a moral victory but the Democrats had at last achieved their goal: enough Iowans, plus Congress and the president, had agreed on statehood for Iowa, with boundaries fully approved, with the slight exception, which no one seemed to notice, that the southern boundary was still an open question. The framework of government was agreeable to a majority of voters, even if that majority was so small as to be hard for some Iowans to accept.

Now Iowans proceeded to create their government, though formal admission was still a thing of the future. On September 9 Governor James Clarke proclaimed the Constitution of 1846 to be ratified and adopted, and set October 26 as the date for the election of state officers. On that date the Democratic candidate for governor, Ansel Briggs of Andrew, was the winner over the Whig, Thomas McKnight. The Democrats likewise won control of the General Assembly.

The remainder of the story is purely perfunctory except for the striking detail that a state government was brought into being before the formalities of admission had been completed! On November 30 the assembly met on Governor Clarke's call and on December 2 he delivered his last official message as governor of Iowa Territory. On December 3 Ansel Briggs was inaugurated as governor of the state of Iowa, though such a state did not really exist. On December 15 Delegate Dodge presented the Constitution of 1846 to Congress; the House passed a bill of admission on December 21 and the Senate passed it on the 24th. On December 28 President James K. Polk signed the bill into law and Iowa thus became the 29th state of the Union.[14]

The Constitution of 1846

An important question about the Iowa constitution of 1846 has to do with the antecedents of the document. In general, it can be said that the men of the two conventions of 1844 and 1846 were practical men who drew on their knowledge of previous territorial and state governments, not brilliant innovators toying with the task of concocting a model constitution. The debates as recorded show that some members had given much thought to the subject of good government and the question of how the best features of government in the older states could be adapted to the needs of Iowa.

More specifically, it has been demonstrated that the principal source of Iowa's supreme law was the Ordinance of 1787 by way of the organic law passed by Congress in creating the Territory of Wisconsin. The basic rights of 1787 were granted to Wisconsin Territory and these were in turn guaranteed to the people of Iowa in 1838. The Convention of 1846 continued these guarantees in their handiwork, with the minor addition of a clause denying the right to hold office to any citizen who had engaged in dueling.[15]

Although a bit anticlimactic, the document of 1846 should be compared with the one of 1844. Changes in the second are not numerous or profound; after all, the chief stumbling block in the path of the 1844 vehicle had been the altered boundaries as set by Congress. If the 1846 document could correct these satisfactorily, few fundamental changes would be required on other points. One change of real significance was the provision for a governor's term of four years, a change which was not allowed to stand very long. Salaries were slightly increased, the pay for governor going from $800 to $1,000, and others proportionately. The amending process provided for was an awkward one: the General Assembly must let people vote on the question whether or not to hold a convention. In case a majority of those voting on the question favored a convention, the legislature must arrange an election. The resulting convention could then accept or reject a proposed amendment or amendments. No provision was made for a referral to the people for ratification. As for "incorporations," the touchiest subject of the day, the General Assembly was given the power to make "general laws" concerning them, but not the power to "create" them by special laws; specifically, *no banks were to be created,* and no banking functions were to be performed by an institution or person.[16] All county government and local government matters were passed over in silence and by inference referred to the legislatures of the future.

CHAPTER 6 THE DEVELOPMENT OF A FRONTIER STATE 1846–1870

NOW THAT IOWA HAD BEEN ADMITTED INTO THE UNION OF states, with her boundary problems virtually settled and most of her land purchased from the Indians, a new surge in her development might be confidently expected. Such was the theme of the speeches and proclamations of her major officials, while those who had land to sell advertised freely in Eastern papers and soon learned to tap European sources of immigration. As pointed out above, Iowa's crying need was for people. Organized campaigns for settlers and investors were conducted on a small scale by state officials.[1] The state's fine farmlands were stressed above all other assets; also likely to be mentioned were her fine citizens, her free and open society under a good government, and the unlimited opportunities for growth and development. It is generally agreed that letters to friends and relatives did more to encourage settlers to leave their familiar haunts and move west than any other form of persuasion.

POPULATION GAINS

Population statistics alone can tell one a great deal about the economic and social development of the new state of Iowa in the years soon after the date of admission as a state. From the figure of 43,112 in 1840 the number jumped to 97,588 in 1846, 192,214 in 1850, and 674,913 in 1860, phenomenal leaps forward of 345.8 percent and 251.1 percent for the successive decades.[2] Obviously such percentages of growth could not be maintained in a state which was primarily agricultural. The number of persons per square mile, on a basis of 55,475 square miles in the state, rose from 0.8 in 1840 to 12.2 in 1860. In 1850 the gross number of farms was 14,805; by 1860 it had risen to 61,136.

An interesting and highly important point about Iowa's popula-

TABLE 6.1: Foreign-born in Iowa, 1850–1970

Country of Birth	1850	1860	1870	1880	1890	1900	1910	1920	1930	1940	1950	1960	1970
All Countries*	20,969	106,077	204,692	261,650	324,069	305,920	273,484	225,647	168,080	117,245	84,582	56,278	40,217
Germany	7,101	35,842	66,162	88,268	127,246	123,162	98,290	70,642	53,901	35,540	22,774	14,368	9,026
Sweden	231	1,465	10,796	17,559	30,276	29,875	26,763	22,493	16,810	11,406	7,080	3,813	1,864
Norway	361	5,688	17,556	21,586	27,078	25,634	21,924	17,344	12,932	8,642	5,531	3,159	1,547
Denmark	19	661	2,827	6,901	15,519	17,102	17,961	18,020	14,707	10,987	7,625	4,864	2,658
Netherlands	1,108	2,615	4,513	4,743	7,941	9,388	11,337	12,471	10,135	7,840	6,078	4,335	3,087
England	3,785	11,545	18,103	22,610	26,228	21,027	16,784	13,036	9,045	5,961	4,931	3,917	3,191
Scotland	712	2,895	5,248	6,885	7,701	6,425	5,162	3,967	2,871	1,829	1,332		
Wales	352	913	1,967	3,031	3,601	3,091	2,434	1,753	1,183	674			
Ireland	4,885	28,072	40,124	44,061	37,353	28,321	17,756	10,685					
N. Ire.									1,778	747	57	395	
Eire									4,179	2,671	2,066	769	
Belgium	4	91	650	357	384	491	929	1,232	932	784	678	565	
Switzerland	175	2,519	3,937	4,584	4,310	4,342	3,675	2,871	2,096	1,414	838	522	
France	382	2,421	3,130	2,675	2,327	1,905	1,618	2,125	1,435	892	793	662	
Austria	13	2,709	9,457	12,027	12,643	13,118	15,136	4,334	1,596	1,558	1,156	845	
Hungary			134	244	213	453	1,178	747	295	325	319	324	
Czechoslovakia†								9,150	8,280	5,552	3,819	2,307	1,198
Poland		100	178	403	453	751	2,115	2,028	1,875	1,284	1,402	1,133	691
Yugoslavia								1,603	1,306	1,086	920	867	
Lithuania						47	140	687	835	775	601	427	
Russia (USSR)	41	40	96	535	782	1,998	5,494	7,319	4,552	3,671	2,774	1,777	986
Italy	1	30	54	122	399	1,196	5,846	4,956	3,834	3,461	2,908	2,254	1,557
Greece	1	1	1	4	1	18	3,356	2,884	1,910	1,535	1,407	1,145	623
Canada	1,756	8,313	17,897	21,062	17,465	15,687	11,596	8,929	6,333	4,962	4,122	2,725	2,342
Mexico	16	6	14	18	41	29	509	2,560	2,517	1,335	1,253	1,038	1,224
Asia	2				151	282	64	170	144	120	869	634	2,880

SOURCE: Figures for 1850–1940 are from the *16th Census* (1940), p. 865; for 1950 from the *17th Census,* vol. 2, pt. 15, p. 47; for 1960 from the *World Almanac* for 1968; for 1970 from the *19th Census,* PC(1)–C17, Iowa, p. 219.

* The figures for "All Countries" make up a larger total than the sum of the countries listed here.

† Bohemians in Iowa numbered 10,423 as of 1885, 9,098 as of 1905, and 9,500 as of 1915.

tion growth is the contribution made by foreigners. (See Table 6.1.) In 1850 there were 20,969 people of foreign birth and 170,931 native Americans, a ratio of approximately 1 in 8.5; in 1860 the respective figures were 106,077 and 568,836, or 1 in 5.3; looking forward, in 1870 the ratio was 204,692 to 989,328, or one in 4.8. These figures give convincing testimony of a considerable debt to the European sources, a debt too great by far to be discharged by a few complimentary references to such colorful communities as the Dutch settlement of Pella (founded 1847), the German Amana Colonies (1855), the Irish town of Emmetsburg (1856), the Swedish town of Stanton (1870), and the English colony in Plymouth County (1878). These exotic communities pale into insignificance when compared with the contributions of thousands of their fellow citizens who scattered out all over the state and became the yeoman farmers and builders and industrial workers who did so much to enrich the whole state.

Of the 106,077 foreign-born residents of Iowa as of 1860, more than half (57,709) lived in the ten Mississippi River counties. Dubuque County with 12,958 was far ahead of its closest rival, Scott County (Davenport), with 9,253; Louisa County was the smallest in this respect with only 832. Two counties in the next tier west, Winneshiek (Decorah) at 5,390 and Johnson (Iowa City) with 4,376, were the only other counties with notably large numbers of foreign-born; the others were scattered through the other eighty-seven counties of the state, in numbers ranging from 0 to 2,131. No one county had a majority of foreign-born residents, Dubuque County coming the closest to that ratio with 12,958 foreign-born and 18,206 American-born, the former divided three to one along German and Irish lines. Most of Scott County's 9,253 foreigners were Germans. Clayton County and Clinton County complete the list of counties with large proportions of foreign-born, mostly Germans.

As of 1860, Iowa's foreign-born residents were mostly from Western and Northern Europe. Not only in the counties indicated but in Iowa as a whole, Germans were by far the most numerous element among the foreign-born—35,846 out of a total of 106,077. (Strictly speaking, there was no "Germany" until 1871.) In second place were the Irish, 28,072 and many more to come, escaping from the oppression of poverty and the rigors of English control of the Irish government, economy, and state-supported church. In third place were the English with 11,522, a number which may surprise some readers. If to the Irish and the English one adds the 2,895 Scots in the Iowa of 1860 and then throws in the 8,313 from British North America, he finds a total of 50,802 settlers in Iowa who once had British ties, even outnumbering the Germans if all could be legitimately grouped under one heading. This all-British number would grow to 79,939 by 1870.[3]

By contrast, the Scandinavian-born population was only 7,814 in

1860. Norway sent the largest number to Iowa (5,688 as of 1860). Sweden was next with 1,465 and Denmark sent only 661. The earliest Norwegian emigrants to Iowa were families which had made earlier settlements in Illinois and Wisconsin. Their scouts found more congenial locations for them in Iowa and so their westward march was resumed, just as later some of these and others would go on to Minnesota and the Dakotas. Soon their letters to relatives and friends in Illinois and Wisconsin and in the "old country" would bring streams of settlers to Iowa. The economic, religious, and cultural influence of the Scandinavians on Iowa has been out of all proportion to their numbers.[4]

In fifth place (if the Scots are counted as British) were the Dutch (Hollanders), 2,615 of them in 1860 and 4,513 in 1870. In 1847 a group of 800 emigrants left Holland in search of economic opportunity and religious freedom. It should be strongly asserted that the first reason has been understated and the second overstressed and misinterpreted. The many references to religious persecution should be interpreted as the efforts of state officials to force all Hollanders to join and support the official state church. Their experience was a duplication in principle of the story of the English Separatists who left their country for the same reasons. The Dutch who came to Iowa were under the leadership of Henry Peter Scholte, a firm opponent of compulsory membership in the state church and at the same time a businessman of the first rank. This aggressive man and his close associates arranged for the purchase of 47,000 acres of land in Marion County and founded the town of Pella, still the chief center of Dutch economic, religious, and cultural activity in Iowa. Offshoots of the Pella colony founded Orange City, Sioux Center, Maurice, Hospers, Remsen, and other towns in northwest Iowa.[5]

Immigration statistics such as those given above can be deceptively complete in appearance. The term "German" or the label "Scandinavian" means something, to be sure, but "East Prussian," "West Prussian," "Bavarian," or "Wurttemberger" means much more to the knowledgeable student of German cultural traits, and similar provincial distinctions can be made within the Norwegian, Swedish, and Danish ranks. Beyond these regional terms one would like to know something about the social and economic class backgrounds of the newcomers: peasant, middle class, urban upper class, landed gentry, and so on. It has been shown, for example, that theological differences, which for a time divided the Norwegian settlers and weakened their church organization, were rooted in class conflict which required two or three generations of living in America to eradicate. In another study it has been demonstrated that by delving into the manuscript census returns on the township level it is possible to account for political action that otherwise must be clouded by loose generalization.

This study of voting records in Carroll County, presumably a stronghold of German and Irish Catholic sentiments, revealed that those townships which were heavily American as to origins, and possessed of a well-known New England pietism, voted overwhelmingly for Republicans and for Prohibition; certain other townships, heavily German as to origins and definitely antipietistic in personal beliefs, were equally enthusiastic in their support of Democratic and anti-Prohibition candidates.[6] Similar studies will be cited below in an effort to account for certain pockets of political behavior.

ORGANIZATION OF IOWA COUNTIES

A corollary to the rapid growth of population in Iowa was the need for attention to the problems of local government, particularly on the level of county government. No topic serves better to illustrate the realities of political evolution. From the division of the Iowa District of Wisconsin Territory into two counties, De Moine and Du Buque, in 1834, the first of which was divided into seven counties, on to the delineation of the present ninety-nine, Iowa achieved a county structure not unreasonable in number and individual size in terms of the means of transportation at the time. (Perhaps some future historian will be called on to describe the reduction from ninety-nine to some smaller number, perhaps the twenty-five as recommended by the Brookings Institution Report in 1933.)

As the people moved westward and filled in the land after 1833, particularly after each of the treaties with the Indians, culminating with the treaty with the Sioux in 1851, the need for new counties grew progressively with the westward movement. Practically all the story of county organization falls between 1834 and 1851, only three counties being formed after the latter date. Summarizing, forty-four counties were established before admission as a state in 1846; these were scattered all the way from the Mississippi to the tier including Polk and Story counties. In 1847 seven counties were formed; in 1851 came the omnibus—forty-five counties in all—followed by one each in 1853, 1856, and 1857, the last one being Humboldt County. The boundary lines were juggled in a bewildering series of acts which are of no importance to the general reader.

A few changes or attempted alterations are of some interest. Cook County was carved up and given to its neighbors, including Scott County. Risley County and Yell County were merged and renamed Webster County. A county named Bancroft was created in 1851 by taking a part of gigantic Kossuth County, but it was blotted out in 1855 before it was ever formally organized. In 1870 a successful attempt was made to create a new county, Crocker, named in honor of the Civil War general, by using the same area as Bancroft, but the success was only temporary. The legislative act of creation was nullified by the Supreme Court on the grounds that its total size was only 408 square miles, 24 less than the minimum prescribed by the Constitution of 1857. In 1874 an effort was made to divide Iowa's other giant, Pottawattomie County, and name the new county for General William W. Belknap, the Iowan from Keokuk who was then the popular secretary of war under President Grant, but the proposal was voted down; a similar effort two years later to take the same area and name the new county after Senator Grimes was likewise voted down. A few counties have managed to change their names: Washington County was once known as Slaughter County; Monroe was once Kishkekosh, Woodbury was once Wahkaw, Lyon was Buncombe, and Calhoun was Fox.[7]

THE LUMBER INDUSTRY

The great leap forward in Iowa's economic and social development came after 1833, when both the government and potential settlers recognized the superior qualities of Iowa's land for farming purposes. A corollary to the resulting growth in settlement was the creation of insatiable demand for lumber suitable for building purposes. The typical settler could bring with him to the frontier practically all the things he needed for existence except good mill-sawn lumber. After arriving at his homestead, his family could live for a time, if necessary, in the covered wagon in which they had made their journey; then a sod or a log cabin could serve as a temporary home until the new settler could arrange for both money and time to make the trip to a market and buy sufficient mill-sawn lumber for his purposes—first for a house, later for barns and outbuildings.

It was soon discovered that Iowa's native hardwoods were not suitable for general building purposes and that the northern white pine was infinitely superior. Such lumber was not available until logging operations could be developed in the pineries of Wisconsin and Minnesota, and the logs floated down the Mississippi to towns where sawmills could process the lumber in sizes to meet the needs of new farmer-settlers in southern Minnesota, southern Wisconsin, and eastern Iowa, eventually in all of Iowa. Viewed from this perspective, nothing is more fascinating than to observe the speed with which entrepreneurs went into the business of meeting this demand for lumber. The raw material was plentiful but getting it out of the forests along the St. Croix, Chippewa, Black, and Wisconsin rivers, and down those rivers to the Mississippi, and then to the mill towns was a challenge which only the hardiest men could meet. First, the trees had to be cut in the dead of winter and dragged on sleds over roads of snow and ice to the small tributary rivers. Then, when the spring thaw came, the logs could be pushed into the rivers and "driven" to a "boom" on or near the Mississippi, where the logs were sorted and marked like cattle with the owners' brands, then formed into a raft and floated, towed, or pushed down the river to the mills. At the boom, if not earlier, the logs would have been bought by millowners, whose saws were hungrily waiting for them in river towns in Minnesota, Wisconsin, or Iowa (Lansing, McGregor, Guttenberg, Dubuque, and the larger towns to the south). Experienced men from Maine or other Eastern states were in great demand as loggers and mill hands. In the 1830s–1850s the techniques were very simple and the operation of all the equipment depended mostly on brute strength; in the late 1850s inventors began to improve the machinery and adapt it to steam power.

The size of the milling operations and the consequent growth of the mill town were largely determined by the amount of settlement in the hinterland which created the market. This is not to deny the personal factors which went into the aggressive and efficient management by some men; it is simply to assert that the fertile lands lying directly west of Dubuque, Clinton, and Davenport would understandably be more attractive to settlers than the rugged terrain west of Lansing, McGregor, and Guttenberg. This advantage was increased by the coming of the railroads in the second half of the 1850s and later. Until this had happened, the inland settler had to haul his produce to the river towns by wagon and sell it, then pick up a load of lumber for the return trip, plus the sugar, salt, flour, textile goods, and any other items which could not be produced on an Iowa farm. Later, shipments by rail made it possible for inland businessmen to buy lumber in the river towns and stock it in their lumberyards for retail selling.

Only owners of the larger mills could arrange for Eastern financing and buy the new high-speed gang saws and all the complementary equipment now needed. This gave the firms in the larger places an edge on those in the small towns, an advantage which grew and grew as the scale of operations expanded and technology developed new methods. Logs had to be bought in gigantic quantities or, better yet, timberlands bought or leased to insure steady supplies for the mills; logging railroads must be built through the forests to replace horse-drawn sleds; steamboats must be bought to serve as towing ships for the rafts. In this fiercely competitive era the natural advantages of Dubuque, Clinton, and Davenport were augmented by Eastern financing. Clinton seems to have been the winner in this battle for power, gaining the reputation for a time as the largest producer of finished lumber in the world.

Certain individuals stand out as leaders in the development of this business: Henry L. Stout and M. H. Moore of Dubuque; W. J. Young of Clinton, an Irish immigrant who somehow arranged for Cincinnati capital and did not rest until he had built the largest one-owner mill in Iowa; Young's very worthy rivals, Chauncey Lamb of Clinton and David Joyce of North Clinton (Lyons); Frederick Weyerhaeuser of Rock Island, Illinois, a German immigrant, who did much of his business through Davenport; the Crossett family of Davenport; Peter M. Musser of Muscatine and his fellow townsman, Ben Hershey; John H. Knapp, originally of Menomonie, Wisconsin, but later the holder of immense investments in Fort Madison and Dubuque, where a partnership with Henry L. Stout of Dubuque, reputedly the richest man of his generation in Iowa, was advantageous to him and to the town of Menomonie, which both men befriended; S. and J. C. Atlee of Fort Madison; and others in Burlington, Keokuk, and lesser towns. These were only some of the men who made great fortunes out of lumber in the second half of the nineteenth century. Clinton alone could at one time boast of seventeen millionaires in lumbering or allied businesses.

It is safe to say that for a comparable number of years, roughly the fifty years from 1850 to 1900, no single business in Iowa's economic history accounted for a greater concentration of wealth than the Mississippi River lumber business in its heyday. The disappearance of the lumber magnates from the Iowa scene can be traced to the destruction of the timber supply at the source. The seemingly inexhaustible forests of Wisconsin and Minnesota were finally used up by wasteful logging methods and a lack of any reforestation program. The peak of the business was reached about 1892, followed by a gradual decline until the pineries were used up in the early 1900s. Most of the lumber barons were shrewd enough to foresee this turn of events and transfer their operations from Iowa to the Southern yellow pine forests or to the fir stands of the Pacific Northwest.[8]

AGRICULTURE

One of the assertions formerly made with great confidence, but now with some uncertainty, concerns the preference of incoming settlers for farms on the wooded lands rather than the prairie sections of Iowa (and other states). According to the traditional view, farmers believed that stands of timber indicated fertility of the soil while prairie soil was assumed to be barren. Countless man-hours of back-breaking toil went into the work of clearing the forests in order to use this timbered soil. After the wooded areas had been largely used up, latecomers were forced on to the prairies where the discovery was made that prairie soils were richer than the woodlands, and, when properly drained, ideal for farming.

In the most exhaustive research yet done on the relations of speculators to actual sale and settlement of the public lands of Iowa, it was found that some incoming settlers, particularly those from Europe such as the Dutch settlers who came to Pella in 1847, preferred the open lands; that many farm purchasers chose to wait and come in on the second wave of settlement and buy farms which had been cleared and on which improvements had already been made. This investigator found that the ideal farm unit was one in which timber, water, and prairie were available in the approximate ratio of three acres of flatland to one of timber.[9]

With so much cheap land available to the early settlers, it is not surprising to find that the first farmers and landlords were indifferent to good farming practices. Extra time, effort, and expense devoted to deep plowing, application of manure, and careful seeding and cultivation seemed wasteful when good land was so plentiful and cheap. Blooded stock was not needed to cater to a market which paid little or no attention to distinctions in quality. Better to let the stock run free, and as for crops, hack away at the soil, drop in some seed for "sod corn," or "sod wheat," and take the meager results. Despite these poor methods, corn was raised on the same ground year after year, a deliberate choice in favor of soil exhaustion which seemed to be a reasonable form of economy to the average small-scale farmer who was operating on a narrow margin at best. One of his more profitable discoveries, however, was the superiority of marketing his grain on the hoof rather than by sale of the grain itself.

In retrospect, the early farmers may be subject to very little criticism in view of the primitive implements still in use, the lack of knowledge about soil science, and the universally held theory that it was better to "skim off the cream" and take the profits than to use intensive methods. Fortunately, several factors combined to change the thinking of these hardy pioneers. By the late 1850s and 1860s, after making some improvements on his homestead and putting down social roots in his community, and after the best land had been taken up, the average farmer found that it paid to listen to the advice of those people who had learned to use better farming methods and raise blooded stock rather than to exhaust the soil and move away in search of virgin lands. This was the beginning of "book farming" in Iowa.

For years a number of progressive farmers who practiced their own preachings had been spreading the gospel of "scientific" farming and setting examples of better methods for all the world to see. Most if not all of them were public-spirited men who combined their professional careers in the law, medicine, and journalism, or banking or merchandising, with some sort of political activity, and still found time to direct their own farming interests. Obviously these men would have to leave the daily chores and the responsibility of daily management to herdsmen and other farm workers, an arrangement which enabled them to travel and observe the work of others and to have leisure for research and for thinking and writing about the problems of farming as a moneymaking activity.

As early as the 1850s such leaders as Peter Melendy of Cedar Falls, a transplant from Ohio, and Coker F. Clarkson of Melrose Township in Grundy County, formerly a successful farmer and publisher-editor in Brookville, Indiana, had come into Iowa almost as farm missionaries as well as practical farmers. Christian W. Slagle of Fairfield and his Ohio-trained law partner, James F. Wilson; Josiah B. Grinnell; George G. Wright of Keosauqua, the eminent jurist; James W. Grimes of Burlington, who took time out of his busy career as a lawyer, banker, railroad promoter, and politician to conduct a page on horticulture for the *Iowa Farmer and Horticulturist,* were other leaders and pace-setters. William Duane Wilson, editor of the *Iowa Homestead,* and Benjamin F. Gue, editor, politician, and farm owner, were active in founding the Iowa State Agricultural College and Model Farm at Ames in 1858; Suel Foster, the Muscatine horticulturist, was an ally in the educational project. All these men and many others were on the alert for new information and better ideas about farming and farm life, and were veritable crusaders for better techniques. Some of them would later support organizations such as the Grange, designed to improve the social aspects of rural and small-town life; until then they worked as individuals. Isolation and monotony were breeders of boredom, especially for women and children; therefore, clubs and county fairs were copied from the older states of the East which in turn had imported them from England and Scotland.

The new steel moldboard plow with a steel share which was invented in 1837 by John Deere at Grand Detour, Illinois, became available in the 1850s. It was perfected in the 1860s by James Oliver of Indiana, who discovered a way to make a chilled iron plowshare. Cyrus McCormick's reapers, mowers, and horse-drawn rakes also came into use. These developments did much to eliminate the backbreaking, bone-searing aspects of frontier farming. It was equally fortunate that better breeds of cattle, horses, sheep, and hogs were now well established in England, Scotland, and France and available for importation into the United States.

Yet one must be careful not to overestimate the progress which resulted from the introduction of labor-saving machinery and from the exemplary preachments and demonstrations from the few leaders mentioned, and their associates. Until certain scientific facts could be turned into commonplace knowledge through the educational facilities of the State Agricultural College and Model Farm at Ames, it could be argued that the improved machinery was a contributor to soil exhaustion rather than an aid to improved techniques of farming. Easier cultivation, unless backed up by restoration of the soil through systematic cultivation, fertilization, and crop rotation, simply made it possible to cover more acres and use up native fertility faster than under the old methods. Peter Melendy, one of the best of the self-educated practitioners of better farming, was one of the first to recognize that voluntary efforts such as farmers' columns in the weekly newspapers, agricultural articles in the *Iowa Homestead,* and annual county fairs and occasional state fairs after 1854 were not sufficient to meet the challenge. Not until the State Agricultural College could begin a formal program of classes in agricultural education in 1869 could the era of "book farming" really take hold in Iowa.[10]

EDUCATIONAL DEVELOPMENTS

Few topics are more difficult to discuss with both authority and interest than the subject of educational beginnings in Iowa. The chief distinguishing factor of today's educational system, the overpowering role of the state, was not present in the territorial period and unevenly applied from 1846 to 1857 under the state's first constitution. Private academies were very common and made a tremendous contribution to the advancement of the youth of the state in this era. To be sure, the early legislatures took some notice of educational needs, and so did Congress when making land grants, usually setting aside Section 16 in each township for the support of public schools. Most of the federal grants for education went to the state, not to the local school district, after which the state could decide when to sell and what to charge for the land. The processes of selecting the lands, surveying, registering, and auctioning were slow at best. Officials had then to decide whether to sell the lands outright or to rent, and then whether to spend the proceeds at once for buildings and routine expenses or to invest the capital funds and spend only the income. Either choice soon developed into a new situation calling for support by taxation.

The Constitution of 1857 created a State Board of Education which functioned rather well until its abolition in 1864; under it the heavy but beneficial hand of the state was omnipresent. The office of state superintendent of public instruction could be a powerful one if that official and the board worked together to prescribe and enforce courses of study and licensing requirements for teachers. Even these signs of progress were not enough to conceal the need for additional improvements to the system. In all but the larger towns and cities the one-room school to accommodate all grades was commonplace.

School terms were brief and intermittently scattered through the calendar year according to road conditions or the seasonal needs for help from the children. The minimum legal school year was twenty-four weeks; local officials were permitted to offer more if they could finance the extra period. Schools of this era were loosely graded. The first "high" school beyond the eighth grade is credited to Tipton in 1856, though some make a prior claim for Muscatine. Usually children simply stayed in school up to a certain age, regardless of advancement by grades, the leaving age depending on a family's economic condition or a youngster's degree of maturity. Girls married at an early age; boys were inclined to leave home and school for an early fling at self-support as soon as the family could spare them. Attendance at college was the exceptional thing and formal training for the professions was brief and sketchy.[11]

Higher Education

Considering the nature of the frontier, it is surprising to find so much attention given to higher education. Many towns and cities boasted of something that was called a college, an institute, or a seminary; fortunately most of them have long since passed into oblivion, but a few have survived.

Catholic higher education in Iowa goes back to the training of young men for the priesthood in a bishop's school at Dubuque. Out of this came eventually Columbia (Loras) College for young men and Clarke College for young women. The roots of Loras College and Clarke College go back to 1834 and 1843, respectively, though it was many years before either institution could lay claim to college status. Iowa Wesleyan College traces its academic lineage back to territorial days when the Mount Pleasant Female Institute was founded in 1842; by 1855 it would evolve into Iowa Wesleyan University, following the pattern of many post–high school institutions of that day in adopting the pretentious title of "university." The school therefore has good authority for describing itself as one of the first institutions of higher learning west of the Mississippi River. The title was changed to Iowa Wesleyan College in 1911.[12]

Discounting the collegiate status of the above-named institutions in their early years, the University of Iowa would have a claim to first place as the oldest institution of higher learning in the state—if paper foundations would suffice. Only fifty-nine days after the state's birth on December 28, 1846, the General Assembly chartered a "State University of Iowa." Not until 1855, however, would classes be held, a fact overlooked by casual or hasty readers, and it would be many more years before a university worthy of the name would come into existence. The principal reason for the delay was the fight put up by various groups who fought through several sessions of the General Assembly to divide the financial resources of the university by establishing branches at Mount Pleasant, Fairfield, and Dubuque and by creating normal schools at Andrew, Oskaloosa, and Mount Pleasant. In 1849 a bill was actually passed creating branches of the university at Fairfield and Dubuque but fortunately nothing came of the plan. In 1848 the trustees of the university were able to make an arrangement with a group of medical doctors at Keokuk to operate a medical school as the "Medical Department of the University of Iowa," without state financial support.

Three state officials should be honored for their influence in persuading the General Assembly to concentrate their financial resources behind one central institution, unhindered by branches and normal schools to share the budget: State Senator George G. Wright of Keosauqua; Thomas Hart Benton, Jr., superintendent of public instruction; and Governor James W. Grimes of Burlington. Governor Grimes, a graduate of Dartmouth College, vetoed a bill which contained a grant of $5,000 to the College of Physicians and Surgeons at Keokuk, partly because he thought that young men should get their professional training at their own expense, and partly because he did not want to see the university's resources dissipated to this extent, even in a worthy cause. The governor also used his official powers in criticism of the idea of branches at the places mentioned above and in warning against proposals for other branches at Glenwood, Fort Dodge, and Delhi.

The matter was settled once and apparently for all time to come by the Constitutional Convention of 1857. Swayed by the not altogether unselfish arguments put forward by William Penn Clarke of Iowa City, the convention voted down a proposal to establish the university at Monroe City, in Jasper County, and, as an alternative, put Article IX, Section 11, in the constitution, providing that the permanent home of the university shall be in "one place, . . . without branches at any other place, and the University fund shall be applied to one Institution, and no other." Clinching the victory for Iowa City was Article XI, Section 8, which "permanently established" the capital at Des Moines and the state university at Iowa City.

Even with the question of location and centralization settled, the progress of the university toward excellence and prestige was slow. A book of praise of the state, issued in 1865 as an enticement to immigrants from abroad and from Eastern states, could only assert that the school had two buildings—Old Capitol and one other—with a third one under contemplation; that the assets of the institution were over $300,000 with an annual income of about $20,000, and "the number of Professors and Teachers, including four female teachers, 18; the number of students for the year, 432."

Through these early years the chief handicap of the university was a lack of adequate high schools in the state to prepare students for admission, necessitating the maintenance of a Preparatory Department at Iowa City to do the subfreshman work which most applicants for admission sadly needed. This not only drained off money needed for the collegiate departments but created an academic climate which was not conducive to high standards. For a time the school was sarcastically nicknamed the "Johnson County High School." Not until 1878 could the trustees bring themselves to the compromise decision to abolish the first year of the preparatory department as of 1878 and the second year in 1879. The decision did not indicate that the "middle schools" (high schools) were now able to prepare students for full admission to the university; for years to come it would be necessary for nearly half of the incoming freshmen to take makeup work at an Iowa City high school or arrange for tutorial assistance. The decision simply informs us that the trustees had cut the Gordian knot by putting the university at its proper place as the head of a unified school system reaching from the elementary schools through the grades and high schools to the baccalaureate degree in the state university. At present this was only a theory but it was a theory which could and would be implemented in practice in the years to come.[13]

Looking at other Iowa colleges whose institutional genealogy begins in this era, some can only be listed; some can be described briefly. One which clearly deserves attention is Grinnell College. It was founded as Iowa College at Davenport in 1847 by members of the Congregational "Iowa Band" in discharge of their pledge, "Each to found a church, all to found a college," after an earlier effort to start a college at Denmark had failed to materialize. Twelve years later the institution at Davenport succumbed to unfavorable conditions. Congregational leaders at once moved the college to Grinnell. Here it was merged with the Reverend Mr. Josiah B. Grinnell's "University," hardly more than a name. Known officially though not in common usage as Iowa College, its name was legally changed in 1909 to Grinnell College. Although never owned by the Congregational Church, there was from the beginning an affectionate relationship of mutual benefit between the college and the church, a relationship never totally obliterated.[14]

The list continues with Dubuque University, a Presbyterian institution, founded in 1852; Wartburg College in Waverly, owned by the American Lutheran Church since 1930, though traceable to small beginnings in 1852; and Central University, in Pella, founded by Baptists in 1854 and taken over by the Reformed Church and named Central College in 1916. Three other pre-Civil War colleges which have shared Grinnell College's standing as a strong liberal arts institution are Cornell College, a Methodist foundation whose roots go back to 1850 though instruction did not begin until 1853, and the name Cornell was not taken until 1855;[15] Coe College, at Cedar Rapids, founded by Presbyterians in 1851, becoming Coe College in 1881; and Simpson College, founded by Methodists in 1860 as Indianola Male and Female Seminary. This name was changed to Simpson Centenary College in 1866 in honor of Bishop Matthew Simpson, President Lincoln's great friend and funeral orator; the word "Centenary" was dropped in 1884. Another Methodist-sponsored college was Upper Iowa University at Fayette, founded in 1857. It became an independent institution in 1928 and changed its name from University to College in 1965.

Luther College in Decorah owes its foundation to members of the Norwegian Evangelical Lutheran Church and was long known as a "preacher" college. About 1857 talk of a college was begun, but for the time being students were urged to go from Iowa to Concordia College and Seminary in St. Louis. On October 14, 1859, a Norwegian missionary, Laur. Larsen (Peter Laurentius Larsen), was appointed Luther College Professor at Concordia, and this date is now treated as Founders Day in the Luther College calendar. In 1861 the Iowa students and Professor Larsen fled to St. Louis and its Civil War riots and returned to Decorah. Luther College was housed temporarily near La Crosse but in 1862 it was firmly established in Decorah, with Laur. Larsen as president, an office he would hold until 1902, after which he remained on the faculty as a professor until 1913, surely one of the most remarkable records in American college history.[16]

One other institution which has had great significance for Iowa was founded during this period, the one presently known as the Iowa State University of Science and Technology. Not always possessed of such a grand title, it was founded in 1858 as the Iowa State Agricultural College and Model Farm, largely as a result of the urging of Benjamin F. Gue, Suel Foster, and William Duane Wilson. For a decade the "college" was hardly more than a demonstration farm in frontier Story County. After the Republican success of 1860, Congress enacted the Morrill Land Grant College Act of June 2, 1862, by which a grant of land was made, 30,000 acres of land for each member of Congress from any state which might choose to participate in a program to create a college for the teaching of agriculture and the mechanical arts, with a very elastic definition of those terms. Iowa's General Assembly quickly decided in special session to accept the offer and to use the money in an upgrading of the State Agricultural College and Farm rather than allocate it to the State University at Iowa City, as some selfishly suggested, or initiate a totally new college, as some others proposed. Iowa's share of lands under the plan should have been 240,000 acres but the grant proved to be for only 203,309.3 acres. Peter Melendy of Cedar Falls, mentioned above, was appointed to select the lands for Iowa. Most of the lands chosen were in Kossuth and neighboring counties in northwest Iowa. Some of them were sold at once to raise money for a cash working fund; the remainder were put on a rental basis to provide an endowment fund. In 1868 a president was selected and the next year saw the beginning of formal instruction.[17]

Two other colleges remain to be mentioned though they were not founded until post–Civil War days. The University of Northern Iowa, at Cedar Falls, was founded as a normal school in 1876 to take advantage of the availability of a building originally built to house orphans of war veterans. It evolved into a teachers college, then a multipurpose state college, then into university status. Drake University, at Des Moines, was founded in 1881 by the Disciples of Christ as the successor to Oskaloosa College. A gift of $20,000 by General Francis M. Drake of Centerville was acknowledged by giving his name to the new institution.

THE SPIRIT LAKE MASSACRE

It may seem strange to interpret the Spirit Lake Massacre of 1857, probably the saddest event in the whole of Iowa history, as merely an incident in the development of a frontier state. This, however, is just what it was. The known facts are quite simple. A few bold—some would say foolish or unreasonable—men had dared to push far beyond the bounds of populated settlements, taking their families with them, in that attitude of mixed daring, hardihood, and foolhardiness which is the ever-present theme of the opening up of our frontier. Where sober fact leaves off, the historian must leave to the poet or novelist the proper description of the motives and the personal qualities of people who persist in defying the ordinary laws of security, abandoning the comforts of a fixed abode in favor of a conquest of the unknown. In 1856 such people, in the persons of Rowland Gardner and Harvey Luce and their families, had pushed far north of Fort Dodge, itself a frontier outpost, into the former lands of the Sioux, all the way to the banks of West Okoboji Lake. Here they were soon joined by others, the most notable being adventurer Dr. Isaac H. Herriott, Alvin M. Noble, J. M. Thatcher, and William Marble, and their families, making up a group of well over thirty persons dwelling in cabins scattered around within a distance of six miles from the lakes. Technically these people were squatters. Cooped up in their little cabins, scarcely more than huts, the very fact that they were able to endure the long hard winter of 1856–1857 with its tremendous snows and bitter cold is a tribute to their fortitude, stamina, and faith.

One more thing must be remembered: the same snow, the same bitter cold, and the same inability to subsist on the land hurt the Indians of the area as much as the white people. Therefore, it should come as no surprise to be told that a band of hungry Wahpeton Sioux, under the renegade chieftain Inkpaduta, outlaws from their own people, swooped down on the badly outnumbered whites, demanded food from them, and started to kill the very family (the Rowland Gardners) which was dividing its meager store of food with them. One killing led to another and soon thirty-two whites had been massacred, only the fourteen-year-old Abigail Gardner, Mrs. Noble, Mrs. Thatcher, and Mrs. Marble being spared. Of these four, Mrs. Thatcher later was pushed into the water to drown and Mrs. Noble was beaten to death. Mrs.

Marble was ransomed and so was Abigail Gardner, who lived to tell her story and to operate a shop for the sale of her book and mementoes of life on the frontier. As for the murderous Indians, they were chased over a good part of southern Minnesota but were never apprehended and punished.

Celebrated in every way from grade school pageant to a 967-page novel by one of Iowa's ablest writers of fiction, MacKinlay Kantor, the Spirit Lake Massacre is usually treated, though not so by Kantor, as a simple act of murder by bloodthirsty Indians led by the repulsive pock-marked Inkpaduta. Adding a trace of emotion to the story are the fact that the Sioux were known as the fiercest of all Indians, and the legend that Inkpaduta was out to get revenge for the murder many years earlier of his brother, Sidominadota, by a trader and whisky-seller, Henry Lott. Kantor rejects this story with the simple assertion that Inkpaduta was a Wahpekute Sioux, the other a Sisseton Sioux.

Perhaps it is too early, though more than a hundred years have passed since the event, for Iowans to be able to see the tragic incident in full historical perspective. The Spirit Lake Massacre which looms so large in Iowa history is only one of many such massacres in the annals of Indian-white relations, not the smallest but far from the largest. It was an outgrowth of bad feelings between the white man and the Sioux Indians, a chapter of a story which began with the treaties of 1851, noted above, by which these proud and warlike Indians had been induced to sell their lands in Iowa and certain lands elsewhere. Since that time they had not found any other available lands which yielded as well for farming or for hunting. Disappointment and anger roused them to retaliate with the only weapon at their disposal, war, including raids on helpless people, scalping the men and raping the women, stealing horses and food, methods of war which the white man had long practiced on them. This particular chapter of bad feelings did not close with the raid at Spirit Lake in 1857 but in 1862, when a massacre of hundreds in the countryside around New Ulm, Minnesota, spurred the government at Washington to furnish sufficient soldiers to suppress the raids and the fighting in this area.[18] Perhaps the most plausible interpretation of the incident is to accept the thirty-four victims as martyrs to the great westward movement of the American people. If this view is correct, the monument near Spirit Lake should be inscribed not only to the thirty-four but to all the thousands who paid the supreme sacrifice so that later generations could follow after them and peacefully inhabit the land.

THE RAILROADS

No other facet of the westward movement is more important than the story of the railroads, an assertion which has particular significance in Iowa history. Certainly no one agency contributed so much to the building up of the state in its entirety. And yet it is possible to claim —or to grant—too much for the role of the railroads. It has been persuasively, though not conclusively, argued that railroads were not indispensable; that had there been no railroads, other means of transportation would have been developed: more and better canals would have been built, better roads would have been built for overland travel, the internal-combustion engine and the diesel engine, both of which had been theoretically described as early as 1824, would have been more rapidly developed, and river highways might have been more largely utilized in answer to the problem of mass transportation. For example, the two great arterial rivers on her eastern and western borders and supplemental feeder canals might have moved vast quantities of freight out of the Iowa granary. Such feeder canals were once proposed for Iowa and other Midwestern states, and justified from an engineering point of view. One was to run from New Boston, Illinois (at the mouth of the Iowa River), inland to Columbus Junction to Cedar Rapids to Waterloo and north to Austin, Minnesota; another would have run from Columbus Junction to Marshalltown; one from Peterson to the Missouri River; one from Ortonville, Minnesota, to Fort Dodge to Des Moines and on to the Missouri River. Even when allowance is made for the closing of the rivers and canals by ice for several months a year, it has been shown that the savings afforded by railroads over the various means of transportation listed above would not have been as great as is usually assumed.[19]

So much for the "might-have-beens" of Iowa's transportation history; the things which actually happened make up quite a different story, a story which goes far beyond economic affairs into the national politics of westward expansion. Although much of this story is beyond the limits of this volume, it must be remembered that, willy-nilly, Iowa was drawn into the politics of transportation by her geographical position. After New York City, Boston, and Baltimore had been linked to Chicago, it was inevitable that Chicago must be linked with the Mississippi, then the Missouri, and, finally, with the Pacific Coast.[20] Iowa's railroad history, therefore, is much tied in with the history of Chicago and Illinois companies that were building roads in a westerly direction; all the great trunk lines across Iowa are merely extensions of roads from Chicago to the Mississippi.

The need to reach California and the Pacific Coast by rail served as a pretext for congressional aid in the form of large land grants, not for just one but for four roads predicated to cross Iowa! An act of Congress, May 15, 1856, made a princely gift to the state of Iowa of alternate sections of land for each prospective road, for a distance of six miles from the right of way, or their equivalent elsewhere (in round numbers about four million acres in all, roughly one-ninth of the almost

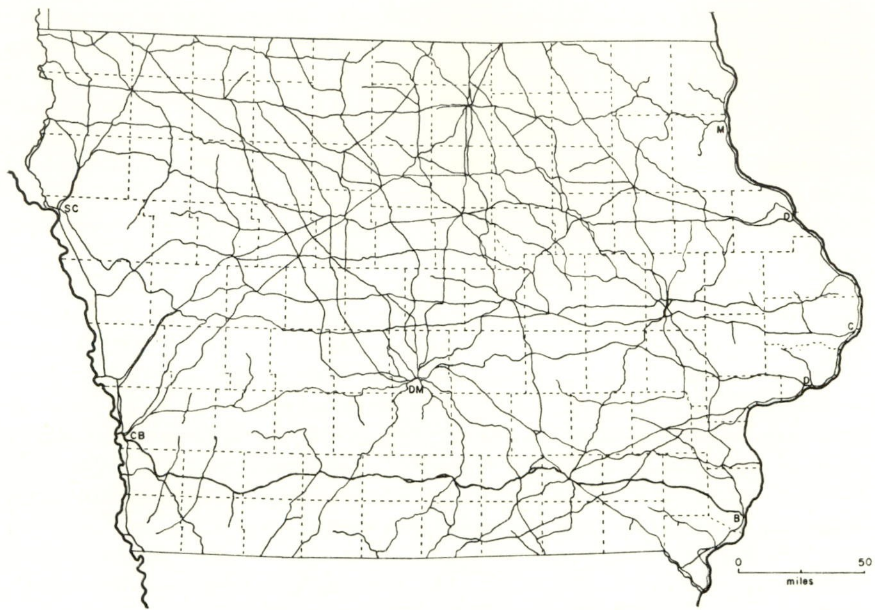

FIG. 6.1. This map shows the approximate structure of the railroad systems of Iowa as of 1960–1970. The initials on the map indicate the location of key termini, as follows: B (Burlington); D (Davenport); C (Clinton); D (Dubuque); M (McGregor); CB (Council Bluffs); SC (Sioux City); DM (Des Moines), an important railroad center. The reader should give special attention to the line from Burlington to Council Bluffs, the route of AMTRAK across Iowa.

thirty-six million acres of land in the state), to be used as bait to railroad builders. It was stipulated that one road was to originate at Burlington, one at Davenport, one at Lyons (North Clinton), and one at Dubuque. The road from Burlington would terminate at a point opposite the mouth of the Platte River, the two middle roads would run to Council Bluffs, and the Dubuque road would have its terminal at Sioux City.[21] The reader who is familiar with later railroad history will know that the four roads were destined to be the main lines in Iowa of the Burlington Road, the North Western, the Rock Island, and the Illinois Central. These and other roads were built, however, in short end-to-end segments such as "Iowa Falls and Sioux City," and "Sioux City and Pacific," which eventually could be joined into trunk lines under the names so familiar to later generations.

Iowa's first operating railroad had humble beginnings, although its name, The Mississippi & Missouri Rail Road, indicated the ambitions of the builders. In 1852 the builders of the Chicago & Rock

Island Railroad had foreseen the advisability of continuing their road across Iowa, once they reached the Mississippi, and they organized a company for this purpose even before their iron touched the banks of the river at Rock Island in February 1854. The names of the promoters are famous in the annals of railroad building in America—hard-driving men who were to usher in a new era of economic activity in Iowa, and, it must be added, a new code of business ethics as well. High on the list of promoters was Henry Farnam of Chicago, who seems to have been an honest operator though not above seeing to it that his road had "friends" in the legislature. Another was Joseph E. Sheffield, an Eastern financier, whose chief interest was an immediate return on his money. Last of the great names was Thomas C. Durant, known everywhere as "Doctor" Durant, of whom it must be said that he was chiefly interested in doctoring sick railroads for his own financial gain. Other well-known men who had prominent parts in Iowa's M. & M. Railroad history were John A. Dix; William B. Ogden, sometime mayor of Chicago; Norman B. Judd; William Walcott; and Ebenezer Cook, the Davenport banker. Some of these men were honored by place names.

The first M. & M. problem was to decide on a route, a matter to be determined chiefly by the choice of a crossing point on the Mississippi; if at Davenport, then whether to go due west, southwest, or northwest. There was some possibility of dropping downriver from Rock Island to cross the river at Muscatine, but this choice was overruled in favor of a due west route, partly because of the aid offered by Iowa City, the state capital, and partly because some of the promoters owned lands along the due west route, lands which could be sold for town lots and farms. Iowa City seemed a sufficient goal for the moment; agents who were sent to Fort Des Moines and to Kanesville (Council Bluffs) failed to stir up interest and donations because of the sparseness of population and the bleak outlook for the development of central and western Iowa.

Actual construction was begun in 1853, if planning, surveying, and grading be allowed as "construction." These steps frequently long preceded the actual laying of iron as a means of stirring up interest and of fulfilling legal requirements for the paying over of funds when and as if "construction" had begun. Peter A. Dey of Iowa City and his young protégé, Grenville M. Dodge,[22] surveyors who were adept at the location of rail routes, began the survey of the route on May 17 and finished as far as Iowa City on May 26. The first shovelful of dirt was not turned until September. From that date through the remainder of 1853, 1854, and the first half of 1855, the work of grading the right-of-way was carried on in desultory fashion. In the meanwhile, Dodge carried out the survey of a tentative route from Iowa City to Council Bluffs in just seventy-nine days, from September 4 to November 22, 1853, in a race with a competing line, the Iowa Central Air Line Rail Road. Dodge won the surveying race but his competitor would be the first to lay its rails all the way across Iowa from river to river, beating the M. & M. into Council Bluffs by two years.

In mid-1855 the tempo of construction activity on the M. & M. picked up. Iron was laid from Davenport to Wilton Junction, and a branch line was run from there down to Muscatine, where, on November 20, 1855, the citizens celebrated in grand style the actual completion of the first link of finished railroad in Iowa. Other crews built the main line from Wilton Junction to West Liberty; from there, urged on by the lure of a promise of $50,000 from Iowa City if the line reached there by January 1, 1856, every resource was devoted to winning that prize. Henry Farnam came out to lend a hand and drove the crews at their work; Iowa City residents volunteered their assistance even though it meant that the city would have to pay the prize money. Just on the stroke of 12:00 P.M., December 31, an engine was inched along on temporary rails the last few rods to the appointed destination. The triumph was properly celebrated a few days later with a great feast and much speechmaking, with bold predictions for the future of railroads to the west.

Farnam and Durant, using promotion methods typical of the times, publicized their grand ideas in the manner of the best modern public relations experts. Articles were planted in newspapers, and mass meetings were held in places along the prospective route. Bond issues and gifts were sought and won from localities and counties; key men were won over by such favors as hot tips for real estate purchases along the right-of-way or advantageous terms for stock purchases. Very fortunately for the promotional campaign, the bridge between Rock Island and Davenport, which the M. & M. would use, was completed in 1856, an event which not only materially improved the physical aspects of efficient railroad operation but served as a symbol of the strength of the railroad companies. Another boon in 1856 was the announcement of the congressional grant of lands for four roads across Iowa, one of which would follow the route of the M. & M. Offsetting these advantages, alas, was the Panic of 1857 and the tightening of money markets all over the country, while the national political situation centering on the slavery issue was another deterrent. For these and other reasons the M. & M. had to endure long periods of standstill, with just enough occasional bursts of activity to keep the company alive and to keep up the hopes and contributions of the communities along the route. The Civil War impeded the work, as might be expected, making it difficult to recruit laborers, secure supplies of iron, and raise the necessary capital funds. Des Moines was not reached until 1867; the entry into Council Bluffs did not come until 1869.[23]

In the meanwhile the other three lines were having their own alternating successes and delays. One, the Burlington & Missouri, was incorporated in 1852 for the purpose of extending C. B. & Q. lines into

Iowa, once that road was completed to a point on the river opposite Burlington. This was done in 1855. The Illinois road and its Iowa satellite, for which James W. Grimes, a Burlington banker and lawyer, was a local booster, were financed in Boston, John Murray Forbes being the principal source of financial support. As a New England man of New Hampshire background, Grimes could appeal to the New England financiers for their support. By July 1856, the rails had reached Mount Pleasant; two more years were required to reach Fairfield and another year to reach Ottumwa (1859). That was the year in which young Charles Elliott Perkins came out from Cincinnati as an assistant to the division mannager, beginning an association with the Burlington Road and the city of Burlington which would not end until 1901, after twenty years as president. By 1869 the road had fulfilled its assignment of reaching the Missouri opposite Plattsmouth. In 1870 a spur was run from Pacific Junction north to Council Bluffs to compete for business through the Omaha gateway.[24]

The road which was the first to complete the full link between the two rivers was the one known to history as the North Western. In its infancy it consisted of roads which operated under a variety of names, against great odds. A gambler watching its competition with the M. & M. and the Burlington & Missouri would probably have bet on it to come in third in the race across the state. The original construction company carried the pretentious title of Iowa Central Air Line Rail Road Company and was organized in 1853 to build a road from Lyons (North Clinton) to Cedar Rapids. When it went bankrupt in early 1856 because of an officer's foul deed of absconding with the company's bonds, the workers were paid off in groceries and dry goods, hence the colorful name, The Calico Road. A new and stronger company, the Chicago, Iowa & Nebraska Rail Road, was organized almost overnight, and yet three years were required to reach Cedar Rapids with rails. Beyond that achievement the future looked dim and hopeless.

A new company, the Cedar Rapids and Missouri Railroad, was set up in 1860, in which John Insley Blair of New Jersey was the driving force. Blair sent out crews in spite of the handicaps of war and other troubles, and by 1862 the rails were laid to Marshalltown. In 1864 the company's bridge over the Mississippi at Clinton was completed, eight years after the one at Davenport. In 1865 the rails reached Boone and in 1866 they were completed almost to Denison. In January 1867 the road was finished all the way to Council Bluffs, more than two years ahead of the M. & M. and three years ahead of the Burlington Road. Historians credit John I. Blair as the man who won the race for the future North Western Road.[25]

Duplicating much of the story of the three roads just outlined is the story of the building of the Illinois Central in Iowa. This Chicago-based company was originally planned as a Galena-to-Chicago road.

Iowa Senators George W. Jones and Augustus Caesar Dodge helped to secure an extension from Galena to Dunlieth, Illinois (now East Dubuque), in 1853. This was the spur to leading Dubuquers such as Platt Smith, Jesse P. Farley, General C. H. Booth, and others to organize the Dubuque & Pacific Railroad Company in April 1853. Nothing of importance happened until 1855 when construction was begun. In 1857 the rails reached Dyersville, only 29 miles from Dubuque. Eight more miles were managed before the company went bankrupt, even though its share of the 1856 land grant was figured at 1,162,373 acres, out of which few sales were made.

In 1859 J. Edgar Thompson, a friend and business associate of Andrew Carnegie, was made president of a new company, the Dubuque & Pacific, which extended the road to Manchester, Independence, and Jesup, a village named in honor of Morris K. Jesup of New York City, who financed further construction to Waterloo, and then to Cedar Falls by April 1, 1861. No more building took place during the war except a short branch line to Waverly; even after the war, construction moved slowly. A new president of the Illinois Central, John M. Douglas, could hope for no better than second place after the North Western in the race to Council Bluffs. His plans called for leasing the Dubuque & Sioux City, employing John I. Blair as a builder, and entrusting the bridging of the Mississippi at Dubuque to young Andrew Carnegie and the Keystone Bridge Company. Even though these measures were taken, the Illinois Central was the last of the four to reach the Missouri, at Sioux City, and a branch down to Council Bluffs.[26]

Mention should be made of a fifth road, which built two lines across Iowa. This was the Milwaukee Road, but it did not start with that name. A company called the Milwaukee & Mississippi had built a line from Milwaukee to Prairie du Chien; following the logic of all other operators, these people wanted to continue the road across northern Iowa, tap the business going up to the Twin Cities, and also solicit business to be gotten from a road continuing into Dakota Territory. A company was organized in 1863 called the McGregor Western, a front for Milwaukee & Mississippi investors but including some Iowans, notably William Larrabee of Clermont, a future governor of Iowa, and Judge George Greene of Cedar Rapids, jurist and capitalist. This company enjoyed considerable success. A road was run west from McGregor to Cresco and on to Owatonna and the Twin Cities; second, by slow stages a road was run on to Estherville and Sioux City, tieing in with an independent road from Sioux City to St. Paul. This track-laying was facilitated by a new company called the McGregor & Sioux City, organized in 1868, and by a land grant promised by Congress as an aid to the line across northern Iowa, a grant for which Representative William Boyd Allison, later a senator, always claimed the chief credit. The

Milwaukee & Mississippi Company was taken over by the road which eventually became the Chicago, Milwaukee, St. Paul & Pacific. By 1879 the McGregor road had built into Dakota Territory to Canton.

Not satisfied with one road in the north, the Milwaukee interests under Alexander Mitchell succumbed to the challenge to build a second road across Iowa, this one from Sabula to Council Bluffs. By 1872 it had reached Marion (not then a suburb of Cedar Rapids) but did not achieve full operation into Council Bluffs until 1882. Under the vigorous leadership of Mitchell it quickly cut into the Omaha-Council Bluffs gateway business; in addition, its officers built or bought many feeder lines all over Iowa. The day would come when it would rank as third in the state with respect to track mileage in Iowa.[27]

CHAPTER 7 ANTISLAVERY POLITICS AND BIRTH OF THE REPUBLICAN PARTY 1846–1856

IOWA'S ADMISSION INTO THE UNION IN 1846 OCCURRED IN A MEMorable year in the nation's history, often called "the year of decision." The war with Mexico, officially declared on May 13, quickly raised the prospect of the acquisition of lands reaching from the Gulf of Mexico to the Pacific, and with every mention of the war came the overpowering question of the day: Will slavery be permitted in any part of the lands presumably to be acquired? Outright abolition of slavery was as yet unthinkable except for a daring few, so the antislavery forces could go only so far as to assert that slave owners must not be allowed to extend chattel slavery as an institution into any territories organized in the lands acquired by the United States. "Extension of slavery" versus "nonextension of slavery" was a debating topic which stirred the passions of the time. Iowans, although safe from slavery itself, were much involved in antislavery politics and the national contest for political power, a contest which would long determine Iowa political history.

THE WILMOT PROVISO

In the years after 1836, when the Texas Question was being agitated and before the Mexican War divided the American people, it was well understood by most thinking citizens that a war involving so much territory would arouse increased interest in the slavery question. Many people, especially New Englanders, and not necessarily all of them abolitionists, opposed the war from the beginning because they anticipated the troubles over territorial organization and slavery which would surely arise. As so often is the case, the fierce debate about the principal issue was complicated by side issues. In this instance, the chief complication was the tariff question. Protariff Northern Democrats resented being asked to subordinate their differences with Southern Democrats over the tariff and slavery for the sake of party solidarity. An opportunity for the expression of their resentment came in August 1846, when President Polk asked for a fund of $2,000,000 to be used at his discretion in peace negotiations. David Wilmot, a high-tariff Pennsylvania Democrat, much to the discomfiture of Southern Democrats, and many Iowa Democrats, moved to amend the appropriation bill by a provisional clause that forbade slavery in any piece of territory acquired from the Republic of Mexico, or the use of the money for the purchase of such territory.[1]

"Wilmotism" became one of those issues which cannot be avoided or postponed. A recent authoritative analysis asserts that the sponsorship of the Proviso was not anti-Southern in spirit but a defensive move by the Van Buren Democrats troubled by antislavery sentiments among their constituents. "In attempting to assure their constituents that the Mexican War was not being waged to spread slavery, they stumbled upon a principle—the non-extension of slavery—which would shape the politics of two decades."[2] In one form or another the Wilmot Proviso came up repeatedly during the war and even after peace was achieved in 1848. It was accepted by the House in 1846 and again in 1847, but defeated by the Senate in 1847.

Iowa could speak with only half a voice, as it were, for or against the measure. The state had no representation in the Senate for the first two years of its existence because a petty dispute among the Whigs, Democrats, and Independents in the First General Assembly prevented the election of anyone. In the House of Representatives Iowa was represented by Shepherd Leffler of Burlington, a Democrat of strong convictions, born and educated in Pennsylvania and later an attorney in Wheeling, Virginia (now West Virginia), and Serranus C. Hastings of Bloomington (Muscatine), a former New York Democrat of judicial temperament. These two spokesmen for Iowa were sworn in on December 29, 1846, one day after Iowa's formal admission into the Union, four months after the Proviso was introduced and passed the first time. When it came up for a second vote, this time under the sponsorship of Preston King of New York, Leffler was one of the 115 in its favor against the 89 who voted nay; Hastings did not vote.[3] (The Proviso was now often called the "Three Million Bill" in reference to the sum of money to be given to the president for his use in making peace.) By the time Iowa had succeeded in electing her two senators and they had been seated, on December 7, 1848, the peace treaty had been made and the matter had lost its urgency. The new senators, Augustus C. Dodge of Burlington and George Wallace Jones of Dubuque, could have been expected to vote against the Proviso.

It has been asserted that the influence of the numerous former Southerners in the eastern river counties of Iowa and in some Iowa-Missouri border counties was great enough to enable them to control the General Assembly, prevent the adoption of resolutions or instructions in favor of the Wilmot Proviso, and otherwise uphold the proslavery point of view. It is true that every state legislature in the North, with the glaring exception of Iowa's General Assembly, passed such a resolution but there are several arguments which can be advanced against the easy acceptance of the idea that ex-Southerners controlled the thinking and the votes of Iowa's legislators or congressmen. For one thing, it is an oversimplification to assume that all or even most ex-Southerners held proslavery beliefs, or, second, that they would continue to vote as their Southern proslavery friends or relatives desired. A greater objection, however, is the assumption that all residents or former residents of so-called Southern states are identical or even similar in their views. As pointed out above, many of the former Kentuckians, North Carolinians, Virginians, and Tennesseans who had moved to Iowa were originally from the mountainous nonslaveholding area of those states; they were opposed to slavery and, as it were, had run away from it since there was no hope of abolishing the institution in the foreseeable future. Admittedly, many of these people were anti-Negro, to use a blunt expression, but this was a far cry from being proslavery. Just why it should be thought these former Southerners would now want the institution of slavery extended into the new territories is something that would be difficult to demonstrate. Other criticisms have also been advanced against this thesis, one in particular which holds that Iowa's representatives and senators were not proslavery, as demonstrated by their very words and deeds.[4]

The debates on the Proviso brought out into the open the constitutional theory of Senator John C. Calhoun of South Carolina, who held that the Union was made up of sovereign states; the states owned the territories; therefore, citizens of states had the right to take their property with them when they emigrated into the territories to live, including their property in slaves, and, therefore, Congress had no right to restrict slavery in the territories. Antislavery people had no alternative but to retaliate with the much older argument that the territories belonged to the United States of America, that is, to the "nation," and Congress, as the legislative agent of the national government, had the right to control the territories by the legislative process, including the right to prohibit slavery therein. If this point of view were ever conceded by the proslavery forces, the antislavery forces of the fast-growing Eastern and Midwestern states would soon be able to elect enough members of Congress to pass restrictive legislation and thus by simple legislative process, not by an amendment, prevent the spread of slavery. Thus the fight over slavery extension became part of a contest for sufficient raw political power to run the country.

Another point of view stressed the "liberty" clause in the Fifth Amendment: "No person . . . shall be . . . deprived of life, liberty or property, without due process of law. . . ." This doctrine as developed by William H. Seward and Salmon P. Chase in 1849–1850 became gospel to the Free-Soilers, who argued that Congress had the duty to enforce this constitutional provision in the District of Columbia and in the territories. A fourth point of view hovered in the background, but inasmuch as it was anathema to proslavery people, its proponents had not dared to bring it forward: the old Lewis Cass theory of popular sovereignty, more often called "squatter sovereignty." Senator Stephen A. Douglas of Illinois did not openly avow this doctrine until 1859. Under its logic the people of the territories would decide all controversial questions for themselves under the name of self-rule; as to slavery, for example, they might vote it in or they might vote it down. Neither the proslavery nor antislavery forces were eager to gamble on the choice such voters might make.[5]

Seeing these clashing points of view clearly, the proslavery advocates were determined to keep as long as possible the advantage they had in the Senate with its balance of slave and free states. No matter what might happen in the House of Representatives, where the growing population of the Eastern and Western states would tend to widen the margin between antislavery and proslavery votes, the principle of equality of representation in the Senate could always be the bulwark of the "peculiar institution" of slavery. If this balance were ever destroyed, the antislavery forces could nibble away at the legal structure now protecting slavery and gradually wipe it out.

THE COMPROMISE OF 1850

Although proponents of the Wilmot Proviso were not able to steer its passage through Congress, the controversy over "free soil" would not subside. As in 1820 and again in 1833, Congress found a solution for an impasse by working out a compromise, in this case one made up of five individual acts known collectively as the Compromise of 1850, by which, presumably, the most pressing problems of the day were solved. California was admitted as a free state; New Mexico and Utah were to be organized as territories, either one or any part of one to be admitted as a state with or without slavery as their future state constitution might provide (an implied acceptance of the principle of popular sovereignty); Texas was to give up disputed territory to New Mexico in return for assumption by the national government of $10,000,000 in debt claims; the slave trade (but not slavery) was abolished in the District of Columbia; and, finally, a more stringent fugitive slave law was enacted, a sop to Southern owners of slaves and their spokesmen in Congress, all passed in September.[6]

Generally speaking, the Democrats of the time favored the compromise. Certainly this was so in Iowa. Both senators, Augustus Caesar

Dodge and George W. Jones, supported in debate and ultimately voted in the affirmative for every one of the five bills making up the compromise package enacted in September 1850, a distinction which only three other senators could claim. It comes as no surprise, then, to learn that the Iowa Democratic Convention, held in the preceding June when passage of the bills seemed assured, strongly endorsed Henry Clay's compromise bills in their entirety as being fair to all concerned. For governor the Democrats nominated Stephen B. Hempstead, a Connecticut-born resident of Dubuque since 1838, who might be more generally acceptable than a man of Southern background. For congressman from the First District they nominated Bernhart Henn, an ex-New Yorker now well established as an Iowan, residing in Fairfield; from the Second District they selected Lincoln Clark of Dubuque, Massachusetts-born but a resident of Alabama for some time. The Whigs accused Clark of being soft on slavery, "infected" by his years in Alabama. Both candidates for Congress could be expected to give support to the execution of the compromise now under discussion.

Against such redoubtable competition, the Whigs could only remain silent on the compromise bills, not daring to promise support for the Fugitive Slave legislation but equally unwilling to repudiate the other four acts. For governor they nominated James Harlan, a recent graduate of Indiana Asbury College (DePauw University) and now an educator in Iowa City. (Shortly after the nomination, it was discovered that the nominee did not quite meet the minimum age requirement of 30 years, and his place on the ticket was given to James L. Thompson.) For congressmen they nominated George G. Wright of Keosauqua, recently arrived from Rockville, Indiana, and William H. Henderson of Johnson County, only recently arrived from Tennessee where he was a prominent Whig politician. The candidates accepted the Whig shibboleths of internal improvements at national expense and a high tariff.[7]

A portent for the future which few voters seemed to recognize was the emergence of the Free-Soil party in Iowa. Successor to the old Liberty party, this small but determined group emphasized their opposition to the extension of slavery into any new territories. Most of its members at this time were incipient abolitionists and would soon espouse the doctrine of "immediatism"—the immediate and unrecompensed emancipation of all slaves. In 1850 they could present for governor an able lawyer and journalist, William Penn Clarke of Iowa City, the kind of party wheelhorse who is almost never elected to office but exerts much influence as the trusted adviser of those who are elected. For congressmen they named George Shedd, one of the pillars of the Congregational flock led by Asa Turner in Denmark, and the little-known John H. Dayton. The infant party would grow rapidly, thanks to the evangelical fervor of Asa Turner, William Salter, and other members of the Iowa Band, and their associates, notably George F. Magoun.[8]

Campaigning in the 1850s called for rugged physical resources. One must ride horseback or in a buggy, surrey, wagon, or stagecoach over poor roads; occasionally there might be the luxury of travel by a steamboat on the Mississippi or the smaller rivers. In this contest matching powers of endurance as well as ideas, the August elections gave victory to the Democrats in every race, largely because of the popularity of the compromise principle which they supported and which would be enacted into law the next month, after months of debate.[9] The margins were narrow but beyond any basis for protest or recrimination. The Free-Soilers deflected a few votes from the major parties, but their votes, added to the losing party's votes, would not have changed the results, race by race.

One did not need to be clairvoyant, however, to foresee troubles ahead for the Democrats; some dramatic and outstanding event might create an issue which would break the peace established by the great compromise and clear the way to victory for their opponents. Such an issue did not arise in 1851 when the Democrats were again victorious. (These were the years of annual elections, some offices being filled one year and some the next.) In 1852 the Democrats felt more pressure. In this election the presidential contest added to the usual excitement over lesser races. Nationally, the Democrats put Franklin Pierce of New Hampshire into the White House; in Iowa, they won the congressional seat in the First District for Bernhart Henn but lost the Second District to the Whig, John P. Cook of Davenport, mostly because of squabbles within the party. The Free-Soilers in Iowa were more active than previously, though as a strategic move they passed up the congressional races and concentrated on other offices. Best of all for the Democrats, their candidates carried the state legislative elections and therefore they were in position to reelect George W. Jones as United States senator. The Whigs tried to emphasize their support of internal improvements at national expense but Senators Jones and Dodge could match them in fervor on this point. Apparently the Democrats could still travel on the momentum of the past plus their reputation as the party of the Compromise of 1850.[10]

THE KANSAS-NEBRASKA ACT, 1854

The spirit of acquiescence in the compromise held over in the 1853 elections—but 1854 was a different story. The events of that year are tied in with the efforts to organize Kansas and Nebraska as territories of the United States. The first move in such a direction was taken in December 1851, followed by other efforts in 1852 and 1853 which failed in one house or the other. A new Nebraska bill was introduced in the Senate on December 14, 1853, by Senator Dodge of Iowa, in his capacity as chairman of the Committee on Public Lands. The bill was based on the assumption that the Missouri Compromise was inviolable, an assumption shared by most people at that time. Much to the consternation of nearly everyone, friend and foe alike, the Dodge bill was replaced on January 4, 1854, by one sponsored by Senator Stephen A. Douglas, and this was replaced on January 23 by still another Douglas measure proposing the division of Nebraska into two territories, Nebraska and Kansas, and the outright repeal of the Missouri Compromise, each territory to make its own decision on slavery by a vote of its own people.

Just how much credit or blame Douglas should have for bringing about the passage of the bill has been much debated. Bypassing here the historical problem of Douglas's motivation, admittedly mixed to a high degree, stress has recently been placed on the tie-in of the bill with Indian policy. As we have seen many times above, acquisition of Indian lands must rest upon a formal treaty with the Indian occupants, providing for compensation and for removal elsewhere. This inconvenient obstacle was attended to by the Treaty of Fort Laramie of 1851, bringing to an end the policy of nonmixture of Indians and whites.[11] For trivial annuities the Indians of this area were to allow the whites to build roads and military posts and were to refrain from attacks on emigrants to the Pacific Coast; by a strained interpretation, "roads" could be made to mean "railroads."

The fight over the bill was destined to occupy a period of several months, from January 23 to May 30, 1854, a period during which political parties would be made and unmade. A leading American historian has satisfactorily demonstrated that Douglas does not deserve the credit which has been showered upon him for guiding the maneuvers and corraling the necessary votes. In the Senate he must share the credit—or blame—with Senator David Rice Atchison of Missouri, a spokesman for the Calhounites in the South, who demanded the explicit repeal of the antislavery clause in the Missouri admission act of 1820 before they would contribute their votes for the measure. In the House it was Alexander H. Stephens of Georgia who delivered the Southern votes on the key test leading to final passage. Stephens, a Southern Whig, found the votes by drawing on a coalition of Southern Democrats and Southern Whigs who saw eye-to-eye on slavery.[12]

For Iowans, the crucial question involved the effect of the debates and the final passage of the bill on the politics of the time, both state and national. Iowa Democrats had begun to reflect the dissension within the national party. Many Northern Democrats were beginning to see that their views and their interests did not at all agree with those of the dominant Southern wing of the party; only the traditions of the past, and the reluctance to destroy a going thing, and the desire for power held the national party together. On the slavery question a revulsion was in evidence, as illustrated by the case of Samuel Jordan Kirkwood. Born and reared in Maryland as a Democrat, he was shocked and disillusioned by what he saw as a youth of the slave trade in Washington, D.C., and was completely won over to antislavery views during his residence in Ohio before coming to Iowa in 1855, so could not in good conscience remain a Democrat. Multiply his experience by the hundreds, then by the thousands, and by 1860 by the hundreds of thousands, and the disruption of the Democratic party is amply explained. Add the tariff issue, free homesteads, internal improvements at national expense, the temperance issue, and some quarreling over the proper attitude toward immigration, and there were enough sources of dissent to wreck any party.

Under these disturbing circumstances, now brought to the front by the Nebraska business, the Democratic party was the first Iowa party to hold its state convention in this trying year. Meeting at Iowa City on January 9, 1854, two weeks before Douglas introduced his amended bill, featured by the proposal to repeal the Missouri Compromise, the Democrats were not too early to escape the effects of the national debate. This was a time for bold action and strong candidates; instead, the slate of nominees proved to be quite colorless, only Curtis Bates of Dubuque, the choice for the race for governor, deserving any favorable notice. The platform makers dealt only in generalities: praise for the Pierce administration, destined to become known as the weakest in our entire national history, and endorsement of the proposal to organize the Nebraska Territory, a necessary formality because their leader, Senator Dodge, was the author of the original bill on the subject.

MORE CONVENTIONS: ANTISLAVERY POLITICS, 1854

Not only the Democrats but the other parties were disturbed by the great issues of the times. Ever since the debates on the Wilmot Proviso, politics had been in a state of flux and the time was ripe for decisive steps in the arena of party action. A "process of disintegration" was going on, "the natural prelude to the reintegration of a series of political elements into a new party."[13]

Indeed, a new party was in the making. From the beginning of the debate on the Douglas bill in January, a "party" began to take form around the concerted opposition to the extension of slavery into the territories, joining in mass meetings regardless of other disagreements. A great deal of editorial comment and a great outpouring of political oratory encouraged the masses to join in these protest meetings. Here is proof that a political party is first formed in the minds of people; the development into an organized party occurs later when the political system undergoes "a crisis of participation."[14] For example, Ohio Senator Salmon P. Chase's "Appeal of the Independent Democrats," issued on January 24 as a blast against the Nebraska bill's proposal of popular sovereignty, evoked a widespread response. It was endorsed by James W. Grimes, who was by now the leader of the radical Whigs.

Not waiting for the outcome of the Nebraska debate, the Free-Soilers held a convention in early February 1854 in the small town of Crawfordsville, in Washington County. Meeting in the Seceder Presbyterian Church and acting under the adopted name of the Free Democracy, these antislavery people performed the two most important acts of any party convention: the nomination of candidates and the adoption of a platform. For governor they named the relatively unknown Simeon Waters of Mount Pleasant, a Congregational minister and agent of the American Home Missionary Society; for secretary of state, J. W. Cattell of Des Moines; for superintendent of public instruction, George Shedd of Denmark, a forthright Abolitionist, perhaps the most active antislavery man in Iowa at the time, with the possible exception of James W. Grimes. Their platform was typically Free-Soilish, specifically opposing the Nebraska bill and extension of slavery into the territories.[15]

So far as we know, no mention was made in the meeting of the word "Republican" as a name for a new party, but the same could be said of many other anti-Douglas, anti-Nebraska meetings held in 1854 all over the country. The word most in use just then was Fusion; some preferred The Coalition. No one was consciously planning a major political party and so the precise name would have to come later. The whole movement was a voluntary and instinctive protest against what they considered to be an evil thing. It was fitting, therefore, that the Free-Soil meeting was held in a church building because religion and moralizing were definitely the source and inspiration of the "antislavery impulse" of the leaders who were present. Other interests might have been represented, then and later: railroads, protective tariffs, internal improvements, free land, antipolygamy, and temperance—but nothing strikes the student of this movement so much as the fact that practically all the leaders were either clergymen or active church laymen, who would have, if possible, legislated an end to slavery. At this Crawfordsville meeting, however, they had to accept and declare for a compromise solution: nonextension of slavery into new territories.

Only a few days after the meeting at Crawfordsville, two similar meetings were held at Ripon, Wisconsin, on February 28 and March 20. The term "anti-Nebraska" covers the sentiments of the Ripon protesters in these meetings where Alvan E. Bovay and his fellow townsmen enunciated the principles which have gained widespread acceptance of the

Wisconsin town as the birthplace of the Republican party. Their declarations differed little if any from those made by George Shedd and his Free-Soil-"Free Democracy" friends at Crawfordsville, or from pronouncements by similar groups meeting at Decatur, Illinois; Logansport, Indiana; Jackson, Michigan; or any one of a countless number of places while the Douglas bill was before Congress and in the months immediately following. Bovay urged Horace Greeley to use the word "Republican" as a name for the protest groups and, finally, on June 24, the word appeared in Greeley's paper, the *New York Tribune,* the bible of people of these sentiments. A mass meeting on July 13 at Jackson, Michigan, seems to have been the first group to call themselves Republican.[16]

As the fight over the Kansas-Nebraska bill waxed hotter and hotter, more and more people found in this issue the force to turn them from a divided Whig party, or the divided Democratic party, or the passionate but numerically weak Free-Soil party, fast becoming an Abolitionist party or society. Not much later the American (Know-Nothing) party would be added to this list of components, and also a host of young voters voting for the first time. Antislavery feeling caused a fusion of all these elements into one new party, dedicated, first of all, to the eventual destruction of slavery by putting an end to its extension into the virgin lands of new territories where it could perpetuate itself for another generation.

The Democratic party was carried along by the momentum of its past successes, plus whatever strength it might derive from honest and sincere support for the Douglas measure. Opponents of the Democrats cautiously moved into the fight against the Illinois senator's proposal. Seeking support from a variety of sources, the Iowa Whigs met in state convention in Iowa City on February 22, 1854, and took a popular stand on a number of causes: provision for a banking system; retention of the Missouri Compromise line of 1820 as a "final settlement of the Question of Slavery" in the area specified; opposition to the Douglas Nebraska bill; internal improvements paid for by federal funds rather than by tonnage duties on internal commerce, as proposed by Douglas; changes to prevent one-third of the state educational funds from going for administrative expenses; support for a congressional gift of public lands "in limited quantities, to actual settlers"; and a stringent state law prohibiting the manufacture and sale of "ardent spirits" as a beverage.[17]

In democratic politics, political parties and platforms must be identified with personalities. In this respect, the Whigs were more fortunate than their Democratic opponents. As their candidate for governor they chose James Wilson Grimes of Burlington, an able lawyer and financier who had been in the thick of affairs since his arrival in the Iowa District of the Territory of Wisconsin in 1836.

The most important thing to note at this point is that Grimes had become thoroughly identified with the Abolitionist wing of the Whig party in Iowa, and at the same time closely associated with the Free-Soil group which was dominated by the Congregational clergymen of the Iowa Band. Grimes was a prominent member of the Congregational Church in Burlington whose pastor since 1846 had been the brilliant William Salter, a member of the Iowa Band, Grimes's pastor until the statesman's death in 1872, and then his biographer.

As a leader, Grimes personified the political-economic-social views of the rank and file Whigs who were unknowingly moving along a straight line toward membership in a new party. He had been a participant in the take-over of the Indian lands by treaties, and in the border dispute and Honey War with Missouri. He was a banker and real estate speculator as well as a lawyer and, like most Whigs, a firm advocate of revision of the Iowa constitution so as to permit banks and banking in Iowa. He was associated with Illinois businessmen in railroad building and was a booster for railroads in Iowa; in the meanwhile he took the next best thing and joined other Iowans in a plank road enterprise from Burlington to Mount Pleasant. He was a strong temperance man though shrewd enough not to push the matter too far and thus antagonize the German vote in Burlington, Davenport, and Dubuque, and the scattered German settlers in northeast Iowa.[18]

The Whigs completed their work in separate district conventions where they nominated Rufus L. B. Clarke, a Mount Pleasant attorney, as their candidate for Congress from the First District, and James Thorington of Davenport from the Second District. Of the two, Thorington was much more the politician. Unbeknownst to most Iowans at the time, Thorington was soon to be a leader in the Know-Nothing circles. Born in North Carolina and educated in Alabama, he is an interesting example of the Southerner who came north to live, bringing with him strong antislavery beliefs.

Unfortunately for the Whigs in this time of flux, an internal squabble weakened them and helped to ruin their chances to dominate the new party then taking shape. Their trend toward disunity was a close parallel to the Democratic split of the same time but with the positions reversed. Just as the Democrats, nationally, were torn asunder by the withdrawal of some members who resented the domination of their party by proslavery leaders, the Whigs were rent in twain by the "traditionalists" who resented the tendency of the radicals in the party to pull away to stronger ground.[19] Even the *Burlington Hawk-Eye* turned against the "radical" Grimes and caused people to wonder why the nominee for governor could not command the support of his own hometown party organ. Only the timely purchase of the *Hawk-Eye* by Clark Dunham, a Vermonter by birth and recently an editor of an Ohio newspaper, prevented the Burlington situation from becoming ruinously embarrassing to Grimes.

In one way or another the Iowa Whigs showed great cleverness. In 1850 they had tried without success to lure the Free-Soilers into a merger or at least an alliance. Now the Whigs used another tactic: for superintendent of public instruction they went into Free-Soil ranks and borrowed their ardent leader, George Shedd, for a nominee, and for secretary of state named the Reverend Mr. Simeon Waters of Mount Pleasant, each of whom had been nominated by the Free-Soilers but for different offices. Disappointingly, however, the Free-Soilers did not go along with the radical Whigs by cooperatively dropping their own party aspirations and their desire to play a part in Iowa antislavery politics.

Until recently Free-Soiler tactics of 1854 have been difficult to explain. Of the two men jointly nominated by Free-Soilers and Whigs, George Shedd was a fairly well-known person of definite views, a man who would have been an asset to any party; selection of the unknown Simeon Waters, on the other hand, has been a source of wonder. Who was this nonentity who seemed so readily expendable for trading purposes by the Free-Soilers?

It is now possible to piece together the known and the hitherto unknown and deduce the likely truth about this bit of undercover 1854 politics. As for the known element, although Grimes later gave Senator Chase a dishonest report on the facts, it has long been on record that in the face of poor prospects for a straight Whig victory, Grimes was forced to take a calculated risk and go to the Free-Soilers (the Free Democrats) to beg for their support at the expense of losing some of the conservative (Silver Gray) Whigs. Hat in hand, figuratively speaking, Grimes journeyed the few miles to Denmark, headquarters of the Free-Soil group, to meet such Abolitionists as George and Curtis Shedd, Asa Turner, and George Frederic Magoun, and make a bid for their help.

It is apparent that Grimes had little trouble in making a deal with these men; perhaps the fact that he was a trusted coreligionist helped. He had the quick satisfaction of seeing a call from their pens for a new Free-Soil convention, to be held at Crawfordsville on March 28. This convention duly met and resolved that two matters were of concern to their members: one, the election of a governor, other state officers, and a state legislature, all dedicated to opposition to the extension of slavery; the other, the enactment of a "Maine Law" (Prohibition) for Iowa. Control of the state legislature by antislavery men who were opposed to the extension of slavery would insure the election of a United States senator in 1855 of like mind. The convention went on to endorse James W. Grimes for governor "because we believe, if elected, that he will maintain and carry out these principles. . . ."

The hitherto unknown element concerned the role of Simeon Waters. The endorsement of Grimes meant, of course, that Waters had been dropped as the Free-Soil candidate for governor. Until the recent discovery of a letter from his pen, it was not known that Simeon Waters had consented to his own political sacrifice. Just after the election, Waters wrote from his temporary residence in Maine to Julius A. Reed, chief agent of the American Home Missionary Society in Iowa, admitting that he (Waters) had helped to arrange the deal which "has resulted in the triumphs of the friends of morality and freedom in Iowa," even though this ruined his own chances for an "occupation."[20]

When to this confession is added Grimes's own reminiscent commentary made four years later in a letter to Senator Salmon P. Chase of Ohio, asserting that only Chase's influence in securing for him the Free-Soil vote saved him from defeat in 1854, the importance of the minor party's marginal vote is made convincingly clear. Grimes's election as governor as a Whig-Republican—it is difficult to decide which is the correct word—was the first notable victory over the Democratic machine in Iowa since the formation of the state, and, as Grimes told Chase, made possible "the succession of anti-Nebraska triumphs" which followed his victory in 1854.[21] Grimes's margin over Curtis Bates was only 2,123—23,325 to 21,202—a margin which could be credited only to the Free-Soil vote.

The next victory for the anti-Nebraska forces followed soon. In 1855 James Harlan of Mount Pleasant, president of Iowa Wesleyan University, was elected senator to replace Augustus C. Dodge. The victory did not come without a struggle. In a divided assembly—Whig House and Democratic Senate—the Democrats tried every stratagem to block Harlan's election. The assembly was kept in a turmoil from December 4, 1854, until the following January 6; finally, in a session of doubtful legality because absent Democrats prevented a quorum, Harlan was declared the winner. Again the antislavery forces, Republican in all but name, had broken into the victory column.[22]

FUSION OF ELEMENTS IN A REPUBLICAN PARTY

Iowans of antislavery views could now take the last formal steps in organizing a new party on a statewide basis. Local meetings here and there passed resolutions calling for some kind of concerted action. In Fairfield, for example, a meeting of such people passed resolutions in favor of organization, one resolve going so far as to furnish a name: the Republican Party of Iowa. A similar meeting took place in Dubuque; in fact, such meetings were common all over the Midwest and were attended by people from all parties without thought just now of anything but opposition to slavery, hence the commonly used title, Opposition party. At the moment these dedicated souls were in the grip of a religious and moral fervor whipped up by orators who spoke by the hour to eager listeners. Disillusioned antislavery Northern Democrats came to realize that they must split once and for all with proslavery Southern Democrats, and liberal Northern Whigs from Southern Whigs and from Northern Silver Gray Whigs. Such self-exiled Democrats and Whigs were natural allies in the making of a new party.

New to the scene were the American party members, better known as the Know-Nothings, who are usually condemned out of hand as narrow-minded anti-Catholics and anti-Europeans who hid behind the secrecy of their lodges, giving the stock answer, "I know nothing," to all inquirers. Recent research has pretty well demolished this convenient stereotype. In a remarkably thorough and cogent study of the Iowa section of this party,[23] it has been demonstrated that the secret, "dark lantern" phase of their existence was very short-lived; as to the character of the membership, the "best people" of many communities were members, as attested by a compilation of over three hundred names of Iowa leaders of the party. Editors of prominent newspapers made no attempt to hide their affiliation or sympathy; names of members and stories of their activities frequently appeared in the scanty news columns of that day. Many members, especially those at the officer level, maintained their membership in the Whig or Free-Soil parties (or the new Opposition party) and apparently found no conflict of loyalties. Their nativism was not harsh, persecutive, or likely to express itself in riots, but was more inclined toward a later philosophy called "America First-ism." Limitation of the suffrage and prescription of longer periods of residence before naturalization were Know-Nothing demands which other Americans found hard to resist. The continental Sunday of the European immigrants, German "beer-swilling" and Irish whisky drinking were severely criticized by the Know-Nothings; perhaps these were a veneer for economic prejudice against any European likely to deprive a native American from a job in this era of hard times concurrent with the Panic of 1857. Anti-Catholicism had nothing to do with such economic prejudice. Prejudice was more prevalent in the cities than elsewhere; foreigners who settled in small towns and on farms suffered very little. Iowa badly needed population and cheap labor and few questions were asked of those willing to work on farms and railroad construction projects.

Two more elements of the new party remain to be named but not much more than that is required. One, the Free-Soil element has been referred to frequently above; the other is the group that may be referred to as the class of 1856, young voters who were about to cast their first ballots. In a growing state like Iowa such voters would make up a considerable addition to the party. Of the two, the former contributed ideas as well as numbers. By 1856 the Free-Soilers were more and more thought of as Abolitionists, once a pejorative but no longer a handicap. From the viewpoint of the builders and leaders of the new unnamed party, the problem was to acquire and hold these voters and their talents without allowing them to take over the party; from the point of view of the Abolitionists, the problem was to infiltrate the new party and thus have an instrument for use in helping the Negro as much as possible until more effective means could be developed.

The practical tactic which the abolition-minded Free-Soilers followed was to accept the *compromise* doctrine of nonextension of slavery for the time being, then gradually work for total abolition of slavery as time and circumstances would permit. In their minds the new coalition party, whatever its name, was a *compromise party* which must be transformed as quickly as possible into a "radical" party, never to be satisfied with anything less than complete freedom for all slaves everywhere. Not for them Lincoln's policy of "nonextension of slavery, but protection of slavery wherever it is already established." Some historians now contend that the non-Abolitionist elements in the Republican party were opposed to the admission of Negroes, either slave or free, into the new territories and that this anti-Negro prejudice was the basis of their antislavery politics. It would be the role of certain Abolitionists to break down this attitude—but this was far into the future. In the 1850s very few Abolitionists were ahead of their contemporaries on the subject of genuine political, social, and economic equality.[24]

BIRTH OF THE REPUBLICAN PARTY IN IOWA, 1856

It was in January 1856, almost twenty-one months after the Kansas-Nebraska Act became law, that a call went out for a state organizational meeting of the antislavery forces of Iowa. The artfully worded invitation appeared almost simultaneously in several newspapers:

> TO THE CITIZENS OF IOWA
>
> Believing that a large majority of the people of Iowa are opposed to the political principles of the present administration, and to the introduction of slavery into the territory now free, and also made free by the compromise of 1820; and that the party, styling itself the "Democratic party," are striving to make slavery a great national institution, contrary to the principles laid down in the Declaration of Independence and the Constitution, as taught by the fathers of the Republic; we would call upon all such free citizens to meet in convention, at Iowa City on the 22nd of February, for the purpose of organizing a Republican party, to make common cause with a similar party already formed in several other states of the Union.
>
> Many Citizens

It is interesting to note that a meeting fraught with so much meaning for the future should have been called in such an informal and impersonal way, so much so that to this day it is difficult to find a great deal of documentary material on the subject. One of the activists who issued the call was beyond any doubt Governor James W. Grimes; other identities are less certain but there is every reason to believe that Senator James Harlan was a coauthor of the call. Presumably one or more of the movement's leaders in every town and county knew or took on faith the genuineness of the notice which appeared under date of January 3, 1856, first in the *Burlington Hawk-Eye,* in Governor Grimes's own place of residence, and the *Mount Pleasant Observer,* in Senator Harlan's hometown. The call was widely copied and it drew favorable comment from many editors.[25]

Unfortunately the Iowa City meeting collided with the national preliminary convention for organizational purposes held on the same date in Pittsburgh to plan for the first national convention of the party to be held in Philadelphia in June, drawing away at least one prominent Iowan, William Penn Clarke of Iowa City. Senator Harlan stayed by his duties in Washington but sent a discourse to be read to the Iowa City meeting. The exact number of delegates in attendance is hard to ascertain because of poor record keeping and because of the fractional method of voting which was employed. Perhaps we may rely on the editor of the *Fairfield Ledger,* presumably a delegate, who wrote that the Hall of Representatives in the capitol was filled to the limit. Of course we have no way of knowing that all who were in attendance were bona fide delegates; surely there were some who were representatives of the press, and some who were influential people who had not been chosen as official delegates.

The list of candidates selected for this first Republican campaign in Iowa was a fairly strong one though no major offices were to be filled. The ticket was headed by Elijah Sells of Muscatine for secretary of state. For chairman of the State Central Committee, the most important party post, a Des Moines lawyer and banker, and former state auditor, Andrew J. Stevens, was chosen. For the party's purposes in 1856, the platform was more important than the slate of nominees. The document was confined chiefly to one topic: opposition to the extension of slavery into the territories. It was a living proof that the Iowa Republican party was founded on the philosophy of Wilmotism—and equally clear proof that Wilmotism was the rock on which the Democracy must split. Other party interests such as temperance, stringent naturalization laws, homesteads, and internal improvements were swept under the rug by the party architects; the platform must not offend this or that group by mention, yea or nay, of pet interests of various groups. The German members wanted some strong statement in favor of the easy system of naturalization then in use; by contrast, the Know-Nothings wanted a longer waiting period, imitating those who in some states were asking for a waiting period of twenty-one years! The gamble of saying nothing was taken—and won; only the aggressive German members from Dubuque walked out, all other German delegates remaining and loyally supporting the party.[26]

Other points in the platform were rather general and could have proved embarrassing in the future if platforms were meant to be taken seriously. This platform declared that it was the "mission" of the Republican party "to maintain the Liberties of the People, the Sovereignty of the States, and the Perpetuity of the Union." The federal government was declared to be one of limited powers. The pretensions of the Democratic party as a national party were denied and the Republican party was declared to be the true "national" party. Such meaningless generalizations can only be interpreted as sops thrown to the old-line Whigs and Democrats to retain their support of the party—events would soon show that the states were not sovereign in any meaningful sense, and, under victorious Republicans, the pendulum of power would swing far to the side of the national government, not to the states.

What the people of Iowa and the nation were witnessing in 1854–1856 was really a revolution in American politics. By a miracle of political biology the Republican party had been conceived and born in a thousand places. As an amalgam of several different parties it succeeded in absorbing in whole or in part their respective characteristics. In the long run, the new party at one time or another revealed the influence of all the separate groups: here the Whigs, there the Free-Soilers, or in another place the Know-Nothings. For a short time the Know-Nothings (American party) threatened to take over the new party but they were absorbed by a process of assimilation which secured their votes but not at the price of accepting all their views—or their name. This element strengthened a strain of nationalism in the new party which poorly equipped it for dealing with the immigration problems and other minority group relations of the future.[27]

"Free men, free land, free schools, and Fre-mont!" made a good slogan for the presidential campaign. Although not incorporated in this slogan, "free labor" might have been included. A convincing case has been made that many founders of the party stressed the role of free labor in the North as opposed to slave labor in the South and the European class system which made advancement difficult. Republican orators appealed to the working classes for their votes by placing great emphasis on the fact that in the North a laborer was not restricted to that lot in life.[28]

It is easy to foretell that in Iowa the Democrats, however well entrenched, could not withstand the challenge of a party which combined humanism with pietism, morality, and economic progress.

JAMES W. GRIMES

JAMES HARLAN

SAMUEL J. KIRKWOOD

JAMES S. CLARKSON

WILLIAM LARRABEE

EMORY H. ENGLISH

ALBERT B. CUMMINS

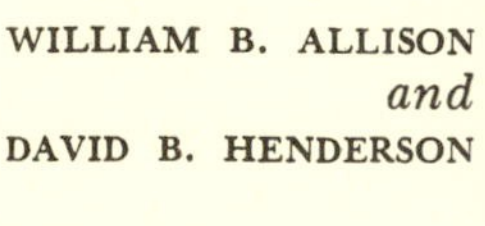

WILLIAM B. ALLISON
and
DAVID B. HENDERSON

WILLIAM B. ALLISON *and* JONATHAN P. DOLLIVER

SMITH W. BROOKHART

JAMES B. WEAVER

DAN W. TURNER

ROBERT D. BLUE

BOURKE B. HICKENLOOPER

ROBERT D. RAY

GEORGE WASHINGTON CARVER

HENRY AGARD WALLACE

HENRY CANTWELL WALLACE

HENRY CLAY DEAN

HORACE BOIES

UY M. GILLETTE

HERSCHEL C. LOVELESS

HAROLD E. HUGHES

RICHARD C. CLARK

CLYDE L. HERRING

RUTH SUCKOW

MACKINLAY KANTOR

JAMES HEARST

PAUL ENGLE

GRANT WOOD

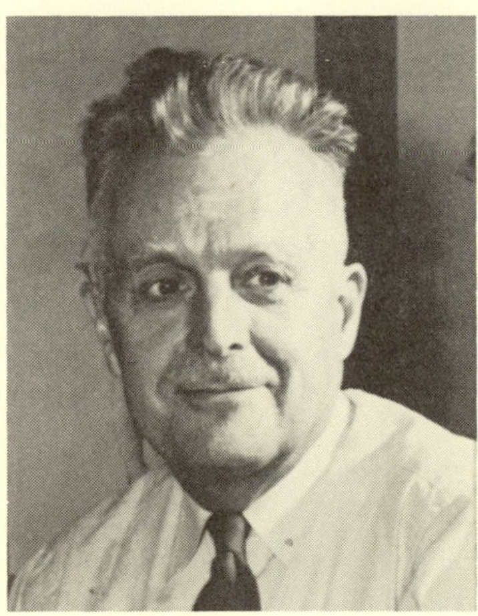

MARVIN CONE

AMELIA BLOOMER

ANNIE WITTENMYER

AGNES B. SAMUELSON

CARRIE CHAPMAN CATT

CHAPTER 8 SUPPORT OF THE REPUBLICAN PARTY 1856–1860

THE NEW REPUBLICAN PARTY IN IOWA ENJOYED ALMOST INSTANT success, thanks in part to Democratic blunders and lethargy. Iowa Democrats were their own worst enemy in 1856. Exaggerating their role as the conservative party, they did not fight back after the defeats of 1854 and 1855, nor did they sufficiently publicize their votes for internal improvements, land grants for railroads, and other public works associated with the idea of progress. They allowed the Republicans to run off with the credit for the act of 1856, noted above, which granted lands to assist in the building of four prospective east-west railroads across Iowa. This act was in no way a Republican monopoly; Democratic members of Congress had been working for it for six years, Iowa Democrats as much as anyone else. But Governor Grimes farsightedly called a special session of the General Assembly, and Iowa Republicans were shrewd enough to manipulate its proceedings so as to make it appear that the donation was a Republican achievement. Another example of Democratic lethargy was the failure of Senator Augustus C. Dodge to return to Iowa to participate in the fight for his own reelection in 1855, and his failure to take a part in the rebuilding of the party in the face of Republican growth. A keen student of Iowa politics of the period sums up the Democratic attitude as "defeatism."[1]

The election results of the August 1856 elections showed that the tide was running with the new party. Republicans Samuel R. Curtis of Keokuk, a West Point graduate turned civil engineer and railroad surveyor, and Timothy Davis of Dubuque won the two seats in the national House. Both houses of the General Assembly were carried, assuring a Republican replacement for Senator George W. Jones in 1858. The minor state offices fell to the Republicans in the train of their major victories, all by the largest margins in the history of the young state. Finally the Republicans elected their four candidates for presidential elector and thus insured four votes for John C. Frémont against Buchanan.

The most outstanding success of the Republicans, however, was the victory of their proposal for a constitutional convention. They merely picked up where the Whigs had left off in criticism of the Constitution of 1846. Democratic leaders, especially outgoing Governor Stephen B. Hempstead, again played their accustomed role of conservatives and opposed the calling of a convention, giving the fledgling Republican party the chance to appear as the party of progress and improvement. The General Assembly of January 1855, under the urging of the new governor, James W. Grimes, took the first step toward a new constitution by putting the question on the ballot for the election of August 1856. At that time the voters opted strongly for a convention, 32,790 for and 14,612 against, and in November the Republicans elected 21 delegates, the Democrats only 15. The convention was called to meet at Iowa City in the new capitol on January 19, 1857.

THE CONSTITUTION OF 1857

The handiwork of the Iowa Constitutional Convention of 1857 has somewhat surprisingly survived far into the twentieth century as the basic framework of Iowa government and there seems small likelihood of a call for a new convention and a completely new document. Iowa's constitutional experience is somewhat typical of the American states in general. Four New England states are still using their first and only constitutions, as amended, of course; these, however, are exceptional. Four other states older than Iowa (New Hampshire, North Carolina, Ohio, and Indiana) are on their second constitutions, and many states younger than Iowa are on these two lists. Three states (New Jersey, Vermont, Tennessee), all older than Iowa, have moved on to their third documents; Illinois has recently adopted (1970) a fourth constitution.

Most of the members of the 1857 convention came from and disappeared into a well-deserved obscurity. Of the thirty-six members, not more than a dozen names are readily recognizable to longtime students of Iowa history. Admittedly, fame and public notice are not proof of ability, but it seems a fair supposition that men deserving of election to a convention of this sort would be men whose leadership had been previously recognized and would continue to be recognized. Using the scanty biographical material available, certain facts about the members emerge. Few offices on the state level were ever held by any of the members, before or after the convention, one notable exception being Jonathan C. Hall of Burlington, who became a judge of the State Supreme Court. No governor, attorney general, or clerical officer ever came from this list of thirty-six men; only a few ever made it to the state legislature for one or two terms. On the national level, two members, James F. Wilson of

Fairfield and Aylett R. Cotton of Clinton, were elected to membership in the national House of Representatives, and Wilson was later elected to the Senate for two successive terms. No cabinet members came from the list.

A study of the available fragments of the debates in the convention shows that three men were the most prominent proposers and defenders of ideas: Rufus L. B. Clarke, a Mount Pleasant attorney; William Penn Clarke, an Iowa City attorney and Supreme Court reporter, 1855–1860; and Jonathan C. Hall, mentioned above, a Burlington attorney and railroad promoter. Not even James F. Wilson seems to have been a frequent speaker. Others offered little except unsung hack work on the committees. The external evidence shows that a very few men did most of the originating work and the others merely voted yes or no.

Iowa's constitution, like those enduring ones in other states, has sufficed only because a feasible amending machinery makes possible constant updating of the original. The amending processes are too difficult to lend themselves to abuse yet not too difficult to block a legitimate majority program. Basically there are two ways of amending: legislative proposal by two successive General Assemblies followed by approval by a majority of the voters, voting thereon, *or* proposal by a convention which has been requested by the voters. (Every tenth year ending in zero the voters *must* be given the question.) As of 1972 the 1857 document has been amended thirty-four times.

The document was put together in forty-six days, most of it a repetition of the 1846 version. The principal motive for writing a new fundamental law was to provide for a banking system. After "freezing" some points which should have been left to the processes of ordinary legislation, Article VIII on banks and banking was finally agreed upon. Basically, it authorized the creation of a "free" (private) banking system, and a State Bank, which was not a state-owned bank at all but a private bank, with branches to be set up in towns and cities wherever a chartering group could meet the requirements. It should be noted that the constitution did not create such banks; it merely authorized their creation. The General Assembly had to pass the necessary enabling acts and these in turn had to be approved by the people in a general election. Thus legislation on one of the most intricate and technical subjects in our economic structure was put at the mercy of a great body of voters who were not prepared by experience or study to pass judgment on such a subject. As matters turned out, a proposal for free banks was carried in 1858 but no banks were founded. A State Bank with its branches came into existence in 1858, enjoyed a fair degree of success, and played a large part in financing the state's activities during the Civil War until the National Banking Act of 1863, as amended in 1865, forced the State Bank and all its branches to convert into national banks.[2]

Another important question concerned the rights of Negroes in

Iowa. The census of 1850 showed only 333 members of that race in Iowa; the Iowa census of 1856 showed only 271. A reading of the fragments of the debates shows how far the people of Iowa, as personified in these delegates, needed to change their thinking before Negroes would acquire even such limited rights as the suffrage, unsegregated schooling, and the holding of property. To put it bluntly, the "first free state in the Louisiana Purchase" was not very free; the Negro was "north of slavery,"[3] just that and little more, with perhaps a small degree of advancement over the views expressed in 1844 and 1846. The people of Iowa (and other Northern states) took much interest in the condition of Negro slaves in the South, and the current probabilities of slavery in Kansas, but little interest in the condition of free Negroes in Iowa (and other Northern states). Many Abolitionists did not go far beyond mere emancipation in their thinking on the Negro problem.

After prolonged debate in which many individuals made statements of personal views remarkable for their anti-Negro bias, the convention retained the constitutional limitation of the suffrage, restricting the vote to "white, male citizens," but adopted a provision to submit to the voters the question of striking the word "white," a proposition which failed by the overwhelming margin of 49,387 to 8,489. Another restriction was the prohibition of Negro membership in the General Assembly. As to property-holding and other personal rights, the 1857 document represents a slight advance over 1846. The "due process" clause as to life, liberty, and property was made applicable to him; a Negro's testimony in court was now acceptable, and the right to trial by jury was given to him not only in criminal cases but for all cases involving the "life or liberty of an individual." This provision applied to fugitive slaves and might be thought of as an extension of the doctrine laid down in the "Ralph" case of 1839.[4] The "white" suffrage qualification had the carry-over effect of barring Negroes from holding offices and from jury duty, a handicap not removed until an 1880 amendment struck the word "white" from requirements for legislative service.

On the subject of racially integrated education, most of the members seemed badly frightened by the idea of mixed schools. One member, apparently a minority of one, was willing to go as far as "separate and distinct schools," quite a bit short of the "separate but equal" doctrine reached by the Supreme Court in 1896. The best that could be obtained from this convention was a clause "for the education of all the youth of the state through a system of common schools." Presumably each community could make its own decisions under that umbrella-type of statement.

In one other decision the convention retained the 1846 provision for a militia limited to "white, male citizens. . . ." R. L. B. Clarke of Mount Pleasant, the convention's most active champion of equal rights for Negroes, utilized the debate to demonstrate the consistency of his logic, arguing that if the privileges of citizenship were not to be given to the Negro, "when by your laws you ostracize him . . . when you deprive him of all its [society's] protection, . . . is it right, is it just, that you should call upon him to serve in the militia to defend that country in which you made him an alien?" The question was answered by holding to the limitation of 1846.

Other items in the new constitution presumably made provisions for improvement in the mechanics of government. Some of the changes, however, do not conform to later ideas of good government. A two-court system, that is, a Supreme Court and a set of district courts, without intermediate courts between these two, was created. Popular election of Supreme Court judges was adopted as being the "right" of the people, a point of view which would eventually undergo limitations. The governor's term of office was changed from four years to two; elections were changed from August to October except in the years of election of a president, when the date would be the Tuesday after the first Monday in November; the beginning date for the biennial session of the General Assembly was changed from December to the second Monday in January. A limit was set on the allowable indebtedness of cities and counties, a principle already in use in the state's government. The limit was set as an amount equal to 5 percent of the value of the taxable property. Finally, as shown above, the location of the state university and the relocation of the state capital were dealt with. The General Assembly of 1855 had already enacted a law requiring the changing of the capital from Iowa City to Des Moines. Now, a move was set on foot to embed this decision in a constitutional ice-block, where it would be almost unchangeable, and accompany it by a mollifying provision naming Iowa City as the permanent home of the state university. This decision was written into Article XI, Section 8, of the new document.

The convention closed its work on March 3, 1857. The new constitution was publicized and debated freely, all too much as a political issue rather than on its merits as a framework of government. Attacked and defended fiercely along partisan lines, the new Republican party managed to gain approval for the document by the slender margin of 1,630 votes, 40,311 to 38,681. The banking issue proved to be paramount. Iowa Democrats had been antibank on principle since the 1840s; to their technical arguments they added the accusation that the Republican party was trying to drag in the Negro question by coupling the proposition to remove the word "white" from various clauses with other provisions. In retaliation the Republicans accused certain Democrats, especially Bernhart Henn, the banker-politician, of opposition to legitimate banking because he was a dealer in "wildcat" Nebraska paper money, just then flooding Iowa.

The margin of ratification, 1,630 votes, was a very puny endorsement as compared with the 18,628 margin originally in favor of calling the convention, indicating the disappointment of some voters in the framework of government which the convention had produced. On September 3, 1857, Governor James W. Grimes, the former Whig now classified as a Republican, a founder of the new party, proclaimed the new constitution to be the "supreme law of the State of Iowa."[5] Surely here is evidence that the newborn party was the party of the progressive businessmen of the era.

"BLEEDING KANSAS"

In the meanwhile the spring and summer of 1856 were filled with something besides political oratory, though there was enough of that and to spare. This was America's own time of troubles, especially the ordeal which gave rise to the term "Bleeding Kansas." Proslavery men and antislavery men with overheated tempers turned this unfortunate territory and nearby states into a battleground for freedom, with enough political tension and fighting to justify the expression, the "war before the war." Proslavery men rode into Kansas from time to time to vote for men or measures favoring slavery, at the same time keeping their eyes open for good lands, while antislavery men from New England, with monetary assistance from the New England Emigrant Aid Society and other sympathizers, came out to save Kansas for freedom with their votes and at the same time acquire sites for future homes and farms. Recent investigators have found two points of real importance to the Kansas story: on both sides of the conflict there was more interest in lands than in the slavery controversy; second, although some lives were lost, Kansas did not "bleed" as much as Northern people were led to believe by Republican orators and editors who found the Kansas troubles, real and imaginary, to be the source of their most effective propaganda.[6]

On their journey to the Kansas "battlefield," the Eastern crusaders came directly across Iowa, usually along a route designed by William Penn Clarke, the Iowa City Abolitionist, to avoid contacts with proslavery Missourians. All routes through Iowa converged on the southwest corner of the state as the best place for men to receive arms and training before making a wild dash into Kansas Territory. Southwest Iowa also served as a rendezvous for those in search of a refuge after fighting in Kansas. The recently founded town of Tabor, Iowa, a would-be "Oberlin of the West," was a familiar name to this generation. Under the leadership of the Congregational minister, John Todd, this little Fremont County town, a little bit of Ohio transplanted to frontier Iowa, served as an arms depot for men going to the battles in Kansas, and a hideout and medical aid station for those coming back from the wars.[7]

THE UNDERGROUND RAILROAD

As part of this system of antislavery activities, an "underground railroad" was put into operation to assist escaping slaves on their way to freedom. Some of the bloom has been taken off this colorful historical perennial by a recent historian who has demonstrated that the U.G. has been overly romanticized and credited with too much effectiveness. It is not necessary, however, for Iowans to give up acceptance of the basic story of the operation of secret escape routes by their forebears; that much of the legend of an Underground Railroad is supported by credible evidence. For example, John Todd of Tabor and William M. Brooks, the president of Tabor College after its founding in 1857, appointed committees to give assistance to the escaping slaves. From Tabor the escapees were sent on their way, most likely via the Quaker village of Earlham to Des Moines, and then Grinnell, where a welcome would be extended by the Reverend Mr. Josiah B. Grinnell or some of his Congregational flock. From Grinnell the route led on to Iowa City, where William Penn Clarke or Samuel Jordan Kirkwood or their deputies or perhaps Governor James W. Grimes himself would furnish assistance. Clinton and Muscatine were the crossing points on the Mississippi most heavily used.

Of course, as time went by, many variations of this route were introduced in an effort to maintain secrecy. Poor indeed would be the town in the southern half of Iowa which could not boast after the war of having been a station on the U.G. Besides Tabor and Grinnell, each a Congregationalist stronghold, the best-known stations were Quaker communities such as Earlham, Salem, Low Moor, and Springdale. The most prominent historian of the U.G. has compiled a list of over one hundred persons in Iowa who assisted in the operation of the escape routes; many of the people on his list, especially the Congregational ministers, are well known for their antislavery work. Undoubtedly many names could be added to his list if all the facts were known. For obvious reasons, many participants in this illegal activity, a clear violation of the Fugitive Slave Laws, kept their part as secret as possible; others wanted to "stand up and be counted" in this cause.[8]

To most of the Abolitionists, in Iowa or elsewhere, the hero of the Kansas antislavery crusade was John Brown, to be addressed in hushed tones as "Captain John Brown" and assisted in every possible way, with few questions asked as to the factual accuracy of the claims he was making. Any doubts as to the legality of his acts could always be allayed by falling back on Seward's "higher law" doctrine, first enunciated in 1850. Men were discovering the roots of a radical treatment of the slavery question, including the use of violence, self-justifying to those who hated slavery. Although John Brown forfeited the support of his Tabor following by his use of force in a sortie into Missouri to free some slaves, other Iowans in and around Springdale and elsewhere befriended him. Iowa was his home and his headquarters during much of the two-year period before the Harpers Ferry incident; troops were trained and much planning for future action took place here on Iowa soil.[9]

POLITICS, 1857–1859

Iowans and Iowa politics could not be isolated from the issues of the times. By 1857 the public debate over slavery had reached the stage where it could not be settled on points. Events rather than ideas must now take over and bring the quarreling sections of the country to one of three decisions: conflict, surrender, or compromise. The people of the time could not know that the country was on a collision course, and that the events of 1856 to 1860 would later be spoken of as "the prelude to war."

The Dred Scott decision in 1857 rocked the country. In the Supreme Court's majority opinion, residence in one or even two free states had not automatically made Dred Scott free; furthermore, since he was a Negro, and Negroes were not citizens, he had no standing before the court. But the greatest bombshell of all was the ruling, usually called an obiter dictum, that Congress had no power to enact such provisions as those embodied in the Missouri Compromise of 1820; the act had therefore been unconstitutional ever since its passage, and the repeal of that provision in 1854 had not been necessary. The ruling was followed by a great uproar in antislavery circles. Perhaps some Iowans recalled the ruling of the Iowa Supreme Court in 1839 in the case of Ralph, wherein Chief Justice Charles Mason had decided a similar case in exactly the opposite way. In Illinois, Abraham Lincoln asserted that his party would obey the decision but would try to obtain control of the government so that eventually the ruling could be reversed. Some others were not so temperate in their remarks. In 1858 the Iowa Senate followed State Senator Samuel J. Kirkwood's leadership in adopting a resolution condemning the Dred Scott decision.

Iowa politics in 1857 was marked by a slight decline in Republican strength; the great success of 1856 was not repeated in proportion. The general feeling seemed to be that even so mild a stand as opposition to the extension of slavery was too radical. Many people seemed to fear that the Republicans were really Abolitionists and Democratic campaigners did all they could to foster that idea. The party was victimized just then by scandals emanating from the location of the new state capitol on Des Moines's East Side rather than the West, and from the misfeasance in office of certain high officials.[10] Republican candidates won by small margins and the new constitution, openly claimed as the handiwork of the new party, barely won ratification. The overwhelming rejection of Negro suffrage by a ratio of 6 to 1, as described above, surely proved that many who were willing to vote against extension of slavery were at the same time not ready to let the Negro have the most elementary symbol of free men in a free state.

Victories of Grimes and Kirkwood

The election of Governor James W. Grimes as senator in 1858 might seem to be an exception to these statements about the decline of Republican strength. Actually, the real battle had taken place in 1856, when the Republicans won a majority of places in the forthcoming General Assembly. This victory assured the election of a Republican to the Senate seat held since 1848 by George W. Jones of Dubuque. Jones not only was now in the minority party but in the minority (pro-Buchanan) wing of that party; Benjamin M. Samuels, also of Dubuque, was the recognized leader of the pro-Douglas majority faction in the party. As for Republicans, several of them ran up trial balloons, principally William Penn Clarke of Iowa City. Clarke received secret encouragement from Senator James Harlan, who all the while was putting up a show of neutrality between Clarke and Grimes. Fitz Henry Warren of Burlington was another who tried to undercut his fellow citizen. The Republican caucus took care of the intraparty bickering and decisively settled on Grimes. The Democrats chose Samuels as their favorite. Grimes went on to win in the anticlimactic election, 64 to 41.

The elections of 1859, especially the gubernatorial election, would be crucial in determining the future orientation of the state in national politics. It was a blessing for the Democrats that their ablest leader, Augustus Caesar Dodge, returned from his ministerial post in Spain to head their ticket in the canvass of the voters. For the Republicans it was equally fortunate that their convention of 1858 had been able to persuade John Adam Kasson, a newcomer to the state, to take the state chairmanship of the party. Kasson had quickly mastered the finer points of sectional politics within the state; moreover, he was a realist who foresaw that his party could never win the governorship with an ineffective candidate such as the present incumbent, Ralph P. Lowe of Keokuk.

By contrast, Samuel J. Kirkwood was the made-to-order man for the Republican candidacy. With his record of transfer from the Democrats to the new party, his standing as a successful businessman, his record of service in the Ohio Constitutional Convention of 1850, his participation in the founding convention of the Iowa Republican party in 1856, and his simple homespun manners of talk and dress, he was the ideal candidate in frontier politics—not right for the effete East, perhaps, but just right for Iowa in 1859. Very fortunately, Governor Lowe, more a jurist than a politician, was easily transferred to a vacancy on the ticket as a candidate for the State Supreme Court, and Kirkwood could be put up for governor. Thus a party fight was avoided, the ticket was strengthened, and the public was none the wiser.

The Kirkwood-Dodge campaign emulated the Lincoln-Douglas series of debates, though far less genteel and less cerebral in manner and content. No such fine shadings of constitutional theory as the Freeport Doctrine emerged from their confrontations. Kirkwood ridiculed Dodge for his immaculate appearance and courtly manners and drew attention to his own indifference to such matters; Kasson and Grimes stood by with advice on the finer points of strategy. On the other side, Dodge was led into foolish attacks on Grimes and Harlan, both safely in office, and forgot to defend his own good record as a friend to railroads and internal improvements. Even so, Dodge won a respectable share of the votes, 53,332, to 56,502 for Kirkwood. For lieutenant governor Kasson had favored Nicholas Rusch, a prominent German leader in Davenport, as a lure to the foreign vote and as proof that the Know-Nothing influence was no longer important in the Republican party.[11]

JOHN BROWN AT HARPERS FERRY, 1859

The peace of the country was shattered by the news of John Brown's attack on the arsenal at Harpers Ferry, Virginia, on October 16, 1859. Iowans felt particularly involved in the incident because of Brown's recent associations with Iowa Abolitionists, because of his protracted stay at Springdale, and because there were more volunteers from Iowa in the plot than from any other state. Six out of twenty-one hailed from Iowa: Edwin and Barclay Coppoc, Stewart Taylor, Jeremiah G. Anderson, George B. Gill, and Charles W. Moffat. The early planning of the Harpers Ferry seizure had taken place at Springdale; only the final details were settled in conferences with Eastern friends, and in a meeting at Chatham, Ontario.

Hastily proclaimed as insane by his counsel for purposes of legal defense, Brown refused to avail himself of this plea. He was found guilty of treason to the state of Virginia, and sentenced to be hanged on December 2. New counsel, hoping for a pardon or a new trial, collected affidavits produced for the purpose, showing insanity on both sides of the family. After some hesitation, Governor Wise refused to examine the insanity evidence, and John Brown went on to his death as scheduled—and probably as he desired.

Later apotheosized as The Martyr, this was not John Brown's immediate status after the incident. Reaction in Iowa and elsewhere was unfavorable in most quarters. Senator Grimes, for example, carefully avoided endorsement of Brown's plan and actions, though paying lip service to his courage and spirit, however illegal the action. Other Republican leaders spoke or wrote in guarded fashion. In 1859 it was good politics to play down the affair; not until later years would the apotheosis take place, to give way in more recent years to a rather heated debate among historians and partisans over the question of Brown's sanity. Some believe him to have been unbalanced; some have made an effort at rehabilitation of Brown's reputation. Of more importance would seem to be the now well-established fact that Abolitionists in New England and in Ohio's Western Reserve, virtually a New England colony at the time, secretly furnished John Brown with money and supplies. They were the ones who were willing for John Brown and his followers, including the six from Iowa, to risk their lives to dramatize the cause of antislavery while they as secret sponsors remained at home in perfect security.[12]

Iowa was thrust into the national spotlight because of the interest aroused in the fate of the two beardless boys from Springdale, Edwin and Barclay Coppoc. The former was captured, tried, and executed. "I hope you will not reflect on me for what I have done, for I am not at fault, at least my conscience tells me so," he wrote to his mother. More fortunate was his brother, who managed to escape and make his way to Iowa. His extradition was demanded by Governor Wise of Virginia and the nation watched as Governor Kirkwood played a shrewd game of quibbling over legal technicalities until the accused young man could again make his escape.

Iowans have been intrigued by the story, widely circulated in 1897 and after by Benjamin F. Gue, once a prominent Quaker Abolitionist in Iowa, about an effort to warn Secretary of War John B. Floyd of Brown's plot to attack Harpers Ferry. It seems that Brown confided his plans to Moses Varney, a Springdale Quaker, who told them to David F. Gue, Benjamin Gue's brother. David Gue and one A. L. Smith wrote separate anonymous letters of warning to Secretary Floyd, who regarded the whole thing as preposterous and ignored the threat. Actually the story of the intercession by the Iowans had been told soon after the event in 1859 but the revelation was unnoticed in the excitement of the times.[13]

PARTY CONVENTIONS OF 1860

The Democrats were the first to hold their national convention. Meeting in late April in Charleston, South Carolina, probably the most inappropriate place that could have been chosen, the social environment, the inadequate hotel facilities, and the weather would prove to be important factors in the deliberations—and the failure—of the delegates. The site had been chosen at the 1856 convention as a concession to the extreme proslavery elements in the party, and now the whole party was to be the victim of that mistake. Iowa Democrats sent a divided delegation, the pro-Douglas faction in the majority but the anti-Douglas people a very militant minority. The Douglas issue was only one of several which had split the Dubuque stronghold of the party into two bitter factions, nicknamed the "Montagues" and the "Capulets," which reached out into the state for support and even beyond the state, thereby dividing the state organization into bitter factions.[14]

After several days of debates, the almost hopeless divergence between pro- and anti-Douglas men in the whole convention, as well as among Iowans, was all too apparent. The split was mainly along sectional lines, with the Northwest firmly against the South, and Northeastern Democrats somewhat divided. At last the majority on the Committee on Resolutions presented a platform embodying the Southern Democratic ideas, built around a plank which demanded a congressional guarantee of slavery in the territories. This was a demand which Senator Jefferson Davis of Mississippi had recently put before the Senate without success. Confidently expecting the convention to go along with their report, the Southern members were painfully surprised by an eloquent presentation of the minority report by the Iowa pro-Douglas leader, Benjamin M. Samuels of Dubuque, stressing the Cass-Douglas doctrine of popular sovereignty. After a bit of skirmishing between the factions, a compromise was voted down and the issue was squarely drawn between the diehards of the South and the equally determined pro-Douglas forces of the Northwest. In a test vote the minority report was adopted as the will of a majority of the delegates. This was too much for the Southern extremists, William L. Yancey, Robert Barnwell Rhett, and Edmund Ruffin, who bolted from the hall followed by their fellow conservatives. The long-feared and much dreaded "disruption of the American Democracy" was complete—the unnatural alliance between urban Northern Democrats, frontier Northwestern Democrats, and slaveholding Southern Democrats was a thing of the past. The convention broke up without making any nominations, necessitating later conventions of the separate factions, and thereby frittering away any advantage the Democrats might have gained from being first in the field.

It is surely a matter of some significance that the revolt against the domination of the Democratic party by Southern extremists was precipitated by Westerners, led by an Iowan. Benjamin M. Samuels was originally from Virginia's Shenandoah Valley but later lived in the western part of Virginia, the nonslaveholding area, a fact which again illustrates the point that not all "Southerners" were proslavery. A man of splendid personal appearance with a magnificent physique stretched over six feet six inches of body, magnetic in manner and conceded by his Iowa political opponents to be the greatest orator in the state, he was the perfect choice as a spokesman for the Douglas views against the firebrands of the South. As might be expected, he was the leader of the Iowa delegation which came to Baltimore in June and helped to nominate Douglas for president on the Northern Democratic ticket.[15]

After the Democratic fiasco at Charleston, the focus of attention turned to other parties. A minor party made up mostly of ex-Whigs and ex-Know-Nothings, under the name of the Constitutional Union Party, met next, on May 9, and nominated John Bell and Edward Everett, but received little more than undeserved sneers and ridicule.

Therefore, when the Republicans met at Chicago on May 16, they could well know that with the opposition so badly divided, victory was a sure thing if only they could play their cards well. In 1856 their defeat had been charged to their failure to carry four states: New Jersey, Pennsylvania, Indiana, and Illinois, which therefore became the pivotal states of 1860. It automatically followed that Republicans must agree to a platform which was not as extreme on slavery as the one of 1856 had been. They must moderate their views and must accept new ideas for the sake of carrying the four doubtful states. Two things especially were needed: a protective tariff plank to please Pennsylvania and a conservative candidate to please almost everybody. Iowa Republicans made a real contribution on the first point. Their party manager, John A. Kasson, was the Iowa delegates' choice for membership on the Committee of Resolutions. Along with Horace Greeley, he virtually wrote the entire final version of the platform, including a tariff plank satisfactory to the Pennsylvanians.[16]

As for the Iowa delegation's voting in the convention of 1860, there has been much misunderstanding. Because a few prominent leaders were for Lincoln, and because Grenville M. Dodge and others helped the Illinois railroad promoters who were so strong for their man, the impression has been nourished that "Iowa" helped to nominate Lincoln. Contributing to this piece of misinformation was the natural desire of all politicians to be on the winning side, especially when that winner leads his country to victory and then becomes a martyred hero. The facts are that Iowa delegates to the convention in The Wigwam were badly split among the several possibilities for the nomination. Their preconvention favorite would seem to have been William Henry Seward of New York. His most recent biographer concludes that Seward's prospects for success at Chicago were nullified by three factors: his managers were outbargained by Lincoln's managers; his well-known anti-Know-Nothing position would lose the votes of the American party members who had joined the Republican party after the slow death of their own party; and his reputation as an extremist on the slavery question combined with his anti-Know-Nothingism to destroy his "availability" in the eyes of party managers.[17]

Another favorite with many Iowans was Salmon P. Chase of Ohio. He and Grimes had been corresponding for years and there is every reason to think that any votes controlled by Grimes would have gone to Chase, at least on the first ballot. Another Iowa delegate, William B. Allison, born and reared in Ohio, was presumably a Chase man. John A. Kasson was for an old St. Louis friend, Edward Bates, even though other Iowans had shied away from the Missouri judge because of his suspected strong Know-Nothing sentiments. John McLean of Ohio had little following in Iowa; he was in the race mostly to cut into the Chase vote. Simon Cameron of Pennsylvania, a convert from Democracy, a wealthy industrialist and machine politician of the worst sort, and Jacob Collamer of Vermont, complete the list of "also rans."

Abraham Lincoln of Illinois was the great hope of the true conservatives of the day. He was on record for his belief in the immorality of slavery and his determination to work for its "ultimate extinction," to use his own terminology. At the same time, he asserted his belief that slavery was *not* to be disturbed in the states where it now was legal and he was willing to uphold and enforce the Fugitive Slave Laws. Most striking of all, he was not a believer in the equality of the races, in which intellectual position he was in accord with an overwhelming majority of the people of his day, Northern as well as Southern. In addition to his "satisfactory" views on slavery, Lincoln pleased a wide variety of delegates and working nondelegates with his stand on railroads, homesteads, internal improvements, and the tariff. Strong railroad men such as Henry Farnam and Norman Judd, who worked closely with Kirkwood and Grenville Dodge in Lincoln's behalf, knew their man, as did Judge David Davis and many others. The most scholarly recent judgment of Lincoln holds that the Lincoln of 1854–1860 had demonstrated "greatness" in the way he had met and coped with many challenges, particularly the shaping of the Illinois Republican party and establishing himself as its leader (much as Grimes had done for the Republican party in Iowa, it might be added). Lincoln was ambitious but his ambition was "notably free of pettiness, malice, and over-indulgence [and] leavened by moral conviction and a deep faith in the principles upon which the republic had been built. The Lincoln of the 1860's was much the same man under greater challenge."[18]

Yet most of the thirty-three Iowans who went to Chicago did not go there pledged to Lincoln or beholden to his managers. Later generations may find this hard to believe but the roll call votes tell the story. The uninstructed delegation of such unwieldy numbers had only eight votes, one-fourth vote for each man, one man not voting. On the first ballot their votes were scattered around with reckless abandon, Lincoln getting only two votes (eight delegates), Seward two, and Chase, Bates, Cameron, and McLean one each. On the second ballot Lincoln's vote from Iowa went up to five (twenty delegates); on the third, five and one-half. A quick count of the third ballot showed Lincoln only one and one-half votes short of victory; an Ohio spokesman supplied four votes and the job was done. Of course, all who could do so now switched their votes and climbed on the bandwagon to claim preferment afterward. Perhaps this delayed action was the source of the persistent claim that Iowa supported Lincoln for the nomination.

The Democrats discovered that the damage done at Charleston was beyond repair. Hopelessly divided into two factions, the Northern or Douglas Democrats met at Baltimore on June 25 and carried out the inevitable nomination of their leader, with Herschel V. Johnson of Georgia as his running mate. The Southern faction met separately and nominated the ticket of John C. Breckinridge of Kentucky and Joseph Lane of Oregon. Such a split presented suicidal aspects but had one redeeming quality, sincerity: for once, men demonstrated that they would put their convictions, right or wrong, above expediency. The one advantage for Douglas was that he no longer had to carry the stigma of "guilt by association" with slaveholders.

ELECTION OF 1860

In the hard-fought campaign which followed, one would not have known that Douglas was moving toward almost certain defeat. Then, and in later historical judgment, he won wide approval for his statesmanlike views on the national crisis. He and the Northern Democrats harped on the radicalism of the Republican position, stressing the inclusion of Abolitionists in the Republican makeup. On their side, the Republicans stressed many points of appeal besides nonextension of slavery into the territories: federal aid to railroads, free homesteads, a protective tariff, and federally sponsored internal improvements. Candidates played down (or up) the party's past attitude toward foreigners, prohibition, and polygamy, as the local situation seemed to dictate. In addition, the Republicans came up with several new devices to enliven the dull routine of political campaigning. One was their men's marching clubs, the Wide-Awakes. Marching usually in night parades, carrying torches held high, they made a splendid appearance in their smart semimilitary attire. The torches lighted up their bright oilskin coats and hats which they wore to protect them from the dripping pitch from the torches. Young women were allowed to get into the act with their clubs known as Liberty Belles, usually riding on floats or in beribboned carriages. Brass bands, male glee clubs, and throngs of ordinary citizens joined in the processions as great rallies were held in county seat towns and market towns of all sizes. Never less than two speakers and usually five or six were advertised as magnets to draw crowds; excursion trains gave special rates; picnics and barbecues were the order of the day. On such gala days who cared if all the speakers said virtually the same things? An orator was judged more by the energy expended and the capacity to excite emotional responses than by his ideas.

Iowa went safely into the Republican column with 70,118 votes for Lincoln and Hamlin, 55,639 for Douglas, 1,763 for Bell, and 1,034 for Breckinridge. Of the ninety-seven counties then organized, Lincoln carried sixty-nine, Douglas twenty-five; two counties had tie votes, and one did not report. Many of the sparsely settled western counties had less than a dozen votes. The Douglas counties were not confined to the southern part of Iowa, but well scattered over the state. The Republicans made a clean sweep of all the other offices which were at stake, the most important being the two seats in the national House of Representatives, which went to Samuel Ryan Curtis of Keokuk and William Vandever of Dubuque.[19]

Two special studies of the election of 1860 in Iowa throw considerable light on this episode of political history. One deals with the German vote in the state and one with the Holland Dutch vote in the township which includes Pella. The former is an analysis of the township voting in the heavily German-populated counties and was designed as a test of two generally and widely held assumptions: that the German vote in Iowa (and six other Northwestern states) supplied the margin of victory for Lincoln, and the foreign-group leaders had the ability to deliver the votes of their ethnic groups at will. A close examination of the vote on the township level revealed facts which summarized county figures cannot supply. The study proved that the German vote in the six most heavily German-populated counties in Iowa went to the Democratic columns; it also showed that the rank-and-file voters did not follow their leaders who were advocating the Republican cause.[20]

In the case of the Pella Dutch, the study showed that Henry Peter Scholte, the founder of the colony in 1847 and its religious and economic leader ever since, was not able to deliver the vote of his ethnic group in the crucial elections of 1859 and 1860, and that this sizable block of votes went to the Democrats. Scholte began his American career as a Whig, then switched to the Democrats in 1854 because of Whig-Republican sponsorship of Prohibition and because of the Know-Nothingism within the new party, then switched back to the Republican party because of the Democratic position on slavery in Kansas. As an early Whig he was able to align most of his followers with that party; likewise, when he went over to the Democrats in 1854, most of his group went with him. Alas, when he went over to the Republicans in 1858, the state leaders of that party, Grimes and Kirkwood, found that the Dominie could not bring his followers with him! The author of the study attributes this to political inertia on the part of the rank-and-file voters.[21]

While many questions remain as to the reasons advanced for the choices made by Iowans, the verdict was clear and unmistakable—and one by which and with which the state would live a long time. Iowa had made her choice in favor of the strongest antislavery party then available; she had strongly vindicated her ranking as the "first free child of the Missouri Compromise." At the same time she had increased her chances for securing federally subsidized railroads, free homesteads carved from federal lands, and federally constructed internal improvements by choosing to support the Republican party. It was not within the power of the voters of 1860 to know that the choice they made that year would lead to a one-party state and would be perpetuated almost solidly through the years down to 1932, and, except for occasional deviations, down to the present writing (1973).

CHAPTER 9 THE CIVIL WAR 1861-1865

THE VICTORY OF LINCOLN AND THE REPUBLICAN PARTY IN IOWA in 1860 was complete, more so than in some states east of the Mississippi. During the long interval between November and March, Republican party leaders everywhere, Iowans no less than others, jumped into the great American game of political jobbery. With eager anticipation they began to plan and scheme for the spoils of political warfare—from cabinet portfolios and federal judicial plums down to postmasterships and bureau clerkships. As applicants from a young state which had only four electoral votes in 1860, Iowans could not hope for a great reward; from now on, Iowa Republicans would have to pay the penalty of residence in a "safe" state, one of small population. No matter how able or zealous Iowa party workers might be, the greatest rewards would go to workers in the pivotal two-party states, and those states whose population earned more weight in the electoral college.

In February 1861 these hungry office seekers and favor seekers betook themselves to Washington and lined up at the trough. The president-elect was besieged from every quarter, first at Springfield and then at Washington. Senators Grimes and Harlan suddenly found themselves indispensable as intermediaries between hungry supplicants from Iowa and the first Republican president in history. Not unexpectedly, because of his recent accomplishments for the party in Iowa and at the Chicago convention, John A. Kasson came away with the highest prize, the first assistant postmaster generalship, a post with vast possibilities for the control of patronage, nationally as well as in Iowa. William Boyd Allison, a Dubuque attorney, like Kasson an Iowan only since 1857, overshot himself in trying for the post of United States district attorney for Iowa and lost out to a Lincoln friend, State Senator William H. F. Gurley of Davenport. Hubert Hoxie of Des Moines was given the job of United States marshal for Iowa. On a lower level, machinery was set in motion for a wholesale switch from Democratic to Republican postmasters, most of these jobs going to editors of Republican newspapers.[1]

FAILURE TO PREVENT WAR

Alas, while such mundane things occupied men's minds part of the time during the awkward four-month interval, other and more serious things were happening. In December, South Carolina carried out her historic threat and seceded from the Union; in January 1861 she was joined by Mississippi, Florida, Alabama, Georgia, and Louisiana, in that order, and on February 1 by Texas. Many people had plans for solving the crisis but no one wanted to listen to anyone else for fear of being labeled "soft" and "unmanly." Senator John J. Crittenden of Kentucky tried to bring men back to their senses by a set of compromise resolutions built around the idea of extending the Missouri Compromise line all the way to the Pacific. President-elect Lincoln placed his own compromise plan in the hands of Senator William Henry Seward of New York, who put it before the Senate's Committee of Thirteen, recently appointed to act for the Senate in trying to find a solution of the problem which was dividing the nation. The Committee of Thirteen accepted only the first of Lincoln's three points: an "unamendable" amendment which would preclude any further amendment which would enable Congress to abolish or interfere with slavery in the states, but nothing came of it or any other suggestion put before them. Senator Grimes of Iowa was a member of this prestigious committee, a distinct tribute to him as a senator with only two years' service. A similar group in the House, the Committee of Thirty-three, made up of one member from each state, also accepted the idea of the "unamendable" amendment guaranteeing noninterference with slavery in the states. The proposed amendment passed both houses but the coming of the war stopped further consideration of the proposition. Seward's latest biographer concludes that these efforts by Seward and others gained time for thought and helped to prevent the border states from making a "close coalition" with the cotton states.[2]

Virginia, still holding aloof from the secession movement, called a Peace Convention, to meet in Washington on February 4. It came to be known as the "Old Gentlemen's Convention," after Horace Greeley's belittling description. Its one hundred and thirty-two attending delegates included a few very able men but their work was doomed before ever they met—extremists from both South and North had created an atmosphere in which compromise was impossible. Governor Kirkwood took the easy way out and asked the Iowa delegation in Congress to serve as Iowa's spokesmen in the convention. Their first response was that their duties in Congress prevented their service; as time went on, they made nominal appearances as individuals in some sessions. True to his position as the leader of Iowa's uncompromising radical Republicans of the time, Senator Grimes deigned to attend very few sessions, as did Senator Harlan. At the end, Iowa's four members voted along with Maine against every one of the seven divisions of the majority report turned in to the convention.[3]

On February 4, the very day of the meeting of the Peace Convention, delegates from six of the seceded states met at Montgomery, Alabama, to organize a government. The tactics of Southern extremists was to rush along toward the organization of a Southern government while the anti-Lincoln, anti-"Black Republican" fever was at its highest pitch. On February 8 Jefferson Davis of Mississippi was elected president of the new Confederate States of America, and in March a constitution was ready. In the meanwhile, individual states had seized all federal properties within their boundaries except Fort Sumter, in Charleston harbor.

In the midst of this flurry of talk and excitement over secession, the last session (December–March) of the Thirty-sixth Congress came under Northern control because of the withdrawal of members from the seceding states. Somewhat as a portent of the future actions of the Thirty-seventh Congress (1861–1863), which would be under solid Republican control, the outgoing Congress passed a mild protective tariff act sponsored by Representative Justin S. Morrill of Vermont. This action was a small step toward the redemption of the Republican platform pledge of 1860. The bill passed the House by a voice vote; in the Senate Iowa's Grimes and Harlan added their votes to the majority. Grimes had previously taken a very strong antiprotection stand; in this case, his only claim to consistency was that the mildness of the protective clauses made them innocuous.[4]

PRESIDENT LINCOLN TAKES OVER

In spite of hot talk and much gossip, Lincoln's closely guarded inauguration went off quietly. The general response to the ideas of the First Inaugural Address was favorable, even in the South where some leaders were resisting the hotspurs who were calling for immediate secession. Lincoln deliberately refused to call a special session of the Congress and took on himself full responsibility for handling the crisis. As the tension mounted, his infinite patience was rather generally mistaken for and denounced as weakness and procrastination. When the fateful decision to relieve Fort Sumter was acted on, on April 12, impetuous Southerners fired the first shot against the flag which they had formerly defended—and the long-dreaded war was a reality.[5]

There was no formal declaration of war. Acting on his powers as commander-in-chief of the nation's forces and his oath to defend the country, President Lincoln called for 75,000 volunteers for ninety-day service. He also summoned Congress into special session—but not to meet until July 4. Virtually all Iowans, including Democrats, responded with enthusiasm and complete approval. In public meetings, editorials, sermons, and letters, people asserted that the time for argument, doubt, or compromise had ended; the flag must be defended.

RESPONSE TO THE WAR

Public declarations of patriotic intentions are one thing; willingness to volunteer for active military duty is another. In the absence of an orderly plan for recruiting under a system of selective service, the War Department fell back on a loose plan of allocation of quotas of soldiers, state by state, with the governors' offices to serve as clearinghouses and headquarters for all activities. Iowa's assigned quota was one regiment made up of ten companies of seventy-eight or more men in each company. The basic plan of recruitment called for acceptance and enrollment of volunteers in towns and cities, such recruits to be transported to a rendezvous such as Camp Franklin in Dubuque. From these points the recruits would be transferred to St. Louis, where, at Jefferson Barracks, they would be processed, assigned to training centers, and ultimately dispatched to their battlefield units or other duties.

Fortunately, Governor Samuel J. Kirkwood showed real executive ability and powers of decision. The governor was allowed four military aides, each of whom was allowed an assistant. The deputy in Dubuque was William Boyd Allison, who turned the job into a political asset. Even more important than the aides was the adjutant general, Nathaniel B. Baker of Clinton. A graduate of Harvard College and a former governor of New Hampshire, General Baker showed a genius for military administration and gave brilliant service throughout the war.

Iowa and Iowans met every call for troops, financial support, and political support for the Union cause ("Mr. Lincoln's War"), with room to spare. All quotas assigned to her throughout the war were met, only one time resorting to the draft, and that in 1864, when the end of the war was in sight. All in all, Iowa furnished forty-six infantry regiments (about 800–1,000 men in each regiment), plus the nucleus for one Negro regiment, plus four companies of light artillery and nine regiments of cavalry; plus thousands of replacement troops. The First Iowa Infantry under Colonel John F. Bates of Dubuque was the first Iowa unit to be activated under the president's call for volunteers for ninety-day service. After that the three-year enlistment was typical. In 1864 four Iowa regiments and one extra battalion, 3,901 men in all, performed guard duty and light tasks under a 100-Day Plan suggested by Midwestern governors to President Lincoln. In addition, a regiment of "Gray Beards" was recruited of men over forty-five, who performed similar duties but without a time limit on their enlistment.

Somewhere between 72,000 and 76,000 men gave some sort of military service. A meaningful figure is the one which tells us that about one-half of the male population of the state took some part in the war; in many a home, the women were left to harvest the crops and do other forms of a man's work. Iowa furnished more men, proportionate to her population, than any other state. Among these were 3 major generals, 6 brevet major generals, 10 brigadier generals, and 28 brevet brigadiers. Other cold but significant statistics inform us that 13,001 Iowans died during their time of service. Of these, 3,540 were killed or mortally wounded in battle; 8,498 died of disease; 515 died while prisoners of war; 227 died from accidents; and 221 from nonmilitary causes. A total of 8,500 were reported as wounded. Twenty-eight men won the Medal of Honor.

Iowans served with distinction at Wilson's Creek in Missouri, their baptism of fire. Here the death of the first Iowan to pay the supreme sacrifice is recorded, Shelby Norman of Company A, First Iowa Infantry, who is memorialized on the Soldiers and Sailors Monument on the Statehouse grounds in Des Moines. This battle also took the life of General Nathaniel Lyon, after whom a county would be named. Other battles or campaigns in which Iowans served were Fort Donelson, with such dubious record that Iowa leaders later asked for a chance to redeem themselves; Pea Ridge, in northwest Arkansas, and campaigns involving Little Rock and Helena; bloody Shiloh, Iuka, and Corinth; the abortive Red River expedition under General Nathaniel Banks; the Vicksburg campaign; Chattanooga, Allatoona, and the Atlanta campaign; Sherman's March to the Sea and then the march north to Columbia, South Carolina.[6]

Iowa's most publicized soldier of the Civil War is undoubtedly Grenville Mellen Dodge of Council Bluffs, who rose from colonel of the Fourth Iowa Infantry to the rank of major general. Impartial study of Dodge's record takes away much of the bloom from his accomplishments—earlier writers forgot to notice that most of the testimony about his bravery and his tactical brillance came from his own memoirs compiled rather late in life when an old man's vanity had gotten the best of his judgment and his wealth had made it possible for him to employ secretaries to take down his self-glorifying dictation. Furthermore, his promotions were secured not from a grateful president eager to recognize his genius, as Dodge would have us believe, but only after much importuning of the president by Congressman John A. Kasson of Des Moines, and others, who begged Lincoln and Secretary Stanton for the stars for Dodge's epaulets. Any notion that he was the hero of the Battle of Pea Ridge, to single out one notorious claim, is quickly dispelled by a reading of the scholarly accounts of that small-scale but important contest. Even so, scholars do not deny him credit for his accomplishments as a wrecker of Southern railroads and a builder of new roads for Grant and Sherman, nor for the spy system which he created.[7]

It is unfortunate that instead of giving so much attention to Dodge,

Iowans have not been told more of Francis Jay Herron of Dubuque, who began his service as a lieutenant colonel and rose to major general at the age of twenty-five; about John M. Corse of Burlington, one of the heroes of Atlanta, who rose to the rank of brevet major general; about William Worth Belknap of Keokuk, who rose from captain to brigadier general and whose rating with General Sherman was such that that tough-minded soldier recommended him to President Grant to succeed General John A. Rawlins, as secretary of war when Rawlins died in office; or Brigadier Generals Cyrus Bussey and Marcellus M. Crocker, and many others. Nor should one overlook the contribution of Mrs. Annie Wittenmyer of Keokuk, who discovered and overcame the great need for better diets for the sick and wounded in military hospitals, for which she won President Lincoln's support and praise;[8] nor Mrs. Ann Eliza Harlan, wife of the Iowa senator, who brought a woman's cheer and encouragement to the lonely soldiers in many camps.

At least a paragraph should be given to the topic of the use of the draft (selective service) in Iowa during this war. The Enrolment [*sic*] Act of March 3, 1863, was invoked only once in Iowa, in September 1864, by which time enthusiasm for the war had waned considerably. The law, which was used only four times in any state, was not intended to be much more than a pressure to encourage volunteering. It should be judged as one experimental effort in the history of modern warfare in Europe and America to find an equitable system of compulsory service. The law gave a draftee two options: commutation by the payment of $300, or furnishing a substitute at his expense. Many men used a simpler plan of evasion: on the day of enrollment they simply went visiting in distant parts. In Iowa's one experience with the draft, 7,548 names were drawn, 5,572 were examined, 2,446 were exempted, 3,126 were held to service, 67 paid the legal commutation fee, and 1,197 furnished substitutes, leaving a total of 1,862 men who were actually drafted. The draft machinery was run by acting assistant provost marshals in the congressional districts. One such marshal and one enrolling officer were reported as fatalities while performing their duties.[9]

THE WAR IN NORTHWEST IOWA

Although barely more than a footnote to the story of the Civil War in the South and East, passing mention should be made of the war in the Northwest, particularly northern Iowa, southern Minnesota, and Dakota Territory. This was, of course, war with the Indians of the region, notably the Santee Sioux. The War Department took cognizance of the danger in this area by creating a Military Department of the Northwest, under Generals Alfred Sully, John Pope, and Iowa's own Samuel R. Curtis, in that order. It was not "war" at all for most of the enlisted men but simply a prolonged period of guard duty. In the larger sense this phase of the war was merely part of the frontier conflict between the Indians and the expanding white population. Very likely some conflict would have occurred had there been no Civil War, though not necessarily at the same time and places.

The New Ulm Massacre in Minnesota on August 17, 1862, and the subsequent raids in that area, had noticeable effects on nearby Iowa. Many people believed the attack on New Ulm to be a part of a planned uprising throughout the Northwest. Thousands of settlers in Iowa, Dakota Territory, and southern Minnesota abandoned their homes and crops and took refuge in the nearest towns. Iowa's Governor Kirkwood authorized Lieutenant Colonel James A. Sawyer to organize a Northern Border Brigade of five companies; other volunteer troops were soon assembled in the area, and Sioux City was selected as the headquarters and command post for the district. Aside from lives lost, property losses were incalculable. Thirty-eight Sioux were hanged as an example to other would-be Indian raiders.[10]

"POLITICS AS USUAL"

The Civil War had its political aspects, both interparty and intraparty varieties. From the moment of South Carolina's secession until long after the last shot was fired, differences of opinion on the treatment of the seceding states caused a bitter clash within the Republican party. Questions on that point led to a restatement of the issue: What is the purpose, the objective, of the war? Early in the war President Lincoln repeatedly stated that the one and only objective was the preservation and restoration of the Union, and many members of Congress held to the same view. In July 1861 Representative John J. Crittenden of Kentucky introduced a resolution to the effect that the war was not being waged for conquest or subjugation but for the preservation of the Union, with all the rights of the states unimpaired. This proposal passed both houses of Congress by a wide margin, Iowa's Curtis and Vandever in the House and Grimes and Harlan in the Senate voting for it. Yet six months later, in December 1861, when Representative Holman of Indiana proposed the reaffirmation of the Crittenden resolution, the motion was laid on the table by a vote of 71 to 65. This time Iowa's Vandever did not vote and Curtis had resigned his seat to accept a commission in the army; his successor, James F. Wilson, had not yet taken his seat.[11]

This change of attitude indicates a sharp change in the thinking of many members as to what the war was all about. Another piece of evidence is the interest in the subject of postwar treatment of the seceded states if the Union cause were victorious. Some spoke of the seceded states as places to be defeated and then governed as "conquered provinces"; others said that the secession was a form of "suicide"; still others, led by Iowa's Senator Harlan, said the seceding states should first be conquered and then reduced to the status of "territories," and governed as such.[12] Bills to suit these theories of the war and the treatment of the rebellious states were introduced in Congress but all failed.

Here one perceives the key to an understanding of Republican politics during and after the war: an understanding of the conflict between the conservatively inclined and the radically inclined elements in the party. The evolution of opinion had caused men to move in one direction or another. There were former Whigs, Democrats, and Know-Nothings in each faction—the Abolitionists made the difference. The events of 1860–1861 emboldened them to press forward to the expression of their true ideas which they had heretofore muted because of their minority status within the Republican party. Now the radical wing began to speak out for a thorough social and political revolution in America which would produce both freedom and the suffrage for the slaves. Here were the true "Black Republicans," although the party as a whole had been given that label, undeservedly, by extreme Southern orators since 1856.

WAR DEMOCRATS AND PEACE DEMOCRATS

Immediately after the Fort Sumter incident there was a spontaneous union of Republicans and Democrats in the North and West in a nonpartisan effort for the preservation of the Union, but this unity was soon dissipated. During that burst of enthusiasm, no less a Democratic leader than Dennis A. Mahony, editor of the *Dubuque Herald,* could write to Governor Kirkwood and offer to recruit and lead an Irish regiment to the front, an offer which was not accepted.[13] Published evidence and items in manuscript collections make it clear that offers of political cooperation, even for the creation of a "Union" party, in 1861, were rejected by Republicans for reasons of their own, apparently because they wanted to reap the advantage of a partisan victory resulting in partisan control of the political, economic, and military situation. The editor of the *Dubuque Times,* a leading Republican organ, was so bold as to say that if the Democrats wanted to cooperate they should join the Republican party. Alas, the Union party which Lincoln needed to *create* in 1864, was rejected by Iowa Republicans in 1861.

The desperate military position brought on by Confederate victories destroyed all hope of a quick and easy ninety-day war. Such desperation made it necessary for men to make up their minds in a hurry; they must either support the war wholeheartedly or risk the charge of treason, a word thrown around with reckless abandon. Not only in Iowa but throughout the North, the great majority of Democrats enthusiastically supported the war effort in every conceivable way, taking for themselves the well-earned title of War Democrats. Their services were eagerly accepted when offered by individuals, and President Lincoln aided his cause by giving them a disproportionate share of military commissions, much to the chagrin and dissatisfaction of Republican aspirants. Among the leading War Democrats were Benjamin M. Samuels, Judge Chester C. Cole, Generals James M. Tuttle, William W. Belknap, Marcellus M. Crocker, John M. Corse, and Cyrus Bussey. Some of these leaders and many rank and file War Democrats sooner or later made their way over to the Republican party.

At the other extreme, a small but zealous and vociferous minority of Democrats soon came to oppose the war and won for themselves the title of Peace Democrats, though later the terminology for them was not so complimentary. Judged in the fairest and most generous terms possible, the Peace Democrats should be thought of as the original hard core of the intellectual opposition to the new Republican party of 1856 and 1860, driven to more extreme positions after the coming of the war. Originally they were nothing more nor less than strict constructionists who felt that the Constitution was being subverted in the name of change and political opportunism. Even before South Carolina led the way to secession and war, these particular Democrats had raised the cry, "The Constitution as it is and the Union as it was," a shibboleth which took on new meaning after the war began.[14]

Discerning in the Republican platforms of 1856 and 1860 a tendency toward a greater concentration of powers in the national government, in order to implement the policies of free homesteads and federal aid for internal improvements, the Peace Democrats fought a losing battle in the face of the politics of the antislavery movement. The coming of the war and its inevitable corollary of the growth of national powers changed nothing for these strong-minded people: what had been wrong before the war was still wrong. Some new points were soon added to their arsenal of arguments: the war was a needless war because other means of a peaceful nature could be found for a solution of the problem of slavery. Freeing the slaves would not really solve the problem of slavery; indeed, freedom would merely create new problems, one of which would be the inundation of the North and West by freedmen who would not be capable of living and working in an industrial and agricultural society for which they had had no training. Moreover, any benefits coming from the war would be bought at too high a price in both blood and money.

Perhaps more importance will be attached to the role of Iowa's Peace Democrats if one remembers that they were not isolated objectors but part of a large segment of opinion throughout the North and West. As time went by and the war became more and more a blood bath and a financial drain, the emotional response on both sides reached the fever stage. Republicans and War Democrats competed in expressions of scorn and hatred of the advocates of peace—and vice versa; if possible, War Democrats outdid Republicans in their contempt for Peace Democrats.

The situation was the kind which breeds a politics of hysteria. As an easy means of political warfare against the advocates of peace, nothing was easier than to resort to the technique of name-calling. In the Republican lexicon every Peace Democrat was now a "Copperhead," a word loosely applied to anyone who criticized or questioned the war. Other favored epithets were "Secesh" and "traitor." At election time, a War Democrat or a moderate who dared to run against a Republican received the same kind of treatment given to a Peace Democrat, in spite of his support of the war.

Two vastly different men led the Peace Democrats. Dennis A. (Aloysius) Mahony, who quickly abandoned his spontaneous support of the war, was an Irish emigrant to Philadelphia who somehow found his way to the hamlet of Garry Owen in Jackson County, Iowa, and then to Dubuque, where he became a prominent businessman, editor, political leader, and Catholic lay leader. Henry Clay Dean was an ex-Marylander, a renegade Methodist preacher who had once been chaplain of the national House of Representatives. Now a frontier lawyer in southeastern Iowa, he was a literary freak who could quote from the Bible or Shakespeare by the hour, but a man so totally indifferent to personal aesthetics that he has come down through history identified (by his opponents, to be sure) as "Dirty Shirt" Dean and "H(eated) C(arrion)" Dean. Republican orators heaped their scorn and ridicule upon him as they sought to divert attention from Governor Kirkwood's rather careless personal habits. Slurs upon Dean were always good for a laugh from a crowd during a campaign and for votes on election day.[15]

Other strong Peace Democrats were John P. Irish, editor of the *Iowa City State Press;* LeGrand Byington, Iowa City lawyer, land speculator, and civic leader; Lysander Babbitt, editor of the *Council Bluffs Bugle;* Stilson Hutchins, Mahony's capable successor at Dubuque in 1863 and later a newspaper publisher at St. Louis and Washington; David Sheward, editor of the *Fairfield Constitution and Union;* Charles Mason, the eminent jurist who had handed down the decision in the *Ralph* case in 1839; and Charles Negus, a lawyer-banker in Fairfield. Augustus Caesar Dodge would seem to deserve inclusion in this group though he remained largely inactive in politics during and after the war. George Wallace Jones of Dubuque was extremely indiscreet in 1861 but apparently quickly learned "the limits of dissent."[16] As a former classmate and friend of Jefferson Davis at Transylvania University, Jones was either so loyal to this friendship or so naive as to write letters to Davis in 1861 and bring himself under suspicion. Although protesting his innocence, he paid the price of two months' imprisonment for his misreading of the public temper, after which he disappeared from the public eye.

A third group of Democrats might be called the "moderates." They were highly respected citizens of their respective communities, neutrals of a sort, yet much nearer the War Democrats than the Peace Democrats, and so firmly established as civic leaders that they were beyond suspicion or attack. It is difficult to pigeonhole them in any narrow category and it would be a mistake to try to do so. Above all else, they were traditional Democrats who wanted to keep their party alive pending the return of peace and the two-party system of politics. A list of their outstanding leaders reads like a bluebook of Iowa's intellectual aristocracy: John Francis Duncombe of Fort Dodge, one of the greatest lawyers in the state's history; Judge E. H. Thayer of Muscatine, later Clinton, editor of the *Clinton Age;* Maturin L. Fisher of Clayton County, a minor office-holder; W. H. M. Pusey of Council Bluffs, an eminent attorney; and Benjamin Billings Richards of Dubuque, attorney and sometime state senator.

THE CONGRESSIONAL PROGRAM OF THE WAR YEARS

The Republican majority in Congress was faced with a two-part challenge: legislative enactment of the promises made in 1856 and 1860, tempered by the need to provide wartime legislation as needed for the successful prosecution of the war. As might well be expected, the first major problem to confront the Thirty-seventh Congress, which President Lincoln called into special session on July 4, 1861, had to do with finances. By the end of 1861 the United States government found itself with an empty purse. Salmon P. Chase, secretary of the treasury, began his wartime regime by insisting on a policy of paying in gold all the bills incurred in running the war, a ruinous practice even though his intentions were laudable. After much pressure from bankers and merchants, and following the leadership of two wealthy businessmen in the House, John B. Alley and Samuel Hooper, both of Massachusetts, Congress was persuaded to enact, and Secretary Chase to accept, a system of unsecured irredeemable paper money with legal tender quality, paper money which soon earned the name of "greenbacks" because the notes were pasted to pieces of green paper backing to increase their physical durability. By the act of February 25, 1862, an issue of $150,000,000 was authorized; later, additional amounts were approved. Iowa's Senators Grimes and Harlan voted for the bill, as did Representative James F. Wilson; William Vandever was on military leave. Thus a matter which was to have far-reaching political as well as economic consequences became the fiscal policy of the government, presumably for the duration of the war.[17]

A promise which was redeemed was the platform plank on free homesteads. On May 20, 1862, the pledges of 1856 and 1860 were fulfilled by the passage of a bill providing a gift of 160 acres of government land to those filling the requirement of five years' residence and payment of a nominal fee. At the time, the act was praised as a great boon to the "little man" who now could become a "free," independent, self-supporting, self-respecting landowner. It proved to be a snare and a delusion, a plan whereby the rich (and the clever) got richer and very few poor men ever emerged as true beneficiaries. On the key vote determining passage of the bill, Representative William Vandever of Dubuque was not there to vote, having become a colonel in the army, though without resigning his seat; James F. Wilson voted yea, as did Senator James W. Grimes. Senator Harlan did not vote, but later acted as a member of the joint conference committee whose report was adopted on a voice vote. No one could know this in 1862 but the day would come when James Harlan would be charged with manipulation of this very homestead plan in such a way that he, along with several other highly placed Iowans, could prevent the bulk of the lands from reaching their intended recipients.[18]

Of great concern to Iowans was an act consummated a few weeks later, on July 1, when President Lincoln signed the Pacific Railroad Act, the climax to years of agitation and promises. Until recently it has been described as an act made possible by the wartime situation and one which would promote the war effort; now it is looked upon as an act passed only as the result of much lobbying by certain interests which had much to gain. The war situation and war needs served only to furnish a screen for the lobbyists and the special interests. Iowans had a real stake in the bill. This was the first step in the formation of what would become the Union Pacific Railroad, with its eastern terminus at Council Bluffs, by President Lincoln's decision, but with Omaha as the effective terminus of the road. The four railroads across Iowa for which assistance had been given by the act of 1856 would tie in with this road to the Pacific. Senator James Harlan played a very active and important part in the vast labyrinth of maneuvers which produced the act of 1862.[19]

On July 2, 1862, the president approved the Morrill Land Grant Act, which was to prove to be of incalculable importance to Iowa as a source of support for the Agricultural College and Model Farm which had been founded at Ames in 1858, as described above. Other states also profited from this assistance to land-grant colleges. Senator Harlan and Representative James F. Wilson voted for the bill, as requested by the Iowa General Assembly, but Senator Grimes voted nay, joining six other senators from the Midwest who feared the lands granted would be sold off to Eastern capitalists who would impede actual settlement of the lands. In view of Grimes's own record as a land speculator, his vote does not reveal the point of view of a statesman.[20]

One of the last acts of this Congress which set the tone of the war years was probably the most far-reaching of all its monumental achievements. This was the act providing for a system of national banks, an act whose effects are still felt today. Designed for permanency as a source of needed currency as well as a temporary outlet for the government's bonds, and sponsored by such distinguished leaders as Secretary Chase, Senator John Sherman, and Representative Samuel Hooper, the principal author of the greenback legislation, one might suppose that the bill would have had easy sailing through a Republican-dominated Congress. Not so. The opposition included two notable Iowans, Senator James W. Grimes and Representative James F. Wilson. In the Senate the vote was a tight 23 to 21, Iowa's Harlan voting with the majority; in the House the margin of victory was a more comfortable 78 to 64.

If one seeks an answer to the question of reasons for opposition to what seems to have been a highly advisable, badly needed war measure, one long overdue as a corrective to the deplorable system of state bank currency then in use, that answer seems to be self-interest. An analysis of the vote reveals that practically all the Republican opposition came from Eastern members of Congress who were responsive to pressure from state banking interests who foresaw their severe loss of income in the face of competition from the new national banks. Grimes and Wilson, allied to banking interests in their hometowns, lent their support to the Eastern interests, two of only a handful of Western members who voted against the bill.[21] (Ironically, Wilson would later become the president of a national bank in his hometown, Fairfield.)

Although not in the congressional program, one should not leave this time period without notice of the presidential Emancipation Proclamation, on which congressional leaders were consulted. The proclamation was issued on a tentative basis on September 22, 1862, and strengthened and confirmed on January 1, 1863. Designed as a military measure, not a humanitarian document, it nevertheless was consonant with the radical Republican philosophy and was claimed as a great victory by the Abolitionist forces. The proclamation announced that slavery could no longer exist in those parts of states or whole states which were still in rebellion against the United States.[22]

ELECTIONS OF 1862 AS A TEST OF WAR SENTIMENT

In 1861 and 1862 the simple way to demonstrate one's belief in the war as a means of preserving the Union was to vote for Republican candidates for office; each election was regarded as a test of attitude toward "Mr. Lincoln's war." The legislative program of 1861 and 1862 also came under this referendum. Iowa was far more consistent in its support of the Republican cause than other Midwestern states. In 1861 Governor Kirkwood easily overcame rivals for the Republican nomination and then went on to defeat Colonel William H. Merritt of Cedar Rapids by an ample margin, definitely a demonstration of prowar sentiment. In 1862, as a result of a jump in population from 192,214 in 1850 to 674,913 in 1860, Iowa's delegation in the House of Representatives was increased from two to six. Some mild gerrymandering of the six districts followed as a matter of course.[23] The six Republican nominees, in the order of their districts, were: James F. Wilson, Fairfield attorney and banker, who had been previously chosen to fill out the term of Samuel R. Curtis, now a general in the army; Hiram Price, Davenport banker and railroad investor; William Boyd Allison, a Dubuque attorney, blessed with the title of lieutenant colonel of cavalry as a deputy to Addison Sanders of Davenport, the governor's military aide in eastern Iowa; Josiah B. Grinnell of Grinnell, whom we have already met as a Congregationalist minister and Abolitionist leader; John A. Kasson of Des Moines, already met on several occasions; and Asahel W. Hubbard of Sioux City, a prominent lawyer in that frontier section of the state.

The most exciting race was in Allison's Third District. His opponent was Dennis A. Mahony, leader of the Peace Democrats in Iowa and well known beyond the borders of the state as editor of the *Dubuque Herald,* which ranked on even terms with the *Chicago Times,* the *Columbus Crisis,* and the *La Crosse Democrat* as an organ of the Peace Democracy. By a remarkable coincidence, United States Marshal Hubert Hoxie of Des Moines appeared in Dubuque only six days before the Democratic District Convention, arrested Mahony, and hustled him off to Washington, without benefit of trial but accused of interfering with the war effort. In spite of or maybe because of this treatment, his cohorts secured his nomination. The voters in the Third District therefore had a choice between a strong supporter of the president and the war effort, on the one hand, and a Peace Democrat now in prison for his antiwar editorials, on the other.[24]

President Lincoln helped his cause in Iowa by the appointment of an Iowan, Samuel Freeman Miller of Keokuk, to the Supreme Court, a tribute to the perseverance and political skill of Senator Grimes and Representative James F. Wilson, who carried out some expert maneuvers to secure the appointment and its confirmation. Lincoln was eager to please the Iowa delegation but hesitated at naming the man from Keokuk who was totally unknown to him. He knew of Daniel F. Miller, an Iowan who had served as a loyal Whig in Congress in 1850–1852, but not this former Kentuckian who had come out to Iowa where his antislavery views would be more welcome. Grimes and Wilson assured the president of the soundness of Samuel Miller's views on the war and John A. Kasson was able to set Lincoln straight on the identities of the two men. It would be good politics, of course, to name someone from Iowa, which was about to vote for six congressmen. And so the appointment was made and duly confirmed.[25]

Every one of the six candidates was successful, a record the party was not able to match in five other Northern states, notably Lincoln's home state, Illinois, and Indiana and Ohio, whose lack of support was alarming because of their proximity to the border state of Kentucky. Iowa thus established a reputation as a dependable Republican stronghold and earned the title of "Vermont of the West." Part of the Republican margin could be attributed to the soldier vote. Instead of mailing absentee voter ballots to the servicemen, election commissioners were delegated to visit the camps in person where they openly solicited soldiers' votes by urging them to "vote as they shot." Continuing the trend of the 1854–1860 elections, strongly augmented by the sentiment of patriotism and a belief in the Republican party as the war party, the party to save the Union, and the party which would support Northern and Western interests against the South, Iowa now became virtually a one-party state.

ELECTION OF 1863

For Iowans and Americans everywhere the years 1863 and 1864 were a great trial of faith in the worthwhileness of the war, and in President Lincoln's determination to see the war through to victory. The casualty lists of 1862 had been bad enough because of heavy losses at Fort Donelson and Pea Ridge, the fearful carnage at Shiloh, and the futile sacrifices at Fredericksburg, where 9,000 men were lost trying to take Marye's Heights; the casualty lists of 1863 were still heavier. The bloody Vicksburg campaign, though victorious, put a damper on enthusiasm for the war; the losses at Chattanooga's Lookout Mountain added to the grieving in many Iowa homes. Iowa regiments were not involved in the great battle at Gettysburg but many a relative or friend of Iowa families lost his life in those three days of fierce charge and countercharge. There was much grumbling, much criticism of Grant and of the seemingly endless waste of life and money, and of the president's soft attitude toward the rebels. His rebuke of federal generals who encouraged slaves to come over to the North and freedom was especially galling to the radicals.

In these trying times the gubernatorial election of 1863 in Iowa did not offer Iowans much of a choice, each candidate being a soldier who advocated relentless pursuit of the war. The Republican nominating convention chose Colonel William Milo Stone of Knoxville, home on sick leave from a wound suffered at Vicksburg. Colonel Stone was no neophyte at politics; a founding father of the Republican party at Iowa City in 1856 and once chairman of the state central committee, he added military prestige to his political reputation. The Democrats overcame Mahony's pleas for a candidate who would support demands for a negotiated peace and nominated a War Democrat, General James M. Tuttle of Keosauqua, as their standard-bearer, apparently a man with a splendid war record. Low level politics reduced the appeal of each man. Stone was the victim of a whispering campaign maligning his personal morals, while Tuttle was subjected to a barrage of accusations about the sale of confiscated cotton in his keeping. Stone emerged as the winner by a margin of about 30,000 votes.

PROWAR AND ANTIWAR ELEMENTS APPROACH A SHOWDOWN

As the election campaign of 1863 reached the boiling point, extreme Peace Democrats drove themselves to new heights of frenzied activity. Now more than ever the Copperheads could feel justified in arguing that the war was not worth the price that was being called for. It has been charged that some Iowans were now members of a secret society, the Knights of the Golden Circle, dedicated to opposition to the war to the extent of using conspiratorial methods. In treating such a serious matter, historians should be very careful to use precise terminology as well as factual proof for their statements. Undoubtedly there were antiwar elements in Iowa—but whether there were any members of the K.G.C., or even if such a society existed in Iowa or elsewhere, is a doubtful matter. Obviously, proof would be hard to find because of the need for secrecy, if such a group existed. Professor Dan Elbert Clark's oft-quoted statement, "This [the K.G.C.] was a secret society or lodge, which in February, 1863, was *said to be* [italics mine] organized in every township in the State and to have as many as 42,000 members," is very doubtful as to factual accuracy. It defies historical method and scholarship to claim, on the authority of "said to be," that such an organization existed *in every township in the state,* with members dedicated to resistance to the draft, forwarding a union of the Northwest and the South, and collecting and storing arms for use against Union forces, as the K.G.C. was accused of doing.[26]

Governor Kirkwood cannot be blamed if he became excited over the reports which he received from southern and central Iowa. He urged one informant, L. B. Fleak, a War Democrat in Brighton, to use deception if necessary in securing helpful information about any secret group in his neighborhood. Another informant was told that "general statements" were not sufficient; he must obtain specific evidence about acts and words attributed to suspected opponents of the war and then make out an affidavit containing the charges. This legalistic attitude is worth noting because the crusty old war governor was not always so tender toward the opposition.

The one overt act by an antiwar group which might have given Governor Kirkwood concern was the little scare known to Iowa history as the "Tally War" or "The Skunk River War," in and around the village of South English, in Keokuk County. Even though most of the reports on this skirmish are from the victorious anti-Tally side, it seems clear enough that a band of opponents of the war, under the leadership of George Cyphert Tally, a young Baptist minister not otherwise known to fame, had some plans to break up a Republican County Convention, scheduled to meet in South English on Saturday, August 1, 1863. The convention members "got wind" of the plan and came well armed for self-defense. When Tally daringly, or foolishly, led a procession of his followers, well armed and defiant, down the principal street of the little town, trouble was certain to ensue. Tally sent word that he only wanted to bring his men through the town but the Union men were prepared for a ruse.

At just the wrong moment, someone on one side or the other fired a shot. Guns suddenly appeared everywhere and shots were exchanged. Tally, standing in a wagon and brandishing a gun and a bowie knife, was immediately shot dead.[27] His followers, generally believed to number a thousand men, were camped near the town and were considered a threat to its safety. There was much loud talk of "war" and messages requesting troops were rushed to Governor Kirkwood. The governor took steps at once to send troops to South English and he went in person to nearby Sigourney, from whence he sent a warning of his intention to deal firmly with any traitors. These moves were sufficient to put an end to the episode. The best testimony available avers that there was more of a threat from the rebels than was generally thought.[28]

RECONSTRUCTION POLICY AND THE POLITICS OF 1864

The matter of reconstruction took on new meaning in 1863–1864. Shortly after the elections of 1863, and in direct response to the Union's military successes in Louisiana, Arkansas, and Tennessee, President Lincoln announced his own reconstruction policy for these states. Lincoln's plan was based on the fact that a significant number of people in the seceded states had remained loyal to the Union and only wanted an opportunity to act in some practical way. The presidential plan gave them this opportunity. Wherever 10 percent of the population of a state now under federal military control was willing to take an oath of loyalty to the Union and proceed with other formalities of readmission, the president would recognize such a state and consider it restored to the Union.[29]

The first response in Iowa to the president's announcement was highly favorable. Both outgoing Governor Kirkwood and incoming Governor Stone fully endorsed the policy. Luckily, the legislative election of a senator was due in January 1864, a good chance to register approval of Republican policy, a chance which was seized by reelecting Senator Grimes by the overwhelming vote of 128 to 5. Republicans in Iowa and elsewhere soon changed their minds, however, and severely denounced the president's "soft" policy of reconstruction. In Congress, where the real decisions would have to be made, the president's "10 percent plan" enjoyed only a brief honeymoon of acceptance before coming under attack by the advocates of congressional reconstruction.

The chief sponsors of the right of Congress to make and manage reconstruction policy were Representative Henry Winter Davis of Maryland and Senator Benjamin F. Wade of Ohio. Davis introduced a bill on February 15, 1864, which was heatedly debated until its passage in July, after which it received a pocket veto. Thus the question of congressional versus presidential reconstruction became an issue in the politics of that year.

Iowans in Congress were not conspicuously for or against the Davis bill. In the House vote on final passage of the main bill, four of the six members—Wilson, Price, Allison, and Hubbard—voted for the bill; Grinnell and Kasson, perhaps significantly, did not vote. In the Senate, Harlan voted for the bill, striking proof that he was not yet the friend of President Lincoln that he has been represented to be. Senator Grimes demonstrated his drifting away from the Radical position by voting against the bill on a test vote on July 1; when the final vote was taken on the next day, he was absent, one of several opponents who were unexplainably absent and whose default enabled the bill to go through.[30]

LINCOLN'S SECOND TERM

Many party regulars were not enthusiastic about Lincoln as their presidential candidate in 1864. In spite of Vicksburg and Gettysburg the war was drifting on and total victory seemed always to be just out of reach. The president was closely associated in the public eye with the long, frustrating search for a victorious general, and severely criticized for the fearful price that had been paid for the few successes so far achieved in battle. When to these points is added the clash over reconstruction policy, it is not difficult to explain the president's unpopularity in some quarters in 1864.

The first overt move to ditch Lincoln was a quiet, almost secretive effort to work up a sentiment for Salmon P. Chase as a man with a long record as a virtual Abolitionist who would still have appeal to those less extreme in their views. Meetings were held and letters were written in late 1863 and early 1864 but without enough success to warrant a campaign to overthrow the man in the White House. Secretary Chase lent his support to these efforts but was shrewd enough to prevent an open break with Lincoln. It is logical to expect that Senator Grimes and Representative William B. Allison would have supported this pro-Chase movement. Both men had been strong allies of Chase in the pre-1860 antislavery movement and there is no reason to believe that they were completely dedicated to Lincoln.

The Chase boomlet played out early in 1864 and Chase himself stated publicly that he was not a candidate for the nomination. Not so easily damped was a brush fire revolt by General John C. Frémont, backed by a few extreme Radicals and egged on by Wendell Phillips, the ultraradical Abolitionist. This little diversionary movement tried to play both ends against the middle by taking a strong "push the war" and "immediate emancipation" position at one extreme and cooperation with the Copperheads at the other. Phillips was so bitterly anti-Lincoln that he could not refrain from support of Frémont, in spite of William Lloyd Garrison's advice to the contrary. The anti-Lincoln, pro-Frémont cause drew four hundred delegates to Cleveland on May 31, 1864, where General Frémont and a Colonel John Cochrane, a prewar Democrat, were set up as a ticket for the Radical War Democrats. Even though the Chase and Frémont lures to Republicans were not very successful, the "ditch Lincoln" movement would not die. Opponents even went so far as to try to postpone the quadrennial convention from June to September but their efforts were defeated.

Senator James Harlan showed his true feelings toward Lincoln to a close friend and supporter, Major William Penn Clarke, the Iowa City attorney and Republican party manager, soon to be a Harlan appointee. On April 2, 1864, Harlan wrote a belittling letter about the president, telling Clarke of many of Lincoln's weaknesses but admitting that if he were renominated, "it will be to the interest of the cause to elect him. We must try to cure as far as possible, by the action of Congress, what he fails to achieve."[31]

In spite of doubts by Harlan and others, the party had no choice but to go to Baltimore in June and proceed with the nomination of Lincoln, this time dropping Hannibal Hamlin in favor of former Senator Andrew Johnson of Tennessee, a War Democrat and the military governor of that state, as the vice-presidential nominee on a Union Republican ticket. It might be of interest to Iowans to know that it was Governor William Milo Stone, a late appointee to the Iowa delegation at Baltimore, who made the nominating speech for Andrew Johnson, and that Iowa gave eight votes to Johnson, four to Daniel S. Dickinson of New York, and four to Hamlin. There is ample evidence that President Lincoln wanted to ditch Hamlin, a Radical Republican from Maine, a safe Republican state, and put in Johnson, a War (Union) Democrat, and that Stone was merely acting as a tool for the president.[32]

All through the summer there was much discontent; the grumbling against Lincoln would not die down. Sherman's victory at Atlanta on September 3 was the turning point in Lincoln's fortunes. Surely few could doubt that victory would come to him and to the Union cause. Many who had been critics suddenly became his "best friends" while only a few skeptics continued to doubt his fitness as a candidate. Among these were Iowa's Governor Stone and Senator Grimes. In early September Stone made a fact-finding tour of Western states to sound out public opinion as to Lincoln's chances for victory. He came home with the opinion that Lincoln would carry Iowa, but not "on his merits"; the consequences of a defeat would be too "disastrous" to make it possible for the Republicans to vote for anyone else.[33] As for Senator Grimes, who had proudly denoted himself as a Radical on earlier occasions, he now plainly revealed that only party loyalty, not admiration for the president, would hold him fast to the Lincoln-Johnson ticket. Writing to Adam Gurowski, the Polish expatriate and confidant of the Radicals and the Lincoln-haters, Grimes asserted that he would vote for Lincoln, but only because of McClellan's Chicago platform. "Few now want to vote for him. He is very far from being a popular man today. He will only be accepted because the *public* are so genuinely loyal to the government, and they are afraid to trust the men who concocted the Chicago platform" and who would surround McClellan if he were elected.[34]

The agony of the 1864 presidential campaign at last came to an end. Lincoln and Johnson attracted 2,213,665 voters to the polls in their behalf, their votes being distributed in such a way as to produce 212 electoral votes. Indicative of the peace sentiment of the country was the astounding popular vote of 1,805,237 for General George B. McClellan. In Iowa there was never any doubt of a Lincoln victory, yet the 49,525 votes for McClellan reveal a surprising anti-Lincoln, propeace strength. In the races for the House, the six stalwart Republicans who had won in 1862 were again winners, in spite of threats of disaster as voiced by the Peace Democrats if the "warmongers" should be returned to Washington to support Lincoln and "Butcher" Grant. Their cries of alarm were of no avail—Iowa voters gave the six Republicans a larger vote than in 1862!

LINCOLN AND HARLAN

During the awkward and agonizing interval of November to March, while waiting for the second inauguration and for the almost inevitable Confederate surrender, the president made several trips from Washington to nearby battlefields and to General Grant's headquarters. Among those likely to be in the president's party were Iowa's Senator James Harlan, his wife, and their daughter Mary, and, either as a member of the group or the object of a visit, young Captain Robert Todd Lincoln, on leave from his studies at Harvard to play at soldiering under the totally undeserved commission which only a presidential father could have arranged. Historians should long ago have wondered at what forces were responsible for the sudden friendship of Lincoln and Harlan after several years of opposition by the senator to presidential measures, particularly Reconstruction policy.

The myth that Harlan was one of the president's great and true friends and counselors can now be laid to rest. The gulf between Lincoln the conservative and Harlan the radical is too great to be ignored.[35] It seems obvious that Robert Todd Lincoln's "love at first sight" courtship of Mary Harlan was the wedge which opened the door for a sudden friendship between the fathers of the young people.[36] As the romance developed, the friendship between their fathers could develop. Now the senator found himself elevated into the Lincoln family circle, the constant companion of the family, the habitué of all White House gatherings, the companion on trips to the battlefields, Mrs. Lincoln's escort to the Second Inaugural, and, finally, a cabinet appointee.[37]

Such pleasantries were rudely interrupted by the terrible tragedy of the president's assassination.

CHAPTER 10 POLITICS IN THE POSTWAR YEARS 1865-1872

IOWANS, NO LESS THAN THE PEOPLE IN OTHER STATES, FOUND THE experiences of 1865 and succeeding years far more than a simple matter of "war and peace." Any notion that the war was over and the country would automatically snap back into its pre-1861 social and political attitudes was soon dispelled. The tremendous economic developments of the war years guaranteed that American society would never again be the same. The situation was aggravated by the change in national leadership occasioned by the terrible tragedy of Lincoln's assassination shortly after Lee's surrender. The great triumphal processions in Washington and other cities were turned into funeral marches—the apotheosis of Lincoln had begun. Radical members of Congress, Iowa's Allison, for example, who had planned to rally their followers and call for a vindictive policy against the defeated South, now found themselves making eulogistic orations at mass meetings, praising instead of criticizing the fallen leader. The Lincoln that no one knew would soon take form.

RECONSTRUCTION POLITICS

In Iowa, more so than in many other states of the North, the Republican party emerged from the war as "the party of the Union," "the party of patriotism," and "the party of victory." As such it enjoyed a sense of superiority, security, and self-righteousness as the undisputed dominant party of the state. It soon found itself divided, however, torn by a factionalism which can be traced to personal factors as much as to clashing ideas, perhaps more so. One naturally expects to find alignments under the labels in current use—"Radicals" and "Conservatives" —but soon finds that such a simplistic terminology is useful but not definitive as a key to political loyalties in Iowa over the next few years.

The label of "Radical," as used here, can be endowed with meaning as early as 1861, connoting belief in a firm, dictated policy of Southern reconstruction, well illustrated by Senator James Harlan's proposal to govern the seceded states as if they were territories belonging to the Union.[1] The refusal of the House in December 1861 to reaffirm the Crittenden Resolution, defining the purpose of the war as the preservation of the Union, after acceptance of that resolution in the previous July, shows a hardening of Northern attitudes. In 1864 the harsh, almost brutal, language of the Wade-Davis Manifesto in response to President Lincoln's pocket veto of the Davis bill for congressional-controlled reconstruction, revealed further development of a vindictive attitude toward the South. There was honest difference of opinion as to whether the Congress or the president should make and execute reconstruction policy, and this clash accounts for much of the bitterness of presidential politics in 1864. Not to be "Radical" was to be "Anti-Radical," better expressed by the word "Conservative." Of course, the Radical Republicans claimed to be the *real* Republicans, who found further justification for labeling their intraparty opponents as "Conservatives" by accusing them of harboring the same economic and social ideas as the Democrats, the acknowledged true conservatives of that era.

The Thirteenth Amendment

One of the first concrete acts of reconstruction, and an expression of the influence of the Abolitionist wing on the remainder of the Republican party, was the enactment of the Thirteenth Amendment, proposed by Congress in February 1865, as the war was dragging to an end, and ratified by the states by December of that year. Although Representative James F. Wilson of Iowa may be regarded as the author of the amendment, the state's claim on a part of the monumental document stops there. Iowa was deprived of a chance to join the parade of ratifying states because Governor William M. Stone refused to call the General Assembly into special session in a nonlegislative year, a small price to have paid for the honor of voting to end human bondage in America.

THE UNFINISHED CIVIL WAR

As the war ended, a great national debate engaged the Abolitionists. In oversimplified terms, the Garrisonian wing or faction of the group took the position that the adoption and certain ratification of the Thirteenth Amendment had triumphantly accomplished the one supreme mission of the American Anti-Slavery Society. Garrison recognized that the freedmen needed and deserved far more than mere freedom from chattel slavery, the franchise first of all, but he was willing to disband the society and allow other groups to finish the fight for the suffrage and other civil rights. Wendell Phillips took a position diametrically opposite; in his view, the fight for true justice to the Negro had just begun, and the Anti-Slavery Society should continue the struggle to go beyond freedom, the immediate objective being the suffrage on the same terms as for the whites. On a test vote, Phillips won by a large margin.[2]

After freedom and the suffrage, other rights would appear desirable and deserved, and so the struggle would go on and each victory and each defeat would generate more determination to fight with greater courage for the rising expectations. The Garrison-Phillips debate, therefore, epitomizes the "unfinished Civil War," a legacy bequeathed by the victors of 1865 to future generations of Americans. Iowa's direct contacts with that fight have not been as extensive as those in some other states, but the movement has never been completely missing from Iowa's history. Certain aspects of the struggle will be noted below and in succeeding chapters.

THE BATTLE FOR NEGRO SUFFRAGE

There is abundant evidence of an ongoing effort in Iowa to increase the political rights of Negroes immediately after the war. As in other Northern states, it had not been necessary to wait for freedom for the blacks, as it was necessary in the South, before granting the right of suffrage. Iowa's total Negro population in 1860 was only 1,069; the 1870 census would show 5,762, and 9,516 in 1880. Each census of the following years would show a slight increase until the number reached 19,005 in 1920. That figure went down in 1930, and again in 1940 when it stood at 16,694. In 1950 the number reached 19,692; in 1960 it was 25,354; in 1970 the number counted was 32,596. Regardless of absolute increases or decreases, until 1970 the Negro population had always been less than 1 percent of the white population of Iowa; in that year the percentage climbed to 1.15 percent.

Of course the people of 1865 could not see into the future and accurately predict these small increases in the Negro population. Fears of "inundation" seemed very real to some orators and platform makers in both parties. Iowa Democrats were positively and unanimously opposed to the vote for the Negro, but insured their defeat by splitting over the question of tactics. One faction could not be restrained from holding a convention under the name of "Soldiers' Anti-Negro Suffrage Party," adopting a single-plank platform to that effect, and nominating Colonel Thomas H. Benton, Jr., for governor. Other Democrats followed the lead of LeGrand Byington of Iowa City, the outspoken Peace Democrat of war days, in preferring to reorganize the party and stand on a more varied platform. Their nominees were inconspicuous citizens except for Lysander Babbitt, editor of the *Council Bluffs Bugle* and a far-out Peace Democrat.

Even the Republicans were somewhat divided and had to overcome the foot-dragging influence of the great war governor, Samuel J. Kirkwood, whose negative attitude is explained by his fears that the issue would split the party. On this point he was acutely sensitive since he was hoping for election to the Senate as successor to James Harlan, now secretary of the interior. Kirkwood had to accept a strong Negro suffrage plank:

> That with proper safeguards to the purity of the ballot box, the elective franchise should be based upon loyalty to the Constitution and the Union, recognizing and affirming the *equality of all men* before the law; therefore we are in favor of amending the Constitution of our State by striking out the word "white" in the article on suffrage.[3]

Parenthetically, it should be noted that an unrelated movement for woman suffrage in Iowa was launched simultaneously with the drive to put in Negro suffrage. Although sponsored and led by well-known women, including the famous Amelia Bloomer of Council Bluffs, the leaders soon realized that their cause was running a poor second to the drive for dropping the word "white." To this set of priorities they bowed with good grace in the face of cruel taunts from some editors and other ungallant members of the opposite sex.[4]

At this point it needs only to be added that the Republicans proved to be the victors, that the two subsequent sessions of the General Assembly passed the proposal for amending the constitution, as the Republicans had pledged, and that the proposition was submitted to the people in 1868 and duly ratified. The details of ratification will be treated below at greater length.

POLITICS, 1865–1872: KEY TO FUTURE POLITICAL CONTROL

Interweaving political ideas and personal inclinations, one finds that *as of 1865* Senators Grimes and Harlan, and Representatives Wilson, Price, Allison, and Hubbard, defined themselves as Radicals and were accepted as such by those redoubtable Radicals, Wade of Ohio and Sumner of Massachusetts. Clearly dominating Iowa politics at the end of the war, their Radicalism can be adduced by their letters and speeches, and by statistical studies of their votes on key legislation.[5] Their Iowa colleagues, Kasson and Grinnell, are not so easily classified. Although claiming to be good Republicans, both men found themselves under fire, for reasons difficult to discern.

It is not too much to say that Iowa politics—and therefore many policy decisions—for the next half-century would be affected by and largely determined by the party maneuvers and electoral results of 1865–1872. Of the eight members of the Iowa congressional delegation,

Grinnell and Kasson would soon feel the political axe; Grimes would undergo a shift of attitude toward "liberalism," a form of party treason just then; Harlan would become the fiercest anti-Southern, anti-Andrew Johnson Radical of the entire group, but would soon lose out as a victim of Iowa factional politics; and William B. Allison would emerge as the long-time leader of Iowa Republicans. Very few if any observers of the Iowa scene in 1865 would have hazarded a prophecy of these results if he had tried to rate these political figures on a scale of ability.

The story of these years begins with an account of Iowa senatorial politics in 1865–1866.[6] As related above, Senator James Harlan was appointed secretary of the interior by President Lincoln, on March 15, 1865. For various reasons Harlan's accession to the post was delayed and whatever prospects for happiness and success he might have had as as a member of Lincoln's cabinet were destroyed by the death of the president on April 15, 1865. The cabinet appointment was continued by President Andrew Johnson and Harlan took office on May 15. Harlan's premature endorsement of President Johnson's presumed Radicalism was soon replaced by total disillusionment with the president and his policies. The Radicals' hatred of Lincoln's successor was so bitter that anyone who enjoyed agreeable relations with him was in their opinion guilty of apostasy to Radicalism. Harlan was caught in an uneasy relationship, torn between sincere belief in Radicalism and loyalty to his chief. For several months Harlan was hardly more than a spy in the Johnson political camp.[7]

The Mount Pleasant man's vacant seat in the Senate immediately commanded the covetous glances of those Iowans who thought of themselves as senatorial timber. The man conceded to be the most deserving of Harlan's place was former Governor Kirkwood. The Grimes faction in the party expected Governor Stone to appoint Kirkwood and thought they had a promise from him to do so. Unfortunately, the indecisive governor dallied until January 1866, when the seat was still vacant as the legislature assembled. Harlan, in the meanwhile having broken with President Johnson, now wanted to return to the Senate, and took his case to the General Assembly. To the great disappointment of Kirkwood and his friends, Harlan was able to corral the votes to get the long term for himself (1867–1873), leaving the short (unexpired) term to Kirkwood as a crumb from the table. In effect, Harlan would simply succeed himself as senator after time out to enjoy the prestige of cabinet status (the first Iowan to be so honored) and a chance to wallow in the fleshpots of the most corrupt and corrupting department of the government.

Harlan's ambition and his presumption that he would always be accepted as the senior statesman of Iowa were to be his undoing. It is a fair assumption that the pro-Kirkwood faction led by Grimes, Wilson, Allison, and Grenville Dodge, must necessarily, perhaps willingly, have shared power with him indefinitely *if* he had never left the Senate for the cabinet, but now they felt rebuffed and cheated by the manner in which Kirkwood had been euchred out of his expectancy of succession to a seat in the Senate. Harlan's stubborn ambition to reclaim "his" seat, about which he spoke with proprietary air, and the upset of the other clique produced disastrous long-run results for the Harlan faction, and determined the control of the Republican party for the next generation. Only the overwhelmingly superior numbers of the Republicans saved them from ruin, now and later. It was now a party with two distinct wings, with what fateful results for Harlan we shall soon see.

There were other momentous and far-reaching developments in Iowa politics in this crucial year of 1866. In high Radical councils, Representatives Kasson and Grinnell were marked for expulsion. Grinnell's case is still somewhat of a mystery as he was an old-time Abolitionist and an ultra-Radical through two terms in Congress. Whatever the source of his undesirability, it was *not* the quarrel with General Lovell H. Rousseau of Kentucky and the humiliating beating administered by Rousseau on the steps of the national capitol, as has been repeatedly stated.[8] That unpleasant piece of business did not take place until after the nominating convention in Oskaloosa, which substituted William Loughridge, a nonentity but an intense and party-serving Radical, for the onetime stationmaster on the Underground Railroad, friend and host to John Brown. It would seem that Grinnell's fault was that he was too much a man of ideas, too much a man of Christian charity, to hold the affections of the hardbitten leaders of the Radical faction.

As for John A. Kasson, certainly a moderate, often pro-Johnson, he had the hard luck to stand in the way of ultra-Radical General Grenville M. Dodge, now chief engineer of the Union Pacific Railroad, who aspired to run for Congress. Even so, only by resort to the dirtiest kind of personal politics, and by securing a delegate's vital marginal vote by promise of a railroad job, was Dodge able to sidetrack Kasson on the 177th ballot.[9] The other four members of the delegation—Wilson, Price, Allison, and Hubbard—were easily renominated and the entire slate of six anti-Johnson Radicals rode to victory without serious trouble.

THE IMPEACHMENT CRISIS

The fight between Radicals and Conservatives was continued in the Thirty-ninth Congress. For better or for worse, after Congress had completed the passage of its Reconstruction program, early in 1867, the president might have been allowed to fade away into a quiet, harmless existence until the end of his term, but his own stubbornness and fighting spirit would not permit this good fortune. Recent scholarship holds Johnson responsible for the manner in which as chief executive he fought against Congress after the elections of 1866 upheld the congressional point of view toward Reconstruction. The fight would not end until the president had been impeached, tried, and almost found guilty in 1868.[10]

Two Iowans, James F. Wilson and James W. Grimes, played key roles in the great drama of impeachment and trial. Wilson, as chairman of the House Committee on the Judiciary, was in a position to hinder or assist the effort to destroy the president. His actions as committee chairman show him in a good light as a statesman rather than a politician. Although considered a good Radical, he proved to be independent in his judgments, defied intimidation, preserved a judicial manner, and refused to go along with the Radicals simply because he was a member of the group. Perhaps for these reasons the impeachment matter was taken from his committee and given over to a special committee, the Committee on Reconstruction.

It proved to be very difficult to secure a formal indictment (impeachment) of the president even in a House dominated by his enemies. Three attempts failed; only Johnson's obtuseness made him vulnerable on the fourth attempt. A series of appointments and resignations under the Tenure of Office Act should have warned Johnson to let well enough alone; if so, the whole matter might have ended as hardly more than a footnote in history. This he would not do. He found a puppet general (Lorenzo Thomas) to take the title of secretary of war, and the quarrel soon reached an impasse. The president's enemies at last had their talking point and could impeach him for "high crimes and misdemeanors." On this test, the Iowa delegation gave unanimous support.

The Senate now became a trial court, though hardly an impartial one, under the presiding hand of Chief Justice Salmon P. Chase. James F. Wilson had only a small part to play as a member of the Board of Managers, who acted as the prosecuting attorneys for the House. Long sessions were devoted to arguments and testimony, followed by two voting sessions, May 16 and May 26. The trial ended in failure to convict by a margin of one vote short of the two-thirds needed, 35 to 19, the same seven Republicans, including Senator Grimes, voting "not guilty" on each occasion. It is an exaggeration to single out Grimes as the one whose vote saved the president. Of the seven, perhaps the greatest honor should go to Senator Edmund G. Ross of Kansas because he knew he was risking his future by his adverse vote. Also of great importance were the influential votes of Senator William Pitt Fessenden of Maine. Both Grimes and Fessenden had announced in a secret session of the Senate on May 11 that they would vote against conviction, exposing them to fierce pressure, but they stood their ground and kept their senatorial oaths "to do impartial justice." Their examples helped to sustain the other five "recusants."

Grimes deserves special credit, of course, regardless of a yea or nay vote, because he rose from a sickbed, a victim of paralysis, to be brought on a stretcher to the chamber to record his vote. Although the point is usually ignored, he was there on May 26 as well as on May 16. For his "not guilty" vote the grand old man of Iowa Republicanism was reviled, cursed, and denounced far and wide, nowhere more so than among his former friends and party colleagues. The name Judas was freely thrown at him without regard to his feelings. The brave man could only explain as best he could and then wait for a return of public sanity. At one time or another he made several different, though not necessarily conflicting, statements in defense of his votes. The most convincing one was that he could not in good conscience do anything which would bring such an unfit man as Senator Benjamin F. Wade of Ohio, president pro tempore of the Senate and next in line of succession, to the White House.

In the larger sense a vote of "not guilty" was more than a vote to save Johnson—it was a vote to prevent the elevation of the legislature above the executive and the undoing of the American system of the balance of powers. This is not to say that all who voted "guilty" were aware of such effects or that all who voted "not guilty" were consciously voting against Old Ben Wade and against the theory of legislative supremacy. Judging by the later remarks of Senator Grimes, one would assume he was aware of the consequences of his vote; he was aware of the fact that if one president, granted that he was the unpopular Andrew Johnson, could be put at the mercy of a hostile legislature, the same thing could happen to any president who dared to cross Congress, and the office would soon be destroyed.[11]

It is good to be able to record that the people of Iowa soon returned to their senses and the senator from Burlington was restored to his place in their affections as an honorable man who had done his duty, had searched for and found the truth according to his own honest convictions and had voted accordingly. Because of his continuing poor health which the best cures of Europe could not relieve, he resigned in August 1869, effective as of December 6 of that year. Added to his physical infirmities there was another reason for his resignation. One needs only to read of his differences of opinion with many Republican colleagues on the subject of the protective tariff, and his agonizing distress over the graft and corruption which were poisoning his party, to come to the conclusion that continuation in Radical Republican ranks was for him impossible. It is not altogether idle speculation to assert that poor health which led to his retirement averted a transfer to the ranks of the Liberal Republicans who were trying to reform the old line party and the government.

Little noticed in the commentary on the side effects of the impeachment contest was the retirement of James F. Wilson from Congress. As early as April 4, well before the climax of the trial going on in the Senate, he wrote to a friend in Fairfield of his determination to retire from the House. Wilson's letters indicate that he, like Grimes, was disgusted with public life and the ways of politicians. Whatever his precise reasons for voluntarily retiring, we know that he rejected various opportunities which came along and that he did not return to public life until 1882.[12]

Before leaving the subject, it should be noted that Senator Harlan was strongly in favor of the Radical position against Johnson. Harlan was the epitome not only of the Radical Republican stance on impeachment but also the attitude of the Methodist Church, of which he was a national leader. In its General Conference held that same year in Chicago, which happened to coincide with the date of the Republican National Convention in the same city, the Methodists voted overwhelmingly in favor of conviction of President Johnson and also endorsed General Grant for the presidency.[13]

THE FOURTEENTH AMENDMENT

While the episode of the impeachment and trial monopolized the headlines, two other closely associated events of great importance were vying with it for attention. The first was the progress of the Fourteenth Amendment toward acceptance. This amendment has had a checkered career in the hands of public men and historians who have found in it varying and sometimes conflicting meanings and interpretations, too numerous and complex to summarize here. A careful study of the opinions of editors and political leaders in the Iowa of 1867–1868 revealed nothing which resembles the interpretations put forward in recent years. Iowans of that era thought that the proposed amendment was intended to assist Negroes in the South to obtain the privilege of voting, to punish the Southern states by curbing their representation in Congress, and to establish the validity of the national debt beyond any doubt. In those years and for many years to come it was *not* thought of as guaranteeing to Negroes such things as "equal protection of the laws" and "privileges and immunities as citizens." Once again we see evidence of the prevailing belief of that era: the ballot would give Negroes a voice in government and would educate them in the ways of citizenship—and that would be sufficient. Perhaps Iowans, who in 1868 were striking the word "white" from their own constitutional requirements for voting and who were only just then abolishing segregated schools, were too ready to assume that the Fourteenth Amendment was primarily a suffrage amendment. What Iowa whites and all other American whites failed to see in 1868 was that the right of suffrage was not in itself a guarantee of improvement in the status of the Negro. The Iowa House of Representatives voted for ratification on January 27, the Senate on March 9; other states did their part and the great Civil Rights Amendment was proclaimed on July 28, 1868.[14]

POLITICS AND ELECTIONS, 1868–1870

Touching off the highly significant moves leading to the elections of 1868 was the nomination by the Republicans of General Ulysses S. Grant as their standard-bearer for president. Like several other soldiers who reached the White House, this one had not known which party he preferred until the moment of decision forced him to affiliate with one or the other. A later generation would adjudge Grant to have been one of the most inadequate presidents in our history, but this was not the attitude of most Republicans toward him during the generation in which his term of office fell. In Iowa, James S. Clarkson and the *Des Moines Iowa State Register* helped to create a veritable Grant cult, and Des Moines Republicans organized a statewide "Grant Club" as the very citadel of the party's staunchest adherents. In 1876 these and other leading Iowa Republicans supported the effort to nominate Grant for a third term.

As in earlier elections, Iowa in 1868 was more loyal to the Republican party than many other Northern states. In general, the GOP did not do well but Iowa gave Grant a good margin and elected all six Republican candidates for the House.[15] In Iowa the local matter of greatest importance was the question of ratification of the Negro suffrage amendment. Between 1865 and 1870 fourteen states in the North rejected such a suffrage extension outright, to the great embarrassment of Radical Republican orators who were calling for the South to enfranchise the Negro. Four states, Illinois, Michigan, Minnesota, and Wisconsin, were able to get the voting clause on the statute books or into their constitutions only by trickery. A perusal of Iowa newspapers of 1866–1868 shows that Radical Republican editors strongly urged Iowa voters to extend the franchise, but confidential letters recently made available show clearly that the state party organization doubted their ability to carry the amendment. For this reason they begged the national organization to leave all Iowa party funds in the state for use in the fight.[16] The amendment, the first to be added to the Constitution of 1857, carried by a vote of 105,384 to 81,119, a 66.5 percent–33.5 percent split of the 186,503 votes on the proposition, a safe margin but nothing to engender enthusiasm in Negro circles.

Be that as it may, Iowa was the only state to adopt such an amendment that year "by means of a single, uncomplicated referendum." A recent analysis of the county and township statistics for all 97 counties and the 437 townships then organized in Iowa reveals some very interesting facts about the decision made by Iowans. The township voting figures reveal a high correspondence between the vote for the Republican presidential candidate and the vote for Negro suffrage: the coefficient of correlation stands at +0.91. This, coupled with the generally sweeping Republican victories, indicates that the party managers had done a good job of convincing the voters that "good" Republicans were also firm believers in the cause of equal rights at the polls. This figure is more astounding when one recalls that in 1857 Iowa voters had turned down Negro suffrage by an overwhelming 85.4 percent to 14.6 percent; now 66.5 percent voted for Negro suffrage and only 33.5 percent against it.[17]

Other comparisons were made in this highly detailed and exhaustive study. Voters in small towns (below 2,500) and in rural areas showed a slightly larger number of pro-Republican and proamendment votes than towns and cities above 2,500. Some relationship between economic conditions and voting patterns was found. Democratic orators, mostly from the larger towns and cities, harped on the Negro worker as an economic threat to white laborers. Therefore it was of some significance that the study revealed a higher degree of support for Negro suffrage in the prosperous rural areas than in the poorer ones, indicating that workers in prosperous areas harbored less fear of the Negro as a competitor than those in the poorer areas. On another point, using the data from the Daniels study of the Iowa foreign vote in the 1860 election, the investigators found that the townships in which foreign groups gave the highest Democratic vote were the very same townships with the lowest vote for the Negro suffrage amendment. Going further, they found that the townships which cast less than 10 percent of their votes for the amendment were the ones with the highest Democratic vote in 1860 and 1868. There were seven townships in this group and all showed over 48 percent foreign-born residents in the census of 1860.

The study proves that in the Reconstruction era, Iowa Republicans, as the dominant voting group in the state, were more consistent than Republicans in other states since they were willing to grant to Negroes in the North the privilege (admittedly at small cost) which they were demanding for Negroes in the South as a condition for readmission of the Southern states into the Union. The study also gives positive evidence, supplementing the platform statements, of a major difference between the two parties. Taken in conjunction with four other amendments which eliminated the word "white" from census and apportionment regulations, and another removing the word from qualifications for membership in the state militia, the Republicans had done as much as could be done *by law* to establish equality in voting. (One other point, the elimination of the word "white" as a qualification for membership in the General Assembly, was overlooked in 1866. This was corrected by amendment in 1880, at which time it was ratified by a 63.4 percent vote.) One further comment is that the 1868 action gives proof, if proof were needed, of the dominance of the Radical faction within the Republican party, and establishes the Democratic party as the true conservative party of the times.

Returning to the topic of factional politics, the senatorial election of 1870 proved to be the forerunner of bitter feelings between the pro-

and anti-Harlan forces, a continuation of the 1866 imbroglio. After James W. Grimes resigned in 1869 because of bad health—and not because of his anti-Radical vote in the Johnson case—the Grenville Dodge faction jumped into the fray in an effort to prevent the Harlan forces from electing one of their men to the vacant seat. Their first choice as a candidate was James F. Wilson. Still sulking in his tent after being passed over by President Grant for a cabinet post, Wilson rejected the call but suggested his colleague, William Boyd Allison of Dubuque, who agreed to run. The Harlan wing recruited and easily elected Judge George Grover Wright, since 1855 a member of the State Supreme Court, but thus insured themselves a bitter fight over Harlan's seat in 1872.[18]

THE FIFTEENTH AMENDMENT

In February 1869, after prolonged debate, Congress proposed to the states the ultra-Radicals' amendment: "The right of citizens of the United States to vote shall not be denied or abridged by the United States or by any State on account of race, color, or previous condition of servitude." Iowans in Congress had a spotty record on this amendment which was really a slap at those states which had denied the vote to Negroes, and the Republican-controlled General Assembly was slow to act. Wilson, Price, Allison, and Dodge voted for it in the national House but Asahel W. Hubbard of Sioux City refrained from voting and William Loughridge of Oskaloosa strangely voted nay, after speaking emphatically in its favor—the same Loughridge whom the Radicals had put in as replacement for the doubtful Josiah B. Grinnell in 1866! Only two other Republicans in the House voted against the proposal, thus putting Loughridge in a bad light. In the Senate Harlan voted for the amendment but Grimes was absent on the decisive ballot, the last of any importance remaining to him. In the fight for ratification, the votes of twenty-eight states were needed and Iowa was the twenty-seventh to ratify. Earlier action was not possible without a special session of the General Assembly, and Governor Samuel Merrill did not yield to the need for haste. When Iowa legislators at last got their chance to vote, January 26–27, 1870, the two houses delivered their overwhelming approval. (Nebraska's vote for ratification on February 17 cleared away all technical doubts as to the required number of ratifying states and the amendment was proclaimed to be a part of the Constitution on March 30, 1870.)[19]

THE HARLAN-ALLISON CONTEST OF 1872

Both Harlan and Allison had been victims of severe criticism in 1868, Allison for some questionable railroad deals and Harlan for the sale of some Cherokee Indian lands in Kansas on allegedly illegal terms during his short tenure as secretary of the interior. Even so, Harlan's candidate against Allison for the Republican nomination for the Senate in 1870 was selected, upholding Harlan as the accepted leader of the Republicans of Iowa. Now, with a friendly senatorial colleague, and in good standing with President Grant because of his strong support of Grant's recent effort to acquire Santo Domingo, and with the strong support of the powerful Methodist Church in Iowa, virtually an adjunct of the Republican party, Harlan appeared to be unbeatable in 1872 for reelection—but there were men with long memories of 1866 and 1870.

This time the Kirkwood-Dodge forces left nothing to chance. Allison was persuaded to run again and Dodge himself assumed full responsibility for the direction of the campaign. Candidates for the General Assembly were judged and assisted not on their merits but on their likelihood as pro-Allison or pro-Harlan voters. After the October elections had determined the membership of the assembly, the second round of the bidding contest began for their votes in the January countdown. Outright purchases by either group were probably rare but many subtle ways were available for winning a doubtful vote, such as a loan on generous terms, assistance in buying a newspaper, or finding a job for a friend or relative. The Allison camp revived the serious charges against Harlan's actions as secretary of the interior and seemingly had documentary proof. The switch of the *Des Moines Iowa State Register* from Harlan to Allison by young James S. Clarkson on December 13, 1871, could not have been anything more than a contributing factor to victory or defeat for "Father" Clarkson's favorite, Harlan, a fellow Hoosier and fellow Methodist. James F. Wilson's belated entry into the race indirectly helped Allison, it would seem, because Wilson as a veteran party member would tend to divide the old-line vote with Harlan.

On the night of January 10, 1872, the Republican members of the Fourteenth General Assembly met in the capitol for their caucus, where nomination was equivalent to election. All three candidates were present to direct their forces in the final drive. On the second formal ballot Allison won the designation by a single vote! Unfortunately for the historian, the caucus voting was "off the record" and beyond analysis. Soon after the caucus came the victory over the Democratic nominee put up for sacrificial slaughter, in this case Joseph F. Knapp of Keosauqua. And thus the great drama which had originated in the 1866 senatorial contest came to its climactic ending.[20]

Far more than a six-year term had been won by Allison. Because a party seldom repudiates an incumbent, Allison had really won a lifetime leasehold on the office. In addition, the power of the office and the party leadership would soon enable him to establish virtual control over the other seat. In four more years Judge Wright would tire of the Senate and return to the practice of law; then, one by one, came Allison's handpicked choices as his colleagues: Samuel J. Kirkwood, James F. Wilson,

John H. Gear, and Jonathan P. Dolliver. He would also have a large voice in the selection of gubernatorial candidates, congressional candidates, and aspirants for the General Assembly, all of whom were selected in easily controlled county, district, and state conventions.

Harlan's defeat was just as significant for him as victory was for Allison. It was a bitter pill for one so long accustomed to power. Never again would he be allowed to win a state or national office. He could not know this in 1872 but a long bleak road of twenty-seven years stretched out ahead of him, with nothing to brighten his gloom except a few empty honors. Sallies were made toward the governorship and again toward the Senate but always the way was barred, the door was closed, by the Allison machine. His help as a party orator was acceptable but aspiration for real power for himself was the signal for the start of another whispering campaign. A more complete example of political ruthlessness cannot be imagined.

In all this intraparty fighting in Iowa there was not even a passing reference to genuine issues, past, present, or future. Radicalism was not the issue in 1872 and the power of the Radicals was not under attack. Southern Reconstruction was a dead issue, of no interest to Iowans. The new Liberal Republican faction, to be discussed below, could have furnished leadership in a fight for reform but Allison was no liberal and neither was Harlan. The major pro-Harlan newspapers such as the *Burlington Hawk-Eye,* the *Sioux City Journal,* and the *Cedar Falls Gazette* editorially thundered against Allison, challenging the Allisonians to prove their charges against Harlan or admit their deceit. The challenge was not answered; it was simply ignored or drowned in a sea of words. When John P. Irish, a leading Democrat and editor of the *Iowa City State Press,* horned in on the Republicans' private fight and introduced a resolution in the Iowa House calling for an investigation by the United States Senate of the charges made against Harlan, the resolution was killed on the motion of John A. Kasson, a neutral in the fight, and Allison was home free.[21]

THE LIBERAL REPUBLICAN MOVEMENT, 1871–1872

A liberal reaction against the excesses of the Radical Republicans took shape in 1871, beginning in Missouri as an effort to drive a wedge into the Radical strength, and by national alliance with the Democrats to bring the country back to a more compassionate attitude toward the South, clean up the corrupt Grant administration, reform the civil service spoils system, and restore a more moderate tariff policy. In Iowa Republican leaders scorned this effort to clean up the Grant Republican administration. For all their interest in tariff reform, Allison, Wilson, and Kasson did not desert the main branch of their party. In Iowa the outstanding Liberal Republicans were Dr. E. A. Guilbert of Dubuque, David C. Cloud of Muscatine, Fitz Henry Warren of Burlington, and Joseph Eiboeck of Elkader, all of whom acknowledged the leadership of Josiah B. Grinnell, the erstwhile Radical until his virtual expulsion from that faction in 1866.[22]

Fate probably deprived the Liberals of a prestigious associate when James W. Grimes was forced by illness to resign from the Senate in 1869 and retire from public life. It is demonstrable that Grimes by 1870–1871 had become a liberal in his thinking and that his sympathies were on the side of the Liberal Republicans. We can never know if he might have assumed public leadership of the movement. His rapidly failing health prevented any political activity except a wide correspondence. In a letter to his old friend and colleague, Senator William Pitt Fessenden, one of the "Seven Martyrs" in the impeachment controversy, he bared his feelings about the "corruption" and "venality" in his party. Another letter to a good friend was equally severe in its condemnation of the moral standards of the party.[23]

The Liberal Republicans met in convention in Cincinnati in April 1872 and nominated Horace Greeley for president. Recent research has shown that this decision was not reached by political amateurs and starry-eyed reformers but by tough-minded professionals who were convinced that Greeley was their best man.[24] In Iowa the Liberal Republicans did not put on an energetic campaign. They carried through their part of the national alliance with the Democrats, even if it did require the impossible in the form of a reconciliation between the old Radical, Josiah B. Grinnell, and Dennis A. Mahony, the once-hated Peace Democrat. The Liberal Republican cause in Iowa was hopeless from the start. In Iowa Grant received 131,000 votes; Greeley, only 71,000. The New York editor carried only three counties in the whole of Iowa: staunchly Democratic Dubuque County, sometimes Democratic Scott County, both by sizable margins, and Fremont County on the western border by 31 votes. Even so, the Republican vote did not keep pace proportionately with the state's increase in population, indicating that many party members went somewhere besides the polls on election day rather than vote for Grant. Some of the Liberals returned to the party fold in 1876, some became Mugwumps in 1884, and their reform movement vanished into thin air.

CHAPTER 11 AGRARIAN RADICALISM: THE GREENBACK PROBLEM AND THE RAILROAD QUESTION 1865–1878

After the Civil War drew to a close, matters other than state politics commanded the attention of Iowans, for whom national affairs now became state affairs. This was not a simple age in which men could accept one challenge at a time, dispose of it, and move to the next one, all in neat chronological order. Nor did men group themselves under chosen political banners and remain there loyally for the rest of their days—it was an age of great political mobility. These were the years of Andrew Johnson and his war with the Radicals, described above; the years of "Grantism" and scandals which cried out for reform; of pronounced tariff controversy, and of the Silver Problem and the Greenback Problem. The Granger Movement idealistically championed many causes, and helped to curtail the economic and political power of the railroads. All the while there was the crying need for timely civil rights legislation.

Sooner or later the monetary problem caught up with everyone. As a wartime question which was bequeathed as a legacy to the postwar generation, it must be thought of as a part of Reconstruction history,[1] using that term to connote far more than mere restoration of the rebellious states to the Union. In this area of thought and action, Iowans were to be more involved than in Southern Reconstruction per se.

GREENBACKS AND GREENBACKISM

Since no nation can finance an extended war on a pay-as-you-go basis, part of the burden must be passed on as a debt to succeeding generations. An even more depressing thought is that this debt must always be an inflated debt, incurred by having to purchase goods and pay out wages, salaries, and interest at artificially inflated prices. The Civil War was no exception to this assertion. As described above, the

Lincoln administration found soon after the war's beginnings that it could not maintain Secretary Chase's policy of paying the government's debts in gold, and had to resort to the use of "printing press" money, that is, inconvertible or irredeemable paper money that could not be converted into specie on demand. These notes were called "legal tenders" in the parlance of the day because they were acceptable in the payment of certain obligations to the government; later they were better known as "greenbacks," pieces of paper printed and issued by the United States government's fiat. An additional measure authorized the floating of government bond issues as a means of borrowing from banks and individual investors, great and small, thereby greatly increasing the national debt. Still another related measure created a national banking system, partly for the purpose of securing a nationwide chain of fiscal agents to assist in the purpose of financing the war.

Of these three measures, it was the first which created the greatest and most enduring postwar economic problem, one which became a political issue, as well. By the war's end the amount of greenbacks in circulation totaled $450,000,000. This "money" had been accepted (though not at par with gold or silver) and used by the public from 1862 to 1865 as the only money readily available. The holders of this fiat money could only hope that someday the completely unsecured irredeemable paper money would become redeemable in specie.[2] (Of course, if that day ever came, the holders would not want to convert it.) At their lowest point, greenbacks were worth only 39 cents on the dollar in terms of gold or silver, except for those who could use them for paying obligations to the government, in the purchase of government bonds, or in subscribing capital for the organization of a national bank.

As soon as peace was achieved, the influence of Congressmen Hooper and Alley was thrown in the direction of "no more greenbacks" and a quick return to orthodox financing, a "stop the presses" policy which was topped by the "cremation" policy of Hugh McCulloch, secretary of the treasury, who burned the greenbacks as fast as they returned from circulation. It was this abandonment of greenbacks that had been anticipated with disfavor by Henry Clay Dean, the famous Iowa Peace Democrat. As early as 1864 Dean ventured beyond denunciation of the war into the realm of postwar economic adjustment. Speaking as a tribune for the debtor classes, Dean countered the Hooper-Alley and McCulloch policies by calling for more, not less greenbacks. He foresaw that retirement of the greenbacks would cause a ruinous deflation, with the debtors as the principal sufferers. By contrast, the bondholder and the shareholder had turned their 39-cent greenbacks into 100-cent dollars by converting them into government bonds or bank shares. Few Iowans noticed the "heretical" ideas of the much despised leader of the Peace Democrats but his plan was picked up by the *Cincinnati Enquirer* and developed into a serious monetary theory in opposition to Secretary Hugh Mc-

Culloch's antigreenback philosophy. From the realm of the printed word it was taken up as campaign material by Ohio's leading Democratic politician, George H. Pendleton, in 1866 and 1868, thus giving rise to the nickname, "Pendleton's Rag Babies," for this paper money.[3] Thus the controversial idea was transferred to the arena of national politics and from 1866 to 1884 the issue was a factor in many congressional races and at least two presidential elections.

THE GRANGER MOVEMENT: GRANGERISM

A great feature of the social and economic history of the postwar years, especially in the Midwestern states, was the influence of the farmers' organization, the Patrons of Husbandry, known far and wide as "The Grange" after the title of the local units. Founded in December 1867 by a Minnesota farmer and journalist, Oliver Hudson Kelley, for the moment a clerk in the Bureau of Agriculture in Washington, the organization enjoyed no real success until Kelley carried the idea to Midwestern states. Social and educational activities such as box suppers, spelling bees, expository essays, and debates served to relieve the monotony of rural life. The appeals of ritual and exclusiveness were not overlooked, Kelley putting his Masonic membership to good use as a source of ideas.[4]

Once the organization was well established, there followed the tendency to stress the economic grievances of farmers against railroads and storage elevators whose high rates and favoritism for certain shippers made farming a precarious business. Then came the decisive question: whether or not to go into politics in an effort to secure relief or remedy for their sufferings. Grange spokesmen on all levels were eloquently vehement as they denounced their economic oppressors but usually the organization stopped short of sponsoring candidates for office. The line between passage of resolutions of protest and actual participation in political party action might be a thin one, indeed, and the line was not the same in all localities. On one occasion certain members were rebuked as violators of the Grange charter and put down by the master of the Iowa State Grange for merely suggesting that he should make the race for governor! Recent research has shown that Kelley made statements before the founding which can be interpreted as anticipation on his part that the society would have a place for political action.[5] A great deal depends on the interpretation placed upon certain words. This much is clear: opponents of government regulation of railroads blamed the Grange for such an idea and called the restrictive legislation Granger Laws. Whether the statutes deserved such a name will be dealt with below.

It is evident that Iowa was a fertile field for the Grange organizers. In the early 1870s Iowa had the largest membership of any state in the

Union. In a decade when national membership approached the phenomenal figure of 1,000,000 members, Iowa's share attained a figure of 100,000, all of them owners or renters engaged in active farming, out of the 116,292 people in that category as reported by the census of 1870. These members were organized into 1,999 local Granges, more units than any other state could boast. The social structure and the economic interests of the Grange organization made a strong appeal to Iowa farm families and the character of the officers and chief recruiters was notably attractive. All thoughts of the promoters as rabble rousers of an agricultural frontier population must be rejected. Such leaders as William Duane Wilson, uncle of the future president; Dudley W. Adams of Cresco, a prosperous horticulturist; and Coker Fifield Clarkson of Grundy County, a prosperous farmer and principal owner of the *Des Moines Iowa State Register,* were not charlatans.[6]

Coker F. Clarkson deserves special notice not only as a Grange organizer but as a very superior type of migrant to Iowa from an older state. In 1855 he left a well-established home and newspaper in Brookville, Indiana, to come to Melrose Township in Grundy County, Iowa, where he and his sons bought land and began farming on an extended scale. Melrose Farm became famous as a model farm. Later Coker F. Clarkson added to his interests by buying the *Register,* which he edited with pronounced success, at the same time using it as a training school for his sons in the art of printing and in newspaper operation. "Father" Clarkson sold his interest in the paper to his sons in December 1871, at the height of the Allison challenge to James Harlan for the senatorship, and turned the editorial direction over to them, henceforth dividing his time and interests between his beloved farm and the writing of a popular column for farmers in the *Register.* He was an indefatigable researcher and experimenter in new methods of farming and stock-raising, ever on the search for ways and means to elevate the standard of living on the farms of Iowa. The Grange was an organization made to order for a man of his interests, and Oliver Hudson Kelley's philosophy was one that he could embrace with enthusiasm, and for which he became a highly successful recruiter. Herbert Quick used him as the prototype for the staunch Anti-Monopolist, Governor Wade, in *The Hawkeye.*[7]

THE ANTI-MONOPOLY MOVEMENT

A passing phase of the protest movement in Iowa against the railroads and other oppressive corporations, real or imagined, was the effort to create an Anti-Monopoly party in 1873–1874. In some respects this party, if such it may be called, would have continued the Liberal Republican effort to form an alliance with the Democrats, this time directing their energies against the forces which were accused of hurting the farmer and the small businessman instead of the more remote agencies of government. Nothing enduring came of the effort to form a new political party. Many leading Democrats were at first rather enthusiastic about the alliance but on second thought remembered that only a strong national government could enforce the laws which might be passed against monopolies—and a strong national government built up at the expense of states' rights was the very Leviathan which they feared and hated. There was nothing for such Democrats to do but retreat in confusion and let the movement die. Even so, the title of Anti-Monopoly would crop up from time to time, though without real meaning.[8] It might be observed that in rejecting this short-lived experiment in cooperation with these largely agrarian reformers the Democrats flubbed a chance to lure a good part of the farm vote away from the Republicans. The missed opportunity of 1873–1874 goes far in explaining the long-standing Republican domination of the rural vote in Iowa.

THE GRANGER LAWS

It was all too obvious that only the Republicans had the power to impose control over the railroads and other powerful corporations. Certain Republican leaders were quick to seize on this opening and assure the voters that the Republican party was the true "anti-monopoly" party of the day. Of course, not many businessmen were able to follow the logic that it was better for the corporations to be regulated by their friends than by their enemies. This did not deter the proponents of limited control from going ahead with their idea.

The problem originated in 1854 when the Chicago roads reached the banks of the Mississippi and then quickly tied in with eastern Iowa roads. The railroad bridges across the great river at Davenport (1856), Clinton (1864), and Dubuque (1868) contributed to a vast increase in traffic. The economy of Iowa was really at the mercy of the new carriers which were able to operate for years with almost no regulation by the state. The problem of regulation did not become serious until the 1860s when the energetic, hard-driving Chicago railroad men challenged the old-fashioned, easy-going methods of the river men. Heretofore, drovers would deliver their herds and farmers would bring their grain to the river ports such as Dubuque, Clinton, Davenport, Burlington, and Keokuk, where commission men and shipping magnates would buy their wares and take over the responsibility for the transportation to St. Louis, Memphis, and New Orleans and for the sales at these river ports. Now all this was changed. Chicago dealers invaded the Iowa market, helped along by Chicago-based railroads which arranged lower rates for the long haul than the short haul, openly favored one town against another, and granted rebates to favored shippers.

During every legislative session from 1860 to 1874 the most active battlers on the side of regulation were the river shippers, backed by merchants and commission men in the "way points" (towns which were located on one railroad only), businessmen whose profits were cut into by the new methods of transportation and the new markets. Farmers and farm organizations were not included in this partnership though undoubtedly some farmers were interested and helpful. Opposing them were the railroad owners and managers who feared any opening wedge of the power to regulate, and who called regulation a "confiscation" of their property rights. Backing up the railroad owners were the people from the western part of the state, as yet not served by railroads, who feared that regulation would drive railroad promoters to refuse to build any new lines. The operators of the roads secured some support by favors, the commonest being the gift of a "free pass" to people of influence.

The proregulation groups were brought together by common interests, not partisan politics. Most active of all proponents of regulation were the business interests of Dubuque, whose chief spokesman was Benjamin Billings Richards, sometime state senator and frequent candidate for governor and United States senator on the Democratic ticket, but on this matter a nonpartisan. Another prominent Dubuque Democrat was William Mills, a member of the legislature who in 1873 introduced and fought for a bill reputedly drafted by the brilliant Richards. This bill failed of passage by one vote.

Victory came at last, in 1874, to the river shippers and their allies. Although universally called the Granger Law, it should not be credited to the Grangers except as boosters for the idea of regulation. The act of 1874, which went on the books on March 19, was not drawn according to their specifications and they were not satisfied with it until some years later when changes were made in its terms. The authors of this misnamed Granger Law borrowed heavily from two Illinois Granger laws of 1871 and 1873. Governor Cyrus C. Carpenter, a Fort Dodge Republican with over two decades of military and civil service to the state, gave the cause a good push in his inaugural address when he recommended the adoption of the Illinois plan for the classification of railroads according to their earnings. Combining the "Dubuque formula," which featured the principle of a maximum rates clause plus the classification of the roads according to their earnings, made it possible to pass the bill. Always heretofore some faction had been able to hold out for its pet idea. This time the final drafting of the bill was the work of a committee of twelve Republicans and eleven Anti-Monopoly men, with Senator Frank T. Campbell, a reform-minded Republican from Newton, generously designated the author. Illinois experience was again called on to furnish a schedule of rates as already issued for roads in that state. Maximum freight rates were set *according to distance,* thus eliminating the long-and-short-haul problem. As for passenger fares, the roads were divided into classes according to their earnings, and fares restricted accordingly. Class A roads were those with earnings of $4,000 or more per year; Class B, those with earnings of $3,000 to $4,000 per year; Class C, those with earnings under $3,000 per year. Passenger fares were limited to three, three and one-half, and four cents per mile, as determined by a road's earning power.

The law did not work out as planned or expected. The railroad owners found that their opposition had been misplaced; instead of expected losses they surprisingly made increased profits. As for the river shippers at Dubuque and other river ports, they soon discovered to their dismay that the new rates did not result in increased inland shipments to the river towns. More and more they saw shipments going on to Chicago and even to Atlantic ports. On the basis of the lessons learned, both sides were willing to modify the law four years later.[9] One prominent Iowan, Representative George W. McCrary, saw that the problem was one demanding federal regulation and introduced a bill in Congress to that effect, thirteen years before such a law could be passed in 1887. James S. Clarkson, editor of the *Des Moines Iowa State Register,* was a convert to federal regulation in 1876.[10]

Iowa was not alone in the drive to bring the railroads under some degree of control. Illinois, Minnesota, and Wisconsin were notable in their efforts in the same direction. As for the roads, they were divided in their attitudes toward the act of 1874; some were loud in their defiance, others somewhat mixed in their views. When the time came for action, only the Burlington Road refused to accept the legislation without a legal struggle. A suit was brought asking for an injunction to prevent the state attorney general from enforcing the law against the road. The case was heard in early 1875 in the United States Circuit Court sitting at Davenport, Judge John Francis Dillon presiding. David Rorer of Burlington, chief of the road's legal staff, assisted by special counsel Orville H. Browning of Quincy, formerly secretary of the interior, and the eminent James Grant of Davenport, prepared the case for the railroad. They argued that the state had violated the law of contracts, violated the federal constitution by regulating interstate commerce, and violated the state constitutional requirement for uniform application of all laws by dividing the roads into three classes. A court decision in Wisconsin in 1874, upholding the Potter Law, which was similar to the Iowa act of 1874, should have been a warning to the railroads that a new philosophy was now sweeping the land. When it came, Judge Dillon's ruling was clear and unmistakable: the right of a state to regulate commerce within the state was affirmed and the prayer for the injunction was denied.[11]

On advice of counsel, the ruling by Judge Dillon was at once appealed to the Supreme Court of the United States. The C.B.&Q. was not challenging the right of a state to regulate a corporation but the directors were convinced that their property rights had been taken away without due process of law. This conviction on the part of the railroad management rested on a new concept of property rights advocated by the new counsel employed by the road. Although not finding fault with the services of Rorer, Browning, and Grant, the directors added as new counsel five of the most eminent attorneys in the whole country, including Senator Frederick T. Frelinghuysen of New Jersey, to join Browning as advocates before the Court. The directors further stated that they were not acting for the benefit of the C.B.&Q. alone but for all property owners everywhere.

The brief drawn up by these attorneys, in conference with other counsel representing all parties which were attacking the Granger laws, incorporated all the points in the Rorer brief in the previous trial but broke new ground by adding an original concept of property, taken from an obscure case entitled *Bartemeyer* v. *Iowa,* in which Justice Samuel F. Miller had stated that a prohibition law might be so rigid that it not only took away a dealer's liquor but even the right to do business. In short, *property* might be more than mere tangible physical substance; it might be thought of as an asset which could rise and fall in value.

The Burlington's counsel went on to argue that the state of Iowa had deprived the C.B.&Q. of its property, defined as a business asset, without due process of law. In this instance, by setting a maximum rate for the railroad's services, the road was prevented from making enough profit to make certain payments which were due to the Burlington & Missouri Railroad, which the C.B.&Q. had leased; also, the rights of holders of C.B.&Q. bonds were impaired by the Iowa act of 1874 because the investors in the bonds had bought them on an understanding of the ability of the road to make payments of interest and principal, an ability now jeopardized by the effects of the law of 1874.

This was a very clever application of the "property as an asset" principle. It proved to be in vain in this particular case. The majority opinion, handed down by Chief Justice Waite, and resting on a rigidly orthodox interpretation of the law of property, upheld Judge Dillon's ruling completely. Much more significant for the future was the dissenting opinion of Justice Stephen J. Field, who boldly accepted the philosophy of property as a business asset, a doctrine which would soon become the concept of the courts of the future. In this sense, the exemplar of judicial competence was not Judge Dillon, whose praises have been so widely sung, but Justice Field. Nor should one forget David Rorer, the brilliant attorney in the small city of Burlington, whose brief before Judge Dillon's court had pointed the way to the new concept of property which was taken over *in toto* by the counsel who prepared the appeal to the Supreme Court.[12]

The railroads now changed tactics. A twofold campaign was carried out to get the 1874 law repealed. Newspapers were supplied with "educational" material in favor of the railroads, mostly to the effect that Eastern moneyed men would not invest a dollar in new railroad ventures in Iowa until the sacred rights of property owners to manage their own businesses without state interference was guaranteed. Figures were cited by the roads to show that there had been almost no new construction since the law of 1874 had been put on the books. (This was true, but the spokesmen for the roads carefully refrained from saying that little building had taken place anywhere since the Panic of 1873.) The other method of fighting the law was to help friendly candidates for the legislature into office, as brought to light many years after the fact by the admission of Charles Aldrich, one of the great names in Iowa newspaper history, that he had spent six weeks assisting candidates in northern Iowa at the request of the Illinois Central Railroad.

These methods were sufficient to secure a repeal vote, 55 to 43 in the House, and 29 to 21 in the Senate. The word "repeal" was widely used but it was a misnomer. The new law was actually not an abandonment but rather a modification of the 1874 law. Regulation was not forsworn; simply the method of regulation was changed. The new law established a Railroad Commission of three appointed members, the very thing that the Grange had wanted in 1874, but now their salaries were to be paid by assessments on the railroads, *a plan which the Grange did not want.* Although the governor would do the appointing, with confirmation by the Senate, the roads could exert much influence in the selections. Much depended on the determination of a governor to see to it that the interests of the people were put first. Most of those who wanted regulation as a protection of the public interests knew that the law was not perfect and that it would have to be amended from time to time as knowledge of the problems grew and legal means were perfected to deal with them.[13]

NEW DEVELOPMENTS IN THE MONEY PROBLEM: TOO MUCH SILVER

In the 1870s the quest for a solution of the money problem took on new aspects. The forces in favor of inflation seemed to be hopelessly deadlocked with those favoring deflation. There were Iowans in both camps but the inflationists were more vocal, probably more numerous. Years of debate and unplanned experimentation had not produced a satisfactory answer in the form of either more or fewer greenbacks. And now, shortly after 1873, a silver problem was added to the fight over greenbacks. It was a matter of indifference to most inflationists whether their goal was attained by one medium or the other. Iowans took prominent parts as champions of each.

A few elementary facts are essential to an understanding of this problem. As far back as 1792 Congress had decreed that a silver dollar should contain 371.25 grains of fine silver (or 412.50 grains with alloys added). For years prior to 1873, that number of grains of fine silver bullion would bring not merely $1.00 but about $1.03 on the open market, measured in terms of gold. The government had to pay this premium to obtain the silver necessary for the small coins needed in business but it had no calls for silver dollars. After consideration by five different sessions of Congress and much public debate, Congress passed a coinage act on February 12, 1873, which, among other things, dropped the silver dollar from the list of mintable coins. At the moment little notice was taken of this routine act of Congress, but such bliss of unconcern was soon to be broken by the loud cries of silver bullion owners and the debtor classes who shouted that a "crime" had been committed—the "Crime of '73."

For many years the standard textbook explanation of this "crime" has been that dropping the silver dollar was the result of a combination of fortuitous events: adoption of the gold standard by Germany in 1871 and the threat of France and other European countries to do likewise (a threat carried out in 1874). When new silver lodes were discovered shortly after the passage of the act, silver mine owners who were eager to sell their product, backed up by spokesmen for the debtor classes everywhere, charged that the new coinage act was the result of a conspiracy between Eastern bankers and British money interests, who had persuaded Congress by devious means to demonetize silver and, in effect, force the United States on the gold standard. For years to come millions of people would repeat this charge with such fervor that it became the emotional basis for widespread political appeal and action. Writers and commentators were content to repeat the charge without investigation of the facts.

Recent research has shown that the charge of an evil conspiracy between British and American bankers was not well founded. Some international bankers and some members of Congress were acting in cooperation, but not with evil intentions. They were better able than the masses to judge the effects of the decision of European countries to go on the gold standard, and for years they had been alarmed by the constantly increasing annual output of American silver mines. They knew that the law of supply and demand would ultimately bring about a decline in the price of silver. Foreseeing clearly the inevitable devaluation of silver and the rampant inflation which would follow if silver coinage were maintained by law, the dropping of the silver dollar was in their opinion a beneficent act, not a "crime." The only "conspiracy" was the collaboration of George A. Boutwell, secretary of the treasury, with Senator John Sherman in persuading Congress to pass an act for the good of the people, that is, "good" for them in terms of the economic laws then prevailing.[14] At the time, however, the masses and many of their better educated leaders sincerely believed that a real conspiracy had been entered into and they acted accordingly.

THE POLITICAL REVOLT OF 1874–1875: THE REJECTION OF GENERAL WEAVER

The general depression, brought on by the Panic of 1873 and the excitement created by the silver situation, bred a small-scale political revolt in the West in 1874. Other states were more seriously affected than Iowa, where the supremacy of the Republicans was so great that the protest coalition party, the Anti-Monopoly–Democrats, could elect only one candidate for Congress, Captain Lucius L. Ainsworth of West Union, a former War Democrat and Civil War veteran of excellent reputation. Other states produced numerous victories for radical spokesmen for agrarian and small-town interests.

In the middle of this decade of unrest, Iowa Republicans enacted a little drama of their own, one which was to help to produce long-range state and national political consequences. In 1875 there were numerous aspirants for the party's nomination for the office of governor, of whom General James B. Weaver of Bloomfield, a prestigious Civil War veteran and orthodox Republican, was the apparent front-runner. His connections with the Greenback movement were not yet very extensive; he was better known for his pronounced enthusiasm for Prohibition. At the time there was a growing sentiment in favor of prohibitory legislation against the sale of alcoholic beverages throughout America. Perhaps a clear majority believed that the people had a right to legislate on the subject, while opponents of the idea said that it was wrong for a portion of the people to dictate the morals of the entire population.

This argument over sumptuary legislation was nothing new, of course; the "Maine Law" of 1846 and its later versions served as models for other states to follow. Most of the founders of the Republican party in Iowa had been favorably inclined toward Prohibition, and they had enacted the mild prohibitory law of 1855 in spite of having to placate the Know-Nothings. Now there was a very vocal anti-Prohibition wing of the party, definitely in the minority but marked by the prestige of its members, led by former Governor Kirkwood. Democrats had no such problems, the German and Irish groups which dominated the party being almost unanimously against Prohibition. These groups, mostly Roman Catholic in religion, regarded Prohibition as a product of evangelical, pietistic Protestantism, whose cultural values were in direct conflict with the European traditions which had shaped the thinking of the immigrants. In this matter, General Weaver had fallen into disfavor with some Republican party regulars, not so much because he was a Prohibitionist but because he was on this subject, as on others, inclined to be an extremist, an emotional idealist rather than a political realist.

When the nominating convention was held on June 30 in Des Moines, it was soon apparent that a strong pro-Weaver sentiment was sweeping the delegates into his camp. The anti-Weaver minority did not dare upset this trend and force another candidate on the party unless they could offer a well-known and popular party regular, such as former Governor Kirkwood, who could overcome the bad feeling which would follow any move to ditch Weaver. The maneuvering which followed would have done credit to any political machine of fact or fancy. First, the anti-Weaver group threw the delegates into an uproar by an unexpected but well-staged nominating speech for Kirkwood, unparliamentary but effective. The convention was then turned to other considerations to gain time while telegrams could be sent to Iowa City imploring the doughty old war governor to accept a nomination. Kirkwood had his heart set on the senatorship which would be filled in the forthcoming legislative session and he was honorably opposed to the idea of taking the governorship for a few months only to abandon it if he could win the higher office, which was pretty well conceded to him. At the same time he was somewhat afraid that the legislature might not elect him to the Senate if he took the governor's office.

As an extreme precautionary measure, certain leaders arranged to use a railroad engine and make the hundred-mile trip to Iowa City under forced draft to call in person on the reluctant veteran of so many political wars and persuade him to save the party from the man they did not like. Much against his wishes and better judgment, Kirkwood gave them grudging consent to use his name. The word was flashed to Des Moines; the convention was stampeded, to use James S. Clarkson's word, Weaver was shunted aside, and Kirkwood was formally nominated.

The sequel followed the scenario precisely. Kirkwood was elected governor, thanks in part to Weaver's good grace in accepting the convention's decision and his willingness to campaign for Kirkwood. Then in January 1876, almost as soon as he had been inaugurated as governor, the General Assembly elected Kirkwood to the Senate over a field of able candidates, including former Senator Harlan, General William W. Belknap, currently secretary of war, and former Representative Hiram Price of Davenport. On February 1, 1877, Kirkwood resigned his governorship after a year of nominal service, to be replaced by Lieutenant Governor Joshua G. Newbold. Very few pro-Weaver people were aware of the details of the clever scheme used to defeat them, and few Republicans were ever aware of this factor in General Weaver's later switch from the Republican party to the vagaries of third-party politics, as a Greenbacker.[15]

THE IMPEACHMENT OF SECRETARY BELKNAP

A totally unexpected dividend from the Kirkwood victory was the escape from a victory by General Belknap. Before the Kirkwood entry into the race for senator, in January 1876, Belknap, who cut a dashing figure and dominated every social occasion, had very likely prospects for victory. The *Des Moines Iowa State Register* under James S. Clarkson was his principal backer. Kirkwood was easily victorious over Belknap and the other aspirants, a very fortunate turn of events for Iowa Republicans because in all innocence they might have made Belknap their senator-elect. Less than two months after the election, Belknap was accused of selling army post traderships. He instantly resigned from office, indicating either a sense of guilt or a great desire to protect the name of his wife, who was accused of complicity in the receipt of kickbacks on the sales. President Grant accepted the resignation with unseemly haste. In spite of his resignation Belknap was impeached. After a lengthy trial by the Senate he escaped conviction, a number of senators taking the ground that he was beyond the Senate's jurisdiction because his resignation was handed in prior to the impeachment. Senator Allison took this technical position while his colleague, George G. Wright, one of Iowa's greatest jurists, took the position that the Senate had jurisdiction but guilt had not been proved "beyond a reasonable doubt."[16]

GREENBACKISM AND RESUMPTION

While the silver question was coming to the front, the agitation for and against greenbacks finally found a partial solution, one which satisfied no one but which was acceptable to all except the diehards at either end of the spectrum. The results of the elections of 1874 may have had something to do with speeding up a decision to do something quickly about greenbacks. Rather than wait and allow the few successful third party radicals to join with the Democrats and the fiscally unorthodox Republicans, such as Iowa's Senator George G. Wright, to produce drastic and upsetting monetary legislation when they came to Congress in December 1875, the Republican leaders of the outgoing Congress hammered out a compromise bill which was passed in January 1875 in an effort to head off the "wild ones." A prominent member of this little knot of Republicans was Iowa's Senator William B. Allison. This act provided for the "resumption" of specie payments, that is, the redemption of greenbacks in specie, on and after January 1, 1879. The four-year delay was written into the bill so that the treasury would have time to accumulate a stock of gold and silver coins to exchange for the hitherto irredeemable paper money. The bill of 1875 provided for retaining $300,000,000 in greenbacks in circulation but in 1878 the unhappy Greenbackers managed to secure a compromise which set the figure at whatever amount of greenbacks might be outstanding at the bill's effective date.[17] This amount proved to be $346,000,000, a figure long carried on the books of the treasury, giving substance to the theory that someday there might be a demand for redemption in specie, an action which has never taken place. Except for a few rare specimens reposing in museums and collectors' vaults, all other greenbacks of this vintage have long since disappeared, victims of attrition in usage. No one presented the notes for conversion, of course, because paper money which is redeemable at par is more convenient to use than specie.

The Greenbackers were not pleased with this development and continued their efforts to flood the country with irredeemable paper money. Many Iowans, notably Dennis A. Mahony, the famous Peace Democrat during the Civil War, and Josiah B. Grinnell, the former Republican congressman, now a man without political moorings, joined in this effort. In 1876 a Greenback party was organized and Peter Cooper of New York was nominated for president, securing only 81,000 votes. After the great railroad strike of 1877, which the C.B.&Q. fought tooth and nail in Iowa, the Greenbackers merged with the labor dissidents to form the Greenback-Labor party which was able to elect two congressmen in Iowa, General James B. Weaver of Bloomfield and Edward H. Gillette of Des Moines, who not only won victories in Iowa but ably assisted candidates in other states by speaking in their behalf. Besides their two victories in Iowa, twelve other Greenback-Labor men were elected to Congress in 1878. This was the peak of the movement. In 1880 Weaver polled only 308,000 votes for president on a Greenback-Labor ticket; in 1884 the eccentric General Benjamin F. Butler polled only 175,000 votes under the same label. In Iowa the Republicans found it necessary to bring home John A. Kasson from his diplomatic post in Vienna to beat Gillette for a second term in 1880. After this flurry of Greenback activity, the movement subsided and the new protest vote was registered under other labels.[18]

CHAPTER 12 AGRARIAN RADICALISM: THE SILVER PROBLEM AND POPULISM

1878–1900

IN SEARCH OF A RETROSPECTIVE VIEW OF THE IMMEDIATE POST-Civil War decades, it would be difficult to find anything credible to say either in high praise or extreme derogation of the general run of Iowa's political leaders and their followers. There was not much to generate excitement except the developments in federal monetary legislation, the beginnings of railroad regulation, and a fight over Prohibition. The Republican party, riding its Civil War reputation, was firmly in the saddle and nomination in its caucuses and conventions was normally equivalent to election. Republicans seldom had any worries except internal disputes; other parties could at best deliver a protest vote. Typical office seekers were average men who were able to parlay a veteran's status and some local distinction into membership in the General Assembly; some managed to move up to office on the state level, and the chosen few won election as governor or congressmen, or worked the spoils system for good appointments. Military rank was an asset, and status as a Civil War veteran and as a member of the G.A.R. was helpful though not absolutely necessary. A veterans' reunion was hardly more than a Republican rally. The quality sought for in nominees might well be expressed in the word "safe," meaning reliability with respect to the preservation of the status quo and immunity against Democratic attacks and exposures.

LATE NINETEENTH-CENTURY IOWA: A PERIOD OF DRIFT

Iowa politics reflected the unexciting nature of life in Iowa in this period, so wonderfully pictured in Ruth Suckow's fiction and James Norman Hall's poems attributed to Fern Gravel.[1] For twenty years or more all the governors after Kirkwood were "safe"—and undistinguished. Their pictures appear in the various "mug books" with the dates of their incumbency; their stereotyped inaugural addresses appear in Shambaugh's *Messages of the Governors of Iowa*—and there is little else to say about them. For the record, here is the list: Colonel William Milo Stone, Knoxville, 1864–1868; Captain Samuel H. Merrill, McGregor, 1868–1872; Colonel Cyrus C. Carpenter, Fort Dodge, 1872–1876; Samuel J. Kirkwood, Iowa City, 1876–1877; Captain Joshua G. Newbold, Mount Pleasant, 1877–1878; John H. Gear, Burlington, 1878–1882; Captain Buren R. Sherman, Vinton, 1882–1886. All were Republicans; all except Gear and Kirkwood were Civil War veterans, and Kirkwood had been in office as governor during most of the war. Omitting Kirkwood, whose name, as has been shown, should never have been on the ballot for 1875, only Gear among the others would ever show the ability to rise to a higher office, and one would be hard put to prove that his record in public office was truly distinguished. Carpenter was a bit above average, making a real contribution to the Railroad Act of 1874. After brief service on the Iowa Railroad Commission in 1878, he had two inconspicuous terms in Congress, followed by an anticlimactic stint as fourth assistant auditor in the War Department.[2] Perhaps Carpenter's experience typifies the dullness and the isolation of Iowa public life. There were no major scandals; there were few major accomplishments. The Iowa of this era might be described as calm, complacent, and comfortable, or, as someone put it, Iowa was one of several states filled with "corn, cattle, and contentment."

The state's population was growing but not at the rapid tempo of earlier decades. In 1880 the total population was 1,624,615, representing a growth rate of only 76 percent for the previous decade, compared with 251.1 percent and 345.8 percent, respectively, for the two previous decades, 1850–1870. An astute student of Iowa population figures has shown that the year 1880 was truly a turning point in Iowa history, the first year in which the census showed that the rural population had stopped growing, indicating that henceforth rural numbers would decline unless some unforeseeable happening should change the trend. This, in turn, would indicate that any increase in Iowa's total population would have to come from the growth of population in the towns and cities.[3] Yet there were no great metropolitan centers as of 1880 and none in prospect. Des Moines was the largest city, at 22,408, having overtaken and surpassed Dubuque and Davenport. The capital city would grow to 50,093 in 1890 and 62,139 in 1900.[4]

Of the total population in 1880, 261,650 were foreign-born, practically all of European origins. In 1890 the state's population had risen to 1,912,297, of whom 324,920 were foreign-born, the highest ratio ever between these two factors.[5] By 1900 the total population had again risen, this time to 2,231,853, but the number of foreign-born had slipped to 305,782. Looking ahead, since that date both absolute and relative numbers of foreign-born have gone down steadily. This constant decline over a period of eighty years indicates that a potent source of population growth for the state has disappeared. As for other minority groups, the Indians were long ago dispossessed and shifted to reservations in other states or territories (except for the small group of Mesquakie near Tama), and until recently Negroes made up less than 1 percent of the population of Iowa.

THE SILVER PROBLEM: THE BLAND-ALLISON ACT OF 1878

The great curse of the 1878–1900 period was the lack of general prosperity. The cure for this condition, according to some, was an increase in (inflation of) the circulating currency. Paralleling the Greenbackers' efforts to secure an unrestricted use of paper currency was an effort after 1875 to secure the unlimited (free) coinage of silver dollars at the ratio of 16 to 1, silver to gold, regardless of the market value of silver. Many Iowans persuaded themselves of the correctness and justice of this proposition and all the members of the Iowa House delegation voted consistently in favor of a greater use of silver.

The chief sponsor and spokesman for free silver, though no advocate of runaway inflation, was a Missouri congressman, Richard Parks Bland. After several unsuccessful efforts to get a free silver bill through the House, Bland finally succeeded in December 1877, all nine Iowa members voting for the bill. The rejoicing of the silverites was of short duration. When the Bland bill went to the Senate the terms were severely modified by the Committee on Finance. For this piece of legislative surgery the chief credit goes to Iowa's Senator William Boyd Allison, though not for the reasons usually assigned for his action. The Iowan, speaking for Midwestern states on this occasion, was not yet the ally of the Eastern financial interests that he tended to become in his later years. Instead, whatever his personal monetary philosophy might have been, he held to the views of a state which was clearly in favor of free silver. In proposing the limitations to the Bland bill which take their name from him, Allison was primarily seeking the smallest degree of legislative compromise which could command the two-thirds vote necessary to pass *any* silver bill over the promised veto of President Hayes. Consequently, the Allison amendments were moderate and restrictive enough to secure the support of some Eastern sources of financial conservatism. Instead of unlimited coinage of silver dollars, the secretary of the treasury was instructed to buy not less than $2,000,000 and not more than $4,000,000 worth of silver bullion monthly, and coin that silver into dollars, regardless of the number. In addition, the bill was made to speak out firmly in favor of bimetalism, and an international conference was prescribed which would deal with this subject.

The Senate passed the Bland bill as thus modified by the Allison amendments by a vote of 48 to 21, 7 not voting; the House accepted the Senate version, 196 to 71, again all Iowans voting in the affirmative. Thus the gauntlet was thrown down to President Hayes. That stern and unbending believer in financial orthodoxy delivered an unhesitating veto which was duly set aside by a larger vote than in the first instance. The whole process was finalized in February 1878. If the Free Silver people felt cheated, just as the Greenbackers had felt cheated by the Resumption Act, it was President Hayes, not Allison, who should have received their rebukes.[6]

The disaster predicted by many if even a limited silver bill were passed, did not materialize. President Hayes instructed his secretary of the treasury, John Sherman, to buy the minimum allowable amount of silver bullion, $2,000,000 worth per month, and Presidents Garfield, Arthur, Cleveland, and Harrison followed suit. At the prevailing price of silver, $2,000,000 would buy enough bullion to make more than two million "dollars" containing the prescribed 371.25 grains of silver per dollar—but not many more. The year-to-year coinage of $24,000,000 worth of silver bullion varied from 28,000,000 to 39,000,000 "dollars." The difference between the annual cost, $24,000,000, and the number of "dollars" coined, represented the amount of inflation caused by the act.[7] Thus it is demonstrable that Allison's prophecy of a moderate and endurable inflation was fulfilled. As seen from a later viewpoint, the 1878 silver act was a mild experiment in deliberate inflation, a pre-Keynesian program of money management long before Keynes was born. It was what a majority of the people of Iowa and the West wanted at the time—and the term "agrarian radicals" thrown at its sponsors and supporters is badly misplaced.

PROHIBITION POLITICS

There was a strong effort in these times to halt the sale and use of alcoholic liquors as beverages, an effort covered by the sweeping and all-inclusive term, "Prohibition." Republican advocates of this policy were able to overcome, or thought they had overcome, the opposition of a minority of their own party, led by ex-Governor Kirkwood, and the opposing Democrats as well, and secure a prohibitory law in the form of a constitutional amendment. After two passages through the General Assembly, in 1880 and 1882, the proposal then met the further requirement of popular ratification, by a vote of 155,436 to 125,677, and the amendment became effective on July 28, 1882. Ratification had been given in a special election in which the prohibition issue had not been confused with any other voting proposition.

Opponents of the amendment lost no time in attacking the new law. Suit was brought in Davenport and an opinion quickly given, in

October 1882, by Judge Walter I. Hayes of Clinton, who ruled against the amendment in the case of *Kohler & Lange* v. *Hill* on the technicality that the House and Senate versions of the amendment were not identical in language. Reacting furiously, the Prohibitionists appealed the case to the State Supreme Court. A brilliant array of legal counsel was recruited to argue the case, notably Senator-elect James F. Wilson and John F. Duncombe for the Prohibitionists, and ex-Senator George G. Wright, a former chief justice of the Court, for the opponents of the amendment. Oddly enough, Duncombe, a Fort Dodge Democrat and attorney for the Illinois Central Railroad, was not a proponent of Prohibition, whereas Judge Wright was a strong temperance man. Duncombe was retained by the Prohibitionists because of his standing at the very top of his profession, while Judge Wright was willing to serve the anti-Prohibitionists because of his belief that Prohibition was an unwarranted interference with personal freedom.

The Supreme Court acted with dispatch. In an opinion handed down by Justice William H. Seevers, the ruling made by Judge Hayes was upheld. The Prohibitionists petitioned for a rehearing but this plea was denied by the Court, Justice James G. Day speaking for the majority. A great volume of abuse was showered on Judge Day, as if he should have violated his judicial oath in order to uphold the Prohibition cause. In the Republican State Convention which met shortly afterward, Justice Day was publicly repudiated and set aside as their nominee in favor of Joseph R. Reed. The Democrats obliged by nominating Judge Hayes as their candidate, and the election became a sort of unofficial referendum on Prohibition. Kirkwood openly advocated a "scratch" of the ticket by anti-Prohibition Republicans, advice which apparently was not followed by enough of the faithful to defeat Reed.

As an important sequel to this action, the Prohibition forces in the next General Assembly were able to put through a strong version of of the old law of 1855, a form of local option plus the use of informers and trials before justices of the peace, both paid according to the number of convictions, a very unsatisfactory arrangement. In 1894 the Mulct Law was passed, a curious law under which a saloonkeeper could be fined $600 or more, if local officials so decreed, for operating a saloon which had been approved by a local option election! This strange law was upheld by the State Supreme Court and somehow served to keep the traffic in liquor at a minimum, which pleased nearly everyone. In the meanwhile Republican allegiance was badly deranged by prolonged arguments and bad feeling over the question, in spite of an effort not to make belief in Prohibition a test of Republicanism.[8]

WILLIAM LARRABEE AND RAILROAD REGULATION

Iowa's actions in the area of railroad regulation were a very important part of the national movement in this direction, though not ahead of those in Illinois, Wisconsin, and Minnesota. The acts of 1874 and 1878 were nationally recognized as important contributions to the problem of control of the roads. On their side, the railroad owners were opposed to even a small degree of regulation, as witness a constant flow of lawsuits and legislative efforts to overthrow the act of 1878 and the supplementary act of 1884.

It is in this atmosphere of conflict that the two terms of Governor William Larrabee (1886–1890) must be studied. A Republican state senator from 1868 to 1885, defeated in a try for his party's nomination for governor in 1881 but successful in 1885, this wealthy landowner, banker, and small-town industrialist of Clermont, who had voted against the act of 1874, might appear to be the last man in Iowa disposed to lead a crusade for railroad regulation.

Although Larrabee's pre-1885 legislative career had not been marked by extreme attacks on the railroads, neither had he been naively on their side. He was aware of their discriminatory practices and he was generally in favor of a system of regulation to correct the worst abuses. He had voted against the act of 1874, not because in his opinion such regulation was not needed, but because he thought the act did not go far enough! He had helped to draw up and had voted for the act of 1878, a fact which illustrates that the "repeal" act, as it is called, was in truth a modification to put teeth into the act of 1874. Keeping the best of the old law, it added provisions for a three-man advisory and supervisory commission and for annual reports by the commission to the governor. (When voting for this bill, Larrabee could not have known what effective use he would one day make of such reports!) In 1884 he had voted for an act which strengthened the Board of Railroad Commissioners. These things should have been known by the railroad owners and managers.

In 1885, when the Republicans were alarmed by the results of the election of Cleveland and other Democrats in 1884, Larrabee was thought of as an "available" candidate for governor: activist enough as a railroad critic to please the masses, yet "safe" in the opinion of James S. "Ret" Clarkson, editor of the *Des Moines Iowa State Register.* As manager for the party affairs for the railroad magnates and other business interests who supplied most of the sinews of political warfare, Clarkson was expected to keep down the worst of the elements who were demanding state regulation of the roads. Neither Larrabee nor Clarkson nor anyone else could prevent the party convention in 1885 from adopting a fairly strong antirailroad platform. The Democrats took a similar stand and therefore the voter had little choice between Larrabee and the Democratic standard-bearer, Charles E. Whiting of Monona County. In their closest call since 1854, the Republicans won, 175,504 to 168,525, in a campaign more notable for mudslinging than rational discussion of the issues.

The legislative session of 1886 went by without anything more exciting than talk about the abolition of "free passes." Late in 1886, however, and carrying over into 1887, a seemingly innocent little hassle between Governor Larrabee and President Charles E. Perkins of the Burlington Road was blown up into a major quarrel. The argument originated in the governor's discovery that this road was charging more for carrying coal from the Lucas County coalfields to Glenwood, where a state institution was located, than for carrying the same freight to Council Bluffs, twenty-three miles farther. A protracted correspondence followed. Larrabee gathered his facts and supporting statistics with great care, virtually handling the case by himself when for some reason the Railroad Commission backed away from the encounter. President Perkins reacted defiantly by raising, not lowering, the charges. Larrabee then gathered more figures, including a bill for $3,326.40 for overcharges, and demanded a hearing before the commission. The governor turned this occasion (April 9, 1887) into a combined exposé of the Burlington Road and an attack on the commission for nonfeasance. At last, but too late, the spokesman for the C.B.&Q. admitted his error and tried to make peace.

It so happened that just as the Larrabee-Perkins quarrel was heating up, Congress completed the passage of the Interstate Commerce Act on February 4, 1887. Instead of alleviating the trouble, the immediate effect was to make it worse. The roads lowered their through rates while increasing their local rates. This proved to be a very shortsighted move. Waves of protest arose and Larrabee suddenly found himself supported by editors throughout the state. In the fall elections, not only did the antirailroad forces, the Iowa Farmers' Alliance, the Grange, and the Union Labor party, elect forty-nine out of the one hundred members of the House but Larrabee himself was reelected by 169,000 to 153,000 for the Democrat, Thomas J. Anderson. Both men were antirailroad, and the prorailroad group could not overlook the sting and the significance of the defeat.

With this endorsement and the support of the state press, Governor Larrabee could and did become more aggressive. The legislature left no doubt of its mood of determination to force the roads to come under stricter control, so much so that reform was almost the victim of its friends as one man after another sought the credit and the honor of the sponsorship of the bills. Several should be singled out for their contributions: J. H. Sweney of Osage, Lafayette Young of Atlantic, James G. Berryhill of Des Moines, John T. Hamilton of Cedar Rapids, Abraham B. Funk of Spirit Lake, and, most of all, Representative Albert Baird Cummins, a young Des Moines lawyer and Independent Republican serving his first and only term in the state legislature. Cummins was truly outstanding as Larrabee's chief lieutenant in the General Assembly and a political partnership was begun here which was to yield handsome dividends to Cummins in later years.

The House passed the bill, 89 to 0, and sent it to the Senate, where it was amended and passed, 44 to 0. The resultant joint conference committee worked out a compromise which the House then approved, 74 to 0, and the Senate, 41 to 0; the governor signed it on April 5, 1888. These details are given in such exactitude not to indicate real unanimity, but rather the fear of the opposition of being placed in an adverse position before the public. During the struggle, Governor Larrabee was the very essence of the "strong" executive rather than the "weak" or passive type envisaged by the makers of most state constitutions in the eighteenth and nineteenth centuries. Indeed, he probably strained the proprieties as he worked with committees and sat in on legislative debates, effectively using the point that he would not be running for office in 1889.

What manner of railroad law was this act of 1888, passed with such show of unanimity after so hard a fight? First of all, Larrabee stressed the nonrevolutionary character of the act as the equivalent on the state level of the federal Interstate Commerce Act of 1887, and its similarity to statutes passed in other states. Although the title of the bill made reference to "passengers and freights," the law did not touch the sore point of maximum passenger rates, a topic which was left for later days. Known as the Railroad Commissioner Law, it was supplemented by an additional act which provided for election instead of appointment of the Board of Commissioners, who were to be paid by the state out of its own tax funds, not by assessments on the railroads, an obvious aid to independent decisions. The board was given powers to carry out its own investigations, hold hearings attendant thereto, and to bring suits. The things that were forbidden, and to which the board would turn its attention, make up a checklist of the complaints heard through the years: all charges must be reasonable and just; no special rates, rebates, refunds, or other devices of favoritism and preference must be used; all railroads must be given the same treatment in the interchange of traffic; the long-and-short-haul grievance was dealt with by outlawing a greater charge for the short haul rather than the long haul *if* the short haul were included in the long haul; pooling of profits was forbidden. All schedules of rates must be printed, posted in public, and a copy furnished to the commission; no increases could be made unless on ten-day notice. The commission itself might make or revise schedules of rates which would then be considered maximum rates unless the defendant could show cause for a change.

The new law went into effect on May 10, 1888. The new board consisted of Peter A. Dey, Spencer Smith, and Frank T. Campbell, the first and last being veterans of the long fight for the principle of public control of the common carriers. Without delay they made a thorough study of freight rates and announced a new schedule, effective July 5, 1888. The "Big Three" among Iowa roads—the North Western, the

Milwaukee, and the Burlington Road—brought suit to secure an injunction against the schedule, which Judge David J. Brewer of the Eighth United States Judicial Circuit Court granted on a temporary basis, on the grounds that the roads had a right to make a profit. In further hearings the board showed that its rate schedule was fair, inasmuch as it did allow a good profit, and showed that the roads were guilty of new acts of discrimination. Judge Brewer now reversed himself and denied a permanent injunction, saying that the rates had not been yet fairly tested. Two days later the fight against the new act collapsed. The Burlington announced its acquiescence and the other roads followed that lead.[9]

A few months later Governor Larrabee could retire at the end of his second term in the good graces of nearly everyone except a few diehards who resisted the whole idea of the right of the state to regulate the operators of a business. As indicated below, Larrabee was brought forward by certain interests in 1889–1890 as a possible opponent of Senator Allison for the oncoming term, a move to which he gave no encouragement. Except for a two-year term on the State Board of Control and an occasional comment on state politics not to his liking, he remained in seclusion at "Montauk,"[10] his magnificent country home near Clermont, or collected books and *objets d'art* while on his distant travels. In many ways he was a forerunner of the Progressive Movement whose leader, Albert B. Cummins, enjoyed his warm support.

IOWA POLITICS, NATIONAL POLITICS, 1888–1890

Iowans, particularly Senator Allison and his friends, found in 1888 that Iowa was not so isolated from national affairs as they might have thought—or wished. That strange anomaly, an Iowa Republican leader from Dubuque, the "Gibraltar of Iowa Democracy," had risen to a position of national leadership and in this crucial year was given serious consideration for the Republican presidential nomination. To be sure, that prize was eventually claimed by Benjamin Harrison, who went on to victory over Grover Cleveland, the Democratic incumbent of the White House, losing the popular vote but winning in the electoral college, 233 to 168. Omitting here the details of Allison's try for the nomination, a story that belongs to national rather than state history and which has been amply covered elsewhere,[11] it should be pointed out that Allison's failure to win the nomination was due in part to the paradox of Iowa's reputation as a safe and sure Republican state which was temporarily in the grip of radical agrarianism. As the reputed home of the Granger laws, and the center of social and political unrest, Chauncey Depew, the New York Central Railroad magnate who aspired to the nomination, convinced himself and his Eastern friends that it was true, and that Iowa and the Midwest should be punished by preventing the nomination of Iowa's "favorite son."

Admittedly, there was a groundswell of feeling which was sweeping the people of the Midwest along in a demand for reform and change. The election in 1889 of a conservative Democrat, Horace Boies of Waterloo, instead of a traditional Republican victor, was the first time the governor's office had not gone to a Republican since Grimes won the spot in 1854. This was only one sign of unrest, an indication of dissatisfaction with the Old Guard. Another sign was the activity of those who wanted to replace Senator Allison in 1890 with William Larrabee. More threatening was the strength of the Democrats, who were able to make their senatorial nominee, Samuel Bestow of Chariton, more than the usual token of the existence of another party; only the votes of the holdover members of the Senate gave the Republicans a majority and the power to send Allison back for another term. Bestow received 63 votes; Allison, 75; Larrabee, 8. Later in the year the Democrats performed the miracle of Iowa history by winning six out of eleven seats in the House and nearly winning three more, proof positive of the economic and social unrest pervading the state. As proof of this assertion, one finds the Democratic total of 194,832 votes in all eleven districts compared with 185,783 for the Republicans the worst congressional election defeat for them between 1852 and 1932.

ANALYSIS OF THE HORACE BOIES LEGEND

The victory of Horace Boies for a second term in 1891, his candidacies in other races, and his role as a serious contender for the Democratic presidential nomination in 1892 and again in 1896 offer ample evidence that here was no ordinary man. Surely these were no mean accomplishments for a Democrat who hailed from a state with such tremendous Republican strength. Yet too much emphasis can be placed on the denomination of Boies as a Democrat or the notion that he was about to restore that party to its pre-1854 standing. After his victory in 1889, one enthusiastic admirer rhapsodized that Boies was "a man who has never been defeated, a leader of the party that changed the politics of the state from a republican majority of 78,000 to a democratic majority of 8,000." Besides noting the fact that a majority of 8,000 is a precarious advantage, there were other factors that should have been noted by this observer.

First, by their split over Prohibition, the Republicans defeated themselves in 1889. By officially adopting Prohibition, the party lost Samuel J. Kirkwood, a former governor, senator, and cabinet member, and George G. Wright, a former chief justice of the state supreme court and United States senator, with all their followers, especially the large number of voters in the populous river counties who scratched their ballots in favor of Boies. Second, against Boies the Republicans put up a political weakling, Joseph Hutchison, a lethargic candidate whose prorailroad position in the recent reform battle cost his party much of the farm vote. Third, one must qualify in labeling Boies, formerly a Whig and then a Republican, as a Democrat. It is not at all certain that he was in full sympathy with many prominent Democrats, especially those who were caught up in the trend toward populism.

Boies was forty years of age when he moved to Waterloo from New York in 1867 and began his law practice, gradually investing his savings in valuable farmlands in Grundy and Hardin counties to become a very wealthy man. His overt break from the Republicans came over the issue of Prohibition. He was a firm believer in and practitioner of temperance, but just as firmly against Prohibition on the grounds that it would deprive persons of their property rights without remuneration, and invade their personal rights as well. In 1884 he cast his first known Democratic vote in going for Grover Cleveland for president. Later, he developed strong views against the protective tariff and built his whole political philosophy and career around that issue. When "free silver" grew to be the dominant interest of the Democrats and their Populist allies, Boies could give only lukewarm support to that cause. Thus it appears that this first, and only, Democrat to break the thirty-two-year string of Republican victories was a political independent, certainly no agrarian radical, certainly no urban reformer, who must have felt as uncomfortable among extreme Democrats as Larrabee had been among extreme Republicans. He accepted the call to office only out of a sense of duty, without compromise of his personal beliefs for the sake of election. Staunch Waterloo Republicans such as Matt Parrott and J. C. Gates, fellow townsmen who knew him well, rose above partisanship and praised him for his integrity and wisdom.[12]

THE SILVER QUESTION AGAIN—AND CIVIL RIGHTS

In the Fifty-first Congress which met in December 1889, the first "billion-dollar" Congress in our history, three issues in which Iowans were concerned and involved stood out above all others: the silver question, still crying for solution; the tariff question; and Negro suffrage in the South, where an elections act was needed to put teeth in the Fourteenth and Fifteenth Amendments. The proposal for enlarging civil rights was called a "Force Bill," because it provided for the use of force if necessary in backing up the registrars whom the bill would provide as supervisors of elections. As the Congress began work on these three points, it became quickly apparent that a powerful coalition had been formed between the Republican senators from the six newly admitted Western states, two of which were large silver producers, and Democrats from the Southern states. In the baffling and wearisome maneuvers which followed, the "silver senators" secured the Sherman

Silver Purchase Act as a replacement for the Bland-Allison Act of 1878.[13] The new act provided for the purchase of 4.5 million ounces of silver monthly, the ore not to be coined into silver dollars but stored, warehouse style, and made available as money in the form of silver certificates circulated as representative money. Under this plan the average person would not quibble over whether the silver represented by the certificate was worth the face amount in gold. One of Iowa's ten Republican congressmen, Edwin H. Conger of Des Moines, was chosen as a staunch party regular to introduce the bill in the House. All ten Republicans from Iowa voted for the bill, as did Representative Walter I. Hayes, the lone Democrat; Senators Allison and Wilson also voted for it.

The McKinley Tariff Act, which was passed as part of the three-cornered deal, erected the highest protective wall yet built by Congress as a response to the plea that the "infant" industries of American manufacturers must be protected against the pauper labor of Europe and Asia. Iowa Republicans gave their all in furnishing votes for the bill. Senator Allison was no longer recognizable as the moderate tariff reformer of the 1860s–1870s. The Iowa votes demonstrated that Iowa's agricultural interests had not yet discovered the value of bargaining on the tariff issue.

As for the Force Bill, or Lodge Bill, named after Representative Henry Cabot Lodge of Massachusetts, a sad tale must be told. Here was a chance to implement many of the brave words of the 1860s about equal rights for all citizens (only male citizens, to be sure), a chance to go far toward finishing the "unfinished War." Instead, the House passed a bill on the subject but the Senate postponed the day of taking a stand until the rush toward adjournment at the end of the session caused the matter to be dropped. It was all too evident that the Republican leaders did not have their hearts in the matter—and no one else would have until the post–World War II movement for full political equality.

THE RISE OF POPULISM

A new factor in the public life of the 1890s was the People's party, a third party which was a considerable force in the elections of 1892 and 1896. This party was of special interest to Iowans because of the Iowa residence (Bloomfield) of its leader, General James B. Weaver, and because it was a medium of agrarian protest. The People's party, better known simply as the Populists,[14] was formed in 1891 at a Cincinnati convention of a baffling variety of factions and splinter groups. The party was nothing new but merely a formal organization of something that had been in existence under one name or another since the early days of the greenback controversy in 1865 and which had grown through the years as new interests and new circumstances bred additional issues to attract the support of agrarian and small-town groups. It was a movement rather than a party, but a movement with a positive program, dedicated to human welfare rather than narrow class interests, and its tragedy was that it could never establish a hard-core political alliance made up of Eastern labor, Western farmers, and Southern farm tenants which could have produced the mass voting strength necessary for success. Even so, the Populists were able to throw a real scare into Republican ranks in the elections of 1892, 1894, and 1896.

Populist leaders were interested in achieving a better balance between the elements of American life. Primarily spokesmen for "dirt farmers," they wanted recognition for the contribution made by agriculture to the total American economy. In their concept of economic life, people were divided into two groups: producers and nonproducers. Farmers were, of course, producers; a man on a Board of Trade dealing in wheat futures was, in their thinking, a nonproducer. Who could blame an Iowa or Kansas or Nebraska farmer for bitterness after sweating through a whole season of back-breaking toil, with great outlay of cash for seed and fertilizer, only to see his planning and his labor come to nought when the railroad took a big slice of his income and a commodities dealer in far-off Chicago or Minneapolis took much of the remainder? One needs only to reread William Jennings Bryan's "Cross of Gold" speech to catch their spirit and their logic.

It is commonplace to say that nearly all of the Populist platform of 1892, in detail or in principle, later became the law of the land, but no one in 1892 would have predicted that outcome. To its contemporary opponents it seemed like a monstrous creation of the devil. Free silver was only one of its heresies but the one most subject to attack, partly because Populists themselves made the mistake of overemphasis of that point. Other planks in their platform called for government issue of paper money instead of allowing the national banks a monopoly of that privilege; government ownership of the railroads and telephone and telegraph facilities; popular election of United States senators; a graduated income tax; postal savings banks; a reformed land system; immigration controls; abolition of strike-breaking agencies; the eight-hour day on all federal work projects; pensions for war veterans; the single-term presidency; and the adoption of the initiative, the referendum, and the recall. The Populist campaign for its 1892 Omaha platform was a part of a larger campaign that went beyond 1892 to 1894 and to and beyond 1896. In their thinking the key issue was the need for more money in circulation; since greenbacks had been disposed of as a solution, the field was clear for silver as the answer to all money problems. Whereas a Republican in 1878 could straddle the issue by supporting silver on two or three conditional safeguards, Populists (and Silver Democrats) rejected the conditional clauses and plumped for "free silver at the ratio of 16 to 1," regardless of consequences.

Politics under Populist Pressure: The Case of Iowa

The elections of 1892 went in favor of gold and "sound money." Grover Cleveland, a Gold Democrat, described by no less an authority than Woodrow Wilson as a "Republican in disguise," easily defeated Bland of Missouri and Horace Boies of Iowa for the Democratic nomination, and went on to defeat Benjamin Harrison and General James B. Weaver, Republican and Populist, respectively. Harrison, his own worst enemy, lost the support of many party wheelhorses, such as James S. Clarkson, now living in the East.[15] Weaver, who was really his party's second choice after Judge Walter Quentin Gresham, made a good showing but some of the luster formerly attached to his accomplishment has been dimmed by a recent study which shows that many of his more than 1,000,000-plus votes, which produced 22 electoral votes in the Far Western states, were cast by Democrats who scratched their own tickets, knowing that their party was hopelessly in the minority vis-à-vis the Republicans, and voted for Weaver just to hurt the Republicans.[16]

Harrison's legacy to Cleveland was the Panic of 1893, one of the worst in our history. A special session of Congress was called to deal with the problem. A last-ditch stand by the silver forces to save some large role for silver ended with the defeat of Bland's effort to revive the Bland-Allison Act, 213 to 136, all eleven Iowa members voting nay; on the following decisive vote for repeal of the Sherman Act, nine voted yea while Colonel William Peters Hepburn of Clarinda and Alva L. Hager of Greenfield, strong Western men, voted for the use of silver. In the Senate, both Allison and Wilson failed to vote but Allison made a pair in favor of repeal, which carried.[17]

In 1893, having healed the split over Prohibition, the Republicans put up Frank D. Jackson of Greene, a party hack, against Horace Boies, trying for a third term. The Waterloo man should never have tried for this honor. For one thing, the "no third term" tradition was against him, Kirkwood's third term, the only one in Iowa history thus far, having come after an interval of twelve years. Second, Boies had switched most of his interest to the tariff issue, an unexciting topic for state politics even though Boies demonstrated that Europeans could not buy Iowa's agricultural produce unless they could sell some of their goods in this country. Finally, he was bucking a positive trend toward the return of the state to normal Republican supremacy. Along with a Republican governor, the General Assembly was returned to safe Republican control and Iowa Republicans could again believe in the merits of mass suffrage. Their throttlehold on the state was strengthened by two big victories in 1894, the election of John Henry Gear to the Senate in January over Horace Boies, and the winning of all eleven seats in the national House in the November elections.

In any discussion of the politics of the 1890s, the historian is constantly challenged to explain why Iowa was not swept into the Populist column as were, to a greater extent, Kansas, Nebraska, the newly formed states of North and South Dakota, and even Minnesota. The economic situation was very acute in these states—not all states were as secure for orthodox economics and politics as Iowa. It has been demonstrated that while Iowa had its troubles, what with low prices for farm produce, heavy mortgage indebtedness at exorbitant rates of interest (sometimes reaching 15 percent), high freight rates, and adverse weather conditions, such factors were not as severely felt in Iowa as in the states just named. A high percentage of the mortgages were of the constructive and investment type, farm tenancy was not the result of a land monopoly in the hands of nonresident owners, and the regulation of the railroads under the new laws of 1878, 1884, and 1888 afforded some relief. The east central counties of the state were developing a new and more profitable type of agriculture which utilized Iowa's grain and hay for hog- and cattle-feeding operations, and the northeast counties added large-scale dairying, thus relieving the dependence on railroads and producing more cash income. Added to these factors was the tendency of the two older parties to accept the ideas of the Populists, though not immediately translated into laws.[18]

PREPARATION FOR THE SHOWDOWN ON SILVER MONEY

National developments in 1894 and 1895 dictated the necessity of coming to some final decision on the money question. A "Battle of the Standards" loomed as one which must be fought out in the political arena to a positive conclusion. William Jennings Bryan of Nebraska, a great orator and virtual Populist, was already campaigning for the 1896 Democratic nomination on a free silver platform, and thousands of people, Iowans among them, heard the essence of the "Cross of Gold" speech long before it was delivered in Chicago. Richard P. Bland of Missouri was just as evangelical as Bryan, though not so emotional, and Horace Boies of Waterloo, Iowa, played along with the free silver advocates, though more concerned with the tariff question. On the antifree-silver side, George Evan Roberts, publisher-editor of the *Fort Dodge Messenger,* a banker and a self-taught economist, established a national reputation as the author of a pamphlet which answered the arguments of "Coin" Harvey's little book, *Coin Goes to School,* point for point, using Harvey's own techniques.[19] Leslie M. Shaw, a banker and lawyer in Denison, and Jonathan P. Dolliver of Fort Dodge, the best speaker in Congress, were other able antisilver propagandists.

THE CAMPAIGN AND ELECTION OF 1896

Iowa's actual participation in the important election of 1896 was more than casual. First, Iowa Republicans put their house in order in 1895 by replacing the weak governor, Frank D. Jackson, with General Francis M. Drake, a banker and railroad builder from Centerville, and the last Civil War veteran to win the governor's office in Iowa.[20] The Republicans also won a safe majority in the legislature, enabling them to reelect Senator Allison in January 1896 and turn the election into a public ceremony for purposes of gaining publicity for his presidential candidacy.

There was much brave talk about winning the nomination for Allison but none from the senator himself. James S. Clarkson, now a resident of Philadelphia, directed his campaign, and a great deal of time and money were invested in the cause before it was conceded that no one had a chance in the St. Louis convention except William McKinley of Ohio. Allison's more realistic friends wanted to withdraw his name earlier to spare him embarrassment, but the diehards went through all the motions of the nominating speeches. McKinley won on the first ballot but not until the adoption of a gold plank caused Senator Henry M. Teller of Colorado, the "defender of the West," and 100 of his prosilver followers to bolt the convention.[21]

The Democrats put on a much better show at Chicago. Horace Boies and Richard P. Bland challenged Bryan but without success. Boies was hurt by his reputation as an antilabor man but twenty-six delegates from Iowa stayed by him loyally until the last moment before climbing on the Bryan bandwagon. As for the Populists, they accepted General Weaver's advice and nominated Bryan.

The election results have been analyzed with great care.[22] Bryan made a heroic effort to carry the Midwest, especially Iowa, which he wanted to hold to its prosilver tradition; his last speech outside Nebraska was made in Ottumwa. It was all in vain: McKinley won 7,104,779 popular votes and 271 electoral votes; Bryan, at 6,502,925 popular votes, ran 601,854 votes behind and received only 176 electoral votes. John M. Palmer, the Gold Democrat, received only 133,148 popular votes; the lesser candidates hardly enough to mention. Bryan's greatest disappointment was his failure to carry the North Central states. He lost Iowa, 289,293 for McKinley and 233,741 for his losing cause.

Presumably, the country could now resume the search for prosperity, with some hope of success.

CHAPTER 13 THE PROGRESSIVE MOVEMENT: THE EARLY YEARS 1897-1904

FOLLOWING THE ELECTIONS OF 1896, CIRCUMSTANCES SEEMED TO conspire in favor of William McKinley, the apostle of gold and Republicanism, and against William Jennings Bryan, spokesman for silver and for Populist-Democracy. The Silverites, like the forgotten Greenbackers, had based their case largely on the theory that prosperity is keyed to the volume of money in circulation. Better times followed, in and after 1897, and Jonathan Dolliver's campaign ballyhoo of McKinley as the "advance agent of prosperity" seemed like an inspired pronouncement. The causes were many, however, and the Silverites could claim no credit for the improvement of the economy. Even so, a waiting period of four years was required before the votes were available for passage of the Gold Standard Act.

THE CHANGING SCENE

Nathan Howe Parker's promotion book, *Iowa as It Is in 1856,* prophesied that the valleys of Iowa's three largest rivers would be filled with "manufactories" in the future. Had he lived until 1905 he would have seen fourteen of the seventeen largest industrial cities of Iowa on the banks of the Mississippi, the Missouri, and the Des Moines rivers. A few years later, William Duane Wilson's book, *A Description of Iowa and Its Resources* (1865), proudly tabulated the number of factories in the various congressional districts and the value of their products. Here is evidence of an early interest in urban economic activity to supplement Iowa's agriculture.

Iowa's urban industrial establishment, then and later, would be keyed to her agricultural economy. After the turn of the century, gasoline-powered machines began to replace manpower, horsepower, and even steam-powered machines on farms in Europe and America, nowhere more than in Iowa. Steam engines, both stationary and portable, had long been used to do farm work, but portable steam engines had many handicaps: proper fuel was sometimes difficult to obtain, sometimes water had to be hauled great distances, and, worst of all, the monsters might bog down in a wet field. As a result of these shortcomings, various manufacturing firms experimented with gasoline engines but none could overcome the problems of satisfactory carburetion and ignition. In 1892, when John Froelich, a farmer-tinkerer in Clayton County, succeeded in harnessing a Van Duzen gasoline engine to a farm implement and made it operative forward and in reverse, he perhaps did not realize the extent of the revolution he had launched.

Others realized that Froelich had hit upon the right idea. He sold his invention to the Waterloo Gas Traction Engine Company in 1893; this firm and others then plodded along for years without coming up with distinct improvements. The real breakthrough was the result of the joint efforts of Charles W. Hart, an Iowan studying at the University of Wisconsin, and his friend and fellow student, Charles H. Parr, a native of Wisconsin. The two engineering students met in 1892 and soon tackled the problem of automotive farm machinery. Staying on at Madison, they continued to experiment and build. In 1900 they moved their operations to Charles City, Iowa, and by 1902 had produced their first tractor, soon to be followed by others, enough to prove that they had conquered the basics of the problem. In 1907 they adopted the name tractor to distinguish their machine from the steam-powered giants; others used the word as a short substitute for "gasoline traction engine."

Concurrent developments in the petroleum industry and in electronics enabled the tractor industry to make enough progress to stay alive and very slowly to demonstrate that the tractor was here to stay. Kerosene and naphtha products were more efficient than gasoline. Henry Ford's entry into the tractor field in 1915 was a notable event and aided in the matter of mass production. For Iowa, the purchase of the Waterloo Gas Traction Engine Company in 1918 by the John Deere Company was a move of the greatest significance, certainly one of the most significant in Iowa economic history. Constant experimentation led to vast improvements in design and efficiency and to virtually complete replacement of horsepower and steam power on the farm.

The decline of Iowa's population by 0.3 percent between 1900 and 1910, though slight, was alarming because Iowa was the only state in the nation to lose population in that decade. Between 1900 and 1910, seventy-one counties lost population and twenty-eight counties, mostly those with urban centers, made gains. Obviously, farmers and farm workers were moving to the towns and cities in Iowa or to other states. Contrary to general opinion, California was not yet the magnet which drew Iowans in vast numbers. A study of the census figures shows that

TABLE 13.1: Native-born Iowans living in other states (selected)

	1870	1890	1900	1910	1920	1950	1960
Arizona	...	617	1,453	2,417	4,087	11,420	26,691
Arkansas	652	3,229	4,526	5,286	6,431	6,280	6,133
California	5,361	18,372	26,789	54,960	87,551	256,390	309,247
Colorado	...	20,008	24,960	44,276	45,253	43,560	51,638
Florida	19	594	706	1,042	3,457	11,630	24,564
Idaho	...	2,938	6,124	16,168	17,779	12,750	11,238
Illinois	11,312	24,522	48,096	57,948	72,989	139,170	136,057
Indiana	3,472	4,539	6,670	7,246	8,864	17,475	19,524
Kansas	12,990	66,148	88,153	64,333	55,062	33,710	30,229
Michigan	1,478	3,534	4,865	6,446	11,532	29,605	30,616
Minnesota	3,956	20,841	42,096	67,100	105,853	117,855	119,054
Missouri	22,383	37,312	52,575	56,893	56,302	58,010	57,286
Montana	...	4,792	9,005	17,455	27,666	17,005	13,309
Nebraska	7,605	95,886	85,807	94,623	92,115	74,355	72,758
Nevada	492	597	601	1,008	1,569	2,885	4,913
New Mexico	...	795	1,268	4,184	3,428	5,535	8,964
New York	886	2,564	4,358	6,126	9,337	15,910	16,485
North Dakota	...	4,559	9,005	30,553	27,631	12,655	9,513
Ohio	2,824	4,433	6,805	7,704	10,691	16,295	18,868
Oklahoma	...	3,013	19,255	41,186	34,004	20,595	16,406
Oregon	3,694	12,478	15,730	28,242	30,309	46,280	41,771
South Dakota	...	26,128	31,047	75,815	71,463	44,410	37,344
Texas	541	3,967	5,986	11,858	15,958	26,880	36,079
Utah	...	2,402	3,035	4,303	4,348	3,580	4,381
Washington	...	14,512	20,015	47,862	49,254	64,630	58,302
Wisconsin	2,416	6,986	11,932	16,312	26,214	40,415	44,145
Wyoming	...	3,636	6,112	10,651	13,903	10,965	10,153

SOURCE: Figures for 1870–1920 are from a study by William L. Harter and R. E. Stewart, "The Population of Iowa: Its Composition and Changes," Bulletin 275, Agricultural Experiment Station, Iowa State College, Ames, Nov. 1930; for 1950 and 1960 from a study by H. C. Chang, "Iowa's Population: Past, Present, and Future," Spec. Rept. 71, Agricultural and Home Economics Experiment Station, Iowa State University, Ames, Mar. 1973.

there were more notable out-migrations to other states during these years. (See Table 13.1.)

Professor John E. Brindley of Iowa State University found two causes for the decline of population: competition from cheaper lands in the West and Canada, and the failure of Iowans to take up the slack in farm employment by creation of urban industries. His study is noteworthy, but two points might be ventured by way of demurrer: he did not make sufficient allowance for the effects of labor-saving machinery on the farms, and he made industrial growth seem too easy, as if factory owners would come to Iowa at the slightest invitation. More than sixty years after the census of 1905 first revealed the decline of rural population, Iowa towns and cities were still seeking urban industry to take up the slack, and, though remarkably successful in this kind of promotion, the state's population is maintained at a barely stable figure. Actually, the state has had ninety years to work on this problem, since, as pointed out above, the real turning point in Iowa's population trends was not 1910 but 1880.

TABLE 13.2: Dollar value of manufactures in the 17 largest cities of Iowa in 1905, the percentage of increase or decrease since 1900, and the comparative ranking of these cities as manufacturing centers in 1900 and 1905

1905 Rank (1900 in parentheses)	1905 Value of Products	Percentage of Increase or Decrease
	(dollars)	*(%)*
1. Cedar Rapids (2)	16,279,706	46.2
2. Des Moines (6)	15,084,958	78.2
3. Sioux City (1)	14,760,751	3.8
4. Davenport (3)	13,695,978	38.7
5. Ottumwa (5)	10,374,183	19.4
6. Dubuque (4)	9,279,414	–3.8
7. Burlington (9)	5,779,337	29.9
8. Muscatine (8)	5,039,640	–3.4
9. Clinton (7)	4,906,355	–20.9
10. Waterloo (12)	4,693,888	124.8
11. Keokuk (11)	4,225,915	35.3
12. Marshalltown (10)	3,090,312	–21.9
13. Fort Dodge (15)	3,025,659	200.8
14. Fort Madison (14)	2,378,892	50.8
15. Council Bluffs (13)	1,924,109	13.7
16. Oskaloosa (17)	779,894	54.7
17. Boone (16)	714,288	13.7

SOURCE: *Census of Iowa,* 1905.

The census of 1856 showed the total value of Iowa's manufactured products to be $4,096,961, measured in 1856 dollars, one should remember; a half-century later the total value was $160,604,161. Clearly, great strides had been taken in the field of industrialism. The number of reporting companies had been cut down by higher standards, but the total capital involved and the value of the total product had increased tremendously. The average production was listed at $33,543 per reporting company. These 4,788 companies listed 7,124 salaried officials and workers, and 49,482 daily wage earners. The principal product lines were meat packing ($29,714,737), butter ($14,766,067), flour ($12,099,493), food preparations ($6,934,724), lumber and lumber products ($11,310,-981), foundry and machine shop products ($5,103,676), and brick and tile products ($3,361,776), and many other lines of lesser value.[1]

Table 13.2 shows the ranking order in 1905 of the cities in the manufacture of goods, their ranking in 1900, the dollar value of their products in 1905, and the percentage of increase or decrease in the dollar value of their production in those five years.

REPUBLICAN DOMINATION, 1892–1932

At the turn of the century, oldsters who were veterans of the Civil War were getting fewer in numbers but, wherever possible, holding on to offices against the challenge of younger men. General Drake was the last Civil War veteran to be governor. On one thing all were agreed:

the supremacy of the Republican party in Iowa must be perpetuated—and this was done. Few Midwestern states could match the Iowa story of one-party domination over a forty-year period. Only a stray Democrat could get himself elected to the House: one in each election of 1892, 1902, 1906, 1908, 1910; three in 1912 when Woodrow Wilson won the White House; one in 1914; and then none until 1930, when one was elected. Only one Democrat, Dan F. Steck of Ottumwa, in 1924, could win election to the Senate, the first since Dodge and Jones in the 1850s, a winner only because he successfully contested the disputed election of a very irregular Republican, Smith W. Brookhart, as described below. All the governors during these years were Republicans. Every General Assembly had a majority, usually an overwhelming majority, of Republican members, and, with rare exceptions, the county courthouses were staffed by Republicans. Little wonder that Jonathan Dolliver once described Republicanism as the religion of the people and predicted that "hell would go Methodist before Iowa went Democratic."

All this Republican power inside Iowa and in its delegation to Congress at the turn of the century was neatly meshed with Republican power in the national administration. It was commonly said to those who wanted something from the federal government, "Ask Iowa!" because so many congressional committees were chaired or dominated by Iowans, thanks to the effects of the seniority system and boss control. A brief catalog of the Iowans who achieved power and influence at Washington should suffice to demonstrate the point.

WILLIAM BOYD ALLISON of Dubuque was a member of the Senate from 1873 to 1908, the "Mr. Republican" of his last two decades. In the era before a Bureau of the Budget was created, as senior Republican member of the Committee on Appropriations from 1897 on, he had the most powerful single voice in Congress on all decisions involving financial support, for example, any increase in naval building or the construction of a Panama Canal had to have the approval of his committee, Allison's first of all. Cabinet members and military and naval men courted him, as did anyone who had an interest in government financing. On the powerful Committee on Finance, he ranked as an expert on tariff matters. He was a member of the Committee on Committees, chairman of the Republican caucus, and chairman of the steering committee. Other sources of power were his as part of the invisible government of the country. Allison of Iowa, Nelson W. Aldrich of Rhode Island, Orville H. Platt of Connecticut, and John Coit Spooner of Wisconsin made up "The Four," truly a *quadrumvirate* as they dominated Congress from their base on the Committee on Finance. Too busy with national affairs to take a hand in routine Iowa politics, he occasionally acted as referee between rival factions.

The courtly gentleman from Dubuque, 71 years of age as of March 2, 1900, made membership in the Senate a way of life. Childless, left a widower in 1883 by his second wife's suicide, he found his work in the Senate almost his only interest in life, especially his duties on the two big committees. He was wedded to his job and wanted to continue in it as long as he lived, even though this meant working at about one-fourth capacity and efficiency during the last years of his life as he struggled against the ravages of prostatic cancer, to which he finally succumbed.[2]

JONATHAN PRENTISS DOLLIVER of Fort Dodge, a member of the House from 1889 to 1900, was appointed to the Senate in 1900 and reelected in 1902 for the remainder of the term, and again in 1906 for a full six-year term which he did not quite finish. He was a member of the Ways and Means Committee in the House; in the Senate he served at various times on the committees on Interstate Commerce, Education and Labor, Agriculture and Forests, and lesser committees. One of the greatest orators in American history, he was one of the founders and leaders of the progressive movement. He was favorably considered for the nomination for vice-president when McKinley was seeking a running mate for 1900, and by Taft in 1908, but each time he politely rejected the honor because of distaste for the job and inability to bear the financial burden.[3]

DAVID BREMNER HENDERSON of Dubuque, a member of the House, 1883–1903, and Speaker of the House, 1899–1903, was the first man from a state west of the Mississippi to gain that honor. A colonel in the Civil War, he carried a wound received at Shiloh and always won the veterans' votes. He was at once Allison's protégé, advisor, and political manager. As successor to "Czar" Thomas B. Reed as Speaker, he was stern and unrelenting in his rulings, openly favoring his own party and using his own judgment as to what was good for his party.[4]

Others can only be listed: Captain JOHN ALBERT TIFFIN HULL of Des Moines, member of the House, 1891–1911; staunch standpatter; high-tariff man; ranking Republican on the Committee on Military Affairs. Major JOHN F. LACEY of Oskaloosa, member of the House, 1889–1891 and 1893–1907; highest ranking Republican on the Committee on Public Lands and strong advocate of national parks. ROBERT G. COUSINS of Tipton, member of the House, 1893–1909; now virtually forgotten, in his prime he was one of the greatest orators in the country; keynoter at the Republican convention in 1904.[5] GILBERT N. HAUGEN of Northwood, member of the House, 1899–1933; a member, sometimes chairman, of the Committee on Agriculture through all thirty-four years, he became a leader in that field of legislation.[6] WALTER I. SMITH of Council Bluffs, member of the House, 1900–1911; member of the powerful committees on Banking and Currency, and Appropriations; took a prominent part in the "revolution of 1910" which destroyed the power of Speaker Cannon. Colonel WILLIAM PETERS HEPBURN of Clarinda, member of the House,

1881–1887 and 1893–1909; a powerful member of the committees on Interstate Commerce, Insular Affairs, and Pacific Railroads.[7]

In addition to these longtime members of Congress, one should remember the unusual situation of two Iowans serving simultaneously in the cabinet: James ("Tama Jim") Wilson, plucked from his position as professor of Applied Agriculture at Iowa State College of Agriculture and Mechanical Arts at Ames to be secretary of agriculture under McKinley and continuing in this position under Theodore Roosevelt and William Howard Taft; and former Governor Leslie Mortier Shaw of Denison, secretary of the treasury under Roosevelt, 1902–1907. In Iowa local history remembered chiefly as an ultraconservative governor, Shaw was a man of great influence in state and national politics, with an eye on the main chance as he coveted the office of president after Roosevelt's retirement.[8]

If these were not enough, there were others. John Adam Kasson, who ably represented Iowa in the House in earlier years and then served as minister to Prussia and then to Austria, was now a resident of Washington, with the rank of minister plenipotentiary in the State Department and head of the Reciprocity Commission, 1897–1901. His was the hopeless task of trying to make a dent in Republican thinking about the virtues of protective tariffs, offering as a substitute a plan of reciprocal trade agreements. Kasson's special contribution was the idea of having such trade treaties ratified by a simple majority of each house of Congress, not by a two-thirds majority of the Senate.[9] George Evan Roberts of Fort Dodge was director of the Mint, and Maurice D. O'Connell of the same city was solicitor for the Treasury Department. In 1910 their fellow citizen, William Squire Kenyon, became assistant attorney general in charge of antitrust cases, and in 1911 was elected to the Senate. Dolliver, Roberts, O'Connell, and Kenyon: What other town in America of 15,000 population could claim four men so highly placed in the government?

Conservative Republicans versus Progressive Republicans

There is a joker, however, in such a description of Republican supremacy. Another wave of bitter factionalism split the party wide open during these years. This time the split was between conservative ("standpat") and progressive ("insurgent") wings of the party, the latter led by the "new" Jonathan P. Dolliver and by Albert B. Cummins of Des Moines, to be discussed at length below. The national political spotlight played upon Iowa as the state took a prominent place, probably just behind Wisconsin, in the standpat-progressive conflicts which were the dominant feature of state and national politics in the early 1900s. Although progressivism was a force in each of the two major parties, the emphasis in this account will be placed on the Republican party because of the negligible strength of the Democrats in Iowa at this time.

Certain assumptions have been made in drawing up this account of Iowa's segment of the national story. One such assumption is that no two standpatters or progressives were exactly alike in their thinking. Another is that both words acquired new shades of meaning as the years went by and sometimes men did not change as fast as the meanings of the words, hence the old saying, "the liberal of today is the conservative of tomorrow." It follows that political labels are meaningless unless defined in the context of the times and of the personal characteristics of the leaders who bear the labels. Most compelling of all is the assumption that ambition, as expressed in a desire for public office, was a far greater motivating factor among both standpatters and progressives than any ideological consideration.

Iowa conservatives have not received from historians as much attention as their more colorful opponents. As the "ins" or "haves" against the "outs" or "have nots," politically speaking, Iowa standpatters were in the unfortunate position of all conservatives at all times in history: they must try to make their defense of the status quo and of their vested interests seem plausible, something more than mere selfishness. Unhappily for his cause, the true conservative must want to conserve not only the values of the present and the past but also the power which he has amassed. It follows that in defending his values and his power, these interests take on for him a sacred air, while the values of his opponents seem to him to be profane, and their power is denounced as dangerous to the welfare of the people.[10]

The standpatters of this era are best understood by examining the attitudes of their leaders. The list must be headed by Senator William B. Allison, not as an articulate exponent of conservative philosophy but as a leader of those long entrenched in power and eager to keep that power. The leading ideological conservative in the state was a railroad attorney, Joseph W. Blythe of Burlington, chief solicitor of the Burlington Road.[11] Known far and wide as the head of the "Regency," a small group controlling the Iowa Republican organization, his political power was especially great in the southern counties of the state which were directly served by the C.B.&Q., so much so that this region was known in political journalism as the "Q Reservation." Well educated, holder of a degree from Princeton University, successful in his profession, and politically allied with his father-in-law, former governor, now senator, John H. Gear, Joe Blythe was the protector of the past and the present, the sworn enemy of the progressive concept of the future. In his view of local history, the railroads had been the chief instrument in Iowa's economic growth in the past and, as the largest taxpayers in the state, the foundation under the state government and Iowa's cultural structure. Closely allied with him were his brother, James E.

Blythe, a successful attorney in Mason City, and Charles E. Perkins, president of the C.B.&Q. Blythe's most powerful ally was also his rival, Judge Nathaniel M. Hubbard of Marion and Cedar Rapids, the Iowa attorney for the gigantic North Western Railroad.

It would be hopeless to try to make up an all-inclusive list of those who supported these leaders but certainly one should begin with Governor Leslie M. Shaw of Denison and continue with Congressmen David B. Henderson, John A. T. Hull, John F. Lacey, and William P. Hepburn, all of whom have been mentioned above. Others of prominence were George D. Perkins of Sioux City, editor of the *Sioux City Journal,* a congressman from 1891 to 1899, and a citizen of the highest order; John T. Adams, Dubuque businessman, who became a professional politician in 1908 when he took over the management of Allison's last campaign; John S. Runnells, Des Moines attorney, later a Pullman Company official in Chicago, to whom the slightest tinge of liberalism was sure proof of socialist beliefs; Ernest E. Hart, Council Bluffs attorney; General Grenville M. Dodge, nominally of Council Bluffs, residing chiefly in New York City; and many others.

A special case was James S. "Ret" Clarkson, from late 1872 to 1888 the powerful editor of the *Iowa State Register* in Des Moines, and then a strong force in Iowa through his brother, Richard P. Clarkson, even though he kept his residence in the East. In 1902 he and Richard sold the *Register* to George E. Roberts and allied interests, then switched the sale to Gardner Cowles of Algona when Roberts decided to let go of his shares.[12] (Under Cowles and his editor, Harvey Ingham, the editorial policy would become progressive and strongly pro-Cummins.) Before and after his change of residence, Ret worked hand-in-glove with Senator Allison and warmly supported Senator Dolliver, whom he loved like a brother. One of his special contributions to Iowa politics was his influence with a former Iowan, his very wealthy friend Leigh Smith James Hunt, whom he persuaded to donate large sums to the campaign war chests of Allison and Dolliver, and occasionally others.[13]

THE PROGRESSIVE MOVEMENT

A very brief statement must be made about the theoretical aspects of progressivism before undertaking an account of the personalities involved in the politics of the progressive movement in Iowa. Progressives have an advantage over conservatives because the very word "progress" is attractive in its implications of change for the better. Their problem is to convince a majority of voters that there is a need for change. Needed changes must be secured through reform rather than revolution; the whole economic and social structure must be regulated for the benefit of the whole society, not for any special classes. This regulation can be performed only by a strong government—city, state, or national—a Hamiltonian government working for Jeffersonian goals. The progressives, then, were reformers for the public good, and they felt justified in working for control of government to put through their reforms. If necessary, progressives were willing for the "people" to be brought into the process to operate the devices of direct government, the initiative, the referendum, and the recall, though some progressives might object to the latter as applied to judges and judicial decisions.

The progressives of the early 1900s were not the first and not the last reformers, by whatever name. Even the most casual observer can discern that a very thin line divides legitimate reformers from "do-gooders" and can further observe that the train of reform might stop with the distaste of its leaders for any further change, or might move on and on into realms of theory and action undreamed of by the founders of the movement. He also may discern that "progress" and "reform" may simply be nice words to cover up the desire of the "outs" to displace the "ins."

It should be flatly stated that these theories of government had nothing to do with the origins of progressivism in Iowa. Any sort of concerted challenge to the conservatives was slow in developing into an open split within the Iowa Republican party. Jonathan Dolliver's biographer, whose studies of this topic are definitive, asserts that the division was rooted in practical politics and isolates the gubernatorial politics of 1897 as the seedtime for the division into two factions. In his view, when Leslie M. Shaw of Denison secured the Republican nomination for governor by a victory over his rivals, Abraham B. Funk of Spirit Lake and Matt Parrott of Waterloo, and in the same campaign Albert B. Cummins of Des Moines interested himself in the legislative elections in anticipation of the senatorial election of 1900, the die was cast for a struggle for power within the party. The surface politics were obviously a part of a power struggle. The Blythe-Hubbard "Regency" originally favored Parrott for governor but switched to Shaw as a means of heading off Funk, a Cummins man. All participants were looking ahead to 1900 by which time Senator Gear would have retired or died in office. Shaw was nominated and elected, and in 1900 played the part which was expected of him in blocking Cummins's ambition for the Senate. From these beginnings the split within the party grew wider and wider.[14]

Albert Baird Cummins

The very capable "front man" of the progressives in Iowa was a Des Moines attorney, Albert Baird Cummins. It would be completely erroneous, however, to put the philosophy before the man. It is at least a defensible speculation that the Old Guard of Iowa politics drove this brilliant and magnetic leader of men into progressivism, much as their counterparts a generation earlier had driven James Baird Weaver into Populism. A courageous man of strong convictions on public issues, as evidenced by his stand with a minority against Prohibition in 1884 and his aid to Governor William Larrabee in 1888 on the railroad question, he nevertheless kept his political fences in good repair by maintaining cordial relations with Senator Allison and other party regulars, even with Joe Blythe! Here was no cynical advocate of a suicidal split within the party, no leader of a revolution—yet.

Beginning his practice in Des Moines in 1878, Cummins grew wealthy as a corporation lawyer. Rather early in his career he attained much fame (and a good fee) as counsel in a suit against a certain firm which was controlling the market in barbed wire. In 1884 he was sought out by "Father" Clarkson and other Grange leaders as counsel in a suit against the "barbed-wire trust." The suit resulted in victory for the Grange forces, although Cummins withdrew from the case before it was finished. It is straining a point to associate this case with Cummins's later posture as a progressive leader in Iowa, as does a leading authority on the history of progressivism, who says that "after gaining a popular reputation as the chief counsel in a legal battle against the so-called barbed-wire trust, he rallied most of the dissident sentiment to his side and began battle against the reigning conservative."[15] Actually there was a twenty-year time lag between the two historical events: the suit against the Moen barbed-wire firm was filed in the early 1880s while the pitched "battle" against the "reigning conservatives" did not begin until the 1904 session of the General Assembly, and then rather mildly as an issue of simple reform. As a young attorney looking for clients, Cummins took the barbed-wire case, just as any lawyer takes a justiciable and litigious case, partly for the fee involved and partly for the satisfaction of performing the duties and functions of his profession. To him it was no crusade on behalf of embattled farmers; his client, the Grange, was a business organization, engaged in manufacturing farm equipment, not farmers as a downtrodden minority group. Furthermore, the leading Cumminsites were not dissident farmers and their guilds; as will be shown below, the leading Cummins supporters were urban, middle-class, fairly well-to-do businessmen, lawyers, and reform-minded editors. Cummins had no special appeal for or contact with small farmers and the working classes, neither of which groups was well organized or politically strong in the Iowa of 1900 or thereabouts. On the contrary, he was a rather aloof, fastidious man of elegant tastes and patrician manner, a member of Des Moines's most exclusive clubs, who somewhat symbolically drove to his office daily in a fine carriage drawn by spirited horses driven by a liveried coachman, a custom which he continued long after the coming of the automobile.[16]

Politically, Cummins might well be described as a young man in a hurry, consumed by ambition. In 1894 he was bitterly disappointed when Blythe preferred his own father-in-law, John H. Gear, for United States senator, and even more bitterly upset when the Blythe-Hubbard-Shaw machine, with Allison's blessing and assistance, reelected the doddering old man in 1900. Everyone, especially Cummins, believed that this was simply a Blythe plot to deprive the aggressive Cummins of the position, thus giving Governor Shaw a chance to appoint Gear's successor. Sure enough, just two months later, Senator Gear died and Governor Shaw, not daring to resign and have himself appointed, passed over several aspirants, including Cummins, and appointed Congressman Jonathan P. Dolliver to the vacancy until the position could be filled by election at the next session of the General Assembly, in 1902. To say that Cummins was overly ambitious and not yet deserving of such a high office—not as deserving as Dolliver, or Shaw—is to overlook the point that Cummins *believed* in his own fitness for the office and, in a fair and open race, could have beaten Gear.

In spite of these two rebuffs and other lesser signs of his unpopularity with Blythe & Co., Cummins remained a good soldier in the ranks, contributing his abilities as a stump speaker in the annual campaigns and in every way giving the appearance of friendship and loyalty to Senators Allison and Dolliver, and the party managers. No one should ever be misled into believing that Albert Baird Cummins was a self-denying evangelist for better government for its own sake, or a self-appointed champion of "the people." He would have been less than human if he had not wanted power so as to show up those who had so long denied him entrance into the inner circle of officeholders and party directors.

In the meanwhile, certain men in the party began to accept his leadership and to demonstrate a new spirit within the party. It would be tedious and probably impossible to trace their transfers, one by one, to the Cummins camp; suffice it to say that by 1901 his following was large enough to secure his election as governor of Iowa and that the number increased from year to year. Like Cummins himself, some of his aides were men on the make; others were public-spirited citizens with no concern except progress toward better government and a better society in Iowa.

A list of the Cummins lieutenants and chief supporters, of varying degrees of progressivism, includes some of the most distinguished names in Iowa history: Abraham B. Funk, publisher-editor of the *Spirit Lake Beacon,* who entered the General Assembly with Cummins in 1888; Harvey Ingham, who came from Algona to Des Moines to be editor of the *Des Moines Iowa State Register;*[17] Frederick M. Hubbell, Des Moines real estate baron and founder of the Equitable Life Insurance Company of Iowa, ranked as the wealthiest man in Iowa history;[18] industrialist Fred L. Maytag of Newton;[19] John C. Hartman, publisher-editor of the *Waterloo Courier* and historian of Black Hawk County; Emory H.

English of suburban Des Moines, for a time editor of the *Mason City Daily Times;*[20] ex-Governor Larrabee; Warren Garst of Coon Rapids, banker and landowner;[21] Nathan E. Kendall of Albia, attorney, legislator, and future governor of Iowa;[22] George M. Curtis of Clinton, wealthy lumberman; Smith W. Brookhart of Washington, Iowa, attorney, newspaper publisher, and landowner, who will appear prominently in the pages below;[23] William E. ("Billy") Hamilton, publisher of the *Odebolt Chronicle;* Thomas A. Way of Mason City, owner of vast farmlands in Iowa and Minnesota; William S. Kenyon of Fort Dodge;[24] State Senator Thomas A. Cheshire of Des Moines; and Charles E. and Robert Santee of Cedar Falls, businessmen and political leaders.[25] Such occupational data uphold the generalization of similar class origins of both groups of Republicans.[26]

Jonathan Prentiss Dolliver

The name of Jonathan Prentiss Dolliver has been omitted from the above list in order to give him fuller treatment and to avoid the impression that he was a mere lieutenant under Cummins. Until recently it has been customary to say that Dolliver acted with the standpatters out of loyalty to Senator Allison until the Dubuque man's death, after which he asserted his true feelings and turned to Cummins and progressivism. With the publication of Dolliver's biography,[27] such a simplification is no longer tenable. It is not fair to Dolliver or to Allison. Dolliver was too honest and forthright to practice any such deception; there was not that much guile in his nature. He felt a filial devotion to the aging senator and gave him undiminished loyalty to the very end of his life, but it was voluntary and personal, not ideological. Nor would Allison have demanded subservience from Dolliver. Allison was a practical politician, not a blind and unthinking conservative ideologue. When the political tides began to run toward new thoughts on the tariff, Allison was able to adjust to the new directions. Most of all, however, Dolliver should be thought of as a co-leader with Cummins of the Iowa progressives; Dolliver's principal arena of action was in Congress while Cummins until 1908 was working in Iowa, all the while gaining fame as an orator with a national audience.

Jonathan Dolliver was a great bear of a man, hale and hearty, bluff, jovial. An attorney by training, he was never one who would have been happy unraveling the intricacies of a case in corporation law, as Cummins was, or even in handling small local cases. He was a man of social ideas, interested in the problem of human justice. He loved the life of the mind. His letters to his friends are sprinkled with comments on his current reading, for example, the moral lessons in Tolstoy's *Anna Karenina,* just published; by contrast, Cummins never spoke of such things. Jonathan was ever the son of his Methodist preacher-father and might well have been a preacher himself. He was an active layman, a delegate to Methodist conferences, a great worker for small church-related colleges. His progressivism rested on the belief that real progress, the improvement in the human condition, could not take place until a man had been "born again." Man-made laws were not enough.

Fortunately he was growing intellectually and in political wisdom. As far back as 1890 Senator Allison had advised him to give up superficial brilliance and concentrate on one subject, becoming master of its content. He chose the tariff as his first love; railway economics later was added to his storehouse of knowledge. His speeches on the Dingley tariff bill in 1897 show how far he had progressed since 1890. Here he revealed that he was no longer a blind believer in the eternal verities of protectionism, predicting that the day would come when a tariff bill would be made with a more enlightened consideration of the economic needs of the whole country. In the area of rough and ready party politics, he demonstrated great skill in remaining a good Republican, ably steering clear of subservience to either the Blythe-Hubbard-Shaw machine or the new grouping around Cummins, yet maintaining a neutrality which was trusted by both factions.

DOLLIVER AND THE "IOWA IDEA"

In 1901 Senator Dolliver, in attendance at the State Republican Convention at Cedar Rapids, was host to his Fort Dodge friend and spokesman, George Evan Roberts, former publisher of the *Fort Dodge Messenger,* now director of the Mint, and others, meeting privately to draw up a tariff plank for the platform. Dolliver's forward-looking friends wanted a plank which would enable the candidate for governor, whoever that might be, to go before the people of Iowa with the best possible statement of mild reform thought on the tariff—and still not offend the national leaders. Roberts claimed to be, and his claim has never been successfully challenged, the principal author of the plank, destined to become known as the "Iowa Idea." The pertinent portion deserves full quotation:

> We favor such changes in the tariff from time to time as become advisable through the progress of our industries and their changing relations to the commerce of the world. We endorse the policy of reciprocity as the natural complement of protection and urge its development as necessary to the realization of our highest commercial possibilities. . . . We favor such amendments of the interstate commerce act as will more fully carry out its prohibition of discrimination in rate making and modification of the tariff schedules that may be required to prevent their affording a shelter to monopoly.[28]

Here was a practical application of progressive philosophy as it would take form: the powers of government must be used to protect all the people instead of the one or the few. At the moment, it was merely good politics.

The convention went on to nominate Cummins for governor over several rivals, chiefly Major Edwin H. Conger of Des Moines, presently minister to China. Although sometimes credited with the authorship of the "Iowa Idea," Cummins was not among those present.[29] Fortunately Cummins gladly and sincerely accepted the tariff plank as a good statement of his own beliefs and he proceeded to utilize the point to good advantage during his campaign. Brilliant speaker that he was, he popularized the plank so well that many people then and later naturally assumed that he, not someone else, had originated the Idea. Like any good politician, Cummins did nothing to destroy this impression; perhaps that is why George Roberts felt called on to write an article for the *Iowa Journal of History and Politics* under the title, "The Origin and History of the 'Iowa Idea,'" setting straight the lineage of the plank.

Albert Baird Cummins as Governor of Iowa

Cummins won a handsome victory over his Democratic opponent, Thomas J. Phillips, by a margin of some 83,000 votes. The General Assembly elected along with him contained many of his admirers, soon to become almost fanatical followers. At the height of the power which he soon attained, he came nearer to the stature of a Roman general in command of his loyal legions, indeed, came nearer to the attainment of a charismatic quality than any other Iowa politician before or since. In the eyes of his chief lieutenants he was the leader of the forces of righteousness against the forces of evil. From this time on, his allusions to "our boys" came often, the "boys" including among others Senators Samuel H. Harper of Ottumwa, Warren Garst of Coon Rapids, Byron W. Newberry of Strawberry Point, James J. Crossley of Winterset, and James A. Smith of Osage; Speaker George W. Clarke of Adel; and Representatives Joseph Mattes of Odebolt, Emory H. English of Des Moines, and John C. Flenniken of Strawberry Point.[30]

In his eagerly awaited inaugural address of 1902, the new governor expressed ideas which were a foreshadowing of the nature and direction of his leadership. After an orthodox statement of the liberal's belief in the beneficial effects of criticism, and the process of orderly reform, Governor Cummins moved on to specific topics: the need for laws against industrial combinations organized only for the hope of financial profit in the sale of stock, not for the constructive purpose of serving the public need; the tariff and reciprocity; the relations of labor and capital; corporations and their overly aggressive lobbyists; taxation, especially railroad taxation; the need for a uniform law of negotiable instruments throughout the nation; greater support for education, especially the three institutions of higher learning at Iowa City, Ames, and Cedar Falls. On the first four topics he expressed the typical progressive's great fear of monopoly. Competition must be maintained, by law if necessary, to protect the public. His ideas on railroad taxation were prophetic as they indicated legislative remedies which would be fairer to the roads and at the same time eliminate the political factor in the determination of tax rates. All in all, it was a constructive message which breathed a new spirit into Iowa government.[31]

The railroad tax bill was the only out-and-out progressive measure passed in 1902. The bill was sponsored, appropriately enough, by one of Cummins's most devoted admirers and loyal lieutenants, Representative Emory H. English of Polk County. The bill was designed to secure more equitable taxation of the railroads of the state. Heretofore, the assessment of the taxes on the roads had been the prerogative of the Executive Council, made up of the governor, the secretary of state, the state treasurer, the secretary of agriculture, and the state auditor. Usually the roads controlled a majority if not all of the members of the council, who performed their duties in almost complete secrecy. By the terms of the new act a formula for reports on earnings was drawn up, such reports to go to the council, which retained its prerogative but must now make the assessments on the basis of something other than the roads' own figures. The new procedure had the effect of making public business out of this tremendous responsibility of determining the amount to be paid by the state's largest taxpayers. Any newspaper reporter enterprising enough to run down the information could now inform the people of the procedures used and the results. A severe penalty was provided for any road which did not conform to the prescribed regulations.[32]

It was this session of the General Assembly (the Twenty-ninth) which renewed the effort to secure passage of a proposed constitutional amendment to provide a new system of biennial elections in place of wearying annual elections. An earlier amendment for this purpose had been adopted but it had been thrown out by the courts on a technicality. Senator George M. Titus of Muscatine was the principal author and promoter of the earlier amendment which had passed the Twenty-seventh and Twenty-eighth General Assemblies in 1898 and 1900. Although no longer a member of the Senate, he came to Des Moines in 1902 and assisted in the fight for a second adoption.[33] In this struggle a great deal of credit should be given to Governor Cummins and his usual progressive Republican supporters. This long-needed reform eliminated elections for any state offices in the odd-numbered years and sensibly lumped all elections in the even-numbered years, choosing the Tuesday after the first Monday in November as election day so as to coincide with national elections on that date. In view of the tardiness of this reform, one wonders at the reluctance of some members to vote for it.

Speaker Henderson's Retirement: A Progressive Victory

An incident which shows the trend of the new politics and the bitterness of the factional dispute between standpatters and progressives was the withdrawal of Speaker David B. Henderson from the congressional race of 1902. The irascible but lovable old veteran of the Civil War, and of the political wars since 1865, when he became Allison's Man Friday, gave only one reason for his act—criticism by younger members of the party—but there were several contributing factors. He had just seen a choice political plum, an oil inspectorship, snatched away and awarded to Robert Santee of Cedar Falls, a strong pro-Cummins man. The doughty old colonel, never one to bear his infirmities and his annoyances with sweet resignation, also felt bitter resentment toward certain Waterloo progressives who had tried to sidetrack his nomination at the district convention and who were continuing to snipe at him about his protectionist tariff views. In addition, he undoubtedly felt some bitterness at his omission from a tariff conference then in session at President Roosevelt's home. Well might the crotchety old man have felt abused at home and neglected by his powerful friends at Washington!

Add to these affronts the pain and distress stemming from his ill-fitting artificial limb and it is easy to understand that his supply of patience and tolerance was exhausted. Any one of the three troubles he could have mastered; all three coming at once were too many for his endurance—hence his withdrawal from politics. All the entreaties of Allison, Clarkson, Dolliver, even the president himself, were of no avail in getting him to change his mind. Perhaps it was just as well. Before many months had passed he became a helpless invalid, though life was prolonged until February 25, 1906.[34]

More Triumphs for Cummins

Doubtless the standpat forces, especially Senator Allison, were severely shocked by the retirement of a party veteran such as Colonel Henderson. Perhaps this Cummins triumph, for such it was when viewed in its full meaning, helps to explain Allison's willingness to meet in great secrecy with Cummins and Joseph W. Blythe in Chicago and serve as an intermediary between these two deadly rivals as they worked out a tariff plank for the Iowa Republican platform in 1903. The statement was a masterpiece of smooth and gentle language, not completely repudiating the tariff policy of the past but advocating more flexibility in the future, and endorsing the principle of reciprocity "as the natural complement of protection."

For a short time the spirit of cooperation between the two factions, as indicated by this conference of rivals, worked encouragingly, long enough, indeed, for Cummins to be renominated and then elected over John B. Sullivan of Des Moines by a vote of 238,804 to 159,725, along with an increased number of progressive Republican legislators. It was this General Assembly of 1904 which gave the second passage to the biennial elections amendment to the constitution and sent it on for its test in the general election in November, when it was ratified by a margin of only 23,000 votes. By this amendment, terms of present office-holders were extended by one year. Thus Governor Cummins, already the bête noire of the standpatters, gained an extra year in office. The amendment also specified that the holdover General Assembly would meet again in 1906, and the Assembly elected in 1906 would meet on the first Monday in January 1907.

The session of 1904 was notable for other things. After failure to pass a bill in 1902 to provide regulation of insurance companies, a real breakthrough in insurance legislation came in 1904 with the passage of a bill drawn up and sponsored by Emory H. English, giving the state the power to license insurance companies, approve their contract forms, and examine them periodically. A full measure of other regulatory provisions for the insurance industry was enacted in 1906 and 1907, whereby Iowa kept company with New York and other states in regulating a business strangely in need of forced accountability to clients and public alike.[35] The success of the industry, so important to Des Moines and all of Iowa, and the splendid record of performance since then would seem to indicate that the regulatory program was reasonable and helpful rather than punitive. In this connection it is interesting to note that one of Governor Cummins's most enthusiastic admirers and strongest supporters was Frederick M. Hubbell, founder and president of the Equitable Life Insurance Company of Iowa.[36]

Great as were Cummins's triumphs up to this point in his career, his best years were ahead of him.

CHAPTER 14 THE PROGRESSIVE MOVEMENT: TRIUMPH AND DECLINE 1905–1916

SAFELY INTO HIS SECOND TERM AS GOVERNOR, WITH TWO SUCCESSful legislative sessions behind him, Governor Cummins found that the times called for more rather than less activity. Although the elections of 1905 were to be omitted under the new biennial elections amendment, that year had to be used for planning the years ahead. The amendment provided for a legislative session in 1906 with the members of the 1904 assembly holding over until the new election system could be used in November 1906. The year 1906, therefore, might be thought of as a bonus year during which Cummins and his cohorts might enact more progressive legislation and, in so doing, promote Cummins's career in state and national politics.

The governor considered at least three possibilities in thinking about his personal career: retirement, leaving to others to carry out his program; a try at displacement of the strong conservative, Captain John A. T. Hull of Des Moines, as congressman from the Sixth District; a try for a third term as governor. The latter choice, if taken, would require a triumph over the "no third term" tradition, a doubtful and risky thing to try. His reform program had created many enemies, some of whom no doubt thought that four years of Cummins plus a bonus year were enough; it would be galling to have to submit to the Cummins version of Theodore Roosevelt's "square deal" through a third term.[1]

THE MEMORABLE THIRTY-FIRST GENERAL ASSEMBLY, 1906

The power of the Cummins progressive forces was well illustrated in the 1906 session of the General Assembly. The Senate, under Lieutenant Governor John Herriott of Guthrie Center, and the House, under Speaker George W. Clarke of Adel, kept to a busy schedule, all the while keeping a watchful eye on the contest then in progress for the Republican nomination for governor.

No less than three bills to provide a direct primary were brought up, and though all suffered defeat, the discussion helped to educate the public on this new idea in Iowa. Also beaten were bills to provide the initiative and the referendum. On other points the progressives were able to have their way. Perhaps with one eye on the current fight in Congress, Senator Byron W. Newberry of Strawberry Point successfully led the fight for a pure food law, raising the standards for dairy products, for example, and won a hearing for a pure drugs bill, a bill which he was able to carry to victory in the following year. The two acts were a splendid testimonial to the perseverance of the brilliant young lawyer in overcoming the arguments that such safeguarding legislation was socialistic in nature. A later student of progressivism has said of this law: "The struggle for dairy reform in Iowa . . . provides yet another example of what is perhaps the dominant theme of the Progressive Era: *the expansion of the role of government to meet the requirements of an industrial society.*"[2]

Better known than these acts, though not of greater importance to the masses of the people, was the bill for the outlawing of the "free pass" system so widely used by the railroads. (The redundancy was part of the usage of the times.) The decision to oppose the widespread issuance of passes was a complete about-face for the progressives as well as all others who now lined up against the system. Every politician of every party and every faction, Governor Cummins included, had for years accepted such favors as a custom of the times. In its origins the practice was perhaps fairly innocuous, but by 1900 this was no longer true. Not only officeholders but many other people of influence in every community came to expect and accept passes without the slightest twinge of conscience. The roads were usually glad to amplify the lists to include all the names recommended by their attorneys and staff physicians, of whom there was one of each in every large town on the road, men whose function it was to keep the road in good standing with the public and ward off adverse legislation. Judges, ministers, municipal officials, anyone who might ever have an opportunity to cast a decisive vote or say a good word in the right place, could expect to receive such a favor. Many unqualified persons had no compunction in boldly asking for a pass, some giving highly ingenious reasons for their requests. In modern language, the practice had become a "racket" of the first order and one would think that the roads would have been glad to be relieved of the burden. Not so, at the time; this was the price they had learned to expect to pay for protection from legislatures and courts, and they fought like tigers for the privilege of continuing the custom.

Frankly admitting that he was changing his position on the subject because of the abuses which had crept into the practice, Governor Cummins attacked the "free pass" system in many speeches over the state and in messages to the General Assembly. Bills on the subject were put up in 1902 and 1904 without success but in 1906 an antipass law of limited scope was passed with great public acclaim. In 1907 a second act was passed, extending the prohibition to cover everyone except a bona fide employee of a railroad.[3] Few would deny that a great impediment to honest government had been removed.

Interestingly enough, at this very time, Senator Dolliver, and to some extent Senator Allison and Representative Hepburn, were also engaged in a battle for a much needed railroad reform. Their fight was aided at times by the "Republican Roosevelt,"[4] who was blowing hot and cold on various items in the progressive agenda, including an act providing for the enlargement of the powers of the Interstate Commerce Commission, and the courts, in dealing with railroads. Oddly enough, the first bill for this was introduced by Iowa's Hepburn, of Clarinda, known far and wide as a "Burlington man" in a "Burlington town," and not considered to be a progressive on railroad matters. Quickly passed by the House, the bill was virtually rewritten during debate in the Senate. There the Hepburn bill became the Dolliver bill, and, finally, the key amendment which guaranteed passage was introduced (real author unknown) *in the name of* the "Wise Old Senator" from Iowa, William Boyd Allison, who may or may not have known that such a provision was put up in his name. With this addition the unsatisfactory Interstate Commerce Act of 1887, hitherto flaunted by the roads and weakly enforced by the government, became an act with teeth in it.[5] The three men had brought much favorable publicity to Iowa while earning the dislike of the diehard conservatives led by Senator Nelson W. Aldrich of Rhode Island.

POLITICS, 1906–1908: CONSERVATIVES VERSUS PROGRESSIVES

In 1906 George D. Perkins, publisher of the *Sioux City Journal* and a moderate standpatter, apparently believed that the way was open for a new governor. Perkins insisted then (and with increasing bitterness for years to come) that he had been asked by party leaders to run, a point verified by Cyrenus Cole, the well-informed editor of the *Cedar Rapids Republican,* and by Dolliver's biographer, who proves that both Abraham B. Funk and Dolliver himself made this suggestion or request to Perkins on the assumption that Cummins would not want a third term. The Blythe ultraconservative forces did not support Perkins as yet. A tit-for-tat game took place, Perkins announcing on January 22, 1906, and Cummins, now convinced that he needed the governorship as a base for future ambitions, on February 10. Now the Blythe forces joined Perkins as anti-Cummins men if nothing else.[6]

Cummins, fearing the loss of the Allison-controlled votes to Perkins, decided that he had to do something drastic, namely, to renounce publicly any intention to run against Allison in 1908. This he did in a letter to a prominent Dubuque Republican, Major William H. Torbert (on which he would later renege).[7] So even was the race that it finally turned on the settlement of contests over a few disputed county delegations at the state convention. Senator Dolliver acted as arbitrator and awarded most of the disputed seats to progressives.[8] The convention went on to nominate Cummins for governor by a vote of 933 to 603 and named Warren Garst of Coon Rapids for lieutenant governor, in a clear-cut victory for the progressives.

The standpatters were beaten but not subdued. Amid cries of a stolen nomination, the race was finished. The standpatters were wild with fear of their complete ruin if the progressives should sweep the elections. All sorts of deals were offered and no man's political life was safe. There is ample evidence that the standpatters offered help to the Democrats if they would nominate their best man for governor, Claude R. Porter of Centerville, in exchange for Democratic votes for standpat congressmen and state legislators. Porter was an extremely able man whose only fault was that he belonged to the wrong party in Iowa.[9] There is no proof that a bargain was made but thousands of standpatters scratched their tickets for Porter and openly boasted of it. How many progressive-minded Democrats voted for Cummins can never be known—the number has been estimated as high as 20,000. If so, these were the votes which saved Cummins, who won by just that margin, 216,995 to 196,123. In addition, the progressives swept the other state offices and won a majority in the General Assembly, their first since the party had begun to split. After this dramatic fight between the factions, it was no longer sufficient or even meaningful merely to say "Republican"; now one must always use the significant adjectives, standpat or progressive.

IOWA ADOPTS THE DIRECT PRIMARY

It was unfortunate that questionable motivation surrounded the supreme triumph of the progressives, the enactment of a direct primary law, including a provision for a preferential vote by each party to name its candidate for United States senator. The ambitious Cummins was accused of being afraid of the traditional nominating convention and of feeling safer with an appeal to the masses. Yet the convention system was condemned by many observers of the political scene because of its presumable susceptibility to manipulation by bosses and greater ease in the purchase of votes. In Iowa and elsewhere progressives held that the only way to purify the political process was by giving nominations to the people. Cummins could argue that the idea of the direct primary had come from others long before the current delicate political balance had been dreamed of. The earliest proposal came as early as 1896, and in 1898 a law had been passed giving counties the option of using this method of selecting candidates. Compulsory statewide use was proposed in 1902 but without success. In 1904 five bills were introduced; the only one the progressives could pass was a limited one which required all counties of 75,000 people or more to use the primary—a criterion which only Polk County could meet at the time.[10]

Agitation for this form of direct government was continued by the reformers despite the fierce opposition of the spokesmen for the railroads, who saw it as an interference with their control of the selection of candidates. The Cummins forces were not to be denied. In late March 1907, progressives won what they considered their greatest triumph to date, a full-fledged direct primary act. By its terms a primary election would be held on the first Monday in June in the even-numbered years. Each qualifying party would select its official candidates for all county and state offices (except judges), for representatives in Congress, and for senators to the extent of expressing a preference among those seeking a party's favor. The act prescribed rules for operating the machinery of a party and for the conduct of primary elections. A very important detail not often mentioned was the prohibition of delegate proxies in the conventions at all levels.[11]

Together with the second antipass bill, and a third bill which forbade contributions by corporations to the campaign of any candidate for office, the victory over the railroads was complete. There might still be ways of evasion of the law and hidden means of influencing officeholders, but at least the formal, obvious ways were now closed and a method of recourse on offenders had been established.

CUMMINS CHALLENGES ALLISON

At the time of the election of Dolliver in January 1907, Cummins had dared to say that while he would not work for the office, he felt free to accept it should it come to him, a hint of his availability which did not pay off against a man of Dolliver's standing. Little by little it became evident that his real thoughts were of a challenge to Allison in 1908, in spite of the Torbert Letter of 1906. The contrast between the vigorous and innovative Cummins and the aging invalid was too apparent to be missed. To put the matter bluntly, when a seventy-eight-year-old man is suffering from prostatic cancer, virtually kept alive by frequent treatments administered by his loyal secretary;[12] when he is a prisoner of his room except for the most urgent calls to the floor of the Senate, should he or should he not ask the voters for another six-year term? The business world has answered this question but the Congress has not.

A gentleman of the filial sentiments of Jonathan Dolliver said frankly that Allison should not run, and could not perform his duties if elected; said frankly that he expected Cummins to inherit the Allison seat very soon—but if Allison wanted to run, he would help him in every way possible. A small coterie of bosses in the standpat Republican faction, who hated Cummins with a consuming passion, would also say yes. Albert Cummins had a different answer. After being a serious contender in 1894 and again in 1900, when he probably would have won had not the standpatters run a "dead" man against him, that is, the incumbent senator, John H. Gear, who was elected and then died, as predicted, two months later, it might be expected that Cummins felt cheated out of his deserved victory. And now, seven years later, after long years of study and experience, and a brilliant record as governor, and in the prime of life, he felt that he deserved the chance rather than the invalid incumbent to represent Iowa in the Senate. It may be added that President Roosevelt, for all his bluster and swagger, ran away from this fight and followed a neutral course.

In the realm of politics, such matters are not decided through rational processes. After much urging from his friends and an ultimatum from Joseph W. Blythe, who said: "I do not think . . . that it ought to be left entirely for Mr. Allison to decide," the aged senator made his announcement of candidacy on August 26, 1907. Although virtually immobilized by his illness, his mind was still clear. He helped to arrange all the details for a great rally to launch his campaign, held at Council Bluffs on November 25, and asked Dolliver to assume the role of orator for the occasion. Dolliver used part of the Torbert Letter as a weapon against Cummins, both here at Council Bluffs and later in the long campaign. Cummins, who had been slow in announcing his plans, had to make a formal announcement. This was carried in the *Des Moines Iowa State Register,* his home newspaper and most prominent supporter, on December 4, a challenge to Allison and the Old Guard of Iowa politics.

It is pretty certain that never before or since have Iowans taken a political race so seriously. Dolliver led a magnificent attack, depending almost wholly on appeals to sentiment for Allison and charges of duplicity against Cummins, who fought back like a wounded lion. Real issues were almost totally neglected though the fight was in the name of progressivism versus conservatism. The Republican State Convention in March foretold the results when a resolution of endorsement for Allison was adopted by a vote of 678 to 510. In the June preferential primary 200,000 Iowa Republicans trekked to the polls to express their choice, Allison winning by a scant 10,000, only 105,891 to 95,256. Warren Garst, a Cummins man, lost the nomination for governor, securing only 63,737 votes against 88,834 for Beryl F. Carroll, a rugged conservative. Nine out of eleven Republican nominees for congressional seats were conservatives, and the standpatters controlled the delegations in fifty-five out of ninety-nine county conventions, which would give them control of the state convention, with the power to write the plaform, dominate the state central committee, and eventually the power to undo many of the progressive achievements. The only victory won by the progressives was in the number of nominations for the General Assembly.[13]

The Republican voters had spoken—and the progressives had been beaten by their own weapon. Their mood changed from elation to despair. Two developments saved them from utter ruin. One, in the state convention, at Waterloo, the progressives very cleverly took advantage of the "no proxies for absent delegates" rule; too many overconfident standpatters had stayed at home. On a district-by-district basis, the progressives were able to slip into a numerical superiority in the convention and preserve their previous accomplishments. For this the standpatters had only themselves to blame.[14]

The other knockout blow to standpat power was the not unexpected death of Senator Allison, two months and two days after his victory in June. The almost universal references to his "sudden" death attest nothing except the power of the standpat press in creating the impression all through the campaign that Allison had been in good health, a rank deceit on the people of Iowa. Actually, he had failed very rapidly and he was under constant care of doctors and friends for several weeks before the end came on August 4, 1908.

AT LAST: ALBERT BAIRD CUMMINS, UNITED STATES SENATOR FROM IOWA

Dolliver could have had the Republican nomination for vice-president in 1908 and this would have opened a place in the Senate for Cummins. Dolliver ran away from the offer,[15] however, thus in effect requiring Cummins to go through a new fight for the Allison seat. Rejecting the easy way of resigning as governor and allowing his successor, Warren Garst, to appoint him, Cummins insisted on a victory from the people. This was not altogether an act of nobility: such an appointment would have been effective only until the next March 4, and in the meanwhile the assembly elected in November 1908 would have to elect someone for the full term of six years, following an expression of preference by the voters at a primary, if the spirit of the law of 1907 were honored.

The tortuous path through the electoral maze of the next few weeks can best be followed by a simple and highly condensed statement of the facts. As soon as decency would allow, on August 25 Governor Cummins called a special session of the assembly to deal with the vacancy. On August 31 the special session amended the Primary Law of 1907, providing for a primary to be held in conjunction with the November election in case of the death, resignation, or removal of a candidate nominated in June. This amendment applied only to the full six-year senatorial term beginning on March 4, not to a short term. On September 4–9, this same special session undertook to elect a successor for the remainder of Allison's term. The standpatters were able to block the election of Cummins, though not able to elect their own man, Major John F. Lacey of Oskaloosa. The assembly then recessed to await the results of the November preferential primary contest between Cummins and Lacey.

On November 3 Cummins won the primary favor by an ample margin—42,000 votes. On November 24 the assembly reconvened and elected Cummins to the vacant seat for the remainder of the Allison term, 107 votes for Cummins and 35 votes for Claude R. Porter, the Democrat. On that same day, Cummins was sworn in as a United States senator. On January 20, 1909, the new General Assembly elected Cummins for the full term over Porter, 143 to 41, and on March 4 Cummins began his full six-year term.[16]

Cummins Joins Dolliver in the Senate

The requirements of realistic politics and the strange ways of politicians were never better illustrated than in the new relations of Dolliver and Cummins. Dolliver made his peace with Cummins and the two proceeded to serve Iowa and the nation brilliantly. It so happened that Cummins's first full term began in a special session called in March to revise the tariff. Everyone else thought that the "revision" called for in 1908 was to be a revision downward—but not Senator Aldrich of Rhode Island. Aldrich's Committee on Finance had taken a fairly good tariff bill from the House and added 847 amendments! Dolliver tore into the amended bill and exposed it as a shameless and needless vehicle of protectionism. Ably backed by Cummins, Dolliver subjected Aldrich to months of grilling before losing. Later, Cummins would say: "You have heard . . . from the man who knows more about the tariff law than any other man in the United States, more truth than ever before fell upon your ears."[17] One has only to read the masterful summary of Dolliver's speeches in the Thomas R. Ross biography, *Jonathan Prentiss Dolliver,* and chuckle over Ding's cartoons in the *Des Moines Register,* to see how much depended on Dolliver's leadership. Better yet, Professor Ross completely demolishes the myth that Dolliver was motivated by a personal pique at Aldrich for refusing him Allison's place on the Finance Committee. Ross clearly shows that Dolliver had already opposed Aldrich on tariff matters, that he had opposed and beaten Aldrich on the railroad rate bill, and that he had shown a mind of his own on the rate bill, the pure food bill, the employers' liability bill, and other matters. Aldrich knew that he could not purchase Dolliver's support by merely doing him the favor of putting him on the Finance Committee. As for

Dolliver, it was sufficient for him to know that his party had promised tariff revision in its 1908 platform; he was now determined to try to keep it to its promise.

The fight was in vain in spite of Dolliver's heroic and exhausting work. There was talk of reading Dolliver out of the party. His own answer was: "I am going to judgment in the next twenty years, and I am going so that I can look my Maker in the face. I do not have to stay in public life. I can take my books, my wife and my children, and if I am dismissed from the service for following my convictions, I will go out to my farm and stay there until the call comes." Dolliver was not driven out of public life by his course of action but carried over into national fame. He and Cummins and their progressive (now usually called "insurgent") allies were defeated by Taft's and Aldrich's willingness to compromise and accept a corporation tax, which they did not want, instead of a provision for an unpopular income tax, which Cummins wanted to restore to the bill, and by the perverse tactics of some Democrats who voted for the bill now with the thought that it would beat the Republicans in 1910. Instead of ignominy and retirement, Dolliver earned the praise of men everywhere, most of all from thousands of people who paraded in his honor when he returned to Fort Dodge. He had fought the fight of the people; Taft and Aldrich had served the special interests and in doing so had doomed the party to certain defeat in 1910 and 1912.[18]

THE DEATH OF DOLLIVER

In the months following the passage of the Payne-Aldrich Tariff Act, the lines were drawn very rigidly between standpatters and insurgents. On such issues as the Pinchot-Ballinger controversy over the policy of conservation,[19] the fight against the tyranny of Speaker "Uncle Joe" Cannon, the fight to set up a system of Postal Savings Banks, and the contest over the Mann-Elkins Railroad Act, especially the first and the last, Dolliver played a prominent part and was recognized by everyone as the leading progressive in the Senate.

As soon as the session was completed in June, Dolliver came home to participate in the 1910 campaign, though too late for the June primary, where Warren Garst, the progressive, had again been defeated by Beryl F. Carroll for the Republican nomination for governor. Dolliver and Cummins took part in the August state convention, Dolliver as permanent chairman. The fight by the Old Guard, led by Lacey, Perkins, and Hepburn, against the two insurgent senators was bitter, heartbreaking, and inhumane. Dolliver loyally went on to make a few speeches in spite of doctors' orders to rest. He had been in ill health much of the time since 1906 with heart trouble and nasal obstructions, and the wonder was that his heart had held up so long under such strain. The end came on October 10, 1910.

The funeral, alas, was as much a politicians' workshop as an occasion for mourning; the talk was of a new day in Iowa politics and new leaders. The elevation of Cummins to the Senate and the death of Dolliver left the progressive wing of the Republican state organization somewhat adrift. By contrast, the conservative faction was in the strong hands of Governor Beryl F. Carroll of Bloomfield (1909–1913), a staunch standpatter whose political backbone, so the wits said, was "reinforced with a ramrod," and Governor George W. Clarke of Adel (1913–1917), once a valuable Cummins man as Speaker of the House, who had gradually moved away from the progressives.[20]

A few progressive items were left over for enactment after 1907 but they were not of a highly partisan nature. One such item was reorganization of the government of the three state institutions of higher learning: the State University of Iowa, Iowa State College of Agriculture and Technology, and Iowa State Teachers College, to use the names of that era. In 1909 the Whipple Act provided for a unified State Board of Education for all three schools instead of separate boards.[21] Another item was the creation of a State Department of Insurance in 1913. Many other helpful acts of a housekeeping nature were passed.

Iowa's progressive legislative record could be compared favorably with Wisconsin's or that of any other state. The decline in strength of the Iowa progressives was not due to local failures or weaknesses alone. A pattern of decline was evident in other states—the reform movement inherent in progressivism had to become national rather than urban or state-centered if its program were to be completed.

THE ELECTION OF WILLIAM S. KENYON TO THE SENATE

Much of the political discussion at Dolliver's funeral concerned the selection of a successor to the deceased leader. To the standpatters the vacancy appeared to be a heaven-sent opportunity to claim the seat and thus offset the disappointment of the recent loss of Allison's seat to Cummins. To the progressives it presented a challenge to search their ranks for a man who could win the election and carry on as a progressive ally and partner to the brilliant Cummins.

The immediate advantage was held by the standpatters inasmuch as Governor Carroll would surely appoint a fellow conservative and thus give him the edge in the legislative election of someone to fill out the term. Carroll's appointee was Lafayette ("Lafe") Young,[22] formerly of Carroll, Iowa, and now the very able editor of the *Des Moines Capital,* who took his seat on December 6, 1910. Young was another former progressive who had gradually tired of that relationship. For the coming election, the standpatters of course favored Senator Young; the progressives were badly divided. The Cummins men in their ranks wanted the honor for Abraham B. Funk, publisher of the *Spirit Lake Beacon,* for years one of Cummins's chief lieutenants; the moderate progressives induced William S. Kenyon of Fort Dodge, formerly an Illinois Central Railroad attorney, presently an assistant to the attorney general in Washington in charge of antitrust cases, to run; and still another progressive faction put up Howard W. Byers of Harlan, attorney general of Iowa. The Democrats relied on their faithful candidate, Claude R. Porter of Centerville.

The new primary law was applicable only if specifically called into use by the General Assembly. All proposals to authorize a primary election were defeated by the divided progressive Republicans to prevent the sure victory of a standpatter, giving the standpatters a chance to ridicule them for repudiating their favorite device of popular government. Under these circumstances the Thirty-fourth General Assembly could only follow the traditional procedure of a caucus by each party to select a nominee. Such a caucus designation was unofficial, but usually the members faithfully followed the party choice. Obviously afraid of the results, Senator Young's backers threw the session into confusion by refusing to enter a caucus, a move which caused Kenyon's backers to retaliate in kind. The assembly was left with no alternative but to hold a formal balloting and put the five publicized names at the head of the list; other candidates could be nominated from the floor.

With Republican votes divided four ways, Claude Porter led the field on the early ballots but no Republicans would give their votes to make possible his election. Day after day the ritual of taking a ballot was performed but no one could obtain a majority. Byers and Funk withdrew their names after a month of such futility, and a month later Lafe Young did likewise in favor of a new nominee, Iowa Supreme Court Justice Horace E. Deemer of Red Oak, a neutral, compromise candidate. Kenyon's men held fast, however, and this strategy failed.

Finally, as the day of adjournment arrived without a decisive ballot, a lone Democrat broke the log jam by switching to Kenyon. Two Republicans then switched their votes to the man from Fort Dodge and this action encouraged a few others to follow suit. Thus belatedly Kenyon received eighty-five votes and victory; adjourment followed on the same day. Kenyon, the antithesis of Dolliver in temperament and manner, was a loyal Dolliver man, and all Iowa progressives could be sure that a worthy successor to Dolliver had been chosen.[23]

The prolonged Iowa contest of 1911 was similar to divisions within the Republican party in other states and on the national level. A fierce three-way contest for the presidential nomination tore the party into bits and pieces. The first challenger to Taft was the Wisconsin progressive, Robert M. La Follette; Theodore Roosevelt came into the race later, elbowing La Follette aside and then attacking his former protégé. Iowa Republicans were caught up in this war of ideas and emotions, and personal loyalties, and in the heat of battle developed tremendous antipathies toward each other. In January 1911, as a part of this campaign, the National Progressive Republican League was organized to divert the support of all progressives into the La Follette mainstream. Senator Cummins was a charter member of this league but became more cautious as the battle continued. By the time of the convention in June 1912, La Follette had lost out and the contest had become a bitter fight between Taft and Roosevelt.

Roosevelt entered the convention with a decided advantage in the preconvention pledges and promises. Such a margin proved to be of no avail at the convention which opened at Chicago on June 18, to which Iowa sent 26 delegates. The real convention had begun on June 7 with the sessions of the Committee on Credentials. Over 200 delegates were under contest and the committee awarded every one of them to the Taft forces. This advantage was augmented by another victory on a motion to allow contested delegates to vote on all matters except the question of their own eligibility. On the motion to table this proposition, Iowans cast 16 votes to 10, figures which may be equated to 16 conservatives and 10 progressives, the 16 joining the Taft forces which opposed giving up this rule. Taft had still two other advantages: complete control of 60 Negro delegates from the South who voted exactly as told, and the favor of the temporary chairman, Elihu Root.

As decision after decision went against Roosevelt, the nomination of Taft was insured. Having gone this far toward the disruption of the party, Roosevelt gave orders to his followers not to vote on the first ballot. A surprising total of 344 delegates obeyed his orders and then walked out as it was announced that Taft had won with 561 votes. Iowans were *not* among those who walked out; they remained to give those 16 conservative votes to Taft and 10 progressive votes to—Cummins! All along the way, Iowa progressives had hoped that Cummins might emerge as a compromise candidate. Senator William S. Kenyon managed the Cummins boomlet but Roosevelt blocked the plan of a compromise. Idaho added 7 votes to Iowa's 10.

Roosevelt announced immediately that a new party would be formed, and set up an organizing committee of eighteen members. There were no Iowans on the committee. Although fully sympathetic with the Roosevelt cause, neither Cummins nor Kenyon would desert the Republican ship, and they were able to hold the Iowa delegates in line. A second committee was formed on which Iowa was represented by John L. Stevens of Boone. On the call of this new group, the convention met on August 5. In the weeks before and after that date, the principal item of daily news was the announcement of this or that Republican leader that he was sticking by Taft or going over to Roosevelt. Senator Cummins announced that he would not join the new party but indicated he would not vote for Taft; Senator Kenyon assured his following that he would stay by Taft; the new chairman of the Republican State Central Committee, Carl Franke of Parkersburg, went on record to urge Iowa Republicans to support the state ticket but not the national slate.

In the meanwhile the Democrats were having their own troubles in the selection of a ticket. The principal candidates were Woodrow Wilson, governor of New Jersey and a recent convert to progressivism, and Speaker Champ Clark of Missouri, spokesman for the more traditional brand of democracy. William Jennings Bryan wanted to be the nominee or the man who named the candidate. Iowa Democrats were divided in their preferences but leaned toward Clark, partly because he was a Westerner and partly because of the influence of his son-in-law, W. W. Marsh of Waterloo, one of the leading Democrats in Iowa. In the Baltimore convention Iowa's 26 delegates stuck by Champ Clark solidly for the first 29 ballots; on the 30th roll call a break came when fourteen Iowans changed over to Wilson. Sixteen ballots later, Wilson won the nomination.

Returning to the Progressives, when Roosevelt arrived in Chicago for his party's convention, he was asked how he felt; his reply was that he felt as "strong as a bull moose." In this chance way a popular name was born for the Progressive party. The first ovation for Roosevelt ran for fifty-two minutes by the clock. Many Iowans were there as delegates or witnesses—but the men who could have guaranteed victory in the fall for the Bull Moose cause were not there: Cummins, Kenyon, and their likes from other strong Republican states, men whose eyes were on their political futures rather than on further reforms which Roosevelt urged. Such repudiation by the party regulars, even those sentimentally well disposed toward Roosevelt, doomed the Bull Moosers to sure defeat.[24]

THE ELECTION OF 1912 AND THE PROGRESSIVE DEMISE, 1912–1916

The election results in Iowa reflected the results in the nation as a whole. As any novice at politics could have foretold, Wilson won going away, winning 435 electoral votes based on 6,286,124 popular votes; Roosevelt won only 88 electoral votes but a very respectable 4,126,020 popular votes; Taft carried only two states, Vermont and Utah, with 8 electoral votes and 3,483,922 popular votes. In Iowa the vote ran 185,325 for Wilson, 161,819 for Roosevelt, and 119,805 for Taft. Iowa Republicans could curse the evil day of the split and point to their combined total of 281,625 votes, which in a normal election would have given them their customary victory over the minority party. Another way of looking at it, however, would show a combined total of 347,144 "progressive" votes against Taft's 119,805. One can never know how the votes would have been distributed in a straightout Wilson versus Taft, or Wilson versus Roosevelt, contest. That Iowa was still heavily Republican was indicated by the fact that Wilson could carry only three Democratic candidates for Congress on his coattails. The governor's office went to a mildly conservative Republican, George W. Clarke, and the General Assembly was, as usual, heavily Republican.

Only a postscript is needed to account for political fortunes in the years after the Republican national debacle of 1912. Theodore Roosevelt's founding of the national Progressive party as his personal property was not alone to blame for the Republican defeat. It is one of the maxims of politics that every party suffers a shake-up after a long period in office and in this case the Republican party had grown so complacent that some of its own members felt the need for a transfer of power. It is only fair to say that there were men in the Iowa Progressive party, formerly regular Republicans, who sincerely and enthusiastically believed that theirs was the only party which could and would carry on the great reform crusade. These Progressive crusaders, however, were not men who had been *leaders* of the old Republican party. They were men who had been camp followers, not leaders. The new men who now suddenly burst onto the scene in places of leadership in the Progressive party were mere amateurs in the great game of politics. Splendid men they might be, well educated, well meaning, leaders in their professions or their businesses, but they were unknown—and they were political amateurs. One is reminded of the Liberal Republicans of 1872.

In 1912, when the rebellion in the Republican party took place, Iowans who were inclined to go along with Teddy Roosevelt and stand at Armageddon with the Lord, were caught short on leadership. John L. Stevens of Boone was one who came forward to give respectable leadership to the Bull Moose forces. He was an engineer who had turned to the law and had risen to a district judgeship. Not a man of the masses, he ran a distant third in the race for governor in 1912. In 1914 Casper Schenk, a brilliant Des Moines attorney who reflected great personal honor on the Progressives, contested for the Progressive nomination for senator. Schenk, formerly of Waterloo, formally educated at Iowa State University, University of Chicago, and Harvard University, had little trouble in winning the nomination. But with these two names, the list of capable leaders with backgrounds of practical experience comes to an end. In the 1914 elections, Cummins received 205,832 votes; Democrat Maurice Connolly of Dubuque won 167,251; and Schenk a mere 15,058. This victory gave Cummins the honor of being the first Iowa senator elected by the people after the ratification of the Sixteenth Amendment. For governor, George W. Clarke won a second term with 207,881 votes; the popular and able John T. Hamilton of Cedar Rapids received 182,036 as a Democrat; George C. White of Nevada won only 16,796 as a Progressive. No Progressive candidate for Congress received more than a token vote. In 1916 the Progressives made only a token appearance in Iowa and none at all nationally. Their candidate for governor, the unknown Stephen H. Bashor of Waterloo, polled only 2,035 votes—and thus the party's history in Iowa ended as a pathetic joke. William L. Harding of Sioux City, a rigidly regular Republican, amassed 313,586 votes; the new leader of the Democrats, Edwin T. Meredith of Des Moines, won 186,832 votes, even though he had added popularity as a Prohibition leader.

For a few years Cummins and Kenyon would sometimes be referred to as Progressives or Progressive Republicans, as would La Follette, Norris, and a few others, but the label was virtually meaningless in the formalities of political organization. Theodore Roosevelt made no effort to run in 1916. Even if the Progressives had been able to find better leaders in Iowa and elsewhere, it is likely that the issues connected with the problems of the day in the realm of foreign policy would have overshadowed any interest in progressive reforms. Certain vestiges of progressivism would linger on for years to come but the great day of the Progressives was over.[25]

CHAPTER 15 THE FIRST WORLD WAR AND ITS AFTERMATH 1914–1928

THE TWENTY-THREE-YEAR PERIOD KNOWN AS THE "GOLDEN AGE of Agriculture," 1897–1920, might have terminated in 1913 had it not been for the coming of World War I. Well before 1914 American farmers were producing surpluses of some crops and there was talk of methods of reducing the excesses of supply over demand. The holocaust in Europe rescued the whole American economy, particularly the agricultural sector, from a noticeable downturn in 1914. By 1915 Europe's misfortune was bringing about a noticeable prosperity in America, which America's entry into the war in 1917 merely served to augment. This unexpected turn of events prevented an attack on the problem of surpluses while it was in its early stages. After the war, American farmers were keyed to a policy and program of all-out production when full production was no longer needed, indeed, when the resultant surpluses were a burden instead of a blessing.

Inflationary bidding for our products helped to raise farm income from $7.8 billion in 1913 to $9.5 billion in 1916; total American exports to Europe rose from $1.5 billion in 1913 to $3.8 billion in 1916; our exports to non-European countries in the same period rose from $1 billion to $1.7 billion, making a total of $3 billion of abnormal exports. Conversely, our imports were almost nil.[1] Many farmers rushed out to buy more land, more equipment, and more fertilizer; they raised bigger crops and bigger and better meat animals, produced more milk and butter, and raked in the profits, giving little heed to tomorrow. In all of this, Iowa, as a leading farm state, was deeply involved. A farm crisis was in the making—but who dared to play the role of Jeremiah?

THE ELECTIONS OF 1916

In Iowa the crucial elections of November 1916 were affected by two diverse issues: neutrality and Prohibition. Many German-Americans gave up their customary habit of voting the Democratic ticket because they doubted the sincerity of President Wilson's policy of neutrality, so bravely announced in 1914; now they voted against Wilson and all who upheld him. Even more dramatic was the politics of Prohibition. In a strange switch of traditional situations, the Democratic candidate for governor, Edwin T. Meredith of Des Moines, publisher of *Successful Farming,* was an ardent Prohibitionist and strongly supported by forces that were usually on the Republican roster: the *Des Moines Register;* the *Marshalltown Times-Republican;* the *Council Bluffs Nonpareil;* the farm family bible, *Wallaces' Farmer;* and several Protestant churches, notably Meredith's own, the powerful Methodist vote. The Republican candidate, William L. Harding, a Sioux City lawyer, opposed Prohibition but was against the return of the saloon. He was openly supported by the liquor interests, who also opposed woman suffrage on the grounds that women would vote for Prohibition. Another issue affecting the race was the good roads movement, then in its infancy. Each candidate spoke in favor of "local" determination of paving needs but Harding succeeded in pinning the label of "big spender" for roads on Meredith, and hurt him by calling him a supporter of the plan for a state highway commission to act as a planning and supervising agency.

In this badly mixed-up situation, eloquent and repeated appeals to party loyalty, notably by Senator Cummins, an anti-Prohibitionist, and Senator Kenyon, a dry, sufficed to put Harding over for governor and carry Iowa for Charles E. Hughes for president. Apparently enough German-Americans, ordinarily Democrats, voted for Harding to offset the Republican drys who voted for Meredith. The Irish vote, such as it was, probably went against Meredith because the Catholic hierarchy and the Catholic press were against Prohibition.[2]

AMERICA GOES TO WAR

Although the country reelected Wilson in 1916, partly on the slogan "He kept us out of war!", Germany's resumption of unrestricted submarine warfare in January 1917 made a shambles out of the idea of neutrality. On February 3 we broke off diplomatic relations with Germany. On February 24 we learned of but did not publish the Zimmerman Note to Mexico, inviting that country to join an alliance with Germany and Japan. On February 26 the president asked Congress for authority to arm merchant vessels. On March 1 the State Department published the Zimmerman Note. This fanned the war fever but not enough to prevent about a dozen senators, a "little group of willful men" in the president's words, from filibustering to death Wilson's request. Senator Cummins was a leader of the "willful" men; Senator Kenyon was sympathetic. In his new term, the president ordered the arming of the ships, acting as commander-in-chief. The Germans kept on with submarine attacks and on April 2 the president asked for war.[3] The Senate agreed, 82 to 6, Cummins and Kenyon reluctantly voting yea; the House voted 373 to 50, the 50 including three Iowans.[4]

Life on the Home Front

The bare statistics of Iowa's unhesitant participation in the first World War are very impressive. In the military sphere, out of an estimated population of 2,400,000, with a male population of 1,200,000, the number of Iowa men between the ages of 21 and 31 (later extended to between 18 and 45) who registered under the Selective Service Act was 523,478. The number who ultimately served, either as draftees or volunteers, was 114,224, distributed as follows: in the army—96,726 enlisted men, 4,975 officers, 20 in the United States Military Academy, and 611 nurses; in the Marine Corps—1,044 enlisted men and 30 officers; in the navy—10,211 enlisted men, 525 officers, 40 nurses, and 42 yeomen. The casualties ran about 2,000.[5] Of all the Iowa units in the armed forces, surely the most famous was the Rainbow Division's 168th Infantry Regiment, commanded first by Colonel Ernest R. Bennett of Des Moines, followed by Colonel Mathew A. Tinley of Council Bluffs. The individual Iowan who acquired the most fame was undoubtedly General Hanford W. MacNider of Mason City. The first Iowan to give his life in this war was Merle Hay of Glidden.[6]

During the period of neutrality, quite a few (an indeterminate number, of course) thought that Germany was no more guilty of causing the war than the Entente Allies, and a few were bold enough to say so publicly. As pro-Entente sympathies grew, especially after the sinking of the *Lusitania* in 1915, pro-German views became unpopular among a majority of the American people. After April 6, 1917, such views were likely to run afoul of the Espionage Act of 1917 or its amended versions. The slightest divergence from "100% Americanism" aroused suspicions of "treason" and brought about vengeful acts designed to prove a man's loyalty. In many Iowa towns (and all over America) self-styled guardians of patriotism forced locally prominent and highly respected German-Americans to carry the flag in parades and, in some cases, prostrate themselves and kiss the flag in the sight of their fellow townsmen. Liberty Bond purchases were watched carefully and German-Americans were threatened with dire punishment if they did not immediately buy their full quotas. Those who "talked too much" about Germany's successes or complained about Germany's losses were physically intimidated and sometimes beaten, sometimes badly mutilated.

Another example of anti-German feeling in Iowa took a vicious turn. In a blanket proclamation applicable to all foreign languages but obviously aimed primarily at the language of our chief enemy, Governor

William L. Harding struck a blow at all groups not using English. On May 23, 1918, he issued an edict requiring them to use English in public and private schools as the medium of instruction; in conversation on trains, all public places, and over the telephones; in public addresses; and in church services, saying that those who could not speak or understand English should worship in their homes. Comparing our cultural pluralism to the Tower of Babel, he urged everyone to "Speak English!" This was a hard blow to many Iowans, especially those who belonged to the largest immigrant and first-generation American group in the state.

The governor was roundly criticized at home and in other states and even in Washington, his critics saying that he was destroying the very freedom that we were supposedly fighting for, and giving the Germans a good talking point against us in the war of propaganda then in progress. Numerous protests by opponents and several conferences on the subject led to a slight modification of his order; now pastors might deliver their sermons first in English and then in the foreign tongue. The governor's second-term bid in November, already endangered by the strength of his able Democratic opponent, Claude R. Porter, was further jeopardized by the threatened loss of many foreign-related voters and their sympathizers. Harding's defenders said that his information had led him to believe that Iowa's failure to meet her quotas in the recent First and Second Liberty Loan drives had been caused by a "latent patriotism" which the use of foreign languages had encouraged; therefore, if the use of these languages were banned, patriotism would be increased.

The humorous aspects of one well-publicized case did much to undermine the governor's cause. In Scott County five women were apprehended for speaking German in a rural telephone conversation, the original number of two conversationalists having grown to five by virtue of the well-known tendency toward eavesdropping over party lines. The women were fined some $225 and the money turned over to the county chapter of the Red Cross amidst much ridicule of the governor's "law." Eventually an act requiring English as the language of instruction was passed in Iowa and in Ohio, Missouri, and Nebraska, but overturned in the United States Supreme Court.[7]

AGRICULTURE DURING WORLD WAR I

After the United States joined the ranks of the combatants, demands on the national economy rose by leaps and bounds. As for Iowa, primarily agricultural, the stimulus for greater crop production was stronger than ever. Now it would be patriotic as well as profitable to increase one's production, aiding America and our European associates as well. Since the Allies' supplies of gold and overseas investments usable as collateral had been virtually exhausted, our government found it necessary to lend them money for making their purchases—and the Congress approved the loans which were made, eventually running into billions; these were the "war debts" which became the topic of much future debate. At the time of the first loans, both Senators Cummins and Kenyon, on totally unsentimental grounds, advocated a "gift" of money to our associates in the war. They recognized the technical point that we were not lending money but goods: the credits which we were extending were simply digits placed on bank books to be drawn upon by purchasing agents. Cummins, virtually a neutralist, said the "money" should not be loaned but advanced as our contribution to the war, inasmuch as it would be a year or more before we would be ready to make a military contribution.[8] This view, which now seems so sensible and which in principle would become our policy in World War II, was summarily rejected.

"Food will win the war!" was the slogan now heard and seen on every hand. Government spokesmen urged the farmers in Iowa and other states to produce to the limit and bankers begged them to borrow money and buy more land for this purpose. Experts showed them how to increase low yields and urged them to plow up pasturelands and roadsides and put them into production. The government announced guaranteed minimum prices for wheat, corn, cotton, and other products needed for the war effort. No one could lose, so it seemed, even if the price of land did shoot up to $800–$1,000 an acre.[9] One could make a down payment, mortgage the farm for the balance, and in a few good years pay off the debt, what with wheat at $2.20–$3.60 per bushel and corn at $2.00–$3.00. Iowa farmers never had it so good.

Parenthetically, an ominous quarrel between Herbert Hoover, head of the Food Administration, and Henry C. Wallace of Des Moines should be noticed. Hoover held to the theory that an appeal to patriotism would be sufficient to get farmers to increase their pork production; Wallace, on leave from *Wallaces' Farmer,* argued for financial guarantees and assured rewards. Henry C. Wallace joined the quarrel well fortified with a new formula, called the corn-hog ratio, for determining the pork price which would control the farmer's decision to feed or sell his corn. This formula was the brainchild of his brilliant son, Henry Agard Wallace, and was built on the hypothesis that a farmer would have to receive a price for 100 pounds of pork at least 13 times the price of a bushel of corn; otherwise, it would be more profitable to sell the corn for cash. Hoover held on to his point of view and Henry C. Wallace ultimately lost the argument, one result of which was a deep-seated dislike and distrust of one another which was never dissolved.[10]

As the war was grinding to an end, Iowa Republicans won an anti-Wilson victory.[11] As soon as the war ended, President Wilson ordered an immediate return to the free enterprise system, but exceptions had to be made. Price supports for American farm products were kept intact through 1919 and well into 1920, and loans to some foreign countries were continued. This grace period was a boon to all and should have provided a cushion for those about to be pushed off the economic ladder. *Wallaces' Farmer* urged its farm readers to "back down the ladder a rung at a time" and warned them that farmers would be the first "to be pushed off the ladder,"[12] yet it seemed to come as a surprise when public announcement was made on May 31, 1920, that the guaranteed price on wheat was being withdrawn and supports under other crops soon went the same way, and loans to European countries were shut off at the same time.

It seems in retrospect that the government officials made every conceivable mistake in dealing with the problem of phasing out the war programs. Without loans the European nations which were still making postwar adjustments could no longer pay American prices that had been on a rising curve since 1914. The exports which had been the key to our farm prosperity now continued in the same or even a slightly increased volume but at only half the former prices. Even before the crash of 1920, farm income had dropped approximately 50 percent, and now, just when the American farmer needed credit to carry him over this rough spot, the Federal Reserve Board raised the rediscount rate. Money tightened up, the country banks could not renew the notes of their customers, and mortgages came due at the very worst time. To add to the farmers' woes, the Esch-Cummins Act of 1920 allowed an increase in freight rates, taking a larger slice out of the farmers' dwindling income.

Most cruel of all, the farmer found that prices and wages in other parts of the economy were holding up while the prices he received were going down. This loss of purchasing power, soon to be expressed as "the loss of parity of income," was the knockout blow. Many a farmer who had followed the advice of the government and his banker to increase his acreage now found that his only relief was through bankruptcy proceedings. Whereas in 1914 only 5.5 percent of such cases involved farmers, in 1920 the national figure rose to 14.4 percent. In North Dakota the figure for farmers reached the fantastic high of 78.5 percent; in more stable Iowa the percentage of increase rose only slightly between 1914 and 1920, the increase being greater in the south than in the north.[13] Another reliable indicator of the severity of the crisis was the number of bank failures. In 1910, by way of comparison, there were 58 suspensions of commercial banks; in 1914, a bad year financially, there were 149 suspensions, and in 1915 there were 152. In 1920 the number jumped to 167 and in 1921 shot up to 505, then fell back to 366 in 1922. All through the remaining 1920s the number hovered well above the 500 mark each year.[14]

WOMAN SUFFRAGE

In the summer of 1919 Iowans took time away from their postwar concerns to join the parade of states which were ratifying the Nineteenth Amendment, which through a negative approach gave women the right to vote. On July 2, in a special session only one hour and forty minutes in length, the General Assembly's ratifying action made Iowa the tenth state to approve.

Iowans had not always been so ready to accept the idea of votes for women. An amendment to the Iowa constitution was discussed in 1867 and afterward, but the dominant Radical Republicans made one excuse after another to delay and then defeat the proposition in 1872. The prior claims of the Negro suffrage proposal, and the unfortunate fact that a few Eastern suffragettes were advocates of free love, gave opponents two convenient talking points. In spite of a growing popular interest in the movement, Iowa officials dragged their feet, encouraged by the liquor interests which feared the effects of the female vote on the question of Prohibition. In 1914 and 1916 the votes-for-women amendment received the necessary blessings from the General Assembly and it was sent on to the voters at large who defeated it by a margin of 10,341 votes. Scott, Dubuque, Clinton, and Des Moines, all with large German anti-Prohibition votes, were the chief nay sayers.

A former Iowan, Mrs. Carrie Chapman Catt, played a major role in the ultimate national victory for the cause. From 1885 to 1900 she was a national speaker and organizer, and from 1900 to 1905 and again from 1915 to 1919 the president of the National Woman Suffrage Association. In 1919 the fifty-year fight in Congress ended in victory; the necessary number of states finished the ratification process by August 26, 1920.[15] On August 27 the first vote cast in Iowa under the new amendment, and probably the first in the nation, was a vote cast by Mrs. Jens G. Thuesen in a rural school reorganization election near Cedar Falls. Also, if we may look ahead, action was completed in 1926 on an amendment to the Iowa constitution to strike out the word "male" from Article III, Section 4, pertaining to the qualifications for membership in the General Assembly. In 1928 the first woman legislator in Iowa's history, Carolyn Campbell Pendray of Maquoketa, was elected to the House of Representatives.

SMITH W. BROOKHART CHALLENGES HIS FORMER IDOL, CUMMINS

In late 1919 and 1920 American farmers were beginning to feel the pinch of the cancellation of government supports and the effect of lower prices on exports to Europe. On top of these setbacks was their concern over a proposed increase in railroad freight rates. The prospect of higher rates added fuel to a postwar debate already raging through the land over the pros and cons of continued government management of the railroads, adopted in 1918 as a war measure. Indeed, some were bold enough to advocate not just management but the Plumb Plan of outright government *ownership* of the carriers, with management of operations by the government, railroad officials, and workers.

In the Iowa senatorial race of 1920, where Republican nomination was equivalent to victory, Albert B. Cummins, as the incumbent since 1908, would normally have had his party's nomination safely nailed down. There were those, however, who counted Cummins among the supporters of government ownership, a prospect which pleased some of his followers and dismayed others. Chief among the former was Colonel Smith Wildman Brookhart of Washington, Iowa. The colonel was a long-time friend and fellow fighter for regulation of the railroads in the early 1900s, but he may have misinterpreted some of Cummins's statements. On one occasion Cummins did say that *if* a certain man's ideas prevailed in the Interstate Commerce Commission, he would retaliate by supporting government ownership. Many people overlooked the conditional clause in his statement.[16]

After President Wilson announced the pending return of the railroads to private control as of December 31, 1919, congressional leaders were forced to come up with an act to supplement previous regulatory legislation. Declining financial resources made it more necessary to assist the roads than to regulate them. As the recognized master of railway economics in Congress, Senator Cummins, chairman of the Committee on Interstate Commerce, led the way in putting a bill through Congress, the Esch-Cummins Act of 1920.[17] Interestingly enough for Iowans, three of the leading participants in the battle for the railroad law were from this state: Cummins, spokesman for the public as a member of Congress; Clifford Thorne of Washington, Iowa (and Chicago), a one-time Brookhart follower and aide, now an attorney for the shippers; and Glenn E. Plumb, born in Clay, Iowa, and an alumnus of the University of Iowa, in a similar role for labor.

Many reasons have been advanced for Cummins's total or partial change of stance. One of the best is that the Cummins-Funk-Maytag-Hartman progressives were political reformers, not economic reformers, and that he took fright when government ownership became a real threat.[18] Cummins left no doubt that his short-lived flirtation with the idea of direct government management and/or government ownership was a thing of the past.

To Brookhart, this shift seemed like treason to the cause for which they had jointly fought for twenty years. Brookhart's personal economic status might make him appear to be a natural conservative—but no! His thoughts were the essence of the James B. Weaver school of Populism, distilled, updated, and carried over into an era of pure progressivism. He was often damned as a socialist but his socialism was nothing more than a merciful humanitarianism, bred by his observations of the helplessness of the little fellow in town and country. His rhetoric reflected his sympathy for the people whom he pictured as victims of an economic system too big for them to fight except through their elected representatives in government.

In early 1920, convinced for some time that Cummins was a lost leader, Brookhart announced his candidacy for the Republican senatorial nomination as an opponent to his former idol. He had always carefully nursed his organizational ties because he was shrewd enough to know that only through the channels of the Republican party could anyone be elected to office on the state level (barring a political revolution which was not in sight). In this race as in other races he soon learned that The Establishment, if we may borrow language from a later day, was dead set against him; his support would have to come from the economically discontented in Republican ranks, mostly small farmers and laborers, and the few Progressives who had gone beyond the 1907 Cummins policies. Among those who strongly supported Brookhart were James M. Pierce, editor of the *Iowa Homestead,* and the Iowa Federation of Labor, a numerically weak organization at the time. The Iowa Farm Bureau Federation would not quite go the distance of endorsing him but neither would it uphold Cummins.

In a campaign notable for bitterness and open threats of repudiation of the ticket if Brookhart were nominated, Cummins came out the winner by a vote of 115,768 to 96,563, Brookhart carrying only 28 counties. Brookhart carried Polk County, though only by 18 votes out of a total Republican vote in that county of 10,836, a bitter blow to Cummins in losing his home county. Cerro Gordo, Webster, Clinton, and Dubuque were other counties with an urbanized labor element which he carried; 20 of his counties were devoted exclusively to farming or agribusiness, and 3 had coal mining operations of local importance.[19] It is possible that some Democrats crossed over and registered as Republicans in these "labor" counties in order to vote for Brookhart against Cummins.

The Republican nominations for Iowa's eleven seats in the national House were not seriously affected by the Cummins-Brookhart duel. In the gubernatorial primaries, the Republicans chose the very able and experienced Nathan E. Kendall[20] of Albia, a moderate. As a Cummins lieutenant he had been a leader in the drives which spread the progressive program on the statute books. Later he served two terms as a congressman from the Sixth District. As for the Democrats, hopelessly in eclipse in this postwar anti-Wilson climate, they made the valuable discovery of a new candidate, Clyde L. Herring of Des Moines, to relieve Claude R. Porter of carrying the entire burden of token races. Well known as a successful automobile dealer, Herring began a crusade in this campaign for a modernized state government along the lines of the recent Lowden reforms in Illinois. Herring's plea was for the adoption of the methods of the business corporation in the day-to-day operation of the state government, stressing better bookkeeping, tighter auditing, and strict adherence to quarterly budget limits. Herring's personality and manner of speaking were the very antithesis of the traditional politician; at the time his was a voice crying in the wilderness.[21]

PRESIDENTIAL POLITICS, 1920

The Iowa primary on June 7 was followed immediately by the Republican National Convention in Chicago on the 8th. At least six men were possibilities for their nomination: Governor Frank O. Lowden of Illinois, on whom Iowa had some claims as a former resident and a graduate of the University of Iowa;[22] General Leonard Wood; Senators Hiram W. Johnson of California and Robert M. La Follette of Wisconsin, each a dedicated progressive; Senator Warren G. Harding of Ohio, who must be thought of as he appeared to his contemporaries of 1920, not the later Harding of the tarnished reputation; and Herbert C. Hoover, the Iowa-born nominal resident of California, who had just completed a very successful assignment as wartime Food Administrator. Iowa's Cummins and Kenyon were occasionally mentioned. Except for Kenyon's firm preference for Hiram Johnson, Iowa Republicans were solidly behind Lowden.

Wood and Lowden were the front-runners and each commanded a loyal following, so loyal, in fact, that neither group would surrender to the other. Neither man could muster a majority, nor would Hiram Johnson, their closest rival, withdraw and throw his support to one of them. After four ballots on Friday, the convention adjourned until Saturday afternoon. It was during this interval that many things were done which contributed to the selection of a candidate, including the Friday night conference of party leaders in the now famous "smoke-filled room" in the Blackstone Hotel. Iowans were not involved in these convention deals, partly because of their unshakable loyalty to Lowden. Moreover, much as one hates to spoil a good story, the nomination of Harding was not sealed, signed, and delivered in that hotel room of unsavory reputation. Six more ballots and much political finagling were necessary before the bandwagon swept Harding into the winner's position.[23] Iowa's delegation, under the leadership of Charles E. Pickett of Waterloo, a former congressman, remained adamant in its stand for Lowden until the last.

Republican victories, nationally and in Iowa, could be safely predicted. Warren G. Harding and Coolidge easily conquered Cox and Franklin Roosevelt, and the Republicans won a safe majority in both houses of Congress. In Iowa, Cummins swept to victory over Claude Porter, all eleven Republican nominees for the House were victorious, and Kendall beat Herring. The Republican triumph in Iowa came in spite of the revelation of the shady dealings in Governor William L. Harding's administration. Impeachment proceedings against Governor Harding failed by a vote of 70 to 34 but a motion to censure was passed by a House dominated by his fellow Republicans. Other members of Harding's official family were implicated in other irregularities, leading to the resignation of the secretary of state, the declaration by the state game warden that he would not seek reappointment, and suits against the state auditor, the superintendent of banking, the governor's private secretary, and two of his close personal friends and advisors.[24]

Now, for four months, while the invalid president and his wife ran the country from his bedside, anxious Iowans and their fellow Americans could do nothing but wait for the Republicans to take over and see what they could do to solve the many problems facing the country, especially the farm mess.

HENRY C. WALLACE, SECRETARY OF AGRICULTURE

Virtually the first indication of a new president's course of action is the selection of his cabinet. Iowans were primarily interested in Harding's choice for secretary of agriculture. Woodrow Wilson, in his last year in office, had selected Edwin T. Meredith[25] of Des Moines for that post. Now President-elect Harding chose another Iowan for the office—Henry Cantwell Wallace, publisher and editor of *Wallaces' Farmer.* This second generation member of a family already well known in farm circles for able journalistic leadership possessed as many of the qualities needed for the office as one might hope to find in one man. He had received a vast amount of informal instruction from his father, the famous "Uncle Henry" Wallace, plus a good technical education at Iowa State Agricultural College in dairy farming; he had been a "dirt farmer"; he had taught at his alma mater, and in his recent years as an editor he had been a keen student of agricultural economics. As Harding's chief advisor on farm problems during the campaign, he was the natural choice for the cabinet post, approved by virtually all interests except the meat-packers, who remembered his opposition to their business practices.

Strangely enough, this strict Presbyterian elder was able to establish a warm and trustful friendship with the convivial Harding. Wallace was a man of firm convictions, and, once persuaded of the correctness of a course of action, utterly fearless in holding to his belief. This trait was of more than passing importance because of one of Harding's other appointments: Herbert C. Hoover as secretary of commerce. The 1917–1918 controversy between Wallace and Hoover over incentives to greater pork production, described above, was repeated over other issues in the years immediately ahead, this time with greater intensity because of the added power each man now enjoyed. Hoover had accepted his portfolio in a very condescending manner and only after serving notice on Harding that he would reach over into several other departments, including agriculture, in carrying out his self-appointed task of restoring order to the postwar economy. Harding's silence had been interpreted as consent and Hoover felt authorized to proceed with his empire-building course of action. President Harding's role was hardly more than that of a referee in the conflicts between these two very able and dedicated public servants.[26]

Granting Hoover's talents and encyclopedic knowledge of world affairs, Secretary Wallace had certain assets not possessed by Secretary Hoover. He had firsthand knowledge of agriculture not possessed by the mining engineer. He knew the farmer's psychology. Best of all, he enjoyed the friendship and cooperation of the strong Iowa delegation in Congress: Senators Cummins and Kenyon, and all the representatives, especially Gilbert N. Haugen of Northwood and Lester J. Dickinson of Algona. Kenyon had been leading out in legislative proposals for farmers' relief since 1914; Haugen, a member of the House since 1899, was a successful country banker and the owner of thousands of acres of choice farmland in the belt of rich land north of Mason City,[27] whose own prosperity was tied to the welfare of agriculture; Dickinson, a lawyer from Algona in the heart of Iowa's cash grain belt, for a time enjoyed the reputation of being the best fighter for farm relief in either house of Congress.

ORGANIZATION OF THE FARM BLOC

Indicative of a new determination of certain leaders to fight for agriculture's equality with other sectors of the national economy was the formation of a "Farm Bloc" in Congress. This proagriculture group (the French word, *bloc,* was not applied until later) had its inception in a meeting in the Des Moines offices of the Iowa Farm Bureau Federation on November 13, 1920, attended by Senator Kenyon and four Iowa congressmen,[28] a meeting called to discuss the legislative needs of farmers but which turned into a strategy session. What the Iowa Farm Bureau wanted was the organization of a coalition of Midwestern members of Congress to coordinate and foster legislation favorable to agriculture.

A more formal step toward organization took place on May 9, 1921, in the offices of Gray Silver, the legislative representative of the American Farm Bureau Federation in Washington. Twelve senators were in the founding group, led by Kenyon, Arthur Capper of Kansas, and "Cotton Ed" Smith of South Carolina. Norris of Nebraska and La Follette of Wisconsin were notable additions to the list of founders; eventually the number came to twenty-two. Lester J. Dickinson of Algona led out in the formation of a similar group of about one hundred members in the House. Secretary Henry C. Wallace gave strong support to the idea but President Harding and Secretary Hoover bitterly opposed it as irregular and disruptive of party machinery, concerned only with "special interest" legislation. President Harding has been accused of deliberately trying to wreck the Farm Bloc by luring Senator Kenyon away with an offer of a circuit court judgeship in 1922.[29]

Although denying total selfishness, the nonpartison Farm Bloc admitted that it was out to redress the balance in the representation of agriculture as against big business and labor. Stated broadly, its policy was assistance to any bills favorable to agriculture and opposition to any bills harmful to agriculture. This they hoped to accomplish by use of the "balance of power" technique. All three of the major farm organizations—the Grange, the Farmers Union, and the American Farm Bureau Federation—closely observed the positions taken by the Farm Bloc but only the last named took the position of a silent partner and virtual patron. In fact, Gray Silver, Washington lobbyist for the AFBF, went so far on one occasion as to announce that his organization was keeping score on congressional votes on farm legislation and would know who were its enemies. This kind of pressure, not yet the commonplace it would later become, brought down official criticism on Silver's head.

Under Kenyon's leadership, the Farm Bloc was able to show an impressive scorecard of achievements: the Packers and Stockyards Act of 1921, providing federal regulation of the rates charged by packinghouses and commission merchants and also aiming a body blow at collusion among packers; the Grain Futures Act of 1921, giving the secretary of agriculture control over grain exchanges; and the Capper-Volstead Act of 1922, exempting farm cooperatives from antitrust laws. Another 1922 achievement was an act which provided for a spokesman for agriculture on the Federal Reserve Board. After Kenyon's resignation from the Senate in 1922 the bloc was held together under Senator Capper's leadership; in 1923 it pushed through the Agricultural Credits Act, creating twelve Intermediate Credit Banks to serve as a mechanism to provide long-term credits to collectives rather than to individuals.

GEORGE N. PEEK TACKLES THE FARM PROBLEM

As one distinguished historian has pointed out, the above list of laws for the benefit of agriculture would in earlier times have been thought of as a "stupendous achievement"; not so, now.[30] Too many things had happened and too many new ideas had been dreamed up which were far beyond the old ideas about self-sufficient, independent farmers. The new thinking revolved around one central theme: the government *must* do something to give agriculture *equality* with urban business and organized labor.

Such a theme was the message of a booklet published in 1922 by two officials of the Moline Plow Company: George N. Peek and Hugh S. Johnson. The title expressed the idea which has never been missing from agrarian polemics from that day to this: *Equality for Agriculture.*[31] By these words the authors meant to suggest the argument contained in their booklet: the government gave many forms of aid to corporate business and to organized labor; now it should equalize the system by giving assistance to agriculture. The point was strongly made that organized agriculture was not asking for special favors at the expense of the other two members of the triangle but only equal consideration. Whereas many lines of urban business and labor profited directly and indirectly from such special favors as the protective tariff, subsidies, and tax breaks, agriculture, so it was asserted, enjoyed no such favors. (The booklet was written before the passage of the Capper-Volstead Act of 1922.) The products of the farm were sold at prices set on exchanges in Liverpool, Tokyo, and New York, the "world price," whereas the farmer had to buy on an "American" market, where prices were higher because of the protective tariff against cheaper European or Asian, chiefly Japanese, products.

The seemingly obvious solution to the problem of surpluses was an increase in exports. Equally obvious was, or should have been, the fact that unless America accepted more European or Asian exports, Europe and Asia could not buy more of our products, especially since higher paid American labor and handling costs added an appreciable margin to the prices of our exports. With these facts in mind, and in disregard of other facts, George N. Peek and his associates came up with a two-price plan for the disposal of American agricultural surpluses: sell at any price they would bring on the foreign market ("dumping" is the technical term), and let the protected home market pay American prices for whatever it could consume. This two-price system was based on the unwarranted assumption that foreign markets would always be open to our products. Peek and his allies seemed to forget that there were European farmers who were distressed over their own problem of surpluses and low prices, and that these farmers would use their political power to secure tariff protection from their respective governments.

The stumbling block in the plan was that someone would have to make up the loss (margin) between the American price and the lower world price. Peek's idea was that this margin must be "equalized" by some device that he called a "tariff equivalent." Ever the conservative in matters of government intervention, Peek did not want the national government to reach into the general tax revenues to make up this difference but he boldly asserted that the government should be helpfully involved in the total process of bringing about the "equality of agriculture" with other sectors of the national economy. As the idea took final form, the difference in prices was to be made up by an "equalization fee" to be derived from a fund to which each seller paid an assessment. Peek wanted the government to assist in these transactions by forming commodity corporations which would take charge of the machinery of conducting the sales and distributing the equalization fee.

HENRY C. WALLACE VERSUS HERBERT HOOVER–AGAIN

This aspect of government intervention was a feature of the Peek plan which brought out all the venom in the smoldering feud between Henry C. Wallace and Herbert Hoover. The former might be thought of as a reluctant believer in a role for the government, accepting the idea out of a desperate desire to see something done to bring relief to farmers; Hoover, on the contrary, was doctrinally opposed to any proposition that even faintly suggested government intervention in private business—but was myopic in applying this philosophy. He could see the intervention only when it applied to agriculture. His voice and his influence in the cabinet were thrown into the balance against the George Peek–Henry C. Wallace way of thinking. What is more, he was able to carry Presidents Harding and Coolidge with him. The death of Secretary Wallace in 1924 was followed by the appointment of William L. Jardine of Kansas as his successor. Jardine proved to be clay in Hoover's hands and joined the opposition to the Peek plan.

It is difficult in the 1970s to fathom the attitudes of the 1920s and think *historically* about the ideas involved in the personal conflict between Hoover and Wallace over the tariff-equivalent plan. It is doubtful if any student of agricultural economics in the 1970s would contend that the Peek-Johnson plan could have been successfully carried out. "Dumping" is never a long-range remedy for the problem of surpluses, whatever the product. In this case, as an act of economic nationalism, it would certainly have invited reprisals, a point which Coolidge's advisors recognized. Furthermore, the plan contained no provisions for limitation of production. Granted that the plan might have worked for one year, it would have invited farmers to increase their production the next year and the surpluses would inevitably have shot up to new heights.[32]

McNARY AND HAUGEN TAKE OVER THE PEEK PLAN

It may be said, therefore, that Hoover, Coolidge, and Jardine were correct in their opposition to the two-price plan—but partly for the wrong reasons. In spite of their opposition it was taken over for legislative action by other Republicans: Senator Charles L. McNary of Oregon, ranking member of the Senate Committee on Agriculture,[33] and Gilbert N. Haugen of Iowa, chairman of the House Committee on Agriculture, and "Peek-ism" became "McNary-Haugenism."

Farmers, and farm interest groups such as implement dealers and country bankers, were not able to match Hoover's rational attitude, living every day as they did so close to the problem of approaching bankruptcy and destitution. In those agonizing years of declining farm fortunes, farmers did not relish the argument that government intervention on behalf of agriculture was a "socialistic" evil. In their eyes McNary-Haugenism was a symbol of the government's willingness to help a depressed segment of the economy, not to be judged strictly on its economic principles or results. They were persuaded by their plight that the government must do something, and they were infuriated by the seeming indifference of President Coolidge and Secretary Hoover. The average farmer could not have explained the technicalities of the McNary-Haugen plan; all he knew was that the president, on Hoover's advice, was against *the only relief bill* that Congress had taken seriously, and that Hoover was not offering any substitute except easier credit arrangements and cooperative marketing. On the other side, so staunch a capitalist as Frank O. Lowden went over to the "radicals," as the supporters of McNary-Haugenism were called; in Iowa, Henry A. Wallace editorialized for the two-price plan, and the Iowa Farm Bureau Federation under staunchly Republican Charles E. Hearst of Cedar Falls strongly supported it, as did the American Farm Bureau Federation, of which Hearst was vice-president.[34] The Farmers Union under Milo Reno gave its valuable support at the other end of the political-economic spectrum.

THE POLITICS OF AGRICULTURE: SMITH BROOKHART IN THE LIMELIGHT

Iowa's congressional votes on farm legislation were in the keeping of the Republican party—but that party was badly divided between conservatives and progressives. For some time the party had been coming apart at the seams, even though in 1921 an Iowan, John T. Adams of Dubuque, was elected national chairman.[35] The United States senators were pulling apart, Cummins becoming more and more conservative, and Kenyon more and more progressive. Kenyon's activities as a champion of farm relief have been indicated above, while, unfortunately for the conservatives, their wing of the party became identified with opposition to a positive farm program. But the real source of trouble was the presence in the party of Smith Brookhart, the radical spokesman for the small farmers and all others who were victims of the farm depression of the 1920s. Kenyon made no secret of his leanings in the direction of Brookhart's radical ideas, which were similar to those held by the Iowa Farmers Union. Brookhart, in turn, although carefully preserving his label as a Republican, was very much aware that he had been an outcast in high party councils ever since his race against Cummins in the 1920 primary.

Brookhart's opportunity to test his strength came about in the most unexpected way. In 1921 President Harding offered Senator Kenyon an appointment as federal judge for the Northern District of Iowa, an honor which Kenyon refused, giving as his reason that his legislative work was not finished. In January 1922, Harding, ever the astute poker player, raised the ante and offered Kenyon a place on the bench of the Eighth Judicial Circuit Court of Appeals, which Kenyon accepted promptly. Both the offer and the ready acceptance aroused suspicions and unkind comment. Whatever the motives, the leader of the Farm Bloc had been disposed of. To fill the post until an election could be held, Governor Nathan Kendall appointed a "safe" man, Charles A. Rawson of Des Moines, who promised not to run in the election.

Brookhart at once entered the primary contest as the odds-on favorite because of his good showing against Cummins in 1920. The only way of stopping him seemed to be by using the Iowa "35% law," that is, if the top candidate in the primary does not win at least 35 percent of the vote, the task of nominating is transferred to a party convention. Five men announced as aspirants for the nomination, each one a challenger to Brookhart: Charles E. Pickett of Waterloo, Burton E. Sweet of Waverly, Claude M. Stanley of Corning, Leslie E. Francis of Spirit Lake, and Clifford Thorne, now of Des Moines, formerly Brookhart's closest friend and aide. Pickett and Sweet, former members of Congress, might be thought of as bona fide candidates, thoroughly deserving the office if chosen; Stanley and Francis offered little but good intentions; Thorne, probably the brainiest man in the lot, was a lawyer and transportation expert who had helped Brookhart get up the facts and ideas for Governor Cummins's fight for regulation of the railroads and the abolition of the free pass system.

After three months of spirited campaigning, Brookhart's coalition of small farmers and labor groups, a companion to the Farmer-Labor party in Minnesota which no other Iowa political leader has ever been able to hold together, emerged victorious with 133,102 votes, 44.1 percent of the total. The nearest rival, Thorne, had only 52,783; then came Pickett, Francis, Sweet, and Stanley. The sum total of all non-Brookhart votes was 189,820, surpassing the Brookhart vote by 56,718, a lesson in politics not lost on Brookhart's enemies. Brookhart's appeal was largely to people in areas of economic distress.[36]

Brookhart was now the official party nominee with the vote-getting label, "Republican," at the head of his column on the ballot. Many conservatives, including Cummins, publicly repudiated him and vigorously advocated the election of the Democrat, Clyde L. Herring of Des Moines. Literature was distributed which instructed voters how to mark their ballots for Herring while otherwise voting the straight Republican ticket. But all this was not enough. Kenyon and Rawson endorsed Brookhart, and Senator Arthur Capper of Kansas came into Iowa to speak in his behalf. Brookhart's personal platform was as innocuous as most American political campaign talk, the difference being that he believed what he was saying, and conservatives were frightened by it. Two points stood out: the income tax should be more extensively used so that wealth would carry its proper share of the cost of government, and railroads, overcapitalized and inefficiently managed, so he charged, should come under government ownership.[37]

The people apparently believed in Brookhart. In November he won an amazing 389,751 votes to Herring's 227,833. In December 1922 he was sworn in, being escorted down the aisle not by Cummins but by Senator "Cotton Ed" Smith of South Carolina, second in command of the Farm Bloc, which Brookhart joined at once. In the two years allotted to him to fill out Kenyon's term, he made a name for himself by his belittlement of Washington's excessive attention to social protocol. For him, an unpressed business suit was sufficient for all occasions. He earned the cordial dislike of Presidents Harding and Coolidge and became the favorite whipping boy of the *New York Times*.

In 1924, running for the full six-year term, he overcame his opponent for the Republican nomination, Burton E. Sweet, a courtly gentleman of the old school, who was everything that Brookhart was not, 199,828 votes to 163,413. The party managers did not dare deny him a seat in the national convention, where he rejected all overtures from the La Follette forces to join in the formation of a third party—but neither would he endorse Coolidge. In November he barely stayed ahead of his Democratic opponent, Daniel F. Steck of Ottumwa, an able lawyer with strong backing from the American Legion. The official count of the vote was delayed from November 5 to November 24, at which time Brookhart was certified to the Iowa Executive Council as the winner, 447,706 votes to Steck's 446,951. Steck immediately announced that he would contest the election.

When Brookhart's new term began on March 4, 1925, the Senate leaders punished him, La Follette, and the two North Dakota senators for their refusal to support Coolidge by denying them their usual committee assignments. Furthermore, they did not begin the recount of the contested votes in the Brookhart-Steck duel until July, and dragged it out until April 12, 1926. In the final vote, hardly a senator voted according to the evidence but rather according to his personal and party ideology. Sixteen proadministration Republicans and 29 Democrats voted to unseat Brookhart; 31 Republicans, 9 Democrats, and 1 Farmer-Laborite voted in his favor, a vote of 45 to 41. Thus Brookhart was undone, Steck was seated, and Iowa had its first Democratic senator since the conclusion of George Wallace Jones's term in 1859.

The Brookhart-Cummins Duel of 1926

Brookhart had previously announced that he would enter the 1926 June primary against Cummins if the contest with Steck went against him. He did so, and made a whirlwind campaign throughout the state, aided by practically all the leading Senate progressives as speakers. On the other hand, Cummins's campaign was managed and carried out largely by others because of the veteran senator's poor health, putting Cummins in the same place which Allison had been forced to occupy in 1908 against him when he challenged the veteran. But this time, unlike Allison, Cummins had no Dolliver to take over for him. Then it was Cummins who was accused of being a Socialist, and a threat to the stability of the government; now it was Cummins who called Brookhart the Socialist whose election would endanger the welfare of the country. As in 1908, the race drew national attention and newspaper coverage. It proved to be a one-sided contest, Brookhart winning by the amazing margin of 208,894 to 137,367, carrying 85 out of the 99 counties. Another progressive, Howard J. Clark of Des Moines, drained off 64,392 votes, many of which might have gone to Brookhart in a two-man race

The victory was generally interpreted as a slap at the Coolidge farm policy. In recognition of this possibility, the Republican bosses made the concession of selecting a pro-Brookhart man, Dan W. Turner of Corning, as temporary chairman of the state convention, in which capacity he could endorse Brookhart. Even more remarkable, they invited Brookhart himself to address the convention, an honor which he rejected. This same Iowa convention endorsed Coolidge but passed a resolution of criticism of three members of the Coolidge cabinet: Mellon, Jardine, and Herbert Hoover.

Less than two months after the June primary, Cummins died, just as the aged and infirm Allison had died soon after the 1908 primary. The party leaders adamantly refused to make Brookhart the party nominee to run for the remainder of the Cummins term. For this honor the party convention voted 1,000 to 385 in favor of David Stewart of Sioux City, rejecting the man who had just won the party's nomination in the direct primary for the full six-year term! This undemocratic act, which cost Brookhart a chance to gain precious seniority in the Senate, was clear proof of the dominance of the party machinery by the conservative forces. In spite of this rebuff, Brookhart took his place as a "regular" member of the party and worked hard in the campaign, even speaking on behalf of Stewart, who had been appointed by Governor John Hammill to serve until November. Stewart had no opponent for the short term and he was given what amounted to a complimentary vote of 336,454. For the full term, Brookhart defeated Claude R. Porter, 323,409 to 247,869.[38]

THE EQUALIZATION FEE BLOCKS McNARY-HAUGENISM

When Brookhart returned to the Senate in 1927 he found that the feeling over the farm problem was more determined, more demanding, than it had been when he was ejected almost a year earlier. In an atmosphere of much bitterness the McNary-Haugen bill had been defeated in 1926, the House vote on May 21 being 212 to 167 and the Senate vote on June 24 being 45 to 39.[39] All of Iowa's members voted for the bill, as might well be expected. In February 1927, just before Brookhart's new term would begin, the bill came up again and Brookhart pulled all the weight he could muster. This time it passed the Senate, on February 11, by a vote of 47 to 39, both of Iowa's senators, Stewart and Steck, voting for it, and on February 17 it passed in the House, 214 to 178, all of Iowa's eleven representatives voting in the affirmative. An unhesitant veto was immediately forthcoming from President Coolidge. In no uncertain language he called the bill unconstitutional, and unworkable even if valid.[40] Presidents of several farm organizations and many other farm spokesmen responded with severe criticism of the man from Vermont.

Coolidge continued to support Hoover's brainchild, the Capper-Williams bill, or the Curtis-Crisp bill, each of which stressed the development of cooperatives as an aid to farm prosperity. The Farm Bureau people and their allies fought for a modified McNary-Haugen bill but one which still included the equalization fee. This was passed in May 1928, with strong support from Iowa members.[41] Again President Coolidge found things wrong with the bill. On May 23 he delivered a stinging veto message, pointing out that the bill would call for price-fixing, that the equalization fee was a special tax for the benefit of one class, that it would be difficult to administer, and that it would result in increased production.[42]

Although terribly disappointed by the veto, which was pronounced a mixture of truth and error, Iowa farm leaders and most of their allies in other states regarded this as the end of McNary-Haugenism. George N. Peek was personally willing to keep up the fight but he was virtually alone in this attitude. Most of the leaders agreed that the fight would have to be transferred to the arena of politics—presidential politics—in the hope of finding a president dedicated to the principle of equality for agriculture, one who would not work with the East against the West and the South.

CHAPTER 16 THE PRESIDENCY OF HERBERT HOOVER 1929–1933

THE IMPORTANCE OF THE DECISIONS MADE BY PRESIDENT CALVIN Coolidge against the McNary-Haugen bills, with Commerce Secretary Hoover's blessing, should not be discounted. Farm relief now became a hot political issue, especially in presidential politics. "Silent Cal's" enigmatic statement of 1927, "I do not choose to run," seemed to leave the field wide open for Republican aspirants. His Iowa-born cabinet member from California, true to his entrepreneurial instincts, foresightedly secured pledges from 400 likely delegates and thus easily became the front-runner in the race for the Republican nomination unless his chief should decide at the last moment to run again. Iowa farm leaders remembered Hoover's solid opposition to McNary-Haugenism and his favoritism for industry, and therefore opposed his nomination. At the time neither Iowans nor others paid much attention to the fact that Iowa was Hoover's birthplace. Legally he was a citizen of California and was so referred to in the publicity given to his candidacy.

Iowa farm spokesmen had no doubts as to the identity of their favorite. Long-time Republicans and farm leaders such as Charles E. Hearst, John W. Coverdale, Lester J. Dickinson, and Gilbert N. Haugen were fully dedicated to the candidacy of Frank O. Lowden of Illinois, who had espoused McNary-Haugenism since 1925. Harvey Ingham, influential editor of the *Des Moines Register,* was another who strongly supported Lowden in preference to either Coolidge or Hoover. The *Register's* front page news and its editorials indicated a belief that Coolidge would emerge as the Republican candidate; therefore he rather than Hoover was the primary target for the paper's editorial criticism and sharp darts from "Ding" Darling, one of America's most perceptive cartoonists.[1]

POLITICAL DECISIONS OF 1928

The June primaries of 1928 again proved the strong position of the Republican party in the state. Governor John Hammill of Britt was renominated for a third term along with nine of the eleven incumbent Republican congressmen, the other two voluntarily retiring. Obviously the leaders of the Republican rank-and-file who bother to vote in primaries were satisfied with their longtime officeholders. It is hardly worthwhile to mention the Democratic nominees who furnished the token opposition.

Fresh from this demonstration of their debt to the past, the party's twenty-seven delegates went to the national convention at Kansas City. The group included Charles E. Hearst of Cedar Falls and Dan W. Turner of Corning as the chief farm spokesmen for Iowa. It is almost impossible in mere words to convey the desperation of the outlook of average Western farmers as they contemplated the spectacle of the convention. It had been predicted that 100,000 Midwestern farmers would make the pilgrimage to Kansas City, a foolish exaggeration, of course. One or two thousand managed to make the trip. Some of the more excitable ones came armed with shovels and pitchforks and took up a position across the street from the convention hall. Most of these men felt driven to change politics, if necessary, in their search for relief.

It was all wasted money and time and energy. The frustrated farm leaders worked hard for Lowden but it was a lost cause from the start. Liberal Progressives such as Brookhart and Norris of Nebraska refused to support Lowden, and Brookhart gave his support to Hoover in the campaign, surely one of the strangest alliances in political history. The platform pledged the party to create a Federal Farm Board to help in the orderly marketing of crops; any reference to the McNary-Haugen type of equalization fee was noticeably missing. Sensing his defeat, Lowden withdrew his name, but twenty-two of the twenty-seven Iowa delegates voted for him anyhow.[2] Hoover was nominated on the first ballot.

It must be repeated: Peek, Hearst, and their followers were not misguided leaders who looked on McNary-Haugenism as a panacea—they used it as a means of doing something to get acceptance of the principles of parity and of government assistance in *managing* the surplus. They were looking for a candidate who could and would recognize that the plight of the farm population was not altogether of their own making and that farmers deserved some measure of relief. They wanted a president who would not veto the only plan that could be put through Congress.

In this spirit many of the farm leaders made a second pilgrimage, this time to the Democratic convention at Houston. Frustration was again in store for them. Alfred E. Smith, the Democratic nominee, knew little about the farm problem. Although many in the South and West regretted his status as a Catholic, a wet, and a Tammany Hall product, it has been demonstrated that Catholicism was not the cause of his undoing.[3]

Such diverse personalities as Brookhart, Dickinson, Dan Turner, McNary, and Haugen supported Hoover; Henry A. Wallace deserted the Republicans and publicly supported Smith. George Peek, a dyed-in-the-wool conservative Republican on every issue except farm relief, was willing to put that cause above everything else. He believed in Smith's good intentions, in spite of Smith's curious vacillation on McNary-Haugenism, and therefore supported him with all his energy and strength. He organized a "Smith Independent Organization Committee" and, with ample financial support from the Democratic National Committee, directed a strong fight throughout the West for the farm vote.

The outcome was never seriously in doubt, least of all in Iowa, where Hoover received 623,570 votes to Smith's 379,311. Nationally, Hoover received 21,391,381 to Smith's 15,016,445 in the popular vote and 444 to 87 in the electoral college. Such figures, however, are easily misleading unless further analyzed. In Iowa, Hoover's gain over Coolidge's 1924 vote was only 86,112 and was a loss of 11,000 compared with Harding's 1920 total, the largest vote ever given to a candidate in Iowa up to that time. By contrast, Smith's 379,311 total was a gain of 218,959 over John W. Davis's weak run in 1924 and 151,390 more than James M. Cox's vote in 1920. Obviously the Democratic party was gaining voters at Republican expense—and not in Iowa alone. In eleven Midwestern states the 1928 figures showed that the Democrats had gained 1,987,218 votes over 1920 while the Republicans were gaining only 1,572,818, this in spite of two very weak Democratic candidates in 1924 and 1928.

THE HOOVER PRESIDENCY AND FARM RELIEF

Iowans had good reasons for a sentimental attitude toward Herbert Hoover as president. He was born in the Quaker village of West Branch and spent his early boyhood there; his wife Lou Henry Hoover, whom he met during his student days at Stanford, was a Waterloo girl. Furthermore, his western campaign manager of 1928 was James W. Good of Cedar Rapids, whom he rewarded with an appointment as secretary of war. His secretary of the interior, Dr. Ray Lyman Wilbur, a native of Boonesboro, Iowa, was an old friend who had risen to the presidency of Stanford University. Former Congressman Albert F. Dawson of Preston, currently a bank president in Davenport, had assisted James W. Good in the campaign.[4] The optimism about the economy which emanated from the inauguration address of the engineer-turned-politician was more noticeable in the cities than in the small towns and the countryside, and pointed up the great paradox of the 1920s: urban prosperity side by side with rural depression.

Hoover's awareness of the problem created by surpluses of farm products led him to accept, somewhat reluctantly, something more radical than cooperatives, his longtime panacea for low prices. The result was the quick passage of the Agricultural Marketing Act on June 15, 1929, just three months and eleven days after he took office. Iowans in Congress and leaders of the farm groups supported the bill. The chief feature was a provision for a Farm Board to assist in the orderly marketing of the major crops, Hoover's chief concern for years. The theory behind the bill was impeccable. The Farm Board was to supervise several government marketing corporations. Armed with $500 million capital, these corporations would enter the market at a time when the offerings were heaviest, on the heels of a harvest, and would buy freely so as to keep prices up to reasonable levels. Then, in the months following, the corporations would withdraw supplies from storage and dribble their holdings onto the market in small amounts so as to prevent a glut of the market and consequent drop in price. The board was not interested in making a profit, of course, but hoped to break even over a period of time. If so, everybody would be happy: the farmer would receive a fair price, commission men would receive their fees, processors could buy their raw materials at a fair price, and the government would recover its capital outlays. Unfortunately, events conspired to break this hypothetical cycle. Good crops brought record-breaking yields just when the hard times of 1929–1930–1931–1932 reduced the effective demand. Try as it would, the Farm Board could not prevent its holdings from piling up in bins and elevators. By 1932 the board was in debt to the tune of $354 million or more, and the end of its troubles was not in sight.

Certain Republicans had managed to insert in the bill a provision which the president (and Eastern senators) despised, called the "export debenture" plan. The idea was strongly favored by the Grange leaders. This was an intricate scheme for the issuance of debentures (certificates) to an exporter to represent the difference between domestic cost of production and the foreign cost of production. Such certificates were to be negotiable and could be used in the payment of import taxes. In theory the plan would accomplish the same thing as the equalization fee of the McNary-Haugen bills but with less red tape. It was this proposal by Western senators which stirred the wrath of Senator Moses of New Hampshire and prompted him to label the farm defenders as "sons of the wild jackasses," an epithet which soon became a badge of honor in farm circles and the source of incalculable damage to Republican candidates in the West. President Hoover's threat to veto any measure containing the debenture provision made it advisable to delete that clause from the bill. Later, this threat was cited, along with preceding actions, as proof that Hoover was against the farmer.[5]

THE PANIC OF 1929

The troubles of the Farm Board were still in their infancy when even greater troubles appeared in another sector. After several flurries during the summer and early fall, in October the New York Stock Exchange collapsed in utter confusion and failure. The event had manifold consequences which were worldwide in scope, the one of special importance to Iowans being the rise of frank and unmitigated economic nationalism, not only in the United States but in western Europe, South America, and Japan, to mention only the places where American trade was heaviest and most directly affected. Iowans who understood the importance of exports could well lament this development.

On the excuse of economic self-defense, the American Congress and the president now gave the country a mixed program of legislation designed to provide national economic security *and* domestic relief. In doing so, President Hoover was forced to abandon his long-cherished ideal of a completely laissez faire economy and venture into a large measure of statism, carrying many likeminded Republicans and Democrats with him. The Agricultural Marketing Act, already referred to, was a step in this direction. The first major item of nationalistic legislation was the Hawley-Smoot Tariff Act of June 17, 1930. Originally conceived and debated in 1929 as a tariff which would help to equalize farm protection with industrial protection, this bill grew bit by bit until it became simply an old-fashioned protective tariff for the benefit of the manufacturing interests, the highest tariff in our history up to that time.

More than a thousand economists petitioned the president not to sign the Hawley-Smoot bill if it passed but this deterred neither the Congress nor the president. Duties on farm goods were raised, and this concession plus party loyalty held most of the Iowa members of Congress in line. Only Ed Campbell of northwest Iowa stood against it on the final House vote. Senator Brookhart voted against it, as might be expected; Senator Steck did not vote, being absent, but was announced as paired against the bill.[6] Forgotten were the elementary economic truths that trade is a two-way street and that a nation can pay its debts in only three ways: gold, goods, and services. European nations, our debtors, had no gold to spare above their reserve needs; if we shut out their goods with a high tariff wall and refused to buy their services, we were making it impossible for them to pay their debts and to continue as our best customers. Few people were ready to follow this logic to its full conclusions.

Although President Hoover advocated many measures helpful to the economy, he could not totally erase the popular impression of aloofness and indifference to the welfare of the common laborer and the little farmer. Certain Democratic leaders were aided by the president of the

Iowa Farmers Union, Milo Reno, in the creation of this impression.[7] Reno was ably assisted by his editor of the *Iowa Union Farmer,* H. R. Gross. Then known as Chuck Gross, his column, "Mustard Seeds, Thistles and Quack Grass," was a feature of the newspaper. In it Mr. Gross regularly fired away with his unrivaled powers of sarcasm at President Hoover, usually denominated as "Doctor" Herbert Clark Hoover. The president was ridiculed for his pretentious advice to farmers and pilloried for his failure to produce prosperity. He was all for Hoover's defeat in 1932, and, when it came, Franklin Roosevelt's victory was a matter for rejoicing.

One result of the widespread anti-Hoover campaign was an increase in the totals of Democratic votes for congressmen in 1930, enough to give the alliance of Democrats and Progressive Republicans control of the House, and increased power in the Senate. Iowa reflected this national sentiment by electing Bernhard M. Jacobsen, a labor spokesman from Clinton, as the first Democrat to be sent to the House since 1914. Also anti-Hoover was the choice of two militant supporters of farm legislation: Lester J. Dickinson of Algona for the Senate, and fiery Dan W. Turner of Corning, perhaps the last of the old-fashioned Cummins progressives, for governor.

THE ADMINISTRATION OF GOVERNOR DAN W. TURNER, 1931–1933

Iowa farmers could not have hoped for a better spokesman as governor than pugnacious Dan Turner. As a state senator from 1904 to 1908, he had helped Governor Cummins put over the progressive legislative program. He possessed a great capacity for sensing the hopeless condition of men who had seen their labor virtually wasted since 1920, as farm prices dropped to the point where it was more economical to burn their corn for fuel than to sell it; to the point where many of them thought that it was no longer worthwhile to try to save their mortgaged farms from foreclosure and the sheriff's sale. His ability to understand the farmers' distress came partly because he was one of them: he was a farmer and stockman in southern Iowa, a distressed area which at best is not as richly endowed as the other sections of Iowa; partly, it came from an inherent ability to sympathize with the victims of misfortune and give sincere expression to his emotional involvement.

This able man has never received his just dues as a reformer. As a true disciple of progressivism, Dan Turner first of all wanted Iowans to help themselves. His inaugural message urged the consolidation of departments and a study of any and all ways to save money in the routine operation of the state government. Both suggestions were aimed at a reduction in taxes. One of the last acts of the General Assembly in 1931 was the creation at his request of a six-man interim committee to make a study and write a report on possible economies in state government. This committee was duly set up with two men appointed by the governor: W. S. Gilman of Sioux City, chairman, and Clark W. Huntley of Chariton; two members from the Senate: Ed R. Hicklin of Wapello and Roy E. Stevens from Ottumwa; and two representatives: Ed R. Brown of Des Moines, chosen as secretary, and Otto J. Reimers of Rock Rapids. Their report was not made until late in 1932 and will be considered below.

THE "COW WAR" OF 1931

Governor Turner's efforts to improve the economic situation were interrupted by a most unfortunate event. Only a time of severe and prolonged depression could have been the setting for the "Cow War" of 1931, an ugly clash between a few farmers and state authorities. Unfortunately, a climactic drive for eradication of bovine tuberculosis coincided with a rash of bank failures in 1931, the long-postponed result of the economic depression of the 1920s. Starting in the late winter and reaching over into the long hot depression summer of that year, when it seemed that man and nature had conspired to ruin the farmer, the program of testing cattle for the presence of the dread disease was seriously resisted in many parts of Iowa. The greatest excitement, however, occurred near Tipton, in Cedar County, only a few miles from the birthplace of Herbert Hoover. A cow war could have been sparked off in any one of a dozen places in the state but the dubious honor of leading the armed resistance to the state veterinarians was reserved for this county, where a tragedy was narrowly averted.

A program of testing, followed by the destruction of all animals found to be reactors, had been authorized by a 1929 law. Nearly everyone agreed that elimination of the disease, by testing and destruction of diseased animals, was necessary, and it was unthinkable that minority resistance could be allowed to stop the campaign. Having said this, a good case remains in defense of the protesters' objections if not their methods of opposing the agents of the law. Officials were guilty of a poor job of pretesting education about the nature of the disease; inexact methods of testing resulted in some clinical failures and enough blunders to give the protesters some good talking points such as inadequate compensation for the confiscated animals, especially at this time of economic distress, and high-handed measures of law enforcement. These errors, in their total effect, go far toward explaining the fact that normally peaceful, law-abiding citizens were brought to the point of armed resistance to the orders of the state. Advice given by a quack promoter over a nearby Muscatine radio deluded some of the protesters and goaded them into action.[8]

The unfortunate governor into whose lap this problem was dropped, however sympathetic he might be, was not the type to run away from a fight. Governor Turner sent three regiments of the Iowa National Guard into Cedar County and several key figures were arrested, enabling the veterinarians to proceed with their work under the cover of military protection. In the *Iowa Union Farmer,* Milo Reno's newspaper, columnist H. R. Gross compared the sending of the militia to the dispatch of the marines to Nicaragua, and severely criticized the *Des Moines Register* for approving the former but condemning the latter,[9] but all to no avail. The program was quickly completed in Cedar County, after which the troops were sent into nearby Henry, Muscatine, Jefferson, and Des Moines counties for similar action. It was never found necessary to declare martial law but for two months the people in this pocket of Iowa farmland, much of it the best in the state, learned at first hand the meaning of military occupation.[10]

PRESIDENT HOOVER VEERS TOWARD MORE STATISM

By the summer of 1931 the national economy appeared to be on the verge of an upturn when news of financial distress began to arrive from Europe. The myth of American isolation was destroyed as it was demonstrated that a bank failure in Europe *could* lead to bank failures in the United States; that war debts and reparations *were* related, presidents and Congresses to the contrary notwithstanding. Under these circumstances the president arranged the one-year "Hoover Moratorium" on International Payments (War Debts and Reparations), in June 1931, an act of splendid courage as well as needed financial statesmanship. It was not enough and it came too late. The suspension of the largest bank in Austria had disastrous repercussions in Germany; the shock passed on from there to Great Britain, already hard hit by the loss of export markets, and in August that country abandoned the gold standard. France, which in 1926 had been the first government to resort to a managed currency and severe devaluation, was nationalistic and obstructionist rather than cooperative.

As economic conditions continued to deteriorate, in late 1931 the president persuaded the Congress to take the most momentous step of his entire term of office. This was the creation of the Reconstruction Finance Corporation (RFC), which received its charter on January 16, 1932. Capitalized at $500 million, with authority to borrow an additional $1.5 billion, this institution could lend on favorable long-term rates to banks, building and loan associations, insurance companies, and railroads. Thousands of such corporations were saved or enabled to gain time for solvent liquidation instead of being forced into bankruptcy. Iowa members of Congress supported this monumental legislation strongly. Additional banking legislation eased the lending provisions of commercial banks and gave aid to building and loan associations and federal land banks.[11]

MILO RENO AND THE FARMERS HOLIDAY ASSOCIATION

The Cow War contributed to consequences far beyond the incident itself; it might well be thought of as a spark dropped into the tinder box created by the depression. With corn at 13 cents per bushel, pork at 3 cents per pound, and beef at 5 cents per pound, no one should be surprised that producing farmers had been driven to the breaking point and were ready to take things into their own hands. Direct action may not be a complete remedy for troubles but it serves as an outlet for pent-up feelings and acts as a release for frustrations which have been building up for years. Under the prevailing economic conditions all that was needed was a leader to act as the spokesman and organizer of the masses who were demanding action.

It was not necessary to go far in searching for such a leader. Since 1921, as president of the Iowa Farmers Union, Milo Reno had been in training for just such a moment as this. Born in southern Iowa and reared in a Populist environment, his mind had fed on a diet of Populist literature and William Jennings Bryan's oratory, with a seasoning of Campbellite theology which qualified him for status as a local preacher. Over the years he had developed the ideas, the vocabulary, the wit to supplement the native genius needed for "hell-raising" among the distressed farmers of Iowa, Nebraska, Minnesota, and the Dakotas; whatever he lacked could be readily supplied by the staff writers in the *Iowa Union Farmer,* most of whom possessed great skill in the use of Populist rhetoric. From such a background it was a natural move for Reno to step into the presidency and field leadership of the National Farmers Holiday Association.

As far back as 1927, Milo Reno had announced his thinking to his colleagues on the Corn Belt Committee: "If we cannot obtain justice by legislation, the time will have arrived when no other course remains than organized refusal to deliver the products of the farm at less than production costs."[12] This was, of course, too drastic for 1927. But in 1931, two years after the Wall Street collapse, John Bosch, a county Farmers Union president in Minnesota, advocated a farm strike in a speech at the annual convention of the Iowa Farmers Union; later, Reno and Bosch joined in asking the National Farmers Union convention to resolve to begin a strike on January 1, 1932.

This date did not prove to be feasible but the idea remained alive. The straw that broke the camel's back of opposition to the farm strike technique was the disillusionment of the Iowa Farmers Union delegation which visited Washington and suffered an exposure to the callous disregard, as they deemed it, of the farmers' welfare. As soon as the delegates returned to Iowa, Reno and his fellow workers began to drum up more sentiment for a farm strike, preaching the word that all other methods of getting higher prices had failed. The organizational meeting for a

Farmers Holiday Association was held on the State Fair grounds in Des Moines on May 3, 1932. Milo Reno was the almost unanimous choice for president; John Bosch, his Minnesota counterpart, was chosen as vice-president. A few simple resolutions sufficed for a "platform" or program of action—and the Farmers Holiday Association was in business. The key decision summing up all their planning, and their emotions as well, was one which set July 4 as the beginning date for a withholding action, to run for thirty days or until "cost of production" was achieved.

Definition of "cost of production" was never made clear, or exactly what methods were to be used to force somebody to grant it to them. It was one of those delightfully vague expressions that made it easy for an orator of the Milo Reno type to appeal to an audience of discontented farmers. If the term meant anything at all, it meant a price which would cover the "rent" of the land, the cost of seed, fertilizer, and labor, and an allowance for a reasonable profit. Presumably, to have any certainty at all, such a price would have to be paid by processors for that portion of the crop consumed domestically; any crop surplus beyond that amount would have to be the responsibility of the farmer-producer. Administration and enforcement, if possible, would require a small army of government employees, a thing which Reno and his followers opposed strenuously. Also it may be presumed that if the supply of produce exceeded the demand, and prices fell accordingly, the government—who else?—would be asked to make payments which would make up the difference.

THE PRIMARIES AND CONVENTIONS OF 1932

The shadow of the month-old Farmers Holiday Association was over Iowans of all parties as they went to the primary polling places on June 6. But there were many other things for them to ponder. A virtual standstill in population (see Table 18.1) had just resulted in Iowa's loss of two of the former eleven seats in the national House of Representatives. Bank failures and farm mortgage foreclosures and farm sales were staples of the daily news. Ominous indeed was a closely related fact: the steady growth of farm tenancy, now at the highest point in the state's history. While farm tenancy is not always a bad thing, and some very able farmers prefer renting to ownership, it is generally agreed that tenancy is not a way of life to be encouraged. Many thought that a rate of 55.4 percent (18,951,634 acres), more than half of the land of the state, and an increase of 1.5 percent since 1928, was too much tenancy. Oddly enough, Northwest Iowa as a region, and Lyon County, in the extreme northwest corner of the state, had the highest rate of tenancy in the state, Lyon County topping all others with a rate of 73.4 percent, and yet this area had the highest corn yields in the state, ordinarily a source of prosperity. Dubuque County, dominated by thrifty Germans and ambitious Irish, had the lowest rate of tenancy, 31.4 percent.[13] These statistics, when related to the general decline of farm population and the economic insecurity of agriculture, indicated that absentee ownership was a matter of serious concern to all.

Another point widely stressed in the thinking of the day was the position of the powerful Anti-Saloon League on each aspirant for nomination. On June 2, just four days before the voting, the league made its pronouncements, all by name rather than party, but few people were in doubt as to the wets and the drys. In the Senate race, Republican aspirants Henry Field, George Cosson, and Smith W. Brookhart were labeled "satisfactory"; Colonel Glenn C. Haynes of Sioux City drew no comment. Without exception the Democratic rivals for the same nomination were labeled "not satisfactory," a list including such stalwart citizens as Daniel F. Steck of Ottumwa, Louis Murphy of Dubuque, Charles F. Lytle of Sioux City, Nelson G. Kraschel of Harlan, and Fred P. Hagemann of Waverly. Louis H. Cook of Des Moines, Independent Republican, a brilliant writer and expert on governmental matters, especially taxation, was categorized as "does not believe in Prohibition." Of the aspirants for the nomination for governor, Republican Dan W. Turner was listed as "satisfactory," whereas all the Democratic hopefuls, Clyde L. Herring of Des Moines, L. W. Hounsel of Humboldt, Otto Lange of Dubuque, and Louis E. Roddewig of Davenport, were blacklisted.[14] Such league pronouncements, backed up by the Women's Christian Temperance Union's national president, Mrs. Ida B. Wise Smith of Des Moines, carried great weight throughout Iowa, especially in rural and small-town areas.

The contests did not furnish many surprises. Henry Field of Shenandoah, well-to-do seed merchant, nurseryman, and mail order merchant, and owner and operator of a radio station specializing in programs of a rustic nature and seed and merchandise catalogs of a similar variety, ran a shrewd campaign. He mixed good business sense with an ample portion of hillbilly music played on a steam calliope, and outran all his rivals. The overpopulated Democratic race was won by an astute retired editor and tax consultant from Dubuque, Louis Murphy. Turner, the incumbent Republican governor, was an easy winner in his contest for renomination, and Clyde L. Herring won the Democratic nomination in spite of the W.C.T.U. and the Anti-Saloon League. To astute observers it was apparent that many Iowans were in a mood for change, and Democratic nominations gave promise of something more than political martyrdom.

There could be no surprises in the Republican National Convention at Chicago. Hoover's renomination was a foregone conclusion; some thought he might find a more attractive running mate than Charles Curtis but the Kansan was again selected. The only big question for the delegates was what to do about Prohibition. The tide was running strongly against that method of controlling the liquor traffic, a method which Republicans, with few exceptions, had officially favored since 1856. Now there was much soul-searching as the party leaders sought some formula which would please all factions.

Such was the setting for a dramatic contrast between the performances of two Iowans who captured most of the headlines during the convention. Senator Lester J. Dickinson of Algona, who was selected to give the keynote address, failed to rise to the opportunity to make a contribution to the needs of the party and the nation and chose rather to stultify himself by the usual keynoter's habit of glorifying his own party and blasting the opposition. The speech contradicted everything that the "hell-raiser for agriculture," to quote Nicholas Longworth, had stood for. There were no allusions to the continuing need for farm relief or for new banking legislation. On his presentation, every proposal of the Republican party for government spending was praiseworthy for its promise of restoration of employment; every Democratic proposal was damned for its creation of "unnecessary and unproductive public works"; Republican spending always produced employment; Democratic spending always rested on the theory that you could "squander yourself into prosperity." C. C. Clifton, correspondent for the *Des Moines Register,* found little to praise in the speech except its brevity and its cleverly designed appeal to the audience; Walter Lippmann's syndicated column called the speech "dull" and "the crudest kind of partisanship," and pitilessly analyzed its violations of fact.[15]

Governor Dan Turner, by contrast, went into the open hearings conducted by the Committee on Resolutions and made an impassioned plea for the unemployed in the cities and the farmers who were approaching ruin. "I implore you to get busy on something else besides this booze question," he shouted belligerently. "We've got eight or nine million people out of work. The Republican party has the greatest opportunity since 1861 and yet you twiddle your thumbs and talk about booze."

In presenting the case for farm relief, Turner was ably supported by Louis J. Tabor, national master of the Grange. The fiery Iowa governor urged more power for the Federal Reserve Board to control credit in order to restore commodity prices to predepression levels. Governor Turner concluded with this challenge: "Iowa has stood by the Republican party since 1861 on the principle that the employment of labor furnished an outlet for farm produce. Let the party continue to stand by that principle." It was a superb performance and should have produced greater results. Instead, the platform had nothing but the usual platitudes about the farm problem. J. N. "Ding" Darling, cartoonist-turned-politician and a member of the Resolutions Committee, frankly confessed that the making of a platform is a work of many compromises; as to agriculture, the Eastern members of the committee refused to make any concessions—and that was that.[16]

Now it was the turn of the Democrats to come to the aid of the country. The Iowa delegation was pledged to Franklin D. Roosevelt although the younger members of the state convention wanted Governor Albert C. Ritchie of Maryland.[17] At the Chicago convention it was not much of a trick for Roosevelt to find his needed marginal votes in the Texas and California delegations. As for farm relief, the Democratic plank for agriculture was not much more satisfactory to Iowa leaders than the Republican document. Farm Bureau President Charles E. Hearst scored both platforms; it was simply a matter of choosing the lesser evil.

THE FARMERS HOLIDAY ASSOCIATION IN ACTION, 1932

Returning to the story of Milo Reno's strategic campaign for direct action on the farm front, nothing was done after May 3 to get the strike program under way on July 4, the date set in the organizing resolutions. There had been much talk about "cost of production" as the farmers' goal but it seems nearer the truth to say that the rank and file members of the association wanted two things, for which no abstract formula was needed: an immediate increase in prices up to a point which would give them a decent living, and a chance to vent their feelings of hatred of the politicians and their agents whom they blamed for their troubles.

Direct action in an effort to boycott the markets was begun at Sioux City on August 11. The rather simple and vague plans of Milo Reno for an orderly, peaceful withholding of farm products were not realized; instead came almost instant violence, marked by picketing of the highways, dumping of milk trucks, and bodily harm to those who would not follow the association members' "advice" to join in the strike. The Sioux City blockade, as well as dumping operations in scattered places, such as Council Bluffs, Des Moines, and the Benson Creamery near Cedar Falls, was designed to prevent delivery of milk and cream to the processors. Hog marketing was another intended victim of the pickets. Although much milk was dumped on the highways and into ditches and although many bruises were sustained, few real gains were made by the strikers.

As John L. Shover, the foremost student of the Holiday Movement, concludes, the strike failed because of a lack of discipline among the striking forces on the picket lines and inadequate economic preparations for a prolonged strike.[18] As to the former point, the authorities in the cities and the governors of the states were firm though not brutal in breaking up the nonpeaceful picketing. Wholesale arrests and jail sentences did much to cool the ardor of the pickets, most of whom were hardworking, law-abiding citizens, temporarily driven to desperate actions. Vast reserves of strike funds would have been necessary to make the holiday successful, and these were not available. Most of the farmers were compelled by hard necessity to market their produce when it was ready, regardless of the price—they needed whatever hard cash it would bring, and furthermore, meat and dairy products must be marketed when a certain point has been reached in their preparation for the market.

The calling of a Governors' Conference for September 9 to consider the problem gave Reno a way out, and on September 1 he called off the strike. Only four governors attended the Sioux City meeting but several others sent substitutes or observers; only Governor Charles W. Bryan of Nebraska refused to budge an inch in dealing with the strikers and their leaders. The conference settled nothing but passed harmless resolutions to be sent to the two presidential candidates. President Hoover's response was to promise a special session of Congress to consider measures to ease the farm mortgage situation; Governor Roosevelt was much more cordial and gave the impression, if not the promise, that if elected he would work for "cost of production" guarantees.

Roosevelt spoke in Sioux City on September 29 and was graciously attentive to the farm leaders who were present. President Hoover spoke in Des Moines on October 4. A large crowd of Farm Holiday Association members, estimated at 5,000 to 10,000, staged an orderly parade preceding President Hoover's arrival in the city and vented their emotions by displaying a wide assortment of anti-Hoover signs, notably lacking in wit and truth. In Des Moines, as elsewhere, the president tried to convince his Western audience that in spite of unfair charges to the contrary, he did have a heartfelt concern for suffering farmers and their families. His Des Moines speech, however, promised no more than an effort to persuade Congress to reorganize the federal land banks and make them helpful in fact as well as in theory. Strangely, the president's chief point was his opposition to the cancellation of the war debts, actually a dead issue now following the Lausanne Conference of the preceding May. As usual, he assured his listeners that he would not accept any bill which would destroy the initiative and the individualism of the American farmer.[19]

RIGHTISTS AND COMMUNISTS OFFER LEADERSHIP TO THE FARM HOLIDAY MOVEMENT

An interesting sidelight on the Farmers Holiday Movement was the effort of outsiders to come into the Middle West, particularly Iowa and Nebraska, and take over the leadership of the strike; if successful in this, presumably they would have taken over the entire Farmers Holiday and Farmers Union organizations back of the strike.

The effort of the right wing extremists was headed by an agitator named Lester P. Barlow, leader of an organization called the Modern Seventy-Sixers. In the hubbub over the Holiday, he was clever enough to form a friendship with Milo Reno and certain local leaders in northwest Iowa, and to convince Wallace Short, a labor leader and former mayor of Sioux City, that his ideas for controlling the strike situations were sound, though they consisted of the use of force and little else. The

Barlow-led Modern Seventy-Sixers movement collapsed in failure and ridicule.

Not so simple, not so easily defeated, was the effort of the Communist party of America to infiltrate the Holiday Movement and use it as a springboard to power over what they fondly but foolishly believed was a peasant economy in the Midwest. No place would seem more unlikely for a Communist attempt at boring from within than the farm communities of the Midwest. Their partial success is a tribute to their skill in recognizing the opportunity which the economic distress in agriculture provided, and their further skill in working anonymously behind a front of the farmers themselves. Three members of the party, Harold Ware, his mother, Ella Reeve Bloor, known widely as "Mother" Bloor, and Lem Harris, came out from New York to take charge of the program of stimulating the protest movement in the hope that the traditional capitalistic system of farming could be destroyed. Technically, their program called for the teaching of the Marxist philosophy of class consciousness and the creation of an agrarian wing of the proletarian movement.

The three agents arrived too late to do much on the picket lines around Sioux City. Now they were there, however, and ready to help behind the scenes when the Farm Holiday Association staged a demonstration on September 9, the day of the Governors' Conference. That same day Mother Bloor managed to corral about fifty farmers in a splinter meeting over which she presided, completely hoodwinking the innocent farmers into calling a "Farmers National Relief Conference" to meet in Washington on December 7–10, 1932. Twenty-six states contributed some 228 delegates; undoubtedly there were Iowans among them. A Farmers National Committee for Action (F.N.C.A.) was set up, with Lem Harris as executive secretary. Probably most if not all of the 228 delegates returned to their homes blissfully unaware that they had been puppets in a Communist-staged play.[20]

THE DOMESTIC ALLOTMENT PLAN

Indicative of the evolution of thinking as the search went on for an effective plan of farm relief was the development of the "domestic allotment" plan. The original idea, built around the then heretical belief that genuine relief would have to come from a control of production rather than from easier credit or from better marketing devices, seems to have sprung from the brain of Dr. W. J. Spillman, a brilliant economist in the Department of Agriculture, who owed much to the support given him by Secretary Henry C. Wallace. The idea of production controls was at first greeted with scorn and derision; any such open interference with the freedom to produce to the limit of one's ingenuity was denounced as evil, un-American, contrary to good economic theory and practice, and impossible to administer. In spite of the adverse criticism, the idea gradually took hold in certain circles. After Dr. Spillman broached it, the first to publicize it was the Minnesota farm paper, *Farm, Stock and Home,* in 1926. Dr. Spillman gave it another boost in 1927 in his book, *Balancing the Farm Output,* and then came a notable convert, Professor John D. Black of Harvard. All the while Henry A. Wallace was giving notice to it in *Wallaces' Farmer* and drawing closer to it. Beardsley Ruml, a Cedar Rapids transplant to New York, was another convert to the idea and a helpful friend to the theorists.

The man who perfected the idea was Professor Milburn L. Wilson, an agricultural economist at Montana State College of Agriculture. "M. L." Wilson was a native of Iowa and a graduate of Iowa State College of Agriculture in the early 1900s, just ahead of young Henry Wallace. Here he learned soil science and then went into large-scale farming, first in Iowa and then in Montana. A bookish man and a bit of a dreamer, he had a vision of better things for farmers and for the American society. Somehow he acquired a place on the faculty at the Bozeman institution and spent his summers in graduate work at Chicago, Wisconsin, and Cornell, and in world travels. He picked up the idea of voluntary control of farm production in his study of the European system of subsidies and bonuses for higher production as an offset to low prices. Wilson (and John D. Black) simply turned the idea around and invented the idea of offering a bonus for nonproduction![21]

Like the George Peek idea which became the nucleus of McNary-Haugenism, the domestic allotment idea had to be tied in somehow with the tariff system. Stated in its simplest form, the Wilson-Black formula was a plan to allot a certain amount of acreage to each established farmer for certain specified basic commodities such as wheat, cotton, corn, and peanuts. Each participating farmer would be given certificates in proportion to the amount he was entitled to produce as his share of the domestic market, known as "domestic allotment" rights. The certificates were negotiable under certain circumstances. At the end of the crop season the farmer would market his crop and processors would buy not only the produce but the allotment rights. The price paid for the allotment rights would be approximately the equivalent of the tariff margin on that commodity. This extra payment was to be obtained from a fund derived from a processing tax, *not* from the funds in the United States Treasury. (Of course the processor would pass this tax on to the consumer.) There is much more about the plan that needs to be explained but any reader with a general knowledge of later farm legislation will recognize at once that here is the source of the New Deal approach to "equality for agriculture."

Admittedly difficult to administer, especially in the initial years of application until the formulas could be well established for each locality and each farmer's allotment, and politically involved as well, what with state, county, and township committees to make the allotments, the

Wilson-Black plan did not come up for a legislative test in the years between 1926 and 1932. Only in the desperation born of the continuing decline of farm prices and the growing list of farm mortgage foreclosures could its adherents secure its adoption, and then in simplified terms and with less complicated procedures. Its chief political asset was that it was considered to be the only viable substitute for the McNary-Haugen plan which most people had abandoned as hopeless after the Coolidge vetoes of 1927 and 1928.

The domestic allotment plan was of major importance, however, for its political effects as well as its theoretical economic effects. It became a factor in congressional politics in the West and South and even in presidential politics and in cabinet selections, as will be seen in more detail below. The idea was abhorrent to President Coolidge and to his advisor and successor, Herbert Hoover, and even many McNary-Haugen supporters thought it was too radical, and shaped their politics accordingly. On the other hand, it was passed on to Governor Franklin D. Roosevelt of New York, who, before and after his nomination for president, with a politician's leeway, embraced it sufficiently for it to become a factor in his speeches on agricultural policy and in his selection of a secretary of agriculture—and thus a point in favor of Henry A. Wallace, who had accepted it. But that is another story, to be told below.[22]

THE ELECTION OF 1932

The election of 1932 proved to be a turning point in American history as it gave a sweeping victory for Roosevelt and his followers in Iowa and throughout the nation. If one may disregard the fluke victory of Woodrow Wilson in 1912 because of a divided Republican party, Iowa now gave its vote to a Democratic candidate for president for the first time since the state began to vote Republican in 1856, giving Roosevelt 598,019 votes to 414,483 for Hoover. Roosevelt carried 93 counties, losing Black Hawk by 86 votes, Warren by 183, Marshall by 219, Linn by 1,040, Story by 1,097, and Polk by 2,506.[23] For senator, Louis Murphy, little known outside the Dubuque Democratic stronghold, was carried in by Roosevelt over Henry Field, a weak and untypical Republican candidate, 538,422 to 399,929; Brookhart received only 43,174 votes. Herring was elected governor by only 53,000 votes over Dan Turner.

In the congressional races, the Democrats won six out of nine contests, a phenomenal showing for them. The most notable acquisition to the Democratic contingent would prove to be Guy M. Gillette of Cherokee; the most notable victim of the upheaval was Gilbert N. Haugen, a veteran of seventeen consecutive terms, and chairman of the House Committee on Agriculture since 1919. So powerful and prestigious had he been that in 1928 the Democrats were unable to find a sacrificial victim to run against him; now he was beaten by Frederick E. Biermann, a

Decorah editor, by a vote of 62,598 to 42,471. Haugen's defeat was a symbol of the failure of the Coolidge-Hoover administrations to cope with the problems of agriculture, a symbolism which he did not deserve. No one had worked harder for the cause of farm relief. After the failure of the McNary-Haugen bills of 1927 and 1928 because of Coolidge's vetoes, Haugen had mounted a personal campaign throughout Iowa at his own expense, speaking widely in an effort to awaken urban interests and make them aware of the need for effective farm legislation.[24] Age and health may have played a part in his 1932 defeat. The grand old gentleman from Northwood was 73 years of age and worn out by his incessant labors. He died on July 18, 1933, having given the best years of his life to the service of his county and district, beginning with election to the Iowa General Assembly in 1894 and to Congress in 1898.

THE AWKWARD INTERVAL: NOVEMBER 8 TO MARCH 4

Franklin Delano Roosevelt was the last president-elect who had to wait the long four-month interval between the November election and inauguration on March 4. Thanks to the "Lame Duck" Amendment (XX) which would become effective in 1933 (the Iowa General Assembly ratified it in January 1933), that awkward interval in the transition of power was cut in half. Bad enough even in good times, the long interregnum was almost unbearable in the parlous time of 1932–1933, as America, perhaps the world, paid a fearful price for the standstill which the eighteenth century governmental timetable prescribed. In the best of all possible worlds President Hoover and President-elect Roosevelt might have "spoken with one voice" as they waited in this time of crisis for the transfer of power—but this was not the best of all possible worlds. As a "lame duck" president, Mr. Hoover was almost powerless as he tried to salvage something from the wreck of his plans. A repudiated president and a poor loser, he was sublimely confident that his policies were correct, and was eager to prove that he was not to blame for the debacle around him. Never an easy man to work with, he was extremely difficult just now. Nor was Roosevelt any better. Self-confident, jaunty, cockily riding the wave of his great victory, he was in honest disagreement with Hoover at many points. He was not willing to cooperate by accepting responsibility for those decisions or plans with which he disagreed, and, being human, he was eager to save for the incoming regime the chance to gain the credit for any successes which might follow.[25]

In the meanwhile there was no standstill in Iowa. Just three days after the election the Interim Committee on the Reduction of the Costs of Government gave out a preliminary sketch of its long-awaited report. The six-man committee, of which Senator Ed. R. Hicklin of Wapello and Representative Ed. R. Brown of Des Moines were the moving spirits, presented a twelve-point program, some of which had been preached by

Herring for many years. In highly condensed form the points were as follows: eliminate the Iowa decennial census, taken in the "5" years; eliminate the annual audit of state institutions; place all finances under the legislature and have a continuous audit; revise all laws about state printing; reduce salaries by 5–25 percent; make the terms of state officers four years instead of two years; extend the terms of drivers' licenses so as to reduce renewal costs; forbid the use of state-owned automobiles except in the most necessary cases; abolish the State Geological Survey; prevent the Finance Committee of the State Board of Education from administering the affairs of the state educational institutions (an obvious personal thrust at someone); curtail convention trips; require central handling and metering of all mail.[26]

It is true that some of these points represented penny-pinching—but most people in 1932 were saving pennies; some were constructive proposals. To cover these proposals, the committee drew up over sixty bills for the attention of the incoming General Assembly. Undoubtedly the study made state officials and servants more economy-minded; it was a reflection of the desperateness in the lives of most people at the time.

CHAPTER 17 THE DEMOCRATIC NEW DEAL COMES TO IOWA 1933-1938

IN THE EARLY 1930s STATE AND LOCAL HISTORY WAS DWARFED BY the tremendous drama occupying center stage in Washington and by happenings in the capitals and chancelleries of Europe and Asia. President Roosevelt saw the necessity of putting his house in order, a process which included three things: the restoration of prosperity and tranquillity at home; the construction of diplomatic alliances and friendships abroad; and the reduction of enmities and frictions which consumed valuable resources and energy.

DAN TURNER'S FAREWELL AND GOVERNOR HERRING'S INAUGURAL ADDRESS, 1933

While the world watched Hitler, Stalin, and Roosevelt, Iowans focused their attention on men at the state capital. It probably is true that Iowans were more concerned over the return of prosperity than with moves and countermoves on the international chessboard. Governor Dan Turner and Governor-elect Herring kept a close eye on the day-to-day developments in Iowa, particularly the financial crisis. Reports of want and suffering were coming in from every town and city; mortgage foreclosures were common occurrences; angry farmers were sometimes taking matters into their own hands in ways such as protecting their friends from losses at a sheriff's sale. In his "farewell" address, Turner urged quick reforms to protect mortgagors but advised the assembly not to put too much power in the hands of the Executive Department.[1]

In his inaugural address two days later, Governor Herring spoke as one whose educational efforts could at last pay off:

> Twelve years ago I first advocated a complete reorganization of state and local government in Iowa. In the campaign just ended I repeated my

advocacy of this same reorganization program. The conduct of public business in Iowa is being carried on under a system devised and adapted to the horseback and stage coach period. If the taxpayer is ever to get his dollar's worth in service from his government, this antiquated system must be completely overhauled and rebuilt. In its place must be set up a compact and efficient method for handling public affairs.[2]

This statement neatly summarizes Herring's philosophy of state government: reorganization on strictly business lines would produce greater efficiency and reduced costs, an idea going back at least as far as the administration of Governor George W. Clarke in 1915. Now the times were right for action.

Governor Herring had the wisdom to use a strictly nonpartisan approach to the problem of reform. During the campaign he cleverly stated his theory of democracy: "Every voter a stockholder, and a stockholders' meeting every two years." Now, in his inaugural address, he said: "I seek no personal power. At best, I am but a fleeting figure in the public life of Iowa, and I would willingly pass to the hands of another . . . the power solicited for the office of governor. . . . I do not regard my election as a purely partisan victory." The new governor then indicated some of his specific ideas about reform: abolition of most of the political boards and commissions; fixed responsibility for the spending of the taxpayer's money upon elected officials directly accountable to the electorate; all moneys to be deposited with the state treasurer and spent only by direct appropriation by the General Assembly.

Such recommendations may sound commonplace but each one was rooted in a situation which needed correction. They were the distillation of Herring's studies and observations over a period of years. He was appealing to businessmen and all persons familiar with business methods.[3] He concluded his remarks on reorganization with a formal statement about a prospective study by an interim committee, the study to cover all aspects of state, county, and municipal government. This committee was to be assisted by experts in the field of state government. (It will be shown below that such a committee was created.) The remainder of the inaugural address dealt with the need for more equitable taxation based on figures to be supplied by the interim committee after its study, the needs of agriculture, especially the halting of foreclosures on mortgages, a close examination and audit of motor vehicle tax refunds, banking legislation, and better methods for the selection of judges.

THE FARM MORTGAGE AND BANKING CRISIS OF 1933

Leaving for a moment the realm of inaugural oratory to return to the world of action, we find Governor Herring faced with a rapidly developing financial crisis. To say that the crisis was national or even universal in scope was of no comfort to Iowans. Two aspects of the situation were most alarming: the farm mortgage problem and the forced closing of many banks which were fundamentally sound but temporarily caught up in the pressures of the regional and national situation.

As for the farm mortgage foreclosures, the rate was the highest in Iowa history. In 1932 there had been 5 forced sales per 100 farms; in 1933 the rate was 8 per 100. In October 1932, briefly noted above, Charles E. Hearst, as president of the Iowa Farm Bureau Federation, had called a conference at Ames at which many of the state's leading bankers and insurance company executives joined forces with state officials and farm leaders to discuss ways and means of stemming the flood of foreclosures which were ruining the farm economy. Spokesmen for the lending agencies made it clear that they did not want to acquire land —that their business was the renting of money. Out of this conference came a State Credit Council and a complete network of County Credit Councils to supplement the work of local banks in trying to carry worthy credit risks over the crisis. Henry S. Nollen, president of the Equitable Life Insurance Company of Iowa, whose portfolios bulged with farm mortgages, was elected president of the State Credit Council; other elected members were B. F. Kauffman, Des Moines banker; L. A. Andrew, state superintendent of banking; J. N. "Ding" Darling; R. K. Bliss of the Extension Service of Iowa State College; and Charles E. Hearst.

Milo Reno was another who was keenly aware of the tragic farm situation. In the early months of 1933, while holding its strike weapon in abeyance until the new administration could show its hand on farm relief, Reno's Farmers Holiday Association turned its attention to the foreclosure situation. The association as such stayed clear of the action but its directors set up an auxiliary called the Loyal Order of Picketeers, made up of those who were the most inclined to resort to physical violence in preventing the dispossession of a mortgagor who was in arrears on his payments. By their very presence at foreclosure sales the pickets intimidated outside bidders; when bids were called for they proceeded to bid in the property for a few pennies (hence "penny auction" and "Sears Roebuck" sales), and then turn the debt-free parcel over to the original owner. This extra-legal technique was used frequently all over Iowa and in other Midwestern states, leading to a decision by the Nebraska Supreme Court that a sale was not invalidated by the inadequacy of the bid.[4]

Indeed, the situation was about as bad as one can imagine it in a rural area such as northwestern Iowa, eastern Nebraska, the Dakotas, and southern Minnesota, normally so far removed from the turmoil and excitement associated with external conflict between the forces of labor and capital. In Iowa the leaders of the Farmers Holiday Association movement were quite sufficient for the occasion without falling back on outside help in their actions of protest and confiscation. In early

January, the Holiday's chairman in Plymouth County led 1,400 farmers to Le Mars, the county seat, and interfered with a sale of a farm on which the New York Life Insurance Company was the mortgagee. The attorney representing the company was forced to send the company a telegram asking for permission to bid the full amount of the mortgage, thus avoiding a deficiency judgment. His request was granted. In the melee the sheriff was slapped and rendered helpless; Judge C. W. Pitts was held a prisoner while demands were made that he promise to sign no more foreclosure decrees. The judge was able to save himself from the mob only by promising to write to Governor-elect Herring. Reports of similar activities in nearby states filled the papers.

One should take note of the responses of those in the seats of power to these circumstances. On January 19, in one of his first acts as governor, Herring issued a proclamation urging no further foreclosures where mortgages were in default. Later he could afford to admit that the proclamation had no legal basis but had the approval of the people of Iowa, and with such sanction it was "as powerful as law itself." This emergency proclamation was followed by a formal statute on February 17, providing a moratorium on foreclosures until March 1, 1935.[5] Not only were these steps taken by the governor and other agencies of the state, but in late January 1933, hard on the heels of the rough treatment of the New York Life Insurance Company's agent at Le Mars, that company announced that it would suspend all foreclosures until remedial legislation on the subject could be passed, frankly admitting that its action was caused by the governor's proclamation and by the fact that the injured person was its own attorney. Five other large national companies immediately followed suit.

As for the banking crisis, sometimes hurting the rich or well-to-do as much as the poor, something had to be done to provide relief; there was little comfort and no profit whatsoever in recrimination. The statement was frequently made that Iowa banks would have been solvent if bankers had not bought so many foreign bonds, especially from Latin American countries, most of which went into default. Granting the justice of this criticism, what could be done now to save the banks—and their depositors? The answer came in late 1932 and early 1933 when fourteen states took it on themselves to declare banking holidays, in an effort to conserve the banks' temporarily frozen assets. Iowa banks and bankers suffered their share of troubles during the 1920s and the early 1930s. There had been a steady decrease in the number of banks during this period, with an alarming jump in the number of suspended banks in 1931 and 1932 (not all of which were failures, to be sure), as the deeper effects of the decline of the 1920s began to show up.

Be it said to the credit of Governors Turner and Herring and the General Assembly, and all others concerned, Iowa's state government acted swiftly and helpfully. Completely nonpartisan in this instance, the record in coping with the banking crisis was a good one. In the first twelve days of 1933, 13 out of the 643 state banks in Iowa found it necessary to close their doors. To meet this growing crisis, one of the first acts of the Forty-fifth General Assembly was the passage in January 1933 of Senate File No. 111 which created machinery for taking over a troubled bank by the state superintendent of banking and keeping the bank under his deputy or under trusteeship until such time as the Iowa Banking Department would permit it to reopen under its old charter, or under a new charter as a reorganized institution. The superintendent's deputy would use his best offices to conduct a serviceable bank, thaw the frozen assets as soon as possible, and protect the interests of all concerned, those of the depositors first of all. One hundred and thirty-five banks were immediately given refuge under Senate File 111. After the national moratorium on *all* banking was declared on March 5, 1933, all state banks and trust companies came under the protection of the state banking department under the terms of the law. No bank could reopen until authorized to do so by the superintendent of banking.

As a result of this beneficent legislation, which was largely the handiwork of Frank Warner of Des Moines, long the secretary of the Iowa Bankers Association, and Fred J. Figge of Ossian, then president of that association, and as a result of the careful and efficient work of the deputies and trustees, 211 banks were reopened at once without restrictions; 48 were allowed to reopen under depositors' agreements which had been made prior to the passage of this law; 10 were voluntarily liquidated by their owners and managers at no loss to the depositors; the remaining number, 359, were continued under S.F. 111 until the superintendent found them ready for release. Of these 359 banks, 245 were released from the superintendent's control after waivers were secured from the depositors, 70 were liquidated by receivers, and 44 were recapitalized or sold, either in full or in part. All in all, 274 depositors' trusts were set up and virtually all paid off in full. A meaningful summary of results, in terms of actual dollars and cents, is as follows: at the time of the passage of S.F. 111, the state banks of Iowa carried deposits of $214,559,413; the actual loss to depositors was $9,479,676, a mere 8.75 percent of the total. The law was designed to allow a bank which was solvent by all ordinary standards time enough to liquidate its assets, while in the meantime it could conduct a banking business under supervision or perhaps under full control by the superintendent of banking. The record speaks for itself. After the crash of 1929 banking everywhere was under severe attack, perhaps rightly so. In Iowa alone, 722 state banks closed, consolidated, or were liquidated during the years 1921–1933, up to the passage of S.F. 111 in January. Thanks to the administration of banking affairs under that law, well supplemented, to be sure, by the benefits of the deposit insurance provided under the Federal Deposit Insurance Corporation, confidence was fully restored.[6]

THE BROOKINGS REPORT

Governor Herring's recommendation, mentioned above, for a committee on greater efficiency in state government and the employment of a body of experts to make a survey of the entire structure of the state government was soon translated into action. Senators E. R. Hicklin of Wapello (Louisa County) and Roy E. Stevens of Ottumwa (Wapello County)[7] sponsored joint Resolution No. 2 which proposed the creation of a special joint legislative study committee on state government operations at all levels, with an eye to the reduction of expenditures. This sweeping proposal was later amended so as to propose "that a going, non-partisan, legislative committee be and is created, to be known as a Committee on Reduction of Government Expenditures and shall be composed of three members to be appointed by the Governor." This resolution passed the Senate by a vote of 41 to 7, with one absent or not voting. The most notable opponents were Senators Leo Elthon of Fertile and George A. Wilson of Des Moines, both future governors of the state. In the House the measure passed by an overwhelming vote.[8] Later the resolution was again changed so as to provide for a five-man committee, reminiscent of the six-man committee under Governor Turner set up for the same general purpose. Special five-man committees on taxation in each house would assist the main committee.

William F. Riley, a prominent lawyer in Des Moines, was made the nonlegislative member and chairman of the group. From the Senate came John K. Valentine of Centerville, Democrat, and David W. Kimberly of Davenport, Republican, a veteran member of many years of service; from the House, Earl M. Dean, Democrat, of Mason City and John Speidel, Republican, of Washington. For all of their ability, this committee was set up largely for window dressing purposes, having neither the time nor the technical training to carry out the details of the assignment. The work was actually to be done by a group of specialists from the Brookings Institution of Washington, D.C.,[9] whose anticipated employment the governor had alluded to in his inaugural address. Fortunately for Governor Herring, the legislature did not let him down but appropriated $25,000 for the expenses of the Interim Committee. Now the contract could be made with this famous research institution to make an exhaustive study and blueprint of the government, together with recommendations of changes.

While the members of the research team were gathering the data for their report, some of their experts took time to draft a bill which became the Budget and Financial Control Act, passed on April 24, which would take effect on the following July 4, 1933. Other items in the legislative program could wait. This particular act was the realization of the twelve-year dream of Clyde L. Herring and constitutes one of the monuments to his career as a worker for state government reform. In his second inaugural address Herring could say: "[Now] all state expenditures are coordinated. Each hand knows what the other is doing. Duplication and waste and inefficiency are prevented, and always the Governor is able to hold expenditures down to revenue."[10]

The findings of the Brookings team of experts took the form of a stout volume of 653 pages, now virtually a collector's item, under the cumbersome title of *Report on a Survey of Administration in Iowa Submitted to Committee on Reduction of Governmental Expenditures,* of which 26 pages were devoted to "Recommendations for the Reorganization and Improvement of Administration in Iowa," and the remaining 627 pages to a "Summary of a Report on a Survey of Administration in Iowa." It is safe to say that this was the most complete study of Iowa's governmental structure which had ever been made up to that time. The *Report* was dated July 25, 1933, but it was not made available to the committee until August 8 and was not released to the public until August 29.[11] Bulky as the principal volume of the *Report* may seem to be, it did not include five chapters, entitled "The Revenue System," which were published as a separate pamphlet on September 25, running to 170 pages.

HENRY AGARD WALLACE: SECRETARY OF AGRICULTURE

The point of greatest long-range interest for Iowans was the policy of Roosevelt toward agriculture. The first indication of his intentions would be his choice for secretary of agriculture. Speculation began even before the election and continued furiously after November 8. Nearly a dozen names were run through the gossip mills at one time or another, including Frank O. Lowden; Henry Morgenthau, Jr.; Governor Harry Woodring of Kansas; Professors M. L. Wilson of Montana State College and George F. Warren of Cornell University; George N. Peek; and Henry Agard Wallace of Iowa, editor of *Wallaces' Farmer,* and experimental scientist and social scientist. It is impossible to piece together all the available evidence, much less the imponderables, which went into the final selection of Wallace, the fourth Iowan and second Wallace to hold the office. For years he had given all of his time to a study of various aspects of the farm problem. As Morgenthau's brilliant biographer points out, in addition to other advantages possessed by Wallace, one was a belief in the Domestic Allotment plan which was rejected by Morgenthau.[12] Wallace himself boosted Peek and then Lowden for the spot, and Lowden boosted Wallace! One of the most helpful points in Wallace's favor was a resolution passed by the Iowa General Assembly strongly urging Roosevelt to appoint him;[13] another advantage was his residence in the Midwest, the most important agricultural section in the country.

So it was not altogether surprising that in mid-February Roosevelt gave Wallace the much-deserved invitation to the cabinet. With becoming humility he accepted the post, wrote his farewell column to the readers of *Wallaces' Farmer,* and made his way eastward to the strange new world of New Deal Washington.[14] For several years to come the history of American agriculture could be written in the form of a biography of this Iowa-born, Iowa-educated scholar now transferred to the world of action. Few would doubt and none could successfully refute his intellectual equipment for the gigantic tasks ahead. Henry Agard Wallace began his new career with three commitments. One was to democracy, not just the arithmetical democracy of "one man, one vote," but a sincere belief in the dignity of the individual, a belief which would eventually express itself in the title of his book, *The Century of the Common Man.* Another was to the belief that American agriculture was in trouble because of its ability to overproduce, the remedy for which was a policy of immediate but temporary "planned scarcity" by means of the Domestic Allotment system. Finally, there was a humane commitment to the mass of small farmers who were the helpless victims of conditions beyond their control. He had observed these people through the years; he had read their letters as they poured out their hearts to him personally or in "letters to the editor" of *Wallaces' Farmer* and similar journals. Ironically, the day would come when some of these people, the sharecroppers of the South, about whom he had much to learn, would be called the "forgotten farmers" under the New Deal, while the large-scale farmers and farm corporations would be accused of profiting too much from the payments for lands put in the soil bank. But such things were not in the plans of Henry Wallace when he took over the department which would soon become the gigantic USDA, subsuming everything from a seminar in agricultural economics to a hot lunch program in the public schools.

Wallace decided that the urgency of the farm situation demanded immediate attention in the special session of Congress which President Roosevelt called for March 9. A farm conference in Washington on March 10 followed calls to men all over the country with whom he had corresponded and worked for years in an effort to secure "equality for agriculture." Fifty leaders pitched in with nonpartisan spirit to do a heroic job of drafting emergency legislation. Economists, lawyers, and bill-drafting experts were at Wallace's beck and call to perform the tricky business of writing a constitutionally sound bill which would incorporate M. L. Wilson's scheme for the payment for lands retired from use. Conspicuously missing from the list of helpful workers and advisers were Milo Reno, busily directing the Farmers Holiday Association activities which were becoming more and more dubious, and John A. Simpson of Oklahoma, president of the American Farmers Union, who had done a quick about-face after campaigning enthusiastically for

FDR the previous year. These two leaders called a national convention of their organizations to meet in Des Moines on March 12–13.

MILO RENO'S FOLLOWERS MARCH ON THE CAPITAL

In a militant mood the Holiday Association met and adopted a series of resolutions and peremptory demands for immediate action. On March 13, in what was surely a "first" for Iowa history, 3,000 members of the convention staged an orderly march on the capitol. By invitation they visited the General Assembly where their spokesmen presented these resolutions and demands:[15]

> We are loyal American citizens who believe in our country and its institutions and we are proud of its history. We do not desire to seek redress of our wrongs and grievances through force except as a last resort. But we are free men and we refuse to become the serfs and slaves of the usurer and money king.
>
> A universal bank holiday has been declared for the protection of banks. Unless we receive legislative justice by May 3, 1933, we shall then prepare for a marketing strike within ten days. . . .
>
> We refuse to pay interest, debts or taxes until the dollar is made to serve as an honest measure of value.
>
> We demand a national moratorium on foreclosures of farm and city property by executive order in the same way as the bank holiday.
>
> We demand passage of the Frazier Bill [for refinancing of farm mortgages with fiat money].
>
> We demand the federal government take over the banking and currency system as a public utility.
>
> We demand legislation to assure farmers cost of production.
>
> We demand a steeply graduated income tax and cessation of issuance of tax exempt securities.
>
> We demand passage of the soldiers' bonus.
>
> We advise Congress not to go to the expense of hearings on the non-sensical [*sic*] domestic allotment plan.
>
> We demand that farmers ought to be represented in the drafting of new agricultural legislation.

At the time, the General Assembly could do no more than give a respectful hearing to these demands. The items were beyond the power of a state legislature acting in isolation; in reality, the Iowa General Assembly was being used as a sounding board in an effort to force action elsewhere.

THE AGRICULTURAL ADJUSTMENT ACT OF 1933

High pressure labors by Henry Wallace and his cohorts, ranging from starry-eyed utopians to "dirt farmers," resulted in a bill, H.R. 3835, tactfully entitled "To relieve the existing national emergency by increasing agricultural purchasing power . . . ," a title which in itself made opposition difficult. On March 22 this bill was passed by the House, 315 to 98, only 18 not voting, and the Roosevelt-Wallace farm relief program was on its way. Of Iowa's nine members, Republicans Dowell, Gilchrist, and Thurston joined Democrats Eicher, Jacobsen, and Willford in the majority, while Democrats Biermann, Gillette, and Wearin withheld their support from the Roosevelt-Wallace leadership.[16] The votes of Gillette of Cherokee, in the northwest Iowa cash corn area, and Wearin of Hastings, in the heavily agricultural Seventh District, are hard to explain.

When the bill went to the Senate, John A. Simpson, the Farmers Union president, backing up the threats of the Des Moines convention, was on hand to work for the "cost of production" formula, supported by the very able liberal, Senator George W. Norris of Nebraska, who led the debate for that provision. For the opposition, Secretary Wallace testified against the idea as impracticable, and impossible to administer.

BITTER INTERLUDE: TRAGEDY AT LE MARS

During the debate on "cost of production," distressing news came in from Iowa. A few Iowa farmers in the western part of the state, almost certainly urged on by outsiders, committed acts which were a disgrace to the state. At Primghar on April 27 a foreclosure sale at the courthouse was broken up, and the sheriff, his deputies, and the attorney for the creditor were forced to kiss the flag. But this was child's play compared to an incident which took place at nearby Le Mars. Many of the participants in the Primghar incident took off for Plymouth County when told of a foreclosure sale there which had been pending for several days. Finding nothing going on at the farm involved, the mob's attention was directed to the courthouse where important proceedings were in progress in the court of Judge Charles C. Bradley. The judge ordered the men to remove their hats and to stop smoking. At this command the tempers of some of the men flared up. The judge was seized, dragged from his bench to a truck, and carried a mile into the country. Here he was removed from the truck, his trousers were taken away, and he was taunted with the threat of mutilation. Then a rope was drawn tight around his neck and an ultimatum delivered to the effect that he must swear not to sign any more decrees of foreclosure. The judge bravely answered: "I will do the fair thing to all men to the best of my knowledge."

Fortunately, the men responded to the restraining influence of Rome F. Starzl, editor of the *Le Mars Globe-Post,* and contented themselves with pouring grease over the victim's head, filling his trousers with gravel, and leaving the poor man by the side of the road in a dazed condition. That night the sheriff asked the governor for the militia. By coincidence a foreclosure sale on a farm near Denison, in Crawford County, was broken up by Holiday members on the same day, in spite of resistance by the sheriff and fifty deputies. This sheriff also asked the governor to dispatch the militia to his county. On the 28th Governor Herring sent troops into both counties to restore order and to arrest the offenders. This was done and thus was brought to an end the last of the excesses in Iowa which could be charged against the Farmers Holiday Association or its allies.[17]

CONGRESS ENACTS THE AGRICULTURAL ADJUSTMENT ACT

The test vote in the Senate on the Simpson-Norris "cost of production" amendment came up on this same April 28, the day after the terrible incident at Le Mars, and carried by a vote of 64 to 20, Iowa's Senators Lester J. Dickinson and Louis Murphy in the majority.

A convention of the Farmers Holiday Association, held in Des Moines on May 3, resolved to launch a strike in ten days unless farmers were given legislative relief! Stories of protests and threats drifted into Washington from all over the Midwest. The House of Representatives met these threats with a resounding defeat on May 9 for the "cost of production" amendment. The vote was 283 to 109, with 40 not voting. In the crucial vote on this clause, so dear to Milo Reno and his followers, Iowa Democrats Eicher, Gillette, and Wearin joined Republicans Dowell, Gilchrist, and Thurston in the majority while Democrats Biermann, Jacobsen, and Willford voted to accept the amendment. On May 10, a key vote in the Senate on acceptance of the ensuing conference report, both Iowa senators voted yea with the majority of 53, against 28 in the negative. But when further debate was called for in the Senate on the question of receding from the amendment, a final determinative vote, Republican Dickinson switched to support for Wallace while Democrat Murphy voted against him! The vote was 48 to recede and 33 against, with 14 not voting.[18]

In the meanwhile, other impediments to smooth passage of the farm bill had to be disposed of. Senators Elmer Thomas of Oklahoma and Burton Wheeler of Montana, perhaps not unresponsive to their distressed constituents, outdid the Populists of the 1880s and 1890s by proposing amendments calling for increased use of silver money and/or greenbacks as an inflationary cure-all for the farm problem. It required all of FDR's cunning to persuade Senator Thomas to back down from his extreme position and become an administration ally instead of opponent. To these obstacles to the bill's progress through Congress one must add the effects of the radical panaceas offered to a vast radio audience by Father Charles Coughlin of Detroit, who was currently pro-Roosevelt but stressing "cost of production" and clearly foreshadowing his National Union for Social Justice; Dr. Francis Townsend's scheme for payments of $200 a month to all citizens over 60 years of age; and Senator Huey Long's ominous slogan of "Share the Wealth!" Roosevelt and Wallace also had to face the bitter opposition of ex-President Hoover, who saw every issue in terms of self-vindication.

In spite of, or perhaps partly because of, such threats from both left and right, Secretary Wallace's middle course finally won the day. In a little less than two months, congressional leaders under his guidance rammed through the domestic allotment plan and persuaded a majority to reject the "cost of production" feature. The president signed the bill on May 12, 1933, just two days after the Senate retreated once and for all from their earlier approval of the Simpson-Norris amendment. On the same day the president issued a plea for a voluntary cessation of foreclosures, using language remarkably similar to Herring's phrases of the previous January. Milo Reno accepted the bill and the proclamation as adequate and called off his threatened strike.[19]

The Triple-A was a fulfillment of Henry Wallace's three commitments, given above. The measure was designed to bring about a limitation on production; second, the system, based on voluntary individual participation and administered by local and county committees, was about as near to democracy in action as one can arrange; finally, the act was a direct response to the desperate needs of human beings and provided immediate cash relief, not more studies by wordy experts, committees, and conferences. Unfortunately, the Agricultural Adjustment Act of May 12, 1933, came too late to forestall or cut down on the spring farrowing of the pig crop and the early spring cotton planting. This necessitated a painful decision on Wallace's part. Unless the good intentions inherent in the AAA were to be nullified until a year or more had passed, there was only one thing to do: Wallace must order the compensated destruction of the pig crop and plowing under of a third of the cotton crop, already well started on its growing season. Full well knowing that he would be severely criticized, the order was nevertheless given.

The real meaning of victory in the passage of the farm bill of 1933 was the triumph of George N. Peek's idea of "equality of agriculture," first publicized in 1922 and stoutly championed for eleven years, though for him the victory was diluted by the inclusion of production controls and payments for unused lands, ideas and devices which were anathema to this conservative gentleman. "Equality" was too elastic as a word and it was replaced by the word "parity." As a technical term, "parity" meant equality of purchasing power for farmers with other segments of the economy. It would be achieved whenever a fair ratio could be established between the prices of things farmers sold and the things which they bought, using a base period of known prosperity as the standard of comparison. The period chosen was 1910–1914, the climax to the "golden years" of American agriculture, referred to above.

"Parity" was to be sought after through a program which farmers would enter *voluntarily* but in which the government would furnish assistance by operating the administrative machinery of the program. The plan rested entirely on the functioning of the economic law of supply and demand: cut down on the number of acres planted and thereby reduce production, thus bringing about higher prices as consumers bid against each other for the available supply. The principal device was to be the domestic allotment system (condemned by the Farmers Union–Farmers Holiday Association as "non-sensical"). Under this system each participating farmer would voluntarily enter into a contract with the government specifying the number of his acres (his "allotment") to be kept in cropland and the number of acres to be idled. These allotments would be determined by a complex formula based on the extent of cropland he had farmed in previous years. In addition, he would receive a promise of rental payment, based on an equally complex formula, for the acres left idle under the program. It was in the making of this contract that local and county committees would function in democratic fashion. Officers of the American Farm Bureau Federation and the county demonstration agents (then partly in the Farm Bureau organization) usually played a prominent part on these committees as ready-made personnel.

With variations and changes necessitated by court decisions or commonsense practice, this idea is still in use (1972). The Triple-A was supplemented by the Commodity Credit Corporations which made cash available to growers of seven basic commodities by loans on their crops, a plan later stabilized into what seemed in 1972 like a permanent program. Such crops were put in storage under seal as collateral for a loan; if the price went above the rate used as a basis for the loan, the debtor could sell his produce, pay off the loan, and pocket the difference. Congress appropriated money to get the scheme going but the future ongoing expenses were to be met by a processing tax paid by the first processor. One provision of the act was designed to prevent enlarged production by means of better cultivation and increased use of fertilizers. This was accomplished by a special tax on any production in 1934 and 1935 beyond the permitted amounts.

THE 45TH GENERAL ASSEMBLY, EXTRAORDINARY SESSION, 1933–1934

Returning to the state and local scene, we find that Governor Herring did not try to secure enactment of his entire program in the first regular session of the General Assembly. Many factors contributed to the policy of postponement of some important issues for consideration by a special session. This was held from November 6, 1933, to March 12, 1934. Some of the relief measures needed in Iowa were federal in character and had to wait on action in Washington; some changes would require amendment of the state constitution; some measures needed the benefit of the data and the logic which the Brookings study would provide. Most of all, however, the delay was the deliberate choice of Governor Herring, a cautious leader who was not by nature one to rush pell-mell into battle. He had no taste for the high pressure methods of an ambitious and frantic "boss" type, and he knew he did not have the support to make such methods work in Iowa.[20]

THE END OF PROHIBITION IN IOWA

A good example of Herring's cautious approach to the problems of his day was his handling of the touchy issue of liquor control, culminating in action by a special session. Repeal of the Eighteenth Amendment was a possibility but antisaloon sentiment was still very strong, so much so that out-and-out advocacy of the open sale of alcoholic liquor for beverage purposes would have been political suicide. When the last session of a Hoover Congress, with a Democratic majority in the House and undoubtedly influenced by the Democratic victory in November 1932, launched Amendment XXI on its way on February 20, 1933, Iowa leaders were ready to act promptly. The General Assembly turned the matter over to the people by arranging for the election of delegates to a state ratification convention. On June 20, the voters chose county delegates pledged to vote yes or no on ratification, according to the results of a statewide popular vote. This vote ran 377,275 for repeal and 249,943 against, thus assuring ninety-nine county delegates for repeal, although only sixty counties voted "wet" while thirty-nine voted "dry." Thus Iowa had broken sharply with her past. The formal casting of the vote at the convention on July 10 was just that—a kind of ceremonial formality.

Foreseeing the imminent adoption of this new constitutional provision, which in Section 2 indirectly provided for state options, Herring wanted Iowa to be ready with some system of liquor control which would avoid the necessity of local option elections on the saloon question. Rather than try to impose his own views on either the legislature or the people, the governor secured an authorization from the legislature for a nine-man committee to study the matter and to make a recommendation for some form of liquor control. A blue ribbon committee with General Mathew A. Tinley of Council Bluffs as chairman and Senator Joseph R. Frailey of Fort Madison as vice-chairman was set up. The canny governor was able to persuade his own pastor, the Reverend

Mr. Stoddard Lane of Plymouth Congregational Church in Des Moines, to become a member; another prestigious member was President Orville R. Latham of Iowa State Teachers College. After diligent study of liquor control systems in use for Canada, Sweden, and elsewhere, the committee made its report in favor of a state monopoly on all alcoholic liquors except beer. By this plan, which recognized the inevitability of some sort of sale of liquor, a State Liquor Commission would operate a system of liquor stores throughout the state, with each county or community to have the privilege of electing to remain without a store or to abolish a store. Any person desiring to purchase liquor *for consumption off the premises* would have to provide himself with a "liquor stamp" (a purchasing permit), and each purchase of liquor would be registered. The plan was submitted to the Extraordinary Session of the General Assembly which passed it into law on March 1, 1934.[21]

THE THREE-POINT TAX REPLACEMENT LAW

Undoubtedly the most far-reaching legislation of this extra session, really one of the most important legislative acts in Iowa history, was the Three-Point Tax Replacement Law. The basic idea of property tax relief was quite familiar because for years students of taxation had argued for a tax that would reach those whose wealth was intangible. This particular proposal owed something to the technical assistance supplied by the Brookings team of experts. The three new taxes adopted were a sales tax, an income tax, and a corporation tax.[22] With amendments based on later experience, all three taxes are still in use, apparently a permanent part of Iowa's fiscal program.

Other acts provided for some administrative changes in the state government, but action on many of the major changes recommended in the Brookings Institution report had to be postponed because the Interim Committee announced that it would not be ready for action on these proposals until the 1935 session. Even so, the governor closed the Extraordinary Session with praise for the members, assuring them that they had passed more important legislation in one session than any General Assembly in Iowa history, a statement not likely to be disputed.

THE ELECTIONS OF 1934

People everywhere, especially politicians, looked toward the elections of 1934 as a test of the popularity of the New Deal. While that political philosophy was not as much of a factor in Iowa, even in Democratic politics, as in many other states, no Democrats in Iowa had openly repudiated affiliation with the Roosevelt forces and, therefore, the election could be considered a referendum on the president and his program in the state. The results were definitely favorable but not a landslide.

In general, it seems that the agricultural relief program, and the various schemes to create jobs, such as the Civilian Works Program under the able administration of E. Hubert Mulock, Des Moines banker and insurance man, were popular. As for the NRA program, it was not as important in Iowa as in the more industrialized states and therefore not as much subject to criticism.

The Democrats again elected six out of nine members of the state delegation to the House, this time losing the Third District to the very able John W. Gwynne of Waterloo (who would be reelected six times), but picking up the Fifth District by unseating Cassius C. Dowell of Des Moines, twenty-year veteran of the House who had had fourteen years of experience in the Iowa House and Senate before his first election to Congress in 1914. The total Democratic vote in the nine districts was 444,065; the total Republican vote was 385,852. Clyde L. Herring was reelected over Dan W. Turner for governor, with a smaller total vote but a margin greater by 11,000 votes than in 1932. In the elections for the General Assembly, the true test of grass roots political sentiment, the Democrats won fifty-nine seats against forty-nine for the Republicans in the House; in the races for the Senate, each of the two parties elected eleven men. Governor Herring could well believe that the voters had approved his first term record. Nationally, the Democrats won a strong endorsement by increasing their membership in each house of Congress, giving President Roosevelt encouragement to go ahead with more radical programs.

Herring's Second Term

Herring's second term was not filled with dramatic achievements; for reasons not readily apparent, the Forty-sixth General Assembly concerned itself mostly with routine legislation rather than with the leftover items from the Brookings Report. There was some improvement in the economy as the corrective measures of 1933–1934 began to work their benefits and the situation seemed to call for corrections and improvements in the laws already passed rather than more innovations. Governor Herring was by nature well adapted to work with the legislature in this kind of gradual reform program which required close attention to details and close cooperation with the federal government on many matters.

THE TRIPLE-A DECLARED UNCONSTITUTIONAL

It must be conceded that the political spotlight was on Washington in 1935–1936, not on Des Moines or any other state capital. Observers were interested in the further development of the New Deal and the success of the recovery plans already initiated. The legislation sponsored by Secretary Henry A. Wallace came in for a severe test because of the very adverse weather in 1934–1936, inadvertently helping to reduce the reserves of farm produce and increasing the need for relief agencies. The summers were long and hot and dry, so much so that in many ordinarily lush areas the crops dried up long before the harvest season. The winters were similarly long, and bitterly cold. In these years, before hybrid corn had come into general use, the 1934 nationwide yield was 1,448,920,000 bushels compared with a normal yield of about 2,600,000,000 bushels; in 1935, the yield was up to 2,299,363,000 bushels; in 1936, down to 1,505,689,000 bushels. The Iowa figures for these years were: 1934: 199,879,572 bushels; 1935: 371,076,289; 1936: 173,003,081. Low yields such as these are part of the background for Secretary Wallace's advocacy of the "ever-normal granary."

On January 6, 1936, the United States Supreme Court dropped a bombshell into the ranks of New Dealers with a 6–3 opinion which declared the Agricultural Adjustment Act unconstitutional on the grounds that the act brought about a federal invasion of the rights of the states, and the processing tax was an illegal use of the taxing power.[23] Secretary Wallace at once assured the public that a way would be found to keep the beneficial parts of the act. Wallace had never looked on the AAA of 1933 as final and unchangeable but rather as emergency legislation which would undergo changes as the need arose and opportunity presented itself. He and his advisors had given much time to the study of these needed changes and the court decision found them ready to draw up a new bill with great speed. Bill-drafting experts were put to work immediately to draw up a measure stressing the conservation aspects of the farm program and by March 1, 1936, a new act was on the books under the name of the "Soil Conservation and Domestic Allotment Act."[24] Thus seeming disaster was turned into a blessing.

AGRICULTURE LOSES TWO IMPORTANT LEADERS

In 1936 two prominent leaders of Iowa farmers died, two whose careers illustrate two widely differing attitudes toward ways and means of solving the farmer's problems. On March 5 the end came for Milo Reno, a leader in Iowa protest politics and an advocate of direct action in the struggle for higher farm prices.[25] Just three days later, March 8, Charles E. Hearst of Cedar Falls came to the end of over thirty years of service to Iowa farmers, the last thirteen in the high office of president of the Iowa Farm Bureau Federation. His career was the epitome of the "organization man" in agriculture. As far back as 1912 he was one of a group of Black Hawk County farmers who brought in a county demonstration agent, the third in Iowa, closely following similar steps in Clinton and Scott counties. Later, in 1918, he was a colleague of John W. Coverdale and others who met in Marshalltown and took the first step which led to the founding of the Iowa Farm Bureau Federation, and ultimately the American Farm Bureau Federation, in 1920. He was one of the early promoters of the "short course" idea which grew into an effective educational device in the hands of the faculty of the Iowa State College of Agriculture at Ames.

His years as president of the IFBF, 1923–1936, span the years of crisis for modern American agriculture. During those years of searching for a solution to the farm problem, there was rarely a meeting of farm leaders—state, regional, or national—in which he did not play a part. His collected correspondence teems with important matters which he discussed by letter with leaders such as George N. Peek, Frank O. Lowden, Henry C. and Henry A. Wallace, with economists, bankers, dirt farmers, and political leaders. Widely read, ever the serious student, his feet were planted firmly on the ground of long years of experience as a dirt farmer, stockman, and cattle feeder. He supported the McNary-Haugen plan as long as there was a possibility of its passage; later he went along with the Domestic Allotment plan and helped to implement it in 1933. A lifelong Republican, he rose high above partisanship in the crisis of 1932–1933, and until his death in 1936 warmly supported the Wallace program for farm relief. He was greatly upset when the Supreme Court threw out the Triple-A in the Hoosac Mills case; fortunately, he could live long enough to learn of its replacement by the act of March 1, 1936. On the day of his funeral, Cedar Falls was the agricultural capital of the United States as national and state leaders came to pay him tribute.[26]

THE POLITICAL DECISIONS OF 1936

Even more than in 1934, observers of the political scene watched the races of 1936, nowhere more than those in Iowa, as a test of the hold of the New Deal on the public, especially in the Midwest. The results were quite satisfactory to the Democrats. President Roosevelt carried the state for the second time; Clyde L. Herring was triumphant over Lester J. Dickinson for the Senate, and former Representative Guy M. Gillette of Cherokee was elected for the short term made vacant by the death of Louis Murphy the previous July. The Democrats won only five of the nine seats in the national House, the Republicans regaining the Sixth District for Cassius C. Dowell of Des Moines. Running nearly 100,000 votes behind Roosevelt, Lieutenant Governor Nelson W. Kraschel of Harlan was a slim victor over State Senator George A. Wilson of Des Moines for governor, a clear indication that Iowa's defection to the Democrats was coming to an end. The elections for the General Assembly also reflected this trend, the GOP winning 20 Senate seats to 12 for the Democrats, and evenly dividing the 108 House seats. An effort to organize a Farmer-Labor party in Iowa produced only a state total of 14,088 votes, widely scattered.

IOWA AND NATIONAL AFFAIRS, 1937–1938

National affairs continued to overshadow state affairs. Only President Roosevelt's effort to purge Senator Guy Gillette drew attention to Iowa. Gillette was a leading opponent of certain parts of the Judiciary Reform bill and, when Congress defeated the president on the proposal, the Iowa senator and several others were marked for ousting in the next election in favor of those better disposed to follow presidential wishes. Otha M. Wearin of Hastings, a liberal, was the choice of the pro-Roosevelt forces to run against Gillette in the primary.

While the court fight was in progress, Secretary Wallace guided the "second AAA" through Congress. The Agricultural Adjustment Administration Act of 1938 was designed to incorporate all the best features of the two previous acts and to add a feature which Henry A. Wallace had been mulling over since 1912, say his biographers: a provision for the "ever-normal granary." In later years, Secretary Wallace would point with pride to this act as the climax to his years of study and campaigning for the welfare of farmers. Drawn from Old Testament writings and Egyptian experience and called the "Joseph Law" by Wallace, the terms of the act provided for a carry-over of a surplus, perhaps building up for years, as insurance that the United States (and the world) would have a surplus to fall back on in case of disaster in a given crop year or years.

Although the safeguarding element of conservation was retained (to make it legal), the act dealt with the need for a controlled production and sought to insure good prices. Producers of five basic crops—corn, cotton, wheat, rice, and peanuts—would continue to take their harvested crops to a licensed dealer who would put the produce under seal; the farmer would receive a government loan for same. Instead of a loan keyed to the number of acres idled, as in the 1933 plan, the new law provided for a loan based directly on an estimated parity price. The secretary of agriculture was empowered to set a base price somewhere between 52 percent and 75 percent of parity; this would be the loan rate.[27] The crop loan and surrender provisions were unchanged. A point of some importance to Iowans was Wallace's choice of an Iowa farmer, Rudolph M. ("Spike") Evans of Laurens, as the administrator of the new AAA.

1938: THE END OF AN ERA

In spite of the prospects for a better farm program, and, in contrast to Democratic success through most of the nation, the traditional supremacy of the Republicans in Iowa was about to reassert itself. The unpopularity of the Roosevelt court-packing plan and its attendant rough politics, the recession of 1937, and a general feeling of malaise over the drift toward too much power in Washington contributed to a desire to switch to the party of the past. Another factor was the growing tendency of the urban elements to dominate the Democratic party and neglect the farm and small town interests.[28] This would be keenly felt in a state such as Iowa.

Senator Gillette's nomination and election made up a test case. He had the reputation of being more of an anti–New Dealer than he deserved, then or later. His antiadministration voting record was not the source of Roosevelt's animosity; on certain key votes selected for a comparison with others, his anti-Roosevelt votes totaled only 25 percent as against several cases in 60 percent and 70 percent range, and one, the bitter 81 percent record of Senator Carter Glass of Virginia. Roosevelt's animus against Gillette was because of the Iowa senator's vote against court reform. Senator Herring supported his colleague in the June primary and Secretary Wallace dared to defy the president by supporting Gillette, then and later, against Wearin.[29] The Cherokee man defeated Wearin badly, 81,605 to 43,044, and then went on to win over Lester J. Dickinson in November by 413,751 to 407,980.

The Democrats were able to elect only two representatives, each one in a district where the organized labor vote overshadowed the farm vote: William S. Jacobsen of Clinton and Vincent P. Harrington of Sioux City. For the office of governor, George A. Wilson ran ahead of his ticket, harvesting a vote of 446,959 to 387,783 for the incumbent, Kraschel. Wallace Short, the former mayor of Sioux City, garnered only 10,214 votes as the Farmer-Labor candidate. The state legislature would now be dominated by powerful Republican majorities in each house. Thus ended six years of Democratic–New Deal leadership in the Iowa of the 1930s.

In this chapter the New Deal label has been used mostly as a chronological indicator. The plain fact is that Iowa was never a strong New Deal state in the ideological sense. The relief program of 1933–1936 was very welcome on the farms and in the cities, and one hesitates to try to reckon the cost in the form of revolution if such relief had not been forthcoming—but there the connection between spending and politics comes to an end. Figures are now available which buttress the point which was once only an impression: the New Deal did not "buy" Iowa's affections or her continued support. On a per capita basis, the only meaningful measuring device, Iowa was far down in the list of states in terms of benefits from New Deal spending on work projects. During 1933–1939, the heyday of the New Deal, at $232 per capita Iowa was 25th in rank in the receipt of federal funds. The states of the Midwest averaged only $224, compared with an average payment of $306 in the states of the West, the favored region, consisting of the Pacific Coast, the Rocky Mountain area, and the Great Plains. In the matter of federal loans to the states, Iowa did better with a rank of 8th. Only on one item, loans to the Rural Electrification Administration, did Iowa approach top ranking; on this item she was 2nd, at $4 per capita. On Works Progress Administration expenditures Iowa was 38th in rank; on Federal Emergency Relief Administration outlays, 44th in rank. In contiguous states, as a matter of comparison, Nebraska was well above Iowa in federal spending per capita, at $291; Minnesota was above, at $272; Missouri was just above, at $238; Wisconsin was virtually equal at $234; and Illinois received less, $207.[30]

Only Senators Herring and Gillette were left to carry on the Democratic banner in the state—and neither was a complete follower of the New Deal philosophy as it had developed since 1932. Herring was the more liberal of the two but never a Harry Hopkins type; Gillette was an old-school Woodrow Wilson Democrat. Herring could look back with justifiable pride on the progress made during his two terms as governor toward a better state government, but his talents, even his interests, ended there. He was not the stuff out of which great senators are made. Gillette's best years were ahead of him as developments in the international sphere of government gave him the opportunity to capitalize on his true interests and talents.[31]

The nature of the times and the anti-Republican landslide of 1932 had given the Democrats of Iowa a great opportunity for service to the nation and the state. It would be difficult, if not impossible, to argue that they had not met the challenge. In addition, although still the minority party, they were able to bequeath to the younger members of the party a status which guaranteed a two-party political system in the Iowa of the future.

CHAPTER 18 THE RECENT YEARS 1938-1972

THE CHALLENGING TASK OF WRITING AN ACCOUNT OF IOWA IN recent years begins with the choice of a minimal list of topics to be covered. In this account an effort will be made to present information about certain topics which have had a noticeable effect on Iowa in the last generation. In the opinion of many, Iowa has undergone a "silent revolution" in the last few decades; it is "a place to grow" and "a place to live." Factual information, rightly interpreted, can help to reveal the "new" Iowa.

POPULATION DEVELOPMENTS AND TRENDS

Much has been written about the standstill and subsequent decline of Iowa's rural population and the growth of its urban population, as revealed by the censuses of 1960 and 1970. Aware of the urban gains in the decades between 1940 and 1960, students were eager to see what the 1970 figures would reveal. The first discovery was that twenty-five counties had gained population and seventy-four counties had lost, most of the gainers being urban counties continuing their growth and most of the losers being rural counties (or semirural) which were merely continuing their decline of previous decades.

Tables 18.1 and 18.2 will be helpful as a basis of interpretation.[1]

COMMENTARY

A glance at these tables will show that Iowa's slow rate of population growth is not a matter of recent origin. After the rapid increases, year by year, between 1833 and 1860, the rate of increase slowed down noticeably, as might be expected. The first census to show a serious retardation in the rate of growth was the census of 1890; it was more obvious in the

TABLE 18.1: Growth of population in Iowa, 1836–1970

Census Year	Population	Increase or Decrease during the Interval	Percentage of Change
1970	2,825,041	67,504	2.45
1960	2,757,537	136,464	5.21
1950	2,621,073	82,805	3.26
1940	2,538,268	67,329	2.72
1930	2,470,939	51,012	2.11
1925	2,419,927	15,906	0.66
1920	2,404,021	45,955	1.95
1915	2,358,066	133,295	5.99
1910	2,224,771	14,721	0.67
1905	2,210,050	—21,803	—0.98
1900	2,231,853	173,784	8.44
1895	2,058,069	145,772	7.62
1890	1,912,297	158,317	9.03
1885	1,753,980	129,365	7.96
1880	1,624,615	274,071	20.29
1875	1,350,544	156,524	13.11
1870	1,194,020	437,811	57.90
1865	756,209	81,296	12.05
1860	674,913	157,038	30.32
1856	517,875	325,661	169.43
1850	192,214	96,126	100.04
1846	96,088	52,976	122.88
1840	43,112	20,253	88.60
1838	22,859	12,328	117.06
1836	10,531		

SOURCE: Adapted from a larger table in the *Iowa Official Register,* 1915–1916, pp. 746–47.

NOTE: The percentages are added. The years chosen for presentation are 1836—the first census taken in Iowa District of the Territory of Wisconsin; 1838—the year of the creation of the Territory of Iowa; 1846—the year of the admission of Iowa to statehood; 1840 and all years ending in "0" show the federal decennial census figures; 1856 and all years ending in "5" show the state of Iowa census figures. (The mid-decade census was abandoned by the state as an economy measure in the depression days of 1933.)

figures for 1900 and 1910. As noted above, a demographic study published in 1912 demonstrated that farm population, the segment which had heretofore been the chief source of population growth, was receding after 1880 instead of expanding, and therefore was the locus of Iowa's population loss.[2] The census of 1910 was the first to show an absolute loss in total population in Iowa's history. The decline was only 7,082, a puny 0.3 of 1 percent, but the loss was solid proof that the population curve had reached a virtual standstill. This diagnosis was borne out by the fact that in the succeeding sixty years, Iowa grew only by 600,000, a growth rate far behind the national average. The burden of growth has been carried by the towns and cities.

Four noticeable factors in American life have affected population trends, in Iowa as much as or more so than in any other state: the national trend toward increased urbanization and industrialization, twin processes which have pulled many farm workers away from the farm and

TABLE 18.2: Population of Iowa counties since 1870

	1870	1880	1890	1900	1910	1920	1930	1940	1950	1960	1970
	1,194,020	1,624,615	1,911,896	2,231,853	2,224,771 -7,082	2,240,021	2,470,939	2,538,268	2,621,073	2,757,537	2,825,041
Adair	3,982	11,667	14,534	16,192	14,420	14,250	13,891	13,196	12,292	10,893	9,487
Adams	4,614	11,888	12,292	13,001	10,998	10,521	10,437	10,156	8,753	7,468	6,322
Allamakee	17,868	19,791	17,907	18,711	17,328	17,285	16,328	17,184	16,351	15,982	14,968
Appanoose	16,456	16,636	18,961	25,927	28,701	30,535	24,835	24,245	19,683	16,015	15,007
Audubon	1,212	7,448	12,412	13,626	12,671	12,520	12,264	11,790	11,579	10,919	9,595
Benton	22,454	24,888	24,178	25,177	23,156	24,080	22,851	22,879	22,656	23,422	22,885
Black Hawk	21,706	23,913	24,219	32,399	44,865	56,570	69,146	79,946	100,448	122,482	132,916
Boone	14,584	20,838	23,772	28,200	27,626	29,892	29,271	29,782	28,139	28,037	26,470
Bremer	12,528	14,081	14,630	16,305	15,843	16,728	17,046	17,932	18,884	21,108	22,737
Buchanan	17,034	18,546	18,997	21,427	19,748	19,800	19,550	20,991	21,927	22,293	21,746
Buena Vista	1,585	7,537	13,548	16,975	15,981	18,556	18,667	19,838	21,113	21,189	20,693
Butler	9,951	14,293	15,463	17,955	17,119	17,845	17,617	17,986	17,394	17,467	16,953
Calhoun	1,602	5,595	13,107	18,569	17,090	17,783	17,605	17,584	16,925	15,923	14,287
Carroll	2,451	12,351	18,828	20,319	20,117	21,549	22,326	22,770	23,065	23,431	22,912
Cass	5,464	16,943	19,645	21,274	19,047	19,421	19,422	18,647	18,532	17,919	17,007
Cedar	19,731	18,936	18,253	19,371	17,765	17,560	16,760	16,884	16,910	17,791	17,665
Cerro Gordo	4,722	11,461	14,864	20,672	25,011	34,675	38,476	43,845	46,053	49,894	49,335
Cherokee	1,967	8,240	15,659	16,570	16,741	17,760	18,737	19,258	19,052	18,598	17,269
Chickasaw	10,180	14,534	15,019	17,037	15,375	15,431	14,637	15,227	15,228	15,034	14,969
Clarke	8,735	11,513	11,332	12,440	10,736	10,506	10,384	10,233	9,369	8,222	7,581
Clay	1,523	4,248	9,309	13,401	12,766	15,660	16,107	17,762	18,103	18,504	18,464
Clayton	27,771	28,829	26,733	27,750	25,576	25,032	24,559	24,334	22,522	21,962	20,606
Clinton	35,357	36,763	41,199	43,832	45,394	43,371	44,377	44,722	49,664	55,060	56,749
Crawford	2,530	12,413	18,894	21,685	20,041	20,614	21,028	20,538	19,741	18,569	19,116
Dallas	12,019	18,746	20,479	23,058	23,628	25,120	25,493	24,649	23,661	24,123	26,085
Davis	15,565	16,468	15,258	15,620	13,315	12,574	11,150	11,136	9,959	9,199	8,207
Decatur	12,018	15,336	15,643	18,115	16,347	16,566	14,903	14,012	12,601	10,539	9,737
Delaware	17,432	17,950	17,349	19,185	17,888	18,183	18,122	18,487	17,734	18,483	18,770
Des Moines	27,256	33,099	35,324	35,989	36,145	35,529	38,162	36,804	42,056	44,605	46,982
Dickinson	1,389	1,901	4,328	7,905	8,137	10,241	10,982	12,185	12,756	12,574	12,565
Dubuque	38,969	42,996	49,848	56,403	57,450	58,262	61,214	63,768	71,337	80,058	90,609
Emmet	1,392	1,550	4,274	9,936	9,816	12,627	12,856	13,406	14,102	14,871	14,009
Fayette	16,973	22,258	23,141	29,985	27,919	29,251	29,145	29,151	28,294	28,581	26,898
Floyd	10,768	14,677	15,424	17,754	17,119	18,860	19,524	20,169	21,505	21,102	19,860
Franklin	4,738	10,249	12,871	14,996	14,780	15,807	16,382	16,379	16,268	15,472	13,255
Fremont	11,174	17,652	16,842	18,546	15,623	15,447	15,533	14,465	12,323	10,282	9,282
Greene	4,627	12,727	15,797	17,820	16,023	16,467	16,528	16,599	15,544	14,379	12,716
Grundy	6,399	12,639	13,215	13,757	13,574	14,420	14,133	13,518	13,722	14,132	14,119
Guthrie	7,061	14,394	17,380	18,729	17,374	17,596	17,324	17,210	15,197	13,607	12,243
Hamilton	6,055	11,252	15,319	19,514	19,242	19,531	20,978	19,922	19,660	20,032	18,383
Hancock	999	3,453	7,621	13,752	12,731	14,723	14,802	15,402	15,077	14,604	13,330
Hardin	13,684	17,807	19,003	22,794	20,921	23,337	22,947	22,530	22,218	22,533	22,248
Harrison	8,931	16,649	21,356	25,597	23,162	24,488	24,897	22,767	19,560	17,600	16,240
Henry	21,463	20,986	18,895	20,002	18,640	18,298	17,660	17,794	18,708	18,187	18,114
Howard	6,282	10,837	11,182	14,512	12,920	13,705	13,082	13,531	13,105	12,734	11,442
Humboldt	2,596	5,341	9,836	12,667	12,182	12,951	13,202	13,459	13,117	13,156	12,519
Ida	226	4,382	10,705	12,327	11,296	11,689	11,933	11,047	10,697	10,269	9,190
Iowa	16,644	19,221	18,270	19,544	18,409	18,600	17,332	17,016	15,835	16,396	15,419
Jackson	22,619	23,771	22,771	23,615	21,258	19,931	18,481	19,181	18,622	20,754	20,839
Jasper	22,116	25,963	24,943	26,976	27,034	27,855	32,936	31,496	32,305	35,282	35,425
Jefferson	17,839	17,469	15,184	17,437	15,951	16,440	16,241	15,762	15,696	15,818	14,774
Johnson	24,898	25,429	23,082	24,817	25,914	26,462	30,276	33,191	45,756	53,663	72,127
Jones	19,731	21,052	20,233	21,954	19,050	18,607	19,206	19,950	19,401	20,693	19,868
Keokuk	19,434	21,258	23,862	24,979	21,160	20,983	19,148	18,406	16,797	15,492	13,943
Kossuth	3,351	6,178	13,120	22,720	21,971	25,082	25,452	26,630	26,241	25,314	22,937
Lee	37,210	34,859	37,715	39,719	36,702	39,676	41,268	41,074	43,102	44,207	42,996
Linn	31,080	37,237	45,303	55,392	60,720	74,004	82,336	89,142	104,274	136,899	163,213
Louisa	12,877	13,142	11,873	13,516	12,855	12,179	11,575	11,384	11,101	10,290	10,682
Lucas	10,388	14,530	14,563	16,126	13,462	15,686	15,114	14,571	12,069	10,923	10,163
Lyon	221	1,968	8,680	13,165	14,624	15,431	15,293	15,374	14,697	14,468	13,340
Madison	13,884	17,224	15,977	17,710	15,621	15,020	14,331	14,525	13,131	12,295	11,558
Mahaska	22,508	25,202	28,805	34,273	29,860	26,270	25,804	26,485	24,672	23,602	22,177
Marion	24,436	25,111	23,058	24,159	22,995	24,957	25,727	27,019	25,930	25,886	26,352
Marshall	17,576	23,752	25,842	29,991	30,279	32,630	33,727	35,406	35,611	37,984	41,076
Mills	8,718	14,137	14,548	16,764	15,811	15,422	15,866	15,064	14,064	13,050	11,832
Mitchell	9,582	14,363	13,299	14,916	13,435	13,921	14,065	14,121	13,945	14,043	13,108
Monona	3,654	9,055	14,515	17,980	16,633	17,125	18,213	18,238	16,303	13,916	12,069
Monroe	12,724	13,719	13,666	17,985	25,429	23,467	15,010	14,553	11,814	10,463	9,357
Montgomery	5,934	15,895	15,848	17,803	16,604	17,048	16,752	15,697	15,685	14,467	12,781
Muscatine	21,688	23,170	24,504	28,242	29,505	29,042	29,385	31,296	32,148	33,840	37,181
O'Brien	715	4,155	13,060	16,985	17,262	19,051	18,409	19,293	18,970	18,840	17,522
Osceola	---	2,219	5,574	8,725	8,956	10,223	10,182	10,607	10,181	10,064	8,555
Page	9,975	19,667	21,341	24,187	24,002	24,137	25,904	24,887	23,921	21,023	18,507
Palo Alto	1,336	4,131	9,318	14,354	13,845	15,486	15,398	16,170	15,891	14,736	13,289
Plymouth	2,199	8,566	19,568	22,209	23,129	23,584	24,159	23,502	23,252	23,906	24,312
Pocahontas	1,446	3,713	9,553	15,330	14,808	15,602	15,687	16,266	15,496	14,324	12,729
Polk	27,857	42,395	65,410	82,624	110,434	154,029	172,837	195,835	226,010	266,315	286,101
Pottawattamie	16,895	39,850	47,430	54,336	55,832	61,550	69,888	66,756	69,682	83,102	86,991
Poweshiek	15,581	18,396	18,394	19,414	19,589	19,910	18,727	18,758	19,344	19,300	18,803
Ringgold	5,691	12,085	13,556	15,325	12,904	12,919	11,966	11,137	9,528	7,910	6,373
Sac	1,411	8,774	14,552	17,620	16,555	17,500	17,641	17,639	17,518	17,007	15,573
Scott	38,594	41,266	43,164	54,558	60,000	73,952	77,332	84,748	100,698	119,067	142,687
Shelby	2,540	12,696	17,611	17,932	16,552	16,065	17,131	16,720	15,942	15,825	15,528
Sioux	576	5,426	18,370	23,337	25,248	26,458	26,806	27,209	26,381	26,375	27,996
Story	11,651	16,906	18,127	23,159	24,083	26,185	31,141	33,434	44,294	49,327	62,783
Tama	16,131	21,585	21,651	24,585	22,156	21,861	21,987	22,428	21,688	21,443	20,147
Taylor	6,480	15,635	16,384	18,784	16,312	15,514	14,859	14,258	12,420	10,288	8,790
Union	5,986	14,980	16,900	19,928	16,616	17,268	17,435	16,280	15,651	13,712	13,557
Van Buren	17,672	17,043	16,253	17,354	15,029	14,060	12,603	12,053	11,007	9,778	8,643
Wapello	22,346	25,285	30,426	35,426	37,743	37,937	40,480	44,280	47,397	46,126	42,149
Warren	17,980	19,578	18,269	20,376	18,194	18,047	17,700	17,695	17,758	20,829	27,432
Washington	18,952	20,374	18,468	20,718	19,925	20,421	19,822	20,055	19,557	19,406	18,967
Wayne	11,287	16,127	15,670	17,491	16,184	15,378	13,787	13,308	11,737	9,800	8,045
Webster	10,484	15,951	21,582	31,757	34,629	37,611	40,425	41,521	44,241	47,810	48,391
Winnebago	1,562	4,917	7,325	12,725	11,914	13,489	13,143	13,972	13,450	13,099	12,990
Winneshiek	23,570	23,938	22,528	23,731	21,729	22,091	21,630	22,263	21,639	21,651	21,758
Woodbury	6,172	14,996	55,632	54,610	67,616	92,171	101,669	103,627	103,917	107,849	103,052
Worth	2,892	7,953	9,247	10,887	9,950	11,630	11,164	11,449	11,068	10,259	8,968
Wright	2,392	5,062	12,057	18,227	17,951	20,348	20,216	20,038	19,652	19,447	17,294

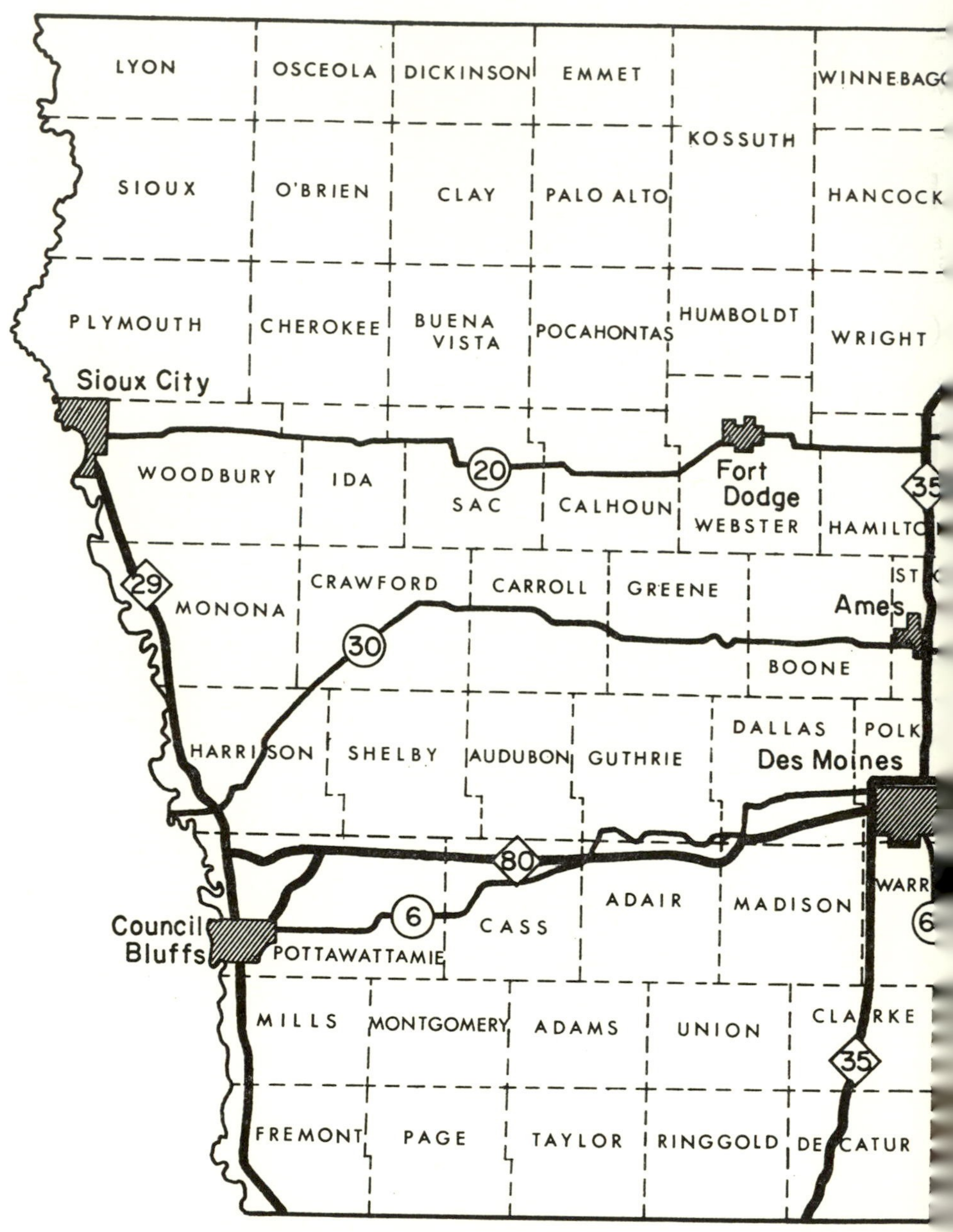

FIG. 18.1. A 1973 map of Iowa showing the counties, principal cities, and principal highways.

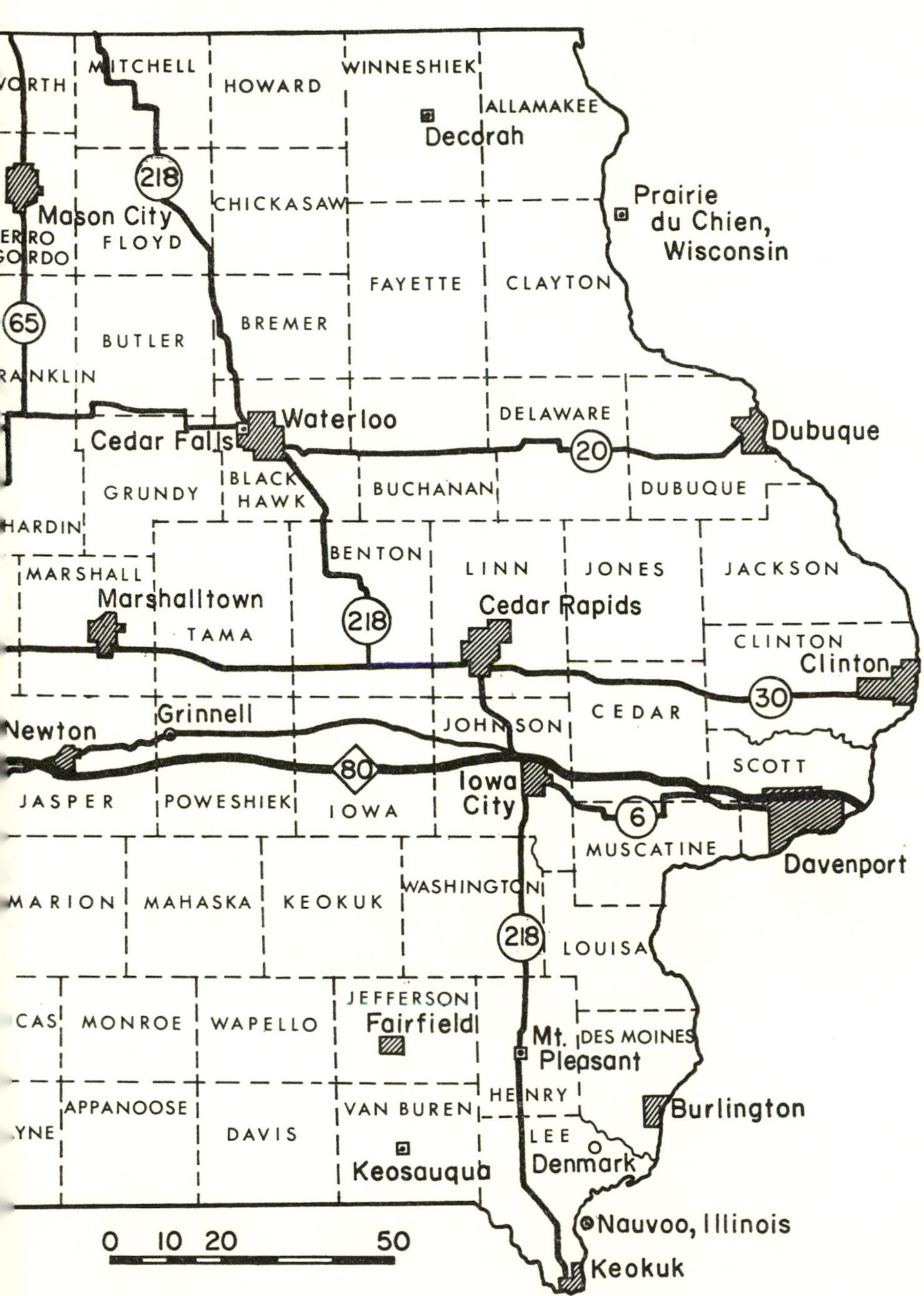
MITCHELL
HOWARD
WINNESHIEK
ALLAMAKEE
Decorah
Mason City
FLOYD
CHICKASAW
Prairie du Chien, Wisconsin
FAYETTE
CLAYTON
BUTLER
BREMER
Waterloo
Cedar Falls
DELAWARE
Dubuque
GRUNDY
BLACK HAWK
BUCHANAN
DUBUQUE
BENTON
LINN
JONES
JACKSON
MARSHALL
Marshalltown
TAMA
Cedar Rapids
CLINTON
Clinton
Grinnell
JOHNSON
CEDAR
Newton
SCOTT
JASPER
POWESHIEK
IOWA
Iowa City
MUSCATINE
Davenport
MARION
MAHASKA
KEOKUK
WASHINGTON
LOUISA
MONROE
WAPELLO
JEFFERSON
Fairfield
Mt. Pleasant
DES MOINES
APPANOOSE
DAVIS
VAN BUREN
HENRY
Burlington
LEE
Denmark
Keosauqua
Nauvoo, Illinois
Keokuk
218
65
20
30
80
6
0 10 20 50

so far have absorbed most of the surplus farm population; the exhaustion of the supply of choice cheap farmlands; the mechanization of the American farm, which has pushed many workers off the farms;[3] and the decline of European immigration to the United States and, for our purposes of analysis, to Iowa. As pointed out above, only 41,217 people of foreign birth were counted in the 1970 census of Iowa.

The year 1956 was a watershed year in Iowa history, the memorable year in which the charts showed the ascending urban line and the descending rural line bisecting each other, a phenomenon which had occurred on the national charts as early as 1920. The estimated population of Iowa at the end of 1956 credited 1,362,000 residents to urban places (those over 2,500) and 1,360,375 to rural homes, that is, residence in towns under 2,500 and on farms. If further proof of a reversal of Iowa's character as a farm state were needed, it came four years later when the census of 1960 showed that out of a total of 2,757,537 people, 1,296,042 (47 percent) were classified as rural, and 1,461,495 (53 percent) as residents of towns and cities above 2,500 in size, of which there were 104 such centers in the state; still further proof came in 1970 with the disclosure that 1,207,971 (42.7 percent) are rural residents and 1,616,070 (57.3 percent) live in urban places, of which there are 111 in the state.

The student of history will be interested in the fact that Iowa's growth came in distinct waves, first to the Mississippi River counties and the southeastern corner counties above Missouri; then westward in waves until the northwestern corner was filled in.[4] This fact can be translated by the sociologist into a wealth of meanings, the most obvious being the overcoming of the culture lag as population grows. Three counties reached the peak of their numbers in 1870 (Cedar, Jefferson, and Van Buren), and Henry County joined them in this distinction in 1875. In 1840 Van Buren County had the largest population of any county in the state; today it is seventh from the bottom.

Other examples of early population peaks are furnished by five counties which reached their peaks in 1880. No county peaked in 1890 but thirty-five reached their zenith in 1900. Monroe County's high in 1910 and Appanoose County's high in 1920 illustrate the rise and fall of the coal mining industry in Iowa, the former falling from 25,429 to 9,357, and the latter from 30,535 in 1920 to 15,007 in 1970. Eight other counties have lost population since 1920, four since 1930, and eleven since 1940, mostly losers because of the trend toward larger farms and the declining need for farm workers. There were three losers in 1950–1960 and eight in 1960–1970, though some were marginal. Of the seventeen counties which peaked in 1970, some owe their growth to industrialization (Linn, Scott, Jasper, for examples), some to the spread of the suburbs into counties adjacent to large cities, and some (Johnson and Story) to the presence of large university student bodies which are now enumerated in the federal censuses. Black Hawk County owes its growth to a mixture of industrial expansion and the numerical growth of the University of Northern Iowa.

In-migration and out-migration are important factors in the rise and fall of population in any state. Whether the in-migration was from eastern and southern states, as in our early decades, or from eastern states and foreign countries later, such inputs were a prime element in Iowa's growth. Happily for Iowa, the period of heaviest in-migration coincided with the period of the least out-migration. In 1920 the in-migration of foreign-born people to Iowa began to decline, partly owing to restrictive national immigration policies, coming down to a trickle from the former flood tides. Net out-migration reached a high of —236,315 in the decade of 1950–1960; some of the total gain since 1960 may be attributed to the decline of that figure to —180,040 in the 1960–1970 decade.[5]

AGRICULTURAL REORGANIZATION AND INDUSTRIAL GROWTH

Profound changes have taken place in Iowa agriculture since the advent of the power-driven tractor, the combine, and the auto truck made possible the replacement of horse-drawn farm implements. Professor Bogue's clever phrase, "how to farm sitting down," would now have to be extended to include "with automatic gearshift, radio, and air-conditioned comfort." Changes in the number and size of farms, a decrease in the number of farm workers but an increase in production per acre, the addition of soybeans to corn as a crop emphasis, the continuing reliance on beef and pork production as moneymakers, and the decline in the number of farms producing and marketing milk, poultry, eggs, and lambs are commonplace information easily grounded in statistical proof.

The most significant figures in terms of social effects are those giving the number of farms, the average size of farm, and the number of people classified as farm population. Looking at the period of the last twenty years as the climax to a longer trend, one finds that in 1950 the number of farms was just over 203,000 and the average size of farm was 169 acres; in 1970 the former number had gone down and the latter figure had gone up: about 135,000 farms and 249 acres in average size. Such figures can be made more meaningful by comparing average farm sizes in specific counties. In 1969 the lowest average farm size was the 176-acre average in Bremer County, long noted for its dairy farms operated by thrifty German and Scandinavian people, closely followed by Linn and Scott counties, both highly industrialized and urbanized, affording excellent markets for dairy products. The highest average size was in Monona County in extreme west central Iowa, a county almost completely devoted to commercial farming, with an average size of 356 acres per farm, closely followed by Fremont County in extreme southwest Iowa, neither county with a town of over 5,000 population. By comparison, in 1935, the peak year for the number of farms in Iowa, the total was 221,986, and the statewide average farm size was 155 acres.[6]

Probably the most remarkable single development in Iowa's recent history has been the enormous increase in urban industrialization, an increase which has reached the point where the dollar size of manufactures has overtaken and surpassed the dollar value of agricultural products. That increase has not been altogether fortuitous but is the end result of a combination of the ingenuity of the manufacturers, the promotional efforts of municipal and state officials, and the contributions of an intelligent and dependable labor force. By their efforts the base of Iowa's economy has been expanded and the unbalanced dependence on agriculture has been reversed. Undergirding these efforts has been the quiet but effective work of the individual who is concerned with the invention and/or design of a product as a profit-making venture, or the individual working as a "tinkerer" who just happens to invent a useful product.

Quite naturally, Iowa's industrial growth has occurred largely but not exclusively in the field of farm machinery and areas allied with agriculture, such as the processing of meat and dairy products. This trend continues, much to the distress of those who would like to see further diversification, and some progress has been made in lines of manufactures not related to agriculture. Now it seems that every town and small city as well as every metropolitan area is able to boast of one or more establishments devoted to the production of farm machinery, capital and consumer goods, household equipment, or the processing of foodstuffs. Many items are shipped to other states and foreign countries, so much so that many firms have their own specialists in the development of foreign trade. One valuable social as well as economic aspect of this phase of the state's economy is that the larger urban factories provide employment not only for local residents but for townspeople and farm families in an extensive area beyond the community where a factory is located. It has been shown, for example, that many farmers who double in outside employment earn more from their off-the-farm jobs than from farming itself, a development made possible by the mechanization of agriculture. This situation has the not unrelated effect of holding down the further concentration of population in the large cities.[7]

IOWA IN WORLD WAR II

Strange as it may seem, World War II did not have the same revolutionary effects on the economy of Iowa as had World War I, nor did it bring on the same degree of social upheaval as had the Civil War. Unlike the attitude in those two war situations, there was almost complete unanimity of support for this war, not only in Iowa but throughout the nation. The prevailing spirit seemed to be one of grim determination to harness all our resources and see the dirty job through, then get back to the business of normal living. This we had done so successfully in World War I, and were about to do again in World War II, that perhaps a false sense of confidence was built up as to our strength and our invincibility.

Militarily, the national government came nearer to success in the implementation of a system of universal military service than ever before, by means of a series of registrations of all available manpower. These enrollments ultimately covered all men from ages 18 to 64, though the 45 to 64 age group was not subject to military service. Consequently, there is no readily available breakdown of the figures to distinguish between voluntary and selective service enlistments. According to the *Iowa Official Register,* a grand total of 882,542 men registered, and 262,638 men *and women* entered upon military service.

As much as in World War I days, "food will win the war" was a viable slogan, supplemented by a great emphasis on industrial production of war goods of every conceivable variety. Iowa's agricultural potential was stretched to the limit and it reached new heights of production with the aid of mechanized machinery and the new hybrid seed corn, just now coming into widespread use. A brief comparison of agricultural statistics for three key years demonstrates the point. In 1930 Iowa had 214,928 farms and the value of all farm products sold or used was $690,302,406; in 1940 Iowa had 212,318 farms and the cash value of all farm products was $561,836,688; in 1945 the number of farms was down to 208,934 but the value of all farm crops sold or used was $1,232,010,705. In 1939 the number of farms chiefly devoted to the raising of corn, the one crop for which Iowa is most famous, was 196,190, with an acreage of 9,330,820; the value of the corn crop was $261,553,211. In 1944 the comparable figures were 189,663 farms, 10,992,786 acres, and a value of $556,496,038.

Iowa's contributions to industrial production make up an important though less well-known story. Many small-town manufacturers of hayloaders, fertilizer spreaders, or aluminum castings, as well as the giant firms in the larger cities, suddenly found themselves called upon to produce the tools of war. It would be well nigh impossible to obtain definitive statistics to indicate what was produced and the quantities and value thereof, partly because some of the articles were of a highly secret nature. A federal statistical study of 1947 provides a basis of comparison. In 1939 there were 2,541 industrial establishments in Iowa, employing 64,773 production workers; the value added by manufacture was $243,390,000; in 1947 the comparable figures were 2,965, 112,490, and $671,100,000. The large number of firms which were awarded the coveted E banner for excellence in production attest the importance of Iowa's industrial contribution to the war effort.

POLITICS IN IOWA, 1938–1972

Throughout the thirty-four years under review, politics on the state level has consisted of a mixture of the traditional and the path-breaking. Iowa's survival of the worst aspects of the Great Depression of the 1920s–1930s was marked by a return to "politics as usual"—meaning the return in 1938 to the supremacy of the Republican party and its customary control of the state and local governments on every level. Striking exceptions were victories in certain older Democratic strongholds, Dubuque and Ottumwa, for example, and certain newer ones, Des Moines and Cedar Rapids; then there were the personalized successes of five outstanding Democratic leaders: Guy M. Gillette of Cherokee,[8] Herschel C. Loveless of Ottumwa, Harold E. Hughes of Ida Grove (the most powerful Democratic spokesman in Iowa in recent times), John C. Culver of Cedar Rapids, and Richard C. Clark of Marion.

The very use of Republican and Democratic labels raises a question as to the meaning of politics in Iowa in this generation. Few need to be reminded that these labels have lost their Civil War meanings, and, in fact, might well be reversed to fit the parties of the 1950s–1960s and the incipient 1970s. Somewhere along the way, certainly as early as the turn of the century, and increasingly so after 1933, the national Democratic party came under the control of its urban elements, as it had always tended to do in the East, with a powerful voice granted to organized labor, a trend that is now evident in the Middle West, including Iowa. If any one point stands out beyond dispute, it is that the new Democratic party accepts the doctrine of strong nationalism in place of the historic doctrine of states' rights, and has taken over the role of the liberals in the advancement of civil rights, a complete switch from Democratic theory of the Civil War era. The national Republican party seems to have undergone profound change on both of these points, enough so to enable it to maintain a working alliance with many present and erstwhile Southern Democrats.[9]

But, as it was observed many years ago, all politics is local politics, and, it might be added, personal politics. It is certainly true that since 1938 the Republicans of Iowa have enjoyed a renewal of their predepression strength, but equally true that exceptions must be noted. From 1938 to 1946 their power was complete across the board except for Guy M. Gillette's victory for senator in 1938. In 1948, apparently because of dissatisfaction with prospective Republican farm policies, many normally Republican farmer voters split their tickets, putting Iowa into the Democratic column for Truman[10] and giving their votes to Gillette for a full term in the Senate, while electing an all-Republican House delegation and a Republican state regime led by William S. Beardsley of New Virginia in his first of three terms as governor. In 1950 Iowa renewed its complete loyalty to the Republican party by reelecting Beardsley and the full Republican House delegation, and continued in the Republican camp through 1972 except for two victories for Herschel Loveless for governor (1956, 1958), three consecutive triumphs for Harold E. Hughes (1962, 1964, 1966) for the same office, and one more victory for him in the contest for the Senate in 1968, and Richard C. Clark's surprising victory over Jack Miller in 1972. Hughes, like Horace Boies, is a former Republican who left that party because of ideological differences. Building on the foundations laid in New Deal days and maintained and strengthened by Herschel Loveless, and profiting from the increase in urban population in Iowa, Hughes has contributed much to the transformation of Iowa into a genuine two-party state.

In Iowa's state and local politics it is impossible to generalize successfully on the basis of conservative and liberal divisions. It is more meaningful to say that some governors, for example, have been more inclined than others to strike out in new directions, but seldom on ideological grounds. Only two Republican governors, Leo Hoegh and Norman Erbe, were unable to take their built-in advantage as incumbents and win second term elections, Hoegh being hurt by his firmness on the need for new taxes, Erbe by his indecisiveness on the question of "liquor by the drink." For the record here are the names, home towns, years of their election, and party identification of the eleven men who have won the governor's office since 1938: George A. Wilson of Des Moines (1938, 1940), Republican; Bourke B. Hickenlooper of Cedar Rapids (1942), Republican, whose great good fortune it was to have to wait only two years instead of the usual four for the easy step from the governor's mansion to the Senate, where a sinecure of four terms was his for the asking;[11] Robert D. Blue of Eagle Grove (1944, 1946), Republican; William S. Beardsley of New Virginia (1948, 1950, 1952), Republican; Leo Elthon of Fertile, interim governor (November 1954–January 1955), Republican; Leo A. Hoegh of Chariton (1954), Republican; Herschel C. Loveless of Ottumwa (1956, 1958), Democrat; Norman A. Erbe of Boone (1960), Republican; Harold E. Hughes of Ida Grove (1962, 1964, 1966), Democrat; Robert D. Fulton of Waterloo, interim governor (January 2–14, 1969), Democrat; Robert D. Ray of Des Moines (1968, 1970, 1972), Republican.

The voting for United States senator from Iowa demonstrates a tendency toward independent choices by the rank and file voters in contrast to party line voting in the old days of legislative elections for this office. The names, home towns, terms of office, and party affiliations are as follows: Guy M. Gillette of Cherokee (1936–1939, 1939–1945, 1949–1955), Democrat; George A. Wilson of Des Moines (1943–1949), Republican; Bourke B. Hickenlooper of Cedar Rapids (1945–1969), Republican; Thomas E. Martin of Iowa City (1955–1961), Republican; Jack Miller of Sioux City (1961–1973), Republican; Harold E. Hughes of Ida Grove (1969–), Democrat; and Richard C. Clark of Marion (1973–), Democrat.

The figures on the elections for the national House of Representatives and the General Assembly of Iowa, where the districts are approximately evenly distributed throughout the state, reveal the true strength of the parties, and here the Republicans have shown their true numerical superiority in Iowa politics. Whereas in congressional elections the Democrats require an outstanding candidate to add to their normal minority vote and thus attract the independent voters necessary for victory, the Republicans have depended on party organization, party discipline, and faithful adherence to sentimental allegiance to the Grand Old Party to hold the line for their candidates. Once elected, it was almost impossible to unseat a Republican from his post without the aid of a political revolution such as 1932 or 1964. With the single exception of H. R. Gross of Waterloo, now in his thirteenth term in the House, no member of the congressional delegation in these thirty-four years has shown the kind of charisma which enables a candidate to rise above national or state trends and win his personal battle for reelection, as Mr. Gross did in 1964 when he was the only Republican candidate of note in Iowa to withstand the anti-Goldwater uprising.[12]

The list of former and present members of the House from Iowa, 1938–1972, is too long to enumerate, but suffice it to say that during those years there was a total of 139 individual regular elections and three special elections, with the Republicans victorious in 112 of the regular elections and all three special elections. In seven consecutive elections, 1942 to 1954, their nominees made a clean sweep of all the contests. Of the 27 Democratic victories, most have come in two districts, the old Second, which includes the Democratic strongholds of Dubuque and Clinton counties, and now Linn County, and the old Fifth, led by Neal Smith and dominated by Polk County and its strong labor vote in Des Moines. The principal additions to these instances of victory were the three victories of Merwin Coad of Boone in the old Sixth District (1956, 1958, 1960) and the near sweep of the state by the Democrats in 1964. The recent successes of John C. Culver (1964, 1966, 1968, 1970, 1972) of Cedar Rapids, in the Second District, indicate that this industrialized city, the second largest in the state, is ready to join Ottumwa, Clinton, Dubuque, and Des Moines in a list of the most reliable Democratic voting centers in the state.

During all these years under discussion, the Republicans have enjoyed preponderant strength in the General Assembly, allowing always for the aberration of 1964. On two occasions, 1946 and 1952, when the elections were unaffected by national issues, Republicans won the astounding totals of 105 out of a possible 108 seats in the House, and lost only one Senate contest in each election. In 1957 and 1959, Democratic Governor Loveless was at the mercy of a Republican-controlled assembly, as was Governor Hughes in 1963 and the Special Session of 1964, though each man was able to achieve considerable success in working with the opposition forces.[13] In only two sessions did the Democrats have a working majority in the Senate, and only once in the House. In only one term, 1965–1967, did the Democrats have full control of the executive and legislative branches of the state government. By contrast, in thirteen elections out of eighteen the voters have provided solid Republican control of the statehouse. This strength at the grass roots shows convincingly the grip of the Republicans on political power in Iowa, and, of course, is the key to Republican eagerness in past years to draw the lines of the General Assembly districts in such a way as to perpetuate that power.

CONGRESSIONAL REDISTRICTING IN IOWA, 1971

Population changes such as those described above could not be permanently ignored. The Sixty-fourth General Assembly, First Session, 1971, under Governor Robert D. Ray, faced three redistricting jobs: congressional, state legislative, and state judicial. Congressional redistricting was the first to be enacted into law. In previous years the decennial congressional revisions were usually the occasions for heavy gerrymandering; this time the redistricting was accomplished with a minimum of excitement and discussion, probably because of the greater interest in the current battle over the state legislative districts. Under S.F. 236, passed in late February 1971, to conform to the congressional reapportionment which reduced Iowa's seats from seven to six, few changes were made in the old First, Second, Third, Sixth, and Seventh districts, though the latter two would have to be renumbered as the Fifth and Sixth. The reduction in districts was accomplished by making up a new Fourth District, chiefly by taking Polk County (Des Moines) from the old Fifth and putting it into the new Fourth, thereby throwing the most populous county in the state into the same district with fairly large Wapello County (Ottumwa), both counties normally Democratic. With a total population of 328,240 in these two counties as against 168,063 in the other nine counties of the district, it would seem that the Republicans on the map-making commission knowingly decided to concede the Fourth, along with Culver's Second, to the Democrats, while presumably keeping the other four. Small wonder that the Republican incumbent of the Fourth, John H. Kyl of Bloomfield, was reported as returning to Iowa to try to dissuade the Republican leadership from making this move. It was done,[14] in spite of his reported protests, and thus it was insured that in 1972 the new Fourth would see a lively contest between two staunch political rivals and equally staunch personal friends, Kyl and Neal E. Smith, the Democratic incumbent of the old Fifth District for nine terms.

REDISTRICTING OF STATE JUDICIAL DISTRICTS, 1971

In the meanwhile, another kind of redistricting problem had drawn the attention of the assembly: the redrawing of the boundaries of Iowa's eighteen district courts, a task which if carried out would make possible a thorough reorganization of the administration of the courts. Vast discrepancies in case loads had crept into the court system, the least active court rendering an average of only 290 decisions per judge in 1970, and the most active, the Tenth (Delaware, Buchanan, Black Hawk, Grundy counties) producing as many as 778 per judge. The spade work for all the studies of the problem was done by representatives of the Iowa Bar Association and the Judicial Association, who submitted a map of new divisional lines drawn to their own satisfaction. The act, effective as of January 1, 1972, provided for eight instead of eighteen districts, although five districts were subdivided for purposes of judicial selection.[15] In each district a chief judge acts as an administrator and endeavors to allocate case loads in an equitable manner.

THE PROBLEM OF REAPPORTIONMENT OF THE GENERAL ASSEMBLY

One of the facts of life in Iowa's recent politics has been the conflict between rural and urban forces. Although preached against as inadvisable and even irrational, the issue has come into the arena of debate without apology and without disguise, as witness the efforts of urban leaders during the last twenty years to secure more representation, in keeping with the new proportions of urban-rural population, and the equally strong efforts of rural leaders to prevent great change. The efforts of the urban spokesmen were given timely though fortuitous aid by the "one man, one vote" doctrine announced by the Supreme Court in 1964.

Until 1888 the assembly reapportioned the state's representation every two years; since 1888 the numerous sessions of the General Assembly have until recently displayed a cavalier attitude toward the people of Iowa on this subject. From 1888 to 1902—eight sessions in all—nothing was done. In 1902 and 1904 the Twenty-ninth and Thirtieth General Assemblies adopted a proposed amendment which had three provisions: to leave the Senate as it was at 50 members; to continue the plan of giving each county one member in the House, but to add nine members, giving each of the nine most populous counties an extra member; and to reapportion after every census (meaning, at the time, the federal census in the years ending in "0" and the state census in the years ending in "5"; the state census was abandoned in 1936 as an economy measure). The voters added their confirmation in November 1904. In the following years, however, nothing was done about reapportioning until 1925 when the Forty-first Assembly passed a proposed amendment setting a maximum of one senator from each county, no matter how populous; this was given second passage in 1927 and ratified in 1928. Two small changes were made in 1941 and 1953.[16]

The root of the trouble was the dependence on area (the "area factor") as the chief source of representation in both houses. A glance at the population table (Table 18.2) explains everything. In the House, Polk County, for example, with 266,315 population in 1960, could have only two representatives, whereas Adams (7,468), Ringgold (7,910), and Clarke (8,222) had one each, as did many others with only slightly higher populations. Thus each Polk County member represented 133,157 people as against the Adams County member who represented 7,468. The senatorial districts were almost as much out of line. As late as 1962 it was demonstrated that only 27 percent of the voters elected a majority of the House and 35 percent elected a majority of the Senate.[17]

The subject would not die, in spite of efforts to ignore it. Governor Hoegh urged fair consideration, as did Governor Loveless in 1957; both parties dealt with it in their platforms. In 1958 Loveless challenged legislative inaction by appointing a sixteen-member bipartisan committee to study the matter and make recommendations. This distinguished "Governor's Reapportionment Action Committee," chaired by Frank T. Nye, Cedar Rapids journalist, unanimously agreed on substitute proposals for the 1904 and 1928 amendments and submitted them to the 1959 session of the General Assembly—which summarily rejected them out of hand.[18]

THE FIGHT FOR A CONSTITUTIONAL CONVENTION

The only way around legislative delays on reapportionment seemed to be the holding of a state constitutional convention, because a great many people doubted that the rural-dominated legislature would ever voluntarily propose or accept from others any legislative plan for reapportionment that would hurt the rural forces, nor take the initiative in calling a convention to do the job. There was a way around this roadblock. Every tenth year the question must be asked of the voters: Shall there be a convention to revise the constitution, and amend the same? If a majority of those voting on the question answer yes, the General Assembly must provide for such a convention. Here was a direct way to secure the amendments which would carry out reapportionment.

Many other concerns of Iowans in recent years can be discovered by reviewing the list of issues under discussion at this time that might have been dealt with by a convention.[19] "Liquor by the drink" was the issue which probably aroused the greatest emotional response. Historically, the Republican party in Iowa had supported Prohibition, even at the expense of a party split, as in 1889; Democrats had opposed it. The repeal of the Eighteenth Amendment in 1933 was paralleled in Iowa by the creation of the state liquor store system. Now the voters were almost indifferent to traditional party alignments as urban Republicans joined urban Democrats to work for a law which permitted the licensed sale of alcoholic beverages by the drink.

Another hot issue, involving millions of dollars and bitter rural-urban arguments, was the division of state road money between cities and counties. Still another topic of the times which complicated the maneuvering of urban-rural forces was the highly controversial "right to work" clause in a 1947 legislative act. This clause guaranteed the right of anyone to work without regard to membership in a trade union, and required the written consent of the worker (and his spouse, if married) before an employer could "check off" a union member's dues from the payroll.[20] Another act limited the conditions which permitted strikes or boycotts. The greatest support for this legislation came from the Iowa Manufacturers Association (IMA) and, of course, organized labor and its friends were bitterly opposed to it. Both principal parties to this argument were urban but in this case the IMA made an alliance with the politically powerful Iowa Farm Bureau Federation (IFBF) to sustain these two laws, thus securing voting power for the numerically weak IMA but driving a wedge between farmers and urban workers.

Other topics were converted into issues but none had the broad appeal of the items named above. The proconvention forces were made up of the urban press, led by the *Des Moines Register*,[21] with the *Council Bluffs Nonpareil* as the most notable exception; the Iowa Federation of Labor; the Iowa League of Women Voters; many municipal officials acting on their own as individuals; academic groups; and countless others acting purely as individuals. The anticonvention forces were led by the IFBF, the IMA, and the rural press, all for the reasons just given. As for political parties, the Democrats were openly and enthusiastically in favor of a convention; the Republicans took an indecisive stand.

The proposition attracted a large vote—90 percent of those who voted for governor voted on the convention question. The yes vote was 400,034 (47 percent); the no vote was a decisive 532,762 (53 percent). In sixteen of the eighteen largest counties, a majority voted for a convention. Polk County, dominated by the Des Moines metropolitan area, gave a tremendous 81 percent of its votes to the yes side. No urban county gave less than 31 percent of its votes for a convention; seven gave between 31 percent and 60 percent; eight gave over 60 percent. By contrast, it was the counties with the least urban population, those in southern Iowa and in the northwest, which registered the greatest opposition to a convention. Forty-four rural counties gave less than 31 percent for a convention; six rural counties gave between 31 percent and 60 percent; none at all gave over 60 percent. Clearly it was a victory for a combination of the farm vote, the small-town vote, and the negative vote in the cities.[22]

THE GENERAL ASSEMBLY'S SEARCH FOR ACCEPTABLE REAPPORTIONMENT

Now that a constitutional convention was no longer a possibility, the fight was transferred to the halls of the General Assembly. Party lines were blurred, sometimes completely obliterated, as urban and rural groupings fought for or against the "Shaff Plan," sponsored by an urban legislator, Senator David O. Shaff of Clinton, but generally regarded as the Farm Bureau Plan. This proposal called for a Senate of 58 members, all districts to be based on population, with county lines to be crossed wherever necessary to make up the 58 districts, but no district to vary more than 10 percent from 1/58th of the state population in the last preceding census; the House would be reduced from 108 to 99 members, one for each county regardless of its population. If adopted, this would eliminate House reapportionment as long as the plan was in use; the Senate would be reapportioned every year ending in "3" by a ten-man commission, five from each party, with a series of deadlines for action which if not met would throw the duty of reapportionment on the Iowa Supreme Court.

Shaff's plan was favored not only by the Iowa Farm Bureau Federation but also by the Iowa Manufacturers Association, who continued the alliance which had worked so well in getting out the vote against a constitutional convention. In the form of a proposed amendment to the state constitution the plan was passed through the Fifty-ninth and Sixtieth General Assemblies in 1961 and 1963, even though the second passage came after the historic *Baker* v. *Carr* ruling by the United States Supreme Court in March 1962, which held that in certain kinds of reapportionment cases the federal courts might assume jurisdiction.[23] The legislature set December 3, 1963, as the date for a referendum on the Shaff Plan amendment.

Before the amendment was put before the people, some of its opponents brought suit in the Federal District Court, a suit which led to the appointment of a three-judge panel to hear the case. In May 1963 this panel held that the 1904 and 1928 amendments were "invidiously discriminatory" and the Shaff Plan was pronounced even more discriminatory, but a decision was withheld because, technically, there would be no Shaff Plan to rule on unless and until the amendment was approved in the coming December election. The panel promised a decision after that event. On this point Judge Edward J. McManus dissented, saying that the Shaff Plan was obviously unconstitutional and that the election would be a waste of the taxpayers' money.[24]

The next round in this marathonic battle consisted of a statewide debate, conducted on a nonpartisan basis. Former State Representative Robert K. Beck of Centerville, a newspaper publisher and staunch Republican, led the pro-Shaff forces, and former State Senator Duane E. Dewel of Algona, a newspaper publisher and equally staunch Republican, led the opponents. Democratic Governor Harold E. Hughes, in his first term of office, took a prominent part in the fight *against* the amendment; Senator Jack Schroeder of Davenport, a Republican leader and prourban businessman, was another prominent opponent. The result was an overwhelming defeat for the amendment, 272,382 to 190,424, with the heaviest opposing vote coming from the state's seventeen largest counties which by themselves contained 50 percent of the state's population. The anti–Shaff Plan vote in these seventeen counties was within 26,000 of the ninety-nine-county yes vote. By adding the no votes from the eleven next largest counties, twenty-eight in all, one finds a larger vote *against* the amendment than all ninety-nine counties cast *for* it.[25]

Now the three-judge panel could make its promised ruling, which it announced on January 14, 1964: the General Assembly in special session *must* apportion its seats on a temporary basis in time for the November 1964 election, and also agree on a permanent plan, pass it as a proposed amendment to the constitution, and thus have it ready for the 1965 General Assembly to act on a second time.[26] The timing involved in these steps would require a special session for quick action on the first point; the second could wait, but not indefinitely. The judicial panel even took it on itself to suggest guidelines: one house must be based on population, and if the plan for the other house deviated from a population basis, it must be a "rational" plan in which population was a factor.

Governor Hughes called a special session to meet on February 24, 1964. Each house set up a special committee on reapportionment. A private citizen, David Belin, a Des Moines attorney, made a strong bid for fame by having a plan ready and waiting when the session got under way, a plan bearing the stamp of approval of Robert D. Ray, Republican state chairman, and Attorney General Evan L. ("Curly") Hultman of Waterloo, the probable Republican candidate for governor in 1964. This blitzing approach was not to be successful, however, as the Belin Plan was shunted aside by nearly 100 rival schemes. Each house had its favorite ideas. The Senate wanted to remain a small body; the House stood up for a Senate using the population factor more heavily than in the past; the Senate wanted a House based completely on population. Back and forth the propositions went and then to joint conference committees, where the work would be undone, and whose substitute would then be rejected. Finally, on March 18, 1964, a compromise bill providing a temporary plan of apportionment was passed and Governor Hughes signed it on March 23.[27] Now the plan could be taken back to the three-judge panel, which had already set March 27 as the day for a hearing. Although the matter was complicated by related suits brought by interested parties, the panel denied the request for a stay order and approved the plan for use in November 1964. Its ruling was appealed to the United States Supreme Court but Justice Byron R. White rejected the request for the high Court to intervene in the Iowa matter. Then on May 5 the appellants asked the Supreme Court to nullify the January 14, 1964, ruling which called for the two plans. This appeal was rejected in no uncertain manner on June 22, 1964, in the case of *Hill* v. *Charles L. Davis et al.* (378 U.S. 565).

THE PERMANENT PLAN OF 1964

Without delay the Special Session of the legislature plunged into the task of drawing up a permanent plan, rejecting the advice of Governor Hughes to take a recess until midsummer by which time the United States Supreme Court would presumably have laid down some guidelines. There was so much disagreement between the two houses that it proved necessary to set up in succession three separate conference committees before agreement could be reached, on April 8, on the third report. The plan, set forth in the form of an amendment to the constitution, called for a Senate of 50 members, 18 to be allocated to the counties with 50 percent of the state's population, 32 to all the others, but no district to contain more than three counties, and all the districts so arranged that a majority (26) would be elected by not less than 36 percent of the population; the House was to have 114 members, with 57 allocated to the big counties with 50 percent of the population, in which the districts must not vary more than 10 percent from the average; the other 57 members would go to districts made up by crossing county lines wherever necessary if a county's population varied 30 percent or more from the average. Another section provided that the General Assembly would carry out a reapportionment every ten years or the task would go to the Iowa Supreme Court. This "permanent plan" bill, frankly a compromise, passed both houses on April 8, 1964,[28] in the form of a constitutional amendment, to be met with the disapproval of both Governor Hughes and his forthcoming opponent, Evan Hultman, but nothing they could do could stop it from coming before the 1965 session of the General Assembly for a second consideration.

"ONE MAN, ONE VOTE"

The Sixtieth Extraordinary Session might well have taken the advice of Governor Hughes to wait for an opinion by the United States Supreme Court about reapportionment, since it was well known that several cases were in the works and would be decided before the Court's summer adjournment. On June 15, 1964, as predicted, the Court handed down its ruling in six different cases on this subject, one of them serving as a prototype for all. By an 8 to 1 vote the Court decided the case of *Reynolds* v. *Sims* in which the epoch-making doctrine of "one man, one vote" was enunciated.[29] The controlling principle in this decision would now have to become the basis of reapportionment in every state in the land if such acts were to be upheld by the courts. The problem of reapportionment would now beset every session of the Iowa legislature until the "one man, one vote" requirement could be satisfied. Iowa's legislators not only had to keep this ruling in mind but also had somehow to compromise the "area versus population" dispute so as to please the contending urban and rural forces.

CHRONOLOGY OF LEGISLATIVE REAPPORTIONMENT, 1965–1972

Now that this account has established the principles of reapportionment, the remainder of this story must be confined to a tracing of the moves and countermoves which were required before a "final" plan could be consummated. With the benefit of hindsight we can know that seven years would be needed before this result could be obtained. Completely bypassing the element of drama in the long fight, a brief outline of the essential facts follows:

In February 1965 the Sixty-first General Assembly was shocked by an order from the 3-judge federal panel, rejecting the 1964 temporary plan, and ordering a new plan for use in 1966.[30] This assembly complied by drawing up a new permanent plan in the form of a constitutional amendment[31] and a new temporary plan[32] for use in 1966.

In 1967 the Sixty-second General Assembly adopted a temporary plan for use in 1968 while waiting for further action on the constitutional amendment, the districts to be drawn by a 10-man commission.[33] It also gave second passage to five amendments, including one for annual sessions, and one containing the 1965 Permanent Reapportionment Plan.[34]

In November 1968 the voters at large approved these amendments.

In 1969 the Sixty-third General Assembly, First Session, the first annual session in Iowa history, enacted H.F. 781 for a 50-person Senate and a 100-person House, to be elected in single-member districts;[35] it also provided for a 14-person commission to draw up districts for use in the 1970 primaries.[36]

In February 1970 the Sixty-third General Assembly, Second Session, was again shocked by a court ruling, this one from the Iowa State Supreme Court,[37] throwing out the 1969 plan because of population variances too great to be allowed, but ordering its use in the 1970 elections because of lack of time to prepare a new plan, and ordering the Sixty-fourth General Assembly in 1971 to draw up a new acceptable plan, or the court would do so.

The Sixty-fourth General Assembly, First Session, 1971, worked five months and in June enacted H.F. 732,[38] providing for a 50-seat Senate and a 100-seat House, their concern being to meet the "one man, one vote" principle and at the same time save as many incumbent members' safe districts as possible. This was admittedly a Republican plan, drawn under the leadership of Representative Elizabeth Shaw of Davenport. In July three suits were brought against the sponsors of the plan.

On January 14, 1972, the Sixty-fourth Assembly, Second Session, was confronted with an Iowa Supreme Court ruling with three points: (1) an order throwing out the 1971 act; (2) an order requiring the election of all 50 senators in 1972; and (3) a statement that it would draw up a new plan of apportionment of its own. On January 19–20 the court heard arguments on its ruling, soon following with a rejection of the complaints.

On March 31, 1972, the court announced its own plan, one which startled many because of its geographically irregular districts, and filed an order for its use.[39] It was used in the 1972 primaries and final elections. Thus ended the drama which really began in the late 1950s with the Shaff Plan.

STATE GOVERNMENT ADMINISTRATIVE REORGANIZATION

Ever since the publication of the Brookings Report in 1933, Iowans, from governors on down, have had access to a blueprint for administrative reorganization. This document was updated by the Report of the Governmental Reorganization Commission, better known as the "Little Hoover Commission," in 1950, and again by a 1966 report prepared by the Public Administration Service of Chicago, the result of a study arranged for by Governor Harold E. Hughes and authorized by the General Assembly. More recently, some far-reaching recommendations were made by a privately financed Governor's Economy Committee, set up by Governor Robert D. Ray and working under the chairmanship of G. LaMonte Weissenburger of Keokuk.

Out of these reports have come several minor changes and at least one major change, the creation at the governor's urging of the Department of General Services in 1971. By this act a number of small boards and agencies, and the office of state comptroller, were brought into one department, all to be administered by a director appointed by the governor with the approval of two-thirds of the Senate and responsible to the governor. By this simple but path-breaking action, more efficiency in the daily operation of the state government is made possible and the power of the governor is enhanced, carrying on a trend which clearly goes back to Governor Hughes and perhaps to the term of Governor Leo A. Hoegh.[40] A new Department of Transportation has been recommended but has not yet been created.

SCHOOL REORGANIZATION

Perhaps the most striking changes in the Iowa scene over the years since the state's beginnings have been in the growth and the quality of the educational facilities, both public and private, provided for the youth of the state. Instead of the one-room rural schools of hallowed tradition, or the all too common hideously ugly and inadequate town and city school buildings, one now finds in almost every town of any size and in many rural locations magnificent new educational plants with ultra-modern equipment, exceeding the wildest dreams of those of an earlier generation. "Reorganization," for that is the magical word, has brought 12,611 rural schools down to the zero mark, and various, assorted school districts to 4,558 in 1953, and these to 452 in 1972, a number which is almost certain to decrease in the near future. Since 1965, in selected places in fifteen geographical areas, one finds new postsecondary "area schools" which are rapidly winning a place high in the favor of Iowans. Four of the fifteen are organized as vocational schools; the others are organized as community colleges, offering the first two years of college work. The latter are, in fact, continuations of previously established municipal or private junior colleges. In some areas the work is offered on two or more campuses and attendance centers. In addition, there are three state universities, one privately supported university, and nearly thirty private colleges. More important, one would find that the curriculum offerings of all the schools are more numerous, better adapted to the future needs of the pupils, and better taught by better trained teachers, by and large, than in the schools of earlier years. Finally, an observer would find that public education is supported by a tax system which though not perfect is more productive and more equitably apportioned than at any time in the history of the state.

All this is a far cry from the crude beginnings in preterritorial, territorial, and early statehood days, when "rate" schools (in which the teacher was paid at a "rate" of the patron's own choosing) and church-supported academies and "seminaries" were the only schools available. Since that time progress has been piecemeal but steady. In his famous Report of 1856, Horace Mann recommended independent township units, which were set up in 1858. Now public education was on its way. The typical township was divided into nine subdistricts, each with its own director; incorporated towns could organize as independent school districts. In 1872 the General Assembly formalized all this by creating the independent school district system, a popular idea as witness the jump from 400 to 2,206 in two years, and to 3,686 by 1900. The most regrettable feature of these schools was the lax system of certification of teachers.

In 1895 the state superintendent of public instruction, Henry Sabin, recommended the then revolutionary idea of publicly supported transportation (a device that in its various technological forms has been the key to much of the progress that has been made since that date). In 1898 Dean Amos N. Currier of the University of Iowa recommended "reorganization" under the township as the administrative unit; central graded schools should be made available to all rural children, with transportation at public expense. His ideas launched a movement for "consolidated" schools, the honor of establishing the first one going to Buffalo Center–Buffalo Township in 1899; Terril set up the second one, in 1901; Marathon could claim the third, in 1903. In 1908 State Superintendent John Franklin Riggs advocated county-wide planning of larger schools and better transportation, thus furthering the consolidation movement; more important, he campaigned for standardization of teacher certification under the control of the state.

From time to time the General Assembly did its part by passing the necessary enabling acts to implement these improvements and provide financing methods for the local districts. In 1933 the Brookings Report (see pages 293; 302) strongly criticized the overdependence on the property tax; the adoption of its three-point tax plan opened the way to relief on property and thus for state central support of education. As examples of implementing acts, the School Reorganization Act in 1945 utilized, perhaps unknowingly, the basic ideas advanced by John Franklin Riggs in 1908; in 1947 a landmark act created the County Schools System, in which an elected County Board of Education would appoint a county superintendent to serve as an executive officer.

In 1953 came two heroic steps: (1) at the urging of State Superintendent J. C. Wright, the Fifty-fifth General Assembly created a nine-member bipartisan Board of Public Instruction which was empowered to appoint the state superintendent, thus presumably removing that office from political pressures, and to exert much control over the schools of the state; (2) the previous law on consolidation was repealed and the "Community School District" became the new unit of public school education in Iowa. In 1957 the assembly passed a law declaring that on certain conditions relative to the payment of Agricultural Tax Credits (a form of property relief) every unit in the state must become a part of a high school district by July 1, 1962, a date which was modified in 1965 by moving it to July 1, 1966.

The increased costs of the above-mentioned reforms have become a major concern of most Iowa taxpayers. Much of the burden has been shifted to the state treasury, to be sure, as a shift away from the sole reliance on the property tax. Undoubtedly a good thing, it has not proved to be a panacea. A separate book would be required to describe all the details of legislation and administration involved in the shift to state support, and the formulas by which state (and sometimes federal) aid is funneled into the local school districts. The obvious pitfall inherent in state support is the temptation to keep local taxes near or above the same old levels, at the same time receiving and spending the state funds, in which case local property relief is not realized. To prevent this very thing, the 1971 legislature passed two bills. One "froze" local tax rates at the point of the yield of property taxes the previous year, the freeze to last for one year, 1971–1972. The other bill provided for a "foundation" plan for the distribution of state aid in the future, a plan originally recommended by a study commission under Governor Hughes. The plan is so far-reaching that it is to be phased in over a ten-year period, beginning in 1972–1973.[41]

EPILOGUE

It is fitting that this account of Iowa's past should end in a discussion of her educational system, past and present. Education, in its various forms from the kindergarten through the graduate schools of the universities, and including some public support for private colleges and parochial schools, is by far the largest single recipient of Iowa's treasury of tax dollars. This support is not perfunctory and unconcerned; a great many Iowans are truly interested in achievement. The culture lag of the past, natural to a frontier state, has disappeared.

Nearly a half-century ago, in 1926, to be exact, in a graceful and highly perceptive essay on the Iowa of that day,[42] Ruth Suckow, a flowering young novelist and keen observer of her fellow Iowans, vouchsafed two salient conclusions about Iowa culture which were the outgrowth of her own experience as well as her study and training. The first point, though not original, was a powerful, sweeping, and confident generalization made possible by a thorough command of the historical sources; the second was an appropriately and completely typical modest venture into the realm of prophecy, modest since her own career and her own work were exemplified in the point she was making.

The first was a statement of Iowa's obeisance to the East, especially to New England and New York City, an attitude of meek submission to the general idea that all worthwhile creative work had come from the East, could only be generated in the East, and must be concerned with Eastern subject matter. To be sure, Hamlin Garland, who had spent his formative years on Iowa farms and in Osage after coming with his parents from the coulee country around La Crosse, Wisconsin, had made the same point many years earlier, and so had John T. Frederick, a University of Iowa junior student, and his mentor, Professor Clark F. Ansley, as far back as 1915, when they were launching *The*

Midland, a literary magazine which flourished until 1934 by publishing Iowa and Midwestern literature.[43] Yet Hamlin Garland and Ruth Suckow, for all their denunciation of Iowans' deference to the East, fled to Boston at the first opportunity, and later to New York.

Miss Suckow's other point was the assertion that a turning point had been reached—the year was 1926—and that henceforth young writers of Iowa *should* and *would* find their subject matter in the lives and the environment of their own people in the West, a sort of declaration of independence of the East just as Emerson had once declared American literary independence from Europe. To illustrate if not to prove that this could be done successfully, she cited Hamlin Garland's *A Son of the Middle Border* (1917) and Herbert Quick's *Vandemark's Folly* (1922) and *The Hawkeye* (1923).[44] She might have cited her own *Country People* (1924) and *The Bonney Family* (1926); a few years later she could have added a whole string of good novels based on the Iowa scene, particularly *The Folks.*

Others contributing to this outpouring of Iowa writing were James Hearst (1900–), who successfully combined the careers of farming and writing poetry until he gave up in part the first for college teaching;[45] Paul Engle (1908–), who first established his place as a poet and novelist and then became the director of the Writer's Workshop at the University of Iowa;[46] MacKinlay Kantor (1904–), who has roamed far afield but in one of his best novels, *Spirit Lake,* has used the incident of the famous massacre as the basis of a case study of white-Indian relations on the advancing frontier;[47] and, more recently, Curtis Harnack (1927–), who has chosen to live in New York but whose novels and an autobiographical essay, *We Have All Gone Away,* are based on farm life in Iowa.[48] Grant Wood and Marvin Cone of Cedar Rapids led a "paint Iowa" movement, though both realized the advantages of study elsewhere and did not hesitate to include some non-Iowa subject matter in their works.[49]

In one sense, this Iowa School was a part of a larger process of cultural evolution, in no sense restricted to Iowa but part of a movement known as "regionalism." It has been the means of growth and development of native art and literature in the state, but no spirit of chauvinism has precluded an interest in national and world culture. Iowa's university and public libraries and museums are creditable repositories of the world's greatest literature and scientific findings; her major galleries in Des Moines, Davenport, Iowa City, and Marshalltown and lesser ones in many other cities contain examples of the world's greatest art of all periods; music is cultivated not only as a performing art but by encouragement to originality. Perhaps no more striking illustration of the difference between the late nineteenth-century Iowa, a land of "corn, cattle, and contentment," and the new Iowa can be found than in the establishment of a modern concert hall at Ames, once derided as a "cow college" town, where now the university community and friends of music from far and wide support an annual music program worthy of any metropolitan center, featured by week-long festivals with the greatest orchestras, conductors, and soloists chosen from all over the world. A similar feast is prepared and served at the University of Iowa in Hancher Memorial Auditorium, and, on a smaller scale, elsewhere in the state.

It is now a truism, amply demonstrated in many communities, that there is and can be no conflict between support for creative and reproductive achievements on the local level and appreciation and support for similar works produced by those who are brought in from the world's capitals of science, music, and art. An exchange of culture is now seen to be as valid and as rewarding as an exchange of agricultural or industrial goods. By its willingness to support such a philosophy, Iowa has demonstrated beyond dispute that it has come of age.

NOTES

ABBREVIATIONS

AHR—American Historical Review
AI—Annals of Iowa (Third Series)
DAB—Dictionary of American Biography
DCB—Dictionary of Canadian Biography
GPO—Government Printing Office
HUP—Harvard University Press
IJHP—Iowa Journal of History and Politics
IJH—Iowa Journal of History
ISUP—Iowa State University Press
JAH—Journal of American History
JSH—Journal of Southern History
MVHR—Mississippi Valley Historical Review
PAL—The Palimpsest
SHSI—State Historical Society of Iowa
SHSW—State Historical Society of Wisconsin
UNP—University of Nebraska Press
UOP—University of Oklahoma Press

CHAPTER 1

1. James Hearst, "Landscape—Iowa," originally published in *Apple,* Autumn 1970. Hearst (1900–), one of Iowa's most honored poets, is a professor of English and Creative Writing at the University of Northern Iowa.
2. Ernest Antevs, *The Last Glaciation* (New York: American Geographical Society, 1928), p. 15.
3. George F. Kay, "Classification and Duration of the Pleistocene Period," *Bulletin of the Geological Society of America* 42 (March 1931): 425–66.
4. Charles S. Gwynne, *The Geology of Iowa* (Ames: ISUP, 1959), p. 10; Gordon R. Willey, *An Introduction to American Archeology. Volume One: North and Middle America* (Englewood Cliffs, N.J.: Prentice-Hall, 1966), p. 28.

5. Nevin M. Fenneman, *Physiography of Eastern United States* (New York: McGraw-Hill, 1938), p. 599; Richard F. Flint, *Glacial Geology and the Pleistocene Epoch* (New York: Wiley, 1942), p. 179.
6. "Local Climatological Data," U.S. Department of Commerce, Weather Bureau.
7. Stephen S. Visher, *Climatic Atlas of the United States* (Cambridge: HUP, 1954), pp. 89–95.
8. Snowden Dwight Flora, *Tornadoes of the United States* (Norman: UOP, 1958), pp. 140, 142. The residents of Oelwein and Charles City might not share the optimism of this statement after the tremendous damage done by a tornado which struck them in May 1967.
9. Allen Walker Read, "The Word Blizzard," *American Speech* 3 (February 1928): 191–217. C. O. Bates, editor of the *Estherville Northern Vindicator,* is credited with the first use of the word in 1871.
10. John Plumbe, Jr., *Sketches of Iowa and Wisconsin* (St. Louis: Chambers, Harris & Knapp, 1839; reprinted by SHSI, Iowa City, 1948), p. 8. There is some controversy over the question of whether the early settlers preferred prairie or timbered lands. The latest and best discussion is to be found in Robert P. Swierenga, *Pioneers and Profits: Land Speculation on the Iowa Frontier* (Ames: ISUP, 1968), pp. 80–98. The topic will be discussed in Chapter 8.
11. John E. Weaver, *North American Prairie* (Lincoln: UNP, 1965), p. 11. One of the best descriptive books about early Iowa is John B. Newhall, *A Glimpse of Iowa in 1846* (Burlington, Iowa: W. B. Skillman, 1846; reprinted by SHSI, Iowa City, 1957).
12. *National Resources Board Report, 1934* (Washington: GPO), p. 127. Iowa has 36,019,000 acres of territory, of which 34,000,000 to 35,000,000 acres are in farms. About 75% of the farmland is Grade 1.
13. The names of the soils in this classification are taken from place names near the spot where the soil was first defined. These names were first used by C. L. Holmes, "Farming Areas in Iowa," Iowa State College *Bulletin 256,* 1929. The scheme was revised in 1938 by C. L. Holmes and C. W. Crickman, "Types of Farming in Iowa," Iowa State College *Bulletin 374.*
14. *Soils & Men: Yearbook of Agriculture, 1938* (Washington: GPO), p. 1054.
15. *1972 Statistical Profile of Iowa* (Des Moines: Iowa Development Commission), p. 7; *World Almanac, 1973,* p. 125.
16. William J. Petersen, *Iowa: The Rivers of Her Valleys* (Iowa City: SHSI, 1941).
17. For a detailed summary of all data regarding the location and licensing of dams in Iowa, see the latest *Report of the Iowa Natural Resources Council,* issued biennially by the Council at Des Moines.
18. For a report on the status at any given time on federal flood control projects on Iowa rivers, see the *Report* described in Footnote 17. A gigantic dam about to reach completion is located at Saylorville, on the Des Moines River.
19. "Economic Impact of Channel Improvement on the Iowa Segment of the Missouri River," *Midwest Research Institute Report for the Iowa Development Commission,* 1961, p. 29. For data concerning traffic on the Missouri, see the most recent *Summary of Missouri River Navigation, Annual Report,* U.S. Army Corps of Engineers, Missouri River Division, Kansas City, Missouri.
20. George F. Kay, "Historical Sketch of Mining," *Iowa Geological Survey* 22 (1912): 91, 116; A. G. Leonard, "Lead and Zinc Deposits of Iowa," ibid. 6 (1896): 66; James E. Wright, *The Galena Lead District: Federal Policy and Practice, 1824–1847* (Madison: SHSW, 1966).
21. Elaine Bluhm Herold, "Hopewell: Burial Mound Builders," *PAL* 51 (December 1970): 497–528; Gordon R. Willey, *An Introduction to American Archeology,* pp. 29–30.
22. Mildred Mott [Wedel], "The Relation of Historic Indian Tribes to Archeological Manifestations in Iowa," *IJHP* 36 (July 1938): 286–91; Marshall McKusick, *Men of Ancient Iowa: As Revealed by Archeological Discoveries* (Ames: ISUP, 1964), and the review of this book by Waldo R. Wedel, *American Anthropologist* 67 (August 1965): 1063–65. Other helpful references are Charles Reuben Keyes, "Prehistoric Indians in Iowa," *PAL* 32 (August 1951); Reynold J. Ruppé, a series of articles in *The Iowan,* 1955–1957; Wilford D. Logan and J. Earl Ingmanson,

"Effigy Mounds National Monument," *PAL* 50 (May 1969); Marshall McKusick, *The Davenport Conspiracy* (Iowa City: University of Iowa, 1970).

CHAPTER 2

1. Marshall McKusick, *Men of Ancient Iowa: As Revealed by Archeological Discoveries* (Ames: ISUP, 1964), pp. 4–7.
2. Mildred Mott, "The Relation of Historic Indian Tribes to Archeological Manifestations in Iowa," *IJHP* 36 (July 1938): 229–30; McKusick, *Men of Ancient Iowa,* pp. 197–203.
3. William T. Hagan, *The Sac and Fox Indians* (Norman: UOP, 1958), especially pp. 57–59, 88–91, 94–100, 124–29, 217–24.
4. Roy W. Meyer, *History of the Santee Sioux: United States Indian Policy on Trial* (Lincoln: UNP, 1967), pp. 1–71.
5. See pp. 71–72; also see William T. Hagan, *The American Indians* (University of Chicago Press, 1961), pp. 81–85.
6. Francis Paul Prucha, *A Guide to the Military Posts of the United States, 1789–1895* (Madison: SHSW, 1964), p. 69; Frank A. Mullin, "Father De Smet and the Pottawattomie Indian Mission," *IJHP* 23 (April 1925), 192–216.
7. McKusick, *Men of Ancient Iowa,* pp. 214–17.
8. Clark Wissler, *Indians of the United States* (Rev. ed. Revisions prepared by Lucy Wales Kluckhohn. Garden City, N.Y.: Doubleday, 1966), pp. 15–18; Hagan, *American Indians,* pp 1–30.
9. Francis Parkman, *La Salle and the Discovery of the Great West* (various editions), Chapter 5, colorfully describes the Jolliet-Marquette expedition. For recent revisionist views on French imperialism, see Sigmund Diamond, "An Experiment in 'Feudalism': French Canada in the Seventeenth Century," *William and Mary Quarterly* 18 (January 1961): 3–34; Gustave Lanctot, *A History of Canada. Volume One: From Its Origins to the Royal Regime, 1663. Volume Two: From the Royal Regime to the Treaty of Utrecht, 1713. Volume Three: From the Treaty of Utrecht to the Treaty of Paris, 1713–1763* (Cambridge: HUP, 1963–1965); W. J. Eccles, *Canada under Louis XIV, 1663–1701* (New York: Oxford University Press, 1964); Marcel Trudeau, "New France, 1524–1715," *DCB* (Toronto: University of Toronto Press, 1960, vol. 1, pp. 26–37.
10. W. J. Eccles, *Frontenac the Courtier Governor* (Toronto: McClelland and Stewart, 1959), p. 82; Eccles, *Canada under Louis XIV,* pp. 105–8.
11. André Vachon, "Louis Jolliet," *DCB,* vol. 1, pp. 392–98.
12. Vachon, "Louis Jolliet," *DCB,* gives the date of the first viewing of the Mississippi as June 15 and says that "eight or ten days later" the party went on shore. This would be the 23rd or 25th, reckoning from the 15th. All other writers known to me except one, Celine Dupré, "Cavelier De La Salle, René-Robert," *DCB,* vol. 1, pp. 172–84, use the date June 17.
13. On Toolesboro and the Iowa River, see Otto Knauth, "The River That Gave Iowa Its Name . . . ," *Des Moines Sunday Register, Picture Magazine,* September 18, 1966; SHSI "News for Members" 19 (July–August 1966), p. 4. Laenas G. Weld, "Joliet and Marquette in Iowa," *IJHP* 1 (January 1903): 3–16, demonstrated the error in Marquette's reckoning. Professor Weld's article has the honor of being the first article in the first volume of Iowa's leading historical journal, now unhappily not being published.
14. J. Monet, "Marquette, Jacques," *DCB,* vol. 1, pp. 490–93, reviews the disputed points about Marquette's career. Father Jean Delanglez, S.J., a well-recognized writer on Marquette, attributes the disputed *Recit* in the *Jesuit Relations* to Father Dablon; so does the author of the sketch on Dablon in the *DCB,* vol. 1, p. 244. Joseph P. Donnelly, S.J., *Jacques Marquette, S.J., 1637–1675* (Chicago: Loyola University Press, 1968) should be supplemented by a reading of Raphael N. Hamilton, S.J., *Marquette's Explorations: The Narrative Reexamined* (Madison: University of Wisconsin Press, 1970), in which the authenticity of Marquette's *Recit* is upheld.

15. Vachon, "Louis Jolliet," *DCB,* vol. 1, pp. 392–98.
16. Dupré, "Cavelier De La Salle"; William R. Taylor, "A Journey into the Human Mind: Motivation in Francis Parkman's *La Salle,*" *William and Mary Quarterly* 19 (April 1962): 220–37. The later story of La Salle's second expedition in which he missed the mouth of the Mississippi and landed at Matagorda Bay, and his subsequent murder, is not given here because it in no way affects the Iowa story.
17. William J. Petersen, "The Spanish Land Grants," *PAL* 47 (March 1966), a reissue of the same material published in earlier issues, with new illustrative material.
18. Dumas Malone, *Jefferson the President: First Term, 1801–1805* (Boston: Little, Brown, 1970), pp. 254–61; E. Wilson Lyon, *Louisiana in French Diplomacy, 1759–1804* (Norman: UOP, 1934), pp. 211–28; George Dangerfield, *Chancellor Robert R. Livingston of New York 1746–1813* (New York: Harcourt, Brace, 1960), pp. 309–94.

CHAPTER 3

1. My treatment of the Lewis and Clark Expedition is based on the following works: Donald Jackson (ed.), *Letters of the Lewis and Clark Expedition with Related Documents, 1783–1854* (Urbana: University of Illinois Press, 1962), pp. 1–66, 654–72; Ernest Staples Osgood (ed.), *The Field Notes of Captain William Clark* (New Haven: Yale University Press, 1964), pp. xiii–xiv and *passim;* Richard Dillon, *Meriwether Lewis* (New York: Coward-McCann, 1965), pp. xi–xiii, 1–5.
2. Osgood, *Field Notes,* p. 80; Reuben Gold Thwaites (ed.), *The Original Journals of the Lewis and Clark Expedition, 1804–1806,* 8 vols. (New York: Dodd, Mead, 1904), vol. 1, pp. 82–83. A helpful reprint of this work was issued in 1959 by the Antiquarian Press of New York.
3. Osgood, *Field Notes,* p. 97. The latest example of confusion over the location of "Council Bluffs" is in John E. Sunder, *Joshua Pilcher: Fur Trader and Indian Agent* (Norman: UOP, 1968). In the index all the references to "Council Bluffs" are listed under the heading: "Council Bluffs, Iowa" yet the context shows clearly that the references are to Council Bluffs on the west side of the river, north of Omaha. For further information on the site and the military use of it, see Roger L. Nichols, *General Henry Atkinson: A Western Military Career* (Norman: UOP, 1965); Francis Paul Prucha (ed.), *A Guide to the Military Posts of the United States, 1789–1895* (Madison: SHSW, 1964), p. 57.
4. Osgood, *Field Notes,* p. 102.
5. Ibid., p. 111, Note 9. Henry Martin Chittenden (ed.), *The American Fur Trade in the Far West,* 2 vols. (Stanford, Calif.: Academic Reprints, 1954), vol. 1, p. 81, is another who rejects the idea that Floyd should be thought of as a "fatality" of the expedition.
6. Perhaps one should add a reference to a memorial highway now under construction or planning. The idea for such a highway originated with Jay N. ("Ding") Darling, the eminent cartoonist for the *Des Moines Register* from 1906 to 1962 and a staunch believer in the conservation and preservation of our natural resources and historic sites. A concurrent resolution by Congress in 1964, *U.S. Statutes at Large,* vol. 78, pp. 1005–7, authorized the marking of the Trail and the creation of the Lewis and Clark Trail Commission, an advisory body. Ding's successor as advocate of the Trail and a sometime chairman of the commission was Mr. Sherry Fisher of Des Moines.
7. Donald Jackson (ed.), *The Journals of Zebulon Montgomery Pike,* 2 vols. (Norman: UOP, 1966), replaces all earlier editions. See vol. 1, pp. 3–131 and notes. Also see W. Eugene Hollon, *The Lost Pathfinder: Zebulon Montgomery Pike* (Norman: UOP, 1949), pp. 51–53.
8. Jackson, *Pike,* vol. 1, pp. 15, 17–19, and notes; pp. 235–37. For a vivid fictional account of the hazards of navigation on this section of the Mississippi, even with the aid of a modern canal around the rapids, see Richard Bissell, *A Stretch on The River* (Boston: Little, Brown, 1950), pp. 97–124.
9. Jackson, *Pike,* vol. 1, p. 19, n.
10. Ibid., p. 23 and note.

11. Hollon, *The Lost Pathfinder,* pp. 87–89; Robert R. Riegel and Robert G. Athearn, *America Moves West,* 4th ed. (New York: Holt, Rinehart & Winston, 1969), p. 305; Donald Jackson, "How Lost Was Zebulon Pike?" *American Heritage* 16 (February 1965): 11–14, 75–80, defends Pike.
12. *U.S. Statutes at Large,* vol. 2, pp. 283–89.
13. John D. Barnhart and Dorothy L. Riker, *Indiana to 1816: The Colonial Period. The History of Indiana,* vol. 1 (Indianapolis: Indiana Historical Bureau & Indiana Historical Society, 1971), pp. 342–44.
14. William T. Hagan, *The Sac and Fox Indians* (Norman: UOP, 1958), pp. 16–25; Charles J. Kappler (ed.), *Indian Affairs, Laws, and Treaties,* 4 vols. (Washington: GPO, 1904), vol. 2, pp. 54–56.
15. *U.S. Statutes at Large,* vol. 2, pp. 331–32.
16. Ibid., pp. 445–46.
17. Bert Anson, "Variations on the Indian Conflict: The Effects of the Emigration Indian Removal Policy, 1830–1854," *Missouri Historical Review* 59 (October 1967): 69; Katherine Coman, "Government Factories: An Attempt to Control Competition in the Fur Trade," *Bulletin of the American Economic Association,* 4 ser., no. 2 (April 1911), 368–88; Paul Chrisler Phillips, *The Fur Trade,* 2 vols. (Norman: UOP, 1961), vol. 2, pp. 497–500. Kenneth W. Porter, *John Jacob Astor: Business Man,* 2 vols. (Cambridge: HUP, 1931), vol. 2, pp. 709–14, tells of the successful effort of Astor and others to persuade Congress to abolish the factory system.
18. Donald Jackson, "Old Fort Madison, 1808–1813," *PAL* 39 (January 1958); reissued as 47 (January 1966), with supplementary material and pictures, and an added article by William J. Petersen. Also see Marshall McKusick, "Exploring Old Fort Madison," *The Iowan* 15 (October 1966): 12–13; 50–51.
19. Louise Phelps Kellogg, "William Clark," *DAB,* vol. 4, pp. 141–44.
20. Glover Moore, *The Missouri Compromise* (Lexington: University of Kentucky Press, 1953); William Salter, *Iowa: The First Free State in the Louisiana Purchase* (Chicago: McClurg, 1905).
21. *U.S. Statutes at Large,* vol. 4, p. 701. The act bears the date of June 28, 1834.
22. Richard G. Wood, *Stephen Harriman Long, 1784–1864: Army Engineer, Explorer, Inventor* (Glendale, Calif.: Arthur H. Clark, 1966), pp. 45–52; 79–84; Dwight L. Clarke, *Stephen Watts Kearny: Soldier of the West* (Norman: UOP, 1961), pp. 23–25.
23. Joseph C. Beltrami, *A Pilgrimage in America* (Chicago: University of Chicago Quadrangle Press, 1962); William J. Petersen, "The Mississippi through Many Eyes," *IJHP* 46 (October 1948): 339–77.
24. Kappler, *Indian Affairs,* vol. 2, pp. 145–46.
25. Clarke, *Kearny,* p. 41; John C. Parish, "The Langworthys of Early Dubuque and Their Contributions to Local History," *IJHP* 8 (July 1910): 315–55.
26. Francis Paul Prucha, *American Indian Policy in the Formative Years* (Cambridge: HUP, 1962), pp. 224–49; Anson, "Variations on the Indian Conflict," pp. 64–89; Prucha, "Andrew Jackson's Indian Policy: A Reassessment," *JAH* 56 (December 1969): 527–39.
27. George Dewey Harmon, *Sixty Years of Indian Affairs* (Chapel Hill: University of North Carolina Press, 1941), pp. 174–75.
28. Kappler, *Indian Affairs,* vol. 2, pp. 177–81.
29. Ibid., pp. 218–21.
30. Nichols, *General Henry Atkinson,* pp. 152–75; unless otherwise noted, my account of the Black Hawk War follows Donald Jackson (ed.), *Black Hawk: An Autobiography* (Urbana: University of Illinois Press, 1964), and Hagan, *The Sac and Fox Indians,* pp. 123–204.
31. Anson, "Variations on the Indian Conflict," 79–81.
32. Hagan, *The Sac and Fox Indians,* pp. 123–40. Kappler, *Indian Affairs,* does not give this treaty. Jackson, *Black Hawk,* p. 114, n., says: "It was not a treaty, but an agreement and a capitulation."
33. Hagan, *The Sac and Fox Indians,* p. 139.
34. Jackson, *Black Hawk,* p. 15, and note.

35. Although the Winnebago had given little help to the Sauk and Fox, they were called to the council and dealt with severely. On September 15, six days before the signing of the treaty with the Sauk and Fox, the Winnebago agreed to cede and leave their lands south and east of the Wisconsin River, and to accept a home in the Neutral Ground as created by the Treaty of 1830. See Kappler, *Indian Affairs,* vol. 2, pp. 251–53. See p. 72 for further details as to the difficulty encountered in the enforcement of the 1832 arrangements.
36. Jackson, *Black Hawk,* pp. 161–64, gives a reprint of the text of an original manuscript of the Treaty of 1832, now on deposit in the Davenport, Iowa, Public Museum. The treaty is given in Kappler, *Indian Affairs,* vol. 2, pp. 253–55. For a good discussion of the treaty, see Hagan, *The Sac and Fox Indians,* pp. 192–97.

CHAPTER 4

1. Jesse Macy, *Institutional Beginnings in a Western State* (Baltimore: Johns Hopkins University, 1884), pp. 7–8; James Alton James, *Constitution and Admission of Iowa into the Union* (Baltimore: Johns Hopkins Press, 1900), has excellent background material; Cyrenus Cole, *Iowa through the Years* (Iowa City: SHSI, 1940), pp. 108–9.
2. *U.S. Statutes at Large,* vol. 4, p 701. Cole, *Iowa through the Years,* p. 115, is the author who has popularized this figure of speech.
3. Mathias M. Hoffmann (ed.), *Centennial History of the Archdiocese of Dubuque* (Dubuque: Columbia [Loras] College Press, 1937), pp. 1–5; Hoffmann, *The Church Founders of the Northwest: Loras and Cretin and Other Captains of Christ* (Milwaukee: Bruce, 1937), pp. 47–67.
4. Aaron W. Haines, *The Makers of Iowa Methodism: A Twentieth Century Memorial of the Pioneers* (Cincinnati: Jennings & Pye, 1900); Ruth A. Gallaher, "The Methodists in Iowa," *PAL* 32 (February 1951): 57–120: Donald G. Mathews, *Slavery and Methodism: A Chapter in American Morality, 1780–1845* (Princeton: Princeton University Press, 1965).
5. Walter R. Houf (ed.), "American Home Missionary Letters from Iowa," *AI* 37 (Summer 1963): 45–76, 37 (Fall 1963): 95–120; Truman O. Douglass, *The Pilgrims of Iowa* (Boston: Pilgrim Press, 1911), pp. 30–32; George F. Magoun, *Asa Turner: A Home Missionary Patriarch and His Times* (Boston: Congregational Sunday School and Publishing Society, 1899).
6. Philip D. Jordan, *William Salter: Torchbearer of the West* (Oxford, Ohio: Mississippi Valley Press, 1939); William Salter, "My Ministry in Iowa," Philip D. Jordan (ed.), *AI* 24 (January 1943): 7–102; Jordan (ed.), "William Salter's Letters to Mary Ann Mackintire, 1845–1846," ibid., pp. 105–85; Frederick J. Kuhns, "Religion on the Iowa Frontier," *IJH* 53 (October 1956): 321.
7. Dwight L. Clarke, *Stephen Watts Kearny: Soldier of the West* (Norman: UOP, 1961), pp. 63–69.
8. *The Book That Gave Iowa Its Name. A Reprint* (Iowa City: SHSI, 1935).
9. *U.S. Statutes at Large,* vol. 5, pp. 10–16; Clarence A. Carter (ed.), *Territorial Papers of the United States: The Territory of Michigan,* vol. 12, p. 1202, n.; John Porter Bloom (ed.), *Territorial Papers of the United States: The Territory of Wisconsin,* vol. 27, pp. 41–52.
10. Alice Elizabeth Smith, *James Duane Doty: Frontier Pioneer* (Madison: SHSW, 1954), pp. 192–208; Louis Pelzer, *Henry Dodge* (Iowa City: SHSI, 1911).
11. The counties were Lee, Van Buren, Des Moines, Henry, Louisa, Muscatine, and Cook. The latter was broken up and distributed. See Frank H. Carver, "The History of the Establishment of Counties in Iowa," *IJHP* 6 (July 1908): 383–93.
12. Francis Paul Prucha, *American Indian Policy in the Formative Years* (Cambridge: HUP, 1962), pp. 250–73, gives the definitive treatment of the Intercourse Act of June 30, 1834, and related matters.
13. Charles J. Kappler (ed.), *Indian Affairs, Laws and Treaties,* 4 vols. (Washington: GPO, 1904), vol. 2, pp. 352–53.

14. Ibid., pp. 367–68.
15. Benjamin F. Shambaugh (ed.), "Maps Illustrative of the Boundary History of Iowa," *IJHP* 2 (July 1904), 369–80; John C. Parish, *George Wallace Jones* (Iowa City: SHSI, 1912); Shambaugh (ed.), *Documentary Materials Relating to the History of Iowa* (Iowa City: SHSI, 1897–1901), vol. 1, pp. 78–99, reprints many pertinent documents for the period of Iowa's inclusion in the Territory of Wisconsin.
16. *Cong. Globe,* 25 Cong., 2 Sess., p. 161; Benjamin F. Shambaugh, *The Constitutions of Iowa* (Iowa City: SHSI, 1934), p. 67.
17. *U.S. Statutes at Large,* vol. 5, pp. 235–41; Shambaugh, *Documentary Materials,* vol. 1, pp. 102–16.
18. Benjamin F. Shambaugh (ed.), *The Messages and Proclamations of the Governors of Iowa,* 7 vols. (Iowa City: SHSI, 1903), vol. 1, p. 77; Bloom, *Territorial Papers: Wisconsin,* vol. 27, pp. 165–66.
19. Roger L. Nichols, *Henry Atkinson: A Western Political Career* (Norman: UOP, 1965), pp. 208–9.
20. John C. Parish, *Robert Lucas* (Iowa City: SHSI, 1907), pp. 155–58, 167–226.
21. Benjamin F. Shambaugh, *The Old Stone Capitol Remembers* (Iowa City: SHSI, 1939), pp. 398–406; Shambaugh, "Charles Mason," *DAB,* vol. 12, pp. 357–58.
22. *U.S. Statutes at Large,* vol. 5, p. 237; Parish, *Lucas,* pp. 175–76; Theodore S. Parvin, "Diary," on deposit in the Masonic Library, Cedar Rapids. Parvin was private secretary to Governor Lucas and his diary is a prime source for the history of this period.
23. Shambaugh, *Old Stone Capitol,* pp. 30–32.
24. Ibid., pp. 13–19, 44–54, 91–110. Earlier, Professor Shambaugh completely demolishes the myth that Father Samuel Mazzuchelli was the architect of the capitol at Iowa City. Professor Margaret Nauman Keyes of the University of Iowa is now engaged in an exhaustive study of the origins and evolution of the Stone Capitol. Regrettably, her study is not yet completed but see her article, "The Gallery Will Be Reserved for Ladies," *AI* 42 (Summer 1973): 1–16.
25. Ibid., pp. 69–77.
26. The road is first mentioned in *Cong. Globe,* 25 Cong., 3 Sess., p. 139. Cardinal Goodwin, *The Trans-Mississippi West, 1803–1853: A History of Its Acquisition and Settlement* (New York: D. Appleton, 1922), p. 251, says: ". . . one Lyman Dillion [*sic*] was employed to plow a furrow between Iowa City and Dubuque, a distance of 100 miles." Others have garbled the facts by saying "from Iowa City to the Mississippi" without specifying a point. Actually the road ran from Dubuque to Iowa City, then on to the Missouri border. An interesting and helpful article is "The Old Military Road," by Marcus L. Hansen and others, *PAL* 51 (June 1970), 249–80, a reprint of the February 1921 issue. Historians will quickly recognize the name of Hansen. Then a graduate student at the State University of Iowa, he went on to become a leading authority on the history of immigration.
27. Through the kindness of Professor William D. Houlette of Drake University, I was allowed to see John Ira Barrett's excellent treatise, "The Legal Aspects of the Iowa-Missouri Boundary Dispute, 1839–1851" (M.A. thesis, Drake University, 1959). One special virtue of Barrett's work is his extensive use of Missouri materials.
28. Duane Meyer, *The Heritage of Missouri—A History* (St. Louis: State Pub. Co., 1963), pp. 180–82.
29. 7 Howard (*U.S. Reports*) 660; Albert M. Lea, "Report made by Albert Miller Lea on the Iowa-Missouri Boundary," *IJHP* 33 (July 1935): 246–59.
30. Louis Pelzer, *Augustus Caesar Dodge* (Iowa City: SHSI, 1908), pp. 86–87.
31. *Missouri* v. *Iowa,* 7 Howard 659.
32. 7 Howard 659; 10 Howard 1. Franklin K. Van Zandt, *Boundaries of the United States and the Several States,* Geological Bulletin 1212 (Washington: GPO, 1966), pp. 212–14.
33. See pp. 50–51. Cole, *Iowa through the Years,* p. 96, uses as a chapter heading these words: "The War Indemnity That Became Iowa."

34. Benjamin F. Shambaugh, "Frontier Land Clubs or Claim Associations," American Historical Association, *Annual Reports,* 1900, 2 vols. (Washington, D.C., 1901), vol. 1, pp. 67–85; Macy, *Institutional Beginnings,* pp. 11–21.
35. Allan G. Bogue, *From Prairie to Corn Belt: Farming on the Illinois and Iowa Prairies in the Nineteenth Century* (Chicago: University of Chicago Press, 1963), pp. 29–39; Bogue, "The Iowa Claim Clubs: Symbol and Substance," *MVHR* 45 (September 1958): 231–53; Bogue, "The Claim Clubs," *The Iowan* 15 (Spring 1967): 38–40, 51–52.
36. Robert P. Swierenga, *Pioneers and Profits: Land Speculation on the Iowa Frontier* (Ames: ISUP, 1968), pp. 210–27.
37. Reproduced from Bogue, *From Prairie to Corn Belt,* p. 30.
38. T. Hartley Crawford, Indian Commissioner, to Joshua Pilcher, March 25, 1841, quoted in Donald J. Berthrong, "John Beach and the Removal of the Sauk and Fox from Iowa," *IJH* 53 (October 1956): 321; Bloom, *Territorial Papers: Wisconsin,* vol. 27, pp. 312–13.
39. William J. Petersen (ed.), "Moving the Winnebago into Iowa," *IJH* 57 (October 1960): 357–76.
40. Quoted in Bert Anson, "Variations on the Indian Conflict," *Missouri Historical Review* 59 (October 1964): 83.
41. Kappler, *Indian Affairs,* vol. 2, pp. 404–7; Berthrong, "John Beach," 322–29; William T. Hagan, *The Sac and Fox Indians* (Norman: UOP, 1958), pp. 205–24. The return of the Fox Indians, under the name of "Mesquakie," to Iowa in 1857 was a dramatic incident. With the assistance of Governor James W. Grimes their leaders came back to Iowa and arranged for the purchase of some 3,000 acres of land near Tama, where their descendants live today as free men.
42. Kappler, *Indian Affairs,* vol. 2, pp. 413–15, for the treaty with the Potawatomi; ibid., pp. 419–20, for the treaty with the Winnebago. Also see Petersen, "Moving the Winnebago."
43. On the Mormons in Iowa, see Robert B. Flanders, *Nauvoo: Kingdom on the Mississippi* (Urbana: University of Illinois Press, 1965); Juanita Brooks (ed.), *On the Mormon Frontier: The Diary of Hosea Stout, 1844–1861,* 2 vols. (Salt Lake City: University of Utah Press, 1964); Wallace Stegner, *The Gathering of Zion* (New York: McGraw-Hill, 1964).
44. The term is from Flanders, *Nauvoo,* p. 28. For an authoritative account of land deals in the Half-Breed Tract, see Irene Neu, *Erastus Corning: Merchant and Financier, 1795–1872* (Ithaca: Cornell University Press, 1960), pp. 136–44.
45. It is Benjamin F. Gue, *History of Iowa,* 4 vols. (New York: Century, 1903), vol. 1, pp. 232, 235–37, who has misled generations of Iowans on this point. Flanders, *Nauvoo,* pp. 28–34, and p. 32, n., has established the facts in the story.
46. The topic of Mormon expansionism is admirably treated in Flanders, *Nauvoo,* pp. 278–305.
47. See Walker D. Wyman, "Council Bluffs and the Westward Movement," *IJH* 47 (April 1949): 99–118.
48. Brooks, *Mormon Frontier,* vol. 1, pp. 171–78, and the voluminous notes supplied by the editor, a leading Mormon historian. Also helpful on the Mormon Battalion episode is David M. Gracy II and Helen J. H. Rugeley (eds.), "From the Mississippi to the Pacific: An Englishman in the Mormon Battalion," *Arizona and the West* 2 (Summer 1965): 127–60.
49. Wallace Stegner, *A Gathering of Zion,* has an extremely vivid account of the trek across Iowa and beyond.
50. This point is taken from Flanders, *Nauvoo,* pp. v–vi.
51. Robert B. Flanders, *The Mormons Who Did Not Go West: A Story of the Emergence of the Reorganized Church of Jesus Christ of Latter Day Saints* (Madison, Wis.: Dane County Title Co., 1967); Inez Davis, *The Story of the Church: A History of the Church of Jesus Christ of Latter Day Saints . . .,* 7th ed. (Independence, Mo.: Herald, 1964).
52. Philip A. M. Taylor, *Expectations Westward: The Mormons and the Emigration of their British Converts in the Nineteenth Century* (Ithaca: Cornell University Press, 1966); William W. Belknap Papers, Princeton University Library.

53. LeRoy and Mary Hafen, *Handcarts to Zion, 1856–1860* (Glendale, Calif.: Arthur H. Clark, 1960) is the definitive work on this subject. Also see Wallace Stegner, *Mormon Country* (New York: Duell, Sloan & Pearce, 1942), pp. 72–83.

CHAPTER 5

1. Benjamin F. Shambaugh (ed.), *The Messages and Proclamations of the Governors of Iowa,* 7 vols. (Iowa City: SHSI, 1903–1905), vol. 1, pp. 94–122, 141–46, 252. Also see Shambaugh, *The Constitutions of Iowa* (Iowa City: SHSI, 1934), pp. 99–114. The overly critical Whig referred to was the future governor, Ralph P. Lowe.
2. See pp. 117–18. My material on the Constitution of 1844 follows closely Shambaugh, *The Constitutions of Iowa,* pp. 114–58; Benjamin F. Shambaugh (ed.), *Fragments of the Debates of the Constitutional Conventions of 1844 and 1846* (Iowa City: SHSI, 1900), pp. 7–204.
3. On this subject see William R. Stanton, *The Leopard's Spots: Scientific Attitudes towards Race in America, 1815–1859* (Chicago: University of Chicago Press, 1960).
4. See Leola Nelson Bergmann, "The Negro in Iowa," *IJHP* 46 (January 1948): 3–90.
5. On all aspects of banking history in Iowa up to 1920, see Howard H. Preston, *History of Banking in Iowa* (Iowa City: SHSI, 1922); also see a recent study by Erling A. Erickson, *Banking in Frontier Iowa, 1836–1845* (Ames: ISUP, 1971), based on his doctoral dissertation, "Banks and Politics before the Civil War: The Case of Iowa, 1836–1865," University of Iowa, 1967. See pp. 39–44 and pp. 130–34.
6. Joseph Nicholas Nicollet, *Report Intended to Illustrate a Map of the Hydrographical Basin of the Upper Mississippi River* (published posthumously, Washington: Blair and Rives, 1843); also published as Senate Document 237, *Cong. Globe,* 26 Cong., 2 Sess.; also published by Blair and Rives in 1845, and as House Document 52, *Cong. Globe,* 28 Cong., 2 Sess. It should be added that one weakness in Shambaugh's use of this document is his failure to take account of the two editions in 1843 and 1845; see Shambaugh, *Constitutions of Iowa,* pp. 157, 162.
7. *Cong. Globe,* 26 Cong., 2 Sess., Appendix, pp. 330–33. It might be added that Florida *accepted* her admission into the Union by the act of March 3, 1845, and thus became the 27th state. Texas was annexed, and then admitted on December 29, 1845, as the 28th state, forcing Iowa to become the 29th. A close examination of the table of dates for all the states admitted between 1821 and 1861 shows that the pairing of free and slave states did not take place after the attempt at pairing Iowa and Florida.
8. Louis Pelzer, *Augustus Caesar Dodge* (Iowa City: SHSI, 1908), pp. 112–27, especially p. 119; Erickson, *Banking in Frontier Iowa,* pp. 44–45.
9. William Penn Clarke Papers, Iowa State Department of History and Archives, Des Moines. Also see Erik M. Eriksson, "William Penn Clarke," *IJHP* 25 (January 1927): 3–61, for an understanding of Clarke's importance in Iowa politics at the time.
10. Shambaugh, *Messages and Proclamations,* vol. 1, p. 319; *Cong. Globe,* 29 Cong., 1 Sess., p. 86.
11. *Cong. Globe,* 29 Cong., 1 Sess., pp. 562, 1203. I am greatly indebted to Professor Robert W. Johannsen, University of Illinois, for an opportunity to read before publication his paper entitled "Stephen A. Douglas and the Territories in the Senate," which he delivered at the Conference on the History of the Territories of the United States, November 3–4, 1969, sponsored by the National Archives and Records Service, in which he gives a valuable interpretation of Douglas as an authority on territorial legislation.
12. Shambaugh, *Constitutions of Iowa,* pp. 204–5, citing the *Journal* of the Iowa Constitutional Convention of 1846.
13. Pelzer, *Augustus Caesar Dodge,* p. 127; *Cong. Globe,* 29 Cong., 1 Sess., pp. 938–41; *U.S. Statutes at Large,* vol. 9, p. 52.
14. Shambaugh, *Constitutions of Iowa,* pp. 210–12; Shambaugh, *Messages and Proclamations,* vol. 1, pp. 358–60; Jacob Swisher, "The First State Governor," *PAL* 27 (December 1946): 357–68. The vote for Briggs was 7,379; for McKnight, 6,626.

15. John Ely Briggs, "A History of the Constitutions of Iowa," *Iowa Code Annotated* (St. Paul: West Pub. Co., 1949), vol. 1, pp. 1–32.
16. Erickson, *Banking in Frontier Iowa,* pp. 46–50. Erickson's description of the business situation which followed bears the colorful title, "Banking in a 'Bankless' State, 1846–1857." See pp. 51–76.

CHAPTER 6

1. See Marcus L. Hansen, "Official Encouragement of Immigration to Iowa," *IJHP* 19 (April 1921): 159–95.
2. The figures given here are taken principally from the *Census of Iowa, 1836–1880* (Des Moines: State of Iowa, 1883); Allan G. Bogue, *From Prairie to Corn Belt: Farming on the Illinois and Iowa Prairies in the Nineteenth Century* (Chicago: University of Chicago Press, 1963), pp. 8–28, has a masterful discussion of the population advances into the West.
3. On the importance of British settlement in Iowa, see Jacob Van der Zee, *The British in Iowa* (Iowa City: SHSI, 1922), pp. 17–53.
4. Leola Nelson Bergmann, "Scandinavian Settlement in Iowa," *PAL* 37 (March 1956): 129–60; Bergmann, "The Norwegians in Iowa," *PAL* 40 (August 1959): 289–368; Bergmann, *Americans from Norway* (Philadelphia: Lippincott, 1950).
5. Jacob Van der Zee, *The Hollanders in Iowa* (Iowa City: SHSI, 1912); Robert P. Swierenga, *Pioneers and Profits: Land Speculation on the Iowa Frontier* (Ames: ISUP, 1968), pp. 96–97, 197, 198; "A Dutch Immigrant's View of Frontier Iowa," *AI* 38 (Fall 1965): 81–118.
6. Samuel P. Hays, "History As Human Behavior," *IJH* 58 (July 1960): 193–206.
7. Frank H. Garver, "The Establishment of Counties in Iowa," *IJHP* 6 (July 1908): 375–456. For the treaty with the Sioux, see Charles J. Kappler (ed.), *Indian Affairs, Laws, and Treaties,* 4 vols. (Washington: GPO, 1904), vol. 2, pp. 438–40.
8. Agnes M. Larson, *History of the White Pine Industry in Minnesota* (Minneapolis: University of Minnesota Press, 1949), might well have added Wisconsin and Iowa to her title. Also see George W. Sieber, "Sawmilling on the Mississippi: The W. J. Young Lumber Company, 1858–1900," Ph.D. diss., University of Iowa, 1960; George B. Hartman, "The Iowa Sawmill Industry," *IJHP* 40 (January 1942): 52–93.
9. Bogue, *From Prairie to Corn Belt,* pp. 38–39; Swierenga, *Pioneers and Profits,* pp. 80–92.
10. Bogue, *From Prairie to Corn Belt,* pp. 148–68, has a brilliant description of technical changes in farming in the 19th century. Also see Mildred Throne, "'Book Farming' in Iowa," *IJH* 49 (April 1951): 117–42; Henry C. Taylor, *Tarpleywick: A Century of Iowa Farming* (Ames: ISUP, 1970); Louella M. Wright, *Peter Memendy: The Mind and the Soil* (Iowa City: SHSI, 1943), pp. 91–98, 113–211.
11. Charles J. Fulton, "The Beginnings of Education in Iowa," *IJHP* 23 (April 1925): 171–91; Vernon Carstenson, "The University as Head of the Iowa Public School System," *IJH* 53 (July 1955): 213–46.
12. Louis A. Haselmayer, "The Mt. Pleasant Collegiate Institute: A Struggle for Existence," *AI* 39 (Winter 1968): 205–32.
13. Harrison John Thornton, "Locating the State University of Iowa," *IJH* 47 (January 1949): 50–62; Carstenson, "The University as Head of School System."
14. John S. Nollen, *Grinnell College* (Iowa City: SHSI, 1953).
15. Marjorie Medary, "The History of Cornell College," *PAL* 34 (April 1953): 145–208.
16. For a reminiscence of early Luther College, see Peer Stromme, *Halvor: A Story of Pioneer Youth,* translated from the Norwegian and adapted by Inga B. Norstog and David T. Nelson (Decorah, Iowa: Luther College Press, 1960), pp. 105–99.
17. Earle D. Ross, *A History of the Iowa State College of Agriculture and Mechanical Arts* (Ames: Iowa State College Press, 1942); Ned Disque, "Iowa State College: 1858–1958," *PAL* 39 (September 1958): 361–76; Clarence H. Aurner, *History of Education in Iowa,* 5 vols. (Iowa City: SHSI, 1914–1920), vol. 4, pp. 193–231.
18. Thomas Teakle, *The Spirit Lake Massacre* (Iowa City: SHSI, 1918); *History of the Spirit Lake Massacre and of Miss Abigail Gardner's three months captivity*

among the Indians according to her own account, as given to L. P. Lee (New Britain, Conn.: L. P. Lee, 1857; reprinted by SHSI, 1971).

19. Robert W. Fogel, *Railroads and American Economic Growth: Essays in Econometric History* (Baltimore: Johns Hopkins Press, 1964), pp. 92–107.
20. Robert R. Russel, *Improvement of Communication with the Pacific Coast as an Issue in American Politics, 1783–1864* (Cedar Rapids: Torch Press, 1948), pp. 1–53, 110–29, 150–232, 262–93; Carter Goodrich, *Government Promotion of American Canals and Railroads, 1800–1890* (New York: Columbia University Press, 1960), pp. 149–74; Earl S. Beard, "Local Aids to Railroads in Iowa," *IJH* 50 (January 1952): 1–34.
21. *U.S. Statutes at Large,* vol. 11, pp. 9–10.
22. Jack T. Johnson, *Peter Anthony Dey* (Iowa City: SHSI, 1939); Stanley P. Hirshson, *Grenville M. Dodge: Soldier, Politician, Railroad Pioneer* (Bloomington: Indiana University Press, 1967).
23. Dwight L. Agnew, "Iowa's First Railroad," *IJH* 48 (January 1950): 1–26; Agnew, "The Mississippi & Missouri Railroad, 1856–1860," *IJH* 51 (July 1953): 211–32; Johnson, *Peter Anthony Dey,* pp. 42–72.
24. Frank P. Donovan, "The Burlington in Iowa," *PAL* 50 (September 1969): 481–87; Richard C. Overton, *Burlington Route* (New York: Knopf, 1965), pp. 93–97.
25. Frank P. Donovan, "The Northwestern in Iowa," *PAL* 43 (December 1962):545–56.
26. Frank P. Donovan, "The Illinois Central in Iowa," *PAL* 43 (June 1962): 265–85; Carlton J. Corliss, *Mainline in Mid-America: The Story of the Illinois Central* (New York: Creative Age Press, 1950), pp. 141–54; Joseph F. Wall, *Andrew Carnegie* (New York: Oxford University Press, 1971), pp. 267–306.
27. Frank P. Donovan, "The Milwaukee in Iowa," *PAL* 45 (May 1964): 177–96.

CHAPTER 7

1. *Cong. Globe,* 29 Cong., 1 Sess., p. 1217 (August 2, 1846). See Chaplain W. Morrison, *Democratic Politics and Sectionalism: The Wilmot Proviso Controversy* (Chapel Hill: University of North Carolina Press, 1967), and Joel H. Silbey, *The Shrine of Party: Voting Behaviour, 1841–1852* (Pittsburgh: University of Pittsburgh Press, 1967), for recent studies of the Proviso.
2. Eric Foner, "The Wilmot Proviso Revisited," *JAH* 56 (September 1969): 278–79.
3. *Cong. Globe,* 29 Cong., 2 Sess., pp. 95, 303, 573. Mildred Throne, compiler, "Iowans in Congress, 1847–1953," *IJH* 51 (October 1953): 331, errs in saying that Leffler was born in Virginia. *The Biographical Directory of the American Congress, 1774–1949* gives Pennsylvania as his birthplace, as does the article in the *DAB,* vol. 11, p. 142, by Bruce Mahan. On Serranus C. Hastings, see *DAB,* vol. 8, p. 342, and Edward H. Stiles, *Recollections and Sketches of Notable Lawyers and Public Men of Iowa* (Des Moines: Homestead Press, 1916), pp. 116–19.
4. Joel H. Silbey, "Proslavery Sentiment in Iowa, 1838–1861," *IJH* 55 (October 1957): 289–318, strongly asserts the pro-Southern, proslavery sentiments of former "Southerners" in pre–Civil War Iowa. I hope my argument against this easy assumption shows that his use of the word "Southerners" is unconvincing. Also see James Connor, "The Antislavery Movement in Iowa," *AI* 40 (Summer, Fall 1970), based on his brilliant M.A. thesis at Drake University. Connor rejects Silbey's conclusions on the basis of political and social views expressed by Senators Dodge and Jones of Iowa, and other Iowans.
5. Edward Younger, *John A. Kasson: Politics and Diplomacy from Lincoln to McKinley* (Iowa City: SHSI, 1955), p. 104, points out that Kasson wrote this point into the Republican platform of 1860. Also see Robert R. Russel, "Constitutional Doctrines with Regard to Slavery in the Territories," *JSH* 32 (November 1967): 466–86.
6. Robert R. Russel, "What Was the Compromise of 1850?" *JSH* 22 (August 1956): 292–309. The five acts were not passed until September but their passage was assured after Daniel Webster's 7th of March speech accepting the principles of compromise, which earned for him the title of "Lost Leader." For the standard book-length presentation of this topic, see Holman Hamilton, *Prologue to Con-*

flict: The Crisis and the Compromise of 1850 (New York: W. W. Norton, 1966).

7. Morton M. Rosenberg, *Iowa on the Eve of the Civil War: A Decade of Frontier Politics* (Norman: UOP, 1972), pp. 38–40; David S. Sparks, "The Decline of the Democratic Party in Iowa, 1850–1860," *IJH* 53 (January 1956): 9–10.
8. Herman R. Muelder, *Fighters for Freedom* (New York: Columbia University Press, 1959), pp. 158–71.
9. Rosenberg, *Iowa on Eve of Civil War,* p. 50, deals with the Democratic victory as a result of Democratic support of the Compromise but does not make clear that the Compromise was not enacted until September, weeks *after* the election. See Note 6 above.
10. Rosenberg, *Iowa on Eve of Civil War,* pp. 56–71.
11. Charles J. Kappler (ed.), *Indian Affairs, Laws, and Treaties,* 4 vols. (Washington: GPO, 1904), vol. 2, pp. 594–96.
12. Roy F. Nichols, "The Kansas-Nebraska Act: A Century of Historiography," *MVHR* 43 (September 1956): 187–212; William E. Parrish, *David Rice Atchison of Missouri: Border Politician* (Columbia: University of Missouri Press, 1961), pp. 121–31, 139–51; Robert R. Russell, *Improvement of Communication with the Pacific Coast as an Issue in American Politics, 1783–1864* (Cedar Rapids: Torch Press, 1948), pp. 150–67; James C. Olson, *History of Nebraska,* 2nd ed. (Lincoln: University of Nebraska Press, 1966), pp. 67–77.
13. Nichols, "Kansas-Nebraska Act," p. 197.
14. See Robert E. Lane, *Political Life: Why People Get Involved in Politics* (Glencoe, Ill.: Free Press, 1959), pp. 74–79, 92–94, 101–14, 299–303.
15. Rosenberg, *Iowa on Eve of Civil War,* pp. 79–109. I am indebted to Dr. Joyce Gault, University of Northern Iowa, for the use of two informative pamphlets: "A History of the United Presbyterian Church, Crawfordsville, Iowa, 1837–1937," and "Historic Crawfordsville and the Republican Party."
16. Ralph R. Fahrney, *Horace Greeley and the* Tribune *in the Civil War* (Cedar Rapids: Torch Press, 1936), p. 21; George H. Mayer, *The Republican Party, 1854–1966,* 2nd ed. (New York: Oxford University Press, 1967), pp. 23–47; S. M. Pedrick, *Life of Alvan E. Bovay, Founder of the Republican Party in Ripon, Wisconsin, March 20, 1854* (Ripon, Wis.: Commonwealth Printers, n.d.); Pedrick, *A History of Ripon, Wisconsin,* George H. Miller (ed.), (Ripon: Ripon Historical Society, 1964), pp. 105–24.
17. Rosenberg, *Iowa on Eve of Civil War,* pp. 91–92.
18. William Salter, *The Life of James W. Grimes* (New York: D. Appleton, 1876); Philip D. Jordan, *William Salter: Western Torchbearer* (Oxford, Ohio: Mississippi Valley Press, 1939), pp. 78–157; Fred B. Lewellen, "The Political Ideas of James W. Grimes," *IJHP* 42 (October 1944): 339–404.
19. Eric Foner, *Free Soil, Free Labor, Free Men: The Ideology of the Republican Party before the Civil War* (New York: Oxford University Press, 1970), pp. 186–225, describes the national conflict between the conservatives and moderates.
20. Simeon Waters to Julius A. Reed, October 3, 1854, American Home Missionary Society Correspondence, Grinnell College Library. I am indebted to Dean Ronald F. Matthias of Wartburg College for calling this important letter to my attention.
21. Grimes to Chase, February 20, 1858, in Salter, *The Life of James W. Grimes,* pp. 116–17.
22. Rosenberg, *Iowa on Eve of Civil War,* pp. 111–14.
23. Ronald F. Matthias, "The Know Nothing Movement in Iowa," Ph.D. diss., University of Chicago, 1966. This essay is a vast storehouse of information on Iowa history as affected by national politics in the 1850s.
24. Eugene H. Berwanger, *The Frontier against Slavery* (Urbana: University of Illinois Press, 1967); James M. McPherson, *The Struggle for Equality: Abolitionists and the Negro in the Civil War and Reconstruction* (Princeton: Princeton University Press, 1964), pp. 3–28; Victor Jacque Voegeli, *Free but Not Equal* (Chicago: University of Chicago Press, 1967).
25. See, for example, the *Fairfield Ledger,* January 17, 1865. See David S. Sparks, "The Birth of the Republican Party in Iowa, 1854–1856," *IJH* 54 (January 1956): 1–34; Rosenberg, *Iowa on Eve of Civil War,* pp. 127–45.

26. Matthias, "Know Nothing Movement in Iowa."
27. Wilfred E. Binkley, *American Political Parties: Their Natural History* (New York: Knopf, 1943), pp. 209–10; Foner, *Free Soil, Free Labor, Free Men,* pp. 250–56.
28. Foner, *Free Soil, Free Labor, Free Men,* pp. 9–39.

CHAPTER 8

1. *U.S. Statutes at Large,* vol. 2, pp. 9–10; David S. Sparks, "The Decline of the Democratic Party in Iowa, 1850–1860," *IJH* 53 (January 1955): 17–25; Sparks, "Iowa Republicans and the Railroads, 1856–1860," *IJH* 53 (July 1955): 279; Earl S. Beard, "Local Aid to Railroads in Iowa," *IJH* 50 (January 1952): 1–34.
2. Erling S. Erickson, *Banking in Frontier Iowa, 1836–1865* (Ames: ISUP, 1971); Howard H. Preston, *History of Banking in Iowa* (Iowa City: SHSI, 1922), pp. 83–125.
3. Leon F. Litwack, *North of Slavery: The Negro in the Free States, 1790–1860* (Chicago: University of Chicago Press, 1965).
4. *Iowa Reports. Reports of Cases Argued and Determined by the Supreme Court of Iowa.* Eastin Morris (ed.) (Davenport: Griggs, Watson & Day, 1870), vol. 1, pp. 1–10.
5. Benjamin F. Shambaugh, *The Constitutions of Iowa* (Iowa City: SHSI, 1934), pp. 213–80, 290–344; Erik M. Ericksson, "The Framers of the Constitution of 1857," *IJHP* 22 (January 1924): 52–88; Russell M. Ross, "The Development of the Iowa Constitution of 1857," *IJH* 55 (April 1957): 97–114.
6. William F. Zornow, *Kansas: A History of the Jayhawk State* (Norman: UOP, 1957), pp. 67–79; James C. Malin, *John Brown and the Legend of Fifty-Six* (Philadelphia: American Philosophical Society, 1942).
7. John Todd, *Early Settlement and Growth of Western Iowa* (Des Moines: Historical Department of Iowa, 1906), pp. 115–33.
8. Larry Gara, *The Liberty Line: The Legend of the Underground Railroad* (Lexington: University of Kentucky Press, 1961). See Todd, *Early Settlement and Growth,* pp. 134–53, for firsthand testimony from a participant in the business of the UG; Josiah B. Grinnell to William Penn Clarke, Clarke Correspondence, for letters from Grinnell about UG passengers. See Wilbur H. Siebert, *The Underground Railroad* (New York: Macmillan, 1898), pp. 409–11; Curtis Harnack, "The Iowa Underground Railroad," *The Iowan* 4 (June–July 1956): 20–23, 44, 47.
9. Stephen B. Oates, *To Purge This Land with Blood: A Biography of John Brown* (New York: Harper & Row, 1970), pp. 242–43, 265; Charles E. Payne, *Josiah Bushnell Grinnell* (Iowa City: SHSI, 1938), pp. 99–115.
10. Stanley P. Hirshson, *Grenville M. Dodge: Soldier, Politician, Railroad Promoter* (Bloomington: Indiana University Press, 1967), pp. 27–30.
11. Louis Pelzer, *Augustus Caesar Dodge* (Iowa City: SHSI, 1908), pp. 235–48; Dan Elbert Clark, *Samuel Jordan Kirkwood* (Iowa City: SHSI, 1917), pp. 123–43; Edward Younger, *John A. Kasson: Politics and Diplomacy from Lincoln to McKinley* (Iowa City: SHSI, 1955), pp. 86–93; Morton M. Rosenberg, *Iowa on the Eve of the Civil War: A Decade of Frontier Politics* (Norman: UOP, 1972), pp. 180–206.
12. C. Van Woodward, "John Brown's Private War," *America in Crisis,* Daniel Aaron (ed.) (New York: Knopf, 1952), pp. 109–30; Allan Nevins, *The Emergence of Lincoln,* 2 vols. (New York: Scribner's, 1950), vol. 2, pp. 5–27, 70–97; Louis Ruchames (ed.), *A John Brown Reader* (New York: Abelard-Schuman, 1959), pp. 11–32. Mary Land, "John Brown's Ohio Environment," *Ohio State Archeological and Historical Quarterly* 57 (January 1948): 24–47, reveals the financial support for John Brown in the Western Reserve district of Ohio, a hotbed of Abolitionism.
13. Clark, *Kirkwood,* pp. 155–62; Benjamin F. Gue, "John Brown and His Iowa Friends," *Midland Monthly* 7 (February, March 1897): 103–13, 267–77. Oates, *To Purge This Land with Blood,* pp. 284–85, cites testimony given by Secretary of War Floyd, given in *U.S. Senate Committee Reports, 1850–1860,* vol. 2, pp. 250–52. Oates warns against trying to make a historical appraisal of John Brown's reputed "insanity." See pp. 331–34.

14. Mildred Throne, "C. C. Carpenter in the 1858 Iowa Legislature," *IJH* 52 (January 1954): 46–49; Sparks, "Decline of the Democratic Party in Iowa"; Richard Allen Heckman, "Out-of-State Influences and the Lincoln-Douglas Campaign of 1858," *Journal of the Illinois State Historical Society* 59 (Spring 1966): 31–34.
15. Roy F. Nichols, *The Disruption of American Democracy* (New York: Macmillan, 1952), pp. 288–305; Owen Peterson, "Ben Samuels in the Democratic National Convention of 1860," *IJH* 50 (July 1952): 225–38.
16. Younger, *Kasson,* pp. 94–107.
17. Glyndon G. Van Deusen, *William Henry Seward* (New York: Oxford University Press, 1968), pp. 220–27.
18. Don E. Fehrenbacher, *Prelude to Greatness: Lincoln in the 1850s* (Stanford: Stanford University Press, 1962), pp. 143–61; Norman A. Graebner, "Abraham Lincoln: Conservative Statesman," in *The Enduring Lincoln,* Norman A. Graebner (ed.) (Urbana: University of Illinois Press, 1959), pp. 67–94. For a view which favors Douglas over Lincoln, see James G. Randall, *Lincoln the President,* 4 vols. (New York: Dodd, Mead, 1946–1955), vol. 1, pp. 154–77.
19. Kenneth F. Millsap, "The Election of 1860 in Iowa," *IJH* 48 (April 1950): 97–120, has a convenient and well-written summary of the campaign and the results in Iowa. For more detail, see Rosenberg, *Iowa on Eve of Civil War,* pp. 207–29. For the national campaign, see Reinhard H. Luthin, *The First Lincoln Campaign* (Cambridge: Harvard University Press, 1944). Luthin stresses the homestead issue as an attraction to Iowa voters. He is probably in error about the Germans as Republican voters. See Note 20 below.
20. George H. Daniels, "Immigrant Vote in the 1860 Campaign: The Case of Iowa," *Mid-America* 44 (July 1962): 146–62.
21. Robert P. Swierenga, "The Ethnic Voter and the First Lincoln Election," *Civil War History* 11 (March 1965): 27–43.

CHAPTER 9

1. See Edward Younger, *John A. Kasson: Politics and Diplomacy from Lincoln to McKinley* (Iowa City: SHSI, 1955), pp. 109–20; Leland L. Sage, *William Boyd Allison: A Study in Practical Politics* (Iowa City: SHSI, 1956), pp. 41–45.
2. Glyndon G. Van Deusen, *William Henry Seward* (New York: Oxford University Press, 1967), pp. 240–44.
3. Robert G. Gunderson, *Old Gentlemen's Convention: The Washington Peace Conference of 1861* (Madison: University of Wisconsin Press, 1961).
4. *Cong. Globe,* 36 Cong., 2 Sess., p. 1065 for the Senate vote, p. 1432 for the House vote. For the act, see *U.S. Statutes at Large,* vol. 12, p. 178.
5. Richard N. Current, *Lincoln and the First Shot* (Philadelphia: J. B. Lippincott, 1963).
6. The most convenient and accurate summary of this subject is by Mildred Throne, "Iowans and the Civil War," *PAL* 40 (September 1959): 369–448. For an account in the immediate postwar style and spirit, see Lurton D. Ingersoll, *Iowa and the Rebellion* (Philadelphia: J. B. Lippincott, 1866).
7. Stanley P. Hirshson, *Grenville M. Dodge: Soldier, Politician, Railroad Pioneer* (Bloomington: Indiana University Press, 1967), pp. 37–109. Younger, *Kasson,* pp. 123, 127–28, 139–40, 156–57, 164, makes clear Congressman Kasson's role in pressuring Lincoln to promote Dodge. Also see Wallace D. Farnham, "Grenville Dodge and the Union Pacific," *JAH* 51 (March 1965): 632–50.
8. Ingersoll, *Iowa and the Rebellion,* pp. 740–43; Ruth A. Gallaher, "Annie Turner Wittenmyer," *IJHP* 29 (October 1931): 518–69.
9. Eugene C. Murdock, *One Million Men: The Civil War Draft in the North* (Madison: SHSW, 1971).
10. Robert Huth Jones, *The Civil War in the Northwest* (Norman: UOP, 1960); Mildred Throne (ed.), "Iowa Troops in Dakota Territory, 1861–1864," *IJH* 57 (April 1959): 97–190.
11. *Cong. Globe,* 37 Cong., 1 Sess., pp. 222–23, 265; ibid., 2 Sess., p. 15.

12. Herman Belz, *Reconstructing the Union: Theory and Practice during the Civil War* (Ithaca: Cornell University Press, 1969), pp. 24–39.
13. Mahony to Kirkwood, April 1861, Samuel J. Kirkwood Correspondence, Iowa State Department of History and Archives, Des Moines. See Sage, *Allison,* p. 53.
14. Richard O. Curry, "The Union As It Was: A Critique of Recent Interpretations of the 'Copperheads,'" *Civil War History* 13 (March 1967): 25–39.
15. Frank L. Klement, *The Copperheads of the Middle West* (Chicago: University of Chicago Press, 1960); Sage, *Allison,* pp. 46–75; Hubert W. Wubben, "Dennis Mahoney and the Dubuque *Herald,* 1860–1863," *IJH* 56 (October 1958): 289–320.
16. The phrase is from Frank L. Klement, *The Limits of Dissent: Clement L. Vallandigham and the Civil War* (Lexington: University of Kentucky Press, 1970), who calls the political conflict "a war within the war."
17. Bray Hammond, "The North's Empty Purse, 1861–1862," *AHR* 67 (October 1961): 1–18; Robert P. Sharkey, *Money, Class, and Party: An Economic Study of the Civil War and Reconstruction* (Baltimore: Johns Hopkins Press, 1959), pp. 15–55; *Cong. Globe,* 37 Cong., 2 Sess., pp. 695, 804, 929, 939.
18. *Cong. Globe,* 37 Cong., 2 Sess., pp. 1035, 1951. The report of the joint conference committee was adopted on May 15, 1862; ibid., pp. 1972, 2061, 2069, 2147–48, 2158. For the subsequent story of the inadequacy of the homestead system, see Fred A. Shannon, "The Homestead Act and the Labor Surplus," *AHR* 41 (July 1936): 637–51. For the story of the manipulation of the homestead law by railroads, politicians, and speculators, see Paul W. Gates, "The Homestead Law in Iowa," *Agricultural History* 38 (April 1964): 67–78.
19. *U.S. Statutes at Large,* vol. 12, p. 489; Wallace D. Farnham, "The Pacific Railroad Act of 1862," *Nebraska History* 43 (September 1962): 141–67; Robert R. Russel, *Improvement of Communication with the Pacific Coast as an Issue in American Politics, 1783–1864* (Cedar Rapids: Torch Press, 1948), pp. 294–308.
20. *U.S. Statutes at Large,* vol. 12, 503–5; *Cong. Globe,* 37 Cong., 2 Sess., p. 2634 for Grimes's vote, p. 2770 for Wilson's vote. Grimes was a leading debater on this topic.
21. For the votes of the Senate and House, see *Cong. Globe,* 37 Cong., 3 Sess., pp. 896–97, 1147–48. For the act of 1863, see *U.S. Statutes at Large,* vol. 12, p. 665; for the 1864 addition, see ibid., vol. 13, p. 99. Also see Leonard P. Curry, *Blueprint for Modern America: Nonmilitary Legislation of the First Civil War Congress* (Nashville: Vanderbilt University Press, 1968), pp. 197–206.
22. See James G. Randall, *Lincoln the President,* 4 vols. (New York: Dodd, Mead, 1946–1955), vol. 2, pp. 126–203.
23. Paul S. Peirce, "Congressional Districting in Iowa," *IJHP* 1 (July 1903): 339–43.
24. Sage, *Allison,* pp. 49–58.
25. David M. Silver, *Lincoln's Supreme Court* (Urbana: University of Illinois Press, 1956), pp. 48–56; Charles Fairman, *Mr. Justice Miller and the Supreme Court, 1862–1890* (Cambridge: Harvard University Press, 1939), pp. 38–39, n.; pp. 40–52.
26. Dan Elbert Clark, *Samuel Jordan Kirkwood* (Iowa City: SHSI, 1917), pp. 262–78. Robert Rutland, "The Copperheads of Iowa: A Re-examination," *IJH* 52 (January 1954): 14–15, citing the *Report of the Adjutant General . . . 1864–1865,* pp. 881–82, indicates the uncertain sources of information which Clark accepted and used with the telltale preface, "it is said."
27. It is unfortunate that there is not more reliable testimony regarding "Tally's War." The latest published item is crudely handled but has a ring of authenticity about it: J. L. Swift, "The Death of Cyphert Tally," *AI* 41 (Winter 1972): 834–42.
28. N. P. Chipman to Kirkwood, May 18, 1865, Kirkwood Correspondence, Iowa State Department of History and Archives, Des Moines. Chipman eventually became commander of the Grand Army of the Republic.
29. James D. Richardson, compiler, *A Compilation of the Messages and Papers of the Presidents, 1780–1899,* 20 vols. (New York: Bureau of National Literature, 1896–1899), vol. 6, p. 179.
30. *Cong. Globe,* 38 Cong., 1 Sess., pp. 2107–8. Also see Belz, *Reconstructing the Union,* pp. 150–243.
31. Harlan to William Penn Clarke, April 2, 1864, William Penn Clarke Correspondence, Iowa State Department of History and Archives, Des Moines; William F. Zornow, *Lincoln and the Nation Divided* (Norman: UOP, 1954).

32. Harry Draper Hunt, *Hannibal Hamlin of Maine: Lincoln's First Vice-President* (Syracuse: Syracuse University Press, 1969), pp. 174–200.
33. Stone to Horace Greeley, September 9, 1864, Theodore Tilton Papers, New York Historical Society. A copy of this letter is in the Iowa State Department of History and Archives, Des Moines.
34. Grimes to Gurowski, September 18, 1864, quoted in LeRoy H. Fischer, *Lincoln's Gadfly: Adam Gurowski* (Norman: UOP, 1964), pp. 109–10.
35. For the uncritical viewpoint on Harlan, see Johnson Brigham, *James Harlan* (Iowa City: SHSI, 1913). Another completely misleading version of the Lincoln-Harlan relationship is in J. Raymond Chadwick, "Lincoln and the Harlan Family," *AI* 35 (April 1959: 610–23. The author was not a historian; at the time he was president of Iowa Wesleyan College, a post once held by Harlan. One can only speculate as to the identity of Chadwick's ghost writer.
36. Ruth Painter Randall, *Mr. Lincoln's Sons* (Boston: Little, Brown, 1955), pp. 172–75, 256–57; John S. Goff, *Robert Todd Lincoln: A Man in His Own Right* (Norman: UOP, 1969); Justin G. and Linda L. Turner (eds.), *Mary Todd Lincoln: Her Life and Letters* (New York: Knopf, 1972), appeared after my account was written.
37. See p. 175. Anyone who takes pride in Harlan's appointment to the cabinet must ignore the circumstances of his predecessor's dismissal. See Elmo R. Richardson and Alan W. Farley, *John Palmer Usher: Lincoln's Secretary of the Interior* (Lawrence: University of Kansas Press, 1960), pp. 51–54, 80–81, 86–91, 127. Reinhard Luthin, *Lincoln and the Patronage* (New York: Columbia University Press, 1943), p. 312, says: "Harlan's selection . . . was truly a personal appointment."

CHAPTER 10

1. Eric L. McKitrick, *Andrew Johnson and Reconstruction* (Chicago: University of Chicago Press, 1960); Herman Belz, *Reconstructing the Union: Theory and Practice during the Civil War* (Ithaca: Cornell University Press, 1969).
2. A good brief account of the quarrel between Garrison and Phillips is found in Russel B. Nye, *William Lloyd Garrison and the Humanitarian Reformers* (Boston: Little, Brown, 1955), pp. 180–87. A good supplementary article is Waldo W. Braden, "Iowa Reactions to Wendell Phillips, 1867," *IJH* 50 (January 1952): 35–46.
3. Carl H. Erbe, "Constitutional Provisions for the Suffrage in Iowa," *IJHP* 22 (July 1924): 363–417. Also see Leola N. Bergmann, "The Negro in Iowa," *IJHP* 46 (January 1948): 21.
4. Louise R. Noun, *Strong-Minded Women: The Emergence of the Woman-Suffrage Movement in Iowa* (Ames: ISUP, 1969), pp. 35–99.
5. Glenn M. Linden, "'Radicals' and Economic Policies: The Senate, 1861–1873," *JSH* 32 (May 1966): 189–99; "'Radicals' and Economic Policies: The House of Representatives, 1861–1873," *Civil War History* 13 (March 1967): 51–65; Allan G. Bogue, "Bloc and Party in the United States Senate: 1861–1863," ibid. (September 1967): 221–41.
6. The brief account here is based on Leland L. Sage, "William Boyd Allison and Senatorial Politics, 1865–1870," *IJH* 52 (April 1954): 97–128; Sage, *William Boyd Allison: A Study in Practical Politics* (Iowa City: SHSI, 1955), pp. 71–75.
7. McKitrick, *Andrew Johnson,* pp. 76–77, 404 n.
8. The error was first made by Paul R. Abrams, "The Assault upon Josiah B. Grinnell by Lovell H. Rousseau," *IJHP* 10 (July 1912): 383–402. Charles E. Payne, usually a scrupulously accurate historian, makes the same error in *Josiah B. Grinnell* (Iowa City: SHSI, 1938), p. 231; so does Cyrenus Cole, *A History of the People of Iowa,* p. 380, and *Iowa through the Years,* p. 315. The *Oskaloosa Weekly Herald,* June 14, 21, 1866, clearly shows that the Rousseau incident came after the nominating convention.
9. On Kasson's contest with Dodge, see Edward Younger, *John A. Kasson: Politics and Diplomacy from Lincoln to McKinley* (Iowa City: SHSI, 1955), pp. 189–209; Stanley P. Hirshson, *Grenville M. Dodge: Soldier, Politician, Railroad Pioneer*

(Bloomington: Indiana University Press, 1967), pp. 132–42. Dodge's tendency in his old age to "amplify" the record was never more apparent than in this matter. In his personal papers and writings he left the impression that the nomination was thrust upon him by a party which was dissatisfied with Kasson; that he was not interested enough to campaign for the nomination. Other writings of his own show that he was eager for the nomination but left the campaign to his expert lieutenants.

10. This account of the impeachment and trial is based largely on McKitrick, *Andrew Johnson,* pp. 3–14, 486–509, and David Miller DeWitt, *The Impeachment and Trial of Andrew Johnson,* with an Introduction by Stanley I. Kutler (Madison: State Historical Society of Wisconsin, 1967).
11. See William Salter, *The Life of James W. Grimes* (New York: D. Appleton, 1876), for an older view of this topic. For a later view, see Hans L. Trefousse, *Benjamin Franklin Wade: Radical Republican from Ohio* (New York: Twayne, 1963), pp. 291–310, especially p. 308; Charles A. Jellison, *Fessenden of Maine: Civil War Senator* (Syracuse: Syracuse University Press, 1962), pp. 239–46; Ralph J. Roske, "The Seven Martyrs?" *AHR* 64 (January 1959): 323–30.
12. Wilson to Christian Slagle, April 4, 1868, in the James F. Wilson Papers, in the custody of the First National Bank, Fairfield, Iowa. This small but valuable collection of letters was discovered in the Fairfield Public Library a few years ago. They were made available to me through the kind intercession of Professor Lewis Wheelock, then of Parsons College.
13. Ralph E. Morrow, *Northern Methodism and Reconstruction* (East Lansing: Michigan State University Press, 1956), pp. 212–13; William Warren Sweet, "The Methodist Episcopal Church and Reconstruction," *Transactions* (Illinois State Historical Society) 20 (1914): 83–94.
14. Robert Rutland, "Iowans and the Fourteenth Amendment," *IJH* 51 (October 1953): 289–300.
15. Charles H. Coleman, *The Election of 1868: The Democratic Effort to Regain Control* (New York: Columbia University Press, 1933), pp. 362–79.
16. John S. Runnells to William E. Chandler, July 25, 1868; James Harlan to Chandler, July 28, 1868, William E. Chandler Papers, Library of Congress.
17. Robert R. Dykstra and Harlan Hahn, "Northern Voters and Negro Suffrage: The Case of Iowa," *Public Opinion Quarterly* 32 (Summer 1968): 202–15. I gratefully acknowledge my debt to these authors.
18. Sage, *Allison,* pp. 91–96.
19. *Cong. Globe,* 40 Cong., 3 Sess., pp. 1563–64, 1639; Appendix, pp. 119–20. Historians have argued the motivation behind the passage of the Fifteenth Amendment. William Gillette, *The Right to Vote: Politics and the Passage of the Fifteenth Amendment* (Baltimore: Johns Hopkins Press, 1965), pp. 9–14, 21–47, 73–78, argues that the sponsors were trying to offset the damage done, in the eyes of some Republicans, by the voting provisions for the benefit of Negroes in the Fourteenth Amendment. The gift of the Fifteenth Amendment would bring in a grateful Negro vote as an addition to the faithful white vote, and thus recapture some of the states lost in 1868. LaWanda and John H. Cox, "Negro Suffrage and the Republican Party: The Problem of Motivation in Reconstruction History," *JSH* 33 (August 1967): 303–30, especially 317–30, challenge Gillette's conclusions and present evidence showing that Republican sponsorship of Negro suffrage was motivated not by political expediency but was supported as a calculated risk. Glenn M. Linden, "A Note on Negro Suffrage and Republican Politics," *JSH* 36 (August 1970): 411–20, gives statistical evidence based on a study of the voting records in Congress and finds that the evidence upholds the Coxes' point of view.
20. This account is summarized from Sage, *Allison,* pp. 99–118. The assertion that James S. Clarkson's switch of the *Register* to Allison won the election for Allison is a myth that dies hard. It is perpetuated in George Mills, "The Fighting Clarksons," *PAL* 30 (September 1949): 283–84.
21. Harlan's case was presented in Johnson Brigham, *James Harlan* (Iowa City: SHSI, 1913).

22. The standard history of the Liberal Republican crusade is Earle Dudley Ross, *The Liberal Republican Movement* (New York: Henry Holt, 1919, reprinted by University Microfilms, Ann Arbor, 1960). On the Iowa aspects of the movement, see Mildred Throne, "The Liberal Republican Movement in Iowa, 1872," *IJH* 53 (March 1955): 121–52. Certain details in both accounts have been corrected by Matthew T. Downey, "Horace Greeley and the Politicians: The Liberal Republican Convention in 1872," *JAH* 53 (March 1967): 727–50, and James M. McPherson, "Grant or Greeley? The Abolitionist Dilemma in 1872," *AHR* 71 (October 1965): 43–61.
23. Grimes to William Pitt Fessenden and Grimes to Jacob Rich, both in Throne, "The Liberal Republican Movement in Iowa," p. 126. See also Fred Lewellen, "Political Ideas of James W. Grimes," *IJHP* 42 (October 1944): 339–404.
24. McPherson, "Grant or Greeley? The Abolitionist Dilemma in 1872."

CHAPTER 11

1. Walter T. K. Nugent, *The Money Question during Reconstruction* (New York: W. W. Norton, 1967), pp. 23–38; Nugent, *Money and American Society, 1865–1880* (New York: Free Press, 1968), pp. 3–13; Bray Hammond, "The North's Empty Purse, 1861–1862," *AHR* 67 (October 1961): 1–18.
2. Of all the mistakes perpetrated by Cyrenus Cole, *Iowa through the Years* (Iowa City: SHSI, 1940), the least excusable was the description of this irredeemable paper money as "merely promissory notes, redeemable at some future time in gold" (p. 350). The Resumption Act of 1875 would not have been necessary if the greenbacks had been, as he says, "promissory notes."
3. Chester McArthur Destler, *American Radicalism, 1865–1901: Essays and Documents* (New York: Octagon Books, 1963), pp. 32–43; Henry Clay Dean, *Crimes of the Civil War and Curse of the Funding System* (Baltimore: Innes, 1868); Robert P. Sharkey, *Money, Class, and Party: An Economic Study of the Civil War and Reconstruction* (Baltimore: Johns Hopkins Press, 1959), pp. 108–9.
4. Rhoda R. Gilman and Patricia Smith, "Oliver Hudson Kelley: Minnesota Pioneer, 1849–1868," *Minnesota History* 40 (Fall 1967): 330–38.
5. W. D. Barns, "Oliver Hudson Kelley and the Genesis of the Grange: A Reappraisal," *Agricultural History* 41 (July 1968): 229–42.
6. Mildred Throne, "The Grange in Iowa, 1868–1875," *IJH* 47 (October 1949): 289–324.
7. Leland L. Sage, "The Clarksons of Indiana and Iowa," *Indiana Magazine of History* 50 (December 1954): 429–46; Herbert Quick, *One Man's Life* (Indianapolis: Bobbs-Merrill, 1925), pp. 218–33; Quick, *The Hawkeye,* pp. 96–105.
8. Mildred Throne, "The Anti-Monopoly Party in Iowa, 1873–1874," *IJH* 52 (October 1954): 289–326.
9. George H. Miller, "The Origins of the Iowa Granger Law," *MVHR* 40 (March 1954): 657–80; Miller, *Railroads and Granger Laws* (Madison: University of Wisconsin Press, 1970), pp. 97–116.
10. Mildred Throne, "The Repeal of the Iowa Granger Law, 1878," *IJH* 51 (April 1953): 117.
11. George H. Miller, "Chicago, Burlington & Quincy Railroad Company v. Iowa," *IJH* 54 (October 1956): 290–304; 5 Fed. Cases, 594 (1875).
12. Miller, "Chicago, Burlington & Quincy Railroad Company v. Iowa," pp. 304–12. For *Bartemeyer* v. *Iowa,* see 18 Wallace 129 (1873). Also see Alfred H. Kelley and Winfred A. Harbison, *The American Constitution: Its Origins and Development,* 4th ed. (New York: W. W. Norton, 1970), pp. 10–13; Richard C. Overton, *Burlington Route: A History of the Burlington Lines* (New York: Knopf, 1965), pp. 152–54.
13. Charles Aldrich, "The Repeal of the Granger Law in Iowa," *IJHP* 3 (April 1905): 256–70; Throne, "Repeal of the Iowa Granger Law," pp. 119–22, 124–29.
14. Allen Weinstein, "Was There a 'Crime of 1873'? The Case of the Demonetized Dollar," *JAH* 54 (September 1967): 307–26, offers a complete revision of the usual sketchy accounts.

15. Leland L. Sage, "Weaver in Allison's Way," *AI* 31 (January 1953): 485–507. In upsetting Weaver, a strong Harlan man, the Allison forces were also striking a blow at the Harlan machine.
16. Philip D. Jordan, "The Domestic Finances of Secretary of War W. W. Belknap," *IJH* 52 (July 1954): 193–202; Roger D. Bridges, "The Impeachment and Trial of William Worth Belknap, Secretary of War," M.A. thesis, University of Northern Iowa, 1963. General Belknap subsequently practiced law in Philadelphia and Washington, with fair success.
17. *Cong. Record,* 43 Cong., 2 Sess., pp. 208, 319, 459; *U.S. Statutes at Large,* vol. 20, p. 87; Nugent, *Money and American Society,* p. 249.
18. Fred E. Haynes, *Third Party Movements since the Civil War with Special Reference to Iowa* (Iowa City: SHSI, 1916), pp. 91–201; Edward Younger, *John A. Kasson: Politics and Diplomacy from Lincoln to McKinley* (Iowa City: SHSI, 1955), pp. 298–303.

CHAPTER 12

1. Ruth Suckow (1892–1960), a native of Hawarden, Iowa, was one of Iowa's most prolific novelists. Her forte was the meticulous portrayal of the lives of farm folk, especially those who had retired and moved to town; often her subjects were immigrants or first-generation Americans. Outstanding in this field was her novel, *The Folks.* James Norman Hall (1887–1951), a native of Colfax and a graduate of Grinnell College, spurned the topic of life in Iowa as a theme for his writing; his only essay into this field was his humorous and lighthearted satire on life in a small Iowa town (Colfax, of course) in the early years of this century: *O Millersville!,* published under the assumed name of Fern Gravel.
2. Mildred Throne, "Cyrus C. Carpenter," unpublished manuscript left in trust with the State Historical Society of Iowa. The writer was privileged to read this manuscript and discuss it with Miss Throne before her untimely death in 1960. Hopefully, it will yet reach publication.
3. *The Census of Iowa,* 1836–1880, 1875, 1895; John E. Brindley, "A Study of Iowa Population As Related to Industrial Conditions," Iowa State College, Bulletin No. 27 (Ames, 1912).
4. Howard J. Nelson, "The Economic Development of Des Moines," *IJH* 48 (July 1950): 193–220. See p. 206 and pp. 219–20, where some of Des Moines's population growth is attributed to annexations of suburbs.
5. Two widely circulated "lure books" were: William Duane Wilson, *A Description of Iowa and Its Resources* (Des Moines: Mills & Co., 1865); A. R. Fulton, *IOWA: The Home of Immigrants* (Des Moines: Mills & Co., 1870; reprinted by SHSI, 1970).
6. Jonas Viles, "Richard Parks Bland," *DAB* 2:335–36; Leland L. Sage, *William Boyd Allison: A Study in Practical Politics* (Iowa City: SHSI, 1956), pp. 143–57; Walter T. K. Nugent, *Money and American Society, 1865–1880* (New York: Free Press, 1968), pp. 221–59; Allen Weinstein, *Prelude to Populism: Origins of the Silver Issue, 1867–1878* (New Haven: Yale University Press, 1970), pp. 301–53.
7. Fred A. Shannon, *America's Economic Growth,* 3rd ed. (New York: Macmillan, 1951), p. 413.
8. For *Kohler & Lange* v. *Hill,* see *Iowa Reports* 60:543. Dan Elbert Clark, "History of Liquor Legislation in Iowa," *IJHP* 6 (January, July, October 1908): 55–87, 339–74, 503–608, traces every move in the long battle. On the importance of Prohibition in Iowa history, see Samuel P. Hays, "History as Human Behavior," *IJH* 58 (July 1960): 193–206.
9. This entire section follows closely J. Brooke Workman, "Governor William Larrabee and Railroad Reform," *IJH* 57 (July 1959): 231–66, based on his M.A. thesis of the same title, State College of Iowa (University of Northern Iowa), 1958. In addition, William Larrabee, *The Railroad Question* (Chicago: Schulte Pub. Co., 1893), is indispensable. Also see Richard C. Overton, *Burlington Route: A History of the Burlington Lines* (New York: Knopf, 1965), pp. 222–25.
10. In 1967 Governor Larrabee's heirs transferred "Montauk" to the management of the State Historical Society of Iowa. It is now open to the public for visits but managed by local officials. See *The Iowan* 16 (Winter 1967–1968): 10–19, 53.

11. Sage, *Allison,* pp. 204–29; Harry J. Sievers, *Benjamin Harrison, Hoosier Statesman: From the Civil War to the White House, 1865–1888* (New York: University Publishers, 1959), pp. 329–56; Robert Marcus, *Grand Old Party: Political Structure in the Gilded Age, 1880–1896* (New York: Oxford University Press, 1971), pp. 101–50.
12. Jean B. Kern, "The Political Career of Horace Boies," *IJH* 47 (July 1949): 215–46; Patty W. Johnson, "Waterloo's Boies: Adroit Genius," *Waterloo Courier,* January 14, 1968.
13. Fred W. Wellborn, "The Influence of the Silver Republican Senators, 1889–1891," *MVHR* 14 (March 1928): 462–80.
14. A vast and highly controversial body of literature on Populism has appeared in recent years. On the Iowa aspects of the topic, I have used Herman C. Nixon, "The Economic Basis of the Populist Movement," *IJHP* 21 (July 1923): 373–96; Nixon, "The Populist Movement in Iowa," *IJHP* 24 (January 1926): 3–107; Fred E. Haynes, *Third Party Movements since the Civil War,* pp. 221–375.
15. Sage, *Allison,* pp. 249–53; Harry J. Sievers, *Benjamin Harrison, Hoosier President: The White House and After* (Indianapolis: Bobbs-Merrill, 1968), pp. 213–33. After the election of 1888, "Ret" Clarkson served a short while as First Assistant Postmaster General, earning the title, "The Headsman," for his ruthless political decapitation of postmasters, then lived in Philadelphia and later New York, seeking greater worlds than Des Moines and Iowa to conquer. See my article, "The Clarksons of Indiana and Iowa," *Indiana Magazine of History* 50 (December 1954): 429–46; Dorothy G. Fowler, *The Cabinet Politician: The Postmasters General, 1829–1909* (New York: Columbia University Press, 1943), pp. 210–15, 220.
16. Robert F. Durden, *The Climax of Populism: The Election of 1896* (Lexington: University of Kentucky Press, 1965), p. 21. Another excellent study of the election of 1896 is in Stanley L. Jones, *The Presidential Election of 1896* (Madison: University of Wisconsin Press, 1964).
17. *Cong. Record,* 53 Cong., 1 (Special) Sess., pp. 1006–8, for the House vote of August 28, 1893; for the Senate vote on October 30, 1893, ibid., 2958.
18. This summary is based on Nixon, "Populist Movement in Iowa," especially pp. 103–7.
19. William R. Boyd, "George Evan Roberts," *AI* 29 (October 1948: 413–24; Emory H. English, "Capable Public Service," ibid., 425–33.
20. *Annals of Iowa* 6 (January 1904): 307–9. His gift of $20,000 to the Disciples of Christ helped this denomination to found a college in 1881 in Des Moines to which they gave his name.
21. Elmer E. Ellis, *Henry M. Teller: Defender of the West* (Caldwell, Idaho: Caxton Press, 1941), pp. 241–64.
22. Edgar Eugene Robinson, *The Presidential Vote, 1896–1932* (Stanford, Calif.; Stanford University Press, 1934), p. 192.

CHAPTER 13

1. See Chapter 18, Note 3; *Census of Iowa,* 1836–1880, 1856, 1895, 1905; *Federal Census,* 1880, 1890, 1900; John E. Brindley, "A Study of Iowa Population As Related to Industrial Conditions," Iowa State College, Bulletin No. 27 (Ames, 1912).
2. Leland L. Sage, *William Boyd Allison: A Study in Practical Politics* (Iowa City: SHSI, 1956); David J. Rothman, *Politics and Power: The United States Senate 1869–1901* (Cambridge: Harvard University Press, 1966), a brilliant study which attributes great power to Allison at the turn of the century.
3. Thomas R. Ross, *Jonathan Prentiss Dolliver: A Study in Political Integrity and Independence* (Iowa City: SHSI, 1958), especially p. 126 and Note 23 on pp. 316–17. Also see Gordon Hostettler, "The Oratorical Career of Jonathan Prentiss Dolliver," Ph.D. diss., University of Iowa, 1947, wherein the study of Dolliver's oratory is built upon a rich historical background.
4. Willard L. Hoing, "David Bremner Henderson: Speaker of the House," *IJH* 55 (January 1957): 1–34, based on his M.A. thesis, "Colonel David Bremner Hender-

son: Speaker of the House," Iowa State Teachers College (University of Northern Iowa), 1956.

5. See Jacob A. Swisher, *Robert Gordon Cousins* (Iowa City: SHSI, 1938).
6. Earle D. Ross, "Gilbert Nelson Haugen," *DAB,* vol. 21, pp. 384–85.
7. See John Ely Briggs, *William Peters Hepburn* (Iowa City: SHSI, 1919).
8. Louis B. Schmidt, "James Wilson," *DAB,* vol. 20, pp. 330–31; Willard L. Hoing, "James Wilson: Secretary of Agriculture," Ph.D. diss., University of Wisconsin, 1964; Earle D. Ross, "Leslie Mortier Shaw," *DAB,* vol. 18, pp. 43–44.
9. Edward Younger, *John A. Kasson: Politics and Diplomacy from Lincoln to McKinley* (Iowa City: SHSI, 1955), pp. 364–79; Mary Jane Thierman, "John Adam Kasson: His Reciprocity Treaties and Their Fate," M.A. thesis, University of Northern Iowa, 1953.
10. George E. Mowry, *The Era of Theodore Roosevelt, 1900–1912* (New York: Harper & Row, 1958), pp. 38–45.
11. Ralph M. Sayre, "Albert Baird Cummins and the Progressive Movement in Iowa," Ph.D. diss., Columbia University, 1958, has an excellent description of Blythe. Regrettably, Professor Sayre's fine monograph has not been published.
12. On James S. Clarkson, see Leland L. Sage, "The Clarksons of Indiana and Iowa," *Indiana Magazine of History* 50 (December 1954): 429–46; John M. Blum, *The Republican Roosevelt,* 2nd ed. (New York: Atheneum, 1963), pp. ix, 43–50. On the sale of the *Des Moines Iowa State Register,* see Sage, *Allison,* pp. 285, 291.
13. Leigh Smith James Hunt is an almost legendary figure in Iowa and American history. This Hoosier-Hawkeye made a fortune in China and then turned social reformer. He was a great admirer of Dolliver. See *National Encyclopedia of American Biography,* vol. 24, pp. 13–14 (1925); *AI* 19 (April 1934): 314–15.
14. Ross, *Dolliver,* pp. 138–41, 155–58.
15. Mowry, *Era of Theodore Roosevelt,* pp. 71, 73–74.
16. My case for a different Cummins is based on Sayre, "Albert Baird Cummins," and Ross, *Dolliver,* neither of which was available to Professor Mowry at the time of his writing. See also Thomas J. Bray, *Rebirth of Freedom* (Indianola: Record and Tribune Press, 1957), especially the Introduction, pp. 1–5, by Emory H. English. Fleming Fraker, Jr., "The Beginnings of the Progressive Movement in Iowa," *AI* 35 (Spring 1961): 578–93, is valuable because it is based on conversations with Emory H. English, an early participant in Cummins's rise to power.
17. Fortunately, the papers of Harvey Ingham (1858–1949) have been deposited with the Iowa Historical Library and will soon be available for use by scholars. See *Des Moines Register,* July 30, 1972.
18. George Mills, *The Little Man with the Long Shadow: The Life of Frederick M. Hubbell* (Des Moines: Trustees of the Frederick M. Hubbell Estate, 1955).
19. Abraham B. Funk, *Fred L. Maytag: A Biography* (Cedar Rapids: Torch Press, 1936).
20. "Emory Hampton English," *Who's Who in Iowa* (Des Moines: Iowa Daily Press Association, 1940).
21. See *AI* 13 (July 1925): 73–74; *AI* 15 (April 1927): 570–76, a tribute by Ora Williams, a longtime Iowa journalist.
22. *AI* 20 (January 1937): 550–51; *Des Moines Register,* November 5, 1936.
23. Ray Smalling Johnston, "Smith Wildman Brookhart: The Last Populist," M.A. thesis, University of Northern Iowa, 1964.
24. Donald L. Winters, "The Senatorial Career of William Squire Kenyon," M.A. thesis, University of Northern Iowa, 1963.
25. On Charles B. Santee, see *AI* 25 (October 1943): 145.
26. E. Daniel Potts, "The Progressive Profile in Iowa," *Mid-America* 47 (October 1965): 257–68, a helpful essay based on the author's master's thesis, "A Comparative Study of the Leadership of Republican Factions in Iowa, 1904–1914," written under Professor Samuel P. Hays, University of Iowa, 1956.
27. See Note 3.
28. This quotation is taken from George E. Roberts, "The Origin and History of the Iowa Idea," *IJHP* 2 (January 1904): 69–70. There seems to be some confusion of subject matter in the literary composition of the full resolution. Why

would the platform makers insert the point "We favor such amendments of the interstate commerce act . . ." into this plank?

29. Ross, *Dolliver,* p. 168, has called attention to the double error by Arthur S. Link, *American Epoch* (New York: Knopf, 1955), p. 105, in attributing the "Iowa Idea" to Cummins as part of the campaign of 1902. Ross points out that the "Iowa Idea" was not originated by Cummins and that the campaign was in 1901, not 1902. I must add that Mowry, *Era of Theodore Roosevelt,* pp. 55, 127, indirectly attributes the authorship to Cummins, saying: "In considerable part, the 'Iowa Idea' accounted for Cummins' popularity in Iowa." For a recent treatment, see James E. Diestler, "The Iowa Idea: Its Origins and Early Development," M.A. thesis, Drake University, 1968.
30. See Note 26.
31. My quotations from the inaugural address are taken from the *Des Moines Iowa State Register,* January 17, 1902.
32. See William L. Bowers, "The Fruits of Iowa Progressivism, 1900–1915," *IJH* 57 (January 1959): 34–60; *Laws of Iowa,* 1902, Chapter 61.
33. George M. Titus, "The Battle for Biennial Elections," *AI* 29 (January 1948): 163–75. Titus makes it clear that opposition to the change was due to the reluctance of some to let Governor Cummins profit from the provision for an extra year in office.
34. This account is based largely on Willard L. Hoing, "David Bremner Henderson: Speaker of the House," *IJH* 55 (January 1957): 1–34.
35. See Robert F. Wesser, *Charles Evans Hughes: Politics and Reform in New York, 1905–1910* (Ithaca: Cornell University Press, 1967), pp. 33–48.
36. Bowers, "Fruits of Progressivism," p. 44. Mills, *Little Man with the Long Shadow,* p. 216, says that Hubbell never interfered with Cummins's political activities.

CHAPTER 14

1. Thomas R. Ross, *Jonathan Prentiss Dolliver: A Study in Political Integrity and Independence* (Iowa City: SHSI, 1958), p. 217. As seen above, Governor Kirkwood's three terms were not consecutive, and Horace Boies's try for a third term had been repulsed.
2. William L. Bowers, "The Fruits of Iowa Progressivism, 1900–1915," *IJH* 57 (January 1959): 50–51; *Laws of Iowa,* 1906, Chapter 166; *Laws of Iowa,* 1907, Chapter 176; Keach Johnson, "Iowa Dairying at the Turn of the Century: The New Agriculture and Progressivism," *Agricultural History* 45 (April 1971): 95–110. On Senator Newberry, see *AI* 26 (July 1944): 74–75. I was fortunate to receive additional information from Professor Donald F. Howard, University of Northern Iowa, who in his youth knew Mr. Newberry well.
3. *Laws of Iowa,* 1906, Chapter 90; *Laws of Iowa,* 1907, Chapter 112; William Larrabee, *The Railroad Question* (Chicago: Schulte Pub. Co., 1893), pp. 205–30.
4. The term is from John M. Blum, *The Republican Roosevelt,* 2nd ed. (New York: Atheneum, 1963).
5. For extensive accounts of the fight for the railroad rate bill, see Ross, *Dolliver,* pp. 191–213; Leland L. Sage, *William Boyd Allison: A Study in Practical Politics* (Iowa City: SHSI, 1956), pp. 294–312.
6. Ross, *Dolliver,* pp. 215–21; Cyrenus Cole, *I Remember, I Remember* (Iowa City: SHSI, 1936), p. 316; Cole, *Iowa through the Years* (Iowa City: SHSI, 1940), p. 435.
7. The letter to Major Torbert is reprinted in Sage, *Allison,* p. 309; Dan E. Clark, *History of Senatorial Elections in Iowa* (Iowa City: SHSI, 1912), pp. 251–52.
8. Ross, *Dolliver,* pp. 217–22; Thomas J. Bray, *The Rebirth of Freedom* (Indianola, Iowa: Record and Tribune Press, 1957), pp. 84–102.
9. Material on Claude R. Porter is difficult to find. He was a perennial candidate for the Democrats and suffered patiently in their hopeless cause. He was three times a candidate for governor: 1906, 1910, 1918; six times for U.S. senator: 1907, 1908, 1909, 1911, 1920, and 1926. He finally received recognition for his faithful service to the party when President Wilson appointed him U.S. district attorney

for the Southern District of Iowa. Later he was appointed counsel to the Federal Trade Commission and President Coolidge gave him an appointment to the Interstate Commerce Commission in 1928, in which place he served until his death on August 17, 1946. See *AI* 28 (October 1946): 161–62; Edgar R. Harlan, *A Narrative History of the People of Iowa,* 5 vols. (Chicago: American Historical Society, 1931), vol. 2, p. 264; *Des Moines Register,* August 18, 1946.

10. *Laws of Iowa,* 1904, Chapter 40, pp. 29–37.
11. *Laws of Iowa,* 1907, Chapter 51, pp. 51–64; Bray, *Rebirth of Freedom,* pp. 109–14.
12. The secretary was Lee McNeely of Dubuque, who gave me this information. As to Allison's age, he was 78 years old when he made his announcement in 1907; had he lived and had he been reelected, he would have been two days beyond his 80th birthday when his new term began on March 4, 1909.
13. This account is based largely on Ross, *Dolliver,* pp. 224–31; Ralph M. Sayre, "Albert Baird Cummins and the Progressive Movement in Iowa," Ph.D. diss., Columbia University, 1958; and Sage, *Allison,* pp. 313–32.
14. Bray, *Rebirth of Freedom,* pp. 127–33; *Waterloo Courier,* June 24–26, 1908.
15. Ross, *Dolliver,* pp. 231–36; William F. Harbaugh, *Life and Times of Theodore Roosevelt,* new rev. ed. (New York: Collier Books, 1963), pp. 226–29.
16. Clark, *History of Senatorial Elections in Iowa,* pp. 250–58; Sayre, "Albert Baird Cummins." It is important to note Professor Ross's correction of Nathaniel W. Stephenson's *Nelson W. Aldrich* (New York: Scribner's, 1930), p. 343, to the effect that Dolliver *immediately* came to the aid of Cummins after Allison's death and helped him to secure election as U.S. senator. Dolliver remained neutral between Cummins and Lacey. Ross, *Dolliver,* pp. 341–42, n. 79.
17. Quoted in Ross, *Dolliver,* p. 283.
18. Ibid., pp. 239–68; George E. Mowry, *The Era of Theodore Roosevelt,* 1900–1912 (New York: Harper & Row, 1958), pp. 241–49.
19. Elmo R. Richardson, *The Politics of Conservation: Crusades and Controversies, 1897–1913* (Berkeley: University of California Press, 1962), pp. 47–104; Samuel P. Hays, *Conservation and the Gospel of Efficiency, 1890–1920* (Cambridge: Harvard University Press, 1959), pp. 150–74; Ross, *Dolliver,* pp. 269–73.
20. Emory H. English, "George W. Clarke," *AI* 33 (April 1957): 553–71, consistently describes Clarke as a progressive. I submit that there was a transition in Clarke's views; in 1912, he supported Taft, not Roosevelt, as did many other progressives who were embarrassed by the necessity of having to make a choice. In 1914, Clarke ran as a regular Republican against the Progressive, John L. Stevens of Boone.
21. *Laws of Iowa,* 1909, Chapter 170, pp. 160–70. I am much indebted to my colleague, Professor Edward Rutkowski, University of Northern Iowa, for help on this subject. See his essay in M. M. Chambers (ed.), *Higher Education in the Fifty States* (Danville, Ill.: Interstate, 1970).
22. Frank Luther Mott, "Lafayette Young," *DAB,* vol. 20, pp. 632–33.
23. Donald L. Winters, "The Senatorial Career of William Squire Kenyon," M.A. thesis, University of Northern Iowa, 1963; Eli Daniel Potts, "William S. Kenyon and the Senatorial Election of 1911," *AI* 38 (Winter 1966): 206–22. Cole, *Iowa through the Years,* p. 440, erroneously describes Kenyon as a conservative. The gentleman was conservative in his personality but distinctively progressive in his politics, as my later references will show.
24. Potts, "William S. Kenyon," asserts that the Kenyon progressives refused to leave the old-line party in 1912 because they had already won control of the Iowa Republican party; why gamble on the loss of that power to another faction of progressives or to the standpatters?
25. Donald L. Winters, "The Persistence of Progressivism: Henry Cantwell Wallace and the Movement for Agricultural Economics," *Agricultural History* 41 (April 1967): 109–20. The continuation of progressive influence beyond World War I is one of the themes in Arthur S. Link, *American Epoch* (New York: Knopf, 1955); the opposite point of view is presented in William E. Leuchtenburg, *The Perils of Prosperity* (Chicago: University of Chicago Press, 1958).

CHAPTER 15

1. Harold U. Faulkner, *The Decline of Laissez Faire, 1897–1917* (New York: Rinehart, 1951), pp. 32–35; Gilbert C. Fite and Jim E. Reece, *An Economic History of the United States,* 2nd ed. (Boston: Houghton Mifflin, 1965), pp. 509–11.
2. I am much indebted to John Thomas Schou, "The Decline of the Democratic Party in Iowa, 1916–1920," M.A. thesis, University of Iowa, 1960, for ideas and data on the election of 1916 and the politics of the war years. For a personal but representative expression of the German-American feelings about American neutrality, see Charles August Ficke, *Memories of Fourscore Years* (Davenport: Graphic Services, 1930). Ficke was an influential lawyer and banker in Davenport. On the point about votes for women, see Louise R. Noun, *Strong-Minded Women: The Emergence of the Woman-Suffrage Movement in Iowa* (Ames: ISUP, 1969), pp. 254–57.
3. For an elaboration of these details, see Wayne S. Cole, *An Interpretive History of American Foreign Relations* (Homewood, Ill.: Dorsey Press, 1968), pp. 382–403. The *New York Times,* March 1–8, 1917, gives ample data on the Senate's votes on armed neutrality. The Iowa House of Representatives, currently in session, considered a resolution of censure of Cummins and Kenyon for their stand against arming merchant ships; the proposal was expunged from the record on motion of Representative Charles B. Santee of Cedar Falls. *Journal of the House,* General Assembly of Iowa, 1917, p. 743.
4. On the declaration of war, see *Cong. Record,* 65 Cong., 1 Sess., p. 261 for the Senate vote; pp. 412–13, for the House vote. The three antiwar Iowa congressmen were Harry E. Hull of Williamsburg, Haugen of Decorah, and Frank P. Woods of Estherville.
5. *Iowa Official Register,* 1967–1968, pp. 308, 311–12.
6. John H. Tabor, *The Story of the 168th Infantry,* 2 vols. (Iowa City: SHSI, 1925); *Des Moines Register,* October 24, 1965; Joan Liffring, "The Many Lives of Hanford MacNider," *The Iowan* 13 (Spring 1965): 33–47, 52; Joan Muyskens, "Merle Hay and His Town," *AI* 39 (Summer 1967): 22–32.
7. William L. Harding Papers, Sioux City Public Museum. See Schou, "The Decline of the Democratic Party"; John E. Visser, "William L. Harding and the Republican Party in Iowa, 1906–1920," Ph.D. diss., University of Iowa, 1957, pp. 231–33. Iowa enacted a law in 1919 requiring the use of English in the schools. Thirty-eighth General Assembly of Iowa, *Journal of the House,* pp. 899–900; *Journal of the Senate,* p. 1572. Ohio, Missouri, and Nebraska enacted similar laws. In 1923 the Supreme Court of the United States struck down the Nebraska statute, in the case of *Robert T. Meyer* v. *Nebraska,* 262 U.S. 390.
8. Ralph M. Sayre, "Albert Baird Cummins and the Progressive Movement in Iowa," Ph.D. diss., Columbia University, 1958; Elbert W. Harrington, "A Survey of the Political Ideas of Albert Baird Cummins," *IJHP* 39 (October 1941): 339–86.
9. William G. Murray, "Iowa Land Values, 1803–1967," *PAL* 48 (October 1967): 441–504.
10. See pp. 259–63. Donald L. Winters, *Henry Cantwell Wallace As Secretary of Agriculture, 1921–1924* (Urbana: University of Illinois Press, 1970); Russell Lord, *The Wallaces of Iowa* (Boston: Houghton Mifflin, 1947), pp. 191–201.
11. Harding defeated Claude R. Porter for governor, 192,662 to 178,815.
12. *Wallaces' Farmer* 54 (January 17, 1919): 112; 54 (February 7, 1919): 312.
13. Fite and Reece, *An Economic History of the United States,* pp. 551–61; Elwyn B. Robinson, *History of North Dakota* (Lincoln: University of Nebraska Press, 1966), pp. 367–78.
14. Board of Governors, Federal Reserve System, *All-Bank Statistics, United States, 1896–1955* (1959), pp. 366–71; *Banking and Monetary Statistics* (1943), pp. 218–92.
15. This section follows closely Noun, *Strong-Minded Women,* pp. 225–61.
16. *New York Times,* February 7, 12; October 23; November 23; December 16, 1919; January 8, 1920. *The Nation,* July 7, August 16, 1919. K. Austin Kerr, *American Railroad Politics, 1914–1920: Rates, Wages, and Efficiency* (Pittsburgh: University of Pittsburgh Press, 1968), pp. 160–78, 222–27.

17. *U.S. Statutes at Large,* vol. 41, pp. 456–99. Senator Cummins did not live to see for himself the effective use of his ideas on consolidation, e.g., the merger of the Pennsylvania and New York Central lines, with the government's blessing, and, more recently, the merger of the Burlington Road with the Great Northern and Northern Pacific railroads. The Transportation Act of 1920 was used as justification for the consolidation. See *United States* v. *I.C.C.* (90 U.S. 708).
18. Ray Smalling Johnston, "Smith Wildman Brookhart: Iowa's Last Populist," M.A. thesis, University of Northern Iowa, 1964.
19. Johnston, "Brookhart," uses statistics from the *Iowa Official Register,* 1921–1922, p. 425, to show that Brookhart carried 28 counties; Cummins, 71 counties. Jerry Alvin Neprash, *The Brookhart Campaigns in Iowa, 1920–1926* (New York: Columbia University Press, 1932), p. 72, gives a map showing 26 counties for Brookhart, 73 for Cummins. Johnston's count seems to be correct. The number of counties carried is not as important as their population and the margin of victory. Brookhart's margin over his opponent in the counties which he carried was only 5,847; he carried 11 counties by margins below 100, one by only 4 votes; five others were carried by 11, 18, 19, 21, and 36, respectively. Such victories are of little importance.
20. On Nathan E. Kendall, see p. 257.
21. *Des Moines Register,* September 16, 1945; *AI* 27 (January 1946): 251–52. The Clyde L. Herring Papers, University of Iowa Library, are of limited value.
22. See the monumental work, a model biography, by William T. Hutchinson, *Lowden of Illinois: The Life of Frank O. Lowden,* 2 vols. (Chicago: University of Chicago Press, 1957), vol. 1, pp. 293–326; vol. 2, pp. 400–406.
23. Wesley M. Bagby, " 'The Smoke Filled Room' and the Nomination of Warren G. Harding," *MVHR* 41 (March 1955): 657–74.
24. See Visser, "William L. Harding and the Republican Party," pp. 260 ff.; Schou, "Decline of the Democratic Party," pp. 256–57; *Des Moines Register,* February 2, 26; April 3, 12, 1919; September 1, 22, 1920. The *Waterloo Evening Courier,* November 4, 1920, in a postelection summary, referred to the "odorous" [malodorous?] administration of William L. Harding. Needless to say, Harding dropped out of political life in Iowa.
25. Concerning Edwin T. Meredith, see the *Des Moines Register,* June 18, 1928; *AI* 16 (October 1928): 473.
26. Winters, *Henry Cantwell Wallace,* pp. 3–8, 27–33, 37–60, 217–46; Earl O. Heady, *Agricultural Policy under Economic Development* (Ames: ISUP, 1962), pp. 26–44.
27. Earle D. Ross, "Gilbert Nelson Haugen," *DAB,* vol. 21, pp. 384–85.
28. *Des Moines Register,* November 14, 1920. Besides Kenyon, those present were William F. Kopp of Mount Pleasant, Burton E. Sweet of Waverly, Cassius C. Dowell of Des Moines, and C. William Ramseyer of Bloomfield.
29. Orville M. Kile, *The Farm Bureau through Three Decades* (Baltimore: Waverly Press, 1948), pp. 99–103.
30. William E. Leuchtenburg, *The Perils of Prosperity, 1914–1932* (Chicago: University of Chicago Press, 1958), pp. 101–3.
31. George N. Peek and Hugh S. Johnson, *Equality of Agriculture,* 1st ed. (Moline: H. W. Harrington, 1922); 2nd ed. (Moline Plow Co., 1922).
32. Leuchtenburg, *The Perils of Prosperity,* pp. 102–3.
33. On Charles Linza McNary, see Roger Taylor Johnson, "Charles L. McNary and the Republican Party during Prosperity and Depression," Ph.D. diss., University of Wisconsin, 1967.
34. Hutchinson, *Lowden,* vol. 2, pp. 553–83. On the career of Charles E. Hearst, see *AI* 20 (July 1936): 395–96; Donald B. Groves and Kenneth Thatcher, *The First Fifty: History of the Farm Bureau in Iowa* (Des Moines: Iowa Farm Bureau Federation, 1968). For an opportunity to see the Charles E. Hearst Papers and for very helpful commentary on Iowa farm history, I am very much indebted to Charles J. and James S. Hearst, sons of Charles E. Hearst. The Hearst Papers are now in the University of Northern Iowa Library.
35. James O. Robertson, "Progressives Elect Will H. Hayes Republican National Chairman, 1918," *Indiana Magazine of History* 64 (September 1968): 173–90. Adams, in Europe at the outbreak of the war in 1914, wrote to friends in Dubuque that

the Germans possessed a vast superiority in manpower and equipment and would easily win the war. Any fair-minded student of the military situation in 1914 can understand why Adams could be misled into making this statement.

36. Neprash, *The Brookhart Campaigns*. My pages on Brookhart closely follow Johnston, "Smith Wildman Brookhart," a more recent, more comprehensive study.
37. *Des Moines Register,* July 22, 1926.
38. Several issues of the *Iowa Official Register* erred in listing Stewart's election as of 1928 instead of 1926. Correction was made in the 1969–1970 issue, p. 33, by Dale L. Ahern, editor.
39. See *Cong. Record,* 69 Cong., 1 Sess., pp. 9862–63, 11872.
40. Ibid., 69 Cong., 2 Sess., p. 3518, for the Senate vote on February 11, 1927; 4,099, for the House vote on February 17; 4771–76, for a copy of President Coolidge's veto message. It is reprinted in George S. McGovern (ed.), *Agricultural Thought in the Twentieth Century* (Indianapolis: Bobbs-Merrill, 1967), pp. 126–35.
41. *Cong. Record,* 70 Cong., 1 Sess., p. 6283, gives the Senate vote, 52 to 23, 17 not voting; pp. 7771–72, the House vote.
42. For President Coolidge's veto of the second McNary-Haugen bill, see Senate Document 141, 70 Cong., 1 Sess. For a sharply critical discussion of the veto message, see *Cong. Record,* 70 Cong., 1 Sess., pp. 9873–79.

CHAPTER 16

1. See the *Des Moines Register* through April, May, and early June, 1928, especially May 4, 5; Gilbert C. Fite, *George N. Peek and Fight for Farm Parity* (Norman: UOP, 1954), pp. 203–7; Charles E. Hearst Papers, University of Northern Iowa Library.
2. Fite, *George N. Peek,* p. 205; William T. Hutchinson, *Lowden of Illinois: The Life of Frank O. Lowden,* 2 vols. (Chicago: University of Chicago Press, 1957), vol. 2, pp. 264, 603.
3. Richard Hofstadter, "Could a Protestant Have Beaten Hoover in 1928?" *The Reporter* 22 (March 1960): 31–33; Herbert Hoover, *The Memoirs of Herbert Hoover: The Cabinet and the Presidency, 1920–1933* (New York: Macmillan, 1952), pp. 207–9.
4. A helpful article on Lou Henry Hoover is by Helen B. Pryor, "Lou Henry Hoover," *PAL* 52 (July 1971): 353–400. The Albert F. Dawson Papers, SHSI, Iowa City, are very rewarding to a student of the 1928 campaign.
5. Murray R. Benedict, *Farm Policies of the United States, 1790–1950* (Berkeley: University of California Press, 1953), pp. 226–29.
6. For data on the economists' petition, see *New York Times,* May 5, 1930; for the voting record, see *Cong. Record,* 71 Cong., 2 Sess., pp. 10635, 10789–90.
7. For more information on Milo Reno, see pp. 277–78, 304.
8. Warren B. Smith, "Norman Baker—King of the Quacks," *The Iowan* 7 (December 1958–January 1959): 16–18, 55.
9. Quoted in Roland White, *Milo Reno: Farmers Union Pioneer* (Iowa City: Athens Press, 1941), p. 61. Reno and H. R. Gross took every mishap in the testing program as proof that the entire program should be abandoned. See the file of the *Iowa Union Farmer* for this period. For a general history of the Iowa Farmers Union, see George Rinehart, "The Iowa Farmers Union," M.A. thesis, University of Northern Iowa, 1955.
10. My account of the "Cow War" follows closely John L. Shover, *Corn Belt Rebellion: The Farmers Holiday Association* (Urbana: University of Illinois Press, 1965), pp. 28–40.
11. Gilbert C. Fite and Jim E. Reece, *An Economic History of the United States,* 2nd ed. (Boston: Houghton Mifflin, 1965), pp. 588–91.
12. On the Farmers Holiday Association, see Shover, *Corn Belt Rebellion.* For the Reno quotation, see p. 27.
13. *Des Moines Register,* May 29, 1932.
14. Ibid., June 2, 1932
15. Ibid., June 15, 1932.

16. Ibid., June 15–16, 1932, concerning Turner and Darling, respectively.
17. This information was given to me by Iver H. Christoffersen, Cedar Falls attorney, who was one of the young delegates to the 1932 state convention.
18. Shover, *Corn Belt Rebellion,* pp. 49–54.
19. *Cedar Falls Daily Record,* October 5, 1932; *Des Moines Register,* October 5, 1932.
20. Shover, *Corn Belt Rebellion,* pp. 58–76, for the full stories about the right-winger, Barlow, and the three Communists; see *Des Moines Register,* January 15, 1933, for picture of Mother Bloor.
21. Benedict, *Farm Policies of the United States,* pp. 229–33; Richard S. Kirkendall, *Social Scientists and Farm Politics in the Age of Roosevelt* (Columbia: University of Missouri Press, 1966), pp. 24–49; William D. Rowley, *M. L. Wilson and the Campaign for the Domestic Allotment* (Lincoln: University of Nebraska Press, 1970), pp. 107–41. An admirable point made by Rowley, not often noticed elsewhere, is the interest taken in the problems of agriculture by insurance companies and banks, which held billions of dollars' worth of farm mortgages. For example, a leading proponent of Wilson's domestic allotment plan was R. R. Rogers, manager of the Farm Mortgage Department of the Prudential Life Insurance Company. Van R. Perkins, *Crisis in Agriculture: The Agricultural Adjustment Administration in the New Deal, 1933* (Berkeley: University of California Press, 1969), pp. 30–32, emphasizes Roosevelt's efforts to please both friends and foes of Domestic Allotment.
22. Rowley, *M. L. Wilson,* pp. 142–99.
23. The loss of six counties to Hoover has been explained on the grounds that they were "urban," and therefore not carried by the discontented farm vote. This theory is not altogether satisfactory as an explanation. Polk, Linn, and Black Hawk counties fully qualify as "urban" (60% or more living in urban areas) and thus support the theory. Marshall and Story counties were mixed urban and rural (31%–60% in the urban class); Warren County was definitely in the rural category in 1930 (less than 31% urban). A counterargument is furnished by the examples of Woodbury (Sioux City) and Pottawattamie (Council Bluffs) counties, both urban. Both voted for FDR, though the latter county had a strong Republican tradition, as did Black Hawk.
24. *Des Moines Register,* June 7, 1928.
25. Harris Gaylord Warren, *Herbert Hoover and the Great Depression* (New York: Oxford University Press, 1959; W. W. Norton, 1967), pp. 269–92; Jordan A. Schwarz, *The Interregnum of Despair: Hoover, Congress, and the Depression* (Urbana: University of Illinois Press, 1970), pp. 230–38.
26. *Waterloo Courier,* November 12, 1932.

CHAPTER 17

1. *Journal of the House,* 45th General Assembly of Iowa, 1933, pp. 38–47. Former Governor Turner died on April 15, 1969, at the age of 92. *Des Moines Register,* April 16, 1969. This issue contained a helpful obituary article and a full page of pictures. An editorial, "Iowa's Courageous Reformer," followed on April 18.
2. *Journal of the House,* 1933, pp. 62–70. All the quotations from this address are taken from this source.
3. William T. Hutchinson, *Lowden of Illinois: The Life of Frank O. Lowden,* 2 vols. (Chicago: University of Chicago Press, 1957), vol. 1, pp. 293–326.
4. John L. Shover, *Cornbelt Rebellion: The Farmers Holiday Association* (Urbana: University of Illinois Press, 1965), pp. 77–102. On the Ames conference, see the *Ames Tribune,* October 21, 1932.
5. The document is in the Herring Papers, University of Iowa Library. The Iowa governor's proclamation, made at the request of the legislative committee on emergency legislation, was similar to one issued by Governor Albert G. Schmedeman of Wisconsin on January 12, 1933. See *Waterloo Courier,* January 13, 20, 1933. For the statute of February 17, 1933, see *Laws of Iowa,* 1933, Chapter 182, pp. 211–12. Shover, *Cornbelt Rebellion,* pp. 86–88, covers this story well but errs in giving Iowa credit for the first state mortgage law. That honor, it seems, should

go to Indiana, where Governor Paul V. McNutt signed such an act on January 19, 1933.

6. See Governor Herring's second inaugural address, *Journal of the House,* 1935, p. 21. Senate File 111 was introduced and passed on the same day, January 20, 1933, and signed by the governor on January 30. *Journal of the Senate,* 1933, pp. 104, 108–11, 188. In the *Iowa Code* it was recorded as Sections 528.90–528.94. Most of my statistical material is taken from two articles in *AI* 30 (July 1949), one by Emory H. English, "Iowa Bank Law a Bulwark of Safety," pp. 39–55, and one by J. H. Redman, "Restored Confidence in Iowa Banks," pp. 55–61. On this topic I am deeply indebted to Mr. Frank Warner, Des Moines, formerly secretary of the Iowa Bankers Association, and to the late V. W. Johnson and to Mr. Wayne S. Mathews, Cedar Falls bankers, for assistance.
7. Either Senator Hicklin (Republican) or Senator Stevens (Democrat) might well stand as the epitome of Herring's ideal legislator: industrious, selfless, nonpartisan when confronted by a severe crisis, completely devoted to the public welfare. Much of the corrective legislation of the session bears their names as joint authors. See the *Des Moines Register,* January 10, 1933, for their pictures and a story about their proposals.
8. *Journal of the Senate,* 1933, p. 176; *Journal of the House,* 1933, p. 14.
9. The Brookings Institution, a strictly nonpartisan and nonprofit research organization in Washington, D.C., specializing in problems of government, was undoubtedly the best of its kind. For a recent history of the Institution, see Charles B. Saunders, *The Brookings Institution: A Fifty-Year History* (Washington: Brookings Institution, 1966).
10. For Governor Herring's second inaugural address, see *Journal of the House,* 46th General Assembly, 1935, pp. 19–30.
11. *Des Moines Register,* August 30, 1933.
12. Russell Lord, *The Wallaces of Iowa* (Boston: Houghton Mifflin, 1947), pp. 323–25; John Morton Blum, *From the Morgenthau Diaries: Years of Crisis, 1928–1938* (Boston: Houghton Mifflin, 1959), p. 31; Edward L. and Frederick H. Schapsmeier, *Henry A. Wallace of Iowa: The Agrarian Years, 1910–1940* (Ames: ISUP, 1968), pp. 160–64.
13. Gilbert C. Fite, *George N. Peek and the Fight for Farm Parity* (Norman: UOP, 1954), pp. 241–42; Hutchinson, *Lowden,* vol. 2, pp. 663–65; *Journal of the House,* 1933, p. 57.
14. The Henry Agard Wallace Papers, University of Iowa Library, are valuable on this subject. In letters to various friends, Wallace confided his hopes and later told of the assurances he had received of appointment.
15. The resolutions are reprinted in Shover, *Cornbelt Rebellion,* p. 96, taken from the *Farm Holiday News,* March 23, 1933. They are given in the *Des Moines Register,* March 13, 1933, together with an excellent picture of Milo Reno, John A. Simpson, and John H. Bosch.
16. *Cong. Record,* 75 Cong., 1 Sess., p. 766.
17. See Shover, *Cornbelt Rebellion,* pp. 117–25; *Des Moines Register,* April 28, 29, 30, 1933; Studs Terkel, *Hard Times: An Oral History of the Great Depression* (New York: Pantheon, 1970).
18. *Cong. Record,* 73 Cong., 1 Sess., pp. 2563, 3079, 3121, 3124.
19. Ibid., p. 3499; *U.S. Statutes at Large* 48:31; Shover, *Cornbelt Rebellion,* pp. 112–13.
20. James T. Patterson, *The New Deal and the States: Federalism in Transition* (Princeton: Princeton University Press, 1969), pp. 129–67, in a chapter entitled "The Governors: Liberals, Conservatives, and Nobodies," comes close to classification of Herring in the latter group. He makes this generalization: "Most Democratic administrations of the decade were neither suspiciously [conspicuously?] conservative nor cautiously liberal—they were practical and uninspired. Preoccupied with state events and more often than not hampered by party factionalism, they accepted as much New Deal aid as they could get, and contented themselves with praising the virtues of the Democratic party at election time. . . . Three such states were Maine, Illinois, and Iowa." Professor Patterson stresses factionalism within the Iowa Democratic fold as an impediment to strong executive

leadership in "putting over" New Deal measures. I hope I have shown Herring in a different light, a leader who chose to use persuasion rather than domineering tactics.

21. *Journal of the Senate,* Extraordinary Sess., 1933–1934, pp. 1284–87; *Journal of the House,* p. 1336; *Laws of Iowa,* 1933–1934, pp. 38–70.
22. *Laws of Iowa,* 1933–1934, Chapter 72, pp. 157–86.
23. *United States* v. *Butler et al., Receivers of Hoosac Mills Corporation,* 297 U.S. 1; Edward and Frederick Schapsmeier, *Henry A. Wallace of Iowa: The Agrarian Years,* pp. 210–23.
24. *U.S. Statutes at Large,* 49:1148.
25. See Shover, *Cornbelt Rebellion,* for the best account of Milo Reno's personality and objectives. In fact, this excellent book might well be subtitled "The Life and Times of Milo Reno." As for H. R. Gross, he left the *Iowa Union Farmer* in 1935, became a well-known radio personality in Des Moines, later in Waterloo, and was elected to Congress in 1948, where he still serves (1973), a convert to conservatism but retaining Milo Reno's crusading spirit and vocabulary.
26. *Cedar Falls Daily Record,* January 13, 16, 1936; March 7, 9, 12, 1936; Donald B. Groves and Kenneth Thatcher, *The First Fifty: The Farm Bureau in Iowa* (Des Moines: Iowa Farm Bureau Federation, 1968), pp. 14, 36, 266; The Charles E. Hearst Papers, University of Northern Iowa Library.
27. *U.S. Statutes at Large,* vol. 52, p. 31.
28. James T. Patterson, *Congressional Conservatism and the New Deal: The Growth of the Conservative Coalition in Congress, 1933–1939* (Lexington: University of Kentucky Press, 1967), especially pp. 272–73, 349.
29. Ibid., p. 352; Edward and Frederick Schapsmeier, *Henry A. Wallace,* pp. 251, 263.
30. Leonard Arrington, "The New Deal in the West," *Pacific Historical Review* 38 (August 1969): 311–16.
31. See pp. 318–19.

CHAPTER 18

1. For my data and for the basis of my comments I have used the various censuses of the State of Iowa and the United States decennial censuses; John J. Hartman, "Characteristics and Structure of Iowa's Population," Special Report 57 (Ames: Iowa State University, 1968); John L. Tait and Arthur H. Johnson, "Iowa Population Trends," Bulletin Pm-517 (Ames: Iowa State University, Cooperative Extension Service, September 1971).
2. John E. Brindley, "A Study of Iowa Population As Related to Industrial Conditions," Bulletin 27 (Ames: Iowa State College, June 1912), pp. 4–11.
3. Reynold J. Wik, *Steam Power on the American Farm* (Philadelphia: University of Pennsylvania Press, 1953), pp. 200–213; Wik, *Henry Ford and Grass-Roots America* (Ann Arbor: University of Michigan Press, 1972), pp. 82–102; E. P. Neufeld, *A Global Corporation: A History of the International Development of Massey-Ferguson Limited* (Toronto: University of Toronto Press, 1969).
4. William L. Harter and R. E. Stewart, "The Population of Iowa: Its Composition and Ranges," Bulletin 275 (Ames: Agricultural Experiment Station, Iowa State College, November 1930), pp. 22 ff.
5. Tait and Johnson, "Iowa Population Trends," p. 6; Richard Doak, "'70 Census Shows Decline in Iowa Outmigration in 1960s," *Des Moines Register,* September 19, 1971. As early as 1964 the *Des Moines Register* editorially raised the question of slow population growth: good or bad? Since that time its answer over the years has been that Iowa is better off with a smaller population and full employment than it would be with a larger population and large numbers of unemployed on the relief rolls.
6. See note 1; Iowa Crop and Livestock Reporting Service, "Number and Size of Farms, 1967–1971."
7. Iowa Development Commission, "Statistical Profiles of Iowa," 1970, 1972; Don Kendall, "Farmers' City Earnings Top On-Farm Sales," *Des Moines Sunday Register,* August 6, 1972.

8. Former Senator Guy Mark Gillette died on March 3, 1973, at the age of 94. See the obituary essay by C. C. Clifton in the *Des Moines Register,* March 4, 1973.
9. For the best recent studies of party history, relevant to the points dealt with here, see George H. Mayer, *The Republican Party, 1854–1966,* 2nd ed. (New York: Oxford University Press, 1967); David Burner, *The Politics of Provincialism: The Democratic Party in Transition, 1918–1932* (New York: Knopf, 1968).
10. Allen J. Matusow, *Farm Policies and Politics in the Truman Years* (Cambridge: Harvard University Press, 1967), pp. 185–90, 220–21.
11. *New York Times,* September 5, 1971.
12. In 1948 H. R. (Harold Royce) Gross, then a Waterloo radio announcer, defeated a veteran congressman, John W. Gwynne of Waterloo, for the nomination for representative on the Republican ticket. A legend persists that the selection of Mr. Gross was made possible only by the votes of labor union members who registered as Republicans in order to vote in the primary against Judge Gwynne. An examination of the voting statistics does not bear this out; Mr. Gross carried 9 out of 14 counties in the district. See *Iowa Official Register* (1949–1951), pp. 290–91.
13. Frank T. Nye, "The 62nd General Assembly of Iowa," *PAL* 48 (November 1967): 539–40, 550–57.
14. *Laws of Iowa,* 1971, 64th General Assembly, 1st Sess., Chapter 94, p. 148; *Des Moines Register,* February 11–26, 1971. Smith and Culver went on to win as expected; the Republicans also lost the First District to Edward Mezvinsky, Democrat.
15. *Laws of Iowa,* 1971, 64th General Assembly, 1st Sess., Chapter 261, pp. 526–28; *Des Moines Register,* September 21, 1971.
16. Frank T. Nye, "Reapportionment in Iowa," *PAL* (June 1964): 244–45.
17. Kenneth Rystrom, "How the Few Control the Legislature," *Des Moines Register,* December 16, 1962.
18. Frank T. Nye, "The 58th General Assembly of Iowa," *PAL* 40 (November 1959): 513–18; Nye, "The 59th General Assembly of Iowa," *PAL* 42 (November 1961).
19. Charles W. Wiggins, "Constitutional Convention Issue in Iowa (1960)," *AI* 40 (Winter 1970): 171–90, has an admirable summary of the details of this subject; I follow his account closely.
20. *Laws of Iowa,* 1947, Chapter 296, pp. 388–90.
21. The *Des Moines Register* ran a series of six historical articles, September 11–18, 1960, by Herbert D. Kelley, a member of its editorial staff. These were reprinted in booklet form and widely distributed.
22. Wiggins, "Constitutional Convention Issue," pp. 188–90.
23. *Baker* v. *Carr,* 369 U.S. 186.
24. The federal panel consisted of Judge Martin D. Van Oosterhout of the Eighth Circuit Court of Appeals, Judge Roy L. Stephenson of the Southern District Court of Iowa, and Judge Edward J. McManus of the Northern District Court of Iowa. Their decision was given in *Davis* v. *Synhorst,* 217 F. Supp. 492 (1963).
25. Much of this is in Nye, "Reapportionment," pp. 241–72, but the last point is my own.
26. *Davis* v. *Synhorst,* 225 F. Supp. 689 (1964).
27. *Laws of Iowa,* 1964, 60th General Assembly of Iowa, Extraordinary Sess., Chapter 1, pp. 1–7.
28. Ibid., Chapter 31, pp. 38–40.
29. *Reynolds* v. *Sims,* 377 U.S. 533.
30. *Davis* v. *Cameron,* 238 F. Supp. 462.
31. *Laws of Iowa,* 1965, 61st General Assembly of Iowa, Chapter 473, pp. 877–78 (June 2, 1965).
32. Ibid., Chapter 88, pp. 149–54.
33. Ibid., 1967, 62nd General Assembly of Iowa, 1st Sess., Chapter 469, pp. 860–62. Charles E. Quirk of Waterloo was the chairman of the ten-person commission.
34. For the five amendments, see ibid., Chapters 461–64, 466, pp. 851–58.
35. Ibid., 1969, 63rd General Assembly of Iowa, 1st Regular Sess., Chapter 89, pp. 109–24.
36. Ibid., Chapter 328, pp. 501–2.

37. *Clark R. Rasmussen* v. *Robert Ray, Northwest Reporter 2nd,* 20. (1971).
38. *Laws of Iowa,* 1971, 64th General Assembly of Iowa, 1st Regular Sess., Chapter 95, pp. 148–81 (H.F. 732).
39. Ibid., 2nd Sess., Chapter 1145, pp. 531–600.
40. *Iowa Official Register,* 1971–1972, pp. 472–73; *Laws of Iowa,* 1971, 64th General Assembly of Iowa, 1st Regular Sess., Chapter 84, pp. 113–42; James Flansburg, " 'Toughness' Seen in Steps Taken by Ray," *Des Moines Register,* May 15, 1972. The data assembled by the Governor's Economy Committee was issued in February 1970.
41. A comprehensive summary in book form is very much needed. I have used a wide variety of sources. A good short treatment is George A. May, "Iowa's Consolidated Schools," *PAL* 37 (January 1956): 1–64. This article, of course, badly needs updating.
42. Ruth Suckow, "Iowa," *American Mercury* 9 (September 1926): 39–45. Also see Suckow, *Some Others and Myself: Seven Stories and a Memoir* (New York: Rinehart 1952), pp. 169–281; Ferner Nuhn, " 'The Orchard Apiary': Ruth Suckow in Earlville," *The Iowan* 20 (Summer 1972): 21–24, 54.
43. Lois T. Hartley, "The Midland," *IJHP* 47 (October 1949): 325–44; Sargent Bush, Jr., "The Achievement of John T. Frederick," *Books at Iowa,* No. 14 (April 1971): 8–30.
44. Allan G. Bogue, "Herbert Quick's Hawkeye Trilogy," *Books at Iowa,* No. 16 (April 1972): 3–13. Also see Roy W. Meyer, *The Middle Western Farm Novel in the Twentieth Century* (Lincoln: UNP, 1965), pp. 47–56.
45. H. Willard Reninger, "James Hearst: A Country Man as Poet," in James Hearst, *Man and His Field* (Denver: Alan Swallow, 1951), pp. 9–15; Ruth Suckow, Foreword to James Hearst, *Country Men* (Muscatine: Prairie Press, 1937).
46. Frank Paluka, *Iowa Authors: A Bio-Bibliography of Sixty Iowa Authors* (Iowa City: Friends of the University of Iowa Libraries, 1967), pp. 214–16; Paul Engle (ed.), *Twenty-five Years of Fiction and Poetry Selected from the Writing Workshop of the State University of Iowa* (New York: Random House, 1961), pp. xxi–xxxvii.
47. Paluka, *Iowa Authors,* pp. 180–86.
48. Curtis Harnack, *We Have All Gone Away* (New York: Doubleday, 1973); Meyer, *Middle Western Farm Novel,* pp. 171–73; Paluka, *Iowa Authors,* pp. 95–104.
49. Hazel Brown, *Grant Wood and Marvin Cone* (Ames: ISUP, 1972).

INDEX